Leonard Gill
January '93

£ 19-50

PBan

ADVANCED TEXTS IN ECONOMETRICS

General Editors

C. W. J. GRANGER   G. MIZON

MODELLING SEASONALITY

Edited by

S. Hylleberg

OXFORD UNIVERSITY PRESS
1992

Oxford University Press, Walton Street, Oxford OX2 6DP
Oxford New York Toronto
Delhi Bombay Calcutta Madras Karachi
Petaling Jaya Singapore Hong Kong Tokyo
Nairobi Dar es Salaam Cape Town
Melbourne Auckland
and associated companies in
Berlin Ibadan

Oxford is a trademark of Oxford University Press

Published in the United States by
Oxford University Press, New York

British Library Cataloguing in Publication Data
Data available

Library of Congress Cataloging in Publication Data

Modelling seasonality / edited by S. Hylleberg.
p. cm. – (Advanced texts in econometrics)
Includes bibliographical references.
1. Seasonal variations (Economics)–Ecibinetruc nideks.
2. Seasonal variations (Economics)–Mathematical models.
I. Hylleberg, S. (Svend) II. Series.
HB141.M597 1992 330'01'5195–dc20 91-38351
ISBN 0–19–877317–X

Typeset by Keytec Typesetting Ltd, Bridport, Dorset
Printed and bound in
Great Britain by Bookcraft (Bath) Ltd,
Midsomer Norton, Avon

Contents

PART I

INTRODUCTION

General Introduction

SVEND HYLLEBERG

The General Introduction has been organized in two sections. The first section discusses the definition of seasonality. In the second section a description of the state of the art is attempted together with an evaluation of the most important and promising ways to model seasonality.

The part (Part I) also contains four 'articles'. The first is an extract from the introduction to Hylleberg (1986) putting the discussion into a historical perspective, while the last article by Bell and Hillmer (1984) adds to this, and in addition, provides a survey and a discussion of some of the major issues involved in the seasonal adjustment of time series data. The two remaining articles by Wallis (1974) and Sims (1974) have since their publication probably become the most influential pieces of research written within this area in the last twenty years.

The definition of seasonality

The concept of seasonality shares a feature with many other concepts used in the daily language. Everyone knows what it is, but very few have ever actually thought about an applicable definition. However, any definition of seasonality must include something like 'a systematic intrayear movement', but 'just how systematic' is the question. The only way to resolve that question is to consider the causes of what we call a seasonal movement, as done by Thomas and Wallis (1971), Granger (1978), and Hylleberg (1986). The basic, and to a varying degree exogenous, causes may be grouped into three classes: (i) weather, i.e. temperature, precipitation, hours of sunshine, (ii) calendar events, i.e. the timing of religious festivals or events such as Christmas, Easter, Ramadan, Yom Kippur, etc., or secular festivals such as the 4th of July, Bastille Day, etc., and (iii) timing decisions such as school vacations, industry vacations, tax years, accounting periods, dates for dividend and bonus payments, etc. Some of these causes may be unchanging over long periods (Christmas), while others may change at discrete intervals (vacations, tax years), and still others are continuously varying but predictable (Easter), while other varying causes are unpredictable (the weather).

These basic causes may have direct effects on economic variables such as the harvest, but they may also have indirect effects through the decisions of economic agents. An economic agent may choose the degree of smoothness of his production and consumption over the year in accordance with his expectations, preferences, the costs, and the physical possibilities. These factors change over the years and, furthermore, the changes may very well be endogenous.

Thus, it is obvious that the seasonal movement in many economic variables is a result of a complex decision process based on varying and changing exogenous causes, but maybe even more important, the intra-year changes and the economic decision problems bear some resemblance to those faced for longer periods.

Although the periodicity of a seasonal economic variable is a weaker concept than often realized, it seems to be natural to include the autocorrelation structure or spectrum in the description: see the important contributions by Nerlove (1964) and Granger (1978). But care must be exercised, as the strict use of a definition of seasonality based on the existence of peaks in the spectrum at the seasonal frequencies may have undesired effects partly because it raises the question of what a peak at the seasonal frequency is, and partly because estimation of spectra for economic time series is a difficult task: see Sims (1978), Tukey (1978), and Hylleberg (1986).

With these arguments in mind we propose the following definition of seasonality in Economics:

Seasonality is the systematic, although not necessarily regular, intra-year movement caused by the changes of the weather, the calendar, and timing of decisions, directly or indirectly through the production and consumption decisions made by the agents of the economy. These decisions are influenced by endowments, the expectations and preferences of the agents, and the production techniques available in the economy.

In order to illustrate the complexities and differences of seasonal processes and also to show how useful simple graphical devices may be, let us consider two quarterly series, the log of quarterly real GDP in Austria and in Taiwan respectively, and a monthly series, the log of monthly real industrial production in Canada.

In Figure 1 the quarterly series for Taiwan and Austria are depicted side by side in order to show the very different nature of the seasonal movement in the two countries. The first and second row show the original data $x_{tj}, j = 1,2$ and the first differences $(1 - B)x_{tj} = x_{tj} - x_{t-1j}$, where B is the lag operator. The following four rows are all based on the decomposition of the fourth difference $1 - B^4$ as $(1 - B)(1 + B)(1 + B^2)$. The operator $(1 - B)$ removes a non-stationary unit root at the long run or zero frequency, while $(1 + B)$ removes a unit root at the semi-annual frequency, i.e. half of a cycle, and $(1 + B^2)$ at the annual frequency, i.e. one quarter of a cycle and the complex conjugate root at three-quarters of a cycle. In case the series is

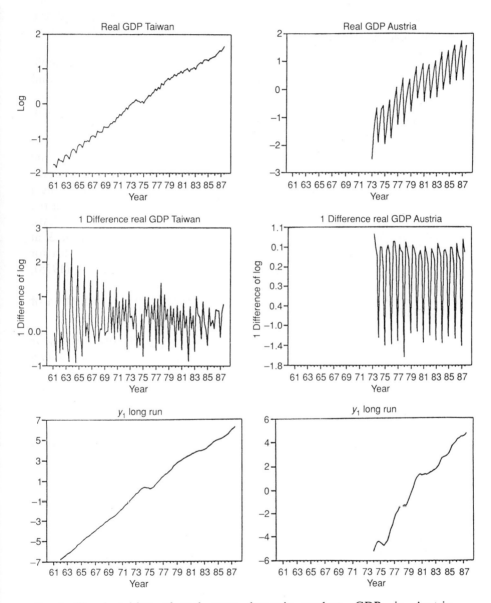

FIG. 1. The logarithm of real gross domestic product, GDP, in Austria 1973.1–1987.3 and Taiwan 1961.1–1987.3. 1. Differences and long-run component y_1.

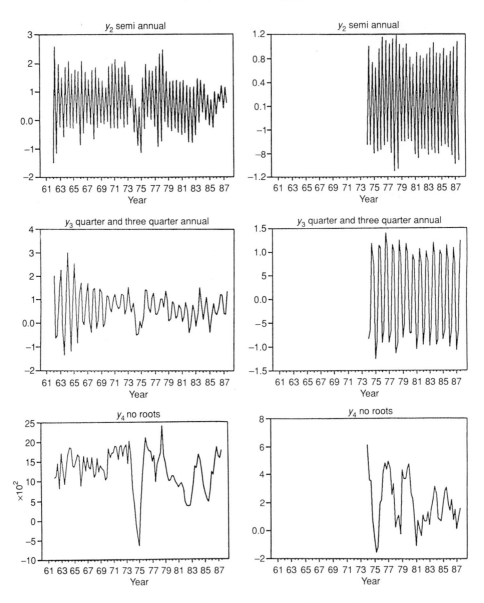

FIG. 1(cont.): Log real GDP in Austria 1973.1–1987.3 and Taiwan 1961.1–1987.3. Semi-annual components y_2 and y_3, and $_4$. Differences y_4.

integrated at the zero and seasonal frequencies transformations such as $y_{1t} = (1 + B)(1 + B^2)x_{tj} = (1 + B + B^2 + B^3)x_{tj}, y_{2t} = -(1 - B)(1 + B^2)x_{tj} = -(1 - B + B^2 - B^3)x_{tj},$ and $y_{3t} =$

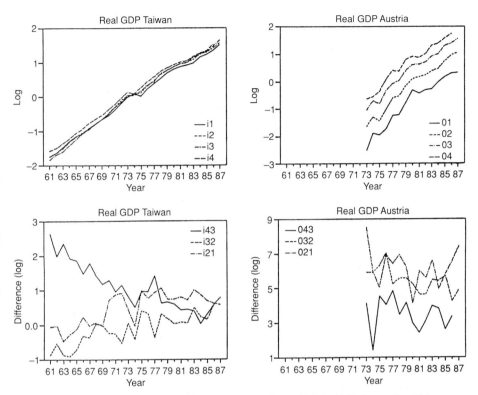

F<small>IG</small>. 1(cont.): Log real GDP in Austria 1973.1–1987.3 and Taiwan 1961.1–1987.3. *i*th quarter, $i = 1,2,3,4$ and differences.

$-(1 - B)(1 + B)x_{tj} = -(1 - B^2)x_{tj}$ retain the unit root at the long run, the semi-annual, and the annual frequency, respectively. In contrast $y_{4t} = (1 - B^4)x_{tj}$ annihilates all the roots.[1] The figures in the four rows depict these transformations and especially the rows showing the y_2 and y_3 transformations clearly indicate the constant nature of the seasonal movement in the Austrian series and the non-constant and changing seasonal movement in the Taiwanese series. Notice, that in case the series have no seasonal pattern the y_2 and the y_3 transformations show no periodicity at all. The last two rows in Figure 1 show the first quarter

---

[1] Series that require a unit root transformation, i.e. a transformation such as $(1 - B)$, $(1 + B)$, etc., in order to become stationary are called integrated. A possible precise definition is that an integrated variable with a pseudo-spectrum of the form

$$f(\omega) = \text{constant}/(\theta - \omega)^2$$

for ω near θ. Technically the series is called integrated of order 1 at frequency θ, and the frequencies of particular interest are zero, i.e. the long-run frequency and j/s, $j = 1,2,\ldots s - 1$ of a cycle, the seasonal frequencies, where s is the number of observations per year, see Hylleberg *et al.* (1990) in Part V.

series q_{1t}, the second quarter series q_{2t}, etc. and the differences between them.[2] In case of a constant seasonal pattern the q_{it} series will be almost parallel, see the Austrian case, while the opposite case where the series may even cross, depicts a varying and changing seasonal pattern, see the Taiwanese case.

Similar transformations can be applied to the monthly case, although figures with 12 series may be difficult to interpret. However, instead of presenting these graphs let us consider some additional valuable trans-formations. In Figure 2 the logarithm of the industrial production in Canada is depicted. The series is clearly seasonal, which is also shown in the log of the spectrum where the peaks at long run and seasonal frequencies clearly shows. Figure 2 also contains so-called Buys–Ballot plots (see below), where the series are depicted against the number of the month.

In case of a constant seasonal pattern the yearly lines should be almost parallel, but they appear not to be. Hence seasonality is an important feature of many economic time series and as such needs to be understood and taken account of in the modelling of time series data. It can be partialled out or jointly modelled as discussed in the next section.

The state of the art and the future

Although many arguments have been put forward against the use of seasonally adjusted data produced by official statistical agencies, the demand for them remains high. This, of course, shows that the private and public sector find the information provided by seasonally adjusted

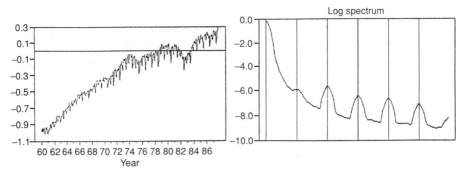

Fig. 2. Logarithm of industrial production in Canada 1960.1–1987.12 and the logarithm of the spectrum.

[2] The application of these figures has been advocated by Franses (1991).

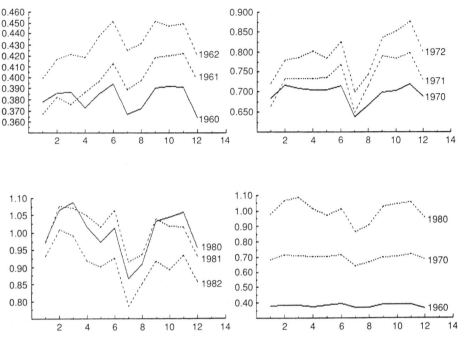

Fig. 3. Logarithm of the industrial production in Canada in selected years. Buys–Ballot plots.

data useful. Furthermore, no serious contender to the X-11 procedure developed by Julius Shiskin[3] and associates at the US Census Bureau has found its way to the market place, and the X-11 program is used all over the world. Therefore it has been a major research topic to describe this complicated procedure and to analyse the effects of using it. The X-11 program is described and analysed in Part III below by Hylleberg (1986) and Burridge and Wallis (1984).[4] It is obvious that a seasonal adjustment procedure such as the X-11 program, which is a complicated program based on a sequential use of moving average filters tailored to the single time series, must possess some less attractive features unless very specific conditions are met. These conditions depend on the specific use envisaged for the seasonally adjusted data. If what is needed is an

[3] See Shiskin, Young, and Musgrave (1967).
[4] Other references are Young (1968), Wallis (1974, see below, 1982, 1983), Cleveland and Tiao (1976), Bell and Hillmer (1984) see Part I below, Laroque (1977), Ghysels (1984, 1990a), Ghysels and Karangwa (1989), and Ghysels and Perron (1990), Hausman and Watson (1985). Notice, that a more detailed presentation and discussion of the book and the articles it includes are provided in the introduction to the four individual parts.

estimate of the non-seasonal components, then X-11 may be sufficient, although it is based on the presumption that the observed time series can be meaningfully divided into at least two unobserved and orthogonal components. However, even this may be too strong an assumption, and several of the references given earlier provide evidence where the seasonal adjustment procedure has affected the results of the estimation of univariate models in a negative way. If the seasonally adjusted data are used in econometric modelling, even stronger assumptions are necessary. These assumptions are concerned with the interdependencies between the components of the series, but again the available evidence (see Sims (1974), Wallis (1974), and Hylleberg (1986) among others) indicates that estimated static and, in particular, dynamic relationships are distorted by the seasonal adjustment. As the degree of the distortion varies the best advice for the researcher is to consider both the seasonally adjusted and seasonally unadjusted series. Obviously this requires both series to be available.

Partly as a reaction to these difficulties, and partly as a sequel to the work of Box and Jenkins (1970), Nerlove (1976), and Grether and Nerlove (1970), the so-called model-based procedures were developed. Part IV contains some of the reports on the work in this area. The articles included are Engle (1978), Hillmer and Tiao (1982), Harvey and Todd (1983), Burridge and Wallis (1990), and Maravall and Pierce (1987).[5]

The model-based procedures use the unobserved components (UC) model as the point of departure. The UC model decomposes the observed series, or its logarithm additively, into a trend, a cycle, a seasonal, and an irregular component. A time series model for each component is then postulated, and in order to be able to identify the model, restrictions are put on the model for each of the components. In some cases the variance of the irregular component is maximized and the other components therefore made as smooth as possible. This model is called the canonical decomposition.

Another difficulty was the use of the Wiener–Kolmogorov framework, which does not allow for non-stationary processes, as for instance integrated processes, i.e. processes that require differencing or other unit root transformations to become stationary. This problem has been overcome by use of the Kalman filter as shown by several of the articles in Part IV.

However, the basic difficulty with seasonal adjustment procedures is their univariate character. A possible solution to the problems of treating each series in isolation would be to build multivariate un-

---

[5] Other important contributions are Hald (1948), Pagan (1975), Burman (1980), Hausman and Watson (1985), and Maravall (1988, 1989).

observed components models, but in practice this road has not been followed by many for obvious reasons. The size of the model, and the number of parameters to estimate, quickly turns out to be prohibitive for such an endeavour.

One possible way out is to base the modelling on structural restrictions, exogeneity assumptions, etc., which again require use of a much larger information set, including economic theory information. In addition, the univariate modelling is best seen as a means of providing valuable information for a more structural analysis, i.e. it has a role similar to graphical tools like data plots, etc.

The articles included in Part V can be seen in this light. Dickey, Hasza, and Fuller (1984), Hylleberg *et al.* (1990), and Osborn *et al.* (1988) all provide tests for seasonal unit roots. As the existence of a seasonal unit root in the data-generating process implies that summer may become winter in the sense that the seasonal pattern may change dramatically, the finding of a seasonal unit root is best interpreted as an indication of a varying and changing seasonal pattern and against a constant seasonal pattern. Whether the seasonal unit root is the result of variation and changes in seasonal causes like the weather, or seasonal mean shifts due to interdependencies between the business cycle and the seasonal pattern (see Ghysels (1990*b*)), or of other changes is a question which requires a much deeper analysis than a univariate test can provide.

The existence of seasonal cointegration as defined in Hylleberg *et al.* (1990) should be interpreted in a similar way, that is as an indication of a parallel but varying seasonal component in a group of time series.

All of this may help in developing a better understanding and description of seasonality, but before further progress can be made we need to develop an empirically applicable economic theory. The articles collected in Part II by Crutchfield and Zellner (1962), Ghysels (1988), Osborn (1988), and Miron and Zeldes (1988) together with articles by Miron (1986), Barsky and Miron (1989), and Todd (1990), and unpublished work by Ghysels (1984) and Hansen and Sargent (1990, 1991) provide a promising beginning.[6]

References

(References marked with a * are included in this volume)
BARSKY, R. B., and MIRON, J. A. (1989), 'The seasonal cycle and the business cycle', *Journal of Political Economy*, **97**, 503–34.

---

[6] For recent surveys see Ghysels (1990*c*) and the discussion by Osborn (1990), and Miron (1990) with the discussion by Hylleberg, Jørgensen, and Sørensen (1991).

BELL, W. R., and HILLMER, S. C. (1984), 'Issues involved with the seasonal adjustment of economic time series', *Journal of Business and Economic Statistics*, **2**, 291–320.*

BOX, G. E. P., and JENKINS, G. M. (1970), *Time Series Analysis: Forecasting and Control*. San Francisco: Holden-Day.

BURMAN, J. P. (1980), 'Seasonal adjustment by signal extraction', *Journal of the Royal Statistical Association, Ser. A*, **143**, 321–37.

BURRIDGE, P., and WALLIS, K. F. (1984), 'Unobserved-components models for seasonal adjustment filters', *Journal of Business and Economic Statistics*, **2**, 350–9.*

—— and WALLIS, K. F. (1990), 'Seasonal adjustment and Kalman filtering: extension to periodic variances', *Journal of Forecasting*, **9**, 109–18.*

CLEVELAND, W. P., and TIAO, G. C. (1976), 'Decomposition of seasonal time series: a model for the X-11 program', *Journal of the American Statistical Association*, **8**, 99–114.

CRUTCHFIELD, J., and ZELLNER, A. (1962), 'Analysis of port pricing of halibut: theoretical and empirical results', chs. 6 and 7 in *Economic Aspects of Halibut Fishery*, United States Department of the Interior, Washington DC.*

DICKEY, D. A., HASZA, D. P., and FULLER, W. A. (1984), 'Testing for unit roots in seasonal time series', *Journal of the American Statistical Association*, **79**, 355–67.*

ENGLE, R. F. (1978), 'Estimating structural models of seasonality', in *Seasonal Analysis of Economic Time Series*. Proceedings of the Conference on the Seasonal Analysis of Economic Time Series, Washington DC, 9–10 Sept. 1976 (A. Zellner, ed.), US Department of Commerce, Bureau of the Census, Washington DC, 281–95.

FRANSES, P. H. (1991), 'A multivariate approach to modelling univariate seasonal time series', *Econometric Institute Report 9101/A*. Erasmus University, Rotterdam.

GHYSELS, E. (1984), 'The economics of seasonality: the case of the money supply', unpublished, Ph.D. Dissertation, Northwestern University, Department of Managerial Economics and Decision Science.

—— (1988), 'A study towards a dynamic theory of seasonality for economic time series', *Journal of the American Statistical Association*, **83**, 168–72.*

—— (1990a), 'Unit root tests and the statistical pitfalls of seasonal adjustment: the Case of U.S. post war real GNP', *Journal of Business and Economic Statistics*, **8**, 145–52.

—— (1990b), 'Are business cycle turning points uniformly distributed throughout the year? Part I: Evidence from descriptive and nonparametric statistics'. Mimeo, C.R.D.E., Université de Montréal.

—— (1990c), 'On the economics and econometrics of seasonality'. Mimeo, C.R.D.E., Université de Montréal (rev. Apr. 1991). Paper prepared for the Invited Symposia lectures of the Sixth World Congress of the Econometric Society, Barcelona, Aug. 1990.

—— and KARANGWA, E. (1989), 'Nominal versus "real" seasonal adjustment'. Paper presented at NBER/NSF Time Series Conference, University of Chicago.

—— and PERRON, P. (1990), 'The effect of seasonal adjustment filters on tests for a unit root.' Paper presented at the C.R.D.E./*Journal of Econometrics* Conference, Montreal, May.

GRANGER, C. W. J. (1978), 'Seasonality: causation, interpretation, and implications', in *Seasonal Analysis of Economic Time Series*. Proceedings of the Conference on the Seasonal Analysis of Economic Time Series, Washington DC, 9–10 Sept. 1976 (A. Zellner, ed.), US Department of Commerce, Bureau of the Census, Washington DC.

GRETHER, D. M., and NERLOVE, M. (1970), 'Some properties of optimal seasonal adjustment', *Econometrica*, **38**, 682–703.

HALD, A. (1948), *The Decomposition of a Series of Observations*. Copenhagen: Gad.

HANSEN, L. P., and SARGENT, T. J. (1990), 'Recursive linear models of dynamic economies'. Manuscript, Hoover Institution, Stanford University.

—— —— (1991), 'Seasonality and approximation errors in rational expectations models'. Manuscript, Hoover Institution, Stanford University.

HARVEY, A. C., and TODD, P. H. J. (1983), 'Forecasting economic time series with structural and Box–Jenkins models: a case study', *Journal of Business and Economic Statistics*, **1**, 299–307.*

HAUSMAN, J. A., and WATSON, M. W. (1985), 'Errors in variables and seasonal adjustment procedures', *Journal of the American Statistical Association*, **80**, 531–40.

HILLMER, S. C., and TIAO, G. C. (1982), 'An ARIMA model based approach to seasonal adjustment', *Journal of the American Statistical Association*, **77**, 63–70.*

HYLLEBERG, S. (1986), 'The historical perspective, in *Seasonality in Regression*. Orlando: Academic Press, 7–14.*

—— GRANGER, C. W. J., ENGLE, R. F., and YOO, B. S. (1990), 'Seasonal integration and cointegration', *Journal of Econometrics*, **44**, 215–38.*

—— JØRGENSEN, C., and SØRENSEN, N. K. (1991), 'Seasonality in macroeconomic time series', *Memo 1991-9, Institute of Economics, University of Aarhus*.

LAROQUE, G. (1977), 'Analyse d'une méthode de désaisonnalisation: le programme X-11 du 'US Bureau of the Census' version trimestrielle', *Annales de l'INSEE*, **88**, 105–27.

MARAVALL, A. (1988), 'A note on minimum mean squared error estimation of signals with unit roots', *Journal of Economic Dynamics and Control*, **12**, 589–93.

—— (1989), 'On the dynamic structure of a seasonal component', *Journal of Economic Dynamics and Control*, **13**, 81–91.

—— and PIERCE, D. A. (1987), 'A prototype seasonal adjustment model', *Journal of Time Series Analysis*, **8**, 177–93.*

MIRON, J. A. (1986), 'Seasonal fluctuations and the life cycle–permanent income model of consumption', *Journal of Political Economy*, **94**, 1258–79.

—— (1990), 'The economics of seasonal cycles'. Mimeo, Boston University. Paper prepared for the Invited Symposia lectures of the Sixth World Congress of the Econometric Society, Barcelona, Aug. 1990.

—— and ZELDES, S. P. (1988), 'Seasonality, cost shocks, and the production smoothing model of inventories', *Econometrica*, **56**, 877–908.*

NERLOVE, M. (1964), 'Spectral analysis of seasonal adjustment procedures', *Econometrics*, **32** 241–86.

—— (1967), 'Distributed lags and unobserved components of economic time series', in *Ten Economic Essays in the Tradition of Irving Fisher* (Fellner, W. et al., eds.), 126–69. New York: Wiley.

OSBORN, D. R. (1988), 'Seasonality and habit persistence in a life cycle model of consumption', *Journal of Applied Econometrics*, **3**, 255–66.*

—— (1990), 'Discussion of Ghysels: on the economics and econometrics of seasonality', Mimeo, Department of Econometrics and Social Statistics, University of Manchester.

—— CHUI, A. P. L., SMITH, J. P., and BIRCHENHALL, C. R. (1988), 'Seasonality and the order of integration for consumption', *Oxford Bulletin of Economics and Statistics*, **50**, 361–77.*

PAGAN, A. (1975), 'A note on the extraction of components from time series', *Econometrica*, **43**, 163–8.

SHISKIN, J., YOUNG, A. H. and MUSGRAVE, J. C. (1967), 'The X-11 variant of the Census Method II Seasonal Adjustment Program', *Technical Paper No. 15*. Bureau of the Census, US Department of Commerce, Washington DC.

SIMS, C. A. (1974), 'Seasonality in regression', *Journal of the American Statistical Association*, **69**, 618–27.*

—— (1978), Comments on: 'Seasonality: causation, interpretation, and implications', by C. W. J. Granger, in *Seasonal Analysis of Economic Time Series*. Proceedings of the Conference on the Seasonal Analysis of Economic Time Series, Washington DC, 9–10 Sept. 1976 (A. Zellner, ed.), US Department of Commerce, Bureau of the Census, Washington DC.

THOMAS, J. J., and WALLIS, K. F. (1971), 'Seasonal variation in regression analysis', *Journal of the Royal Statistical Society Ser. A*, **134**, 67–72.

TODD, R. (1990), 'Periodic linear-quadratic methods for modeling seasonality', *Journal of Economic Dynamics and Control*, **14**, 763–95.

TUKEY, J. W. (1978), Comments on: 'Seasonality: causation, interpretation, and implications, by C. W. J. Granger, in *Seasonal Analysis of Economic Time Series*. Proceedings of the Conference on the Seasonal Analysis of Economic Time Series, Washington DC, 9–10 Sept. 1976 (A. Zellner, ed.), US Department of Commerce, Bureau of the Census, Washington DC.

WALLIS, K. F. (1974), 'Seasonal adjustment and relations between variables', *Journal of the American Statistical Association*, **69**, 18–31.*

WALLIS, K. F. (1982), 'Seasonal adjustment and revision of current data: linear filters for the X-11 method', *Journal of the Royal Statistical Society, Ser. A*, **145**, 74–85.

WALLIS, K. F. (1983), 'Models for X-11 and X-11-FORECAST procedures for preliminary and revised seasonal adjustments', in *Applied Time Series Analysis of Economic Data* (ed. A. Zellner), Washington, DC: U.S. Bureau of the Census, 3–11.

YOUNG, A. H. (1968), 'Linear approximation to the census and BLS seasonal adjustment methods', *Journal of the American Statistical Association*, **63**, 445–71.

1

The Historical Perspective

SVEND HYLLEBERG

The Historical Perspective[1]

The notion that a time series is composed of several unobserved components of different periodicities was an essential part of many of the theories put forward by seventeenth-century astronomers. It was therefore natural that the first person to explain periodicities in economic time series was the British astronomer William Herschel (1801), who tried to find a relation between sunspots and wheat prices.

The first to study seasonal patterns in economic time series was the banker James W. Gilbart (1854, 1856, 1865), who found that the demand for Bank of England notes was high in January, April, July and October, due to periodic payment of dividends, while the circulation of the country banks was high in April and low in August. Based on this evidence, Gilbart argued against any attempts by the country banks to have their issuance of notes parallel that of the Bank of England.

Charles Babbage (1856), who made contributions in the fields of mathematics, physics, meteorology, astronomy, economics, and several other areas and whose main interest was the construction of a calculating machine, found a seasonal pattern in the average daily clearings of the Clearing House during the year 1839. He made adjustment for this pattern by computing average values for the single days after removal of the days on which some special disturbing factors were at work.

William Stanley Jevons, who was a meteorologist as well as an economist, is famous for his sunspot theory, the essence of which can be found in the sentence, 'Now, if the planets govern the sun, and the sun governs the vintages and harvests, and thus the prices of food and raw materials and the money market, it follows that the configuration of the

---

[1] See Nerlove *et al.* (1979) for a more extensive exposition of the historical development of the analysis of economic time series.

Printed with permission of: *Seasonality in Regression*, 7–14. Orlando: Academic Press.

planets may prove to be the remote cause of the greatest commercial disasters' (Jevons, 1875, p. 205). However, Jevons was deeply interested in seasonal variations as well, as can be seen from his study of the money market and the policy of the Bank of England (Jevons, 1866), in which the large withdrawal of coins from the Bank of England in the month of October was explained by a chain reaction starting by the payment of wages to the outdoor workers. The workers did not use banks and the reserves of the commercial banks were consequently depleted, implying that the Bank of England was forced to act as the lender of last resort.

The attitudes of Jevons and his contemporaries are properly expressed by Jevons (1862, p. 4), 'Every kind of periodic fluctuation, whether daily, weekly, monthly, quarterly or yearly, must be detected and exhibited not only as a subject of study in itself, but because we must ascertain and eliminate such periodic variations before we can correctly exhibit those which are irregular or non-periodic, and probably of more interest and importance', and the problems of seasonality were handled either by use of a structural explanation, i.e. by referring to causal factors such as the time of the harvest, or by use of average values for the single weeks or months.

In the search for periodicities in economic time series, more or less visual methods were applied, while the work of the Dutch meteorologist Buys Ballot (1847) did not have any significant influence of the economic literature even though it provided a relatively simple tool of analysis.

The most simple part of the analysis of Buys Ballot is based on a table (the Buys Ballot table) in which the quarterly (monthly) data are arranged in four (12) columns, one for each quarter (month), and in as many rows as there are years in the sample. Column averages or sums are calculated to provide a picture of the seasonal pattern. Some of the ingredients of the analysis of Buys Ballot can be illustrated by the following example.

Consider a series of length 60 with period $n = 4$ arranged in a table with $c = 4$ columns:

	1	2	3	4
	1	2	3	4
	1	2	3	4
	1	2	3	4
	1	2	3	4
	⋮	⋮	⋮	⋮
Sum	15	30	45	60

If the series is arranged in a table with only three columns, we get

1	2	3
4	1	2
3	4	1
2	3	4
1	2	3
4	1	2
3	4	1
2	3	4
⋮	⋮	⋮

Sum	50	50	50

and if the series is arranged in a table with five columns, we get

1	2	3	4	1
2	3	4	1	2
3	4	1	2	3
4	1	2	3	4
1	2	3	4	1
2	3	4	1	2
3	4	1	2	3
4	1	2	3	4
⋮	⋮	⋮	⋮	⋮

Sum	30	30	30	30	30

In a case with three columns corresponding to a guess of too small a period, the figures are displaced to the right, while the figures are displaced to the left if the number of columns chosed is greater than the actual period. Notice that the column sums for, say, the first three rows are the same as the column sums of the rows five (equal $1 + 4$) to seven (equal $3 + 4$) in all three tables. This, in fact, is an illustration of one of the theories of Buys Ballot (1847). [See Nerlove *et al.* (1979) for an excellent exposition of the theorems of Buys Ballot.] In Appendix D, use will be made of the Buys Ballot table as a descriptive measure.

With the growth and systematization of the gathering and publication of economic statistical information at the beginning of this century a lot of work was put into the construction of methods for deseasonalizing economic time series.

The time-series models applied most frequently in those studies were either the additive model in which the series X_t is seen as a sum of four unobservable components called the trend T_t, the cycle C_t, the seasonal S_t, and the irregular component I_t, i.e.

$$X_t = T_t + C_t + S_t + I_t \tag{1.1}$$

or the multiplicative model

$$X_t = T_t \cdot C_t \cdot S_t \cdot I_t \cdot \qquad\qquad (1.2)$$

In the textbook by Mills (1924, p. 357) the trend is defined to be the smoothed, regular, long-term movement of a statistical series, while the seasonal variations are fluctuations that are definitely periodic in character with a period of one year, i.e. 12 months or 4 quarters. The cyclical variations are 'less markedly periodic, but nevertheless characterized by a considerable degree of regularity', while the remaining part constitutes the irregular component.

Similar definitions are given by Westergaard and Lomholt (1925) and by Persons (1919), who was one of the first to state explicitly some definitions of the unobserved components. Most of the literature on seasonality in the 1920s and 1930s accepts this model without much discussion, and the main attention is directed towards the more technical problems of the methods of seasonal adjustment. In order to give the main ingredients of the methods applied in this period, two suggestions [one by Persons (1919) and one by the Federal Reserve Board (1922)] will be presented.

Persons suggested a method based on link relatives, i.e. the relations among the observations computed for successive months (or quarters) in a number of years. The medians for each month were computed, and a chain index was found from these monthly average values. The January index was arbitrarily fixed at one, and the index for the following month was computed as the January index multiplied by the average value for February and so on. A new index for January was computed by multiplying the December index by the average value for the month of January. In case of a positive trend this new index for January will be greater than one, i.e. greater than the 'old' index value. To correct for such trends (or cycles) the difference between the two January indices was distributed over the 12 indices according to an exponential trend. Finally, the corrected seasonal indices were adjusted to sum to one and divided into the original data to give the seasonally adjusted figures.

The method applied by the Federal Reserve Board (1922) was based on the computation of a 12-month centered moving average. The ratios between the actual values and the moving-average values were then used as the first estimates of the unobserved seasonal values. In order to eliminate the irregular component, the medians (or the arithmetic averages) of the seasonal values for each month were computed and adjusted to sum to one. Finally, the seasonally adjusted figures were found by dividing the actual values by the seasonal indices.

Methods analogous to the link relative method applied by Persons (1919) and the ratio-to-moving-average methods applied by the Federal Reserve Board (1922) can be constructed in cases in which the additive model is thought to be the appropriate one.[2] The moving-average method applied in case of an additive model is similar to that applied in the multiplicative case with the exception that differences are used instead of ratios and the seasonal indices are adjusted to sum to zero rather than to one.

Whereas the methods applied in the case of an additive model assume that the seasonal movement is nonvarying over the years, the multiplicative model assumes that the ratio of the seasonal component to the trend/cycle component is nonvarying over the years. However, both assumptions seem to be quite inappropriate in many cases.

Such a critique was also launched in several articles in the 1920s, and the discussion and the suggested improvements were surveyed in detail by Mendershausen (1937a), who classified the methods for dealing with a seasonal movement as either mechanical methods or causal methods. The causal methods were preferred by Mendershausen (1937a, p. 237) because they have greater values from a scientific point of view, while the mechanical methods were considered a necessary step in the development towards the more satisfactory methods. Mendershausen's main criticism of the mechanical methods was that the nonvariation assumptions on which they heavily rely are seldom, if ever, fulfilled in practical situations. In Fig. 1.1 the survey by Mendershausen is presented in a schematic way, but the reader is referred to the article itself for a more detailed description.

Another line of criticism raised especially against the application of moving-average filters was based on the discovery of the so-called Slutzky–Yule effect by Slutzky (1927) and Yule (1927), who showed that it is possible to insert a spurious cycle into a white-noise series by using an adjustment procedure such as a moving-average filter. Their findings were of major concern in the 1920s and 1930s but fortunately it can be shown that the effect of the adjustments can be evaluated, at least, for simple moving-average filters, whereby misinterpretations due to the generated periodicity can be precluded [see Granger and Newbold (1977)].

Since the Second World War the development in, and application of, seasonal adjustments of economic time series have been heavily dependent on the introduction and development of the electronic computer. The most popular methods have been developed at the Bureau of the

---

[2] Of course, the multiplicative model can be transformed into an additive model by a logarithmic transformation. However, a seasonal adjustment based on a computation of a centered-moving average of the logarithm of the series followed by a computation of 12 seasonal indices, and an adjustment made by subtracting the seasonal indices from the logarithms of the series, is not the same method as the ratio to moving-average method suggested by the Federal Reserve Board. The use of logarithms is comparable to a method applying geometric-moving averages.

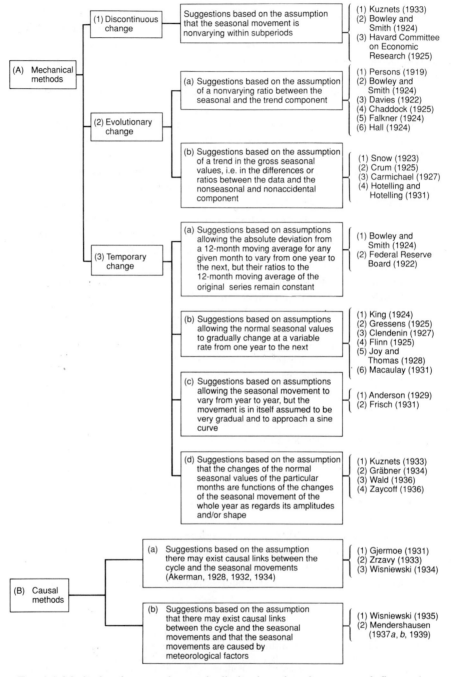

FIG. 1.1 Methods of computing and eliminating changing seasonal fluctuation surveyed by Mendershausen (1937a).

Census, US Department of Commerce, by Julius Shiskin and his associates. The latest offspring of those methods is the X-11 method [see Shiskin *et al.* (1967)]. Besides the Census methods several others are currently applied, and even more have been dropped and replaced by, for instance, the X-11 method.

The common features of most of the work on seasonal adjustment mentioned and of all the methods applied by the data-'producing' agencies are that they consider the series one by one without any concern for the interrelationships among series, and furthermore they do so in a very mechanical way. The main argument in favor of such procedures is that the adjusted data are going to be used either to appraise current economic conditions or to study historical business cycles. [See Nerlove *et al.* (1979).] In both cases the methods applied are like those used at the National Bureau of Economics Research (NBER) by people such as Burns and Mitchell (1946) and Moore (1961), which are methods that do not rely on econometric models and methods but on the study of business-cycle indicators and so on. For a good survey of recent developments, see Pierce (1980).

Due partly to the increased popularity of econometric methods and partly to the growth in the number of daily, weekly, monthly, and quarterly data published, there has been a growing interest in the problems of seasonality in regression [see, for instance, Lovell (1963, 1966), Jorgensen (1964, 1967), Kukkonen (1968), Thomas and Wallis (1971), Engle (1974, 1980), Sims (1974), Wallis (1974, 1977, 1978), Hylleberg (1977, 1979), Gersovitz and MacKinnon (1978), Bunzel and Hylleberg (1982), and Nerlove *et al.* (1979)].

The view taken in most of these studies is that seasonality in one economic variable cannot be considered an isolated phenomenon, but may be related to the seasonality in other economic variables with which that variable interacts, and furthermore that the seasonal components themselves may contain information about the relationships among series.

In general, the results of the studies on the application of the officially seasonally adjusted figures in econometric analysis are that they increase the danger of obtaining misspecified models with spurious dynamic relationships and poor forecast performance. None the less, most quarterly macroeconometric models applied actually use the deseasonalized data that are produced at the official agencies.

In this study it will be argued that methods that treat seasonality as an integrated part of the structural econometric modeling should be preferred. However, less ambitious methods based on the application of time-varying parameter models or the methods of Box and Jenkins (1970) must be seen as an important step in the right direction, and even the application of relatively simple and transparent seasonal adjustment methods allowing tests of hypothesis about the constancy of the structural coefficients between the seasonal and the nonseasonal part of the model are better than the use of the deseasonalized data available in statistical publications.

References

(References marked with a * are included in this volume)

ANDERSON, O. (1929), 'Die Korrelationsrechnung in der Konjunkturforschung', *Veröffentl. Frankf. Ges. Konjunkturforsch*, **4**.

BABBAGE, C. (1856), 'Analysis of the statistics of the clearing house during the year 1990', *Statistical Journal*, **19**.

BOX, G. E. P., and JENKINS, G. M. (1970), *Time Series Analysis: Forecasting and Control*. San Francisco, California: Holden-Day.

BOWLEY, A. L., and SMITH, K. C. (1924), 'Seasonal variations in finance, prices, and industry', *London Cambridge Econ. Serv., Spec. Memo*, **7**, 15.

BUNZEL, H., and HYLLEBERG, S. (1982), 'Seasonality in dynamic regression models. A comparative study of finite sample properties of various regression estimators including band spectrum regression', *Journal of Econometrics*, **19**, 345–66.

BURNS, A. F., and MITCHELL, W. C. (1946), 'Measuring business cycles'. New York: National Bureau of Economic Research.

BUYS BALLOT, C. H. D. (1847), 'Les Changements Périodiques de Température'. Utrecht: Kemink et Fils.

CARMICHAEL, F. L. (1927), 'Method of computing seasonal indexes, constant and progressive', *Journal of the American Statistical Association*, **22**, 339–54.

CHADDOCK, R. E. (1925), *Principles and Methods of Statistics*. Birton: Houghton-Mifflin.

CLENDENIN, J. C. (1927), 'Measurement of variations in seasonal distribution', *Journal of the American Statistical Association*, **22**, 213.

CRUM, W. L. (1925), 'Progressive variation in seasonality', *Journal of the American Statistical Association*, **20**, 48–64.

DAVIES, G. R. (1922), *Introduction to Economic Statistics*. New York: Century.

ENGLE, R. F. (1974), 'Band spectrum regression', *International Economic Review*, **15** 1–11.

—— (1980), 'Exact maximum likelihood methods for dynamic regressions and band spectrum regression', *International Economic Review*, **21**, 391–407.

FALKNER, H. D. (1924), 'On the measurement of seasonal variations', *Journal of the American Statistical Association*, **19**, 167–79.

FEDERAL RESERVE BOARD (1922), *Federal Reserve Bulletin*, 1415–18.

FLINN, H. M. (1925), 'Meeting on the measurement of seasonal variation of May 22, 1925', *Journal of the American Statistical Association*, **20**, 431.

FRISCH, R. (1931), 'A method of decomposing an empirical series into its cyclical and progressive components', *Journal of the American Statistical Association*, **26**, 73–8.

GERSOVITZ, M., and MACKINNON, J. G. (1978), 'Seasonality in regression: an application of smoothness priors 2', *Journal of the American Statistical Association*, **73**, 264–73.

GILBART, J. W. (1854), 'The law of the currency as exemplified in the circulation of country bank notes in England since the passing of the act of 1844', *Statistical Journal*, **17**.

GILBART, J. W. (1856), 'The laws of currency in Scotland', *Statistical Journal*, **19**.

—— (1865), *Logic for the Million, a Familiar Exposition of the Art of Reasoning*. London: Bell and Daldy.

GJERMOE, E. (1936), 'The seasonal movements of employment in their relation to business cycle', *Nord. Statist. J.* **3**, 532.

GRANGER, C. W. J., and NEWBOLD, P. (1977), *Forecasting Economic Time Series*. New York: Academic Press.

GRESSENS, O. (1925), 'On the measurement of seasonal variations', *Journal of the American Statistical Association*, **20**, 203–10.

GRÄBNER, G. (1934), 'Der "bewegliche" Saisonindex', *Algemein. Staatliches Arch.* **24**, 143.

HALL, L. W. (1924), 'Seasonal variation as a relative secular trend', *Journal of the American Statistical Association*, **19**, 156–66.

HARVARD COMMITTEE ON ECONOMIC RESEARCH (1925), *Review of Economic Statistics*, **7**, 44–7.

HERSCHEL, W. (1801), 'Observations tending to investigate the nature of the sun in order to find the causes or symptoms of its variable emission of light and heat with remarks on the use that may possibly be drawn from solar observation', *Philos. Trans.* **91**, part 2.

HOTELLING, H., and HOTELLING, F. (1931), 'Causes of birth rate fluctuations', *Journal of the American Statistical Association*, **26**, 135.

HYLLEBERG, S. (1977), 'A comparative study of finite sample properties of band spectrum regression estimators', *Journal of Econometrics*, **5**, 167–82.

—— (1979), 'Saesonvariation i regressionsdata', in *Anvendt Økonometri* (B. S. Jensen and A. Høskuldsson, eds.), 336–69. Copenhagen: Nyt Nordisk Forlag.

JEVONS, W. S. (1862), 'On the study of periodic commercial fluctuations', in *Investigations in Currency and Finance*, 2–11. London 1884: MacMillan.

—— (1866), 'On the frequent autumnal pressure in the money market, and the action of the Bank of England', in *Investigations in Currency and Finance*, 160–93. London, 1884: MacMillan.

—— (1875), 'The solar period and the price of corn', in *Investigations in Currency and Finance*, 194–205. London, 1884: MacMillan.

JORGENSON, D. W. (1964), 'Minimum variance linear unbiased seasonal adjustment of economic time series', *Journal of the American Statistical Association*, **59**, 681–724.

—— (1967), 'Seasonal adjustment of data for econometric analysis', *Journal of the American Statistical Association*, **62**, 137–40.

JOY, A., and THOMAS, W. (1928), 'The use of moving averages in the measurement of seasonal variations', *Journal of the American Statistical Association*, **23**, 241–52.

KING, W. I. (1924), 'An improved method for measuring the seasonal factor', *Journal of the American Statistical Association*, **19**, 301–13.

KUKKONEN, P. (1968), 'Analysis of seasonal and other short-term variations with applications to Finnish economic time series', Helsinki: Bank of Finland, Institute for Economic Research Publications Series B(28).

KUZNETS, S. (1933), *Seasonal variations in industry and trade*. New York: National Bureau of Economic Research.

LOVELL, M. C. (1963), 'Seasonal adjustment of economic time series', *Journal of the American Statistical Association*, **58**, 993–1010.

—— (1966), 'Alternative axiomatizations of seasonal adjustment', *Journal of the American Statistical Association*, **61**, 800–2.

MACAULAY, F. R. (1931), *The Smoothing of Time Series*. National Bureau of Economic Research, New York.

MENDERSHAUSEN, H. (1937*a*), 'Annual survey of statistical technique: Methods of computing and eliminating changing seasonal fluctuations', *Econometrica*, **5**, 234–62.

—— (1937*b*), *Les Variations du Mouvement Saisonnier dans l'Industrie de la Construction*. Geneve: George et Cie.

—— (1939), 'Eliminating changing seasonals by multiple regression analysis', *Review of Economic Statistics*, **21**, 171–7.

MILLS, F. C. (1924), Statistical methods, London: Pitman.

MOORE, G. H. (ed.) (1961), *Business Cycle Indicators*. New York: National Bureau of Economic Research.

NERLOVE, M., GRETHER, D. M., and CARVALHO, J. L. (1979), *Analysis of Economic Time Series, A Synthesis*. New York: Academic Press.

PERSONS, W. M. (1919), 'Indices of business conditions', *Review of Economic Statistics*, **1**, 5–107.

PIERCE, D. A. (1980), 'A survey of recent developments in seasonal adjustment', *American Statistician*, **34**, 125–34.

SHISKIN, J., YOUNG, A. H., and MUSGRAVE, J. C. (1967), 'The X-11 variant of the census method II seasonal adjustment program'. Washington DC: Technical Paper no. 15. Bureau of the Census, US Department of Commerce.

SIMS, C. A. (1974), 'Seasonality in regression', *Journal of the American Statistical Association*, **69**, 618–27.*

SLUTZKY, E. F. (1927), 'The summation of random causes as the source of cyclical processes', in 'Problems of Economic Conditions' by the Conjuncture Institute Moscow 3 (in Russian); *Econometrica*, **5**, 105–46 (1937).

SNOW, E. C. (1923), 'Trade forecasting and prices', *Journal of the Royal Statistical Society*, **86**, 334.

THOMAS, J. J., and WALLIS, K. F. (1971), 'Seasonal variation in regression analysis', *Journal of the Royal Statistical Society Series A*, **134**, 67–72.

WALD, A. (1936), *Berechnung und Ausschaltung von Saisonschwankungen*, *Beiträge zur Konjunkturforschung 9, Wien*. Vienna: Julius Springer.

WALLIS, K. F. (1974), 'Seasonal adjustment and relations between variables', *Journal of the American Statistical Association*, **69**, 18–31.*

—— (1977), 'Multiple time series analysis and the final form of econometric models', *Econometrica*, **45**, 1481–97.

—— (1978), 'Seasonal adjustment and multiple time series analysis', in *Seasonal Analysis of Economic Time Series*. Proceedings of the Conference on the Seasonal Analysis of Economic Time Series, Washington DC, 9–10 Sept. 1976

(A. Zellner, ed.). Washington DC: U.S. Department of Commerce, Bureau of the Census.

WESTERGAARD, H., and LOMHOLT, E. (1925), 'Periodiske Bevaegelser i det økonomiske Liv', *Nationaløkonomisk Tidsskrift,* **63**, 14–39.

WISNIEWSKI, J., 1934. 'Interdependence of cyclical and seasonal variation', *Econometrica,* **2**, 176–81.

—— (1935), 'Les fluctuations saisonnières dans l'industrie du batement' (in Polish with French résumé), *Kwart. Statyst.,* **2**, 239.

YULE, G. U. (1927), 'On a method of investigating periodicities in disturbed series with special reference to Wolfer's sunspot number', *Philos. Trans. Roy. Soc.* **226**, 267–98.

ZAYCOFF, R. (1936), 'Über die Zerlegung statistischer Zeitreihen in drei Komponenten'. Statistical Institute for Economic Research, State University of Sofia.

ZRZAVY, F. I. (1933), 'Ausschaltung von Saisonschwankungen mittels Lag-Correlation', *Mon. Österreichischen Instit. Konjunkturforsch.,* Beilage nr. 2 Vienna.

ÅKERMAN, J. (1928), Om det ekonomiska livels Rytmik, Nordiska Bokhandelm, Stockholm.

—— (1932), Economic Progress and Economic Crisis, MacMillan, London.

—— (1934), Konjunkturtcomtiska Problem, Fahlbeckska Stifhela, Malmö.

2

Seasonal Adjustment and Relations between Variables

KENNETH F. WALLIS*

This article studies the effect of official seasonal adjustment procedures on the relations between variables. By considering time-invariant linear filters, and in particular a linear approximation to the Census Method II adjustment program, the effect of adjusting one or both of the variables in a distributed lag relation is examined, and the distortions which can arise are described. Applying the actual (nonlinear) adjustment procedure to artificial data indicates that at least for the particular x-series used, the results of the linear filter analysis provide a good guide to the behaviour of estimates obtained from data adjusted by the official method.

1.   Introduction

Discussion of seasonal adjustment procedures has generally proceeded in terms of their effect on a single economic time series. Official statisticians (Brown, *et al.* (1971), Burman (1965, 1966), Shiskin *et al.* (1967), US Bureau of Labor Statistics (1966)) have been concerned with designing seasonal adjustment procedures which satisfy various criteria, and they, together with others (Godfrey and Karreman (1967), Nerlove (1964, 1965), Rosenblatt (1963, 1968)), have evaluated by various means the extent to which these and other criteria are met. Underlying much of this work is the 'classical' additive or multiplicative components model, where the time series is taken to comprise trend-cycle, seasonal, and irregular components. Seasonality is seldom defined rigorously; one

* Kenneth F. Wallis is with the London School of Economics, Houghton Street, London WC2A 2AE, England. A preliminary version of this article was presented at the European meeting of the Econometric Society, Budapest, September 1972. The author wishes to thank David Elliot for computational assistance, the Central Statistical Office for making their program available, and an anonymous referee, J. P. Burman, E. J. Hannan, A. Lancaster, and C. A. Sims for helpful comments. Related, contemporaneous, but independent work by Sims is described in Sims (1974).

Printed with permission of: *Journal of the American Statistical Association*, **69**, 18–31.

of the more explicit statements is that of Nerlove (1964), who defines
seasonality as 'that characteristic of a time series that gives rise to
spectral peaks at seasonal frequencies'. In the time domain, following
Thomas and Wallis (1971), 'by seasonal variation we understand those
systematic though not necessarily regular intra-year movements in economic time series which are often caused by non-economic phenomena,
such as climatic changes and the regular timing of religious festivals'.
Broadly speaking, the objective of seasonal adjustment is to remove the
seasonal component without distorting the remainder, which perhaps
provides an ex-post definition of the seasonal component as the difference between the original and adjusted series. The predominant uses are
those of short-term forecasting and policy analysis, where the implicit
view seems to be that the seasonal component is of little interest, being
not only exogenous to the economic system but also uncontrollable, yet
predictable. Thus, most macroeconomic aggregates are appraised in
their adjusted forms. However, there are exceptions to this, such as
total unemployment, which is taken to be politically sensitive irrespective of season, and at a less aggregated level, various stock-flow
relationships, where the existence of a seasonal peak in demand is
explicitly acknowledged (as with banks' reserve ratios and retailers'
inventories).

In general, little attention has been paid to the effect that seasonal
adjustment of separate time series has on the relations between them,
although changes in dynamic specification when moving between adjusted and un-adjusted data have been observed.[1] Perhaps this neglect
results from the view that the seasonal component of a given series is
noise, and even if correlated with the seasonal component of another
series, it is still noise. Also, the nonlinear nature of the official
adjustment procedures, largely based on ratio-to-moving-average
methods, makes theoretical investigation difficult, although at the simplest level it is clear that they preserve neither sums nor ratios, so that
an adjusted aggregate is not generally equal to the total of the adjusted
components, and an adjusted unemployment rate is not generally equal
to the ratio of the adjusted number unemployed to the adjusted labor
force. Regression methods of seasonal adjustment are easier to investigate, and Lovell (1963) has developed a rationale for their use; a number

[1] For example, in the London Business School quarterly model of the UK economy, on
switching from unadjusted to adjusted data, the consumption function for nondurables
moved from an equation containing current and one- and two-quarter lagged values of
income, estimated in four-quarter differences, to a more conventional form with current
income and the one-quarter lagged dependent variable, the implied adjustment of
consumption to income becoming much slower. At the same time the consumption
function for durable goods became a static equation, the stock of durable goods dropping
out, being highly collinear with income in the adjusted data. (Source: various discussion
papers of the LBS Econometric Forecasting Unit.)

of their implications for the regression analysis of the relations between variables in adjusted or original form are described by Thomas and Wallis (1971). However, such techniques have found little use, 'since no regression models have yet been demonstrated empirically to provide sufficiently accurate estimates of the trend-cycle and the seasonal, particularly in the current period' (Shiskin *et al.* (1967)).

This article studies the effect of official seasonal adjustment procedures on the relations between series. For the present purposes, 'official' means the US Bureau of the Census Method II, Variant X-11 (Shiskin *et al.* (1967)), as modified by the British Central Statistical Office. The view taken is that seasonality in one economic variable is not necessarily an isolated phenomenon, but may be related to the seasonality in other economic variables with which that variable interacts. Thus the seasonal components themselves may contain information about the relationships between series. Various possibilities are considered, and the effects of separate seasonal adjustments on the underlying relationship between two series and on the statistical estimation procedures employed to detect that relationship are investigated. The investigation proceeds by means of a linear filter approximation to the official procedure in Section 2, and by the analysis of artificial data in Section 3, where the actual official method is applied. Some concluding remarks are presented in Section 4.

2.   Linear Filters and Relations between Variables

2.1   *An approximation to the official adjustment procedure*

A linear filter approximation to the official adjustment procedure is first presented, and then the characteristics of the actual procedure which are neglected in the approximation are described. Given an original series $\{x_t\}$, the adjusted series is obtained as

$$x_t^a = \sum_{-m}^{m} a_j x_{t-j} \quad (a_j = a_{-j}) \tag{2.1}$$

and the linear filter or adjustment coefficients $\{a_j\}$ summarize the following steps (a monthly series is assumed, and 'moving average' is abbreviated m.a.):

a. Compute the differences between the original series and a centered 12-term m.a. (a 2×12 m.a., that is, a 2-term average of a 12-term average), as a first estimate of the seasonal and irregular components.

b. Apply a weighted 5-term m.a. to each month separately (a 3×3 m.a.), to obtain as estimate of the seasonal component.

   c. Adjust these seasonal components to sum to zero (approximately) over any 12-month period by subtracting a centered 12-term m.a. from them.

   d. Subtract the adjusted seasonal component from the original series, to give a preliminary seasonally adjusted series.

   e. Apply a 9-, 13- or 23-term Henderson m.a. to the seasonally adjusted values, and subtract the resulting trend-cycle series from the original series to give a second estimate of the seasonal and irregular components.

   f. Apply a weighted 7-term m.a. (a 3×5 m.a.) to each month separately, to obtain a second estimate of the seasonal component.

   g. Repeat step (c).

   h. Subtract these final estimates of the seasonal component from the original series, giving the seasonally adjusted series.

The net effect of these eight steps is represented as the $2m + 1$ term m.a. given in (2.1), where the 'half-length' m is the sum of the half-lengths of the component m.a.'s, namely, 82, 84, or 89, depending on the choice made at (e). In actual practice this choice depends on the relative contributions of the trend-cycle and irregular components to the variability of the preliminary seasonally adjusted series obtained at (d)—the greater the irregular contribution, the longer the moving average used. With quarterly data this choice is not available, and step (e) comprises a 5-term Henderson m.a.; otherwise, replacing centered 12-month m.a.'s by centered 4-quarter m.a.'s where appropriate gives the linear filter approximation for the adjustment of quarterly data ($m = 28$). The coefficients for the monthly ($m = 84$) and quarterly adjustment filters are shown in Figure A.[2] In both illustrations a seasonally adjusted observation is obtained as a moving average of original observations up to seven years before and after, although the weights attached to the more distant observations are very small.

   There are four important features of the official adjustment procedure which are not captured in this representation.

1. *Multiplicative models* are often employed in place of the additive model implicit above. Thus, seasonal components are estimated as average ratios to, rather than average differences from, the trend-cycle, and the result is a set of seasonal adjustment factors which average 100.0 percent over a year.

2. *Graduation of extreme values* is undertaken in order to improve the estimation of seasonal and trend-cycle components by preventing the moving averages from responding 'too much' to a single outlier. Each value of a preliminary estimated irregular component is compared to the standard deviation, σ, computed over a moving 5-year period. Values between $1\frac{1}{2}\sigma$ and $2\frac{1}{2}\sigma$ distant from 0.0 (100.0 for multiplicative models) are weighted, decreasing linearly from full weight at $1\frac{1}{2}\sigma$ to zero weight at $2\frac{1}{2}\sigma$, and values outside $(-2\frac{1}{2}\sigma, +2\frac{1}{2}\sigma)$ are discarded as extreme. The original series is then modified by adding this graduated irregular component back to the other two

---

[2] These coefficients are analogous to the weights for seasonal factor, trend-cycle, and irregular estimates in the present method and the BLS method presented by Young (1968).

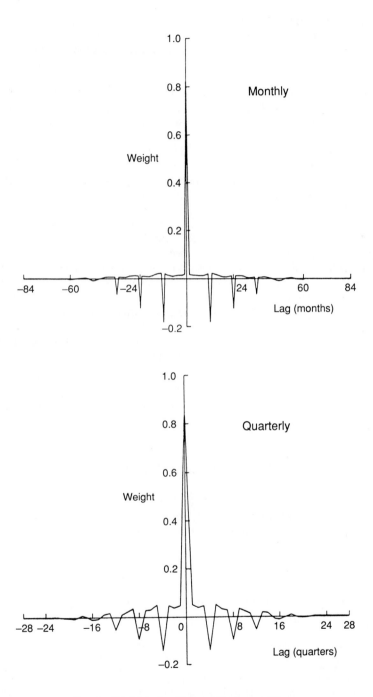

FIG. 1. Weights for linear adjustment filters

components, and trend-cycle and seasonal components are re-estimated. The new irregular component is studied for extreme values once again, and after this second modification of the original series, final estimates of the trend-cycle and seasonal are developed. Thus steps (a)–(h) or their multiplicative equivalents are followed three times, each time beginning with a slightly different input series; the choice of $1\frac{1}{2}$ and $2\frac{1}{2}$ as σ limits is in practice optional, and if these limits were set sufficiently wide, no irregular component values would be considered extreme, and identical calculations would result at each of the three iterations.

3. *Calendar-year totals* of the adjusted series are constrained to equal the calendar-year totals of the original series by making a further adjustment to the output from step (h). This could be done by simply adding one-twelfth of the discrepancy to each month's figure, but the actual corrections are smoothed by a piecewise cubic to avoid discontinuities at year-ends.

4. *End-corrections* are necessary, since seven years of data on either side of an observation to be adjusted are never available; hence, asymmetrical 'equivalent' moving averages are constructed. This general heading covers the important problem of the adjustment of current observations, and the possible need to revise estimated or extrapolated seasonal factors as subsequent observations become available. That problem is not considered in this article, where the focus of interest is the econometric analysis of historical time series. Nevertheless, in Section 3 it is assumed that a limited series of original observations is available over, say, 15 years, and a corresponding adjusted series is required over the whole period.

These four features will be of no further concern in Section 2 of this paper, but are described here to emphasize those elements of the official procedure to be used in Section 3 that the linear filter approximation does not capture.[3]

2.2 *Filtering a single time series*

The properties of the linear filter (2.1) can be described in a number of ways, and it is convenient to introduce some further time series concepts and notation. The generating function or z-transform of a sequence $\{a_j\}$ is defined as

$$A(z) = \sum a_j z^j.$$

The backward shift or lag operator L is defined by $L^j x_t = x_{t-j}$, hence (2.1) may be written

---

[3] 'Trading-day' corrections also feature in practical seasonal adjustment programs, variations in the number of working days per month having an impact on certain 'flow' variables, and changes in the day of the week on which accounts are closed being relevant for certain 'stock' variables. In the Census Bureau method, the necessary correction can be either imposed *a priori* or estimated by regression; for the present purposes it is assumed that any required corrections have been made.

$$x_t^a = A(L)x_t.$$

The effect of the filter on particular frequencies ω of the input series is given by the frequency response function

$$A(\omega) = \sum a_j e^{-i\omega j} = |A(\omega)|e^{i\theta(\omega)}.$$

$|A(\omega)|$ represents the gain of the filter and $\theta(\omega)$ the phase shift; the latter is zero for the symmetric moving averages considered here, as $A(\omega)$ is real:

$$A(\omega) = a_0 + 2\sum_{j=1}^{m} a_j \cos \omega j.$$

The autocovariances of a zero-mean stationary time series are given by

$$\gamma_k = E(x_t x_{t-k}), \quad \gamma_k = \gamma_{-k},$$

with generating function

$$\Gamma(z) = \sum \gamma_k z^k.$$

The autocorrelation coefficients γ_k/γ_0, $k = 0,1,\ldots$ give the correlogram of the series. The autocovariance generating function of a filtered series is obtained from that of the input series and the coefficients of the filter as

$$\Gamma(z)^a = A(z)\Gamma(z)A(z^{-1}). \tag{2.2}$$

The spectral density function is given by

$$f(\omega) = \frac{1}{2\pi} \sum \gamma_k e^{-ik\omega} = \frac{1}{2\pi} \Gamma(e^{-i\omega}),$$

thus the spectra of the original and filtered series are related by

$$f^a(\omega) = |A(\omega)|^2 f(\omega).$$

The squared gain $|A(\omega)|^2$, or transfer function of the filter, represents the extent to which the contribution of the component of frequency ω to the total variance of the series is modified by the action of the filter, and the transfer function of the monthly filter is plotted in Figure 2.[4] It is seen that the filter completely removes the seasonal frequencies $\pi k/6$, $k = 1, \ldots, 6$, all of them being treated equally. Of course if a particular seasonal pattern can be adequately represented by sine and cosine waves at fewer than six seasonal frequencies,[5] then the filter is in effect overadjusting by unnecessarily modifying certain frequencies.

---

[4] Similar functions are calculated for two other seasonal adjustment procedures by Hext (1964).

[5] For an example, see Brown et al. (1971).

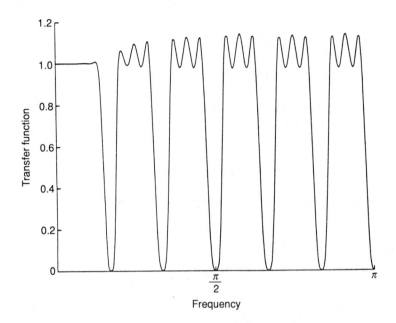

FIG. 2. Transfer function of monthly filter

In the time domain the effect of the quarterly version of the filter is illustrated in Figure 3, which compares the correlograms of original and filtered series, computed as in (2.2), for three simple examples. The first is a 'white noise' or independent input series, with $\gamma_k = 0$ for $k \neq 0$; the resulting 'adjusted' series has small positive autocorrelation coefficients at lags of 1–3, 5–7, ... quarters, and somewhat larger negative correlations between observations 4, 8, ... quarters apart. The second illustration uses as input series the familiar first order autoregression or AR(1) process, with autocorrelation coefficients $\rho^{|k|}$, and the correlograms when $\rho = 0.7$ are shown in the central panel of Figure 3. The moving average increases the autocorrelations overall, inducing little seasonal effect. As ρ decreases from this value, the picture moves towards that of the first illustration, thus when $\rho = 0.5$, the autocorrelations at multiples of 4 lags are negative, though small. The final example takes the simple AR(4) process

$$x_t = \rho x_{t-4} + \epsilon_t,$$

for which the autocorrelation coefficient is zero unless k is an integer multiple of 4, in which case it is $\rho^{k/4}$. It can be seen from the final panel of Figure 3 (where $\rho = 0.9$) that the autocorrelation at lags 4, 8, ... is

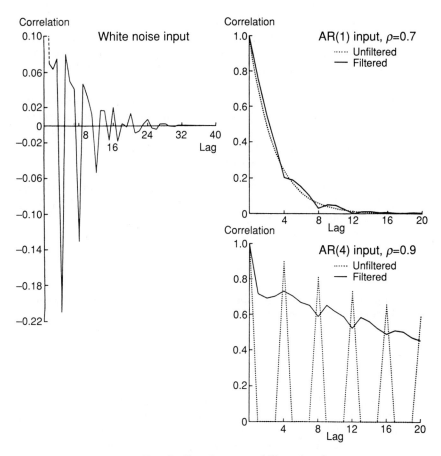

FIG. 3. Correlograms of filtered series

reduced, but substantial autocorrelation at all other lags is introduced by the moving average procedure. The first-order autocorrelation coefficient is almost equal to the fourth; indeed, for $\rho \leq 0.65$, the largest coefficient is the first, which might result in a filtered fourth-order scheme being identified as a first-order scheme.

The correlogram values at $k = 1$ are the (asymptotic) expected values of least squares coefficients when fitting a first-order autoregressive model. Thus if the correct model, as used in the second illustration, is

$$x_t = \rho x_{t-1} + \epsilon_t,$$

then the filtered data give

$$x_t^a = \rho x_{t-1}^a + \epsilon_t^a,$$

and the least squares coefficient $\sum x_t^a x_{t-1}^a / \sum x_{t-1}^{a2}$ provides an asymptotically biased estimate of ρ, for although x_{t-1} and ϵ_t are independent, the same is not true for the moving averages x_{t-1}^a and ϵ_t^a. The extent of the asymptotic bias is given by the difference between the two correlogram values at $k = 1$, and is reported for a range of values of ρ and both monthly and quarterly versions in Table 1. This indicates that the parameter ρ will always tend to be overestimated (asymptotically). However, the opposite is true when the simple fourth-order autoregression is considered, as suggested by the comparison at $k = 4$ in the final panel of Figure 3; the parameter estimate calculated from filtered data is downward biased, and this applies for all values of ρ.

The same effects as those described in the preceding paragraphs are obtained with the monthly filter, provided that 4 is replaced by 12 at appropriate points in the discussion.

2.3   Relations between variables

The relation between two variables is represented by the distributed lag model, familiar in econometrics, of the general form

$$y_t = \sum_0^{\infty} \beta_j x_{t-j} + u_t. \tag{2.3}$$

It is assumed that x_t and u_s are independent for all t and s, and the relationship between y and x is generally represented as a *one-sided* time invariant filter, as indicated. The sequence of distributed lag coefficients $\{\beta_j\}$ is required to converge to zero at some suitable rate for theoretical reasons, and further restrictions are often imposed for practical estimation purposes, such as requiring the coefficients to be functions of a small number of parameters. If the coefficients are all positive, an 'average lag' is given by $\sum j\beta_j / \sum \beta_j$, and estimates of this quantity are often reported in empirical work.

TABLE 1.   Asymptotic bias in estimates of first order autoregression from filtered data

Filter	ρ									
	$-.9$	$-.7$	$-.5$	$-.3$	$-.1$	$.1$	$.3$	$.5$	$.7$	$.9$
Monthly										
(m = 84)	.033	.011	.013	.018	.024	.029	.033	.037	.036	.019
Quarterly	.184	.110	.075	.062	.066	.076	.080	.070	.047	.017

Following previous notational conventions, the model can be written

$$y_t = \sum \beta_j L^j x_t + u_t = B(L)x_t + u_t$$

and the distributed lag frequency response function is

$$B(\omega) = \sum \beta_j e^{-ij\omega}.$$

Introducing the cross-covariance function

$$\gamma_{yx}(k) = E(y_t x_{t-k}) \quad \text{(independent of } t\text{)}$$

and the spectral density functions

$$f_{yx}(\omega) = \frac{1}{2\pi}\sum \gamma_{yx}(k)e^{-ik\omega}, \quad f_{xx}(\omega) = \frac{1}{2\pi}\sum \gamma_{xx}(k)e^{-ik\omega},$$

then

$$f_{yx}(\omega) = B(\omega)f_{xx}(\omega).$$

Assuming now that the two series are adjusted or filtered, possibly using different filters

$$y_t^a = A_y(L)y_t, \quad x_t^a = A_x(L)x_t,$$

then the relation between the adjusted variables is

$$y_t^a = \frac{A_y(L)B(L)}{A_x(L)}x_t^a + A_y(L)u_t,$$

i.e.

$$y_t^a = \sum \beta_j^* x_{t-j}^a + u_t^a,$$

where

$$B^*(L) = \frac{A_y(L)B(L)}{A_x(L)}. \tag{2.4}$$

Although $B(L)$ is one-sided, $B^*(L)$ is in general doubly infinite. The spectral functions for filtered data are

$$f_{yx}^a(\omega) = A_y(\omega)\overline{A_x(\omega)}f_{yx}(\omega), \quad f_{xx}^a(\omega) = |A_x(\omega)|^2 f_{xx}(\omega),$$

and the frequency domain expression corresponding to (2.4) is

$$B^*(\omega) = \frac{A_y(\omega)B(\omega)}{A_x(\omega)}, \tag{2.5}$$

which is not defined at seasonal frequencies. It is seen that the effect of the filtering operations is to change the lag function to $B^*(L)$ and the error term to u_t^a. Of course if the same linear filter adjustment procedure is applied to both series ($A_y = A_x$), then the relationship between them is not changed, and the only effect is on the error term—if u_t is nonautocorrelated, then u_t^a is a high-order moving average process, and least squares estimates with adjusted data will not be fully efficient.[6] This is virtually the situation which applies in this section, for the adjustment procedure under consideration amounts to the application of the same linear filter to both series.[7]

A further consequence of converting an independent u-series to an autocorrelated u^a-series is that the usual formula for calculating the covariance matrix of the estimated coefficients is invalid when applied to adjusted data. As indicated by Malinvaud ((1966) Sect. 13.5), whether the application of the standard least squares formula leads to an underestimate or overestimate of the actual variances depends on the product of the autocorrelation coefficients of the error term and the explanatory variable. The first panel of Figure 3 indicates that if u is an independent series, then u^a has small positive autocorrelation coefficients at lags of 1–3, 5–7, ... quarters, offset by rather larger negative coefficients at lags of 4, 8, ... quarters. Since an adjusted x-series will typically exhibit positive autocorrelation, with low-order coefficients dominating, in determining the net effect on the variance matrix some cancelling will occur. Thus the overall effect may be positive or negative but is likely to be small, so that in this situation the standard inference procedures are unlikely to go seriously awry when applied to adjusted data.

A simple case in which B^* differs from B, corresponding to one which is often found in empirical work occurs when the explanatory variable is nonseasonal and hence is not adjusted. Examples are found with prices or interest rates as explanatory variables, displaying no

---

[6] This corresponds to the case discussed by Thomas and Wallis ((1971), Sect. 3), where the loss in efficiency due to the unnecessary inclusion of seasonal variables in a regression equation is evaluated. In the framework introduced by Watson (1955), the lower bound to the efficiency of least squares estimates with adjusted data is zero, being attained when x is composed only of seasonal harmonics, so that the filter not only produces an autocorrelated error term but also annihilates the explanatory variable!

[7] The only departure from this lies in the choice of a 9-, 13-, or 23-term weighted moving average at Step (e), with monthly data, and different choices for the x and y series would be made if the relative contributions of the irregular components of the two series differed substantially. The distributed lag functions found in empirical work are generally very smooth, hence the irregular component of x contributes relatively little to irregularities in y, the main source being the random error term u. Thus the longer options will tend to be selected the greater the relative variance of u, or the proportion of variance in y unexplained by x (assuming u to be white noise). Nevertheless the overall differences between the three options at this stage are very small, this being only one of many steps in the procedure. The main effect is on the rate of decline of the transfer function to the value of 0 at the seasonal frequencies from the value of 1 at frequencies $\pi/30$ on either side (see Figure B), but even here there is little variation, and consequently B^* is very close to B even when one filter has $m = 82$ and the other $m = 89$.

seasonality, while the dependent variable is used in its adjusted form, seasonality arising from the error term. Thus $A_x(L) = 1$ and (2.4) becomes

$$B^*(L) = A_y(L)B(L).$$

The estimated relationship differs from the true relationship, and an illustration of the distortion is given in Figure D, where the original distributed lag function is the familiar geometrically declining function, $B(L) = 1/(1 - \lambda L)$, with $\lambda = 0.7$, and $A_y(L)$ is the quarterly adjustment filter. While $B^*(L)$ appears to be longer and flatter than $B(L)$ for positive lags, the most striking features are the pronounced seasonal dips in the new lag function, and the coefficients which appear at negative lags and which might suggest to the unwary that x_{t+j} influences y_t. A simpler example is obtained if the original model is static $[B(L) = 1]$, whereupon adjusting y produces a 'dynamic' model. As already seen, these distortions can be avoided by applying the same filter to both or neither of the series, and which course is adopted depends on the postulated nature of the error term. It is assumed in this

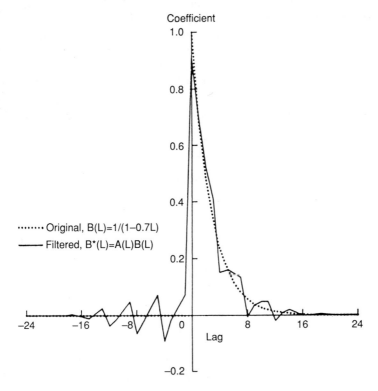

FIG. 4. Distributed lag function for adjusted Y-series

case that u is seasonal, this being the source of the seasonality in y, and so direct estimation (say by ordinary least squares) using the original data will not be fully efficient. The efficient estimator is a generalized least squares-type estimator, which is usually implemented in the time domain by applying OLS to transformed data, the transformation being that required to convert $\{u_t\}$ to an independent series. Thus to the extent that the adjustment filter deseasonalizes u, adjusted data provide more efficient estimates.[8] Note that in order to accomplish these objectives, the same filter is applied to both series irrespective of their nature. Although the success of this procedure requires successful adjustment of the unobservable error term, in the present context of linear models and methods this is achieved whenever the y series is successfully adjusted.

2.4   Seasonal and nonseasonal components of the x-variable

To analyse further the possible effects of seasonal adjustment on the various relations between series, the notion that the different components of the two series may be related differently is introduced, following Nerlove (1967): 'It is plausible, for example, that a manufacturer deciding on inventory levels will react somewhat differently to a change in sales he regards as being purely seasonal in character than he will to one he regards as more permanent or longer lasting or one he regards as exceptionally ephemeral.' For present purposes the x-variable is divided into two unobservable components, the seasonal and other-than-seasonal components,

$$x_t = x_t^o + x_t^s,$$

and the distributed lag model is written

$$y_t = \sum \beta_{1j} x_{t-j}^o + \sum \beta_{2j} x_{t-j}^s + u_t. \tag{2.6}$$

(It might be assumed that the second term gives the seasonal component of y, and the first term the rest, but little is gained by separating these, which would ignore the role of the error term.) Assuming that x^o and x^s are uncorrelated, the spectral density function of x can be similarly split up,

$$f_{xx}(\omega) = f_{xx}^o(\omega) + f_{xx}^s(\omega),$$

[8] It is interesting that in this case there does not appear to be a regression counterpart, for if the true regression model is $y = X\beta + D\alpha + u$, where D is a matrix of seasonal variables, but these are erroneously excluded and y is simply regressed on the X-variables, then the resulting coefficient estimates are not only unbiased but also efficient when D and X are orthogonal, that is when X is nonseasonal.

whereupon

$$f_{yx}(\omega) = B_1(\omega)f^o_{xx}(\omega) + B_2(\omega)f^s_{xx}(\omega).$$

As before, the filtered series obey the relation

$$y^a_t = \sum \beta^*_j x^a_{t-j} + u^a_t,$$

but now

$$B^*(\omega) = \frac{A_y(\omega)}{A_x(\omega)}\left(\frac{f^o_{xx}(\omega)}{f_{xx}(\omega)}B_1(\omega) + \frac{f^s_{xx}(\omega)}{f_{xx}(\omega)}B_2(\omega)\right). \qquad (2.7)$$

This provides an extension of (2.5), which represents the special case $B_1 = B_2$. The situation discussed in the preceding paragraph arises when $f^s_{xx}(\omega) = 0$. One further special case is now discussed.

If $B_2 = 0$, then the seasonal component of x is truly noise, being unrelated to y. In terms of observable variables, (2.6) now becomes

$$y_t = \sum \beta_{1j} x_{t-j} + (u_t - \sum \beta_{1j} x^s_{t-j}), \qquad (2.8)$$

which is of the standard errors-in-variables form. Whether y is seasonal (which depends on u), setting $B_2 = 0$ in (2.7) indicates that the relation between the observed variables provides underestimates of B_1. If no adjustment is made, then the observed variables give the relation

$$B(\omega) = \frac{f_{yx}(\omega)}{f_{xx}(\omega)} = B_1(\omega)\left(\frac{1}{1 + f^s_{xx}(\omega)/f^o_{xx}(\omega)}\right)$$

where f^s_{xx}/f^o_{xx} is the noise-to-signal ratio for x. Thus estimates of B_1 obtained by replacing f_{yx} and f_{xx} by their sample equivalents are inconsistent. An obvious possibility is the adjustment of x so that the actual regressor is 'closer' to the true explanatory variable; however, this does not entirely work. From (2.7), the observed relation between y and x^a is then

$$B^*(\omega) = B_1(\omega)\frac{f^o_{xx}(\omega)}{A_x(\omega)f_{xx}(\omega)}, \qquad (2.9)$$

and since $f^a_{xx}(\omega) - |A_x(\omega)|^2 f_{xx}(\omega)$, whether the ratio on the right side is close to 1 depends on (a) whether $A_x(\omega) \simeq A^2_x(\omega)$, which is approximately true since A is in general close to either 0 to 1, and (b) whether $f^a_{xx}(\omega) \simeq f^o_{xx}(\omega)$. This raises the general question of how 'good' the seasonal adjustment is, and although not much can be said in the absence of specific time series models, it is clear that the relationship will not hold exactly, for $x^a = Ax^o + Ax^s \neq x^o$.

In (2.6), the distributed lag function relating the observable variables is a hybrid, whether or not the adjustment assumed in (2.7) is applied.

While it might be convenient to assume that B^* is given by B_2 at seasonal frequencies and by B_1 elsewhere, i.e. that the ratios f^o_{xx}/f_{xx} and f^s_{xx}/f_{xx} are accordingly zero or one, this can only be an approximation. In practice, there is not a single seasonal frequency but a narrow band of frequencies around $k\pi/6$ at which seasonal effects are manifested. This also applies to the models of seasonal components introduced by Hannan (1964) and Grether and Nerlove (1970), which moreover have non-zero power at all frequencies; on the other hand, the typical spectral shape (see Granger (1966)) which might represent x^o certainly has power at seasonal frequencies. Nevertheless, an analysis at separate frequencies with unadjusted data might indicate whether B_1 and B_2 differ substantially, although a sample of the size common in applied econometrics might not offer sufficient resolution.

For adjusted data, the lag function is given by (2.7), with attendant difficulties and distortions already discussed. As before, some distortion can be avoided by using either the same adjustment filter ($A_x = A_y$) or none at all, and which course is adopted depends, for reasons of efficiency, on the nature of the error term. This can be assessed by tests such as that described by Wallis (1972) or, more generally, by means of the cumulated periodogram of regression residuals (see Durbin (1969)). The observation that were the unobservable x^o and x^s suddenly to become available then (2.6) could be estimated directly (either as it stands or taking x^o and x^s separately, for they are assumed independent) might suggest that the components x^o and x^s be replaced by their estimates x^a and $(x - x^a)$. However, not only are these estimates inexact, as indicated above, but the assumed independence of the components, used in deriving (2.7), is not reproduced in the estimates.[9] The adjusted series has spectral density function $|A(\omega)|^2 f_{xx}(\omega)$, that of the estimated seasonal component is $|1 - A(\omega)|^2 f_{xx}(\omega)$, and their cross-spectrum is $A(\omega)\{1 - A(\omega)\} f_{xx}(\omega)$,[10] which is, however, small except within $\pi/30$ on either side of the six seasonal frequencies (monthly data).

Implicit in (2.6) is the assumption that, while the components x^o and x^s are unobservable by the investigator, they are nevertheless known to the economic agent, and form the basis of his separate reactions. However, in some situations it might be more plausible to assume that the components are equally not observed by the economic agent, who consequently has to form his own estimates; such an assumption seems more in keeping with the previously cited quotation from Nerlove (1967). Thus actual decisions are based on estimates of the seasonal and

[9] This precludes the use of x^a as an instrumental variable in the errors-in-variables problem (2.8), for although it is clearly correlated with x, it is not independent of x^s.

[10] Note from Figure 2 that erroneously assuming independence and calculating the spectrum of the estimated seasonal component as $\{1 - A^2(\omega)\} f_{xx}(\omega)$ would result in some negative values.

nonseasonal components, calculated from the observed past of the series in a manner which can be represented as a *one-sided* filtering operation, current estimates being based on current and past data. Writing $C(L)$ for the agent's 'adjustment' filter, so that

$$\hat{x}_t^o = C(L)x_t = \sum_0^\infty c_j x_{t-j}, \; \hat{x}_t^s = \{1 - C(L)\}x_t,$$

then replacing the unobserved components in (2.6) by these estimates yields the following relation between observable variables:

$$y_t = [B_1(L)C(L) + B_2(L)\{1 - C(L)\}]x_t + u_t.$$

This can be regarded as a generalization of the simple adaptive expectations model, which arises when $B_1(L) = \beta$, $B_2(L) = 0$, and $C(L)$ is the exponentially weighted moving average operator. The overall effect is a one-sided lag function of the initial form (2.2), though rather complex. Separate estimation of B_1 and B_2 would require knowledge of C, or an assumption about the prediction method applied. For the 'official' adjusted series x^a to be of use, it would be necessary to assume that the two filters produced similar results, or that the economic agent reacted to the current value of the official seasonally adjusted series, re-introducing considerations of end-corrections and one-sided m.a.'s previously discussed.

In Section 3 the linear filter approximation is replaced by the official adjustment procedure, and the various cases discussed in the preceding paragraphs are constructed from artificial time series.

3.   A Simulation Study

In this section we describe simulation experiments carried out by generating data according to the various models discussed in Sections 2.3 and 2.4, adjusting the series where appropriate by the official procedure described in Section 2.1, and comparing the results of estimation using adjusted and unadjusted data.

A single x-process is used, namely that designed by Grether and Nerlove (1970) and employed by Stephenson and Farr (1972):

$$x_t = \frac{(1 + 0.8L)}{(1 - 0.95L)(1 - 0.75L)}\zeta_t + \frac{(1 + 0.6L)}{(1 - 0.9L^{12})}\eta_t + \xi_t,$$

where $\{\zeta_t\}$, $\{\eta_t\}$, $\{\xi_t\}$ are mutually uncorrelated normally distributed random variables, with variances chosen so that the three terms have variances 8.5, 1.0, and 0.5, respectively. Where separate components are required, the second term is taken as the seasonal component x_t^s, and the first and third terms as x_t^o. While it is conceptually helpful to keep the three components separate, by giving the rational lag operators a common denominator $(1 - 0.95L)(1 - 0.75L)(1 - 0.9L^{12})$ it can be seen that the x-process has a standard autoregressive-moving average representation, of order $(14, 14)$, although one subject to considerable restrictions on its parameters. The effective sample size is 180, corresponding to 15 years of monthly data, and each experiment consists of 50 replications, in each of which a new x-series is generated. On inspecting the x-series, it is immediately clear that the seasonal pattern changes much more rapidly than is observed in practice. This feature could be removed by making the coefficient of 0.9 in the x_t^s lag operator much closer to 1, but it presents no difficulty in the present circumstances since the adjustment procedure is designed to cope with changing seasonal patterns; nevertheless it would render useless any comparison with simple dummy variable methods, which assume a fixed seasonal pattern. The adjustment procedure is applied incorporating all the features omitted from the linear approximation as described earlier. Thus the filter is truly symmetric only in the eighth of our fifteen years, for only then are there seven years of data on either side of an observation, and the adjustment procedure is entirely one-sided for the first and last observations. Since the multiplicative form is used, a constant term is added to the model presented above, in order to ensure that the series is positive-valued. The estimated spectrum of the x-process, calculated by averaging the periodograms of the fifty series, and the implied transfer function of the seasonal adjustment procedure are presented in Figure 5. The latter is calculated as the ratio of the 'before' and 'after' estimated spectral density functions, thus the spectrum presented on the left of Figure 5 is the denominator of this ratio. The actual transfer function differs from the linear filter approximation (Figure 2) in not reaching zero at seasonal frequencies, although the correspondence is close.

The distributed lag functions used are the simple geometric $1/(1 - \lambda L)$, and an inverted V (see de Leeuw (1962)), beginning with $\beta_1 = 6/12$, increasing linearly to $\beta_6 = 6/12$, and decreasing to $\beta_{11} = \frac{1}{12}$. The independent random error term ϵ_t has unit variance throughout. For a parameter θ, the mean and standard deviation of the 50 estimates, $\bar{\hat{\theta}}$ and $SD(\hat{\theta})$ are reported, thus $\bar{\hat{\theta}} - \theta$ is an estimate of the bias $E(\hat{\theta}) - \theta$, with standard error $SD(\hat{\theta})/\sqrt{50}$. In some cases the inconsistency plim $(\hat{\theta}) - \theta$ has been evaluated to provide a yardstick for the finite sample results. The estimation methods employed are ordinary least squares (OLS) and the spectral distributed lag estimator (see Hannan (1963)). In all cases an intercept term is estimated, although its value is not reported.

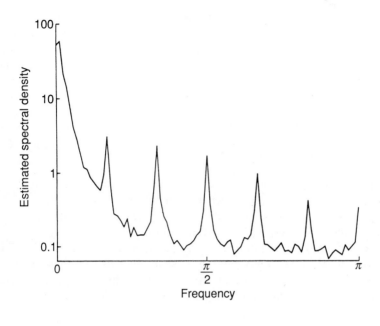

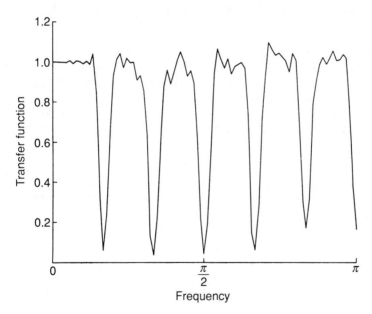

FIG. 5. Estimated spectral density and adjustment transfer function for Grether–Nerlove model

3.1   Experiment A

$$y_t = B(Lx_t + \varepsilon_t$$

We begin with the general case of Section 2.3, and consider the adjustment of both x and y series.

(i) $B(L) = \beta/(1 - \lambda LS), \quad \beta = 1.0, \quad \lambda = 0.7.$

Equation estimated: $y_t = \lambda y_{t-1} + \beta x_t + u_t$:

This is the familiar geometric lag function for which OLS provides inconsistent estimated, the estimated equation having a first-order moving average error $u_t = \varepsilon_t \, \lambda \varepsilon_{t-1}$. The probability limits of OLS estimates are 1.093 and .666, and the results with the original data (sample size 180) correspond very closely,as shown in Table 2. The effect of the seasonal adjustment is a small increase in these biases, although the observed biases are smaller than the asymptotic biases calculated assuming that the linear filter approximation is employed.

(ii) $B(L) = \sum_{j=1}^{11} \beta_j L^j, \quad \{\beta_j\} = \frac{1}{212}\{1, 2, \ldots, 6, 5, \ldots, 1\}.$

The equation is estimated by OLS ignoring information about the shape of the distribution, and the results are presented in Table 3. The original data produce unbiased estimates, as expected. Although the estimated biases with adjusted data are slightly greater, the estimates remain unbiased overall. The variances increase, thus the linear filter result that adjustment in this case reduces efficiency without inducing bias is

TABLE 2.   Experiment A(i), geometric lag function

Statistic	Parameter			
	β	λ	β	λ
	Original data		Adjusted data	
Mean estimate	1.093	.663	1.108	.658
Bias	.093	−.037	.108	−.042
SD	.051	.019	.057	.020
Inconsistency	0.93	−.034	.146[a]	−.049[a]

[a] Calculated for linear filter.

TABLE 3. Experiment A(ii), inverted V lag function

Statistic	Parameter											
	β_1	β_2	β_3	β_4	β_5	β_6	β_7	β_8	β_9	β_{10}	β_{11}	$\sum\beta_j$
Original data												
Mean estimate	.082	.173	.235	.348	.430	.480	.417	.324	.258	.166	.084	2.997
Bias	−.001	.006	−.015	.015	.013	−.020	.000	−.009	.008	−.001	.061	
SD	.063	.078	.076	.081	.079	.069	.049	.080	.069	.065	.061	
Adjusted data												
Mean estimate	.089	.166	.254	.325	.434	.473	.400	.350	.249	.155	.103	2.998
Bias	.006	−.001	.004	−.008	.017	−.027	−.017	.017	−.001	−.012	.020	
SD	.072	.095	.100	.113	.102	.085	.081	.110	.092	.094	.087	
Mean std error	.078	.090	.092	.093	.093	.093	.093	.093	.092	.090	.078	

reproduced by the official adjustment procedure.[11] The final row of Table 3 presents the eans of the coefficient standard errors calculated by applying the usual OLS formula in each replication. A comparison with the standard deviation of then estimated coefficients indicates a slight tendency for the standard errors to underestimate, but overall the correspondence is close, as suggetsed in Section 2.3.

3.2 Experiment B

$$y_t = B(L)x_t^0 + x_t^s$$

This gives an example of a nonseasonal explanatory variable and a seasonal dependent variable, being the special case discussed in Section 2.3. The seasonal component of the Grether–Nerlove model serves as the 'unobservable' error term, while x_t^0 is the observed explanatory variable.

(i) $\qquad B(L = \beta/(1 - \lambda L), \quad \beta = 1.0, \quad \lambda = 0.7.$

---

[11] A substantially greater increase in the variances is observed when simple dummy variables are used in conjunction with the original data. However, the present x-series exhibits a changing seasonal pattern, as noted above, and so simple dummy variable adjustment is not appropriate. Studies with more extensive sets of seasonal variables (such as those employed by Stephenson and Farr (1972)) have not been performed, for the main point of interest is the behavior of the official procedure, nor has an x-series with a constant pattern been constructed, for such a series is somewhat unrealistic.

Equations estimated: (a) $y_t = \lambda y_{t-1} + \beta x_t^o + u_{1t}$
(b) $y_t^a = \lambda y_{t-1}^a + \beta x_t^o + u_{2t}$
(c) $y_t^a = \lambda y_{t-1}^a + \beta(x_t^o)^a + u_{3t}$.

Again OLS estimates of Equation (a) are inconsistent, and from the results given in Table 4 we see that the probability limits once more provide a good guide to the finite sample results. Adjusting only the dependent variable, the sole seasonal variable, retains substantial biases, although the signs are reversed and the variance is somewhat reduced. Finally, adjusting both variables, despite the nonseasonal nature of the explanatory variable, substantially reduces the biases and further reduces the variances to about one quarter of the original variances.

(ii) $B(L) = \sum_{j-1}^{11} \beta_j L^j,\ \ \{\beta_j\} = \frac{1}{12}\{1, 2, \ldots, 6, 5, \ldots, 1\}$.

The results presented in Table 5 show that here the original data produce unbiased estimates, as in Experiment A(ii). If just the dependent variable is adjusted, conforming to a commonly observed practice, significant biases result, the general tendency being a flattening of the inverted V shape. Adjusting both variables not only restores unbiasedness but also reduces the variances, in accordance with the linear filter results, noting that as the error term is seasonal, the efficient estimator is a generalized least squares-type estimator.

3.3   Experiment C

Errors-in-variables:

$$y_t = B_1(L)x_t^o + u_t.$$

Turning to the situations discussed in Section 2.4, the case $B_2 = 0$ is first

TABLE 4.   Experiment B(i), geometric lag function, nonseasonal x

Statistic	Parameter					
	β	λ	β	λ	β	λ
	Original data		Adjusted y-series		Adjusted y and x^o	
Mean estimate	1.067	.675	.928	.720	.991	.702
Bias	.067	−.025	−.072	.020	−.009	.002
SD	.053	.018	.034	.011	.026	.009
Inconsistency	.065	−.022				

TABLE 5.   Experiment B(ii), inverted V lag function, nonseasonal x

Statistic	Parameter											
	β_1	β_2	β_3	β_4	β_5	β_6	β_7	β_8	β_9	β_{10}	β_{11}	$\Sigma\beta_j$
	Original data: y on x°											
Mean estimate	.078	.173	.273	.333	.402	.483	.421	.325	.247	.177	.088	3.000
Bias	−.005	.006	.023	.000	−.015	−.017	.004	−.008	−.003	.010	.005	
SD	.076	.063	.088	.083	.109	.091	.087	.073	.078	.067	.078	
	Adjusted y-series: y^a on $x°$											
Mean estimate	.113	.190	.263	.321	.391	.462	.395	.317	.251	.184	.121	3.008
Bias	.030	.023	.013	−.012	−.026	−.038	−.022	−.016	.001	.017	.038	
SD	.040	.034	.028	.033	.039	.042	.031	.036	.037	.033	.043	
	Adjusted data: y^a on $(x°)^a$											
Mean estimate	.085	.175	.259	.329	.413	.487	.411	.330	.253	.164	.093	2.999
Bias	.002	.008	.009	−.004	−.004	−.013	−.006	−.003	.003	−.003	.010	
SD	.034	.034	.031	.036	.030	.042	.032	.043	.040	.031	.045	

considered. The observed explanatory variable exhibits seasonal variation, but the seasonal component is unrelated to the dependent variable, which is nonseasonal given the nature of the error term, thus the relative seasonality of x and y is the reverse of that in Experiment B.

(i) $B_1(L) = \beta/(1 - \lambda L)$ $\beta = 1.0$, $\lambda = 0.7$, $u_t = B_1(L)\epsilon_t$.

Estimated equation (original data):

$$y_t = \lambda y_{t-1} + \beta x_t + (\epsilon_t - \beta x_t^s)$$

(adjusted data):

$$y_t = \lambda y_{t-1} + \beta x_t^a + v_t.$$

To focus attention on the errors-in-variables problem, this experiment is run with a first-order autoregressive error term $u_t = \lambda u_{t-1} + \epsilon_t$, to give an estimated equation of the partial adjustment form with independent error, and the results are presented in Table 6. The estimates with the original x-series are badly biased as expected, with $\hat{\beta}$ coming off worst. The estimated average lag $\hat{\lambda}/(1 - \hat{\lambda})$ has a mean of 4.3 months, compared with the true value of $2\frac{1}{3}$ months. The use of the adjusted x-series improves matters considerably, reducing the biases to less than one-third of their former values although they are still by no means

TABLE 6. Experiment C(i), geometric lag function, nonseasonal y

Statistic	Parameter					
	β	λ	β	λ	β	λ
	Original data		Adjusted data		x^a as instrumental variable	
Mean estimate	.624	.807	.885	.732	.879	.734
Bias	$-.376$	.107	$-.115$	.032	$-.121$	.034
SD	.100	.030	.072	.023	.070	.021

negligible. An improvement also occurs in the variance of the estimates. Using x^a as an instrumental variable in estimating the original equation achieves results which show slightly greater biases than those obtained when x^a is used directly, although the correspondence is close. The essential elements in determining the biases, namely the covariances of y_{-1} and x^a with the equation's error term, are very similar in the two approaches, given the relatively small seasonal variance, thus this particular instrumental variable has little to commend it (see note 9).

(ii)
$$B_1(L) = \sum_{j=1}^{11} \beta_j L^j,$$

$$\{\beta_j\} = \tfrac{1}{12}\{1, 2, \ldots, 6, 5, \ldots, 1\} \quad u_t = \epsilon_t$$

As shown in Table 7, the original estimates are again badly biased, the inverted V being considerably flattened, although the total multiplier is surprisingly well-estimated on average. The adjusted x-series (note that the y-series is nonseasonal) achieves a great improvement: taking coefficients singly, only $\hat{\beta}_6$ is significantly biased, although the variances have increased. Thus the ratio on the right side of (2.9) is apparently close to 1 when the official adjustment procedure is applied to this particular x-series.

3.4 Spectral distributed lag estimation

The results to be reported here, based on runs with unadjusted data, are less conclusive. Spectra and cross-spectra are estimated by applying a modified Daniell window to the corresponding periodograms, calculated by a fast Fourier transform algorithm.

TABLE 7.   Experiment C(ii), inverted V lag function, nonseasonal y

Statistic	Parameter											
	β_1	β_2	β_3	β_4	β_5	β_6	β_7	β_8	β_9	β_{10}	β_{11}	$\sum \beta_j$
Original data												
Mean estimate	.207	.195	.250	.317	.338	.381	.343	.295	.266	.255	.193	3.010
Bias	.124	.028	.000	-.016	-.079	-.119	-.074	-.038	.016	.058	.110	
SD	.088	.076	.079	.072	.082	.100	.102	.082	.076	.091	.094	
Adjusted x-series												
Mean estimate	.100	.166	.250	.354	.396	.452	.399	.317	.251	.201	.101	2.987
Bias	.017	-.001	.000	.021	-.021	-.048	-.018	-.016	.001	.034	.018	
SD	.104	.080	.110	.091	.096	.121	.135	.107	.099	.105	.111	

First, the 'Hannan inefficient' estimator is applied, calculating coefficients as in Hannan (1963, Sect. 7) for lags of 0-19 months. The results given in Table 8 are based on the original data of Experiment A(ii), with $B(L) = \sum_{j=1}^{11} \beta_j L^j$, but are not directly comparable to those given in Table 3, where an efficient method and a correct specification were employed.

In general, the method performs moderately well. The overall pattern of coefficients emerges somewhat smoothed, with relatively little noise introduced at lags where the true coefficient is zero. However, a number of the individual coefficients appear to be biased, and the sum of the coefficients β_1 and β_{11} of 2.872 underestimates the true value of 3, even neglecting the negative estimates on either side of the inverted V.

The method is then applied to (2.6),

$$y_t = B_1(L)x_t^o + B_2(L)x_t^s + \epsilon_t,$$

where $B_1(L)$ is the geometric lag function ($\beta = 1.0$, $\lambda = 0.7$) and $B_2(L)$ is the inverted V. Estimation of B_1 is attempted by omitting seasonal frequencies from the calculation of distributed lag coefficients using unadjusted data.[12] The periodograms are calculated at frequencies $\pi k/90$, $k = 0$, ..., 90, and in smoothing these to obtain spectral estimates prior to calculating $\hat{\beta}$'s the (seasonal) points $k = 15, 30, \ldots$ together with one point on either side are omitted. Of course this method does not provide efficient estimates of β and λ; the main objective is to see how well the general form of B_1 is estimated.

The results in Table 9 indicate that the general shape of B_1 is reproduced, although the initial values after the first are underestimated and the subsequent geometric decline is correspondingly too slow. The relatively large downward bias at lag 12 suggests that deleting the seasonal frequencies in an attempt to pick out B_1 alone may nevertheless produce seasonal dips in the estimated distribution analogous to those obtained in Figure 4. The possibility remains, however, that the Grether–Nerlove x-process is not well suited to an investigation of this particular point, for the seasonal component has spectral peaks not only at seasonal frequencies but also at the origin, and some contamination of the estimate of B_1 may result. In the context of this model an alternative approach is to use adjusted data and regress y on x^a and $x - x^a$ by least squares without constraining the lag functions. The resulting estimate of B_2 is very erratic, the high variances of the estimates corresponding to the relatively small contribution of the seasonal component, but as indicated in Table 10 the estimate of B_1 corresponds a little more closely to the true geometric lag function and

---

[12] Frequency-band regression analysis is described by Groves and Hannan (1968). An example of spectral distributed lag estimation in which 'seasonal adjustment' is accomplished by omitting bands of seasonal frequencies is presented by Sims (1972).

TABLE 8. Hannan inefficient estimates of inverted V lag function

Statistic	Lag																			
	0	1	2	3	4	5	6	7	8	9	10	11	12	13	14	15	16	17	18	19
Mean estimate	-.005	.118	.196	.255	.346	.428	.465	.385	.294	.215	.115	.055	-.007	-.006	-.023	-.009	-.015	-.014	-.026	.006
Bias	-.005	.035	.029	.005	.012	.011	-.035	-.031	-.039	-.035	-.052	-.028	-.007	-.006	-.006	-.009	-.015	-.014	-.026	.006
SD	.099	.104	.075	.096	.094	.092	.081	.106	.087	.086	.093	.086	.085	.082	.088	.087	.089	.089	.078	.084

TABLE 9. Hannan inefficient estimates of 'seasonally adjusted' geometric lag function

Statistic	Lag																			
	0	1	2	3	4	5	6	7	8	9	10	11	12	13	14	15	16	17	18	19
Mean estimate	1.047	.598	.384	.287	.186	.141	.128	.096	.091	.078	.060	-.006	-.089	-.033	-.003	.019	-.008	.001	.008	.011
Bias	.047	-.102	-.106	-.056	-.054	-.027	.010	.014	.034	.038	.032	-.026	-.103	-.043	-.009	.015	-.012	-.001	.006	.010
SD	.258	.146	.121	.166	.151	.134	.148	.143	.155	.130	.116	.132	.138	.107	.108	.124	.099	.101	.106	.094

TABLE 10. Regression estimates of 'seasonally adjusted' geometric lag function

Statistic	Lag												
	0	1	2	3	4	5	6	7	8	9	10	11	12
Mean estimate	.942	.642	.485	.349	.246	.230	.146	.115	.074	.071	.036	.002	−.029
Bias	−.058	−.058	−.005	.006	.006	.062	.029	.032	.016	.031	.008	−.018	−.043
SD	.130	.108	.109	.097	.121	.099	.113	.104	.106	.116	.122	.111	.105

TABLE 11. Hannan efficient estimates of inverted V lag function

Statistic	Lag												
	0	1	2	3	4	5	6	7	8	9	10	11	12
Mean estimate	.010	.117	.173	.214	.324	.364	.431	.420	.343	.289	.206	.108	−.029
Bias	.010	.033	.006	−.036	−.009	−.053	−.069	.003	.009	.039	.039	.025	−.029
SD	.497	.233	.234	.188	.178	.218	.203	.213	.202	.209	.211	.175	.375

the variances are slightly smaller than those of the spectral estimator using unadjusted data, although a direct comparison is not possible since fewer coefficients could be estimated in the OLS approach.

On turning to the 'Hannan efficient' estimator (see (1963, Sect. 1)) further difficulties emerge. Calculation of spectra and cross-spectra for each individual explanatory variable, in this case each lagged x-value, is required. When these are obtained by the short-cut method of estimating $f_{yx}(\omega)$ and $f_{xx}(\omega)$, and then calculating the cross-spectrum between y_t and x_{t-k} as $e^{ik\omega}f_{yx}(\omega)$ and that between x_{t-j} and x_{t-k} as $e^{i(k-j)\omega}f_{xx}(\omega)$, a significant spurious contemporaneous coefficient ($\hat{\beta}_0$) appears in the estimated lag function. This disappears when separate spectral and cross-spectral estimates for x_t, x_{t-1}, ..., x_{t-12} are calculated,[13] as indicated in the results presented in Table 11, which again are based on the original data of Experiment A(ii). Overall, the biases are little different from those given by the Hannan inefficient estimator, and the inverted V is again rather smoothed.[14] But the standard deviations are most striking. Not only are they substantially greater than those obtained in Experiment A(ii) (OLS estimates are best linear unbiased in finite samples in this model), they are also greater than those of the inefficient estimator,[15] notwithstanding differences in the number of coefficients estimated. This feature, together with the high computational burden of this estimator, has precluded further investigation of its behavior.

4.   Conclusion

The foregoing discussion has considered the problems which arise in estimating a distributed lag relation using seasonally adjusted data. In

---

[13] The author is indebted to Christopher A. Sims for the suggestion that the short-cut method biases $\hat{\beta}_0$ via its biased spectral estimates. Frequency-domain methods treat a series as wrapping around back on itself, and the short-cut method of calculating the cross spectrum between y_t and x_{t-k} implicity aligns the sequence $y_1, \ldots, y_T$ with the sequency $x_{T-k+1}, \ldots, x_T, x_1, \ldots, x_{T-k}$, creating a bias if the values at the end of the series are substantially different from those at the beginning (as is often the case). This problem does not arise in the direct estimate of the cross-spectrum, for the offending observations are deleted, and the effective sample size becomes $T - k$.

In computing the coefficient estimates, a direct estimate of the OLS residual spectrum is used.

[14] This smoothing of lag functions in the Hannan estimates is present in the simulation results of Cargill and Meyer (1971). They also find that in cases with an autocorrelated error term, the efficient procedure gives little improvement over the inefficient procedure in terms of bias in samples of 100 observations.

[15] E. J. Hannan has pointed out that the number of frequency bands used in computing the estimates is rather larger than would normally be recommended for samples of this size, but recomputing with a much smaller number did not lead to any improvement. However, the present combination of a white noise error and a sharp-peaked regressor spectrum is the worst possible case for the Hannan efficient estimator.

Section 2 the argument was constructed in terms of linear filters, and various distortions which might result from filtering one or both of the series were described. While most of the results are perfectly general, and not specifically concerned with filters designed for seasonal adjustment, the introduction of spurious 'future' coefficients as illustrated in Figure 4 is a direct consequence of the two-sided nature of the filter under consideration. A one-sided adjustment filter would not produce this particular distortion, and would also enable one to answer the question, 'For what autoregressive-moving average input series is the filtered series white noise?' The 'optimal' seasonal adjustment of Grether and Nerlove (1970), based on the theory of minimum mean-square error extraction and prediction, can indeed produce a one-sided adjustment filter, though the optimal prediction theory argument is not so compelling when parameters have to be estimated from a finite sample of data and, moreover, the correct autoregressive-moving average representation of the series is not known. So to retain practical relevance we concentrated on the official adjustment procedure. In Section 3 the actual official method was applied, in contrast to the linear filter approximation, but the conclusion in the cases studied is that the approximation is a good guide to the performance of the actual nonlinear method. In particular the nonlinearities were not sufficiently pronounced to negate the argument of Section 2 that applying the same linear filter to both series prevents distortion of the lag relationship. The problem of detecting different (non-zero) relations for the seasonal and nonseasonal components requires further investigation; while some success was achieved with the nonseasonal relationship, the particular seasonal component used presented difficulties.

The practical investigator typically has little prior knowledge of the nature of the seasonal relationships, and which of our experimental results is most representative or relevant must be determined in the specific context. The economist's usual *a priori* theorizing, if specifically focussed on short-run adjustment problems, would be helpful in some applications, such as the theory of the behavior of firms. More generally, which of our cases is likely to apply can be determined by examining the x and y series themselves, to see what seasonality they exhibit—this would allow one to discriminate between the cases considered in experiments A, B, and C, for example. Second-stage diagnostic devices such as examination of the residuals of the first estimates, or reestimation subject to high-order autoregressive error terms, then permit further discrimination. As we have seen, filtering or the use of adjusted data is appropriate in some circumstances, although it should be seen more as an adjustment to the model than an adjustment to the data. The indiscriminate use of filter, or the non-availability of unadjusted data, will inevitably lead to mistaken inferences about the strength and dynamic pattern of relationships. Naturally, other techniques such as the use of dummy variables should be included in the list of possible approaches, and it should be noted finally that such variables can be used to relax one particular assumption of the foregoing analysis, namely that the distributed lag relationship is time-invariant. Cases in which the seasonality in y is caused by coefficients changing from season to season remain to be investigated, although some empirical instances have already been noted.[16]

References

(References marked with a * are included in this volume)

BROWN, R. L., COWLEY, A. H., and DURBIN, J. (1971), *Seasonal Adjustment of Unemployment Series*. Studies in Official Statistics, Research Series No. 4, London: HMSO.

BURMAN, J. P. (1965), 'Moving seasonal adjustment of economic time series', *Journal of the Royal Statistical Society, Ser. A,* 128, Part 4, 534–58.

—— (1966) 'Moving seasonal adjustment of economic time series: additional note', *Journal of the Royal Statistical Society, Ser. A,* 129, Part 2, 274.

CARGILL, THOMAS F., and MEYER, ROBERT A. (1971), 'A simulation study of Hannan's procedures for estimating a distributed Lag Process', *Proceedings of the Business and Economic Statistics Section.* American Statistical Association, 316–23.

DE LEEUW, FRANK (1962), 'The demand for capital goods by manufactures: a study of quarterly time series', *Econometrica,* 30 (July), 407–23.

DURBIN, J. (1969), 'Tests for serial correlation in regression analysis based on the periodogram of least-squares residuals', *Biometrika,* 56 (Mar.), 1–15.

GODFREY, MICHAEL D., and KARREMAN, HERMAN F. (1967), 'A spectrum analysis of seasonal adjustment', in Martin Shubik, ed., *Essays in Mathematical Economics in Honor of Oskar Morgenstern,* 367–421. Princeton: University Press.

GRANGER, C. W. J. (1966), 'The typical spectral shape of an economic variable', *Econometrica,* 34 (Jan.), 150–61.

GRETHER, D. M., and NERLOVE, M. (1970), 'Some properties of "optimal" seasonal adjustment', *Econometrica,* 38 (Sept.) 682–703.

GROVES, GORDON W., and HANNAN, E. J. (1968), 'Time series regression of sea level on weather', *Reviews of Geophysics,* 6 (May), 129–74.

HANNAN, E. J. (1963), 'Regression for time series', in Murray Rosenblatt, ed.,

---

[16] For example, Tony Lancaster has shown that the problems of handling seasonality in the US cement industry example of Wallis (1972, Sect. 3.4) can be resolved by considering output-sales-inventory relations which differ between quarters. This approach was used by Modigliani and Sauerlender (1955), but they did not complete the analysis of all four quarters.

Time Series Analysis, 17–37. New York: John Wiley and Sons, Inc.

—— (1964), 'The estimation of a changing seasonal pattern', *Journal of the American Statistical Association*, **59** (Dec.), 1063–77.

HEXT, GEORGE R. (1964), 'Transfer functions for two seasonal adjustment filters', Technical Report No. 3 under NSF Grant GS-142. Institute for Mathematical Studies in the Social Sciences, Stanford University.

LOVELL, MICHAEL C. (1963), 'Seasonal adjustment of economic time series and multiple regression analysis', *Journal of the American Statistical Association*, **58** (Dec.), 993–1010.

MALINVAUD, E. (1966), *Statistical Methods of Econometrics*. Chicago: Rand McNally and Co.

MODIGLIANI, FRANCO, and SAUERLENDER, OWEN H. (1955), 'Economic Expectations and Plans of Firms in Relation to Short-Term Forecasting', in *Short-Term Economic Forecasting* (NBER Studies in Income and Wealth, Vol. 17), 261–351. Princeton: University Press.

NERLOVE, MARC (1964), 'Spectral analysis of seasonal adjustment procedures', *Econometrica*, **32** (July), 241–86.

—— (1965), 'A comparison of a modified "Hannan" and the BLS seasonal adjustment filters', *Journal of the American Statistical Association*, **60** (June), 442–91.

—— (1967), 'Distributed lags and unobserved components in economic time series', in W. Fellner *et al.*, *Ten Economic Studies in the Tradition of Irving Fisher*, 127–69. New York: John Wiley and Sons, Inc.

ROSENBLATT, HARRY M. (1963), 'Spectral analysis and parametric methods for the seasonal adjustment of economic time series', *Proceedings of the Business and Economic Statistics Section*, 94–133. American Statistical Association.

—— (1968), 'Spectral evaluation of BLS and census revised seasonal adjustment procedures', *Journal of the American Statistical Association*, **63** (June), 472–501.

SHISKIN, JULIUS, YOUNG, ALLAN H., and MUSGRAVE, JOHN C. (1967), *The X-11 Variant of the Census Method II Seasonal Adjustment Program*. Bureau of the Census Technical Paper No. 15 (revised). Washington DC: US Department of Commerce.

SIMS, CHRISTOPHER A. (1972), 'Are there exogenous variables in short-run production relationships?', *Annals of Economic and Social Measurement*, **1** (Jan.), 17–36.

—— (1974), 'Seasonality in regression', *Journal of the American Statistical Association*, **69** (Sept.), 618–26.*

STEPHENSON, JAMES A., and FARR, HELEN T. (1972), 'Seasonal adjustment of economic data by application of the general linear statistical model', *Journal of the American Statistical Association*, **67** (Mar.), 37–45.

THOMAS, J. J., and WALLIS, KENNETH F. (1971), 'Seasonal variation in regression analysis', *Journal of the Royal Statistical Society, Ser. A*, **134**, Part 1, 57–72.

US BUREAU OF LABOR STATISTICS (1966), *The B.L.S. Seasonal Factor Method*. Washington, DC: US Department of Labor.

WALLIS, KENNETH F. (1972), 'Testing for fourth order autocorrelation in quarterly regression equations', *Econometrica*, **40** (July), 617–36.

WATSON, G. S. (1955), 'Serial correlation in regression analysis I', *Biometrika,*
42 (Dec.), 327–41.
YOUNG, ALLAN H. (1968), 'Linear approximations to the census and BLS
seasonal adjustment methods', *Journal of the American Statistical Association,*
63 (June), 445–71.

3

Seasonality in Regression

CHRISTOPHER A. SIMS*

Abstract

The effects of seasonal noise on regression estimates are considered as a type of errors-in-variables problem. The natures of asymptotic biases due to the presence of seasonal noise and to the nature of seasonal adjustment in regressions using adjusted and unadjusted data are explored. Methods for recognizing such biases and for attenuating their effects are suggested.

1. Introduction

Recent work by D. Grether and M. Nerlove (1970) and H. M. Rosenblatt (1968), among others, has again addressed the old question of how best to seasonally adjust economic time series. This work has not, however, considered the question of how seasonal adjustment or the failure to adjust series contaminated by seasonal noise might affect analysis of relations between series. Other recent work which has dealt with seasonality in regression models (J. J. Thomas and Kenneth F. Wallis (1971), D. Jorgenson (1964), M. C. Lovell (1963)) has given specific guidance only for narrower definitions of seasonality than that now commonly used in considering seasonal adjustment of individual series.[1]

* Christopher A. Sims is professor, Department of Economics, University of Minnesota, Minneapolis, Minn. 55455. This research was mainly supported by the National Bureau of Economic Research with additional support provided by NSF Grant GS 36838. The author is grateful to the referees and R. Shiller for helpful comments.

[1] In particular, none of the latter three papers considers the effects of seasonal components in the independent variables which are not purely deterministic. Lovell anticipates some of the practical conclusions of this article by suggesting that interactions of seasonal variables with polynomial or trigonometric trends be used to allow for evolving seasonal patterns, and suggests degrees of freedom corrections similar to those suggested here. But the ideas that the number of seasonal interaction-with-trend variables required depends on sample size and that the theory of the normal linear regression model can be only approximate when seasonality is present were not explicit in Lovell's paper and are incompatible with the more precise statistical model of Jorgenson.

Printed with permission of: *Journal of the American Statistical Association,* **69.** 618–27.

This article develops useful results for regression in the presence of seasonal noise which evolves slowly, producing sharp but not infinitesimally narrow peaks at seasonal frequencies in the spectral densities of the variables.[2] Seasonal components are treated as errors in variables; the model is approximately identified by the assumption that the errors have power concentrated at seasonal frequencies and that the true lag distribution's Fourier transform is smooth across the seasonal frequencies. Methods are suggested for using this identifying assumption to reduce bias due to seasonal noise or due to previous seasonal adjustment.

The article's analytical parts assume the reader is familiar with the theory of covariance-stationary stochastic processes, though at some point there is an attempt to recapitulate briefly in less technical language. A bivariate distributed lag model is the basis for discussion throughout. Extensions to multivariate distributed lag regressions are obvious, and time series regression models in which no lags appear are a special case of the article's general distributed lag model.

Section 2 examines the nature of asymptotic bias in least-squares estimates of lag distributions when seasonal noise is present and seasonal adjustment is either not attempted or incomplete.[3] It is shown that the bias is likely to be either small or, if large, to be clearly recognizable as 'seasonal' if the regression is estimated as a long, two-sided lag distribution with no strong a priori smoothness constraints. Imposition of the usual sorts of a priori constraints on the length or smoothness of the lag distribution is likely to increase the asymptotic bias and make it less obvious in form.

Section 3 develops a procedure which reverses the effect of a priori constraints. If both independent and dependent variables are in a certain sense 'overadjusted', using the same linear procedure to adjust both series, then even quite weak a priori constraints which are approximately valid for the true lag distribution will reduce bias due to seasonality to negligible proportions.

Section 4 considers the case where independent and dependent variables are adjusted by different procedures, as must frequently be the case if published adjusted series are used. In this case there is no

[2] Contemporaneous work by Wallis (1974) arrived independently at some of the theoretical conclusions of this article, particularly expression (2.5) and an analogue of (4.1) below. Wallis's theoretical explorations do not extend into the area of interactions between adjustment methods and approximate a priori restrictions, which take up a major part of this article. Wallis's simulation studies have verified that at least in a certain class of applications the Census X-11 method of seasonal adjustment behaves like a linear filter. Hence, the relevance to practical work of theory based on treating seasonally adjusted data as linearly filtered is given indirect support.

[3] 'Incomplete' seasonal adjustment results, e.g. when data are adjusted by regression on seasonal dummy variables but the seasonal noises actually evolve slowly over time rather than holding the fixed form implied by the use of seasonal dummies.

presumption that use of adjusted data will yield smaller biases than use of original data.

Section 5 takes up the case, probably rare in practice, where seasonal noises in independent and dependent variables are independent of each other. In this case Grether–Nerlove optimal adjustment of the independent variable proves to be part of an unbiased estimation procedure.

2. Effects of Seasonal Noise

2.1 Effects on the unconstrained lag distribution

Suppose we have a true dependent variable y and a true independent variable x contaminated by seasonal noises z and w, respectively. The variables are related by the following distributed lag regressions:

$$y = x*b + u, \tag{2.1}$$

$$z = w*c + v, \tag{2.2}$$

where u is orthogonal[4] to x, v is orthogonal to w, and all the stochastic processes in (2.1) and (2.2) (y, x, u, z, w, and v) are jointly covariance-stationary. The notation '$x*b$' is defined by

$$x*b(t) = \sum_{s=-\infty}^{\infty} b(s)x(t-s). \tag{2.3}$$

Assume further that the noises z and w are orthogonal to x and y.

If we observed, instead of y and x, the contaminated variables $y' = y + z$ and $x' = x + w$, then there will be a distributed lag relation analogous to (2.1) relating y' and x', namely

$$y' = x'*b' + u', \tag{2.4}$$

with u' orthogonal to x'.[5]

How is b' related to b? From what we have assumed it follows that $\tilde{b}' - S_{y'x'}/S_{x'}$, where $\tilde{b}'$ in terms of the underlying variables of (2.1) and (2.2) gives us

$$\tilde{b}' = \tilde{b}[S_x/(S_x + S_w)] + \tilde{c}[S_w/(S_x + S_w)]. \tag{2.5}$$

---

[4] A stochastic process u is orthogonal to a stochastic process x if and only if Cov $[u(t), x(s)] = 0$, for all t, s.

[5] That we can write (2.4) with u' and x' orthogonal is not a unique characteristic of the problem addressed in this article. The random variable $x'*b'(t)$ is the projection of $y'(t)$ on the space spanned by $x'(s)$, $s = -\infty, \ldots, \infty$ under the covariance inner product. We can form such a projection for any covariance-stationary pair of processes to arrive at a relation like (2.4) or (2.1). Hence, any errors-in-variables problem for distributed lag relations (not just seasonal errors in variables) can be approached by comparing b' for a relation like (2.4) with the true b. I have applied essentially this same approach to a problem similar to an errors-in-variable problem in an earlier paper (Sims 1971).

Hence, *in the frequency domain* we have $\widetilde{b}'$ a weighted average of $\widetilde{c}$ and $\widetilde{b}$, with weights which vary with frequency. We shall see that this is not at all the same as having b' a weighted average of b and c in the time domain.

Note that if $c = b$, then $b' = b$, and the 'errors in variables' are irrelevant. That is, when the seasonal component of the observed independent variable affects the dependent variable according to the same distributed lag as the nonseasonal component, the bias problem we examine in this article does not exist. Thus the fact that the series in an applied problem show seasonal oscillations does not imply that seasonal bias will be present, and some reflection on why we might have $c \neq b$ in the problem at hand ought to precede estimation.

By analogy with traditional analysis of errors in measurement, one might think that $c = 0$, the case of independent 'errors' in y and x, is a natural assumption. But in economic data, the causes of seasonal oscillation are likely to be similar in different series, and therefore, the evolution of seasonal oscillation in different series is likely to be related. The hypothesis that $c = 0$ would be useful in estimation if true, but ought not to be treated as a maintained hypothesis except in those rare circumstances where it can be firmly justified. It seems unlikely, for example, that the assumption can be justified in work with aggregate quarterly US economic time series.

If w is a seasonal noise, then S_w will be small relative to S_x except in narrow bands of frequencies near the seasonal frequencies. Thus the first term on the right side of (2.5) is the Fourier transform of b multiplied by a function which is near one except near seasonal frequencies, where it is less than one. In other words, this first term is the Fourier transform of b after a partial 'deseasonalization' through a symmetric linear filter. Of course where $|\widetilde{c}|$ is small relative to $|\widetilde{b}|$, this first term dominates the expression; so it is worthwhile initially to ask how this deseasonalized b differs from the original. It might be expected that, since b is unlikely to have a periodic form in most applications, deseasonalization should not have any substantial effect on the form of b. As a rough first approximation this is true, as can be seen from the examples displayed in Figure 1.

The top panel of Figure 1 shows the spectral density of a hypothetical x' process obtained by adding to an x which has $E[x(s)x(s - t)] = R_x(t) = .9^{|t|}$ (a first-order Markov x with parameter .9) a w satisfying

$$S_w = \left(\frac{\sin(10\omega)}{5\sin(2\omega)}\right)^2 \cdot \left(\frac{17}{16} - \frac{\sin(8.5\omega)}{\sin(.5\omega)}\right)^2 \cdot K, \quad [6] \qquad (2.6)$$

[6] This formula was arrived at by taking the weights of a symmetric moving average representation of the process to be the convolution of $(1/5)(\sum_{s=-2}^{2}L^{4s})$ with $(1 - (1/16)\sum_{s\neq 0s=-8}^{8}L^s)$. The first term of this convolution gives peaks at the seasonals of width about $\pi/5$, while the second term eliminates the peak at 0 in the first term.

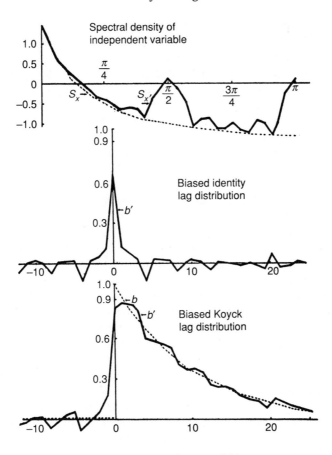

FIG. 1. Examples of seasonal bias

where K is a constant chosen to give w a variance one-fourth that of x. In the two lower panels we see the b' from a true lag distribution b which is an identity lag distribution [$b(0) = 1$, $b(t) = 0$ for $t \neq 0$], and a Koyck lag distribution [$b(t) = 0$, $t < 0$, $b(t) = .9^t$, $t \geq 0$], respectively, on the assumption that $c = 0$ with the S_x and $S_{x'}$ displayed.

In both examples of Figure 1 because of the $c = 0$ assumption, the basic shape of the true lag distribution is only mildly distorted. Because of the assumption that seasonal noises have negligible power at very low frequencies, the sums of coefficients in the lag distributions show little bias. Yet even for these relatively mild examples of bias, fallacious inferences might result. In the case of the identity distribution, the coefficients on future and lagging variables are non-negligible. Even in samples of moderate size, a test of the null hypothesis that the full effect of the independent variable is felt in the current quarter might strongly reject the hypothesis. For both distributions, coefficients on future values are large enough that the hypothesis of one-sidedness might be rejected in samples of moderate size.

Of course this possibility of fallacious inference is mitigated by the fact that unconstrained estimates of the biased distributions would reveal the presence of bias due to the periodic patterns in the coefficients. Note that even in the examples of Figure 1, where seasonal power has been *removed* from the true distributions to give the biased distributions, the effect is to *introduce* seasonal fluctuations into the sequence of coefficients. The reason is that seasonal bias, because it is concentrated at seasonal frequencies, makes the difference between the true and biased distributions large in absolute value only in the neighborhood of seasonals. Hence, this difference must itself show a pattern of slowly evolving seasonal fluctuations. Unless the true lag distribution itself shows seasonal fluctuations, the biased distribution must therefore show seasonal fluctuations around its true form.

When c is zero, i.e. when the seasonal noises are uncorrelated, the magnitude of the seasonal bias is limited. At worst $\tilde{b}' = \tilde{b}/S_{x'}$ will fall near zero in absolute value near the seasonals. But when $c \neq 0$, bias can be much larger if $|\tilde{c}|$ is greater than $|\tilde{b}|$ near seasonals. As can be seen from (2.5), in that case $|\tilde{b}'|$ will tend toward $|\tilde{c}|$ near seasonals, then return to $|\tilde{b}|$ away from seasonals.

Seasonal bias is probably widespread in econometric work. Since becoming aware of its possible existence and likely form, I have found it in several pieces of applied work, both by myself and others. An apparent[7] example of such bias, resulting from a distributed lag regression of GNP on money supply using only three standard quarterly dummies with otherwise unadjusted data, appears in Figure 2. But such bias reveals itself directly only when a lag distribution is not constrained *a priori* to be short and/or smooth. Most econometric work has imposed such *a priori* constraints, and as we shall now see, the use of such constraints with seasonally noisy data is likely to make bias worse as well as conceal it.

2.2   Effects on the bias of constraints

To get an intuitive feel for why *a priori* constraints on the estimate make matters worse, consider the plots in Figure 1. What would happen

---

[7] The supposition that the seasonal oscillations apparent in the estimated lag distribution of this example reflect bias rests on the notion that in this example the identifying assumption that b is smooth across seasonal frequencies is correct. In some applications, e.g. where the lag distribution is thought to be a set of optimal weights for projecting a seasonally varying series from its own past, this assumption will not be appropriate.

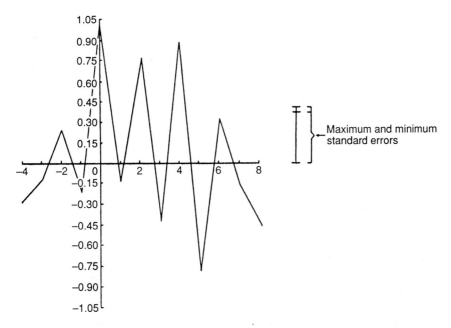

FIG. 2. Estimated lag distribution for GNP on M1, seasonally unadjusted
quarterly data (1951 I-1965 IV)[a]

if we estimated these biased lag distributions by least squares, subject
only to the constraints that for the estimated lag distribution $\hat{b}$, $\hat{b}(s) = 0$
for $s < 0$ and, say, for $s > 8$? In doing this we would be omitting a large
number of variables. In the presence of a strong quarterly seasonal,
$x(t + 4s)$ will tend to show strong positive correlation with $x(t)$ for
integer s of moderate size. If $x(t)$ is an included variable in our
restricted regression, the excluded variables of the $x(t + 4s)$ type will
tend to have coefficients whose sign matches that of the seasonal bias in
the coefficient of $x(t)$, as is clear from inspection of Figure 1. Hence, by
excluding these variables we amplify the bias.

   A tight but not obviously unreasonable prior restriction would, in the
case of the example in the middle panel of Figure 1, require $\hat{b}(s) = 0$ for
all $s \neq 0$. Using the same x' employed in computing the unconstrained
lag distribution of the bottom panel of Figure 1, we find that the
constrained estimate would in large samples give a coefficient on $x(t)$ of
.80. The lag distribution in the bottom panel of Figure 1 has a greater
bias in the zero-order coefficient than this constrained estimate but
yields a better estimate of the sum of coefficients. If we were to relax
the constraint slightly and add $x(t - 1)$ as well as $x(t)$ to the regression,
the coefficients would tend to .58, .31, on current and lagged x,
respectively. If these were estimates of, say, a short-run demand

function for labor the evidence for 'short-run increasing returns to scale' would appear very strong, and by keeping the lag distribution short, evidence of the presence of seasonal bias would be suppressed.

A clearer idea of the reasons for the bad effect of imposing *a priori* restrictions when using unadjusted data can be obtained by looking at the problem in the frequency domain using the apparatus of Sims (1972). That paper shows that when we estimate b' in (2.4) by least squares subject to prior constraints, the estimate $\hat{b}$ will minimize, subject to the constraints, the quantity

$$\int_{-\pi}^{\pi} S_{x'}(\omega)|\widetilde{b}(\omega) - \widetilde{b}'(\omega)|^2 d\omega. \tag{2.7}$$

This is a weighted average of the squared differences between the Fourier transforms $\widetilde{b}$ and $\widetilde{b}'$ of $\hat{b}$ and b', with weights given by the spectral density of x', $S_{x'}$. Constraints of the type usually imposed on estimated lag distributions, requiring that $\hat{b}(t)$ vanish for large t or that $\hat{b}(t)$ decay rapidly (say exponentially), amount in the frequency domain to smoothness constraints on $\hat{b}$. They will, in other words, prevent $\hat{b}$ from displaying sharp peaks or dips of the type $\widetilde{b}'$ has at the seasonal frequencies. Since we do not expect the true $\widetilde{b}$ to display such sharp peaks and dips, preventing $\hat{b}$ from doing this would be all to the good, were it not that $S_{x'}$ itself has sharp peaks at the seasonals. Therefore, because $|\hat{b} - \widetilde{b}'|^2$ at seasonal frequencies is given especially strong weight in the criterion function (2.7), constraints preventing *sharp* peaks or dips in $\hat{b}$ at seasonals only result in estimates which have *wide* peaks or dips at seasonals, trading relatively more error at values away from the seasonal for a good fit very close to the seasonal.

It is evident that one useful way to proceed would be to impose the prior restrictions but, at the same time, be sure that the spectral density of the independent variable is small near the seasonals instead of large. We consider such a procedure in Section 3.

2.3   Seasonal Noise in the Dependent Variable

From the analysis to this point it might appear that if w is zero, the seasonal noise z in y will produce no bad effects. The only effect considered up to this point, however, has been asymptotic bias. Seasonal noise in y does not by itself produce asymptotic bias, but it does produce bad effects in small samples by introducing a seasonal pattern of serial correlation in residuals. Seasonal serial correlation is only a special case of the general serial correlation problem and raises no special theoretical problems. In practice, however, most econometricians use estimation and testing methods which allow for only low-order

autoregressive patterns of serial correlation. Thus, seasonal serial correlation is likely to go undetected by the usual tests and uncorrected by
the usual methods of modifying least squares to allow for serial
correlation. Some consideration of how to proceed when seasonal noise
appears in y can only be found in Sims (1972).

3. Correcting for Seasonal Bias

3.1 Deseasonalizing to reduce bias

If we choose some sequence $a(s)$, $s = -\infty, \ldots, \infty$, and 'filter' both y'
and x' through it to obtain $y'' = a*y'$ and $x'' = a*x'$, then we can still
write, analogous to (2.4),

$$y'' = x''*b' + u'', \tag{3.1}$$

where x'' and u'' are orthogonal and b' is the same lag distribution that
appears in (2.4). If $|\tilde{a}|$ is chosen to have sharp dips at the seasonal
frequencies, then x'' and y'' will be deseasonalized versions of x' and y'.
By deseasonalizing the data, we have left unchanged the asymptotic bias
in the lag distribution.

However, this result depends on the assumption that no constraints
are placed on b' in the estimation process. If the estimate $\hat{b}$ is
constrained, then estimation will again minimize (2.7), but with the
difference that now the weighting function $S_{x'}$ is replaced by the
weighting function $S_{x''} = |\tilde{a}|^2 S_{x'}$. Since the common types of prior
constraints on $\hat{b}$ will prevent it from showing the sharp peaks or dips at
seasonals we expect in $\tilde{b}'$, we can, by making $S_{x''}$ small near the
seasonals, ensure that our estimate $\hat{b}$ will fit closely to the true $\tilde{b}$ over
frequencies away from the seasonals and simply cut across the bases of
the seasonal peaks and dips in $\tilde{b}'$.

The two major questions which arise in implementing the proposed
procedure are (1) how to choose a, and (2) how to decide whether
strong enough prior constraints have been imposed. Consider first the
choice of a. Ideally, one would choose a so that $\tilde{a}$ is 0 in some band of
width δ about the seasonal frequencies and 1 elsewhere. The number δ
would be chosen larger than the width of the largest seasonal peak in
the spectral density of x'. With δ chosen equal to π/k, the implication is
that correlation between annual seasonal patterns may become small
within as little as $2k/S$ years, where S is the number of observations per
year (four in the case of quarterly data). A δ of $\pi/8$ is probably
adequate for most quarterly data. One might start with this choice of δ,
then examine the estimated spectral density of the resulting x'' to be
sure that the desired deep dips in $S_{x''}$ at seasonals have been achieved.[8]

Unfortunately, no filter of finite length can have $\tilde{a} = 0$ over any interval of nonzero length. Hence, the best we can hope for is to make $\tilde{a} = 0$ at the seasonal frequencies and to keep $|\tilde{a}|$ small over the intervals of length δ (henceforth called the 'seasonal bands'). There is a doubly infinite a which has $\tilde{a} = 1$ except in intervals of length of δ about the seasonals. We will call this ideal a, a_δ. For quarterly data its form is

$$a_\delta(t) = -[2 \sin (\delta t/2)]\alpha(t)/t, \quad t \neq 0 \qquad (3.2)$$
$$1 - 3\delta, \ t = 0$$
$$\alpha(t) = 3, \quad \text{when } t = 4s \text{ for integer } s,$$
$$\alpha(t) = -1, \quad \text{all other } t.$$

One reasonable way to proceed would be to truncate a_δ at some length which avoids loss of too high a proportion of the data at the ends of the sample and apply the truncated a_δ as the deseasonalizing filter.

Other easier-to-compute deseasonalizing filters may give practical results as good as truncated versions of (3.2). In order that the filter have Fourier transform near zero at the seasonals, it is only necessary to be sure that the same-month or same-quarter means, $(S/T)\sum_{j=0}^{T/S} x''(k + Sj)$, $j = 1, \ldots, S$, where S is observations per year and T is sample size, are all close to the overall sample mean. For example, choosing $a(0) = 1$, $a(4) = -1$, $a(t) = 0$ for other values of t gives a filter with zeroes at the quarterly seasonals.

However, given that our identifying assumption is that seasonal noise is relatively small outside certain seasonal bands, it is apparent that the form of a good deseasonalizing filter must depend on sample size. The four-quarter difference filter just described creates very broad, yet very gradual, dips at the seasonal frequencies. Even in samples of moderate size, the four-quarter difference will remove more power than necessary and leave unacceptably large local peaks on either side of seasonal frequencies with most economic time series. As we shall see shortly, a corollary of this criticism of simple *ad hoc* time domain filters to remove seasonality is that, because they are not generated by a theory which relates the complexity of the filter to sample size, it becomes difficult to determine the appropriate degrees-of-freedom correction to regression statistics.[9]

[8] The reverse procedure, examining an estimate of $S_{x'}$ to determine δ, may not be reliable. If there is a narrow seasonal peak in $S_{x'}$, the smoothing inherent in spectral windowing may make the peak appear much broader than it is in fact.

[9] A second problem with the fourth-order difference filter given as an example is that it removes power near the frequency 0 in exactly the same way as at the seasonal frequencies. In much applied work it makes sense to remove trend from the data for the same reasons that it makes sense to remove seasonal variation. But where long-run effects are of central importance, a filter which removes power only at the seasonal frequencies is preferable.

An alternative to explicitly filtering the data is to remove seasonality by regression. A procedure which will, as sample size approaches infinity, remove all power in x' and y' in a band of width δ about each seasonal is to estimate the seasonal in, e.g., x', by regressing $x'(t)$ on the set of functions $\cos(\omega_{jk}t)$ and $\sin(\omega_{jk}t)$ for all ω_{jk} of the form $\omega_{jk} = v_j + (2\pi k/T)$, $(-\delta/2) < (2\pi k/T) < (\delta/2)$, $v_j = (2\pi j/S)$, $0 < j \leq (S/2)$.[10] If both y' and x' have seasonal power removed this way, the result is equivalent to including the set of cosine and sine functions explicitly in the regression. Hence the implied loss in degrees of freedom is easily computed. Note that the loss in degrees of freedom (df) is proportional to sample size so that, e.g. with 80 quarters of data and a δ of $\pi/8$, 15 df are lost. In some applications a δ of $\pi/12$ might suffice, allowing a loss of only nine df. To get back to a loss of only three df, the situation equivalent to using standard seasonal dummies requires assuming a δ smaller than $\pi/20$, or that seasonal patterns remain strongly correlated over more than half the full sample of 20 years.

This suggested procedure of using cosine and sine functions to deseasonalize by regression is equivalent to estimating the regression in the frequency domain, suppressing entirely the observations occurring in the seasonal bands.[11]

3.2 Serial correlation

Whenever estimation is carried out with deseasonalized data, it would seem reasonable to correct the degrees of freedom of the regression where possible by determining δ and reducing the degrees of freedom by a factor of $[1 - (3\delta/2\pi)]$. This procedure is justified theoretically by the assumption that use of the adjusted data corresponds to frequency-domain regression with observations in the seasonal bands omitted.

[10] This is not quite the same as removing all harmonic frequencies $(2\pi k/T)$ in the seasonal bands from the frequency domain regression (see note 12), as the seasonal frequencies v_j may not be harmonic frequencies. Since in some instances the seasonal may contain a practically unchanging component, the seasonal noise might have a near-discrete component at the v_j. This discrete component will not be removed even in large samples unless the frequency components removed from the regression include the exact v_j values. Also, there is no need to compute Fourier transforms at exactly the ω_{jk} values given in the text. When Fast Fourier transform methods are used it will be natural to compute the Fourier transforms at some set of frequencies $2\pi j/P$, where $P > T$ is a number with a simple prime factorization and P/S is an integer. Then removal of all the $2\pi j/P$ frequencies in the seasonal bands from $\tilde{x}'$ and $\tilde{y}'$, followed by inverse Fourier transformation to get adjusted x' and y', is in large samples, equivalent to including the $\cos(\omega_{jk})$ and $\sin(\omega_{jk})$ variables of the text in the regression.

[11] Such 'band-limited regression' has been suggested by R. F. Engle (1974) as a way to handle other types of errors in variables as well.

Notice that the residuals from the estimated regression in the time domain will, like the adjusted data from which they are computed, have nearly zero power in the seasonal bands. This means that the time domain residuals from regressions using adjusted data are serially correlated. The frequency-domain interpretation of seasonal adjustment as regression with observations in seasonal bands omitted shows that the serial correlation in the time domain residuals is fully accounted for simply by making the degrees of freedom correction, as long as the spectral density of the residuals is flat outside the seasonal bands (so the frequency-domain regression is homoscedastic). In practice, there will be doubt that the residuals do have flat spectrum outside the seasonal bands, yet serial correlation properties of the time domain residuals cannot be used in any direct way to test or correct for this possibility.

A feasible way to handle seasonality and nonseasonal serial correlation together in a regression is to apply the Hannan efficient procedure in the frequency domain, omitting the seasonal bands from the regression. A convenient way to do this, relying mostly on a packaged ordinary least-squares regression program, would run as follows. Fourier transform x' and y', setting the transforms $\tilde{x}'$ and $\tilde{y}'$ to zero for frequencies in the seasonal bands. Inverse Fourier transform, and estimate the regression by OLS. Fourier transform the resulting residuals and obtain an estimate $\hat{S}_u$ of the spectral density of those residuals over the nonseasonal frequencies. Divide $\tilde{x}'$ and $\tilde{y}'$ by $\hat{S}_u$, and inverse Fourier transform, again with values in seasonal bands set to zero. Repeat the OLS regression. This final regression should have residuals with flat spectral density over the nonseasonal frequencies, and after the degrees of freedom correction the usual OLS regression statistics should be approximately correct.

3.3   Polynomial trend in the seasonal pattern

It may be more convenient in some instances to use, instead of the suggested set of cosine and sine functions, a set of equivalent size of interactions of polynomial terms with seasonal dummy variable. These would be variables of the form

$$D_{pj}(t) = 3st^p, \quad t = j + 4s$$
$$D_{pj}(t) = -t^p, \quad t \neq j + 4s \text{ for integer } j \text{ and } s, \quad (3.3)$$
$$j = 1, 2, 3, \quad p = 1, \ldots, P.$$

Note that to maintain a constant δ, P must be allowed to increase in proportion to sample size. Otherwise we implicitly impose a slower rate of change on the seasonal in large samples than in small samples. If one has chosen δ, a reasonable choice of P is probably $\delta T/2\pi$. Thus in a sample of size 80 and $\delta = \pi/8$, a P of 5 is appropriate. In practice it may sometimes be easier to choose P by inspecting the raw data.

There are some drawbacks to using polynomial-seasonal interactions rather than a corresponding number of trigonometric terms for removing seasonal power. If P is large, the polynomial terms may be highly collinear if used in the form given in (3.3). Collinearity can be avoided by using orthogonal polynomials in place of t^p, but this is at the cost of the algebraic simplicity which is the main appeal of the method. Furthermore, to use the trigonometric deseasonalization method, one can draw on packaged Fourier analysis programs, within which the method amounts to taking the Fourier transform of $x(t)$, $t = 1, \ldots, T$, setting the components of the transform in the seasonal band to zero, then taking the inverse transform. This is much more efficient computationally than using packaged regression programs to remove seasonality with the polynomial-seasonal interactions. Finally, it remains an open question whether, if P is allowed to increase linearly with T, the limiting effect is the desired one of removing all power in a set of seasonal bands and no power elsewhere.

3.4 Including seasonal regressors vs. adjusting the data

The regression methods for deseasonalization are preferable to time domain filtering mainly on grounds of neatness. It may appear that, because the interpretation of the former of the two regression methods as a frequency-domain regression involves completely ignoring observations in the seasonal bands, this method avoids the difficulty that $\tilde{a}$ cannot be zero over intervals of nonzero length. But this is a fallacy, since eliminating the finite number of observations in the seasonal bands in frequency domain regressions cannot prevent leakage of a powerful seasonal noise into the remaining observations.

It may also appear that the regression methods allow an 'exact small sample theory', since they involve no ambiguity in the degrees of freedom correction. But this too is an illusion. Even if the seasonal noise has power *only* in the seasonal bands, not just primarily in the seasonal bands (which is unlikely), the seasonal pattern will not be exactly a linear combination of the regression variables we use to estimate it. Hence, even with the inclusion of seasonal variables in the regression, some error remains in the independent variables and the statistical theory for regression with independent errors can apply only approximately.

The important distinction is not between 'regression' and 'stationary filter' methods or between 'time domain' and 'frequency domain' methods, but between methods which do and which do not refer explicitly to a judgement about δ. The former allow an approximate but logically consistent degrees-of-freedom correction to regression statistics, the latter do not.

3.5 The role of restrictions on length or smoothness

Recall that the asymptotic bias in the unrestricted lag distribution is unaffected by linear seasonal adjustment of the forms suggested here. If the *a priori* restrictions we place on the lag distribution are too weak, the seasonal adjustment will not prevent the asymptotic bias from showing itself. The question is what criteria can determine when restrictions are 'too weak'? Where our restrictions are truncations, restricting $b(s)$ to be zero for $s > M_1$, $s < M_2$ it is not hard to show that the width of peaks in $\hat{b}$ is implicitly restricted to be no smaller than about $4\pi/(M_1 - M_2)$. Thus in our example of quarterly data, $\delta = \pi/8$, truncation restrictions which hold $M_1 - M_2$ below 16 (four years) may suffice to prevent asymptotic bias from showing itself if seasonal power in the independent variable has been removed.

Statistically insignificant but numerically substantial seasonal bias may appear in appropriately adjusted regression when lag distributions of more than about four years length are estimated or when the ratio of nonseasonal noise power to S_x is large for frequencies near but outside the seasonal bands. In such a situation, imposition of probabilistic smoothness restrictions, using, e.g. Robert Shiller's (1973) convenient procedure, would suffice to prevent asymptotic bias from appearing.[12]

Alternatively, one might follow Shiller in using the Theil mixed estimation procedure, but use it to assert that second differences of the Fourier transform of the estimated lag distribution across the seasonal bands are known *a priori* to be small. This uses directly *a priori* information that there should not be large seasonal components in the lag distribution, rather than relying on smoothness constraints to achieve the same effect.

Deterministic smoothness constraints of the common Almon polynomial or 'rational distribution' type will prevent sharp seasonal peaks in $\hat{b}$ if the number of parameters estimated is kept small. Obviously a polynomial lag distribution spread over M quarters can produce no sharper peaks in $\hat{b}$ than a distribution constrained to cover the same quarters without the polynomial constraints. Furthermore, since a poly-

---

[12] Shiller's procedure introduces prior information that fluctuations in $b(t)$ are unlikely. Seasonal fluctuations in the estimated lag distribution can, if the data have been adjusted in one of the ways suggested here, be eliminated with only very small effect of the sum of squared errors in the estimated regression. Hence even weak prior information that the lag distribution is likely to be smooth will flatten seasonal oscillations.

nomial of degree p can have only $p - 1$ local maxima, it is clear that if a peak of width as narrow as δ can be produced only with a lag distribution k years long, a peak that narrow must require a polynomial lag distribution of degree at least $k + 1$.

Rational lag distributions are somewhat trickier in this respect. If the degree of the denominator of the generating function for the lag distribution is as high as S, the number of observations per year, then the parametric family of lag distributions is capable of generating arbitrarily narrow peaks at the seasonals. These peaks are of a special type, of course, and will not appear in the estimates, unless the peaks or dips in $\hat{b}'$ happen to be of the same special type. Nonetheless, even fairly low-order rational lag distributions may admit substantial seasonal bias.

4.   Use of Published Adjusted Data

When a lag distribution estimated from seasonally unadjusted data shows obvious seasonal bias, more often than not reestimation with adjusted data removes the seasonal pattern in the estimates. This, however, is a result which cannot be relied on to hold generally.

Occasionally it may happen that official adjustment procedures are close approximations to the kind of 'a' filter suggested in Section 3. However, we must expect that official adjustment procedures will be deficient for regression work in two respects: they will not in general eliminate all or even most of the power in x' at the seasonal frequency; and the width of the band of frequencies in which they reduce variance may differ between y' and x'. Evidence that official procedures do not produce the required deep dips in the spectral density of the adjusted series appears, e.g., in Rosenblatt's paper (1968).[13] Grether and Nerlove's (1970) criteria for optimal seasonal adjustment of an individual series imply that in long data series we will have approximately $\tilde{a}_x = S_x(S_x + S_w)$ for adjustment of x', and

$$\tilde{a}_y = S_y/(S_y + S_z)$$

for adjustment of y'. Application of a_x to x' would yield an $S_{x''}$ which, on a log scale, would show dips at the seasonals of the same size and shape as the peaks at the seasonals in $S_{x'}$. Thus, optimal adjustment of a single series never produces a drop to zero in $S_{x''}$.

---

[13] Note that Rosenblatt used a spectral window whose width at the base exceeded $\pi/6$, so that if, e.g. seasonal patterns are stable over spans of five or six years and official procedures are Grether–Nerlove optimal, Rosenblatt would have seriously underestimated the depth and sharpness of seasonal dips.

The Grether–Nerlove criterion also implies that the width of the dips at seasonals in $|\tilde{a}_x|$ and $|\tilde{a}_y|$ will differ if the widths of the seasonal peaks in $S_{x'}$ and $S_{y'}$ differ. It is unclear whether agencies publishing adjusted data do in fact commonly allow the width of the dips in their adjustment filters to vary in this way. Posed in the time domain, the question is when the actual seasonal pattern appears to change only very slowly over time, are more years used to estimate it? In any case, I have encountered examples where data from different agencies clearly show differences in the widths of the seasonal dips.[14]

If for whatever reason different procedures are used on y' and x', the adjustment procedure itself may introduce or amplify seasonal bias in b'. Suppose both y' and x' are deseasonalized by linear filters, g and h, respectively. Then the distributed lag regression of $y'' = g*y'$ on $x'' = h*x'$ is given by

$$y'' = g*h^{-1}*b'*x'' + u'' \tag{4.1}$$

assuming that h has an inverse under convolution.[15] Comparing (4.1) and (3.1) one can see that the use of distinct deseasonalizing filters for the two variables has resulted in a change in the asymptotic bias in the lag distribution. If we call the lag distribution relating y'' and x'', b'', then we can write $\tilde{b}'' = \tilde{g}\,\tilde{b}'/\tilde{h}$. If, say, $|\tilde{b}'|$ has dips at the seasonals and $|\tilde{g}/\tilde{h}|$ has peaks of the right size and shape at the seasonals, b'' may be less biased than b'. However, if $|\tilde{b}'|$ has peaks at the seasonals and $|\tilde{h}|$ approaches nearer to zero than $|\tilde{g}|$ or remains small in a wider seasonal band, the bias in b' may be made many times worse. Expression (2.7), showing the least squares criterion for estimation subject to restrictions, now becomes

$$\int_{-\pi}^{\pi} S_{x''}(\omega)|\tilde{b}(\omega) - \tilde{g}(\omega)\,\tilde{b}'(\omega)/\tilde{h}(\omega)|^2 d\omega = \int_{-\pi}^{\pi} S_{x'}|\tilde{h}|^2|\tilde{b} - \tilde{b}''|^2 d\omega,$$

$$(4.2)$$

so that besides the change in bias resulting from replacing b' by b'', there is a reduction in the weight given the seasonal bands due to replacement of $S_{x'}$ in (1.7) by $S_{x''} = S_{x'}|\tilde{h}|^2$ in (4.2). The change in bias may not always be for the worse and the change in weights is always for the better, so more often than not use of adjusted data may reduce bias in the estimates, even when independent and dependent variables have been adjusted by different methods.

Unless we have prior information about the nature of the bias in b'

---

[14] Wallis (1974) shows that the Census X-11 method behaves like linear filter of fixed bandwidth.
[15] If $\tilde{h}$ is everywhere nonzero, h does have an inverse under convolution, given by $\tilde{h}^{-1} = 1/\tilde{h}$.

(as assumed in Section 5), it is clearly better to hold bias constant and force the estimation procedure to ignore seasonal frequencies, adjusting y' and x' by the same filter, than to risk making matters worse by using separately adjusted series.

5. The Case of Independent Seasonal Noises

Seasonal noises in economic time series are probably rarely independent of one another. In aggregate time series certain identifiable factors affect most seasonal fluctuations—weather, seasonal habits of retail customers, influence of annual budget cycles on spending patterns of large institutions. The reason for excluding seasonal 'noises' in estimating a regression, then, is not that the 'true' components of independent and dependent variables are related and the 'noise' components are unrelated, but rather that the two components are related in different ways. In the notation of Section 2, c in (2.2) is not zero; it is just different from b in (2.1).

None the less, there may be situations where seasonal factors in the variables of a regression are known to be unrelated. In such a situation it is possible to make the asymptotic bias small by appropriate seasonal adjustment. From (2.5) we can see that if $c = 0$, $\tilde{b}' = [S_x/(S_x + S_w)]\,\tilde{b}$. From (4.1) we know that use of different adjustment filters on x' and y' alters the bias to give us $\tilde{b}'' = \tilde{g}\,\tilde{b}'/\tilde{h}$. Suppose we take $\tilde{h} = S_x/(S_x + S_w)$ and $\tilde{g} \equiv 1$. Then $b'' = b$ and asymptotic bias has been eliminated.

This particular form for $\tilde{h}$ is, as Grether and Nerlov (1970) pointed out, the optimum seasonal adjustment filter when a doubly infinite sample is available. In long but finite time series, optimal seasonal adjustment will be approximately in the form of this h except at the beginnings and ends of the series. Hence, in this case of uncorrelated seasonal noises, asymptotically unbiased regression estimates can be obtained by adjusting the independent variable only, using the Grether–Nerlove optimal procedure. If there is a seasonal component in y', then least-squares regression estimates will be inefficient, but this now is only a standard problem in correcting for serial correlation.[16]

---

[16] To be precise, if $\tilde{h} = S_x/(S_x + S_w)$ is known exactly and applied to x' to yield x'', the regression of y' on x'' will be $y' = b*x'' + u'$, with b the same as in (2.1), which applies to uncontaminated data. But h cannot be applied to x' unless an infinite sample on x' is available. If truncated versions of h are applied to finite samples on x' with the truncation points for h allowed to grow with sample size, least-squares regression estimates are undoubtedly asymptotically unbiased under weak regularity conditions on x, y, z, and w, but a rigorous proof of this seems more trouble than it's worth, especially since, as noted later, h itself will in general be known only to a good approximation.

Grether and Nerlove propose that the ratio $S_x/(S_x + S_w)$ can be estimated if we have finite parameterizations for both S_x and S_w, making them both rational functions. But choosing such finite parameterizations is an extremely hazardous business. Having estimated rational forms for both S_x and S_w, it would always be prudent to compare the implied $S_{x'} = S_x + S_w$ with a less tightly parameterized estimate of $S_{x'}$. A better way to carry out the estimation would be to estimate $S_{x'}$ directly (taking care not to let a broad spectral window give misleadingly wide spectral peaks), then to estimate S_x by interpolating $S_{x'}$ across the bases of spectral peaks, finally taking $\tilde{h}$ to be $S_x/S_{x'}$.[17]

6. Seasonality in Frequency-Domain Estimation Techniques

As already noted, if we Fourier transform all variables to arrive at a frequency-domain regression, the natural interpretation of the suggestions in Section 3 is that observations falling in the seasonal bands simply be ignored. The 'Hannan efficient' estimation procedure[18] is just weighted regression in the frequency domain, so we already have a recommendation for handling seasonality in this estimation method.

The Hannan inefficient procedure, which takes $\tilde{b} = S_{y'x'}/S_{x'}$ with unadjusted data, must be handled somewhat differently. In my own work with the Hannan inefficient procedure, it has always been possible to eliminate seasonality while taking the seasonal bands to be smaller than the width of the window used in forming spectral estimates. In this case, there is little danger in applying the Hannan inefficient method directly to data adjusted by any of the methods proposed in Section 3. There will be moderate dips at the seasonals in both $S_{y''x''}$ and $S_{x''}$, but as long as the same window is used in forming both estimates, the dips should be parallel and have the effect of interpolating the estimate $\tilde{b}$ across the seasonal bands. Where the seasonal bands are too wide relative to the spectral window, one can instead use the estimated $\tilde{b} = S_{y''x''}/S_{x''}$ only at the nonseasonal frequencies, interpolating values for $\tilde{b}$ in the seasonal bands before taking the inverse transform to get $\hat{b}$ itself.

The method suggested in this section does not make the usual formulas for the covariance structure of the Hannan inefficient pro-

---

[17] While this procedure is adequate for the application proposed here, a good low-order rational parameterization of S_x and S_w, if it can be found, is certainly more convenient for some of the more refined applications Grether and Nerlove have in mind, e.g. finding the best one-sided deseasonalizing filters to apply at the ends of the series.

[18] The 'Hannan Efficient' procedure is described in Hannan (1970), Chapter VII, Section 4, the 'Hannan Inefficient' procedure in Section 7 of the same chapter.

cedure valid. To obtain tests and confidence intervals with asymptotic validity in this situation would require computations elaborate enough to cancel the advantages of Hannan inefficient over Hannan efficient estimation methods.

7. Practical Suggestions

The deseasonalization methods of Section 3, while feasible, are not trivial computations. Time series regression work in the past has proceeded without the use of these methods, and certainly not all such previous work is seriously distorted by seasonal bias. Is there any way to decide when these procedures are necessary?

I would argue that whenever the seasonally unadjusted data contain noticeable seasonal variation, the methods of Section 3 should be applied at least as a check in the final stages of research. But when large numbers of time series regressions are being computed on an exploratory basis, this elaborate treatment of seasonality is not always necessary. The following classification of types of regression equations may help to indicate when use of unadjusted or officially adjusted data may be relatively safe. This is meant as a guide not only to research practice, but to critical evaluation of existing time series regression estimates where seasonality has been treated more casually.

There are two dimensions of variation to the classification—sample size and nature of prior restrictions on the lag distribution. In a large sample (exceeding k years when the seasonal pattern is known to remain stable only over periods of k years), use of the usual $S - 1$ seasonal dummies will not suffice to remove seasonality. If seasonal bias is an important possibility, there is no choice but to determine an appropriate δ for the seasonal bands and apply one of the Section 3 methods. In a small sample, on the other hand, the standard seasonal dummies will adequately protect against seasonal bias in the regression.

But when the lag distribution is only very weakly restricted *a priori* (as is more likely in larger samples), in particular when the only restriction is a truncation that still leaves the lag distribution more than two years long, strong seasonal bias can often be discovered by inspection of the estimated lag distribution. The bias will show up as a pattern of seasonal oscillations in the estimate.[19] Hence, with such a loosely restricted estimation procedure, there is less danger in proceeding with a casual treatment of seasonality, using unadjusted or officially

---

[19] Again, note that in some applications the assumption that $\tilde{b}$ is smooth across seasonal frequencies will not hold, so that seasonal oscillations in the estimate of b might not represent bias.

adjusted data, as long as results are checked carefully for seasonal patterns.

Detecting seasonal bias by eye from time domain plots or listings of coefficients is an acquired skill, however. In some cases, e.g. when the estimated lag distribution contains large oscillations at a nonseasonal frequency, detecting oscillations at a seasonal frequency from time domain statistics may be nearly impossible. A safer procedure is routinely to compute the absolute value of the Fourier transforms of estimated lag distributions; seasonal bias will then show up as sharp peaks or dips at the seasonal frequencies.[20]

More elaborate methods are unavoidable in a heavily restricted distributed lag regression estimated from a reasonably long sample. By the criterion just given, the more than 20 years available in postwar data is a long sample, and the commonly employed rational or Almon polynomial types of prior restrictions are strong enough to prevent seasonal bias from showing plainly. Thus, much existing econometric research with postwar quarterly or monthly time series is potentially affected by hidden seasonal bias. If we are lucky, official adjustment procedures may have been such as to keep the bias small in most instances.

References

(References marked with a * are included in this volume)

ENGLE, R. F. (1974), 'Band spectrum regression', *International Economic Review*, **15** (Feb.), 1–11.

GRETHER, D. M., and NERLOVE, M. (1970), 'Some properties of "optimal" seasonal adjustment', *Econometrica*, **38** (Sept.), 682–703.

HANNAN, E. J. (1970), *Multiple Time Series*. New York, London, Sidney, Toronto: John Wiley & Sons, Inc.

JORGENSON, D. W. (1964), 'Minimum variance, linear, unbiased, seasonal adjustment of economic time series', *Journal of the American Statistical Association,* **59** (Sept.), 681–724.

[20] As an example of the difficulty of detecting seasonal bias by eye in the time domain, consider the estimated lag distribution including future coefficients for GNP on $M1$ in Sims (1972). Though no seasonal pattern leaps to the eye, seasonal effects probably are biasing downward the O-order coefficient.

[a] The regression equation which produced this lag distribution was:

$$y(t) = \sum_{s-1}^{3} a_s D_s(t) + c + b*x(t) + u(t),$$

where $y(t) = g*Y(t)$, $x(t) = g*X(t)$, Y is the log of nominal GNP, and X is the log of nominal $M1$, currency plus demand deposits. The prewhitening filter g has the values 1, -1.5, .5625, for $t = 0$, 1, 2, and the value zero for other values of t. T is a linear time trend and D_j is the j'th quarter seasonal dummy. The estimated equation thus corresponds exactly to those used in Sims (1972). The reader may verify for himself that the severe seasonal bias apparent here does not appear in the regressions with properly adjusted data.

LOVELL, M. C. (1963), 'Seasonal adjustment of economic time series and multiple regression analysis', *Journal of the American Statistical Association*, **58** (Dec.), 993–1010.

ROSENBLATT, HARRY M. (1968), 'Spectral evaluation of SBLS and census revised seasonal adjustment procedures', *Journal of the American Statistical Association*, **63** (June), 472–501.

SHILLER, ROBERT (1973), 'A distributed lag estimator derived from smoothness priors', *Econometrica*, **41** (July), 775–89.

SIMS, C. A. (1971), 'Discrete approximations to continuous time distributed lags in econometrics', *Econometrica*, **39** (May), 545–63.

—— (1972), 'The role of approximate prior restrictions in distributed lag estimation', *Journal of the American Statistical Association*, **67** (Mar.), 169–75.

—— (1972), 'Money, income and causality', *American Economic Review*, **62** (Sept.), 540–52.

THOMAS J. J., and WALLIS, KENNETH F. (1971), 'Seasonal variation in regression analysis', *Journal of the Royal Statistical Society*, Ser. A (General), **134**, 57–72.

WALLIS, KENNETH F. (1974), 'Seasonal adjustment and relations between variables', *Journal of the American Statistical Association*, **69** (Mar.), 18–31.*

4

Issues Involved with the Seasonal Adjustment of Economic Time Series

WILLIAM R. BELL* and STEVEN C. HILLMER†

Abstract

In the first part of this article, we briefly review the history of seasonal adjustment and statistical time series analysis in order to understand why seasonal adjustment methods have evolved into their present form. This review provides insight into some of the problems that must be addressed by seasonal adjustment procedures and points out that advances in modern time series analysis raise the question of whether seasonal adjustment should be performed at all. This in turn leads to a discussion in the second part of issues involved in seasonal adjustment. We state our opinions about the issues raised and review some of the work of other authors. First, we comment on reasons that have been given for doing seasonal adjustment and suggest a new possible justification. We then emphasize the need to define precisely the seasonal and nonseasonal components and offer our definitions. Finally, we discuss criteria for evaluating seasonal adjustments. We contend the proposed criteria based on empirical comparisons of estimated components are of little value and suggest that seasonal adjustment methods should be evaluated based on whether they are consistent with the information in the observed data. This idea is illustrated with an example.

Keywords: seasonal adjustment; model-based seasonal adjustment; seasonality; signal extraction; time series; Census X-11.

When most consumers of seasonally adjusted data—and that includes nearly every economically literate person—are confronted by the question of why they prefer such a series to the original, the most common and natural reaction is that the answer is obvious. Yet on further reflection the basis for such a preference becomes less clear, and those who give the matter extensive thought often finish by becoming hopelessly confused. (Grether and Nerlove 1970, p. 685.)

Printed with permission of: *Journal of Business and Economic Statistics*, **2**. 291–320.
* Statistical Research Division, US Bureau of the Census, Department of Commerce, Washington, DC 20233.
† School of Business, University of Kansas, Lawrence, KS 66045.

Introduction

The impact of seasonally adjusted data on modern US society is pervasive. The Federal Reserve Board sets monetary policies based in part on seasonally adjusted data; presidential and congressional economic policies are influenced by seasonally adjusted economic indicators; and seasonally adjusted values are routinely reported by the news media. Although unadjusted figures are also published, they do not receive the attention of the adjusted data. Thus society is conditioned to expect and even demand seasonally adjusted data.

Even though the public appears for the most part to be comfortable with seasonally adjusted data, we doubt that many users understand the methods by which the data are produced. It may be too much to expect the statistically unsophisticated person to understand the procedures underlying seasonal adjustment, but even statistical experts are often mystified by these procedures, including the most widely used method, Census X-11. This method uses a set of moving averages to produce seasonally adjusted data; and although the basic idea of moving averages is simple enough, the method in which they are applied in the X-11 program is extremely complex. Moreover, the theoretical statistical underpinnings of X-11 and many other seasonal adjustment methods are not understood by many users. Thus many users of adjusted data merely trust that the adjustment procedure is providing useful data, and critics have advocated the abolishment of seasonal adjustment.

The purposes of this article are to express some ideas about seasonal adjustment, to attempt to clarify certain aspects of the subject, and to stimulate discussion in areas that need more attention. Our thinking on seasonal adjustment has been structured around three questions:

1. Why has seasonal adjustment been done in the past, and why have the current procedures evolved into their present forms?
2. Why should one do seasonal adjustment?
3. Given that seasonal adjustment is desirable, how should it be done?

In Section 3 we will attempt to answer the first question by giving a historical overview of developments in seasonal adjustment and relating them to developments in time series analysis. We shall see that seasonal adjustment was initially developed in the 1920s and 1930s as a tool for the analysis of seasonal economic time series in the absence of suitable statistical models for such series. The methods were developed empirically, using tools such as moving averages. Adequate models for seasonal series were not used until the 1950s, and they did not come into widespread use until after the publication of the time series book by Box and Jenkins in 1970 and the subsequent development of computer software for time series modeling.

In the 1950s Julius Shiskin started doing seasonal adjustments on electronic computers at the Bureau of the Census, which permitted the adjustment of large numbers of time series. This advance also marked a transition for seasonal adjustment from a tool used by analyzers of data to a requirement of data publishers.

As time series models and related computer software have become widely used in recent years, seasonal adjusters have looked to time series modeling to solve some of the problems in seasonal adjustment. This search has led to the development of such approaches as the X-11 ARIMA method and various model-based methods. Considering, however, that seasonal adjustment developed as an analytic tool in the absence of suitable models for seasonal time series, and that it is now possible to adequately model many seasonal time series, it is not clear what is gained in general by seasonal adjustment. The use of models in connection with seasonal adjustment raises questions about whether seasonal adjustment should be done at all.

This leads us, in Section 4, to investigate the reasons for seasonal adjustment. In our view, reasons that have been given in the past for seasonal adjustment have tended to be too vague. We suggest that consumers of adjusted data should be concerned that simplifications resulting from seasonal adjustment not be at the expense of a significant loss of information. Seasonally adjusted data are useful to the statistically unsophisticated user only if information loss is small. We review the literature related to information loss in the seasonal adjustment process and contend that the results to data are inconclusive and that more research into this area is desirable.

Since the question of whether to do seasonal adjustment is a difficult one, and since seasonal adjustment is presently a requirement of data publishers, we also consider how one should do seasonal adjustment given that it is desirable. Methods of seasonal adjustment are determined by the assumptions made, explicitly or implicitly, about the components. We thus argue that it is essential to define rigorously the components being estimated. This has not been done in the past. We present an approach to defining the components and attempt to justify our definitions. A rigorous definition of the components makes it possible to examine critically the assumptions underlying an adjustment method and to compare the differences in assumptions for different methods.

Finally, we discuss the evaluation of seasonal adjustment procedures. Reviewing approaches that have been suggested, we argue that empirical comparisons based on criteria for a 'good' adjustment are for the most part useless in evaluating competing methods. We recommend examining the assumptions underlying adjustment methods, which must remain subjective to an extent but can be partially checked against the data. We therefore believe that the most important criterion is that a seasonal adjustment method be consistent with the information about seasonality present in the data being adjusted. We present an approach to assessing whether this is the case.

We emphasize to the reader that we will not attempt to answer all questions involved with seasonal adjustment. Many of the issues involved are complex, some are nonstatistical, and there will always remain some arbitrary elements. We do feel, however, that insufficient attention has been given to several of these issues. We hope to shed new light on some of them and, perhaps most important, to stimulate further discussion and research, ultimately leading to a better understanding of seasonal adjustment.

2.   Definitions and Notation

Seasonal adjustment involves the decomposition of an observed time series, Z_t, into unobserved seasonal and nonseasonal components, S_t and N_t. The underlying decomposition is usually viewed as either additive, $Z_t = S_t + N_t$, or multiplicative, $Z_t = S_t \cdot N_t$. By taking logarithms, the multiplicative decomposition becomes additive; thus for the purpose of analysis, we shall use the additive decomposition. The nonseasonal component can be further decomposed into trend and irregular components if desired; however, we shall not consider this decomposition, for reasons of simplicity.

Many approaches to seasonal adjustment use symmetric moving averages in estimating S_t and N_t. A symmetric moving average of Z_t (of length $2M + 1$) is $(2M + 1)^{-1} \sum_{j=-M}^{M} Z_{t+j}$, or more generally $\sum_{j=-M}^{M} \alpha_j Z_{t+j}$ (sometimes called a weighted symmetric moving average), where $\alpha_j = \alpha_{-j}$ and $\sum_{j=-M}^{M} \alpha_j = 1$. In estimating S_t, it is relevant to use seasonal moving averages that use only values of a time series for the same calendar month. For t near enough to the end of the observed data so that not all of Z_{t+j} in $\sum_{j=-M}^{M} \alpha_j Z_{t+j}$ are available, either an asymmetric ($\alpha_j \neq \alpha_{-j}$) moving average is used, or the data are augmented with forecasts so that the symmetric moving average may be used.

We shall use the seasonal autoregressive integrated moving average (ARIMA) time series model (Box and Jenkins 1970):

$$(1 - \Phi_1 B^s - \ldots - \Phi_p B^{sP})(1 - \phi_1 B - \ldots - \phi_p B^p)$$
$$(1 - B^d)(1 - B^s)^D Z_t$$
$$\times (1 - \theta_1 B - \ldots - \theta_q B^q)(1 - \Theta_1 B^s - \ldots - \Theta_Q B^{sQ}) a_t$$

or

$$\Phi(B^s)\phi(B)(1 - B)^d(1 - B^s)^D Z_t = \theta(B)\Theta(B^s)a_t.$$

Here, B is the backshift operator $(BZ_t = Z_{t-1})$; the seasonal and nonseasonal autoregressive (AR) operators, $\Phi(B^s)$ and $\phi(B)$, have zeros outside the unit circle; the seasonal and nonseasonal moving average (MA) operators, $\Theta(B^s)$ and $\theta(B)$, have zeros outside or on the unit circle; and the a_t's are independent and normally distributed with zero mean and variance σ_a^2. For short, we will write this as $\phi^*(B)z_t = \omega^*(B)a_t$, where $\phi^*(B) = \Phi(B^s)\phi(B)(1 - B)^d(1 - B^s)^D$ and $\theta^*(B) = \theta(B)\Theta(B^s)$. We assume that we are dealing with monthly time series, so $s = 12$; however, our remarks apply equally well to series of other seasonal periods such as quarterly $(s = 4)$ series.

When Z_t follows the ARIMA$(p, d, q)x(P, D, Q)_{12}$ model given above, its spectral density, $f_Z(\lambda)$, is given by

$$f_Z(\lambda) = \frac{\sigma_a^2 \theta^*(e^{i\lambda})\theta^*(e^{-i\lambda})}{2\pi\phi^*(e^{i\lambda})\phi^*(e^{-i\lambda})}\lambda\epsilon[-\pi, \pi]$$

$$= \frac{\sigma_a^2}{2\pi\Pi(e^{i\lambda})\Pi(e^{-i\lambda})},$$

where

$$\Pi(B) = \phi^*(B)/\theta^*(B).$$

The model $\Pi(B)Z_t = \sum_{j=0}^{\infty} \Pi_j Z_{t-j} = a_t$ is the infinite autoregressive form of the ARIMA model. Strictly speaking, $f_Z(\lambda)$ expressed here is not correct when $d > 0$ or $D > 0$, since then Z_t is nonstationary and does not have a spectral density. As defined in this case, however, $f_Z(\lambda)$ is still useful in theoretical manipulations if one is careful to make sure the end results are correct. In particular spectral densities defined in this way are useful in doing signal extraction, which is used in model-based seasonal adjustment. Bell (1984) discussed the assumptions under which such results are correct.

Notice that $f_Z(\lambda)$ given here is well defined when $d > 0$ for all $\lambda\epsilon[-\pi, \pi]$ except for $\lambda = 0$, and when $D > 0$ except for $\lambda = 0$ and for the seasonal frequencies $\lambda = k\pi/6k = \pm 1, \ldots, \pm 6$. The denominator in $f_Z(\lambda)$ is zero for these λ, and at these values we will define $f_Z(\lambda)$ to be $+\infty$.

Our use of ARIMA models in this discussion of seasonal adjustment does not imply that we could not have used other types of time series models. ARIMA models are widely used and are convenient for our purposes, but our comments would generally apply when other types of time series models are used. We are more interested in drawing distinctions between time series modeling and seasonal adjustment than between different approaches to time series modeling.

3.   Historical Perspectives

To investigate the first question posed (concerning past justification for and evolution of seasonal adjustment procedures), it is useful to examine the historical development of both seasonal adjustment and time series analysis. By comparing the development of both, we can see how seasonal adjustment and time series analysis dealt with various problems presented by economic time series and why seasonal adjustment might have been preferred to other methods of analysis. We shall also review model-based adjustment methods to see why empirical methods of adjustment may have been preferred to these and to understand what recently proposed model-based methods may have to say about seasonal adjustment today.

In considering the historical development of seasonal adjustment, we must admit that tradition doubtless played an important role. Many seasonal adjusters, even those currently practicing, may have studied unobserved components in time series because this was the traditional approach, not worrying about whether techniques other than seasonal adjustment might better serve their ultimate objectives. To shed some light on issues surrounding seasonal adjustment today, we will examine what options were available to early seasonal adjusters and ask how the choices made among available methodologies could have been justified, though these alternatives may not have been seriously considered by some people.

3.1   Historical development of seasonal adjustment

This discussion of developments in seasonal adjustment concentrates on work done in the United States. This is partly justified by the fact that the Census X-11 seasonal adjustment method is today the most widely used method; therefore, it is relevant to look at the progression of events leading up to X-11, most of which took place in the United States. Baron (1973) and Burman (1979) discussed seasonal adjustment methods used in other countries, and Dagum (1978) and Nerlove, Grether, and Carvalho (1979) gave historical discussions of seasonal adjustment from somewhat different points of view than the one given here. Pierce (1980*a*) discussed recent work in seasonal adjustment.

Nerlove, Grether, and Carvalho (1979) pointed out that the idea that an observed time series comes from several unobserved components is an old one that came originally from astronomy and meteorology and became popular in economics in England during the period 1825–75. They also gave an extensive discussion of the work of Dutch meteorologist Buys Ballot (1847), who is frequently cited as an early seasonal adjustment reference. For our purpose, it is appropriate to begin our survey somewhat later.

3.1.1   1920s and 1930s

There was a substantial amount of work on seasonal adjustment in the 1920s and early 1930s, much of it inspired by the work of Persons (1919). He viewed time series as being composed of (a) a long-time tendency or secular trend, (b) wave-like or cyclical movements, (c) seasonal movements, and (d) residual variation. He presented a method, called the link-relative method, for isolating the components and used detrended and seasonally adjusted data to construct business indexes. (For a concise description of Persons's method, see Persons 1923, pp. 714–16.) Persons was not the first to do seasonal adjustment or to specify the four basic components. (Persons (1919) referred to a 1910 study by E. W. Kemmerer in which seasonal adjustment was done. Yule (1921) said that the four components were fixed by 1914 and quoted March (1905) as saying that one must distinguish 'des changements annuels, des changements polyannuels (décennaux par exemple), des changements séculaires, sans parler des périodes plus courtes qu'une année', which roughly translates to the seasonal, cyclical, secular trend, and residual components.) Persons may, however, have been the first to come up with a method that people felt could adequately decompose economic series. At any rate, his work led to an explosion of interest in seasonal adjustment.

Several important concepts regarding seasonal components and adjustment became fixed in the 1920s and early 1930s. These included (a) the idea that seasonality changes over time, (b) the need to account for trends and cycles when estimating the seasonal component, (c) the impossibility of describing trends and cycles by explicit mathematical formulas, and (d) the need to deal with extreme observations.

Changing seasonality was noted as early as 1852 by Gilbart (1852; quoted by Kuznets 1933), who found it in the circulation of bank notes. Persons observed, 'Although we wish to ascertain if a systematic variation exists it is not accurate to think of seasonal variation (or, for that matter, the other types of fluctuations) as being exactly the same year after year' (1919, p. 19). Persons used fixed seasonal factors, however, when adjusting, probably because he did not see a convenient way to produce varying seasonal factors. According to King (1924), the first researchers to adjust data with varying seasonal factors were Sydenstricker and Britten of the US Public Health Service, who were investigating causes of influenza. Their graphical method is briefly described in Britten and Sydenstricker (1922). King (1924) modified

Sydenstricker and Britten's method retaining some graphical elements but also using moving medians (taking the median of successive sets of $2M +1$ data points), and reemphasized the need to account for changing seasonality. Snow (1923) suggested fitting straight lines to each quarter (or month) separately and checking for varying seasonality by examining the lines to see whether they were parallel. Crum (1925) gave a general discussion of varying seasonality and modified Persons's link-relative method to handle changing seasonality. Other methods of dealing with changing seasonality were suggested by Hall (1924), Gressens (1925), Clendenin (1927), and Joy and Thomas (1928). Kuznets (1932) suggested a method to detect and adjust for changes in seasonal amplitude from year to year assuming the seasonal pattern remained constant. Mendershausen (1937) reviewed efforts made theretofore to deal with changing seasonality.

The early writers discovered it was necessary to adjust data for the effects of trend before, or at the same time as, estimating the seasonal component. (For example, direct estimation of seasonal effects, using complete calendar year data with an upward trend, results in seasonal factors that are too low in January and too high in December. Furthermore, seasonality in a series makes direct estimation of trend difficult.) We will refer to this problem (which eventually led to iteration between trend and seasonal estimation—something currently done in X-11) as nonseasonal nonstationarity. Several different approaches to this problem were used. Some authors made simple transformations of the data to remove trend, then obtained seasonal estimates and converted these to estimates of seasonal effects in the original series. In this group, Persons (1919) took the ratio of each monthly value to the preceding value—'link relatives'—and Robb (1929) took second differences of the original data. Other authors estimated trend first and then removed it, usually by division (i.e. $Z_t/\hat{T}_t$); this is called the *ratio to trend* approach. Here Falkner (1924) used a straight line trend; King (1924), a trend curve drawn freehand; and Joy and Thomas (1928) and Macauley (1931), moving average trend estimates (*ratio to moving average* method). Carmichael (1927) suggested a hybrid approach, taking first or second differences of the ratio of the data to a trend estimate. Finally, some authors (Snow 1923 and Clendenin 1927) estimated the trend separately for each series of values for a particular calendar month to simultaneously deal with both trend and seasonality.

Although there was initially some use of specific trend functions such as the linear trends of Snow (1923) and Falkner (1924) previously mentioned, it was generally felt by the 1930s that one should not specify a functional form for the trend. The prevailing attitude was reflected by Macauley: 'The type of smooth curve which might be expected to appear in any particular time series if the series were unaffected by the minor or temporary factors which give rise to seasonal and erratic fluctuations is not necessarily representable throughout its length by any simple mathematical equation' (1931, p. 38). Thus it was natural for Macauley and others to consider using moving averages and actuarial graduation formulas to obtain trends, rather than using explicit functions of time.

Finally, there was concern about the influence of extreme observations. For example, Falkner objected to the use of monthly means in seasonal adjustment primarily for this reason, stating, 'The arithmetic average is peculiarly subject to extreme items, and it is for that reason that a monthly seasonal index obtained by this method may be governed more by an exceptional irregular deviation than by the systematic seasonal movement' (1924, pp. 168–9). Concern about the effects of outliers led Persons (1919) and others to use medians instead of means in deriving seasonal factors (some replaced moving averages by moving medians). Crum (1923a) suggested using medians or trimmed means, and Falkner (1924) and Joy and Thomas (1928) also advocated the use of the latter. These trimmed means involved considerable trimming, with the mean being computed using as few as two or three observations. Although the need to deal with extreme observations was recognized early, the problem of how to do it has continued to the present day.

3.1.2   Impact of computers on seasonal adjustment

The next major development in seasonal adjustment did not come until 1954, when Julius Shiskin started doing seasonal adjustments (Method I) on the Univac 1 computer at the Bureau of the Census (see Shiskin 1957, 1978). Method II was introduced in 1955, with successive variants culminating in the development of X-11 in 1965 (Shiskin, Young, and Musgrave 1967). Soon after Shiskin's efforts in 1954, other organizations in the United States and abroad began using the Census method or developing their own computer methods. As a result of the interest in doing seasonal adjustment on electronic computers, a conference on the subject was held in Paris in 1960 (Organization for Economic Cooperation and Development 1960).

One of the objectives in doing seasonal adjustment on computers was to increase the number of series that could be adjusted. Shiskin stated that in 1954,

Principal users of current economic series—for example, the chairman of the Council of Economic Advisers and the chief economist of the National Industrial Conference Board—complained that many of the monthly series published by the government were not adjusted for seasonal variations at all; that many others were adjusted by crude methods; and that for still others the seasonal adjustments did not reflect the most recent experience. (1957, p. 245)

He further noted that this was 'attributable primarily to the huge amount of computation required and to the large costs involved' and that 'the large-scale digital electronic computer has brought an end to this situation'. With electronic computers, literally thousands of time series could be seasonally adjusted by government agencies. This capability had important implications for the procedures that were developed: the calculations required could now be complicated, but the amount of time that could be spent in determining how best to adjust each particular series was reduced. This was something of a reversal of the situation prior to computers. The adjustment methods developed (including X-11) were basically complex modifications of previously used methods that attempted to incorporate automatically, at least to a degree, the professional judgement that was previously required. This automation helped lend an air of objectivity to the seasonal adjustment process, so seasonal adjusters would not be accused of tampering with the data, a consideration that has become even more important in recent years. In this respect, the situation today is much different from that of the 1920s, when some people advocated freehand smoothing (e.g. King 1924) as part of their adjustment method.

Another important development in seasonal adjustment methodology facilitated by computers was the use of regression techniques to account for trading day variation. Important work on this was done by Eisenpress (1956), Marris (1960), and Young (1965), whose approach was incorporated into the X-11 program. Before this work, adjustments for trading day effects were generally based on a priori evidence or opinions about the proportion of activity occurring on each day of the week; Young (1965) discussed some of the difficulties with such an approach. Holiday effects, too, are important in some series and have been considered for many years (e.g. see Joy and Thomas 1927 and Homan 1933). Even today, however, adjustments for holiday effects tend to be made on an *ad hoc* basis, although recently Hillmer, Bell and Tiao (1983*a*) suggested a modeling approach for dealing with holiday effects in seasonal adjustment.

3.1.3. Recent developments

In recent years, there have been many attempts to improve the seasonal adjustment process. The most important recent development is the X-11 ARIMA method of Dagum (1975), which involves forecasting the data one year ahead using an ARIMA model. The forecasted values are used as if they were actual data so that the filters used in adjusting current data are closer to the symmetric filter that will eventually be used when more data are available. Similar approaches using autoregressive models were investigated by Geweke (1978a) and by Kenny and Durbin (1982). The idea of forecasting the series for this purpose is not new; it was recommended by Macauley (1931, pp. 95–6). Statistics Canada and the US Federal Reserve Board use X-11 ARIMA. In the United States the Bureau of Labor Statistics also uses it on many of their series, and the Bureau of Economic Analysis applies it to some of their series, too. It remains to be seen what action the bureau of the Census will take. Eventually (typically after three years) the X-11 ARIMA adjustments converge to the X-11 adjustments, so discussion of the characteristics of X-11 is relevant to X-11 ARIMA as well.

3.2 Historical development of time series analysis and its relation to seasonal adjustment

In considering historical developments in time series, we are interested in the question of why people used seasonal adjustment as an analysis technique rather than other time series methods. The developments mentioned here were chosen with this in mind. We concentrate on relevant developments in time series modeling but also mention some important developments in spectral analysis and signal extraction. In reviewing the history of time series analysis, it is useful to keep in mind the following essential problems presented by data being seasonally adjusted: (a) changing seasonality, (b) nonseasonal nonstationarity (trends and cycles), (c) the impossibility of describing seasonality, trends, and cycles by simple mathematical functions of time, and (d) outliers.

3.2.1. Time Series Modeling

The first important developments in time series modeling were the introduction in 1927 of autoregressive models by Yule and moving average models by Slutsky. Yule (1927) discussed properties of auto-regressive models, introduced partial autocorrelations, and fitted low order models to Wolfer's annual sunspot series by least squares. In his 1927 paper, Slutsky (1937) introduced moving average models and investigated how these models could lead to cyclical series. Wold (1938) was the first to fit moving average models to data, and he introduced the important innovations representation for stationary series and solved the prediction problem.

During the 1940s, progress was made in the area of inference for time series models. Mann and Wald (1943) derived asymptotic theory for parameter estimation in autoregressive models. Champernowne (1948) suggested the use of least squares estimates for autoregressive models and autoregressive models with regression terms, although he did not derive properties of the estimators. Cochrane and Orcutt (1949) suggested autoregressive filtering or differencing of the dependent and independent variables when using a regression model with autocorrelated errors. The asymptotic theory for sample autocorrelations was developed by Bartlett (1946) and Moran (1947).

Whittle (1952) seems to have been the first to use high lags in time series models to account for seasonality. Using a model discrimination procedure, he arrived at a model of the form

$$Z_t - \phi_1 Z_{t-1} - \phi_2 Z_{t-2} - \phi_8 Z_{t-8} = a_t$$

for the Beveridge (1921, 1922) wheat price series. In Whittle (1953a, 1954a) he used the model

$$Z_t - \phi_1 Z_{t-1} - \phi_{22} Z_{t-22} = a_t$$

for six-month sunspot data with a cycle of 22 periods. At about the same time, Whittle (1953a, b) derived properties of approximate maximum likelihood parameter estimates for a general model including autoregressive moving average models as a special case. He then (Whittle 1954b) obtained results for simultaneous estimation of regression and time series parameters. In an effort to find simpler procedures than Whittle's, Durbin suggested another approach and obtained results for moving average models (1959), models with regression terms and autoregressive errors (1960a), and mixed autoregressive moving average models (1960b). Walker suggested still another approach and obtained results for moving average models (1961) and autoregressive moving average models (1962).

More recently, the publication of the book by Box and Jenkins (1970) and the development of suitable computer software have led to the growing popularity and widespread use of ARIMA models in the analysis of time series data. ARIMA models use nonseasonal and seasonal differencing to deal with nonseasonal and seasonal nonstationarity. Although differencing was suggested many years before in other contexts by Carmichael (1927), Robb (1929), and many others (e.g. see the literature on the 'variate-difference method', Tintner 1940), and seasonal differencing was even considered by Yule (1926), Box and Jenkins popularized it as part of a modeling procedure for nonstationary series. Furthermore, for ARIMA models to be useful in the analysis of seasonal time series, lags as high as the seasonal period are needed. Other than Whittle's attempts in the 1950s, this type of model appears not to have been used prior to the introduction of the multiplicative seasonal model by Box and Jenkins. The multiplicative seasonal model provided a representation involving relatively few parameters, which was a good approximation for many seasonal time series.

Finally, approaches to handling outliers when modeling time series were presented by Fox (1972), Abraham and Box (1979), Denby and Martin (1979), Martin (1980), Chang (1982), (see also Hillmer, Bell, and Tiao 1983a), and Bell (1983). For outliers with an assignable cause, the intervention analysis of Box and Tiao (1975) is relevant. Historically, outliers have presented more of an obstacle to time series modeling than they do today. Still, more work needs to be done on outliers both for time series modeling and seasonal adjustment.

3.2.2 Spectral analysis

Spectral analysis actually became available before time series modeling and the work on seasonal adjustment discussed earlier, with the introduction of the periodogram by Schuster (1898). Since spectral analysis can be used to look for periodic components in time series, it would seem to be useful to investigators of economic cycles. Beveridge (1921, 1922), in fact, used the periodogram to look for cycles in a detrended series of wheat prices. Fisher (1929) suggested a significance test for detecting periodicity in a time series. Daniell (1946), Bartlett (1950), and Tukey (1950) suggested smoothed periodogram spectral estimators, and many other spectral estimators have been developed since then. Furthermore, spectral analysis has become more practical in recent years with the advent of electronic computers and improved computational techniques, especially the fast Fourier transform (Cooley and Tukey 1965). Spectral analysis for nonstationary time series was investigated by Priestley (1965) and Hatanaka and Suzuki (1967). For a more extensive historical survey of spectral analysis, see Robinson (1982).

Despite Beveridge's work, spectral analysis was not widely used on economic time series in the early days of seasonal adjustment. One problem, as noted by Kendall (1945), was that people used the periodogram to look for exact periodicities, but economic cycles are not exactly periodic. This problem was overcome with the development of improved spectral estimators and a better understanding of spectral analysis. A more permanent problem was identified by Crum (1923b), who criticized use of the periodogram on economic series, saying that seasonality influences the appearance of cycles in the periodogram, thus making them more difficult to detect. (Crum advocated seasonal adjustment.) In modern terms, this is known as 'leakage'. A typical approach today to doing spectral analysis with seasonal series is to remove or reduce the seasonal effects by prefiltering the data, which leads right back to seasonal adjustment.

3.2.3   Signal extraction

The signal extraction problem is to estimate the signal S_t in $Z_t = S_t + N_t$ when the observations Z_t contain 'noise' N_t. Kolmogorov (1939, 1941) and Wiener (1949) independently solved this problem for stationary time series, obtaining $\hat{S}_t$ to minimize $\mathrm{E}[(S_t - \hat{S}_t)^2]$ for any linear function, $\hat{S}_t$, of the observations, Z_t. Hannan (1967), Sobel (1967), Cleveland and Tiao (1976), and Bell (1984) extended this result to nonstationary time series. Identifying S_t and N_t as the seasonal and nonseasonal components, signal extraction can be used, in conjunction with suitable models for Z_t, S_t, and N_t, to do seasonal adjustment. This approach has been taken in recent years by a number of authors, whom we discuss in the next section.

3.3   Model-based seasonal adjustment

Some early authors criticized the popular empirical approaches to seasonal adjustment. For example, Snow criticized Persons's approach, saying, 'The method of allowing for seasonal variations seems cumbersome and the logic of it is not clear' (1923, p. 334). Fisher said,

> To the student of mathematics it appears strange that economists and statisticians have adopted such rather primitive methods in measuring seasonal variations when, as a matter of fact, more elegant and also more practical mathematical tools, requiring a far smaller amount of tedious arithmetical calculations than the methods of the gifted academic schoolmen, have been available for more than half a century. (1937, p. 179)

(The more elegant and more practical tools Fisher refers to are the orthogonal polynomials of J. P. Gram and the quasi-systematic theory of T. N. Thiele.) This dissatisfaction with the empirical nature of many seasonal adjustment methods led these and later authors to investigate the use of time series models to do seasonal adjustment. We shall refer to such methods of seasonal adjustment as model-based methods.

Model-based methods of seasonal adjustment generally use an additive decomposition, $Z_t = S_t + N_t$, or an additive decomposition for some transformation of Z_t (such as $\ln Z_t$), and use explicit statistical models (or spectral densities) for Z_t, S_t, and N_t. The model for Z_t can be estimated from observed data, but since S_t and N_t cannot be observed, their models depend on arbitrary assumptions (see Sect. 4 of this article). The various methods differ in the type of model fit to the observed Z_t's and in the assumptions used in specifying models for S_t and N_t. S_t and N_t are estimated either directly when fitting the model for Z_t (as in regression methods) or after fitting the model for Z_t by using signal extraction theory.

Regression methods provided the first model-based approaches to seasonal adjustment. The basic approach consists of specifying functional forms for the trend and seasonal components that depend linearly on some parameters, estimating the parameters by least squares, and subtracting the estimated seasonal component from the data. The most popular specifications use polynomials in time for the trend component and seasonal means for a stable seasonal component (with modifications for handling changing seasonality). The error terms are generally assumed to be white noise, although Rosenblatt (1965) pointed out that the regression residuals tend to be autocorrelated and that this should be allowed for.

Regression methods of seasonal adjustment were proposed by Hart (1922), Snow (1923), Fisher (1937), Mendershausen (1939), Cowden (1942), Jones (1943), Hald (1948), Eisenpress (1956), Hannan (1960, 1963), Lovell (1963, 1966), Jorgenson (1964, 1967), Rosenblatt (1965), Henshaw (1966), and Stephenson and Farr (1972). These efforts seem to have had little effect on the way US government agencies perform seasonal adjustment. It may be that the regression approach was doomed from the start, since it requires explicit specification of the mathematical forms of the trend and seasonal components. We have indicated that as early as the 1930s, seasonal adjusters felt that this could not be done effectively.

Recently there has been considerable interest in using either stochastic models or spectral estimates to do seasonal adjustment by signal extraction. The first such model-based approach to seasonal adjustment was that of Hannan (1964), who filtered the data to remove trends and chose a model for the seasonal component, consisting of trigonometric terms at the seasonal frequencies multiplied by independent time series following first-order autoregressive models. These models were stationary but the approach was extended to nonstationary (random walk) models by Hannan (1967) and Hannan, Terrell, and Tuckwell (1970), where the approach is described in detail (see also Sobel 1971). The method required *ad hoc* specification of the relative magnitude of the seasonal and nonseasonal spectral densities near the seasonal frequencies.

Methods based on spectral estimation were suggested by Melnick and Moussourakis (1974) and Geweke (1978*b*). Melnick and Moussourakis estimated the spectrum of the data after detrending it with a least squares straight line and then determined empirically the neighborhoods of the seasonal frequencies that they assumed contained all of the seasonal power. They used spectral ordinates outside these neighborhoods in estimating the (detrended) nonseasonal spectrum within the neighborhoods and thus obtained their seasonal adjustment filter. Geweke estimated the spectrum of the original data at the seasonal frequencies by the periodogram ordinates and at other frequencies by smoothing the periodogram while leaving out the seasonal ordinates. The spectrum of the nonseasonal component was estimated by smoothing the periodogram with ordinates at and near the seasonal frequencies left out. He also used this approach with spectral density matrices to do multivariate seasonal adjustment via multivariate signal extraction—simultaneously seasonally adjusting several time series.

Several authors have suggested seasonal adjustment methods that involve fitting an ARIMA model (possibly with deterministic terms) to Z_t and using this along with some assumptions to determine models for S_t and N_t. Pierce (1978) suggested using ARIMA models and deterministic terms to allow for both stochastic and deterministic trends and seasonality. After estimating and removing the deterministic effects, he filtered the resulting series (the filter usually included differencing) to remove stochastic trends and specified a seasonal ARIMA (1, 1) model for the filtered stochastic seasonal component when stochastic seasonality was present. This model was identified using assumptions, including an assumption that the variance of the seasonal be the minimum value consistent with the model. Wecker (1978) suggested an extension to Pierce's approach. Box, Hillmer, and Tiao (1978) started with the model

$$(1 - B)(1 - B^{12})Z_t = (1 - \theta_1 B)(1 - \theta_{12} B^{12})a_t$$

and derived models for the seasonal, trend, and irregular components consistent with this overall model, using certain assumptions including an assumption that the variance of the irregular component should be maximized, which in turn minimizes the variance of both the seasonal and the trend components. This approach was later extended to more general ARIMA models by Burman (1980) and by Hillmer and Tiao (1982), who discussed some properties of the approach (see also Hillmer, Bell, and Tiao 1983a). Cleveland (1979) fit ARIMA models to the observed data after removing seasonal means and used simple ARIMA models for the components. He chose the component models' moving average parameters in an attempt to make these models approximately consistent with the model for the original series (the autoregressive parameters were determined by assumptions).

The preceding methods all involved determining ARIMA models for the components and then using signal extraction theory to estimate them. Brewer, Hagan, and Perazzelli (1975) took a different approach, fitting an ARIMA model to Z_t and then decomposing interpolated values of Z_t (estimates of Z_t, using the data other than the observation at t) into seasonal and trend–cycle components. This was done by considering a seasonal-trend-cycle-irregular decomposition of the filter that procedures one-step-ahead forecasts. A modification of this approach was later suggested by Brewer (1979). Roberts (1978a) suggested a related method in which part of the fitted ARIMA model is identified as a seasonal adjustment filter.

The final model-based approach we shall mention involves specifying parametric models for the components, which leads to a model for Z_t subject to constraints. Estimating the model for Z_t subject to the constraints also yields models for S_t and N_t that can then by used to perform seasonal adjustment by signal extraction. Engle (1978) used ARIMA models for the components; but finding estimation of the model for Z_t subject to the constraints to be computationally burdensome, he relaxed some of them. Others used models for the components that made the constrained estimation somewhat simpler. Abrahams and Dempster (1979) used fractional Brownian motion for the trend component and a modification of this for the seasonal component. Fractional processes generalize the idea of differencing a time series to stationarity, thus providing a generalization of ARIMA models (see Granger and Joyeux 1980 for a discussion). Akaike (1980) took a smoothness priors approach (related to that of Schlicht 1981), which led to ARIMA models for the components, and used an information criterion to select from among alternative models. Kitagawa and Gersch (1984) further developed this approach, extending it to allow a wider variety of ARIMA component models.

3.4   Summary and conclusions

Seasonal adjustment developed in the early part of this century out of a tradition of looking for unobserved components in time series. Early seasonal adjusters found that their time series contained nonstationary trends and changing seasonality and that this behavior could not be described by explicit mathematical functions of time. They empirically developed seasonal adjustment methods, using such tools as moving averages to deal with these problems. Some early authors criticized the empirical nature of the early adjustment methods. Time series models capable of dealing with the series being adjusted, however, were not available at that time; thus early attempts at modeling and model-based adjustment failed.

In the 1950s Whittle began using models suitable for the sort of time series being seasonally adjusted. Widespread use of such models followed the publication of the book by Box and Jenkins in 1970. While these models were being developed, government agencies started using electronic computers to seasonally adjust large numbers of time series. This made model-based methods impractical by comparison, at least until the recent development of computer software for use in modeling time series.

Whereas seasonal adjustment was originally done as part of the analysis of time series data by statisticians and economists, computerized seasonal adjustment has come to serve the needs of government officials, business managers, and journalists—on the whole, a statistically unsophisticated group with little interest in time series modeling. Furthermore, the responsibility for performing seasonal adjustments has shifted from the analyzers of the data to the publishers of the data.

In recent years, with the further development of time series models and associated computer software, seasonal adjusters have looked to time series models to improve seasonal adjustment methods. Examples are the X-11 ARIMA method, which is now being used by several government agencies, and the recently proposed stochastic model-based methods. We shall see in the next section, however, that if one can model a time series, then it is not clear what is gained by arbitrarily decomposing the series into seasonal and nonseasonal components. Thus the use of modeling in connection with seasonal adjustment raises the basic question of whether seasonal adjustment should be done at all.

4.   Current Issues in Seasonal Adjustment

Although seasonal adjustment has become a well-established practice for the historical reasons discussed in Section 3 it is time to take a fresh look at seasonal adjustment and seasonal adjustment methods. Thus in this section, we will address the second and third questions listed in the Introduction—those regarding the why and how of seasonal adjustment today. We will not dwell on technical details but, rather, hope to stimulate discussion about some of the broader issues. We will express some opinions about the issues raised and attempt to provide the reasoning that shaped our opinions. Our hope is not that everyone will agree with our opinions but, rather, that readers will see that there are a number of important issues that require extensive thought and discussion before they can be satisfactorily resolved.

4.1   Reasons for seasonal adjustment

In Section 3 we noted that seasonal adjustment was developed in the 1920s and 1930s as a tool for analyzing seasonal economic time series in the absence of suitable statistical and economic models for such series. In recent years, as new modeling procedures have become available, the reasons for doing seasonal adjustment have become less clear. Reasons given for seasonal adjustments have typically been rather vague, but they seem to follow three main themes: (a) to aid in doing short-term forecasting, (b) to aid in relating a time series to other series, external events or policy variables, and (c) to achieve comparability in the series values from month to month.

Shiskin argued that adjusted data are useful in short-term forecasting when he said,

A principal purpose of studying economic indicators is to determine the stage of the business cycle at which the economy stands. Such knowledge helps in forecasting subsequent cyclical movements and provides a factual basis for taking steps to moderate the amplitude and scope of the business cycle. (1957, p. 222).

He went on to say that knowledge of the seasonal pattern in sales of products 'is needed by all companies to determine the level of production that is most efficient' and suggested that forecasts of a series can be obtained by taking forecasts of annual totals and allocating these to months in proportion to the seasonal factors. Burman said that the most common purpose of seasonal adjustment 'is to provide an estimate of the current trend so that judgemental short-term forecasts can be made' (1980, p. 321).

Several authors have argued that seasonal adjustment is useful because seasonality in a series can obscure the relationships between the time series and other series, external events, or policy variables. It is hoped that seasonal adjustment will make these relationships easier to investigate and, in the case of relationships with policy variables, make them easier to exploit. With regard to using adjusted data in relating several series, Burman said that seasonal adjustment 'may be applied to a large number of series which enter an economic model, as it has been found impracticable to use unadjusted data with seasonal dummies in all but the smallest models' (1980, p. 321). Furthermore, Granger saw a possible advantage in that 'by using adjusted series, one possible source of spurious relationship is removed' (1978a, p. 39). An example of the use of seasonally adjusted data to examine the effect of external events on a series was provided by BarOn (1978), who related several seasonally adjusted economic series to unusual external events. Finally, governments use seasonally adjusted data in setting policy variables designed to control various aspects of their economies. According to Dagum, 'The main causes of seasonality, the climatic and institutional factors, are exogenous to the economic system and cannot be controlled or modified by the decision makers in the short run' (1978, p. 10). Thus the nonseasonal component may be what can be controlled, to some degree, by government intervention, and so seasonally adjusted data are useful because they 'provide the basis for decision making to control the level of the economic activities' (Dagum 1978, p. 14). Note that for some series, however, seasonality may also be controllable. For example, the Federal Reserve Board has effectively removed seasonality from interest rates through monetary policy.

The third reason given for seasonally adjusting data is that it makes values comparable from month to month. This may be true; but do we really want comparability, or should observations for different months be regarded differently? For instance, atmospheric temperature data are highly seasonal, but people seem comfortable with the original data. We suspect the desire for comparability has something to do with the two points discussed above—forecasting series and relating series to other series, external events, or policy variables.

4.1.1 Justification for signal extraction

Seasonal adjustment may be viewed as a signal extraction problem. In both cases, we observe $Z_t = S_t + N_t$, where S_t and N_t are unobserved components that we wish to estimate using the observed series Z_t. In signal extraction, S_t and N_t are 'signal' and 'noise', whereas in seasonal adjustment they are 'seasonal' and 'nonseasonal'. Z_t can be a transformation of the original series, such as the logarithm, in which case we can view the decomposition as multiplicative. To put the issues regarding justification of seasonal adjustment in perspective, let us consider how one might justify doing signal extraction in general. That is, if we observe Z_t, why should we try to estimate S_t and N_t? To answer this in any given situation, we must consider three basic questions:

1. Is there reason to believe that the observed data Z_t are generated as $Z_t = S_t + N_t$?
2. Given $Z_t = S_t + N_t$, are we really intersted in S_t and N_t, rather than Z_t or something else related to Z_t?
3. Given that we are interested in S_t and N_t, how can we estimate them?

For signal extraction to be appropriate, we must be able to answer adequately these three questions. In connection with the third question, it should be noted that standard signal extraction results on estimating the components require that the models for S_t and N_t be known.

Much of the original motivation for studying signal extraction came from problems in the field of communications engineering. In this field there are physical reasons that imply $Z_t = S_t + N_t$ (see, e.g., Blanc-Lapierre and Fortet 1965, chap. 13, sect. 7). Here, S_t is an emitted signal, and the received signal, Z_t, is corrupted by noise, N_t. The problem is to produce an estimate, $\hat{S}_t$, as close as possible to the emitted signal S_t by attempting to remove the noise N_t. It is obvious that in communications engineering (a) the decomposition $Z_t = S_t + N_t$

makes sense, and (b) the interest is in the signal S_t rather than the observed data Z_t. Furthermore, Yaglom noted:

1. The model for Z_t is calculated (or estimated) from observed data.

2. The model for N_t 'can be determined by using the same measuring device and the same observer ... to make a series of measurements of any quantity whose value is known precisely, e.g., which equals zero because of the conditions of the experiment' (1962, p. 127).

Thus the models for Z_t and N_t, and hence for $S_t = Z_t - N_t$, can be obtained, so standard signal extraction results can be used to estimate the components. Therefore, the use of signal extraction methods in communications engineering is sensible.

Consider now how seasonal adjustment of economic time series fits into the framework of the three questions. Question 1 can always be answered affirmatively, in that the decomposition $Z_t = S_t + N_t$ is always mathematically possible. Whether Z_t was actually produced—by certain economic forces generating S_t and N_t separately and then combining them (additively or otherwise) to get Z_t—is another question. Some writers have regarded the seasonal, trend, and irregular components as arising from different economic factors. In particular, Mendershausen (1937, 1939) advocated this point of view and attempted to model seasonality in terms of meteorological and social variables. Factors generating seasonality in financial data are discussed in a report to the Board of Governors of the Federal Reserve System (1981). Trading day adjustments, as done today, provide a causal explanation for some of the seasonality in economic series. Moreover, the idea that the non-seasonal component is subject to control through manipulation of policy variables, whereas the seasonal component is not, relates to the idea of S_t and N_t being generated separately. Today, however, little emphasis is placed on physical causes when adjustment is actually done; so without physical justification we view the decomposition as a mathematical one.

For seasonal adjustment, the answer to question 2 depends on the components' ultimate use and our ability to define the components precisely. For instance, if the purpose is short-term forecasting of Z_t, then S_t and N_t are not of direct interest, and some would argue that seasonal adjustment is unnecessary. We shall argue in Section 4.2 that the components have not been precisely defined. Until a more rigorous definition of the components is provided, it is difficult to justify the proposition that the components are of interest as ends in themselves.

The question is not difficult to answer if the components can be precisely defined. If not, then it is difficult to construct estimators, since we do not know what is being estimated. With precisely defined components, it seems logical to use signal extraction theory to estimate them.

4.1.2   Justification of seasonal adjustment

We favor modeling series in terms of the original data, accounting for seasonality in the model, rather than using adjusted data. Others have voiced similar opinions. For example, Watts stated, 'I have yet to be convinced that seasonal adjustment is the best thing to do to a series. I believe, rather, that the aim of time series model building should be to develop forecasting models that yield white-noise residuals' (1978, p. 307). Furthermore, Roberts said, 'It appears to me that seasonal adjustments can be only a source of trouble to a statistician interested in forecasting unadjusted values' (1978b, p. 164) and 'surely the route to better scientific understanding is to incorporate the seasonality directly into multivariate models that are formulated in terms of unadjusted data so the source, transmission, and effects of seasonal variations can be better understood' (p. 164). Some econometricians have argued that knowledge of a series' underlying economic structure can provide an understanding of the nature of seasonality in specific time series (see Crutchfield and Zellner 1963, Plosser 1978, and Wallis 1978). This knowledge permits the incorporation of seasonality directly into an economic model, eliminating the need to work with seasonally adjusted data. In fact Plosser (1978) argued that use of adjusted data could lead one to misspecified models, misleading inferences about parameters, and poor forecasts.

In light of these remarks and the previous discussion, is is relevant to ask whether seasonal adjustment can be justified, and if so, how? It is important to remember that the primary consumers of seasonally adjusted data are not necessarily statisticians and economists, who could most likely use the unadjusted data, but people such as government officials, business managers, and journalists, who often have little or no statistical training. We thus offer the following *possible* justification for seasonally adjusting time series:

Seasonal adjustment is done to simplify data so that they may be more easily interpreted by statistically unsophisticated users without a significant loss of information.

We say 'possible' justification because its validity has not yet been established. They key phrase is 'without a significant loss of information'. Obviously, many people have found seasonally adjusted data simpler to use than unadjusted data; but to establish that the above justification is valid, we need to know that the amount of information lost in adjusting is not excessive. In general, there will be some information loss from seasonal adjustment, even when an adjustment method appropriate for the data being adjusted can be found. The situation will be worse when the seasonal adjustment is based on incorrect assumptions. If people will often be misled by using seasonally adjusted data, then their use cannot be justified.

4.1.3 Loss of information from seasonal adjustment

There has been some work on the consequences of using seasonally adjusted data. It has concentrated on how seasonal adjustment affects (a) forecast accuracy, and (b) relating one series to another.

Makridakis and Hibon (1979) forecast 111 time series by various methods and compared the overall accuracy of the forecasts produced by different methods. They used methods that handled seasonal series directly (such as ARIMA modeling) and nonseasonal methods applied to seasonally adjusted data. With the latter methods, forecasts were reseasonalized by applying seasonal factors. Makridakis and Hibon used their own method of seasonal adjustment, which produced fixed seasonal factors. Their results do not permit direct assessment of the effects of seasonal adjustment on forecast accuracy because (a) the forecast results for seasonal and nonseasonal series were not separated, and (b) most of the methods used directly on the seasonal series were not used in nonseasonal form with the adjusted data. Still, they found the methods that used seasonally adjusted data did somewhat better than the methods that handled seasonality directly—including forecasting with ARIMA models. Their results may have been influenced by the use of constant seasonal factors and measures of forecast accuracy that aggregate over series differing in how accurately they may be forecast (thus giving undue influence to series that are inherently difficult to forecast).

Plosser (1979) forecast five economic time series with seasonal ARIMA models and forecast the X-11 adjusted series with nonseasonal ARIMA models. Instead of reseasonalizing the forecasts of the adjusted data, he converted the monthly forecasts to annual totals to compare forecast accuracy. He used fully revised seasonally adjusted values, which could favor the use of the adjusted data because they are obtained by using future values of the series. He found that the seasonal ARIMA models performed substantially better on two series, slightly better on two series, and slightly worse on one series. These results seem to be inconclusive, since direct comparisons were not made in the Makridakis and Hibon paper and Plosser examined only five series.

There is, however, an important aspect of forecasting not considered in these two studies. This is the estimation of forecast error variances and the subsequent provision of forecast intervals for the future observations. There are well-established procedures for estimating forecast error variances and obtaining forecast intervals when using ARIMA or other time series models (Box and Jenkins 1970, chap. 5). Use of seasonally adjusted data in forecasting, however, whether the forecasting is done formally through a model or informally, seems to preclude estimation of forecast error variances and production of forecast intervals. This is obviously true for forecasting the unadjusted data, but it is also true if one wishes to forecast the adjusted data (though we question why anyone would want to do this). Future adjusted values depend on future values of the seasonal components through the future unadjusted data; hence forecast error variances for adjusted data should allow for errors in forecasting the seasonal component, but there is no way to do this with adjusted data. These problems will not be solved if, as has been recommended, government agencies start publishing standard errors for seasonally adjusted data, because it is not clear how to use these to produce forecast error variances.

Seasonally adjusted data have been used in relating time series (as in econometric modeling) presumably on the assumption that their use would eliminate the need to deal explicitly with seasonality in the model without altering the relationships between the series. We now survey some of the work that has been done on the consequences of using adjusted data for this purpose. A more detailed discussion of some of this work is given by Nerlove, Grether, and Carvalho (1979, pp. 162–71).

Lovell (1963, 1966) and Jorgenson (1964, 1967) investigated regression approaches to seasonal adjustment and the appropriateness of seasonally adjusting time series before subsequently using them in a regression analysis. Lovell (1963) showed that prior adjustment by regressing the dependent and explanatory variables on seasonal dummy variables can be appropriate, since this gives the same results as including the seasonal dummy variables in a regression with the unadjusted data. He also noted that adjusting effectively uses up some degrees of freedom and that results with the adjusted data should be modified accordingly. Jorgenson (1964) discussed optimal (i.e. minimum mean squared error) estimation of the seasonal component (in a regression model). Their subsequent papers (Lovell 1966 and Jorgenson 1967) point out that the optimal estimate of the seasonal component is not generally appropriate for adjusting series prior to relating them in a regression model.

Sims (1974) considered the estimation of a distributed lag relation between the nonseasonal components of two time series, y and x, when they are observed with seasonal noise added. He observed that the estimated lag distribution can be biased (especially if a smooth, one-sided—rather than long, two-sided—lag distribution is estimated) and that seasonal adjustment of both y and x by a linear filter that removes seasonality in x can reduce the bias. He considered adjustment filters for this purpose, noting that official procedures (or seasonal differencing or removal of seasonal means) may not be suitable. He found that if y and x are adjusted with different filters, then the bias may be reduced;

but it may be made much worse, so it is usually safer to use the same filter on y and x. The exception to the rule occurs when the seasonal components of y and x are unrelated, in which case optimal (i.e. minimum mean squared error) adjustment of x alone will remove the bias.

Wallis (1974) also observed that adjusting y and x with different filters can distort the lag relationships between them, so using the same filter is safer. He further observed that using the filter that reduces to white noise the residuals in the distributed lag regression of y on x will produce efficient estimates, since this is equivalent to doing generalized least squares. He then used simulated time series to verify his conclusions regarding the effect of seasonal adjustment on estimated relations between series and to ascertain that a linear filter approximation to X-11 that he had devised behaved similarly in this respect to X-11 itself.

An additional point was made by Granger (1978a). He showed that if the seasonal components of two series are correlated and the nonseasonal components are independent, then the adjusted series will be correlated if both series are adjusted separately with linear filters. Thus the adjusted series will exhibit a relationship even though the nonseasonal components are unrelated.

Newbold (1980) illustrated some problems that can arise when relating one adjusted series to another through a transfer function (distributed lag) model. In his example, nonseasonal models were inadequate for his adjusted series and led to distortions in the estimated transfer function and noise models. He remedied these problems by putting 'antiseasonal' terms (leading to negative correlations at seasonal lags) in his model. His example illustrates that it is dangerous to assume, at least without checking, that nonseasonal models will be appropriate for seasonally adjusted data, and he shows how one might proceed when a nonseasonal model is inappropriate.

From these studies, we might conclude that it is hard to say what effect using seasonally adjusted data has on forecast accuracy. Using seasonally adjusted data, however, has a severe disadvantage in forecasting, since it prevents estimation of forecast error variances and production of forecast intervals—something that can be done with the unadjusted data. Adjusted data can be useful in relating series; here, it is usually safer to use the same adjustment filter on all series, unless the seasonal components on the series are known to be unrelated. Sims (1974) and Wallis (1974) offer guidance, the latter pointing out that using X-11 (with standard options) on all series is close to using the same linear filter on all of them. It should be kept in mind, however, that the simplicity of using adjusted data is bought at some risk of biased or inefficient estimation of relationships between series, that degrees of freedom need to be modified if adjusted data are used, and that as illustrated by Newbold (1980), even the simplicity of adjusted data is sometimes illusory.

4.2   Defining the components

It is surprising that so many people have provided estimates of seasonal, trend, cyclic, and irregular components without bothering to define what they were estimating. Statements made about the components have tended to be vague—really descriptions rather than definitions. For example, Falkner said, '*Seasonal variation* is that part of the fluctuation due to the persistent tendency for certain months of each year to be regularly higher than certain other months of the year' (1924, p. 167), and '*Secular trend* is the long-time tendency of the items of the series to grow or decline' (p. 167). Shiskin, Young, and Musgrave stated, 'The seasonal component(s) is defined as the intrayear pattern of variation which is repeated constantly or in an evolving fashion from year to year' (1967, p. 1). Although few would argue with these statements, they are certainly not enough to define what is being estimated.

In recent years, there have been efforts in the direction of more mathematically precise definitions of the seasonal component based on spectral considerations. The first of these was by Nerlove, who defined seasonality as 'that characteristic of a time series that gives rise to spectral peaks at seasonal frequencies' (1964, p. 262). Granger (1987a) gave a reasonably precise definition of when a series is seasonal and when it is strongly seasonal. He suggested taking intervals of width δ (for some small $\delta > 0$) about the seasonal frequencies $2\pi k/12$, $k = 1$, ..., 6; then he defined a seasonal time series as one whose spectral density has peaks somewhere in these intervals and a strongly seasonal time series as one whose spectral density integrated over all of these intervals almost equals the integral of the spectral density over $[0, \pi]$. The problem is that these definitions only tell us when a series has a seasonal component, not what the seasonal component is.

It is essential that the component models be precisely specified; otherwise it is not known what is being estimated in seasonal adjustment. We now present an approach to defining the seasonal and nonseasonal components for the additive decomposition $Z_t = S_t + N_t$. Z_t may, of course, be transformed data. We assume that trading day and other deterministic effects have been removed from Z_t. The definitions of the components are based on the following assumptions, grouped for purposes of discussion.

Basic Assumptions

   1. $Z_t = S_t + N_t$.

2. $\{S_t\}$ and $\{N_t\}$ are independent of each other.

Harmless Assumptions

3. Z_t follows a known ARIMA model $\phi^*(B)Z_t = \theta^*(B)a_t$.
4. S_t follows an unknown ARIMA model $\phi_S(B)S_t = \theta_S(B)b_t$.
5. N_t follows an unknown ARIMA model $\phi_N(B)N_t = \theta_N(B)c_t$.
6. $\phi_S(B)$ and $\phi_N(B)$ have no common zeros.

Arbitrary Assumptions

7. $\phi_S(B) = 1 + B + \ldots + B^{11}$.
8. The order of $\phi_S(B) \leq 11$.
9. $\sigma_b^2 = \text{var}(b_t)$ is as small as possible, consistent with assumptions 1–8.

Under these assumptions, the results of Hillmer and Tiao (1982) can be used to show that the models for S_t and N_t are uniquely determined. (It is mathematically possible for the model for Z_t to be such that a decomposition according to these assumptions does not exist; however, we have rarely found this to happen in practice.) We then define the components S_t and N_t to be the unobserved time series satisfying these assumptions. This definition does not allow exact calculation of S_t and N_t from Z_t, nor should it; but it does tell us what models they follow, which allows us to use signal extractions theory to estimate them. It is vital to discuss why it might be reasonable to make the above assumptions.

The basic assumptions, 1 and 2, define the problem. Someone who does not want to make these assumptions is working on a different problem. (Actually, with respect to assumption 2, note that since S_t and N_t will be nonstationary, they will require starting values. We may want to allow these starting values to be correlated, and only assume that b_t and c_t are independent.) In assumption 3, it is assumed that an ARIMA model can be built from the observed data to aproximate adequately the covariance structure of Z_t. This allows us to handle a wide range of time series, since data that are seasonally adjusted can often be modeled with ARIMA models. A larger class of models than pure ARIMA models is actually allowed, since it is assumed that deterministic effects, such as trading day variation, have been subtracted out. With regard to assumptions 4 and 5, if Z_t follows an ARIMA model, then it seems harmless to assume that S_t and N_t also follow ARIMA models. For all of the ARIMA models here, we assume that the autoregressive and moving average polynomials for a given model have no common zeros and the white noise series (a_t, b_t, c_t) have zero mean and constant variance. If assumption 6 does not hold, then the spectral densities of S_t and N_t will have peaks of similar intensity at the same frequency, which seems unreasonable.

Based on our experience with series that are seasonally adjusted, appropriate models for these series typically have

$$\phi^*(B) = \phi(B)(1 - B)^d(1 - B^{12})$$
$$= \phi(B)(1 - B)^{d+1}(1 + B + \ldots + B^{11}),$$

where $d \geq 0$ and $\phi(B)$ is of low order in B (say, ≤ 3). Given assumptions 1–6, Findley (1985) has shown that $\phi^*(B) = \phi_S(B)\phi_N(B)$, so for the above $\phi^*(B)$, we let

$$\phi_S(B) = 1 + B + \ldots + B^{11}$$

and

$$\phi_N(B) = \phi(B)(1 - B)^{d+1},$$

which leads to assumption 7.

Hillmer and Tiao (1982) show that our choice for $\phi_S(B)$ leads to a spectral density for the seasonal component that has infinite peaks at the seasonal frequencies and relative minima between them. Furthermore, assumption 7 implies that summing S_t over 12 consecutive months produces a stationary series with mean zero, which is consistent with the general belief (as in X-11) that in an additive decomposition the seasonal component should sum to something near zero over a year. The nonseasonal component will be nonstationary, and its spectral density will have an infinite peak at zero frequency. Thus assumption 7 leads to reasonable seasonal and nonseasonal component models.

One case not addressed in our choice of autoregressive operators in assumption 7 is that of models with stationary seasonal autoregressive operators. For models including a factor $1 - B^{12}$, we invariably find seasonal moving average terms to be more appropriate than seasonal autoregressive terms. We have modeled a few series without a $1 - B^{12}$, using instead a seasonal autoregressive operator, $1 - \phi_{12}B^{12}$, where ϕ_{12} is not near 1. We have chosen not to adjust such series because the seasonal pattern of the data tends to change quickly—the highest month could become the lowest month after four or five years. A similar choice was made by Hannan (1964). It is possible to make a different choice of $\phi_S(B)$ and still use the preceding framework if a set of rules replacing assumption 7—for specifying $\phi_S(B)$ and $\phi_N(B)$ given $\phi^*(B)$—is provided.

Hillmer, Bell, and Tiao (1983a) noted that assumption 8 implies that the forecast function in the model for S_t follows a fixed annual pattern that sums to zero over 12 consecutive months. In contrast, if the order of $\theta_S(B)$ exceeds 11, then the forecast function for the seasonal component will change its annual pattern. The forecastable change in the seasonal pattern should be part of the trend and hence included in N_t.

Given assumptions 1–8, Hillmer and Tiao (1982) showed that σ_b^2 must lie in some known range $[\bar{\sigma}_b^2, \tilde{\sigma}_b^2]$ and that the models for S_t and N_t are uniquely determined once a choice of σ_b^2 is made. They called the decomposition corresponding to a σ_b^2 in $[\bar{\sigma}_b^2, \tilde{\sigma}_b^2]$ an admissible decomposition, with corresponding admissible seasonal and nonseasonal components; and they called the decomposition corresponding to the choice $\sigma_b^2 = \bar{\sigma}_b^2$ the *canonical decomposition*. Thus we have defined the seasonal component to be the *canonical seasonal component*, $\bar{S}_t$, corresponding to the choice $\sigma_b^2 = \bar{\sigma}_b^2$. The *canonical nonseasonal component*, $\bar{N}_t$, is then $Z_t - \bar{S}_t$. Hillmer and Tiao (1982) demonstrated that choosing $\sigma_b^2 = \bar{\sigma}_b^2$ minimizes $\text{var}[(1 + B + \ldots + B^{11})S_t]$, making the seasonal pattern as stable as possible. In addition, they established that for any other choice of σ_b^2, the corresponding seasonal component, S_t', can be written $S_t' = \bar{S}_t + e_t$, where e_t is white noise. Thus any admissible seasonal component is the sum of the canonical seasonal component (which follows as stable a pattern as possible and is as predictable as possible) and white noise (which is totally unpredictable and nonseasonal). We see no reason to add white noise to $\bar{S}_t$, when defining the seasonal component.

Assumptions 1–9 lead to precise definitions of the seasonal and nonseasonal components. If we have built a model for the observed data Z_t and assumptions 1–9 are made, then we know the models for $\bar{S}_t$ and $\bar{N}_t$ and can use signal extraction theory to estimate these components. This is the approach to seasonal adjustment taken in Burman (1980), Hillmer and Tiao (1982), and Hillmer, Bell, and Tiao (1983a). Of course, assumptions other than 1–9 can be made about S_t and N_t, even while remaining consistent with the model for Z_t; in particular, a choice of σ_b^2 in $[\bar{\sigma}_b^2, \tilde{\sigma}]$ other than $\bar{\sigma}_b^2$ could be used. Different assumptions will lead to different definitions and models for the components, which, when used in signal extraction theory, will lead to different methods of seasonal adjustment.

This discussion points out the arbitrariness inherent in seasonal adjustment. Different methods produce different adjustments because they make different assumptions about the components and hence estimate different things. This arbitrariness applies equally to methods (such as X-11) that do not make their assumptions explicit, since they must implicitly make the same sort of assumptions as we have discussed here. (The assumptions implicit in additive X-11 with standard options are investigated by Cleveland and Tiao (1976), by Burridge and Wallis (1984), and in Sect. 4.3.4.) Unfortunately, there is not enough information in the data to define the components, so these types of arbitrary choices must be made. We have tried to justify our assumptions but do not expect everyone to agree with them. If, however, anyone wants to do seasonal adjustment but does not want to make these assumptions, we urge them to make clear what assumptions they wish to make. Then the appropriateness of the various assumptions can be debated. This debate would be more productive than the current one regarding the choice of seasonal adjustment procedures, in which no one bothers to specify what is being estimated. Thus if debate can be centered on *what* it is we want to estimate in doing seasonal adjustment, then there may be no dispute about *how* to estimate it.

4.3   Evaluating seasonal adjustments and seasonal adjustment methods

Given the arbitrary nature of seasonal adjustment, people have found it difficult to decide when a 'good' adjustment has been done or when one method is 'better' than another. In this section, we discuss the problems with approaches that have been used to evaluate adjustments and adjustment methods, including criteria for evaluating adjustments, simulation studies, and revisions comparisons. Finally, we make some suggestions about how seasonal adjustment evaluation might be approached.

4.3.1   Criteria for evaluating seasonal adjustments

Various criteria have been proposed for assessing the adequacy of a seasonal adjustment and for deciding when one method does a better job of adjusting a series than another. Attempts at designing such criteria have failed, so today there are no accepted standards by which adjustments can be judged.

Criteria proposed for evaluating seasonal adjustments have generally reflected properties that were thought to be desirable for nonseasonal components. These criteria have been phrased in both spectral and time domain terms. It has been thought that a method performed adequately if the adjusted series exhibited properties similar to those of the 'true' nonseasonal component, and the performances of different adjustment methods have been compared, based on this belief. Unfortunately, although the suggested criteria may reflect desirable properties for the nonseasonal component of a series, this does not mean that they reflect desirable properties for the adjusted series, which is an *estimate* of the nonseasonal component. Anderson (1927) emphasized long ago that the estimated components are not the same as the true components. Furthermore, even if models for Z_t, S_t, and N_t are not known, the true underlying components cannot be calculated; and the best estimates of the components will behave differently enough from the true components to make the proposed criteria of little or no value in evaluating seasonal adjustments. To substantiate this, we cite two examples.

First, Nerlove (1964) suggested various spectral criteria that a good adjustment should satisfy, including (a) high coherence between original and adjusted series, except at seasonal frequencies, (b) minimal phase shifts in the cross spectrum between the original and adjusted series, and (c) removal of peaks at the seasonal frequencies in the spectral density of the original series, without producing dips at these frequencies or greatly affecting the spectral density at other frequencies. Subsequently, Grether and Nerlove (1970) investigated empirically (by simulating series from known component models) and theoretically the perform-ance of the optimal (i.e. minimum mean squared error linear) method of adjustment. They discovered that the optimal method did not look good in terms of these criteria. It reproduced all of the undesirable features that Nerlove (1964) had noted for X-11. Since the minimum mean squared error linear estimator is a reasonable choice if it is available, they concluded that the criteria in Nerlove (1964) left much to be desired.

Second, Granger (1978a) reviewed some criteria that could be used for evaluating adjustments, including (a) and (c) of Nerlove (1964), which he referred to as 'highly desirable'. In their discussions of Granger's paper, both Sims (1978) and Tukey (1978) showed that the spectral properties he suggested have unreasonable parallels in other situations and that the minimum mean squared error linear adjustment need not satisfy these properties. (Wecker (1978) made similar com-ments about why 'overadjustment', the production of dips at seasonal frequencies in the spectrum of the adjusted series, should not be regarded as a problem.) Granger then responded, 'The criteria I suggested have been shown to be impossible to achieve in practice, and thus, should be replaced by achievable criteria. However, I am at a loss to know what these criteria should be' (1978b, p. 55).

Empirical studies comparing the performance of different adjustment methods on various sets of data using the previously proposed criteria are of little value in determining which methods of adjustment are 'better' than others. We doubt that useful criteria that are functions of the adjusted data only can be found. There may be a role, however, for the previously mentioned criteria. Since these criteria are reasonable when applied to the true nonseasonal component, they may be useful in evaluating the assumptions made about the components by adjustment methods. Thus in our approach to defining the components discussed in Section 4.2, we used some criteria to evaluate the properties of the assumed underlying component models. These and other criteria might be applied to the assumptions underlying other seasonal adjustment methods. Efforts would be better spent evaluating the assumptions underlying adjustment methods, rather than trying to evaluate methods by looking at adjusted data.

4.3.2   Simulation studies

Another approach that has been suggested for evaluating seasonal adjustment methods is to check their performance on simulated series. The S_t and N_t components are generated and an adjustment method applied to $Z_t = S_t + N_t$ to see how accurately the method estimates the components. In general, little will be learned from such studies.

The basic problem with this aproach is that the results depend heavily on what the adjustment methods being considered are actually estimating. This can vary considerably from method to method. If one method makes assumptions about S_t and N_t that are similar to those used in generating them and a second method makes different assumptions, then the first method will estimate the components more accurately than the second. This phenomenon is reflected in the results of Godfrey and Karreman (1967). Comparing different methods on simulated data will merely verify that the methods make different assumptions.

To illustrate the preceding remarks, we generated S_t and N_t series of length 900 from each of the following two models, the rationale for which will become apparent.

1. Min Seasonal Model

$$(1 + B + \ldots + B^{11})S_{1t} = (1 + 1.45B + 1.50B^2$$
$$+ 1.44B^3 + 1.24B^4$$
$$+ .99B^5 + .72B^6$$
$$+ .45B^7 + .23B^8$$
$$+ .002B^9 - .11B^{10}$$
$$- .43B^{11})b_{1t}, \ b_{1t} \text{ iid } N(0, .0107)$$

$$(1 - B)^2 N_{1t} = (1 - 1.38B + .39B^2)d_{1t}, \ d_{1t} \text{ iid } N(0, .8223)$$

2. Max Seasonal Model

$$(1 + B + \ldots + B^{11})S_{2t} = (1 + 1.10B + 1.10B^2$$
$$+ 1.05B^3 + .99B^4$$
$$+ .96B^5 + .94B^6$$
$$+ .94B^7 + .86B^8$$
$$+ .80B^9 + .83B^{10}$$
$$+ .87B^{11})b_{2t}, \ b_{2t} \text{ iid } N(0, .4422)$$

$$(1 - B)^2 N_{2t} = (1 + .01B - .98B^2) d_{2t}, \ d_{2t} \text{ iid } N(0, .0740)$$

For both of these models, the resulting model for the sum $Z_{it} = S_{it} + N_{it}$

is the same and is given by

$$(1 - B)(1 - B^{12})Z_{it} = (1 - .4B)(1 - .8B^{12})a_{it}, \quad a_{it} \text{ iid } N(0, 1).$$

Actually, the Min Seasonal Model corresponds to making assumptions 1–9 given in Section 4.2 (lowest possible σ_b^2), and the Max Seasonal Model makes assumptions 1–8 and then chooses the maximum possible σ_b^2. The series were generated in such a way that in fact the same series was obtained from both models; that is, we have $Z_t = S_{it} + N_{it}$, $i = 1, 2$. The following model was identified and estimated for the observed data Z_t:

$$(1 - B)(1 - B^{12})Z_t = (1 - .41B)(1 - .85B^{12})a_t, \quad \sigma_a = .967$$

Using signal extraction theory and the estimated model for Z_t, S_{it} and N_{it} ($i = 1, 2$) were estimated from Z_t under two assumptions:

1. that the true model for S_{it} had minimum σ_b^2, and
2. that the true model for S_{it} had maximum σ_b^2.

Thus, as can be seen in Table 1, there are four cases. In cases A and C, the correct models for S_{it} and N_{it} (within parameter estimation error) have been used, and in cases B and D, incorrect models have been used. The error series

$$e_{it} = S_{it} - \hat{S}_{it} = \hat{N}_{it} - N_{it}$$

were computed in each of the four cases, and the e_{it}'s were standardized by dividing them by their standard deviation from signal extraction theory under the correct model. The results are shown in Figure 1 for the middle 100 observations.

When the correct model is used, as in Figure 1A and C, the standardized e_{it}'s vary about zero reasonably within ± 2 limits. When the incorrect model is used, however, as in Figure 1B and D, the e_{it}'s are considerably larger. This does not tell us that either the Min Seasonal or Max Seasonal method of adjustment is better; it merely illustrated how the accuracy of the estimator depends heavily on what is being estimated.

TABLE 1.   A simulation experiment with model-based seasonal adjustment

	Model used	
Case	To generate data	To construct $\hat{S}_{it}$, $\hat{N}_{it}$
A	Min seasonal	Min seasonal
B	Min seasonal	Max seasonal
C	Max seasonal	Max seasonal
D	Max seasonal	Min seasonal

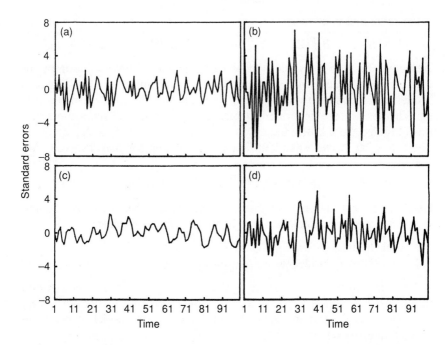

FIG. 1. Standardized signal extraction errors for model-based seasonal adjustment with data simulated from model $(1 - B)(1 - B^{12})Z_t = (1 - .4B)(1 - .8B^{12})a_t$. (A, B, C, and D refer to Table 1.)

4.3.3   Revisions

Most seasonal adjustment methods are based on symmetric two-sided filters. When the observation for the current time period is adjusted, future observations are not available; thus near the end of the series, one-sided filters must be used. As more observations become available, one can come closer to using the symmetric filter. The changes in the seasonally adjusted values as additional observations are added are called revisions.

Many researchers who have conducted empirical studies of seasonal adjustment methods have used measures of the magnitude of revisions as one criteria for evaluating the different methods. This makes sense when comparing adjustment methods that give the same final adjustment, such as X-11 and X-11 ARIMA, or X-11 in year-ahead and concurrent modes. In this case the different methods are all shooting at the same target value—the final X-11 adjustment. Comparisons of the magnitudes of total revisions (changes from the initial to the final adjustment) reflect how close the initial adjustments come to the target. Since the final adjustment is, presumably, better than the earlier adjustments (or we would not bother to revise as additional data became available), lower total revisions are better. Studies comparing total revisions for X-11 and modifications to X-11 that still yield the same final adjustment were done by Dagum (1978), Geweke (1978a), Kenny and Durbin (1982), and McKenzie (1984).

There is a fundamental problem, however, with using revisions as a standard of comparison when the methods being compared produce different final adjustments and thus estimate different nonseasonal components. In this case the magnitude of revisions can be greatly affected by the choice of nonseasonal components. This choice should be based on information in the data and beliefs about seasonality (see Sects. 4.2 and 4.3.4), not on the magnitude of revisions. In the extreme, one could use a method based exclusively on one-sided filters, which leads to no revisions—an approach that has seldom been adopted.

To illustrate the dependence of the size of revisions on the final adjustment used, we shall consider additive X-11 with standard options, the model-based method of Section 4.2 (min seasonal model), and the max seasonal model variant of this discussed in Section 4.3.2. Suppose these methods are used by applying their symmetric filters to data extended with minimum mean squared error forecasts and backcasts. This minimizes the mean squared revisions (MSR) (Geweke 1978a) and Pierce 1980b), so differences in MSR between the methods for a given model for Z_t are only due to the different final adjustment targets. Using the results of Pierce (1980b), we computed mean squared total revisions for the particular case where Z_t follows the model

$$(1 - B)(1 - B^{12})Z_t = (1 - \theta_1 B)(1 - \theta_{12}B^{12})a_t$$

for various values of θ_1 and θ_{12}, with $\sigma_b^2 = 1$. Table 2 presents some illustrative results. Notice that the magnitude of revisions for a given model depends dramatically on the relevant final adjustment. It also depends on the characteristics of the data, so that no one method gives the lowest MSR for all series. These results point out the inappropriate-

TABLE 2. Mean   squared   total   revisions   when $(1 - B)(1 - B^{12})Z_t = (1 - \theta_1 B)(1 - \theta_{12}B^{12})u_t(\upsilon_a^2 - 1)$

θ_1	θ_{12}	X-11	Model-based (min seasonal)	Model-based (max seasonal)
.3	.5	.123*	.133	.177
.5	.9	.059	.032*	.114
.9	.7	.130	.079	.049*

* Minimum across the row.

ness of using total revisions to evaluate seasonal adjustment methods that give different final answers.

We might also consider how the behavior of yearly revisions—the changes in the adjusted values as each additional year of data is added—depends on the final adjustment underlying a method. It might be argued that first-year revisions are relevant, since some users will not be concerned about revisions more than a year or two after the initial adjustment and thus will not be concerned with the actual final adjustment. (For X-11 with standard options, the final adjustment is effectively obtained three years after the initial adjustment; see Young 1968. For the model-based methods considered—min and max seasonal —the filters can be quite long, so the final adjustment comes much later or is effectively never achieved.) Using the assumptions and model given above, Hillmer, Bell, and Tiao (1983a) found that theoretical first-year MSR's were smaller for the min seasonal model-based method when $\theta_{12} > .4$ and smaller for X-11 when $\theta_{12} < .4$, with the difference being more pronounced the further θ_{12} was from .4. (The max seasonal method was not considered.) These theoretical calculations were confirmed empirically by studying the first-year revisions of 76 times series that were modeled and adjusted by both approaches. They found that the model-based approach gave substantially lower first-year revisions and argued that this was because the estimated values of the seasonal moving average parameter (θ_{12}) for the 76 series were almost always substantially larger than .4. Since the model-based method effectively uses longer filters than does X-11 when $\theta_{12} > .4$ and shorter filters when $\theta_{12} < .4$, this leads to the conclusion that longer filters lead to smaller first-year revisions. The filters used to adjust the most recent observations for both methods are modifications of the symmetric filter used for the final adjustment, and the lengths of the filters used for recent data correspond to the lengths of the filters used for the final adjustments. Thus the final adjustment underlying a method has a profound effect on first-year revisions.

To re-emphasize our point: these results illustrate that it is inappropriate to use measures of revisions to judge the relative merits of seasonal adjustment methods giving different final adjustments. The decision about which final adjustment is appropriate should be based on information in the data, beliefs about seasonality, and when possible, on the objectives of the seasonal adjustment. Therefore, in choosing a seasonal adjustment method it is important that attention be concentrated on what is being estimated—the target—rather than on revisions. Evaluating seasonal adjustment methods that yield different final adjustments by using revisions is like judging a parameter estimator by how rapidly it converges as the sample size increases, even if it converges to the wrong value.

4.3.4   Consistency with the data

Consider the ideal situation, in which we know the spectral densities for Z_t, S_t, and N_t: $f_Z(\lambda)$, $f_S(\lambda)$, and $f_N(\lambda)$, respectively. From $Z_t = S_t + N_t$, the spectral densities (and hence the models) are constrained by the relation

$$f_Z(\lambda) = f_S(\lambda) + f_N(s\lambda). \tag{1}$$

The minimum mean squared error estimator, $\widehat{N}_t$, of the nonseasonal component is obtained by applying a symmetric linear filter, $W_N(B)$, to the observed data:

$$\widehat{N}_t = W_N(B)Z_t, \tag{2}$$

where

$$W_N(e^{-i\lambda}) = \sum_{-\infty}^{\infty} W_{N,k} e^{-i\lambda k}$$
$$= f_N(\lambda)/f_Z(\lambda) = 1 - f_S(\lambda)/f_Z(\lambda).$$

(Bell (1984) discusses the assumptions under which (4) provides the minimum mean squared error (linear) estimator of N_t when S_t or N_t or both are nonstationary.) Notice that any two of $f_Z(\lambda)$, $f_S(\lambda)$, $f_N(\lambda)$, and $W_N(B)$ are sufficient to determine the other two, using (1) and (2), but no one of them is sufficient to determine the other three.

In practice, although we will not know $f_Z(\lambda)$, we can at least approximate it by modeling Z_t. Let $\widetilde{f}_Z(\lambda)$ be our estimate of $f_Z(\lambda)$. Now suppose that we have a linear filter, $W_N(B)$, to be used in adjusting Z_t. From (2), the implied spectral densities for S_t and N_t are

$$\hat{f}_S(\lambda) = \hat{f}_Z(\lambda)[1 - W_N(e^{-i\lambda})], \quad \hat{f}_N(\lambda) = \hat{f}_Z(\lambda)W_N(e^{-i\lambda}). \tag{3}$$

By examining $\hat{f}_S(\lambda)$ and $\hat{f}_N(\lambda)$ we can investigate the assumptions that are implicit when Z_t is adjusted with $W_N(B)$.

Suppose $W_N(B)$ results from signal extraction theory for some set of models for Z_t, S_t, and N_t, which we assume are expressed in infinite autoregressive form as

$$\Pi_Z(B)Z_t = a_t, \quad \Pi_S(B)S_t = b_t, \quad \Pi_N(B)N_t = c_t. \tag{4}$$

$W_N(B)$ then satisfies the equation

$$W_N(e^{-i\lambda}) = f_N(\lambda)/f_Z(\lambda) = \frac{\sigma_c^2/\Pi_N(e^{i\lambda})\Pi_N(e^{-i\lambda})}{\sigma_a^2/\Pi_Z(e^{i\lambda})\Pi_Z(e^{-i\lambda})}.$$

We cannot say adjustment with $W_N(B)$ implies the models in (4) because if all of the models in (4) are replaced by the models

$$\sigma(B)\Pi_Z(B)Z_t = a_t,$$
$$\sigma(B)\Pi_S(B)S_t = b_t,$$
$$\sigma(B)\Pi_N(B)N_t = c_t, \tag{5}$$

where $\alpha(B) = 1 + \sum_1^\infty \alpha_j B^j$ has all of its zeros on or outside the unit circle, then the adjustment filter is

$$\frac{f_N(\lambda)/\alpha(e^{i\lambda})\alpha(e^{-i\lambda})}{f_Z(\lambda)/\alpha(e^{i\lambda})\alpha(e^{-i\lambda})} = W_N(e^{-i\lambda}).$$

Thus the adjustment filter stays the same. This reflects the fact that $W_N(B)$ alone cannot determine the models for Z_t, S_t, and N_t. If we have an estimated model $\hat{\Pi}_Z(B)Z_t = a_t$ and an estimate $\hat{\sigma}_a^2$, however, then setting $\alpha(B) = \hat{\Pi}_Z(B)/\Pi_Z(B)$ in (5) leads to implied models for S_t and N_t:

$$\hat{\Pi}_S(B)S_t = \hat{b}_t \qquad \hat{\Pi}_N(B)N_t = \hat{c}_t$$

$$\hat{\Pi}_S(B) = \frac{\hat{\Pi}_Z(B)\Pi_S(B)}{\Pi_Z(B)} \qquad \hat{\Pi}_N(B) = \frac{\hat{\Pi}_Z(B)\Pi_N(B)}{\Pi_Z(B)}$$

$$\hat{\sigma}_b^2 = (\sigma_b^2/\sigma_a^2)\hat{\sigma}_a^2 \qquad \hat{\sigma}_c^2 = (\sigma_c^2/\sigma_a^2)\hat{\sigma}_a^2 \tag{6}$$

Of course, if (4) uses the estimated model for Z_t, then $\Pi_Z(B) = \hat{\Pi}_Z(B)$, $\sigma_a^2 = \hat{\sigma}_a^2$, and the models in (6) are the same as those in (4). The implied spectral densities for S_t and N_t are obtained from the relation

$$\hat{f}_S(\lambda) = \hat{\sigma}_b^2/2\pi \hat{\Pi}_S(e^{i\lambda})\hat{\Pi}_S(e^{-i\lambda}),$$

$$\hat{f}_N(\lambda) = \hat{\sigma}_c^2/2\pi \hat{\Pi}_N(e^{i\lambda})\hat{\Pi}_N(e^{-i\lambda}). \tag{7}$$

The preceding discussion suggests an approach to evaluating the suitability of any linear adjustment method for a particular time series. The overriding consideration is that any method of seasonal adjustment should be consistent with the information in the data, which is summarized, at least approximately, by the estimated model (spectral density) for Z_t. If the implied models (spectral densities) for S_t and N_t in (3), (6), and (7) are seen to be unreasonable, such as if the model for N_t is seasonal, we would conclude that seasonal adjustment using $W_N(B)$ is *inconsistent* with the information in the data. If the implied models (spectral densities) appear reasonable, we would say the seasonal adjustment with $W_N(B)$ is *consistent* with the information in the data. This leads us to propose the following criterion for evaluating a method of seasonal adjustment with respect to a given set of data: *A method of seasonal adjustment should be consistent with an adequate model for the observed data.* This condition is not sufficient for a 'good' seasonal adjustment, since although a method may satisfy the condition for a given set of data, it does not follow that the resulting seasonal adjustment is 'good'. Since many different seasonal adjustments can be consistent with an adequate model for the data (see Sect. 4.3.2), judgements about whether a method that is consistent with the data is 'good' must either be made subjectively, or be based on additional information, such as the intended use of the adjusted data. The criterion is necessary for a good seasonal adjustment, however, in that any method not consistent with the information contained in an adequate model for a given set of data is certainly bad for that set of data. Application of the criterion depends on arbitrary judgements regarding the adequacy of the fitted model for Z_t and the reasonableness of the implied models (spectral densities) for S_t and N_t. Even with these difficulties, application of the criterion can be informative and sometimes the conclusions will be obvious, as we shall illustrate with an example.

We should point out that (3) may not be defined at $\lambda = k\pi/6$, $k = 0$, $\pm 1, \ldots, \pm 6$, since $\hat{f}_Z(\lambda)$ may well be $+\infty$ at these frequencies, whereas $W_N(e^{-i\lambda})$ or $1 - W_N(e^{-i\lambda})$ may be zero at any given one of these frequencies. Depending on $\hat{f}(\lambda)$ and $W_B(B)$, it may be sensible to set $\hat{f}_S(\lambda) = +\infty$ at the seasonal frequencies and $\hat{f}_N(\lambda) = +\infty$ at $\lambda = 0$. This problem does not arise if $W_N(B)$ corresponding to models (4) and (6) are used. We present our criterion as a general approach to evaluating the consistency of a seasonal adjustment method with a model for the data and hope to investigate the computational considerations further.

Example. We evaluate the use of the X-11 method (additive version with standard options) on the series $Z_t = $ employed nonagricultural males, aged 20 and older (ENM20) from January 1965 through August 1979 (data from the Bureau of Labor Statistics). Young (1968) found a linear filter that approximates additive X-11. Cleveland and Tiao (1976) then found approximately the same filter results from signal extraction theory, using the following models for S_t and N_t:

$$(1 - B^{12})S_t = (1 + .64B^{12} + .83B^{24})b_t,$$
$$(1 - B)^2 N_t = (1 - 1.252B + .4385B^2)c_t,$$
$$\sigma_c^2 \, \sigma_b^2 = 24.5. \tag{8}$$

(They actually gave models for the trend (T_t) and irregular (I_t). The model for $N_t = T_t + I_t$ can be obtained from these.) The models in (8) lead to a model for Z_t:

$$(1 - B)(1 - B^{12})Z_t = (1 - .337B + .144B^2$$
$$+ .141B^3 + .139B^4$$
$$+ .136B^5 + .131B^6$$
$$+ .125B^7 + .117B^8$$
$$+ .106B^9 + .093B^{10}$$
$$+ .077B^{11} - .417B^{12}$$

$$+ .232B^{13} - .001B^{20}$$
$$- .003B^{21} - .004B^{22}$$
$$- .006B^{23} + .035B^{24}$$
$$- .021B^{25})a_t$$
$$= \eta(B)a_t; \quad \sigma_a^2/\sigma_b^2 = 43.1 \tag{9}$$

(For alternative models for X-11, see Burridge and Wallis 1984.) For ENM20, we obtained the model

$$\frac{(1 - .26B)(1 - B)(1 - B^{12})}{1 - .88B^{12}} Z_t = a_t$$
$$\hat{\sigma}_a^2 = 16{,}150. \tag{10}$$

The sample autocorrelations of the residuals, $\hat{a}_t 6$, from (11) are reported in Table 3. The statistics

$$Q_L = n(n + 2) \sum_{k=1}^{L} r_k(\hat{a})^2/(n - k)$$

(Ljung and Box 1978) are approximately distributed as X_{L-2}^2 if the model is adequate. For this example, none of the $r_k(\hat{a})$'s is larger in magnitude than two standard errors (.16), and $Q_{12} = 10.2$, $Q_{24} = 20.6$, and $Q_{36} = 33.9$ are all insignificant. We proceed with the estimated model (10).

The logarithm of $\hat{f}_Z(\lambda)$, the estimated spectral density corresponding to (10), is plotted in Figure 2. It has infinite peaks (truncated at 20 for the graph) at $\lambda = 0$ and at the seasonal frequencies $\lambda = \pi k/6$, $k = 1, 2, \ldots, 6$. From (6) and (8)–(10), the implied models for S_t and N_t are

$$\frac{(1 - .26B)(1 - B^{12})\eta(B)}{(1 - .88B^{12})(1 + .64B^{12} + .83B^{24})} S_t = \hat{b}_t$$
$$\hat{\sigma}_b^2 = 374.7 \tag{11}$$
$$\frac{(1 - .26B)(1 - B)^2\eta(B)}{(1 - .88B^{12})(1 - 1.252B + .4385B^2)} N_t = \hat{c}_t$$
$$\hat{\sigma}_c^2 = 9{,}176.1 \tag{12}$$

The implied spectral densities, $\hat{f}_S(\lambda)$ and $\hat{f}_N(\lambda)$, were obtained and their logarithms plotted in Figures 3 and 4. ($\hat{f}_N(\lambda)$ was computed directly, using (12), but $\hat{f}_S(\lambda)$ was obtained as $\hat{f}_Z(\lambda) - \hat{f}_N(\lambda)$ to satisfy (1). Because of the small number of significant digits provided by Cleveland and Tiao (1976), computing $\hat{f}_S(\lambda)$ directly from (11) would not have satisfied (1).) $\hat{f}_S(\lambda)$ has infinite peaks at the seasonal frequencies and may appear reasonable. (There is also an infinite peak at $\lambda = 0$ due to

TABLE 3.   Autocorrelations of residuals from model (10) for ENM20

k	1	2	3	4	5	6	7	8	9	10	11	12
$r_k(\hat{a})$	.00	.00	.11	−.06	.02	.13	−.07	.07	.02	−.02	.06	.09
k	13	14	15	16	17	18	19	20	21	22	23	24
$r_k(\hat{a})$	−.03	.04	−.01	−.13	−.08	−.02	.10	−.08	−.08	−.01	−.03	−.05
k	25	26	27	28	29	30	31	32	33	34	35	36
$r_k(\hat{a})$	−.02	−.01	−.01	.01	−.12	−.02	.00	−.14	−.02	−.03	−.14	−.07

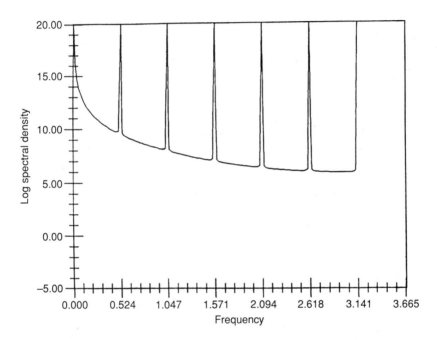

FIG. 2. Spectral density for ENM20 from model (10) ($\log \hat{f}_z(\lambda)$).

the $(1 - B)$ factor implied by the $1 - B^{12}$ in (8). It would not necessarily appear if another set of models, for example, Cleveland 1972 or Burridge and Wallis 1984, were used to approximate X-11.) $\hat{f}_N(\lambda)$, however, has (finite) dips at the seasonal frequencies, which is unreasonable. This is *not* the same as the overadjustment phenomenon referred to in Section 4.3.1, which has to do with dips in the spectral density of the adjusted data. Here we have dips in the implied spectral density for the underlying nonseasonal component, which is unreasonable. Thus we conclude that X-11 is inconsistent with the information in the data for this series.

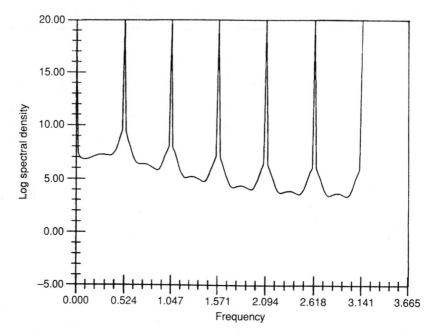

FIG. 3. Seasonal spectral density for ENM20 implied by X-11.

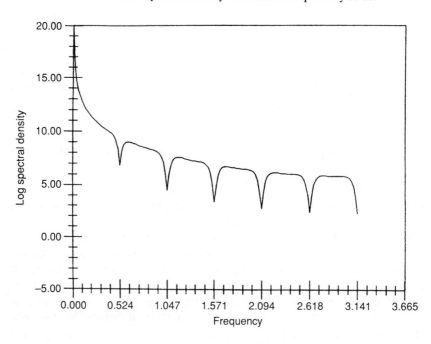

FIG. 4. Nonseasonal spectral density for ENM20 implied by X-11.

To see why the dips arose in $\hat{f}_N(\lambda)$, notice that to a rough approximation, $\eta(B)$ in (9) is

$$\eta(B) \doteq (1 - .35B)(1 - .4B^{12}),$$

so (12) becomes

$$\frac{(1 - .26B)(1 - .35B)(1 - B)^2(1 - .4B^{12})}{(1 - 1.252B + .4385B^2)(1 - .88B^{12})}\, N_t \doteq c_t.$$

Thus $\hat{f}_N(\lambda)$ contains

$$\frac{(1 - .88e^{12i\lambda})(1 - .88e^{-12i\lambda})}{(1 - .4e^{12i\lambda})(1 - .4e^{-12i\lambda})} = \frac{1.774[1 - .992\cos(12\lambda)]}{1.16[1 - .690\cos(12\lambda)]}.$$

This function is plotted in Figure 5. It is near zero at the seasonal frequencies because the $1 - .992\cos(12\lambda)$ in the numerator is quite small, whereas the $1 - .690\cos(12\lambda)$ in the denominator is at least .31 at all frequencies. This results in dips at the seasonal frequencies in $\hat{f}_N(\lambda)$. All of this follows from the estimate (.88) of the seasonal moving average parameter in (10) being considerably larger than .4, the value implicitly used by X-11. Thus this behavior can be expected whenever the estimate of θ_{12} is much greater than .4, which seems to be the case most of the time (see Sect. 4.3.3).

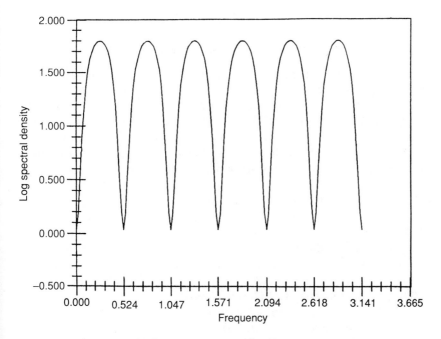

FIG. 5. $1.7744[1 - .992\cos(12\lambda)]/1.16[1 - .69\cos(12\lambda)]$.

In contrast, we examine the canonical decomposition. For the model (10), the component models turn out to be

$$(1 + B \ldots + B^{11})S_t = (1 + 2.093B$$
$$+ 2.722B^2 + 2.977B^3$$
$$+ 2.869B^4 + 2.581B^5$$
$$+ 2.169B^6 + 1.670B^7$$
$$+ 1.206B^8 + .745B^9$$
$$+ .411B^{10} - .007B^{11})b_t, \quad \sigma_b^2 = 82.11,$$

$$(1 - .26B)(1 - B)^2 N_t = (1 - .990B + .001B^2)c_t, \quad \sigma_c^2 = 14,412. \quad (13)$$

The logarithms of the implied spectral densities for S_t and N_t are plotted in Figures 6 and 7. $\hat{f}_S(\lambda)$ has infinite peaks at the seasonal frequencies and minima in between, as was noted in general in Section 4.2. $\hat{f}_N(\lambda)$ has an infinite peak at $\lambda = 0$ and decreases smoothly after that, with no dips or peaks at the seasonal frequencies. This is reasonable behavior for the implied spectral density of an underlying N_t series. Thus the canonical adjustment appears reasonable in this case, whereas additive X-11 with standard options does not.

4.3.5   Classification of linear seasonal adjustment methods

As a general aid to comparing linear methods of seasonal adjustment and assessing their consistency with observed data, we present a scheme for classifying them. Since model-based approaches are linear and Young (1968) and Wallis (1974) showed X-11 (and hence X-11 ARIMA) to be approximately linear, this scheme covers a large number of proposed adjustment methods. The linear filter used is the most important element in a linear adjustment method, so our classifications are based on the derivation of the various linear filters. Our scheme and some of the methods that fall in each group are as follows:

1. Methods that choose filters directly are (a) X-11, (b) X-11 ARIMA, and (c) SABL.

2. Methods that directly choose models for the components S_t and N_t are (a) Hannan, Terrell, and Tuckwell (1970), (b) Engle (1978), (c) Abrahams and Dempster (1979), (d) Cleveland (1979), (e) Akaike (1980), and (f) Kitagawa and Gersch (1984).

3. Methods that model the observed data and deduce models for the components from that model are (a) Melnick and Moussourakis (1974), (b) Brewer, Hagan, and Perazelli (1975), (c) Geweke (1978b), (d)

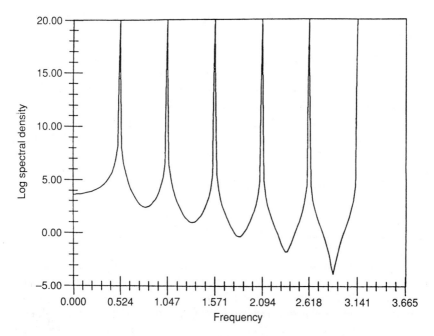

FIG. 6. Canonical seasonal spectral density for ENM20.

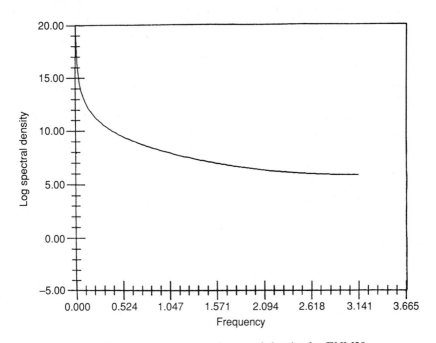

FIG. 7. Canonical nonseasonal spectral density for ENM20.

Pierce (1978), (e) Cleveland (1979), (f) Burman (1980), and (g) Hillmer and Tiao (1982).

Actually, SABL is not really linear, since it uses moving M estimates instead of moving averages. According to Cleveland, Dunn, and Terpenning (1978), however, 'the philosophy of its overall approach is exactly the same as that used in the X-11 procedure' (p. 203); so it can be viewed as a robust analogue of a linear method, and the considerations we will discuss here should apply to it. Cleveland (1979) used elements of both 2 and 3; his approach is to fit a model to Z_t, directly choose component models, and then set the parameters in the component models to approximate the overall model for Z_t.

It should be obvious that for methods in group 1, one would have to be extremely lucky to make a choice of filter that would imply reasonable component models and hence be consistent with an adequate model for Z_t. Section 4.3.4 illustrates this point for X-11. The use of nonstandard options in X-11 or other methods in group 1 may increase the chances that an adjustment method will be consistent with the data; but the number of options in such methods is necessarily limited and options are generally selected subjectively, not based objectively on a model for the data. Thus methods in group 1 are at a disadvantage when it comes to being consistent with the data.

The methods in group 2 afford the opportunity to begin with reasonable component models. Because the model for Z_t (up to parameter estimates) is determined by the specified component models, it is important when using these approaches to perform diagnostic checks on the adequacy of the resulting model for Z_t. Even when the originally specified component models appear reasonable, if the model for Z_t is deficient in some way, then these component models may not be consistent with an adequate model for Z_t. To determine whether the resulting seasonal adjustment is consistent with the data, one would first have to find an adequate model for Z_t and then proceed in the manner discussed in Section 4.3.4.

Another point to consider about methods in group 2 is that the overall model for Z_t should be estimated subject to the constraints imposed by the component models. Depending on the complexity of the component models, this may be a difficult task—Engle (1978) was unable to estimate his model for Z_t subject to all of the constraints of his component models, whereas Akaike (1980), using simpler component models, was able to do this.

In striving for consistency with the data, methods in group 3 have a potential advantage, in that they begin with a model for the observed data. This advantage will be completely lost, however, if the starting-point is an inadequate model for Z_t; hence diagnostic checking of the model is important here, too. The reasonableness of the assumptions leading from the model for Z_t to the component models should also be considered. Usually these assumptions are spelled out explicitly for these methods, which allows them to be readily evaluated.

In Section 4.3.4 we saw that a seasonal adjustment filter does not completely determine models for the components and Z_t. This makes it somewhat difficult to evaluate the assumptions being made about the components for methods in group 1, requiring an analysis like that of Section 4.3.4 for each series. Typically, methods in group 1 are applied without knowing what is being assumed. Regarding methods in group 2 and 3, there generally exist multiple sets of component models leading to the same model for Z_t. To avoid this identification problem, a particular choice must be made. Problems arise when this process is given insufficient attention and the choice is not justified, which is why we attempted to justify our choices in Section 4.2. Again, methods in group 3 have a potential advantage here, in that this approach forces consideration of the range of possible component models consistent with the model for Z_t. Methods in group 2 often employ component models based on considerations other than the suitability of their expression of beliefs about seasonality—considerations such as simplicity of the resulting estimation of the model for Z_t.

In conclusion, we favor adjustment methods in group 3 because we believe that the model for Z_t is a logical starting-point in developing an adjustment method that will be consistent with the data, and because we feel that acceptable assumptions, such as those offered in Section 4.2, can be made leading from the model for Z_t to component models.

Acknowledgements

This article is based on work supported by National Science Foundation (NSF) Grant SES 81-22051, 'Research to Improve the Government-Generated Social Science Data Base'. The research was partially conducted at the US Bureau of the Census while the authors were participants in the American Statistical Association/Census Bureau Research Program, which is supported by the Bureau of the Census and through the NSF grant. In addition, Hillmer was partially supported by NSF Grant SES 82-19336. Any opinions, findings, and conclusions or recommendations expressed here are those of the authors and do not necessarily reflect the views of the National Science Foundation, the American Statistical Association, or the Bureau of the Census.

References

(References marked with a * are included in this volume)

ABRAHAM, B., and BOX, G. E. P. (1970), 'Bayesian analysis of some outlier problems in time series', *Biometrika*, **66**, 229–36.

ABRAHAMS, D. M., and DEMPSTER, A. P. (1979), 'Research on seasonal analysis', ASA/Census Research Project Final Report, US Bureau of the Census, Statistical Research Division.

AKAIKE, H. (1980), 'Seasonal adjustment by a Bayesian modeling', *Journal of Time Series Analysis*, 1, 1–13.

ANDERSON, O. (1927), 'On the logic of the decomposition of statistical series into separate components', *Journal of the Royal Statistical Society*, Ser. A, **90**, 548–569.

BARON, R. R. V. (1973), *Analysis of Seasonality and Trends in Statistical Series. Vol. 1: Methodology, Causes and Effects of Seasonality*, Technical Publication No. 39 Jerusalem: Israel Central Bureau of Statistics.

—— (1978), 'The Analysis of Single and Related Time Series Into Components: Proposals for Improving X-11', in *Seasonal Analysis of Economic Time Series*, ed. A. Zellner. Washington, DC: US Dept. of Commerce, Bureau of the Census, 107–58.

BARTLETT, M. S. (1946), 'On the theoretical specification and sampling properties of autocorrelated time series', *Journal of the Royal Statistical Society*, Ser. B, **8**, 27–41.

—— (1950), 'Periodogram analysis and continuous spectra', *Biometrika*, **37**, 1–16.

BELL, W. R. (1983), 'A computer program for detecting outliers in time series', *Proceedings of the Business and Economic Statistics Section, American Statistical Association*, 634–9.

—— (1984), 'Signal extraction for nonstationary time series', *Annals of Statistics*, **12**, 646–64.

BEVERIDGE, W. H. (1921), 'Weather and harvest cycles', *Economic Journal*, **31**, 429–52.

—— (1922), 'Wheat prices and rainfall in western europe', *Journal of the Royal Statistical Society*, **85**, 412–59.

BLANC-LAPIERRE, A., and FORTET, R. (1965), *Theory of Random Functions*, New York: Gordon & Breach.

BOARD OF GOVERNORS OF THE FEDERAL RESERVE SYSTEM (1981), *Seasonal Adjustment of the Monetary Aggregates: Report of the Committee of Experts on Seasonal Adjustment Techniques*, Washington, DC: Federal Reserve Board.

BOX, G. E. P., HILLMER, S. C., and TIAO, G. C. (1978), 'Analysis and modeling of seasonal time series', in *Seasonal Analysis of Economic Time Series*, ed. A. Zellner, Washington, DC: US Dept. of Commerce, Bureau of the Census, 309–34.

—— and JENKINS, G. M. (1970), *Time Series Analysis: Forecasting and Control*. San Francisco: Holden Day.

—— and TIAO, G. C. (1975), 'Intervention analysis with applications to economic and environmental problems', *Journal of the American Statistical Association*, **70**, 70–9.

BREWER, K. R. W. (1979), 'Seasonal adjustment of ARIMA Series', *Économie Appliquée*, **1**, 7–22.

——, HAGAN, P. J., and PERAZZELLI, P. (1975), 'Seasonal adjustment using Box–Jenkins models', in *Bulletin of the International Statistical Institute, Proceedings of the 40th Session (Vol. 31)*. Warsaw: Central Statistical Office, 130–6.

BRITTEN, R. H., and SYDENSTRICKER, E. (1922), 'Mortality from pulmonary tuberculosis in recent years', *Public Health Reports*, **37**, 2843–58.

BURMAN, J. P. (1979), 'Seasonal adjustment—a survey', in *TIMS Studies in the Management Sciences, Vol. 12: Forecasting*. Amsterdam: North Holland, 45–57.

—— (1980), 'Seasonal adjustment by signal extraction', *Journal of the Royal Statistical Society*, Ser. A, **143**, 321–37.

BURRIDGE, P., and WALLIS, K. F. (1984), 'Unobserved-components models for seasonal adjustment filters', *Journal of Business & Economic Statistics*, **2**, 350–9.*

BUYS BALLOT, C. H. D. (1847), *Les Changements Périodiques de Température*. Utrecht: Kemink et Fils.

CARMICHAEL, F. L. (1927), 'Methods of computing seasonal indexes: constant and progressive', *Journal of the American Statistical Association*, **22**, 339–54.

CHAMPERNOWNE, D. G. (1948), 'Sampling Theory Applied to Autoregressive Sequences', *Journal of the Royal Statistical Society*, Ser. B, **10**, 204–31.

CHANG, I. (1982), 'Outliers in time series', unpublished Ph.D. dissertation, University of Wisconsin–Madison, Dept. of Statistics.

CLENDENIN, J. C. (1927), 'Measurement of variation in seasonal distribution', *Journal of the American Statistical Association*, **22**, 213–20.

CLEVELAND, W. P. (1972), 'Analysis and forecasting of seasonal time series', unpublished Ph.D. dissertation, University of Wisconsin–Madison, Dept. of Statistics.

—— (1979), 'Report to the Review Committee of the ASA/Census Project on Time Series', ASA/Census Research Project Final Report, US Bureau of the Census, Statistical Research Division.

—— and TIAO, G. C. (1976), 'Decomposition of seasonal time series: a model for the X-11 program', *Journal of the American Statistical Association*, **71**, 581–7.

CLEVELAND, W. S., DUNN, D. M., and TERPENNING, I. J. (1978), 'SABL: a resistant seasonal adjustment procedure with graphical methods for interpretation and diagnosis', in *Seasonal Analysis of Economic Time Series*, ed. A. Zellner. Washington, DC: US Dept. of Commerce, Bureau of the Census, 201–31.

COCHRANE, D., and ORCUTT, G. H. (1949), 'Application of least squares regression to relationships containing autocorrelated error terms', *Journal of the American Statistical Association*, **44**, 32–61.

COOLEY, J. W., and TUKEY, J. W. (1965), 'An algorithm for the machine calculation of complex Fourier series', *Mathematics of Computation*, **19**, 297–301.

COWDEN, D. J. (1942), 'Moving seasonal indexes', *Journal of the American Statistical Association*, **37**, 523–4.

CRUM, W. L. (1923a), 'The use of the median in determining seasonal variation', *Journal of the American Statistical Association*, **18**, 607–14.

—— (1923*b*), 'Cycles of rates on commercial paper', *Review of Economics and Statistics*, **5**, 17–29.

—— (1925), 'Progressive variation in seasonality', *Journal of the American Statistical Association*, **20**, 48–64.

CRUTCHFIELD, J., and ZELLNER, A. (1963), *Economic Aspects of the Pacific Halibut Fishery*. Washington, DC: US Government Printing Office, Dept. of the Interior.*

DAGUM, E. B. (1975), 'Seasonal factor forecasts from ARIMA models', *Bulletin of the International Statistical Institute, Proceedings of the 40th Session* (Vol. 3). Warsaw: Central Statistical Office, 203–16.

—— (1978), 'A comparison and assessment of seasonal adjustment methods for employment and unemployment statistics', National Commission on Employment and Unemployment Statistics, Background Paper No. 5, Washington, DC: Government Printing Office, 1–94.

DANIELL, P. J. (1946), 'Discussion of paper by M. S. Bartlett', *Journal of the Royal Statistical Society*, **8**, (Suppl.), 27.

DENBY, L., and MARTIN, R. D. (1979), 'Robust estimation of the first order autoregressive parameter', *Journal of the American Statistical Association*, **74**, 140–6.

DURBIN, J. (1959), 'Efficient estimation of parameters in moving average models', *Biometrika*, **46**, 306–16.

—— (1960*a*), 'Estimation of parameters in time series regression models', *Journal of the Royal Statistical Society*, Ser. B, **22**, 139–53.

—— (1960*b*), 'The fitting of time-series models', *Review of the International Statistical Institute*, **28**, 233–43.

EISENPRESS, H. (1956), 'Regression techniques applied to seasonal corrections and adjustments for calendar shifts', *Journal of the American Statistical Association*, **51**, 615–20.

ENGLE, R. F. (1978), 'Estimating structural models of seasonality', in *Seasonal Analysis of Economic Time Series*, ed. A. Zellner. Washington, DC: US Dept. of Commerce, Bureau of the Census, 281–97.*

FALKNER, H. D. (1924), 'The measurement of seasonal variation', *Journal of the American Statistical Association*, **19**, 167–79.

FINDLEY, D. F. (1985), 'On backshift-operator polynomial transformations for nonstationary time series and their aggregates', *Communications in Statistics*, Ser. A. 49–61.

FISHER, A. (1937), 'A brief note on seasonal variation', *Journal of Accountancy*, **64**, 174–99.

FISHER, R. A. (1929), 'Tests of significance in harmonic analysis', *Journal of the Royal Statistical Society*, Ser. A, **125**, 54–9.

FOX, A. J. (1972), 'Outliers in time series', *Journal of the Royal Statistical Society*, Ser. B, **43**, 350–63.

GEWEKE, J. (1978*a*), 'Revision of seasonally adjusted time series', SSRI Report No. 7822, University of Wisconsin, Dept. of Economics.

—— (1978*b*), 'The temporal and structural aggregation of seasonally adjusted time series', in *Seasonal Analysis of Economic Time Series*, ed. A. Zellner. Washington, DC: US Dept. of Commerce, Bureau of the Census, 411–27.

GILBART, J. W. (1852), 'On the laws of the currency in Ireland, as exemplified in the changes that have taken place in the amount of bank notes in circulation in Ireland, since the passing of the Acts of 1845', *Journal of the Statistical Society of London*, **15**, 307–25.

GODFREY, M. D., and KARREMAN, H. (1967), 'A spectrum analysis of seasonal adjustment', in *Essays in Mathematical Economics in Honor of Oskar Morgenstern*, ed. M. Shubik. Princeton, NJ: Princeton University Press, 367–421.

GRANGER, C. W. J. (1978a), 'Seasonality: causation, interpretation, and implications', in *Seasonal Analysis of Economic Time Series*, ed. A. Zellner. Washington, DC: US Dept. of Commerce, Bureau of the Census, 33–46.

—— (1978b), 'Response to discussants', in *Seasonal Analysis of Economic Time Series*, ed. A. Zellner. Washington, DC: US Dept. of Commerce, Bureau of the Census, 55.

—— and JOYEUX, R. (1980), 'Introduction to Long-Memory Time Series Models and Fractional Differencing', *Journal of Time Series Analysis*, **1**, 15–30.

GRESSENS, O. (1925), 'On the measurement of seasonal variation', *Journal of the American Statistical Association*, **20**, 203–9.

GRETHER, D. M., and NERLOVE, M. (1970), 'Some properties of "optimal " seasonal adjustment', *Econometrica*, **38**, 682–703.

HALD, A. (1948), *The Decomposition of a Series of Observations Composed of a Trend, a Periodic Movement, and a Stochastic Variable*. Copenhagen: G. E. C. Gads Forlag.

HALL, L. W. (1924), 'Seasonal variation as a relative of secular trend', *Journal of the American Statistical Association*, **19**, 156–66.

HANNAN, E. J. (1960), 'The estimation of seasonal variation', *Australian Journal of Statistics*, **2**, 1–15.

—— (1963), 'The estimation of seasonal variation in economic time series', *Journal of the American Statistical Association*, **58**, 31–44.

—— (1964), 'The estimation of a changing seasonal pattern', *Journal of the American Statistical Association*, **59**, 1063–77.

—— (1967), 'Measurement of a wandering signal amid noise', *Journal of Applied Probability*, **4**, 90–102.

—— TERRELL, R. D., and TUCKWELL, N. (1970), 'The seasonal adjustment of economic time series', *International Economic Review*, **11**, 24–52.

HART, W. L. (1922), 'The method of monthly means for determination of a seasonal variation', *Journal of the American Statistical Association*, **18**, 341–9.

HATANAKA, M., and SUZUKI, M. (1967), 'A theory of the pseudospectrum and its application to nonstationary dynamic econometric models', in *Essays in Mathematical Economics in Honor of Oskar Morgenstern*, ed. M. Shubik. Princeton, NJ: Princeton University Press, 443–66.

HENSHAW, R. C. (1966), 'Application of the general linear model to seasonal adjustment of economic time series', *Econometrica*, **34**, 381–95.

HILLMER, S. C., BELL, W. R., and TIAO, G. C. (1983a), 'Modeling considerations in the seasonal adjustment of economic time series', in *Applied Time Series Analysis of Economic Data*, ed. A. Zellner. Washington, DC: US Dept. of Commerce, Bureau of the Census, 74–100.

—— (1983b), 'Response to discussants', in *Applied Time Series Analysis of*

Economic Data, ed. Z. Zellner. Washington, DC: US Dept. of Commerce, Bureau of the Census, 123–4.

—— and TIAO, G. C. (1982), 'An ARIMA-model-based approach to seasonal adjustment', *Journal of the American Statistical Association,* **77**, 63–70.*

HOMAN, J. (1933), 'Adjusting for the changing date of Easter in economic series', *Journal of the American Statistical Association,* **28**, 328–32.

JONES, H. L. (1943), 'Fitting polynomial trends to seasonal data by the method of least squares', *Journal of the American Statistical Association,* **38**, 453–65.

JORGENSON, D. W. (1964), 'Minimum variance, linear, unbiased seasonal adjustment of economic time series', *Journal of the American Statistical Association,* **59**, 681–724.

—— (1967), 'Seasonal adjustment of data for econometric analysis', *Journal of the American Statistical Association,* **62**, 137–40.

JOY, A., and THOMAS, W. (1927), 'Adjustments for the influence of Easter in department stores sales', *Journal of the American Statistical Association,* **22**, 493–6.

—— (1928), 'The use of moving averages in the measurement of seasonal variations', *Journal of the American Statistical Association,* **23**, 241–52.

KENDALL, M. G. (1945), 'On the analysis of oscillatory time-series', *Journal of the Royal Statistical Society,* Ser. B, **108**, 93–129.

KENNY, P., and DURBIN, J. (1982), 'Local trend estimation and seasonal adjustment of economic and social time series', *Journal of the Royal Statistical Society,* Ser. A, **145**, 1–28.

KING, W. W. I. (1924), 'An improved method for measuring the seasonal factor', *Journal of the American Statistical Association,* **19**, 301–13.

KITAGAWA, G., and GERSCH, W. (1984), 'A smoothness priors-state space modeling of time series with trend and seasonality', *Journal of the American Statistical Association,* **79**, 378–89.

KOLMOGOROV, A. N. (1939), 'Sur l'interpolation et extrapolation des suites stationnaires', *C. R. Acad. Sci. Paris,* **208**, 2043–5.

—— (1941), 'Interpolation und extrapolation von Stationären Zufälligen Folgen', *Bull. Acad. Sci. U.R.S.S. Ser. Math.* **5**, 3–14.

KUZNETS, S. (1932), 'Seasonal pattern and seasonal amplitude: measurement of their short-time variations', *Journal of the American Statistical Association,* **27**, 9–20.

—— (1933), *Seasonal Variations in Industry and Trade.* New York: National Bureau of Economic Research.

LJUNG. G. M., and BOX, G. E. P. (1978), 'On a measure of lack of fit in time series models', *Biometrika,* **65**, 297–303.

LOVELL, M. C. (1963), 'Seasonal adjustment of economic time series and multiple regression analysis', *Journal of the American Statistical Association,* **58**, 993–1010.

—— (1966), 'Alternative axiomatizations of seasonal adjustment', *Journal of the American Statistical Association,* **61**, 800–2.

MACAULEY, F. R. (1931), *The Smoothing of Time Series.* New York: National Bureau of Economic Research.

MAKRIDAKIS, S., and HIBON, M. (1979), 'Accuracy of forecasting: an empirical investigation', *Journal of the Royal Statistical Society,* Ser. A, **142**, 97–125.

MANN, H. B., and WALD, A. (1943), 'On the statistical treatment of linear stochastic difference equations', *Econometrica*, **11**, 173–220.

MARCH, L. (1905), 'Comparison numérique de courbes statistiques', *Journal de la Société de Statistique de Paris*.

MARRIS, S. N. (1960), 'The measurement of calendar variation', in *Seasonal Adjustment on Electronic Computers*. Paris: Organization for Economic Cooperation and Development, 345–60.

MARTIN, R. D. (1980), 'Robust estimation of autoregressive models', in *Directions in Time Series*, eds. D. R. Brillinger and G. C. Tiao. Hayward, Calif.: Institute of Mathematical Statistics, 228–54.

MCKENZIE, S. (1984), 'Concurrent seasonal adjustment with census X-11', *Journal of Business & Economic Statistics*, **2**, 235–49.

MELNICK, E. L., and MOUSSOURAKIS, J. (1974), 'Filter design for the seasonal adjustment of a time series', *Communications in Statistics*, **3**, 1171–86.

MENDERSHAUSEN, H. (1937), 'Annual survey of statistical technique: methods of computing and eliminating changing seasonal fluctuations', *Econometrica*, **5**, 234–62.

—— (1939), 'Eliminating changing seasonals by multiple regression analysis', *Review of Economics and Statistics*, **21**, 171–7.

MORAN, P. A. P. (1947), 'Some theorems on time series', *Biometrika*, **34**, 281–91.

NERLOVE, M. (1964), 'Spectral analysis of seasonal adjustment procedures', *Econometrica*, **32**, 241–86.

——, GRETHER, D. M., and CARVALHO, J. L. (1979), *Analysis of Economic Time Series: A Synthesis*. New York: Academic Press.

NEWBOLD, P. (1980), 'A note on relations between seasonally adjusted variables', *Journal of Time Series Analysis*, **1**, 31–5.

ORGANIZATION FOR ECONOMIC COOPERATION AND DEVELOPMENT (1960), *Seasonal Adjustment on Electronic Computers*. Paris: Author.

PERSONS, W. M. (1919), 'Indices of Business Conditions', *Review of Economics and Statistics*, **1**, 5–107.

—— (1923), 'Correlation of Time Series', *Journal of the American Statistical Association*, **18**, 713–26.

PIERCE, D. A. (1978), 'Seasonal adjustment when both deterministic and stochastic seasonality are present', in *Seasonal Analysis of Economic Time Series*, ed. A. Zellner. Washington, DC: US Dept. of Commerce, Bureau of the Census, 242–69.

—— (1980a), 'A survey of recent developments in seasonal adjustment', *The American Statistician*, **34**, 125–34.

—— (1980b), 'Data revisions with moving average seasonal adjustment procedures', *Journal of Econometrics*, **14**, 95–114.

PLOSSER, C. I. (1978), 'A time series analysis of seasonality in econometric models', in *Seasonal Analysis of Economic Time Series*, ed. A. Zellner. Washington, DC: US Dept. of Commerce, Bureau of the Census, 365–97.

—— (1979), 'Short-term forecasting and seasonal adjustment', *Journal of the American Statistical Association*, **74**, 15–24.

PRIESTLEY, M. B. (1965), 'Evolutionary spectra and nonstationary processes', *Journal of the Royal Statistical Society*, Ser. B, **27**, 204–37.

ROBB, R. A. (1929), 'The variate difference method of seasonal variation', *Journal of the American Statistical Association,* **24**, 250–7.

ROBERTS, H. V. (1978a), 'Comments on paper by Estela Bee Dagum', in *A Comparison and Assessment of Seasonal Adjustment Methods for Employment and Unemployment Statistics.* National Commission on Employment and Unemployment Statistics, Background Paper No. 5, Washington, DC: US Government Printing Office, 116–22.

—— (1978b), 'Comments on "The analysis of single and related time series into components: proposals for improving X-11" by Raphael Raymond V. BarOn', in *Seasonal Analysis of Economic Time Series,* ed. A. Zellner. Washington, DC: US Dept. of Commerce, Bureau of the Census, 161–70.

ROBINSON, E. A. (1982), 'A historical perspective of spectrum estimation', in *Proceedings of the IEEE* (Special Issue on Spectral Estimation), **70**, 885–907.

ROSENBLATT, H. M. (1965), 'Spectral analysis and parametric methods for seasonal adjustment of economic time series', Working Paper No. 23, US Dept. of Commerce, Bureau of the Census.

SCHLICHT, E. (1981), 'A seasonal adjustment principle and a seasonal adjustment method derived from this principle', *Journal of the American Statistical Association,* **76**, 374–8.

SCHUSTER, A. (1898), 'On the investigation of hidden periodicities with application to a supposed 26-day period of meteorological phenomena', *Terrestrial Magnetism and Atmospheric Electricity,* **3**, 13–41.

SHISKIN, J. (1957), 'Electronic computers and business indicators', Occasional Paper No. 57, National Bureau of Economic Research.

—— (1978), 'Seasonal adjustment of sensitive indicators', in *Seasonal Analysis of Economic Time Series,* ed. A. Zellner. Washington, DC: US Dept. of Commerce, Bureau of the Census, 97–103.

——, YOUNG, A. H., and MUSGRAVE, J. C. (1967), 'The X-11 variant of the census method II seasonal adjustment program', Technical Paper No. 15. US Dept. of Commerce, Bureau of Economic Analysis.

SIMS, C. A. (1974), 'Seasonality in regression', *Journal of the American Statistical Association,* **69**, 618–26.*

—— (1978), 'Comments on "seasonality: causation, interpretation, and implications" by Clive W. J. Granger in *Seasonal Analysis of Economic Time Series,* ed. A. Zellner. Washington, DC: US Dept. of Commerce, Bureau of the Census, 47–9.

SLUTSKY, E. (1937), 'The summation of random causes as the source of cyclic processes', *Econometrica,* **5**, 105–46.

SNOW, E. C. (1923), 'Trade forecasting and prices', *Journal of the Royal Statistical Society,* **86**, 332–76.

SOBEL, E. L. (1967), 'Prediction of a noise-distorted, multivariate, non-stationary signal', *Journal of Applied Probability,* **4**, 330–42.

—— (1971), 'Approximate best linear prediction of a certain class of stationary and nonstationary noise-distorted signals', *Journal of the American Statistical Association,* **66**, 363–72.

STEPHENSON, J. A., and FARR, H. T. (1972), 'Seasonal adjustment of economic data by application of the general linear statistical model', *Journal of the American Statistical Association,* **67**, 37–45.

TINTNER, G. (1940), *The Variate Difference Method*. Bloomington, Ind.: Principia Press.

TUKEY, J. W. (1950), 'The sampling theory of power spectrum estimates', in *Proceedings of the Symposium on Applications of Autocorrelation Analysis to Physical Problems*. Washington, DC: Dept. of the Navy, Office of Naval Research, 47–67.

—— (1978), 'Comments on "seasonality: causation, interpretation, and implications" by Clive W. J. Granger', in *Seasonal Analysis of Economic Time Series*, ed. A. Zellner. Washington, DC: US Dept. of Commerce, Bureau of the Census, 50–4.

WALKER, A. M. (1961), 'Large sample estimation of parameters for moving-average models', *Biometrika*, **48**, 343–57.

—— (1962), 'Large sample estimation of parameters for autoregressive processes with moving-average residuals', *Biometrika*, **49**, 117–31.

WALLIS, K. F. (1974), 'Seasonal adjustment and relations between variables', *Journal of the American Statistical Association*, **69**, 18–32.*

—— (1978), 'Seasonal adjustment and multiple time series analysis', in *Seasonal Analysis of Economic Time Series*, ed. A. Zellner. Washington, DC: US Dept. of Commerce, Bureau of the Census, 347–57.

WATTS, D. G. (1978), 'Comments on "estimating structural models of seasonality" by Robert F. Engle', in *Seasonal Analysis of Economic Time Series*, ed. A. Zellner. Washington, DC: US Dept. of Commerce, Bureau of the Census, 303–7.

WECKER, W. E. (1978), 'Discussion of "seasonal adjustment when both deterministic and stochastic seasonality are present" by David A. Pierce', in *Seasonal Analysis of Economic Time Series*, ed. A. Zellner. Washington, DC: US Dept. of Commerce, Bureau of the Census, 274–80.

WHITTLE, P. (1952), 'Tests of fit in time series', *Biometrika*, **39**, 309–18.

—— (1953a), 'The analysis of multiple stationary time series', *Journal of the Royal Statistical Society*, Ser. B, **15**, 125–39.

—— (1953b), 'Estimation and information in stationary time series', *Arkiv für Matematik*, **2**, 423–34.

—— (1954a), 'A statistical investigation of sunspot observations with special reference to H. Alfven's sunspot model', *Astrophysical Journal*, **120**, 251–60.

—— (1954b), 'Some recent contributions to the theory of stationary processes', in *A Study in the Analysis of Stationary Time Series* (2nd edn.). Herman Wold, Uppsala: Almqvist and Wicksells, 196–233.

WIENER, N. (1949), *The Extrapolation, Interpolation and Smoothing of Stationary Time Series With Engineering Applications*. New York: John Wiley.

WOLD, H. (1938), *A Study in the Analysis of Stationary Time Series*. Uppsala: Almqvist and Wicksells.

YAGLOM, A. M. (1962), *An Introduction to the Theory of Stationary Random Functions*. Englewood Cliffs, NJ: Prentice-Hall.

YOUNG, A. H. (1965), 'Estimating trading-day variation in monthly economic time series', Technical Paper No. 12, US Dept. of Commerce, Bureau of the Census.

—— (1968), 'Linear approximations of the Census and BLS seasonal adjustment methods', *Journal of the American Statistical Association*, **63**, 445–71.

YULE, G. U. (1921), 'On the time correlation problem, with especial reference to the variate-difference correlation method', *Journal of the Royal Statistical Society,* **84**, 497–526.

—— (1926), 'Why do we sometimes get nonsense-correlations between time-series?', *Journal of the Royal Statistical Society,* **89**, 1–64.

—— (1927), 'On a method of investigating periodicities in disturbed series, with special reference to Wolfer's sunspot numbers', *Philosophical Transactions of the Royal Society,* Ser. A, **226**, 267–98.

PART II

Fragments of an Economic Theory of Seasonality

Introduction

Although seasonal fluctuations account for a major part of the variation in many quarterly and monthly economic time series, the attitude of many economists has been and still is well expressed in the following citation from William Stanley Jevons (1862), p. 4: 'Every kind of periodic fluctuation, whether daily, weekly, monthly, quarterly or yearly, must be detected and exhibited not only as a subject of study in itself, but because we must ascertain and eliminate such periodic variations before we can correctly exhibit those which are irregular or non-periodic, and probably of more interest and importance.'

Implicit in this attitude is the belief that seasonality is periodic to such a degree that it is relatively easy to eliminate, but also that economics has little to say about the seasonal movements and conversely that seasonal variation tells us very little of interest about economic theory. However, both views are incorrect but none the less persistent.

In their analysis of the port pricing of halibut along the north-west Pacific coast, Crutchfield and Zellner (1962) show in this early contribution that both economic theory and statistics form important building stones in a serious description of such a market, which is characterized by seasonal variations in supply and by two sources of demand. In some ports the daily landings are used for both consumption and inventory build up, while only inventory investments play a role at other places. In the fresh-fish markets the price and the size of the daily landing is negatively correlated, while there is no correlation between these two variables in markets, where the landings are bought solely to store. The formulation of an econometric model enables these features to be brought into the analysis. Similarly, the use of structural econometric models makes it possible to analyse effects on prices of conservation measures like quotas and of the creation of special seasons.

In the article by Ghysels (1988) it is proved within the context of a dynamic optimizing model of production that seasonality in an exogenous variable may induce spectral power at seasonal as well as non-seasonal frequencies of the endogenous variables. In economic terms if there exist costs of adjustment, it may pay to smooth production. The simple model applied is one where the demand consists of two components: an exogenous seasonal component and a non-seasonal price dependent component. The intertemporal maximization of the profit of the producer then implies that the exogenous seasonal component of the demand spills over into the non-seasonal components of the production series unless costs of adjustment are negligible. It may therefore be quite misleading to seasonally adjust the production series, and in addition, only by analysing the problem within the framework of a multivariate model based on the seasonally unadjusted series may we have chance of a congruent modelling of the demand and supply. This point was also made by Wallis (1974) and Sims (1974), but Ghysels makes it within the formal context of a theoretical maximizing model.

By the replacement of a single period utility function with a function varying over the seasons and by the inclusion of seasonal habit persistence, Osborn (1988) extends the analysis of Hall (1978) to the seasonal case.

The utility function applied has the form

$$U_t = (C_t)^{1-\beta_q}/(1 - \beta_q), \qquad 0 < \beta_q < 1,$$

$$q = 1, 2, 3, 4, \ t = 1, 2, \ldots, T \qquad (1)$$

when t falls in quarter q, and C_t is consumption. By maximizing

$$V_t = \sum_{i \geq 0} \alpha_q^i U_{t+i} \qquad (2)$$

subject to the period to period budget constraint $C_{t+1} = Y_{t+1} - A_{t+1} + (1 + r)A_t$, and by a few manipulations we obtain the equation

$$(1 - \varphi_{q+1}B) \ln C_{t+1} = \gamma_{q+1} + u_{t+1} \qquad (3)$$

$$\text{where} \quad \gamma_{q+1} = [\ln \alpha_{q+1} + \ln (1 + r) + \sigma^2/2]/\beta_{q+1}$$

$$\text{and} \quad \varphi_{q+1} = \beta_q/\beta_{q+1}$$

α_{q+1} is the discount rate, Y_t real income, A_t end of period real assets, r a constant real rate of interest, σ^2 a constant, u_t a disturbance term, while $\varphi_1\varphi_2\varphi_3\varphi_4 = 1$, a constraint which imply that c_{t+1} is equal to c_{t-3} plus a constant and a disturbance term, i.e. the constraint produces the seasonal difference $(1 - B^4)$.

The model is rejected by the UK data, but by introducing seasonal habit persistence in the form of a seasonally changing 4th-order lag of the left-hand side of (3) more favourable results are obtained. The study by Osborn underlines the importance of a careful and integrated treatment of seasonality.[1]

In the context of a theory model for a representative intertemporal cost minimizing firm, Miron and Zeldes (1988) investigate the production-smoothing hypothesis of finished goods inventories and assess the overall negative findings in the literature. Seasonality is seen to be important in two respects. First, most empirical investigations of the model have incorrectly used seasonally adjusted data, and secondly, the relative ease in predicting the seasonal fluctuations makes it an obvious testing ground for a production smoothing hypothesis.

---

[1] See also Winden and Palm (1990) and Engle *et al.* (1991).

The estimating equation suggested by their theory implies that the growth rate of output depends on the real rate of interest, the growth of the capital stock, the level of inventories, and productivity growth. The productivity measure is determined partly by observable seasonal variables such as precipitation and temperature and partly by unobservables, which then are considered part of the error term. However, the mean is also corrected by use of seasonal dummy variables. The inclusion of unobservable changes in productivity implies that the error term cannot be assumed uncorrelated with the regressors and therefore an instrumental variable estimator is applied. In addition to seasonally unadjusted data Miron and Zeldes also apply data seasonally adjusted by X-11, but then without use of seasonal dummies.

Based on this estimated model and some graphical evidence indicating a parallel seasonal movement in sales and production, Miron and Zeldes conclude by dismissing the production smoothing model of inventories both in case of X-11 seasonally adjusted data and in case of data adjusted by seasonal dummies.

The articles presented above may be seen as an important step towards the development of economic theories which give an integrated explanation of different components such as the trend, the cycle, and the seasonal components. The recent article by Todd (1990), and papers by Hansen and Sargent (1990, 1991) provide an interpretation of seasonality within the context of a dynamic equilibrium model, and they may therefore be seen as a step further in the right direction, i.e. in the direction where model building is based on both economic theory and sound statistical practice.

References

(References marked with a * are included in this volume)

CRUTCHFIELD, J., and ZELLNER, A. (1962), 'Analysis of port pricing of halibut: theoretical and empirical results', chs. 6 and 7 in *Economic Aspects of Halibut Fishery*. Washington: United States Department of the Interior.*

ENGLE, R. F., GRANGER, C. W. J., HYLLEBERG, S., and LEE, II. S. (1991), 'Seasonal cointegration: the Japanese consumption function', *Journal of Econometrics*, forthcoming.

GHYSELS, E. (1988), 'A study towards a dynamic theory of seasonality for economic time series', *Journal of the American Statistical Association*, **83**, 68–72.*

HALL, R. E. (1978), 'Stochastic implications of the life cycle–permanent income hypothesis: theory and evidence', *Journal of Political Economy*, **86**, 971–86.

HANSEN, L. P., and SARGENT, T. J. (1990), 'Recursive linear models of dynamics economies'. Manuscript, Hoover Institution, Stanford University.

—— —— (1991), 'Seasonality and approximation errors in rational expectations models'. Manuscript, Hoover Institution, Stanford University.

JEVONS, W. S. (1862), 'On the study of periodic commercial fluctuations', in *Investigations in Currency and Finance*, 2–11. London 1884: MacMillan.

OSBORN, D. R. (1988), 'Seasonality and habit persistence in a life cycle model of consumption', *Journal of Applied Econometrics*, **3**, 255–66.*

MIRON, J. A., and ZELDES, S. P. (1988), 'Seasonality, cost shocks, and the production smoothing model of inventories', *Econometrica*, **56**, 877–908.*

SIMS, C. A., (1974), 'Seasonality in regression', *Journal of the American Statistical Association*, **69**, 618–27.*

TODD, R. M. (1990), 'Periodic linear-quadratic methods for modelling seasonality', *Journal of Economic Dynamics and Control*, **14**, 763–95.

WALLIS, K. F. (1974), 'Seasonal adjustment and relations between variables', *Journal of the American Statistical Association*, **69**, 18–31.

WINDEN, C. C. A., and PALM, F. C. (1990), 'Stochastic implications of the life cycle consumption model under rational habit formation', Mimeo, University of Limburg.

5

Analysis of Port Pricing of Halibut: Theoretical Considerations and Empirical Results

J. CRUTCHFIELD and A. ZELLNER

Theory of Intrayear Port Pricing

Since halibut fishing takes place over a short part of the year, many dealers find it profitable to build up inventories of halibut in order to supply consumers when fishing is prohibited. Thus one type of demand for halibut at the port is to fill inventories. A second type is the demand for fresh fish; this element of demand is present at some ports but not at all of them. A rough quantitative estimate of the relative importance of these two types of demand may be obtained by noting that the seasonal inventory build-up is about 40 million pounds, whereas total annual production is about 60 million pounds. The difference, 20 million pounds, represents sales of frozen fish from inventories and of fresh fish. Unfortunately, no figures are available to permit separate estimates of these two latter items. It is clear, however, that inventory demand is extremely important.

Since inventory demand is important and since those buying to fill inventories can and do buy at any of a number of ports in Washington, British Columbia, and Alaska, prices at various ports would be expected to exhibit a similar temporal pattern within any given year. At ports where there is a demand at the wholesale level for fresh fish, however, the pattern of port prices within a year should differ in certain respects from the pattern at ports where buyers purchase fish solely for inventory purposes. In particular, when landings are very light at a 'fresh-fish' port, those buying halibut for the fresh-fish market will bid up the port

Printed with permission of: *Economic Aspects of Halibut Fishery*, chs. 6 and 7. United States Department of the Interior, Washington DC.

price. When the price has risen above a certain level, those buying for inventory purposes will refrain from buying at this port and will purchase at other ports, particularly at those where the price has not risen. Thus at ports where there is a demand for fresh fish, a negative correlation between daily volume of landings and daily price should exist.

Buyer mobility also implies that at a particular port where the demand is purely to fill inventories, there may be no significant correlation between daily landings at that port and daily port price. That is, if landings at an 'inventory' port are heavy, the price there does not necessarily drop, because buyers from other ports move in and bid up the price, which action by buyers keeps it in line with prices being paid at other ports. On the other hand, when landings are light at a particular port, the inventory buyers do not bid up the price but shift their purchases elsewhere. In what follows, this hypothesis of no correlation between price and landings at inventory ports will be tested with data relating to the market at Ketchikan, Alaska, where the demand is purely an inventory one.

It was stated above that prices at the various ports would exhibit a similar temporal pattern within a particular year, a pattern that is determined in the main by those purchasing fish for inventory purposes. A theoretical explanation of this intrayear pattern will now be developed.

At the beginning of each season, those who plan to buy halibut for inventory purposes face a number of given conditions. First, they know the inventory carryover from the previous year. Second, they know the quota or catch limit, since it is announced by the Commission prior to the opening of the fishing season. Third, they know what storage costs are. These three factors, taken together with a set of expectations regarding future prices for halibut, determine a desired level of end-of-season holdings that will be called H^d.

Relation Between Port-Price Change and Excess Inventory Demand

With the introduction of H^d, the total end-of-season holdings desired by all holders of inventories, it is now necessary to postulate a relation between port-price change and excess inventory demand. Excess inventory demand at any time during the season, say time t, is measured by the difference between H^d and actual holdings of inventories; that is, excess demand equals $(H^d - H_t)$, where H_t represents actual inventory holdings at the beginning of the t'th day. An excess of inventory demand over actual holdings at a particular time will exert an upward pressure on price. This statement is formalized mathematically as follows:

$$p_t - p_{t-1} = k (H^d - H_t),\qquad(1)$$

where $p_t - p_{t-1}$ is the change of port price from day $t - 1$ to day t and k is a positive proportionality factor. An interpretation of the quantity k is that it represents the fraction of total excess demand that is effective on the t'th market day.

Variability of the Proportionality Factor k with Time t

That k is undoubtedly not constant throughout a single season is a reasonable inference in the light of the following analysis:

1. It may be argued that a particular amount of excess demand would exert more pressure on price if it were present late in the season than if it were present earlier. This greater pressure would exist because of a number of reasons involving particularly the effects of uncertainty and of imperfections in the capital market. Suppose that inventory holders as a group are 15 million pounds short of the amount with which they would like to end the season. If they are 15 million pounds short near the middle of the season, a certain amount of pressure will be exerted on the price at the middle of the season. On the other hand, if they are 15 million pounds short near the end of the season, the price would be subjected to much more pressure than in the former instance. One reason is that an individual planning to increase his holdings at the middle of the season realizes that he has to bear all the uncertainties associated with price throughout the other half of the season as well as the uncertainty associated with it in the out-of-fishing period. Those increasing their holdings at the end of the season bear only the latter uncertainty and therefore are willing to pay more to fill their desired inventory; in fact, the market forces them to pay more through competitive bidding on the exchange. Those who bought earlier are not going to permit latecomers to buy fish at bargain prices—prices so low that they do not cover the costs involved in bearing the additional uncertainty associated with buying earlier in the season.

Further, it may be that some of the smaller holders find it impossible to get sufficient capital to finance the carrying of inventories over an extended period. Buying late in the season is one way of reducing inventory-holding time and the amount of capital tied up in inventories. Even with a 15-million-pound difference at the middle of the season between actual holdings and the desired end-of-season holdings, some of these smaller holders may decide to wait until near the end of season to buy because of capital restrictions. With the 15-million-pound shortage present near the end of the season, both small and large inventory holders are in the market, and the effect on price of such a shortage is much greater.

These considerations make it plausible to assume that k increases during the season; therefore, equation 1 is modified as follows:

$$p_t - p_{t-1} = (k_0 + k_1 t)(H^d - H_t) \qquad (2)$$

where k_0 and k_1 are positive parameters. (In what follows, the formulation, $p_t - p_{t-1} = (k_0 + k_1 t + k_{2t}^2)(H^d - H_t)$ is also tested.)

2. The factor k in equation 1 might depend on the level of price. That is, the higher the price, the smaller might be the influence of a given amount of excess demand in forcing price change. Conversely, the lower the price, the larger will be the pressure of a given amount of excess demand. These propositions, however, neglect the role of expectations. If a high price is viewed as an indicator of still higher prices on subsequent market days, the higher the price, the greater will be the influence on price change of a given amount of excess demand. Reciprocally, if a low price is regarded as an indicator of still lower prices in the future, the pressure of a given amount of excess demand will diminish.

Although these expectational effects may be operative, very probably they are not systematic or important enough to produce a significant positive correlation between price change and the level of price with excess demand held constant. Rather, one might expect that the higher yesterday's price was, the more cautious buyers with a given amount of excess demand will be in pushing the price still higher, since they want to avoid being loaded with high-cost inventories. On the other side, if yesterday's price is low, a given amount of excess demand will exert a good deal of pressure on today's price because buyers rush in to stock up on low-priced fish. These considerations make it advisable to elaborate equation 2 in the following way:

$$p_t - p_{t-1} = -\lambda p_{t-1} + (k_0 + k_1 t)(H^d - H_t) \qquad (3)$$

with λ being a positive parameter.

No a priori restriction can be placed on the size of λ; however, if the market is to exhibit prices that do not 'run away' in an upward or downward direction, $1 - \lambda$ will have to be less than one. In fact, the size of $1 - \lambda$ is intimately bound up with the degree of price stability exhibited in the market. This line of thought will be developed later.

Introduction of a_1 or holdings

The next step in translating equation 3 into a form suitable for statistical treatment is the introduction of an empirical relationship. The seasonal inventory build-up during the regular season (roughly from the middle of May to the beginning of August) can be represented fairly well by a linear function; that is, by

$$H_t = a_0 + a_1 t \tag{4}$$

where a_0 = beginning of season holdings, t = time measured from the first market day, and a_1 = daily increase in inventory holdings. (Plots of cumulative landings against time are almost linear, which is the basis for this statement. If all landings went into inventories, this is all that would be needed. In the present situation, it is also necessary to assume that sales of fresh fish and sales from inventories are made at a constant rate during the fishing season in order that equation 4 be valid. As a precaution, some calculations have been made under the assumption that equation 4 actually should involve a term in t^2.)

Introduction of C_1 the carryover

A few words must be said about a_0, beginning of season stocks. In this analysis, it is important to differentiate a_0 from the carryover from the prior year, since there is an important quality difference between the current year's inventories and inventories carried over from the prior year. H_t is a measure of new holdings. To a certain extent, the carryover is substitutable for new holdings but not perfectly so. To make this consideration explicit, one finds it desirable to write,

$$a_0 = bC \tag{5}$$

where C is the carryover from the previous year and b is some positive fraction between zero and one.

Deterministic relationship

Upon combining equations 3, 4, and 5, one obtains the following relation:

$$p_t = (1 - \lambda)p_{t-1} + [k_1(H^d - bC) - k_0 a_1]t - k_1 a_1 t^2$$
$$+ k_0(H^d - bC). \tag{6}$$

As it stands now, in deterministic form, this relation embodies the considerations presented above. It indicates, if as is to be expected, λ is less than one and greater than zero, that today's price is positively correlated with both yesterday's price, p_{t-1}, and time, t, and negatively correlated with time squared, t^2. (The coefficient of t is expected to be positive, since H^d is much larger than any of the other quantities involved.) As is reasonable, equation 6 indicates that on a particular day, the port price p_t will be higher the larger is H^d, all other things being constant. Further, again all other things constant, the larger H^d, the faster will be the rate of price increase (that is, the coefficient of t will be bigger). These conclusions are reversed with regard to the carryover, C. The larger the carryover, all other things constant, the lower the price level and the lower the rate of price increase. Finally, a supply consideration, the faster the fish are being landed, at all ports taken together, which means a larger a_1, the lower the rate of price change, again under the assumption that everything else is unchanged. These inferences relate to the general price pattern for all inventory ports. Relaxation of the ceteris paribus conditions surrounding these inferences will be treated later.

Problem of stability

To look at the problem of stability, we must recognize that equation 6 is a first order difference equation, say, $p_t = \alpha p_{t-1} + \beta_1 t + \beta_2 t^2 + \beta_0$, where α and the β's may be associated with the coefficients in equation 6. The solution of this difference equation (see any text on difference equations for the simple mathematics) takes the following form $p_t = A\alpha^t + \alpha_0 + \alpha_1 t + \alpha_2 t^2$, with the constant A related to the initial price at the beginning of the season ($t = 0$); that is, $A = p_0 - \alpha_0$, so that the expression for price on the t'th day becomes:

$$p_t = (p_0 - \alpha_0)\alpha^t + \alpha_0 + \alpha_1 t + \alpha_2 t^2. \qquad (6a)$$

In this form, it is seen that if the initial price of the season departs from α_0, this deviation of the price from the underlying pattern given by $\alpha_0 + \alpha_1 t + \alpha_2 t^2$ will gradually disappear in a non-oscillatory manner if α is less than one and greater than zero. If, statistical estimation yields an α outside the range zero to plus one, the possibility of systematic oscillations or explosive prices exists. Since this condition was not encountered in the work to be presented, no further discussion of this possibility will be given. Note that the smaller is α, the more quickly a departure from the 'trend' disappears.

Introduction of the stochastic term, u_t

So far, the discussion has been carried forward in a deterministic framework. It is worthwhile to introduce a stochastic term to take account of the multitude of factors affecting port pricing that have not been introduced explicitly in the analysis. Further, upon analyzing pricing at a particular port, one may find that the seasonal price pattern at this port departs from the overall pattern because of market imperfections, such as lack of information regarding all port prices on the part of buyers. Such informational effects are probably best represented stochastically. Finally, in connection with pricing at a particular port, the influence of prices being paid at other ports must be considered. Since there are many port markets, the influence of prices at other markets on the demand at the market under consideration is a composite effect. Some prices elsewhere are out of line with the seasonal pattern in an upward direction and others in a downward direction, and therefore it seems that the net effect on pricing at the port under consideration can best be represented stochastically. That is, equation 6 should be rewritten to include a random disturbance term that incorporates the effects of market imperfections and of a multitude of outside factors affecting pricing at a particular port that have not explicitly been introduced. This is done in equation 6b where:

$$p_t = (1 - \lambda)p_{t-1} + [k_1(H^d - bC) - k_0 a_1]t - k_1 a_1 t^2$$
$$+ k_0(H^d - bC) + u_t. \tag{6b}$$

The term u_t is a stochastic element introduced to take account of all outside factors not explicitly included in the analysis. The statistical results will provide certain characteristics of this random element.

Since little is known about the probability distribution of u_t and of the probability distribution of the initial price of the season, it does not seem worthwhile to speculate about the properties of the solution to the stochastic difference equation in equation 6b. It is interesting to note, however, that the solution to 6b takes the following form: $p_t = u_t + \alpha u_{t-1} + \alpha^2 u_{t-1} + \ldots + \alpha^{t-1} u_1 + \geq 1^t p_0 + f(t)$, where $f(t)$ is a nonstochastic function of time and $\alpha = 1 - \lambda$. Thus the variance of p_t depends on the variances and possibly the covariances of $u_1, u_2, \ldots, u_t$, the magnitude of $\alpha = 1 - \lambda$, and the variance of p_0, the initial price of the season. Further, the contribution of p_0 to the variance of p_t depends on the size of α, which will be estimated in what follows.

Equation 6b should provide a good representation of the intrayear pricing pattern at ports where the demand is an inventory demand. In view of the widespread interest in the possible effect of daily landings at a particular port on the price at that port, a further variable will be included in the statistical calculations; namely; daily volume of landings at the particular port under consideration. As mentioned above, it is quite probable that heavy landings at a particular inventory port do not depress price at that port because buyers from other ports move in to bid up the price. On the other hand, light landings are not accompanied by high prices, since buyers move to buy at other ports rather than bid up the price at a port with light landings. Thus, in the calculations relating to an inventory port, the daily volume of landings at that port may not exert a significant effect on price at that port. Relevant for the pricing pattern are total landings up and down the coast and the amount going into inventories each day, considerations that are included in equation 6b.

Inventory and fresh-fish demand

Where there is both an inventory demand and a fresh-fish demand, as at the port of Seattle, daily landings will exert a direct effect on the level of port price, primarily through the demand for fresh fish. If landings are very light on a particular day, buyers of fresh fish will bid up the price to such a level that some or perhaps all inventory buyers will switch their purchases to other ports. With heavy landings on a particular day, the purchasers of fresh fish do not have to bid the price above the seasonal pattern in order to get the fish they need; the price is at a level set by inventory demand. Under this view, demand conditions at a fresh fish port are as shown in Figure 1. It will be noted that the bend or kink in the curve represents the point at which inventory buyers shift out of this market. In the statistical calculations, attempts have been made to establish that such a bend or kink exists and to locate its position.

Implications of the Analysis

Further implications may be drawn from the analysis leading to equation 6b, assuming that the quota fixed by the Commission is set at a particular level and that the carryover from the previous year is given. What then can be said about the seasonal price pattern in a short as compared with a long season? This question is particularly relevant for the halibut fishery, since the International Pacific Halibut Commission has been criticized for adopting a method of regulation that has led to an extreme shortening of the fishing season (Gordon, 1954; Crutchfield, 1955 and 1956), and has been urged to adopt measures that would lengthen it. Also, the American and Canadian halibut fleets have adopted a voluntary layover program that has as one of its effects a lengthening of the halibut fishing season. The actual and potential availability of institutional measures that are capable of varying the duration of the fishing season make it of the utmost importance to

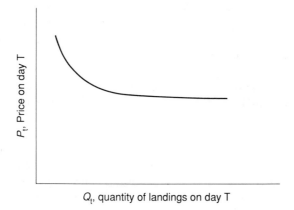

FIG. 1. Demand conditions at a 'fresh-fish' port on a particular day of the season. As the season progresses, this curve shifts upward.

assess the effects of such measures on the intrayear temporal pattern of port prices.

Given the catch limit or quota for a particular year and the carryover from the previous year, a change in the duration of the fishing season can affect the temporal pattern of pricing by its effects on: (1) the quantity a_1, the daily rate of inventory buildup, which appears in equation 6b, (2) the factor k in equation 1, which factor was set equal to k_0 plus $k_1 t$ in developing equation 6b, and (3) H^d, the desired inventory holdings at the end of the fishing season. The variation of each of these quantities accompanying a change in the duration of the fishing season will now be considered.

a_1, Daily rate of inventory buildup

It is not difficult to establish that a_1, the daily rate of inventory accumulation during the fishing season will be larger for a short season than for a long season under the assumptions of the preceding analysis. Suppose that the fixed quota is denoted by $\bar{X}$ (the bar indicates that the variable is fixed or already determined by the conservation authorities); then the following relationship connecting $\bar{X}$ and a_1 holds:

$$\bar{X} = (a_1 + s)m, \tag{7}$$

where s = the daily rate of sales from inventories plus the daily rate of fresh fish sales (assumed constant during the fishing season) and m = the number of days in the fishing season. Under these assumptions, it is clear that a lengthening of the season, an increase in m, will be accompanied by a decrease in a_1; conversely a shortening of the season will result in a larger a_1. (If data were available on daily forward prices, a more general analysis could be pursued that does not involve the assumption that a_1 and s are constant during a particular year. That is, equation 7 would be written: $X = \sum_{i=1}^{m}[a_1(t_i \ldots) + s(t_i \ldots)]$, where now a_1 and s are permitted to be functions of t and other variables.) Examination of equation 6b indicates that both the coefficients of t and t^2 will be affected in the following way: the coefficient of t will be reduced, and the coefficient of t^2 will become more negative, the shorter the season. That is, with a shorter season, more fish goes into inventories each day; the port price will rise less rapidly; and the rate of increase of the port price will be diminished. These effects were noted above under an 'all other things unchanged' assumption. In making a comparison between a short and a long season, we find, as will be seen, that the 'all other things unchanged' assumption is not satisfied. Therefore, some of the effects of a change in a_1 may be intensified or counteracted by other effects. This point will become clear from the considerations included in the following paragraphs.

k, the fraction

It seems reasonable to expect that the quantity k, the fraction of excess inventory demand exerting a pressure on price on a particular day, in equation 1 will be greater in a short season than in a long one. That is, if the same desired level of inventories is present in a long season as is present in a short season (the validity of this assumption will be considered below), it is clear that, say, 10 days after the opening of the season, buyers in the short season with a given amount of excess demand will exert more pressure on the price than will buyers in a long season possessing the same excess demand. Thus in $k = k_0 + k_1 t$, used above, the parameters k_0 and k_1 will be larger (particularly the latter) in a short season than in a long season. (Actually k could be larger throughout a short season as compared with a long one if only k_0 were larger and k_1 remained unchanged. Given a shortening of the season, however, it is also very likely that k_1 also increases. See the earlier discussion concerning the introduction of k_1.) Such changes affect all terms but one in equation 6b. The rise in k_1 with a shortening of the season supplements the effect of the rise in a_1 to make the coefficient of t^2 more negative. Since these are the only two quantities involved in the coefficient of t^2, it is to be expected that the coefficient of t^2 will be more negative the shorter the fishing season (this without any qualification). The effects of changes in k_0 and k_1 on the coefficient of t are in opposing directions, so no such unqualified statement is possible; and further, since other quantities are involved in the coefficient of t, the situation is more complicated than that regarding the coefficient of t^2.

H^d Desired end-of-season holdings

Finally, it is necessary to analyze the effects of changes in the duration of the season on the desired end-of-season holdings, H^d. Since this quantity plays an important part in the analysis and since its determination in a particular year is vitally connected with the conservation authorities' policies, special sections will be devoted to its determination and effects on pricing.

In-fishing-season and out-of-fishing-season. The analysis of the supply and demand for storage presented in this section follows, with some modifications, the work developed by Kaldor (1939), Working (1948), and Brennan (1958).

To get at the determinants of H^d, it is useful to consider two periods; namely, the regular fishing period (involving m time intervals) and the period outside the regular fishing season (involving n time intervals). For each of these periods, there will be a consumer demand for halibut. Let the two demand functions be represented as follows:

$$P_T = f_T(Q_T^D) \tag{8a}$$

$$P_{T+1} = f_{T+1}(Q_{T+1}^D) \tag{8b}$$

where

P_T = the retail price of halibut during the fishing season
P_{T+1} = the retail price of halibut during the period outside the fishing season
Q_T^D = the quantity demanded at retail per time interval during the fishing season
Q_{T+1}^D = the quantity demanded at retail per time interval during the out-of-fishing-season period.

It will be noted that the demand relation within the fishing season, f_T, is different from that relating to the period outside the season, f_{T+1}. This difference may arise because of changes in exogenous factors, such as consumer income, the price of meat, and the prices of other fish products.

The following equations define supply conditions in the two periods:

$$Q_T^S = \frac{X_T - (H_T - H_{T-1})}{m} \tag{9a}$$

$$Q_{T+1}^S = \frac{X_{T+1} - (H_{T+1} - H_T)}{n} \tag{9b}$$

Equation 9a states that the quantity of halibut supplied to consumers per time interval during the fishing season (Q_T^S), is equal to total production (X_T) minus the inventory build-up during the season (end-of-season stocks, H_T, less beginning-of-season stocks, H_{T-1},) all divided by the number of time intervals in the fishing season (m). Similarly, equation 9b states that the quantity supplied to consumers in the out-of-season period per time interval Q_{T-1}^S, is equal to production (X_{T-1}, which may be zero) plus the liquidation of holdings all divided by the number of time intervals, n, in the out-of-season period. Note that $H_T - H_{T-1}$ is out-of-fishing-season liquidation of holdings, since H_{T-1} represents holdings at the end of the out-of-season period (or the carryover for the following year). On the assumption that the retail price adjusts to equate quantity supplied and quantity demanded in both the within-fishing-season period and in the outside-the-fishing-season period, then $Q_T^S = Q_T^D$ and $Q_{T-1}^S = Q_{T-1}^D$ and equations 9a and 9b may be inserted in equations 8a and 8b, respectively, to obtain

$$P_T = f_T[(X_T - H_T + H_{T-1})/m] \qquad (10a)$$

$$P_{T+1} = F_{T+1}[(X_{T+1} - H_{T+1} + H_T)/n] \qquad (10b)$$

In equations 10a and 10b, certain variables may be regarded as predetermined. For example, X_T, production within the regular fishing season, is fixed by the International Pacific Halibut Commission. X_{T-1}, production outside the regular season, will be close to zero in all years without special seasons. In years with special seasons, production in the special seasons can be estimated fairly accurately, since the duration of special seasons is announced by the Commission. Finally, H_{T-1}, planned carryover for the next year, will be approximately zero, since there is substantial quality deterioration associated with keeping halibut in storage over long periods of time. Of course, in actuality, H_{T+1} may depart from zero because of errors in planning or unforeseen events during the year. Hereafter, variables that are considered as being predetermined will be written with a bar over them.

From equations 10a and 10b, it is possible to write:

$$P_{T+1} - P_T = f_{T+1}[(\bar{X}_{T+1} - \bar{H}_{T+1} + H_T)/n]$$
$$- f_T[(\bar{X}_T - H_T + \bar{H}_{T+1})/m] \qquad (11)$$

It is seen that the price change from period T to $T+1$ is a function of just one endogenous variable, H_T, (end-of-fishing-season holdings), since all the remaining variables in equation 11 are predetermined. (Here n and m are considered predetermined; later, this assumption will be relaxed.) The price change is in general a decreasing function of H_T, a fact that is easily established from the usual properties of demand curves. Equation 11 represents the 'demand for storage'.

The fact that inventories of halibut are carried into the out-of-season period means that consumers are supplied with halibut over the entire year. Individuals who hold inventories thus supply a service to the economy. This function is usually referred to as 'supplying storage'. We now turn to the review of the determinants of the supply of storage.

Review of the determinants of the supply of storage

The amount of halibut that a particular individual will want to hold at the end of a fishing season is, of course, determined by profit considerations. For each pound held, the revenue gain will be just the change in the forward price from period T to period $T + 1$, or $P_{T+1} - P_T$. Then to maximize profits from holdings, the volume of holdings, H_T, will be pushed to the point where the expected price change is just equal to the marginal net storage cost (which can be derived from the total net storage cost). Total net storage cost is equal to the physical costs of storage, $O(H_T)$, plus cost associated with risk and uncertainty, $R(H_T)$, minus a convenience benefit derived from holdings, $C(H_T)$. Brennan (1958) has developed the following excellent definitions of the three components of total net storage cost and descriptions of the behavior of these cost components as the level of holdings changes:

The total outlay on physical storage is the sum of rent for storage space, handling or in-and-out charges, interest, insurance, etc. As the quantity of stocks held by a firm increases, the total outlay increases. Although for any single firm this cost may increase at either a constant or an increasing rate, it seems reasonable to suppose that the marginal outlay is approximately constant until total warehouse capacity is almost fully utilized (each firm can store all it wishes without affecting the cost per unit of the commodity stored). Beyond this level marginal outlay will rise at an increasing rate.

We should expect total risk aversion to be an increasing function of stocks. If a comparatively small quantity of stocks is held, the risk involved in undertaking the investment in stocks is also small. An unexpected fall in the price at which stocks must be sold will result in a relatively small loss to the firm holding stocks for later sale ... However, given the total capital resources of the firm, the greater the quantity of stocks held, the greater will be the loss to the firm from the same unexpected fall in the future price. There is probably some critical level of stocks at which the loss would seriously endanger the firm's credit position, and as stocks increase up to this point the risk incurred in holding them will steadily increase also—the risk of loss will constitute a part of the cost of storage. The marginal risk-aversion factor may be assumed to be either constant or, more likely, an increasing function of stocks held.

The costs of storage must be considered as charged against the business operation as a whole. Given day-to-day fluctuations in the market, a producing firm can meet a sudden and 'unexpected' increase in demand by filling orders out of finished inventories or by adjusting its production schedule or by some combination of these. The convenience yield is attributed to the advantage (in terms of less delay and lower costs) of being able to keep regular customers satisfied or of being able to take advantage of a rise in demand and price without resorting to a revision of the production schedule. Similarly, for a processing firm the availability of stocks of raw materials permits variations in production without incurring the trouble, cost and perhaps delays of frequent spot purchases and deliveries. A wholesaler can vary his sales in response to an increased flow of orders only if he has sufficient stocks on hand.

The smaller the level of stocks on hand the greater will be the convenience yield of an additional unit. It is assumed that there is some quantity of stocks so large that the marginal convenience yield is zero.

The above considerations are represented graphically in Figure 2 where marginal net storage cost ($MNSC$) is plotted against level of stocks (H_T). Also shown in Figure 2 are the components of $MNSC$; namely, the marginal physical outlay curve (dO/dH_T), the marginal risk-aversion curve (dR/dH_T), and the marginal convenience curve (dC/dH_T). The $MNSC$ is equal to $dO/dH_T + dR/dH_t - dC/dH_T$; that is, to the sum of the marginal physical outlay and marginal risk aversion minus the marginal convenience yield. The curves in Figure 2 relate to an individual firm.

With pure competition and no external economies or diseconomies in the storage industry, the aggregate supply curve of storage is the horizontal sum of all individual $MNSC$ functions. This aggregate supply of storage relation, SS, is shown in figure 3, along with a curve designated DD to represent the demand for storage. The intersection of these two curves determines an equilibrium end-of-fishing-season level of holdings, H^d, and an equilibrium forward price change (OA in Figure 3). The quantity, H^d, was referred to above in connection with equation 1, as a desired level of end-of-season holdings. The analysis involving

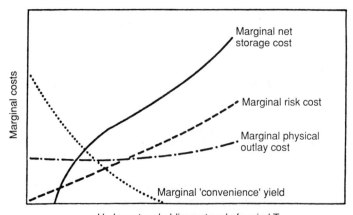

H_T Inventory holdings at end of period T

FIG. 2. Marginal net storage cost and its components.

consideration of the demand for storage and the supply of storage indicates why this level of holdings will be an equilibrium level.

Effect of five variables on the size of H^d

With this analysis set forth, it is not difficult within the present framework to study the effects of the following on the size of H^d:

1. Changes in the duration of the fishing season (that is, variations in m in equation 11).
2. Changes in the catch limit or quota imposed by the International Pacific Halibut Commission; that is, changes in $\bar{X}_T$.
3. Changes in the carryover, $\bar{H}_{T-1}$.
4. Changes in production in special seasons, $\bar{X}_{T+1}$.
5. Changes in certain other exogenously determined variables.

Clearly it is difficult to consider all changes together. The discussion therefore will be carried through under the assumption that only one specified change occurs and that everything else remains constant. Later on, several changes occurring together will be considered.

Changes in duration of season

As mentioned earlier, the duration of the fishing season has been lengthened by the voluntary layover program instituted by the American and Canadian fleets in 1956 and continued to the present. A lengthening of the fishing season involves an increase in m and a decrease in n in equation 11, the demand-for-storage equation. Such variation in m and

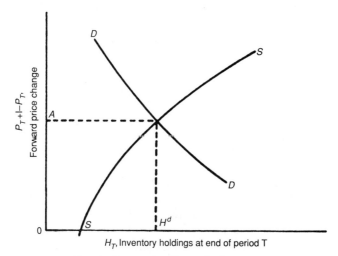

FIG. 3. Demand and supply for storage.

n leads to a downward shift of the demand-for-storage curve DD in Figure 3. Also a lengthening of the fishing season will affect storage costs and thus the supply of storage. That is, the average time inventories are held will be affected by a change in the duration of the fishing season, and this will alter the elements that combine to give total storage costs and marginal storage costs.

(In an arithmetic sense, total storage costs equal the number of pounds held times the length of time these are held times the storage rate. The storage rate is, of course, so many cents per pound per month. Thus, since average holding time is affected by a change in the duration of the fishing season, total and marginal costs will be affected.)

In particular, it seems reasonable to expect that a lengthening of the fishing season will reduce the important absolute and possibly marginal risk costs associated with the holdings of halibut inventories from the fishing period into the out-of-season period. Given that marginal storage costs decrease, the supply of storage curve, SS in Figure 3, should shift downward to the right. Thus the point of intersection is lower, which implies a smaller forward price change from the fishing period to the out-of-season period. It is our conjecture that, with a significant lengthening of the season, the shift in the demand curve DD is more pronounced than is the shift in the supply curve. (Note that the total volume of halibut carried is but part of the inventory holdings of those providing storage, and probably not a very large part for the larger storage suppliers. This conjecture implies that with a lengthening of the season, both the forward price change, $P_{T-1} - P_T$, and H_T^d decline. Thus with a lengthening of the fishing season, a smaller volume of holdings will be carried over to the out-of-fishing-season period, and the forward price will show less variability over the year. This result should be of great value to forward purchasers of halibut and should facilitate port dealers' selling operations to forward buyers.

Changes in carryover ($\bar{H}_{T-1}$)

An increase in beginning of season holdings, $\bar{H}_{T-1}$, all else constant, will produce an upward shift in DD and thus lead to an increase in H^d. That is, the larger the carryover the more the demanders of storage will want carried out of the fishing season period (T) into the out-of-season period ($T + 1$). In actuality, the effect of an increase in $\bar{H}_{T-1}$, the carryover, on H^d may be counteracted by a lengthening of the season. That is, a large carryover will depress the level of port prices and will divert some boats from fishing halibut. With a given quota, this means that the season will tend to be lengthened with the associated effect on H^d described earlier.

Changes in regular season quota ($\bar{X}_T$)

An increase in the regular season quota ($\bar{X}_T$) will lead to an upward shift in DD, the demand for storage, and so to a larger H^d. Then the coefficient of t in equation 1 should increase with an increase in $\bar{X}_T$. However, this tendency may be counteracted if the increase in $\bar{X}_T$ is so great as to produce a lengthening of the fishing season.

Changes in production outside the regular season ($\bar{X}_{T+1}$)

If production outside the regular season ($\bar{X}_{T+1}$) increases, this increase will shift the demand for storage curve downward and so lead to a smaller H^d; that is, the amount of halibut carried out of the regular fishing season (T) into the period $T + 1$ will be diminished. Also, such a change will reduce the forward price change, $P_{T+1} - P_T$. The results are summarized in Table 7.

Effects of Current Conservation Policy on Intrayear Pricing

With the results shown in Table 1 and the former considerations regarding the port pricing pattern embodied in equation 6b, it is now possible to consider the effects of a lengthening of the fishing season, alone or in conjunction with other measures, under only moderately restrictive assumptions. It has been established that with a lengthening of the season with a given quota, the amount of fish going into holdings each day will be smaller than in a short season. That is, a_1 in equation 6b will be smaller the longer the season is, and this inverse relation means a larger coefficient of t and less negative coefficient of t^2. The effect of lengthening the season on k_1, discussed above, also leads one to expect a less negative coefficient of t^2 the longer the season. As regards the coefficient of t, since it is likely that k_1, H^d, k_0, and a_1 all decrease the longer the season is, the net effect on the coefficient is left in doubt. Finally, with regard to the term $k_0 (H^d - bC)$ in equation 6b, the longer the season, the smaller will be this term, on the assumption that the carryover, C, is given.

If a lengthening of the season is accompanied by an increase in the regular season's permitted catch, there will be little change in the seasonal pattern of pricing, since the effects on a_1 and H^d of a lengthening of the season will be counteracted by an increase in the total volume of landings during the regular season. Further, the 'forward

TABLE 1.   Summary of effects of different production conditions

Increase in	Effect on forward price change $(P_{T+1} - P_T)$	Effect on H^d (celeris paribus)	Qualification[1]
Duration of regular season (m)	Decrease	Decrease	
Carryover $(\bar{H}_{T+1})$	Increase	Increase	If fishing season lengthened, this will lead to a smaller H^d.
Quota $(\bar{X}_T)$	Increase	Increase	Some offset to the increase in H^d may occur if the fishing season's duration is lengthened due to the increased quota
Production outside regular season $(\bar{X}_{T+1})$.	Decrease	Decrease	

[1] In all cases it is assumed that net marginal storage costs do not change.

price change', $P_{T+1} - P_T$, which would tend to be reduced, given a lengthening of the season, will now be increased by heavier production during the regular season. Thus the analysis suggests that some of the effects of a lengthening of the season on the price pattern will be offset if at the same time the regular season's quota is increased significantly. On the other hand, the effects of a lengthening of the regular season will be enhanced by an increase in production in the special seasons. That is, increased production in the special seasons $(\bar{X}_{T+1})$ is associated with a decrease in H^d and a decrease in the forward price change $P_{T+1} - P_T$, two changes that are also associated with a lengthening of the season. Thus, the Commission, by establishing special seasons, has produced effects on the price pattern during the regular season, effects that resemble those associated with a lengthening of the season. That total output has been increased by the institution of special seasons rather than merely by an increase in the regular season's quotas has been fortunate, since this course of action, among other things, probably has led to less variable forward prices and a less sharply rising pattern of port prices during the regular season.

In the following we turn to the statistical calculations to determine to what extent these theoretical considerations are supported by the facts.

Data Employed

The port market data underlying the calculations relate to the years 1953 through 1957 and to the ports of Seattle and Ketchikan. Data for Seattle were collected from the records of the Seattle Fish Exchange, which show the hailed weight and the price per pound for each boat's catch. Similar data for Ketchikan (1955) through 1957, were obtained from the Bureau of Commercial Fisheries Market News reporter in Ketchikan. For each market day, an average price for medium halibut was calculated by weighting the price received by individual boats by their respective hailed weights of medium halibut. The 1953 and 1954 data for Ketchikan were obtained from the Bureau's Seattle Market News Service daily fishery products reports. In these reports, the daily volume of medium halibut landed at Ketchikan is given, together with a range of prices paid on each market day. The midrange price was employed to represent the daily average Ketchikan port price for these 2 years.

The analyses of daily data refer to market days included in Table 2.

Results of Calculations

The purpose of this section is to determine how well the model of pricing that was developed above fits the data for Ketchikan and Seattle during individual years. The results at Ketchikan are of particular interest because the price pattern there is not complicated by the demand for fresh fish. Results at Seattle offer an instructive contrast to those at Ketchikan because the price pattern is complicated by a large demand for fresh fish.

Ketchikan

In Table 3 are shown the results of calculations pertaining to pricing at Ketchikan during the years 1953–7. All relations have been estimated by employing the method of least squares. The values of the coefficient of determination demonstrate that the fits obtained are very good. In addition, it will be noted that almost all parameters appear to be significantly different from zero except for the coefficient Q_t, daily volume of medium halibut landed at Ketchikan. As mentioned earlier, this result is consistent with the notion that buyers are mobile and thus do not bid up the price at Ketchikan when landings are light and that they do not permit the price to sag much when landings are heavy relative to landings elsewhere. It will also be noted that all other

TABLE 2. Periods included in the analysis of port pricing at Seattle and Ketchikan

Year	Seattle		
	Period	Number of days in period	Number active market days
1953	21 May–17 July	58	38
1954	19 May–22 July	65	38
1955	16 May–12 Aug.	89	59
1956	25 May–31 Aug.	99	52
1957	3 May–26 July	85	55

Year	Ketchikan		
	Period	Number of days in period	Number active market days[1]
1953	May 1–July 14	75	30
1954	May 19–July 19	62	37
1955	May 16–Aug. 12	89	35
1956	May 24–Aug. 30	99	64
1957	May 5–Aug. 16	104	67

[1] The number of active market days is the number of days in the periods shown above on which medium halibut were sold. In the periods shown above there were landings on almost every market day. With the closing of particular areas, landings fall to zero until the opening of special seasons. Since this represents a break in the continuity of seasonal port pricing, a break that differs from year to year, it was thought advisable to limit the analysis to the periods shown in Table 2.

estimates of coefficients are in agreement with the theoretical considerations presented earlier. The coefficient of p_{t-1} is between zero and one, roughly 0.7, which indicates that the effect of a temporary element of demand that raises price by 1 cent per pound will largely be dissipated after 3 or 4 days. Also, the coefficients of t and t^2 have their expected signs, positive in the first instance and negative in the second. Lastly, the coefficients of t^2 are more negative in the short seasons (see Table 2) 1953 and 1954 than during the longer seasons of 1955–7, a result that is consistent with the theoretical arguments.

To check further the appropriateness of the model, we thought it advisable to test for a possible effect of p_{t-2}. The price lagged 2 market days, on current price. A significant influence of p_{t-2} on current price

TABLE 3. Results of calculations relating to daily port pricing of medium halibut at Ketchikan, 1953–7

Year	N^1	Estimated relationships[2]	$\bar{R}^{2\,3}$	d^4
1953	30	$p_t = 2.76 - 0.122Q_t + 0.791p_{t+1} + 0.0701t - 0.00107t^2$ (0.0885) (0.107) (0.0409) (0.000649)	0.950	1.648
1954	37	$p_t = 5.45 - 0.0264Q_t + 0.600p_{t+1} + 0.0985t - 0.00143t^2$ (0.0486) (0.139) (0.0408) (0.000553)	0.960	2.027
1955	35	$p_t = 5.13 - 0.0242Q_t + 0.472p_{t+1} + 0.0966t - 0.00813t^2$ (0.176) (0.141) (0.0259) (0.000276)	0.927	1.919
1956	64	$p_t = 6.82 - 0.130Q_t + 0.604p_{t+1} + 0.0782t - 0.000548t^2$ (0.173) (0.0912) (0.0239) (0.000184)	0.980	1.942
1957	67	$p_t = 3.65 - 0.0150Q_t + 0.737p_{T+1} + 0.0351t - 0.000272t^2$ (0.0987) (0.0868) (0.0137) (0.000104)	0.965	1.940

[1] N is the number of observations or the number of active market days included in the analysis.

[2] Figures in parentheses are standard errors.

[3] $\bar{R}^2$ is the adjusted coefficient of determination.

[4] d is the Durbin–Watson test statistic employed to test the error term for possible autocorrelation. In every case it is possible to reject the hypothesis of autocorrelation. A 'two-tailed' test at the 5 per cent level of significance was employed. (Durbin and Watson, 1950–1).

Notation:

P_t = Average price of medium halibut on the t'th day (in cents per pound).

Q_t = Landings of medium halibut on the t'th day (measured in units of a hundred thousand pounds).

p_{t+1} = Average price of medium halibut on market day preceding the t'th day.

t = Time measured in days from the first market day.

would mean that a second-order-difference-equation adjustment process is operative rather than the first-order one considered earlier. Calculations with the data relating to Ketchikan, 1954–6, indicate no statistically significant effect of p_{t-2} on p_t. Further, the adequacy of the assumptions leading to terms in t and t^2 was tested by including a term in t^3. The coefficient of this term was not found to be significantly different from zero when 1953 and 1954 data for Ketchikan were employed.

Seattle

In Table 4 the first set of results pertaining to pricing at Seattle during 1953–7 are presented. As with the analysis of Ketchikan port pricing, all coefficient estimates have the expected algebraic sign and, in contrast to the Ketchikan results, daily landings at Seattle exert a statistically significant negative effect on the level of price.

Early in every year, the price at Seattle is very high, a phenomenon

TABLE 4. Results of calculations relating to daily port pricing of medium halibut at Seattle, 1953–7

Year	N^1	Estimated relationships[2]	$\bar{R}^{2\,3}$	d^4
1953	38	$p_t = 8.88 - 0.574Q_t + 0.549p_{t+1} + 0.0776t - 0.00110t^2$ (0.189) (0.109) (0.0718) (0.00115)	0.662	2.374
1954	38	$p_t = 11.86 - 0.543Q_t + 0.436p_{t+1} + 0.122t - 0.00141t^2$ (0.0783) (0.0765) (0.0273) (0.000383)	0.878	1.825
1955	59	$p_t = 8.23 - 0.752Q_t + 0.533p_{t+1} + 0.0554t - 0.00418t^2$ (0.112) (0.0744) (0.0184) (0.000177)	0.877	2.152
1956	52	$p_t = 13.17 - 0.800Q_t + 0.479p_{t+1} + 0.0942t - 0.000589t^2$ (0.193) (0.0700) (0.0218) (0.000589)	0.908	1.953
1957	55	$p_t = 13.08 - 0.517Q_t + 0.338p_{T+1} + 0.0801t - 0.000422t^2$ (0.163) (0.0729) (0.0342) (0.00370)	0.710	2.073

[1] N is the number of observations or the number of active market days included in the analysis.

[2] Figures in parentheses are standard errors.

[3] $\bar{R}^2$ is the adjusted coefficient of determination.

[4] d is the Durbin–Watson test statistic employed to test the error term for possible autocorrelation. In every case it is possible to reject the hypothesis of autocorrelation. A 'two-tailed' test at the 5 per cent level of significance was employed. (Durbin and Watson, 1950–1).

Notation:

p_t = Average price of medium halibut on the t'th day (in cents per pound).

Q_t = Landings of medium halibut on the t'th day (measured in units of a hundred thousand pounds).

p_{t+1} = Average price of medium halibut on market day preceding the t'th day.

t = Time measured in days from the first market day.

not noted in the Ketchikan data. In large part, this high price at Seattle is due to the fact that landings are light during the first few days of the season and buyers are eager to be the first to send the new catch to market. Such early delivery undoubtedly provides the seller with a high return in money, in goodwill, and in prestige, which offsets the high price he pays for the fish.

Further, the high opening price at Seattle, year after year, gives individual primary producers a chance to get a high return. That is, the first boats landing fares get substantially more for their halibut than do boats landing several days later. Hence, every year, many boats try to be the first to return with a full hold. Of necessity, only a few can be the first to reap the benefits of high prices; the remaining fishermen land their catches under almost glut conditions about 8 to 12 days after the first market day. This peak in landings, which appears every year, is associated with a subsequent substantial decline in price. Calculations indicate that an additional 100,000 pounds thrown on the market will depress prices at Seattle by a maximum of 0.9 cents per pound. If daily landings remain up by 100,000, the full effect will amount to a maximum of 1.7 cents per pound fall in price, which would be established in about 2 to 4 days. This is labelled a maximum effect because of the kink or bend thought to be present in the demand curve at Seattle. That is, the price at Seattle on a particular day cannot drop below the value consistent with the inventory pattern of pricing. Thus there is a floor under Seattle prices, and as long as this floor is not encountered, the effect on price of an additional 100,000 pounds on the market will be roughly as stated above. If the floor is encountered, the effect will be less.

Several considerations, in addition to the qualitative ones presented above, support the contention that there is probably a kink or bend in the Seattle demand function. Note that with the use of linear functions, the fits obtained with the Seattle data are not as good as those obtained with the Ketchikan data. For the Ketchikan analyses, every coefficient of determination was over 0.9; whereas for the Seattle analyses, four out of five such coefficients were computed to be less than 0.908, with a range from 0.662 to 0.908. One reason for this difference could be that it is more difficult to 'explain' variability of port prices at Seattle, since this market is inherently more unstable than is the one at Ketchikan. Although this difference in stability is a possibility, it was felt worthwhile to pursue the alternative hypothesis mentioned earlier; namely, that there is a kink or a bend in the function, so the linear function fitted to the data is not entirely appropriate.

The first step in checking this point was to plot the calculated residuals for the Seattle-fitted functions against daily volume of landings. For both light and heavy landings, the residuals tend to be positive; whereas for medium landings, the residuals tend to be negative. The kink or bend appears to be encountered when daily landings are about 50,000 pounds.

A more objective measure of this departure from randomness in the residuals is provided by the values of the Durbin–Watson statistic computed with the residuals ordered according to the volume of daily landings. For the 5 years included in the analysis, the results shown in Table 11 were obtained:

Interyear Changes in the Price Pattern

The results just shown indicate that the model of pricing developed fits the data for Seattle and Ketchikan rather well in individual years. The results now will be viewed to determine how well year-to-year changes in the pattern of pricing can be explained in terms of the theoretical considerations developed earlier. The results relating to Ketchikan will be given most attention, since the price pattern there is not complicated

TABLE 5.   Values of Durbin–Watson statistic[1]

Year	Seattle[2]	Ketchikan
1953	1.091	1.884
1954	1.639	2.055
1955	1.767	2.634
1956	2.018	1.817
1957	1.116	2.071

[1] Here in computing the statistic $d = \sum_{t=2}^{m}(u_t - u_{t-1})^2 \sum_{t=1}^{m} u_t^2$, the residuals have been ordered according to the size of the volume of daily landings.

[2] The results for 1953 and 1957 are consistent with the hypothesis of positive autocorrelation at the 5 per cent level of significance, whereas the Durbin–Watson (1951) test fails to produce a conclusive result with regard to the value of d for 1954. A 'one-tailed' test was employed utilizing tables given in Durbin and Watson (1950–1).

by the presence of a demand for fresh fish. From Table 3, the following appear to be the most salient features of year-to-year variation in the pattern of pricing at Ketchikan:

1. The estimated coefficients of t^2 are more negative in the years 1953 and 1954 than in the years 1955–7.
2. The constant terms for 1953 and 1957 are smaller than are those for other years.
3. There is variation in the estimated coefficients of t over the period covered by the analysis.

The discussion of these year-to-year changes will be carried forward within the context of equation 6b, which is reproduced here for convenience.

$$p_t = (1 - \lambda)p_{t-1} + [k_1(H^d - bC) - k_0 a_1] t - k_1 a_1 t^2$$
$$+ k_0(H^d - bC) + u_t \qquad (6b)$$

Upon comparing the values of the Durbin–Watson statistic in Table 11 with those in Tables 3 and 4, one sees that ordering the residuals according to volume of daily landings has reduced the value of the statistic in four of five cases in Seattle, whereas there was no such systematic effect in Ketchikan. This finding suggests that there is a bend or kink in the demand relation for Seattle.

To explore this point further, we fitted a logarithmic formulation of the demand relation for Seattle to the same data that were employed in estimating the linear functions. It is seen from the results in Table 6 that the fits for the logarithmic formulation are better than are those for the linear formulation (see Table 4). It is to be noted that, as with the linear formulation, the results for 1953 are such that the estimates of the

TABLE 6. Results of calculations relating to daily port pricing of medium halibut at Seattle, 1953–7

Year	N[1]	Estimated relationship[2]	$\bar{R}^2$[3]	d[4]
1953	30	$\log p_t = 1.218 - 00131t + 0.00002777t^2 - 0.102 \log Q_t + 0.304 \log p_{t-1}$ $(0.000981)\ (0.01200)$ (0.0769)	0.887	2.189
1954	38	$\log p_t = 0.917 - 00198t + 0.0000213t^2 - 0.0485 \log Q_t + 0.408 \log p_{t-1}$ $(0.000476)\ (0.00000668)\ (0.00566)$ (0.0680)	.911	1.844
1955	59	$\log p_t = 0.737 - 00171t + 0.0000132t^2 - 0.0540 \log Q_t + 0.510 \log p_{t-1}$ $(0.000436)\ (0.00000425)\ (0.00742)$ (0.0716)	.894	2.456
1956	52	$\log p_t = 0.772 - 00157t + 0.0000105t^2 - 0.0318 \log Q_t + 0.503 \log p_{t-1}$ $(0.000338)\ (0.00000317)\ (0.00653)$ (0.0729)	.866	2.116
1957	59	$\log p_t = 0.982 - 00161t + 0.0000964t^2 - 0.0448 \log Q_t + 0.336 \log p_{t-1}$ $(0.000551)\ (0.00000601)\ (0.00867)$ (0.0684)	.781	2.157

[1] N is the number of observations or the number of active market days included in the analysis.

[2] Figures in parentheses are standard errors.

[3] $\bar{R}^2$ is the adjusted coefficient of determination.

[4] d is the Durbin–Watson test statistic employed to test the error term for possible autocorrelation. In every case it is possible to reject the hypothesis of autocorrelation. See Durbin and Watson (1950–1).

coefficients of t and t^2 are accompanied by large standard errors—so large that it is not possible to reject the hypothesis that the coefficients t and t^2 are zero. Why this is the case will be explored in the next section.

The estimated relations in Table 6 indicate that for Seattle, a 10-per cent increase in landings on a particular day will result in about a 1/2-per cent decrease in price on that day. This indicates that the demand at Seattle is quite elastic. If, of course, daily landings rose by 10 per cent and remained 10 per cent higher, the effect on price would be greater than for landings that rose by 10 per cent for a single day. In the case of a permanent increase of landings by 10 per cent, the results in Table 6 indicate that price would finally be lowered by about 1 to 2 per cent. The fact that price falls far less than proportionately with an increase in landings is an extremely important finding, since it indicates that higher landings although associated with slightly lower prices, provide a larger gross stock or gross revenue to the entire fishing fleet.

Coefficient of t^2

Equation 6b indicates that the coefficient of t^2 depends on a_1, the daily rate of inventory build-up during the fishing season, and k_1, the rate of increase in the fraction of excess stock demand exerting pressure on price at the beginning of the season.

With regard to a_1 in the years covered by the analysis, the best that can be done, given the available data, is to use the monthly figures on United States (including Alaska) and Canadian holdings to estimate the rate of inventory build-up in the years 1953–7. These figures are shown in Table 7.

It is seen that the monthly rate of build-up is greatest for 1954 and next highest for 1953, whereas the rates for 1955–7 are somewhat smaller. Thus these figures are compatible with a higher a_1 for 1953 and 1954 than in the years 1955–7. Also, Table 2 reveals that 1953 and 1954 were short season, whereas 1955–7 were long season, a fact that should make for a larger k_1 (as argued above) in 1953 and 1954 than in 1955–7. Thus the findings that the estimated coefficients of t^2 are more negative in 1953 and 1954 than in the years 1955 to 1957 is in good agreement with the specific theoretical considerations underlying the calculations.

Constant Terms

The constant terms in the relations for Ketchikan (see Table 3) will next be considered. (For this discussion the Seattle results are not included,

Table 7.   US and Canadian peak and trough holdings of frozen halibut and computed monthly rate of inventory buildup, 1953–7

Year	Trough holdings[1]	Peak holdings[1]	Rate of inventory buildup
	Thousand pounds	Thousand pounds	Thousand pounds per month
1953	8,191	42,335	8,536
1954	5,054	45,945	10,223
1955	8,242	37,168	7,232
1956	2,957	38,631	7,135
1957	8,026	34,367	6,585

[1] In each of the years covered by the table, trough-holdings figures are beginning-of-May holdings while peak-holdings are beginning-of-September holdings except for 1956 in which peak holdings occurred at the beginning of October.

Sources: 1953–6 holdings for the United States and Alaska are taken from Anderson and Power (1956a, 1956b, 1957) and Power (1958). Canadian holdings are from Pacific Fisherman.

since the presence of a demand for fresh fish complicates matters.) The constant terms for 1953 (2.76) and 1957 (3.65) are smallest, whereas that for 1956 (6.82) is the largest. Equation 6b indicates that the constant term is $k_0 (H^d - bC)$, where H^d is the desired equilibrium level of holdings at end of fishing season, C is the carryover, k_0 is the fraction of excess stock demand exerted at the beginning of the season, and b is the fraction applied to the carryover to take account of quality changes. Most important in accounting for year-to-year changes in this term will be changes in C and H^d (k_0 and b are regarded as being fairly constant over the years covered). The figures in column 1 of Table 7 showing trough holdings in the years 1953–7, are a close approximation to the carryover in each year. For convenience, these figures are presented in Table 8 alongside values of the constant terms.

The carryover in 1956 was much smaller than in the other years shown and in this year the constant term (6.82) is much greater than for the other years. The carryover in 1954 is smaller than that in the remaining years (excluding 1956), and the constant term for 1954 is second highest. For the other three years—1953, 1955, and 1957—the carryover is about 8 million pounds, and the constant terms are lowest for these 3 years. Thus, the carryover plays an important role, as indicated by equation 6b, in determining the size of the constant term. To explain the variation in the constant term for the years 1953, 1955, and 1957 in which the carryover was about constant, one must give

TABLE 8.   Trough holdings and constant term (in equation 6*b*)

Year	Trough holdings[1]	Constant term[2]
	Thousand pounds	
1953	8,191	2.76
1954	5,054	5.45
1955	8,242	5.13
1956	2,957	6.82
1957	8,026	3.65

[1] Taken from Table 7, column 1. These figures are close approximations to the carryover (C) in each year.
[2] Taken from Table 3 in which estimated price relationships for Ketchikan are presented.

consideration to the factors producing year-to-year variation in H^d, the desired equilibrium level of end-of-season holdings. This quantity will also play a role in the discussion of the estimates of the coefficients of t.

In the previous discussion of the determination of H^d, emphasis was placed on isolating the influence of certain factors (carryover, length of season, size of quota, and catch in special seasons) while holding other things constant. Clearly, in year-to-year changes, other things such as consumer income, prices of products competing with halibut, and storage costs do not necessarily remain constant, and this fact must be taken into account in discussing variation in H^d from year to year. It is to be remembered that H^d represents the holdings that consumers wish carried over from the fishing period (T) into the out-of-fishing-season period ($T + 1$) in a particular year and also the amount that holders of inventories find profitable to carry over. Looking at the demand or consumer side of the market, one sees that if consumer income rises substantially from T (the period roughly from May through August) to $T - 1$ (the period from September to April of the next year), consumers will want a substantial amount of halibut carried over from the period from May to August into the period from September to April, much more than would be the case if consumer income were to remain constant or to fall between these two periods. If consumer income goes up between these two periods, holders of inventories will find it profitable to increase the amount of halibut carried over, provided that there is not an offsetting increase in storage costs or other factors. Conversely, if income is expected to go down, holders will find it advisable to reduce the amount they carry over.

Similar considerations regarding the prices of competing products are also relevant. That is, if prices of meat, chicken, or fish other than halibut are expected to rise substantially between the periods from May to August and from September to April, holders of halibut inventories will find it profitable to carry over greater inventories in anticipation of some shifting of purchases from meat to halibut. Conversely, an expected fall in prices of these competing products will produce the opposite effect; namely, a lowering of the amount of halibut carried over. It thus is pertinent to view the behavior of consumer income, prices of competing goods, and storage costs in discussing year-to-year variation in H^d.

Table 9 shows the behavior of personal disposable income over the period covered by the price analyses. Of particular interest are the figures for 1953–4 compared with those for other years. It is seen that in 1953, income hardly changed in contrast with other years in which substantial increases in income were registered, particularly in 1955 and 1956. This would make for a substantially lower H^d for 1953 than in other years, providing that other factors did not operate to offset the influence of changes in income.

The behavior of the prices of products competing with halibut is shown in Figure 4. It is to be noted that a general break in the prices of meat, fish, and chickens set in, beginning about 1951 or 1952. This trend of prices was probably the result of revised national farm policies coupled with rising imports of fish products. In 1953, these price effects intensified the effects of the income factor to lower further the amount of inventories that holders desired to carry over from the production period into the out-of-production period. Taken together with a carry-over of about 8 million pounds at the beginning of the 1953 fishing season, it is not surprising that the constant term in the price relation-ship for 1953, given by k_0 $(H^d - bC)$ in equation 6b, was lowest in 1953. In 1955 and 1957, when the carryovers at the beginning of the fishing season were again about 8 million pounds, the income factor was acting powerfully to offset the effects of price declines in other products

TABLE 9.   United States personal disposable income, seasonally adjusted annual rates, 1953–8

Quarter	1953–4	1954–5	1955–6	1956–7	1957–58
	Billion dollars	Billion dollars	Billion dollars	Billion dollars	Billion dollars
April-June	251.0	252.3	260.1	285.8	299.9
July-September	251.7	254.6	267.8	288.8	308.7
October-December	251.0	258.4	273.2	294.0	306.8
January-March	252.3	260.1	278.6	295.5	306.1

Source: 1953–6: *Survey of Current Business* (July 1957), 28–9. 1957–8: ibid., passim. (Some of these figures will be revised slightly in future issues of the *SCB*.)

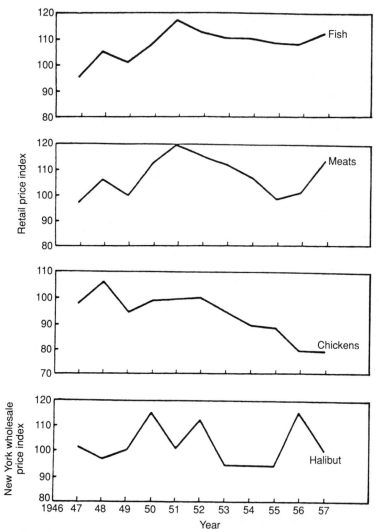

FIG. 4. Retail price index of selected foods and index of New York wholesale
price of halibut for the seasonal years 1947–57, with 1947–9 = 100.

(note too that in 1957, meat prices and prices of other fish had begun to
rise). The rise in income in 1955 was particularly strong, amounting to
$18.5 billion at the annual rate over the production years, as compared
with rises of about $6 billion in 1957 and $1.3 billion in 1953. The strong
effect of income in 1955 probably accounts for the fact that the constant
term in the price relation for that year is somewhat larger than is the
similar term for 1957, particularly when storage costs are taken into
account (see below).

The behavior of storage costs will affect the volume that holders of inventories will wish to carry over from the production period to the out-of-production period. The cost, for example, of cold storage for halibut (Table 10) remained unchanged from May 1953 to January 1956, rose slightly in the period January 1956 to April 1957, and then jumped considerably after May 1957. Also, interest rates for 1956 (Table 11)

TABLE 10.   Cost of cold storage for halibut, Seattle, 1947–59[1]

Effective dates	Fresh to freeze[2]		Received frozen[2]	
	Carload	Under carload	Carload	Under carload
	Cents per 100 lb	Cents per 100 lb	Cents per 100 lb	Cents per 100 lb
1 January 1947 to	85	100	42	50
15 December 1950	16.5	20	16.5	20
16 December 1950 to	95	110	45	55
1 May 1953	18	22	18	22
2 May 1953 to	100	115	50	60
1 January 1956	18	22	18	22
2 January 1956 to	110	125	55	65
30 April 1957	20	25	20	25
1 May 1957 to	127	144	63	75
1959	23	29	23	29

[1] Rates may vary from plant to plant within a range of a few cents, but ordinarily tariffs of various plants are about the same.
[2] The first figure is for the first month, the figure directly underneath it rate monthly thereafter. A carload lot consists of 20,000 pounds or more.
Source: Courtesy of Diamond Ice and Cold Storage, Seattle.

TABLE 11.   Business loan rates—averages of interest rates charged on short-term loans to business by banks in 19 selected cities of the United States, 1953–7[1]

Quarter	1953	1954	1955	1956	1956
	Percent per year	Percent per year	Percent per year	Percent per year	Percent per year
January-March	3.54	3.72	3.54	3.93	4.38
April-June	3.73	3.60	3.56	4.14	4.40
July-September	3.74	3.56	3.77	4.35	4.83
October-December	3.76	3.55	3.83	4.38	4.85

[1] Estimates based on statistics reported by large banks in 19 leading cities. Short-term loans comprise loans maturing in 1 year or less.
Source: Board of Governors, Federal Reserve System (1958).

and particularly 1957 were higher than over the years 1953–5. Thus, in 1957, storage costs rose to offset in some degree the positive influences on H^d of the income factor (which was much weaker than in 1955) and the rise in meat and other fish prices. For these reasons, the fact that the estimate of $k_0(H^d - c)$ for 1957 is somewhat higher than that for 1953 and yet not as great as that for 1955 appears reasonable.

Coefficient of t

Now view the estimates of the coefficient of t in the results for Ketchikan (Table 3). Equation 6b indicates that this coefficient is $k_1 (H^d - bC) - k_0 a_1$. It is seen that the quantity $H^d - bC$, which figured in the discussion of estimates of the constant terms, also appears in the coefficient of t. In addition, the quantity a_1, the rate of inventory buildup, appears. A simple calculation will indicate the relative magnitudes of k_0 and k_1. Suppose the constant term $k_0(H^d - bC)$ is equal to 3.0, a value in line with those appearing in the estimated relations for 1953, 1955, and 1957 shown in Table 3. Assume further that $H^d - bC$ is equal to 35 million pounds (this assumption is reasonable, since peak inventories are in the vicinity of 40 million pounds and the carryover is in the neighborhood of 3 to 8 million pounds—see Table 6). Then k_0 would be about 3/35. Now if the estimate of the coefficient of t is found to be 0.06, it is possible to determine k_1 from the following relation: $0.06 = k_1(H^d - bC) - k_0 a_1$, provided that a_1 is known. The figures in Table 6 indicate a daily rate of inventory buildup of one-third of a million pounds per day. Therefore, $0.06 = k_1(H^d - bC) - k_0 a_1 = k_1 (35) - (3/35)(1/3)$. Since k_1 is the only unknown appearing in this last relation, its value can be calculated. The rough estimate, an order of magnitude estimate, is $k_1 = 0.0025$, about one-tenth the value of k_0. Thus, an approximate way to write the coefficient of t would be: $0.0025 (H^d - bC) - 0.029\, a_1$. This rough estimate provides an indication of the relative weights to be applied to changes in $(H^d - bC)$ and in a_1 in assessing year-to-year variation in the coefficient of t.

Again the discussion will revolve about the results for 1953, 1955, and 1957—years in which the carryover (see Table 7) was about 8 million pounds. Table 7 indicates that the rate of inventory buildup was largest in 1953, next largest in 1955, and smallest in 1957. The difference, however, between 1955 and 1957 is small. Thus on this count alone, the coefficient of t for 1953 should be smallest. As regards the quantity $H^d - bC$, as argued above, this quantity was smallest in 1953, next largest in 1957, and largest in 1955. The tentative conclusion from these considerations is that the coefficient of t for 1953 should be smaller than those for 1955 and 1957. In Table 3, the following estimates are given for this coefficient (figures in parentheses are standard errors): 1953, 0.0701 (0.0409), 1955, 0.0966 (0.0259), and 1957, 0.0351 (0.0137). For 1953, the estimate, 0.0701, is accompanied by a large standard error—so large that is not possible to reject the hypothesis that the true value of the coefficient is zero. This is not the case for either the coefficient for 1955 or for 1957. However, the standard errors are so large so that it does not appear possible to reject the hypothesis that these three coefficients are the same; additional results, comparable to the ones presented, are much to be desired.

Summary of Intrayear Port Pricing Analysis

Perhaps the most valuable contribution of the analysis is that it provides a theoretical framework, in large measure empirically tested, for consideration of problems relating to port pricing of halibut (and possibly of other primary products). The framework is broad enough to incorporate the effects of certain important changes in conservation measures, the effects of the voluntary layover program, and the effects of changes in economic factors such as income and prices of other products. In essence, an important part of the structure within which halibut is priced has been revealed. Given knowledge of this structure, it is possible to talk more confidently of the probable effects on pricing of specific policy measures.

The major results flowing from the analysis of immediate relevance for pricing problems in the halibut fishery are the following:

1. A lengthening of the fishing season will provide a more gradual rise in port price during the season. Thus, the boat owner and crew who happen to miss a trip at the end of the season, when price is high relative to price earlier in the season, will not suffer as great a financial loss as they otherwise would. Also, and very important, a longer season will make for more stability in the wholesale price of halibut throughout the year. Such stability will greatly facilitate the business of dealing in halibut. The risk and costs associated with holding large inventories, a necessary state of affairs in short seasons, will be much reduced by a lengthening of the season.

2. Insofar as the voluntary layover program of the Fishing Vessel Owners' Association has resulted in lengthening the season, it has contributed to producing the effects mentioned above. Further, the effects of this program on the average level of port price should not be overemphasized, since (a) the amount by which the program has lengthened the season has not been large, and (b) other economic factors, particularly consumer income, prices of meat, poultry, and other

competing products, are much more important determinants of the average price in a particular season.

3. The Commission, bound as it is by provisions of the Treaty, has acted to lengthen the season in a special way; namely, by the creation of special seasons. The more halibut taken in these special seasons, the more gradual will be the rise in port price in the regular season. It would be desirable, however, to eliminate the break in the continuity of port deliveries made necessary by the special seasons, since it introduces an element of uncertainty for both boat owners and dealers. By having one continuous long season, the objectives underlying the institution of the special seasons (a more even rate of exploitation of the halibut stocks throughout the year and fishing banks at periods of peak abundance) would be achieved and also the uncertainty associated with a discontinuous season would be removed.

4. Finally, in setting the quota, the Commission should realize that it is affecting both the pattern and level of port prices. If there is some latitude in setting the quota, taking biological considerations into account, then the Commission should pursue policies that foster both intrayear and interyear price stability. The difficulties surrounding the framing and application of such measures should not be minimized. In terms of the above analysis, knowledge of H^d, the desired end-of-season stocks, would have to be known in advance. This knowledge could only be obtained (and then with difficulty) if forecasts of consumer income and prices of other products were available at the time when the quota is determined. It is hoped that the analysis presented above will serve usefully in an approach to this important problem.

Summary

An empirically verifiable theory of intrayear port pricing of halibut is developed that provides a framework within which to appraise the effects of various regulatory measures on the seasonal price pattern. Further, the analysis provides a basis for explaining year to year changes in both the level and seasonal pattern of pricing.

First in the theoretical considerations is a price-adjustment equation that relates daily change in price to excess inventory demand for halibut; that is, an equation that relates daily change in price to the difference between desired holdings and actual holdings of inventories on a particular day. Generally, the larger the deviation between desired holdings and actual holdings, the more rapidly will price change. It is recognized also that a given positive excess of desired stocks over actual stocks will exert more upward pressure on the port price if the price is at a low level than if it is at a high level and if this given positive excess is present late rather than early in the season. These considerations, as well as others, have been incorporated in a relationship explaining the observed temporal pattern of port price within the regular fishing season.

Second, in the theoretical consideration is an exposition and application of the theory of storage to bring together in a meaningful fashion the factors determining the desired equilibrium end-of-season holdings of halibut. Among the factors that determine this quantity are several policy variables, such as the regular season's quota, the catch in the special seasons, and the duration of the regular season. Since the effect of these variables on the desired level of holdings can be predicted under ceteris paribus conditions and since the desired level of holdings appears in the relationship explaining the seasonal pattern of price, qualified inferences regarding the effects of changes in the policy variables on the intraseasonal pattern of pricing can be made.

Statistical data relating to daily pricing at Ketchikan and Seattle for the years 1953 through 1957 have been employed to estimate and test the price-formation relation. The results are quite satisfactory in that the relation fits the data rather well, and all estimated coefficients have algebraic signs consistent with theoretical considerations. Thus, a statistically tested explanation of many aspects of the pricing of halibut is the major contribution embodied in this article.

Some interesting findings of the empirical analysis are the following: fluctuations in daily landings at Ketchikan, where there is only an inventory demand, exert no significant influence on the daily average Ketchikan price. At Seattle, however, where there is demand for fresh fish, fluctuations in daily landings do exert a significant influence on daily average price. The effects of, say, a 10-per cent increase in daily landings amount to about a 1- to 2-per cent decline in average price. These findings indicate that increased landings at Seattle are associated with slightly lower prices there and with higher aggregate fleet gross revenue, all other things being constant.

Analysis of year-to-year changes in the level and pattern of seasonal price movements suggests that beginning-of-year inventory carryover, consumer income, prices of other food products competing with halibut for the consumer's dollar, and costs of storing halibut play a role in explaining year-to-year changes in the seasonal pattern of pricing. It is also likely that lengthening of the season as a result of the voluntary layover program has tended to produce a more gradual rise (abstracting from the usual price decline that takes place early in the season at Seattle but not at Ketchikan) in prices during the season. Since, however, the duration of the regular season has not been increased substantially, this effect is not pronounced. Similarly, one effect of the special seasons instituted by the Commission is probably a slower rate of price rise during the regular season. It appears likely that a further lengthening of the regular season would result in a still more slowly rising port price throughout the regular season and that the institution of one long season would reduce substantially some of the price uncertainties for those who buy and sell halibut.

References

ANDERSON, A. W. and POWER, E. A. (1956a), 'Fishery statistics of the United States, 1953', *US Fish and Wildlife Service, Statistical Digest 36*, 312 pp.
—— —— (1956b), 'Fishery statistics of the United States, 1954', *US Fish and Wildlife Service, Statistical Digest 39*, 374 pp.
—— —— (1957), 'Fishery statistics of the United States, 1955', *US Fish and Wildlife Service, Statistical Digest 41*, 446 pp.
BOARD OF GOVERNORS, FEDERAL RESERVE SYSTEM (1958), *Federal Reserve Bulletin* (July), 886 pp.
BRENNAN, M. J. (1958), 'The supply of storage', *American Economic Review* **48** (Mar.), 50–72.
CRUTCHFIELD, J. A. (1955), 'Conservation and allocation in the Pacific Coast fisheries', *Proceedings of the Western Economic Association*, 69–72.
—— (1956), 'Common property resources and factor allocation', *Canadian Journal of Economics and Political Science*, **22** (Aug.), 292–300.
DURBIN, J., and WATSON, G. S. (1950), 'Testing for serial correlation in least squares regression. I', *Biometrika*, **37** (Dec.), 409–28.
—— (1951), 'Testing for serial correlation in least squares regression. II', *Biometrika*, **38** (June), 159–78.
GORDON, H. S. (1954), 'The economic theory of a common-property resource: the fishery', *Journal of Political Economy*, **62** (Apr.), 124–42.
KALDOR, N. (1939), 'Speculation and economic stability', *Review of Economic Studies*, **7** (Oct.), 1–27.
Pacific Fisherman (1959) International Yearbook, **57**: 2, 260 pp. Portland, Oregon: Miller Freeman Publications, Inc.
WORKING, H. (1948), 'The theory of the inverse carrying charge in future markets', *Journal of Farm Economics*, **30** (Feb.), 1–28.

6

A Study Toward a Dynamic Theory of Seasonality for Economic Time Series

ERIC GHYSELS*

Abstract

Several economists, notably Plosser (1978), Sargent (1978), and Wallis (1978) refuted the assumption that the seasonal component of endogenous variables in a dynamic economic model has almost all of its power restricted to what is termed seasonal frequency and its harmonics. In this article, a model with a closed-form solution is formulated to provide more insight into the arguments put forward by economists. It is concluded that univariate seasonal adjustment cannot be considered a harmless simplification of data without loss of information, neither for the interpretation of economic time series nor for regression analysis.

Key words: Unobserved component models; Dynamic economic models.

1. Introduction

Most statisticians accept a number of fundamental assumptions that allow them to identify seasonality in economic time series. One of these 'basic assumptions', as they were termed by Bell and Hillmer (1984),

* Eric Ghysels is Assistant Professor, Department of Economics and Centre de Recherche et Développement en Économique, Université de Montréal, Montréal, Québec H3C 3J7, Canada. The author wishes to thank William Bell, Lars Hansen, Robert Hodrick, John Taylor, and George Tiao for their comments, as well as Thomas Doan, Robert Lucas, and Peter Rossi for their advice throughout the author's dissertation. Comments from an associate editor and referees led to a substantially improved presentation of the arguments in the article. Parts of the text were written while the author was an ASA/Census/NSF fellow visiting the Statistical Research Division of the U.S. Bureau of the Census under National Science Foundation Grant SES 84-01460. Helpful assistance was also provided by Carol Jones of the US Bureau of the Census.

Printed with permission of: *Journal of the American Statistical Association*, **83**. 168–72.

states that the seasonal component has almost all of its power restricted
to the seasonal frequency and its harmonics. Several economists, notably
Plosser (1978), Sargent (1978), and Wallis (1978) have refuted this
assumption on the basis of the interpretation of dynamic economic
theory. In dynamic models, the seasonality in exogenous variables may
induce power at all spectral frequencies of the endogenous variables.
Until now, economists have only provided theoretical arguments that
lacked a clearly specified closed-form analytical model. This article
presents a closed-form solution that should make the arguments particularly clear for statisticians, since the model allows for the computation
and decomposition of the spectrum and its decompositions of the
endogenous variables. Furthermore, the model allows one to evaluate
the origin of the leakage across frequencies. After having read the
section that presents the formulation of the example, the question
should arise as to the purpose of currently practiced seasonal adjustment. Almost all economic time series are the outcome of a complexity
of dynamic interactions. Hence any attempt to base the component
structure of one isolated series on arbitrary identification assumptions is
bound to give erroneous interpretations of economic time series.
Moreover, if we accept the principle that simplifying data without major
loss of information could justify univariate seasonal adjustments, as
suggested by Bell and Hillmer (1984), we ought to conclude that, since
considerable damage to interpreting series is more than likely, there is
no justification possible. A logical outcome of these observations is that
the treatment of seasonality ought to be made in a multivariate context.
The orthogonality assumption is not discussed in this article. This second
basic assumption is considered in Ghysels (1987a), where it is shown
that for a certain class of dynamic models one may prefer nonorthagonal
decompositions.

2.   A Market Equilibrium Model of Production

2.1 The model

Let us suppose that there is a market with seasonally fluctuating
demand, made up of two components.

$$D_t^s = \theta_1 D_{t-12}^s + \mu_t^s, \qquad \mu_t^s \text{ iid } N(0, \sigma_s^2), \qquad (2.1)$$

$$D_t^c = a_0 - a_1 P_t + \mu_t^c, \qquad \mu_t^c \text{ iid } N(0, \sigma_c^2), \qquad (2.2)$$

with $|\theta| < 1$ and $a_i > 0$ for $i = 0, 1$. The first component, denoted by
D_t^s, is a purely exogenous monthly seasonal autoregressive (AR) process. A seasonal AR process was selected to facilitate analytical deriva-
tions. The second component, denoted by D_t^c, corresponds to demand

responding to market price P_t. The sum of the two components is observed market demand:

$$D_t = D_t^c + D_t^s, \qquad (2.3)$$

with $\{D_{t-k}, P_{t-k}\}_{k=0}^{+00}$ observed at time t. Using (2.1), (2.2), and (2.3), a standard inverse demand function is obtained as follows:

$$P_t = A_0 - A_1 D_t + \mu_t, \qquad (2.4)$$

with

$$A_0 = a_0 a_1^{-1}, \; A_1 = a_1^{-1},$$

and

$$\mu_t = a_1^{-1}(1 - \theta_1 L^{12})^{-1}\mu_t^s + a_1^{-1}\mu_t^c.$$

The stochastic shock to demand μ_t will normally have an ARMA (12, 12) structure (ARMA denotes autoregressive moving average) (see Granger and Morris 1976).

The supply side of the market is based on a model of a firm that represents a typical production unit. The entrepreneur of a production unit faces an intertemporal maximization problem characterized by

$$\max_{\{q_{t+j}\}} E_0 \lim_{T \to \infty} \sum_{j=0}^{T} \beta^j (P_{t+j}q_{t+j} - dq_{t+j} - (e/2)q_{t+j}^2 - (f/2)(q_{t+j} - q_{t+j-1})^2),$$

$$(2.5)$$

with output at time t being donoted by q_t and $0 < \beta < 1$. β represents the discount factor, whereas d, e, and f are strictly positive coefficients. Hence the entrepreneur plans future production, starting from $t = 0$, with the objective to maximize the expected value, given information at zero, of the infinite horizon stream of discounted profits. A rational expectations market equilibrium for a replica of N competitive firms characterized by the condition $D_t = Q_t = Nq_t \forall t$ is derived. The actual derivation of the calculations are included in the Appendix. The analytic results for the endogenous variables of the model are

$$Q_t = D_t = - N(1 - \rho_1 L)^{-1}(1 - \rho_2^{-1}L^{-1})^{-1}\rho_1 f^{-1}$$
$$\times [\theta(L) - L^{-1}p_2^{-1}\theta(p_2^{-1})](\theta(L))^{-1}\mu_t, \qquad (2.6)$$
$$P_t = A_0 + [1 + A_1 N(1 - \rho_1 L)^{-1}(1 - \rho_2^{-1}L^{-1})^{-1}\rho_1 f^{-1}$$
$$\times [\theta(L) - L^{-1}p_2^{-1}\theta(p_2^{-1})](\theta(L))^{-1}]\mu_t, \qquad (2.7)$$

where ρ_1 and ρ_2 are the roots of the characteristic polynomial obtained from the derivation in the Appendix and $\theta(L)$ is the polynomial of the fundamental moving average representation of the μ_t process. The exogenous variables of the model are the stochastic building blocks $\{\mu_t^c\}$ and $\{\mu_t^s\}$.

The exogenous cyclical and seasonal processes enable us to define a composition for Q_t that is based on a distinction between that part of Q_t originating from the exogenous cyclical shocks versus that part originating from the exogenous seasonal shocks:

$$Q_t = Q_t(\mu_t^c) + Q_t(\mu_t^s), \tag{2.8}$$

with

$$
\begin{aligned}
Q_t(\mu_t^c) = & - a_1^{-1}N(1 - \rho_1 L)^{-1}(1 - \rho_2^{-1}L^{-1})^{-1}\rho_1 f^{-1}\mu_t^c \\
& + a_1^{-1}N(1 - \rho_1 L)^{-1}(1 - \rho_2^{-1}L)^{-1}L^{-1} \\
& \times \rho_2^{-1}\theta(\rho_2^{-1})(\theta(L))^{-1}\mu_t^c
\end{aligned}
$$

and

$$
\begin{aligned}
Q_t(\mu_t^s) = & - a_1^{-1}N(1 - \rho_1 L)^{-1}(1 - \rho_2^{-1}L^{-1})^{-1}\rho_1 f^{-1} \\
& \times (1 - \theta_1 L^{12})^{-1}\mu_t^s + a_1^{-1}N(1 - \rho_1 L)^{-1} \\
& \times (1 - \rho_2^{-1}L^{-1})^{-1}L^{-1}\rho_2^{-1}\theta(\rho_2^{-1}) \\
& \times (\theta(L))^{-1}(1 - \theta_1 L^{12})^{-1}\mu_t^s.
\end{aligned}
$$

This particular decomposition of Q_t is unique, given the exogenous sources of cyclical and seasonal fluctuations. A similar decomposition for p_t can be defined, mutatis mutandis, along the same lines of reasoning. Decomposition (2.8) does not correspond to the decomposition of Q_t, according to the principles of univariate seasonal time series analysis. The component $Q_t(\mu_t^c)$ has power at all frequencies, including possibly the seasonal frequency and its harmonics. $Q_t(\mu_t^s)$ not only has power at the seasonal frequency but also at all other frequencies as well. The cause of the 'spillover' effects that occur is the adjustment costs that characterize the intertemporal dynamics of the model. Therefore, when the adjustment costs are absent, that is, $f = 0$, the spillover effects across frequencies will disappear and the decomposition (2.8) will take on the properties of the standard univariate time series model:

$$Q_t = N(1 + a_1 e)^{-1}(a_0 - a_1 d + \mu_t^c + (1 - \theta_1 L^{12})^{-1}\mu_t^s), \tag{2.9}$$

with

$$Q_t(\mu_t^c) = N(1 + a_1 e)^{-1}(a_0 - a_1 d + \mu_t^c)$$

and

$$Q_t(\mu_t^s) = N(1 + a_1 e)^{-1}(1 - a_1 L^{12})^{-1}\mu_t^s.$$

Hence, when the profit maximization problem and, therefore, the model is no longer intertemporally dynamic, we obtain the traditional decomposition. Four numerical examples that show the effects of adjustment costs, that is, the dynamic effects, further illustrate this point.

2.2 Some numerical examples

Models 1 and 2

$$D_t^s = .5D_{t-12}^s + \mu_t^s, \quad \mu_t^s \sim N(0, 1).$$

$$D_t^c = 10 - P_t + \mu_t^c, \quad \mu_t^c \sim N(0, 1).$$

$$\max_{\{Q_{t+j}\}} \lim_{T \to \infty} \sum_{j=0}^{T} (.9)^j [P_{t+j}Q_{t+j} - Q_{t+j}$$
$$- (e/2)Q_{t+j}^2 - (f/2)(Q_{t+j} - Q_{t+j-1})^2],$$

with $e = 18$, $f = 2$ for Model 1 and $e = 2$, $f = 18$ for Model 2.

Model 3 and 4

$$D_t^s = .5D_{t-1}^s + \mu_t^s, \qquad\qquad \mu_t^s \sim N(0, 1).$$

$$D_t^c = 1 - P_t + \mu_t^c.$$

$$\mu_t^c = .9\mu_{t-1}^c + \zeta_t, \qquad\qquad \zeta_t \sim N(0, 1).$$

$$\max_{\{Q_{t+j}\}} \lim_{T \to \infty} \sum_{j=0}^{T} (.9)^j [P_{t+j}Q_{t+j} - Q_{t+j} - (e/2)Q_{t+j}^2 - (f/2)(Q_{t+j} - Q_{t+j-1})^2],$$

with $e = 18$, $f = 2$ for Model 3 and $e = 2$, $f = 18$ for Model 4.

Models 1 and 3 are identical except for the μ_t^c process, which is white noise in the former and AR(1) in the latter case. The same difference appears between Models 2 and 4. On the other hand, the difference between Models 1 and 2 (and 3 and 4, respectively) is that the first has relatively low adjustment costs whereas the latter has relatively high ones. With relatively low adjustment costs, $\rho_1 = .093$ and $\rho_2 = .080$. As can be seen in Equation (2.6), ρ_1 and ρ_2 determine equilibrium output Q_t. When adjustment costs are relatively high, $\rho_1 = .935$ and $\rho_2 = .840$.

The spectral densities of $Q_t(\mu_t^s)$ and Q_t for Models 1 and 2 appear in Figure 1. The underlying shocks are the same; namely, μ_t^s is the fundamental process of the seasonal first-order AR process and μ_t^c is white noise. In one case, however, there are relatively few adjustment costs, whereas the opposite is true for the other model. When adjustment costs are low, the spectrum for Q_t with narrow peaks is obtained. The same pattern appears in the spectrum of $Q_t(\mu_t^s)$, where the latter almost corresponds to a spectrum of the process $(1 - .5L^{12})^{-1}\mu_t^s$. With relatively high adjustment costs, this is no longer true. Indeed, $Q_t(\mu_t^s)$ has considerable power at the low frequencies.

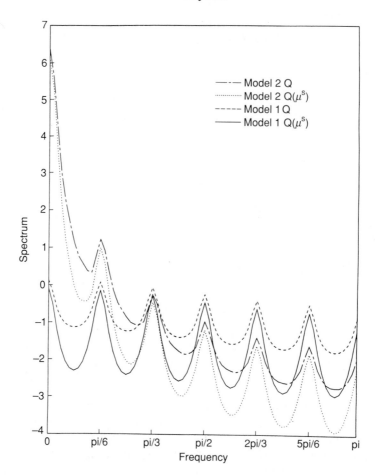

FIG. 1. Log spectrum, Models 1 and 2.

The difference between the spectrum of Q_t and $Q_t(\mu_t^s)$ yields $Q_t(\mu_t^c)$. Note that in both models $Q_t(\mu_t^c)$ is characterized by dips at the seasonal frequencies. For models 3 and 4 appearing in Figure 2, the conclusions are similar. When adjustment costs are relatively low, the power of Q_t at the lower frequencies is that of $Q_t(\mu_t^c)$, since μ_t^c is an AR(1) process whereas $Q_t(\mu_t^s)$ very closely resembles $(1-.5L^{12})^{-1}\mu_t^s$. When we have relatively high adjustment costs, resulting in ρ_1 and ρ_2 getting closer to unity rather than 0, then $Q_t(\mu_t^c)$ and $Q_t(\mu_t^s)$ gain power at the low frequencies. As a matter of fact, there is a point at which one would be led to believe, according to peaks in the Q_t process, that there is no major seasonality occurring in the series.

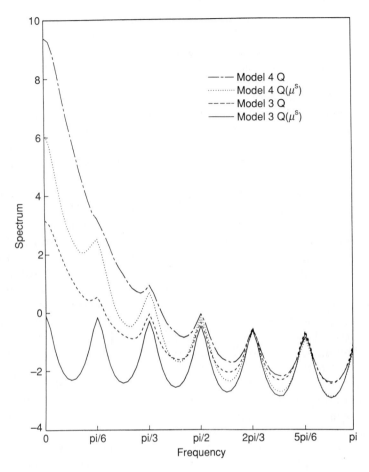

FIG. 2. Log spectrum, Models 3 and 4.

In summary, we have discussed the decomposition of an endogenous variable along the lines of the seasonal versus nonseasonal fluctuations in exogenous variables. This decomposition does not correspond to the standard identification assumptions and is unique, given the decomposition of the exogenous process. Furthermore, the decomposition of exogenous variables can only be done according to the standard identification assumptions common to univariate seasonal adjustment procedures, which is known not to be unique. The model formulated in this section has latent exogenous shocks. The same principle applies, however, to models with observable exogenous variables and stochastic disturbances.

2.3 Can univariate seasonal adjustment be justified?

In light of the proceding discussion it is pertinent to ask whether
univariate time series seasonal adjustment procedures, such as X-11 or
model-based approaches, can be justified. It is also relevant to ask why
we want to seasonally adjust time series in the first place. Seasonal
adjustment can be justified by the desire to find, for example, the
response of inventories to a market demand shock of nonseasonal
nature, such as a subsidy, an oil-price shock, and so on. The model can
either be one in which inventories are endogenous with market demand
assumed to be exogenous, such as in Blanchard (1983), or one in which
both demand and inventories are endogenously determined by a full
market equilibrium model, such as Eichenbaum (1984). Separating out
shocks of a particular nature is often a desirable experiment, but does
this justify the use of univariate seasonally adjusted time series to study
the co-movements of inventories and market demand in order to make
hypothetical projections? As the previous analysis has illustrated, the
answer to this question is clearly negative. The predictions and interpretations based on incorrectly identified decompositions will very likely be
misleading. Moreover, if we accept a principle that could justify univariate seasonal adjustment as simplifying data without major loss of
information, as Bell and Hillmer (1984) suggested, we ought to conclude
again that defining seasonality as peaks at the seasonal frequencies and
harmonics can cause considerable damage to the interpretation of
economic time series and, in principle, cannot be justified, contrary to
what many seem to believe or argue. Sometimes it is also said that
series are seasonally adjusted because economists have no 'theory' about
seasonality. The problem with such an argument is that we actually
apply a particular theory, which is not acceptable, when identifying the
nonseasonal part. A decomposition of an endogenous variable according
to the traditional identification assumptions corresponds to a static
environment, as shown by (2.9) and by the numerical examples.

3.   Conclusion

Although seasonal adjustment has become a well-established practice it
has been difficult for statisticians to develop and justify suitable models
for seasonal time series. This article has attempted to stimulate discussion of one of the basic assumptions in the current statistics literature.
Some critics will say that economists lack knowledge of the structure of
dynamic models and, therefore, will ignore the observations that were
made in this article. My hope is not that everyone will agree with the
opinions expressed here. It is hoped, however, that the reader will

recognize a number of important issues that clearly contradict current practice. Research on seasonality in explicity formulated causal dynamic models should enable us to improve economic time series models that would also be of use to the layperson. This article has, therefore, attempted to make modest progress in this regard. Some critics will also say that the 'leakage' of power across frequencies is negligible and can be ignored. Empirical evidence reported in Ghysels (1987b) shows that, for inventory data linked with industrial production and shipments, there is considerable leakage, which if ignored yields misleading co-movements among series.

Appendix: Model Solution

This Appendix elaborates on the computations of the equilibrium of the model discussed in the text. Lucas and Prescott (1971) pointed out that a rational expectation competitive equilibrium for a model of this type solves a particular type of social planning problem. It consists of considering the area under the demand curve:

$$\int Q_t[A_0 - A_1 X_t + \mu_t] \, dX = [A_0 + \mu_t]Q_t - (A_1/2)Q_t^2$$

$$= [A_0 + \mu_t]NQ_t - (A_1/2)N^2 Q_t^2. \qquad (A.1)$$

N is set equal to 1 for simplicity. The social planning problem corresponding to the competitive equilibrium consists of maximizing the expected discounted area (A.1), minus the social cost of producing the output, which, therefore, implies

$$\max_{\{9t+j\}} \lim_{T \to \infty} E_0 \sum_{t=0}^{T} \beta^t [(A_0 + \mu_{t+j})Q_{t+j} - (A_1/2)Q_{t+j}^2 - dQ_{t+j}$$

$$- (e/2)Q_{t+j}^2 - (f/2)(Q_{t+j} - Q_{t-j-1})^2]. \qquad (A.2)$$

The foregoing expression leads to the Euler equation, for any j, as follows:

$$\beta F_{t+j} Q_{t+j+1} + \phi Q_{t+j} + Q_{t+j-1} = f^{-1}(a_0 a_1^{-1} + \mu_{t+j} + d) \qquad (A.3)$$

with $\phi = -[1 + \beta + (a_1^{-1} + e)f^{-1}]$. The equilibrium output satisfying the Euler conditions (A.3) and the transversality condition (compare Hansen and Sargent 1980, 1981) can then be expressed as (up to a constant)

$$Q_t = \rho_1 Q_{t-1} - \rho_1^{f-1} \sum_{j=0}^{+\infty} \rho_2^{-j} E_t \mu_{t+j}, \qquad (A.4)$$

with ρ_1 and ρ_2 the roots of the characterized polynomial obtained from

the Euler equation (A.3). The conditional expectations appearing in
(A.4) can be solved by using the Wiener–Kolmogorov prediction
formula. Based on the assumption that the fundamental moving average
representations of the $\{\mu_t\}$ process can be written as

$$\mu_t = \theta(L)\xi_t, \tag{A.5}$$

and assuming that entrepreneurs do not observe any series which
Granger causes ξ_t, the closed-form solution for equilibrium out-put can
be written as

$$Q_t = -(1 - \rho_1 L)^{-1}(1 - \rho_2^{-1}L^{-1})^{-1}\rho_1 f^{-1}$$
$$\times [\theta(L) - L^{-1}p_2^{-1}\!\star\! p_2^{-1})](\theta(L))^{-1}\mu_t, \tag{A.6}$$

as Hansen and Sargent (1981) have shown. Equation (A.6) corresponds
to (2.6) in the text with $N = 1$.

References

(References marked with a * are included in this volume)

BELL, W. R., and HILLMER, S. C. (1984), 'Issues involved with the seasonal adjustment of economic time series', *Journal of Business & Economic Statistics*, **2**, 291–320.*

BLANCHARD, O. J. (1983), 'The production and inventory behavior of the American automobile industry', *Journal of Political Economy*, **91**, 365–400.

EICHENBAUM, M. S. (1984), 'Rational expectations and the smoothing properties of inventories of finished goods', *Journal of Monetary Economics*, **14**, 71–96.

GHYSELS, E. (1987a), 'Seasonal extraction in the presence of feedback', *Journal of Business & Economic Statistics*, **5**, 191–4.

—— (1987b), 'Cycles and seasonals in inventories—another look at nonstationarity and induced seasonality'.

GRANGER, C. W. J., and MORRIS, M. J. (1976), 'Time series modelling and interpretation', *Journal of the Royal Statistical Society*, Ser. A, **139**, 246–57.

HANSEN, L. P., and SARGENT, T. J. (1980), 'Formulating and estimating dynamic linear rational expectations models', *Journal of Economic Dynamics and Control*, 2. Reprinted in *Rational Expectations and Econometric Practice*, eds. R. E. Lucas, Jr., and I. J. Sargent. Minneapolis: University of Minnesota Press, pp. 91–125.

—— (1981), 'Linear rational expectations models for dynamically interrelated variables', in *Rational Expectations and Econometric Practice*, eds. R. E. Lucas, Jr., and I. J. Sargent. Minneapolis: University of Minnesota Press, pp. 127–56.

LUCAS, R. E., and PRESCOTT, E. (1971), 'Investment under uncertainty', *Econometrica*, **39**, 659–81.

PLOSSER, CHARLES I. (1978), 'A time series analysis of seasonality in econometric models', in *Seasonal Analysis of Economic Time Series*, ed. A. Zellner.

Washington, DC: US Department of Commerce, Bureau of the Census, pp. 365–97.

SARGENT, T. J. (1978), Comments on 'Seasonal adjustment and multiple time series analysis', by K. F. Wallis, in *Seasonal Analysis of Economic Time Series*, ed. A. Zellner. Washington, DC: US Department of Commerce, Bureau of the Census, pp. 361–4.

WALLIS, K. F. (1978), 'Seasonal adjustment and multiple time series analysis', in *Seasonal Analysis of Economic Time Series*, ed. A. Zellner. Washington, DC: US Department of Commerce, Bureau of the Census, pp. 347–57.

7

Seasonality and Habit Persistence in a Life Cycle Model of Consumption

DENISE R. OSBORN*

Abstract. The allocation of non-durable consumers' expenditure over the four quarters of the year reflects choices made by consumers, implying a utility function exhibiting seasonality. Incorporating such a function, the life cycle model fails to explain fully the observed dynamics in UK seasonally unadjusted data. Seasonal habit persistence effects are introduced and found to be significant. Although this generalized model stands up well to testing in a univariate context, it fails to exclude a predictive role for lagged income changes.

1. Introduction

Seasonality is inherent in many economic time series, but it is rarely considered to be an issue of interest in econometric model-building. Rather than explicitly investigating the economics underlying seasonal variation, modellers typically try to remove its effects either by using seasonally adjusted data or by including seasonal intercept dummies in their equations. The former practice is criticized by Wallis (1974), who shows that it may distort the relationship between variables, while the latter assumes that the function simply shifts up or down with the season. However, except for degrees of freedom considerations, there seems to be no *a priori* reason why the same parameters or functional form should apply at different times of the year: indeed, Gersovitz and MacKinnon (1978) argue that realistic utility, cost or production functions result in models in which seasonal influences cannot be separated out in a simple fashion.

* Department of Econometrics, University of Manchester, Manchester M13 9PL, England.

Printed with permission of: *Journal of Applied Econometrics*, **3**. 255–66.

In the present study seasonality is treated as one of the features to be explained within the economic model. Thus, in the particular application to non-durable consumers' expenditure, it is argued that the allocation of expenditure over the year reflects seasonal tastes and hence seasonality in the underlying utility function: the implications of this are explicitly investigated.

The framework for our analysis is the influential paper by Hall (1978), who derives a random-walk model for real non-durable consumers' expenditure when rational expectations are combined with a life cycle theory of consumption. Hall does not investigate seasonality at all, and employs seasonally adjusted values in his empirical analysis: although subsequent US authors have examined many aspects of this theory, the type of data used has rarely been questioned. On the other hand, the UK studies of Muellbauer (1983) and Wickens and Molana (1984) use seasonally unadjusted data, but neither attempts an analysis of how seasonality should influence model specification.

In a recent study, Miron (1986) examines seasonality in the components of consumers' expenditure for the United States in a life cycle context. Although he incorporates seasonal preferences in a slightly different way, and adopts a different approach to estimation, there is much in common between his investigation and that undertaken here. Contrary to the many earlier US studies which employ seasonally adjusted observations, Miron finds support for the life cycle model in his analysis of unadjusted data.

Seasonality is considered in section 2 in relation to a specific utility function which, in the absence of seasonal preferences, implies a random-walk model in the logarithm of consumption. This (static) function does not, however, fully explain the observed dynamics, leading to the introduction of habit persistence terms in section 3. Habit persistence is a relatively novel feature in the time-series modelling of aggregate consumption data, so that the integrated treatment of seasonality reveals a new aspect to an often-studied macroeconomic variable. The habit persistence model is subjected to testing in section 3. Conclusions complete the paper.

2.   Seasonality and Utility

Studies of real non-durable consumers' expenditure in the UK almost invariably use data in logarithms because changes appear to be approximately multiplicative. Muellbauer (1983) derives the random-walk model of Hall in logarithmic terms by assuming the single period utility function

$$U_t = \frac{C_t^{1-\beta}}{1 - \beta}. \qquad 0 < \beta < 1. \tag{1}$$

In a life cycle context, with utility additive and constant discounting over time, total utility is

$$V_t = \sum_{i=0}^{T} \alpha^i U_{t+i}, \qquad 0 < \alpha \leqslant 1 \tag{2}$$

while the period-to-period budget constraint is given by

$$C_{t+1} = Y_{t+1} - A_{t+1} + (1 + r)A_t, \tag{3}$$

where Y is real income, r is the (assumed constant) real rate of interest and A is the end-of-period real value of assets. Treating A_t as the decision variable, maximization of total utility under certainty then yields

$$C_{t+1}^{-\beta} = C_t^{-\beta}/\{\alpha(1 + r)\}, \tag{4}$$

or, on taking logarithms and rearranging,

$$\Delta \ln C_{t+1} = \gamma, \tag{5}$$

where $\gamma = [\ln \alpha + \ln(1 + r)]/\beta$.

In the real world the future is not known; expectations and information therefore have a role in the implementation of this model. Thus, in particular, when consumers' decisions are based on expected lifetime utility, the left-hand side of equation (4) is replaced by its expectation at time t and a stochastic disturbance is introduced into (5). It is also worth noting at this stage that, with the assumption of a constant real interest rate, income drives consumption: consequently the relevant information set consists of income and its determinants.

The theory just outlined is, however, incompatible with the allocation of expenditure over the year in a definite pattern, as in Figure 1. The simple assumption of a seasonal disturbance in (5) to cope with this cannot be justified, because if this were the case the disturbance would be to some extent predictable, hence C_t would not contain all information available at t, as implied by rational expectations.

Putting aside the rate of interest, the only possible sources of seasonality in this framework are the parameters α and β. To investigate the implications of such seasonality, replace the single period utility function (1) by

$$U_t = \frac{C_t^{1-\beta_q}}{1 - \beta_q}, \qquad 0 < \beta_q < 1, \qquad q = 1, \ldots, 4 \tag{6}$$

when t falls in quarter q. In substituting (6) into (2), and throughout the paper, the obvious notation is adopted that $q + i$ is replaced by

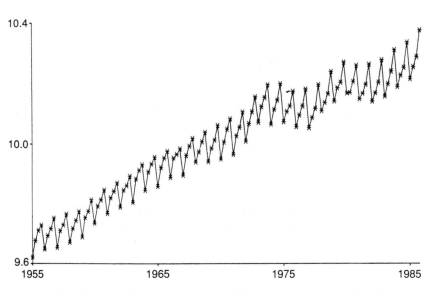

FIG. 1. Logarithm of real non-durable consumers' expenditure

$q + i - 4$ when $q + i > 4$ for any i; similarly, $q - i + 4$ replaces $q - i$ when the latter is negative. Also, (2) must be modified in the obvious way if the discounting parameter α is seasonal.

The rationale for the explicit inclusion of seasonal parameters in the utility function is that the allocation over each year, to the observed in Figure 1, is a matter of choice on the part of the consumer: it therefore must have a basis in the satisfaction derived from expenditure in the various seasons of the year. Although it may be argued that part of the high fourth quarter spending is associated with winter—requiring, for example, additional lighting and heating—the first quarter (the lowest spending period) involves similar expenditure. The component categories which are particularly large in the last quarter compared with the first are alcoholic drink and tobacco, clothing and footwear, and other goods. At least for the first and third of these, this allocation must be ascribed to choice rather than necessity, leading to the parameter β changing over the year. Such a specification treats purchases in the four quarters as, in effect, different commodities.

Maximizing lifetime utility (possibly with seasonal discounting), subject to the period-to-period budget constraint (3), leads to

$$\frac{C_{t+1}^{-\beta_{q+1}}}{C_t^{-\beta_q}} = \frac{1}{\alpha_{q+1}(1 + r)}, \tag{7}$$

in place of (4). Adding a disturbance to this equation and taking logarithms yields

$$\beta_{q+1} \ln C_{t+1} = \beta_q \ln C_t - \ln \{1/\alpha_{q+1}(1 + r) + \varepsilon_{t+1}\}. \tag{8}$$

If expectations are rational, ε_{t+1} represents the response of agents to new information available during period $t + 1$: this disturbance, therefore, has a mean of zero and is uncorrelated with information available at t.

If we further assume that, conditional on information at t, the stochastic term in (8) is NID, that is,

$$\ln \{1/\alpha_{q+1}(1 + r) + \varepsilon_{t+1}\} \sim N(\mu_{q+1}, \sigma^2),$$

then, using the properties of the log-normal distribution,

$$E_t\{1/\alpha_{q+1}(1 + r) + \varepsilon_{t+1}\} = \exp(\mu_{q+1} + \tfrac{1}{2}\sigma^2).$$

Since the left-hand side expectation obviously equals $1/\alpha_{q+1}(1 + r)$,

$$\mu_{q+1} = \ln \{1/\alpha_{q+1}(1 + r)\} - \tfrac{1}{2}\sigma^2.$$

Therefore, equation (8) is approximated by

$$\ln C_{t+1} = \gamma_{q+1} + \phi_{q+1} \ln C_t + u_{t+1}, \tag{9}$$

where

$$\gamma_{q+1} = \frac{1}{\beta_{q+1}} \{\ln \alpha_{q+1} + \ln (1 + r) + \tfrac{1}{2}\sigma^2\}, \tag{10}$$

and

$$\phi_{q+1} = \beta_q/\beta_{q+1}. \tag{11}$$

Notice that the definition of ϕ_{q+1} implies that $\phi_1\phi_2\phi_3\phi_4 = 1$, which is the seasonal generalization of the first differencing in (5).

Two other points should be noted about (9). Firstly, there is no reason why the disturbance need be homoscedastic across quarters. Indeed, even if the disturbances in (8) have constant variance, this will not generally be the case for those in (9) when the coefficients are seasonally varying. Nevertheless, u_{t+1} remains uncorrelated with any information available at t. Secondly, in addition to seasonality in preferences, and in the rate of discount, any seasonal pattern in r and σ^2 will contribute to the shift dummy γ_{q+1}.

The model derived in (9) is a first-order periodic autoregressive process (Tiao and Grupe, 1980). Although such processes have been relatively neglected to date, Osborn (1987) analyses the statistical implications of periodic (or seasonally varying parameter) processes, while Osborn and Smith (1988) demonstrate their usefulness in forecasting seasonal non-durable consumers' expenditure. The model derived here provides an economic rationale for considering periodic processes when the data are seasonal.

As just noted, the white-noise random variable u_{t+1} is, under rational expectations, independent of all variables dated prior to $t+1$. This does, however, presume that the quarterly observation period coincides with the planning period of consumers. Wickens and Molana (1984), and others, have shown that time aggregation over planning periods shorter than a quarter leads to positive first-order moving-average errors in the estimating equation. Due to the inconsistency of least-squares estimation in a dynamic equation such as (9) when the disturbances follow an MA(1) process, the important results are checked using instrumental variables and are quoted in Appendix II. Also, tests for serial correlation are carried out for the least-squares estimations.

Turning to the testing of the model, Table 1 presents unrestricted estimates of equation (9) obtained by four separate ordinary least-squares regressions for $q = 1, 2, 3, 4$. These separate regressions by quarter permit seasonally varying coefficients and seasonally varying disturbance variances. For purposes of comparison the model is also estimated allowing γ_q to vary but imposing constant ϕ and homoscedasticity. This latter case employs seasonal shift dummy variables only, as is common in empirical econometrics using seasonally unadjusted data.

Although no restriction is imposed on any ϕ_q in these estimations, the four separate quarters yield $\hat{\phi}_1\hat{\phi}_2\hat{\phi}_3\hat{\phi}_4 = 0.982$: this value and the

TABLE 1. Estimates of seasonal utility model

	Quarter				
	1	2	3	4	All observations
γ_1	0.557 (0.136)				-0.028 (0.092)
γ_2		0.684 (0.138)		0.120	(0.091)
γ_3			-0.188 (0.084)		0.101 (0.091)
γ_4				-0.941 (0.154)	0.120 (0.092)
ϕ_q	0.935 (0.013)	0.936 (0.014)	1.022 (0.008)	1.098 (0.015)	0.993 (0.009)
$\sigma_u(\times 100)$	1.29	1.24	0.71	1.32	1.62
LMAC[a]	1.49	1.91	-1.18	3.54	9.65

Estimated standard errors are given in parentheses.

[a] MAC is a Lagrange multiplier test, expressed as a t-statistic, for seasonal residual autocorrelation, the degrees of freedom are 27 each quarter separately and 110 for the all observations estimation.

estimate of 0.993 in the constant ϕ equation are very close to one, especially as least-squares estimation of unit roots is biased downwards (Evans and Savin, 1981). Nevertheless, the shift dummy variable regression contains substantial seasonal residual autocorrelation; while the seasonal utility function improves matters, the dynamics of fourth quarter expenditure, in particular, is still not captured adequately.

The point was made above that the disturbances in (9) may be MA(1). Appendix Table A reports instrumental variable estimates directly comparable to, and very little different from, those of Table 1. Also, a Lagrange multiplier test for autocorrelation to order 4 was carried out by adding the residuals lagged one to four quarters inclusive to the regression which uses dummy variables to estimate all coefficients γ_q and ϕ_q $(q = 1, \ldots, 4)$ simultaneously, correcting for heteroscedasticity using the estimated σ_u reported in Table 1. This procedure yielded t-statistics of -0.44, -1.48, -0.38 and 2.20 for the residuals lagged 1 to 4 respectively, and an overall statistic $F(4, 102) = 2.24$. These statistics and those of Table 1 are, of course, only approximately t or F under the null hypothesis of no autocorrelation. Although not sufficiently strong to lead to rejection according to the overall F test, the significant seasonal autocorrelation here accords with the seasonally varying annual autocorrelation test results of Table 1. Also of interest is the t-statistic on the first-order lagged residual, which does not indicate the presence of positive first-order autocorrelation. This, and the instrumental variable estimates, indicate that the potential aggregation problem does not appear to be serious in practice for this data.

Hall (1981) mentions the use of data for one quarter of each year only as a way of avoiding problems associated with seasonality. To write (9) in an appropriate form, successively substitute on the right-hand side of the equation for C_{t-i} $(i = 0, 1, 2)$. Expressed in terms of $\Delta_4 \ln C_t$ for notational simplicity, this yields, after a little manipulation,

$$\Delta_4 \ln C_t = \delta_q + u_t + \theta_{q1} u_{t-1} + \theta_{q2} u_{t-2} + \theta_{q3} u_{t-3}, \qquad (12)$$

where

$$\delta_q = \sum_{i=0}^{3} \theta_{qi} \gamma_{q-i} \quad \text{and} \quad \theta_{qi} = \frac{\beta_{q-i}}{\beta_q} \text{ for } i = 1, 2, 3.$$

When the u_t are independent, $\Delta_4 \ln C_t$ is MA(3) and hence uncorrelated with $\Delta_4 \ln C_{t-4}$: therefore, any series of observations corresponding to one quarter only $(q = 1, \ldots, 4)$ follows a random walk with drift, confirming the validity of Hall's suggested procedure in this context.

Regressing the seasonal difference of UK log non-durable consumption by quarter on its seasonal lag and an intercept, the lag coefficients (with standard errors in parentheses) are: 0.113 (0.191), 0.250 (0.187), 0.167 (0.190) and 0.332 (0.187). Here the persistently positive (although in no individual case significant at the 5 per cent level) seasonal autocorrelation in $\Delta_4 \ln C$ casts doubt on this version of the random-walk model. It is also worth noting that with time aggregation u_t is MA(1), but this will imply only a very small positive seasonal autocorrelation in $\Delta_4 \ln C$. Thus, time aggregation is not sufficient to explain the values obtained.

Our conclusion is that UK seasonally unadjusted data do not support the seasonal rational expectations/life cycle model in either of the forms (9) or (12). In particular, unexplained positive seasonal autocorrelation is present in the estimated models.

3. Habit Persistence and Seasonality

The empirical results of the previous section indicate that the single-period utility function does not account fully for seasonality in consumption. Dynamics arise in the model tested in Table 1 only through the life cycle assumption and the period-to-period budget constraint, rather than through the utility function. Changing patterns in consumption may, however, make this unrealistic. A simple, but plausible, assumption is that consumption is, in part, dictated by habits.

Pursuing the notion that consumers regard expenditure in the different quarters of the year as effectively relating to distinct commodities, we would anticipate that habit persistence may be seasonal. It is particularly notable in Table 1 that the simple seasonal utility model fails principally in explaining expenditure in the Christmas quarter, which is compatible with strong resistance to change at this time of the year.

A generalization of equation (9) to incorporate seasonal habit persistence is provided by the multiplicative process

$$(1 - \phi_{q+1}L)(1 - \lambda_{q+1}L^4)\ln C_{t+1} = \gamma_{q+1} + u_{t+1}, \qquad (13)$$

in which L denotes, as usual, the lag operator. Multiplicative seasonal/non-seasonal processes have been popular for describing seasonal variables since the work of Box and Jenkins (1970): here the multiplicative autoregressive process is generalized to permit seasonally varying (or periodic) coefficients. The properties of periodic multiplicative process are analysed in Osborn (1987). Although (13) has not been derived from a specific dynamic utility function, the unit root restriction $\phi_1\phi_2\phi_3\phi_4 = 1$ is again indicated by viewing this equation as a generalization of (9). Also, as discussed in Osborn (1987), this restriction remains the natural analogue of first differencing when the coefficients are seasonally varying.

Table 2 reports the results obtained when (13) is estimated by nonlinear least-squares imposing the unit root restriction and assuming homoscedasticity. Then, in the first part of Table 3, the restrictions explicitly or implicitly imposed in this estimation are verified. Before returning to Table 2, note that any quarterly heteroscedasticity revealed by the F statistic computed using the squared residuals of (13) is not marked, while no residual autocorrelation at all is indicated by the Lagrange multiplier test (denoted $\rho_1 = \rho_2 = \rho_3 = \rho_4 = 0$). Indeed, in relation to the latter, the t-statistics of the added residuals, lagged 1 to 4, are -0.25, -0.71, -0.33 and -0.31 respectively. The statistic for $\phi_1\phi_2\phi_3\phi_4 = 1$ verifies that there is no question about the statistical acceptability of the unit root. Notice that the problems associated with testing unit roots do not arise here because conventional t-tests reject too often, whereas here the unit root is accepted.

TABLE 2.   Estimates of habit persistence model

	Quarter			
	1	2	3	4
γ_q	0.372	0.435	-0.254	-0.421
	(0.131)	(0.139)	(0.135)	(0.171)
ϕ_q	0.938	0.936	1.023	1.113
	(0.014)	(0.017)	(0.010)	
λ_q	0.286	0.367	-0.227	0.613
	(0.158)	(0.158)	(0.287)	(0.147)
$\sigma_u(\times 100)$			1.06	

Estimated standard errors are given in parentheses.

TABLE 3.   Testing restrictions in the habit persistence model

Restrictions	F	d.f.
Restrictions imposed		
$\sigma_{u1} = \sigma_{u2} = \sigma_{u3} = \sigma_{u4}$	1.65	3, 112
$\rho_1 = \rho_2 = \rho_3 = \rho_4 = 0$	0.20	4, 101
$\phi_1\phi_2\phi_3\phi_4 = 1$	0.40	1, 104
Restrictions not imposed		
$\lambda_1 = \lambda_2 = \lambda_3 = \lambda_4 = 0$	6.54[a]	4, 105
$\lambda_1 = \lambda_2 = \lambda_3 = \lambda_4$	2.43	3, 105
$\phi_1 = \phi_2 = \phi_3 = \phi_4 = 1$	7.54[a]	3, 105

[a] Statistic is significant at the 1 per cent level.

It is notable, in comparing Tables 1 and 2, that the ϕ_q estimates are robust to the addition of the seasonal autoregressive lags and to the imposition of the unit root. The latter is, however, not surprising in that the unrestricted estimates of Table 1 almost exactly imply the unit root as, indeed, do the unrestricted estimates (not reported) corresponding to (13). Despite the invariance of the AR(1) coefficients to the inclusion of the habit persistence terms, the test of $\lambda_1 = \lambda_2 = \lambda_3 = \lambda_4 = 0$ in Table 3 shows that these terms are certainly jointly significant. Once again, this indicates the inadequacy of equation (9) deriving from the static seasonal utility function.

From the point of view of seasonal modelling, the last two tests reported in Table 3 are of particular interest because they examine the importance of allowing seasonal variation in the λ and ϕ coefficients. The evidence here for seasonal habit persistence is not especially strong in that the λ are not significantly different from each other at the 5 per cent level, although constancy is rejected at 10 per cent. Nevertheless, seasonally varying λ have been retained for the later analysis, both because of the statistical support for this and because Table 2 estimates plausibly imply that habit persistence effects are strongest in the Christmas quarter. Once this decision is taken, setting $\lambda_3 = 0$ becomes obvious, since the negative coefficient does not indicate habit persistence and the coefficient is, in any case, statistically insignificant.

Finally, the first difference form of (13) (that is, with each $\phi_q = 1$) is rejected, supporting the proposition that utility is inherently seasonal. Incidentally, this first difference equation yields $\hat{\lambda}_1 = 0.943$, indicating that first differencing fails to remove the non-stationarity in fourth quarter consumption.

The model of equation (13) with $\lambda_3 = 0$ is therefore the basis of our subsequent testing.

Viewed in the light of rational expectations, and Hall (1978) in particular, a correctly specified univariate time-series model for consumption should leave no predictive role for additional lagged variables. The obvious variables to consider adding here in lagged form are income and prices, due to their importance in studies of UK non-durable consumers' expenditure, such as Davidson et al. (1978).

Some care is needed in carrying out tests of significance in this context, since hypothesis testing for non-stationary variables is fraught with difficulties (see Park and Phillips, 1989, Nankervis and Savin, 1987). Although Hall (1978) conducts his tests in terms of the levels of consumption and income, and Stock and West (1987) have recently argued that his test procedure is valid because consumption and income are cointegrated, testing in levels is not pursued here. This is because our seasonal consumption and income variables cannot be cointegrated at seasonal frequencies: this is discussed in Hylleberg et al. (1990), who are using UK data similar to that of the present study. Here we add income as $\Delta_1 \ln Y$ and prices as $\Delta_1\Delta_4 \ln P$: all variables in the equation are then stationary (Osborn et al., 1988) and conventional hypothesis testing results consequently apply.

Table 4 reports the estimated coefficients and standard errors for the added variables, together with the F-tests computed for their inclusion. The coefficients of (13) change relatively little, and consequently are not reported. Initially, income and prices at t and $t-3$ (lags 1 and 4 respectively) are added: these lags are selected in order to capture possible omitted non-seasonal and seasonal influences. The resulting overall F statistic is marginal compared to the 5 per cent critical value. As lagged prices appear to have no predictive content, they are dropped in order to focus on the role of income: the resulting test statistic is then significant.

Table 4 also displays the results when the additional variables are lagged 2 and 4 quarters. The lag 2 replaces lag 1 to check the sensitivity of the test to problems arising from time aggregation. Although both computed F statistics are reduced in value, income retains its additional explanatory role when included on its own. In all cases in the table it is clear that the predictive content of income is in its seasonally lagged value, with the effect being negative.

Another point of interest for UK data is whether a change in the role of income occurs in the early 1970s. Muellbauer (1983) finds evidence of such a change, with lagged variables (income and consumption) being highly significant, but of opposite signs, in the subperiods. He detects no influence for these lagged variables when constant parameters are imposed. Following Muellbauer, Table 5 splits our sample in mid-1972.

TABLE 4.   Testing lagged information in the habit persistence model

$\Delta_1 \ln Y$		$\Delta_1\Delta_4 \ln P$		F	d.f.
Lag 1	Lag 4	Lag 1	Lag 4		
0.061	− 0.099	− 0.085	− 0.007	2.43	4, 101
(0.051)	(0.052)	(0.069)	(0.068)		
0.070	− 0.106*			4.43*	2, 104
(0.051)	(0.051)				
Lag 2	Lag 4	Lag 2	Lag 4		
− 0.042	− 0.103	− 0.064	0.005	1.79	4, 101
(0.052)	(0.053)	(0.073)	(0.071)		
− 0.028	− 0.121*			3.59*	2, 104
(0.051)	(0.050)				

Estimated standard errors are given in parentheses.
* Statistic is significant at the 5 per cent level.

TABLE 5.   Subperiod tests of lagged information in the habit persistence model

Period	$\Delta_1 \ln Y$		F	d.f.
	Lag 1	*Lag 4*		
1957(1)–1972(2)	− 0.076	− 0.171*	3.15	2, 50
	(0.074)	(0.072)		
1972(3)–1985(4)	0.198*	− 0.037	4.55*	2, 42
	(0.074)	(0.079)		
	Lag 2	*Lag 4*		
1957(1)–1972(2)	0.018	− 0.161*	2.59	2, 50
	(0.079)	(0.076)		
1972(3)–1985(4)	− 0.139	− 0.060	2.14	2, 42
	(0.083)	(0.085)		

Estimated standard errors are given in parentheses.
* Statistic is significant at the 5 per cent level.

The coefficients provide some evidence of a structural break, with the seasonal lag of income being important only in the first subperiod. It is the one-quarter lag of income which has predictive content in the second subsample. Unlike our other results, however, this predictive role for income in the recent period does not carry over when the lag 1 is replaced by lag 2.

4.   Concluding Remarks

This study has examined the importance of seasonal modelling and of habits in the life cycle model of consumption. For UK seasonally unadjusted data at least, our specification dominates the original random-walk model of Hall (1978) in the significance of both the seasonal variation in the coefficients and of the habit persistence terms. An appropriate treatment of seasonality is necessary for the interpretation of the habit persistence effects here. This is so because the imposition of constant slope coefficients, as in conventional modelling of seasonal data, pushes any seasonal variation in the true autoregressive coefficients into the seasonal lag terms (Osborn, 1987). Thus, one-quarter and four-quarter dynamics will be confused, which will then not permit the separation of period-to-period life cycle and seasonal habit persistence implications.

Since we find a predictive role for lagged income, our results do not support the generalized life cycle model. On the other hand, none of the t or F statistics for lagged income is significant at the 1 per cent level, so that its predictive content is relatively small. This finding is in contrast to Muellbauer (1983), where the rejection of the life cycle model for the UK up to mid-1972 is a great deal more decisive. Thus, while we cannot confirm Miron's (1986) conclusion that previous rejections of the theory can be attributed to the treatment of seasonality, we can support his view that the modelling of seasonality is important for the analysis of consumption.

Acknowledgements

This study is based on research funded by the Economic and Social Research Council (ESRC), reference number B00232124. I am grateful to an anonymous referee for his stimulating comments, and to John Nankervis and Peter Phillips for their advice on hypothesis testing. My colleagues Chris Birchenhall and Alice Chui have also provided invaluable assistance to this work.

Appendix 1:   Data

Quarterly real non-durable consumers' expenditure, as used here, excludes rent, rates and water charges because data on this category consist of an annual series (based on rateable value) interpolated quarterly; see *United Kingdom National Accounts Sources and Methods* (1985, Paragraph 6.588). The values used have been obtained as the sum of the remaining six categories. Observations from 1955(1) to 1986(2) in 1980 prices are available from *Economic Trends Annual Supplement* (1987), but the last two quarters are omitted from the analysis since these are the most recent and hence the most liable to revision. Almost all estimations quoted commence from the beginning of 1957, using previous observations to provide initial lagged values as required. The only exceptions relate to the two estimations of Table 4 where $\Delta_1\Delta_4 \ln P$ lagged four quarters is required: estimation here is from 1957(2).

Real personal disposable income, in 1980 prices, and the retail price index are used as the income and price variables respectively in Section 3.

Appendix 2:   Instrumental Variable Estimation Results

As noted in the text, the basic equation (9) will contain MA(1) disturbances if the planning period of agents is shorter than the quarterly observation period used in estimation. To check on the possible inconsistency of least squares in this case, Table A reports instrumental variable estimates of this equation: the values here can be compared with those in Table 1 of the text.

TABLE A. Instrumental variable estimates of the seasonal utility model

| | Quarter | | | | |
	1	2	3	4	All observations
γ_1	0.566				− 0.034
	(0.136)				(0.092)
γ_2		0.679			0.114
		(0.139)			(0.091)
γ_3			− 0.188		0.095
			(0.085)		(0.092)
γ_4				− 0.947	0.114
				(0.154)	(0.092)
ϕ_q	0.934	0.937	1.022	1.099	0.993
	(0.014)	(0.014)	(0.008)	(0.015)	(0.009)
$\sigma_u(\times\ 100)$	1.29	1.24	0.71	1.32	1.62
LMAC*	1.51	2.09	− 1.19	3.70	9.68

Estimated standard errors are given in parentheses.
* LMAC is a Lagrange multiplier test, expressed as a t-statistic, for seasonal residual autocorrelation; the degrees of freedom are 27 each quarter separately, and 110 for the all observations estimation.

Since, with MA(1) disturbances, u_{t+1} is uncorrelated with information available at $t − 1$ or earlier, the logarithm of consumption dated $t − 1$ and earlier provides valid instruments. Note that the ability of the model to capture the seasonal characteristics of consumption is of interest here: in order to obtain the seasonal autocorrelation Lagrange multiplier test (here computed as the MLM test of Breusch and Godfrey, 1981), sufficiently long lags on the dependent variable need to be included among the instruments. Here $\ln C_{t-i}$, $i = 1, 2, 3, 4$ are used as instruments for $\ln C_t$ in each case.

It should be noted that the quoted standard errors are consistently estimated in Table A for the series by quarter, even when the disturbances are MA(1). This is because u_{t+1} is correlated with u_t, but not with u_{t-3}: the model implies no disturbance autocorrelation when (9) is estimated on annually sampled data.

Instrumental variable estimation corresponding to Table 2 of the text was also carried out, with the same instruments as in Table A. As all coefficients were estimated in one equation, the instruments were constructed by multiplying each lagged consumption value by each of the four seasonal dummy variables. The results were, however, so similar to those of Table 2 that they are not repeated here. Nevertheless, it is worth noting that the results show no evidence of first-order moving average errors as the instrumental variable residuals yield a Durbin–Watson statistic of 2.015.

Finally, instrumental variable estimation confirms the significance of lagged income. When the two- and four-quarter lagged changes in income are added to equation (13) and to the above instruments, the estimated coefficients and standard errors are almost identical to those of Table 4. The overall test for the two income variables yields $\chi_2^2 = 6.89$, which is again significant at the 5 per cent level.

References

Box, G. E. P. and Jenkins, G. M. (1970), *Time Series Analysis, Forecasting and Control*. San Francisco: Holden-Day.

Breusch, T. S. and Godfrey, L. (1981), 'A review of recent work on testing for autocorrelation in dynamic simultaneous models', in D. Currie, R. Nobay and D. Peel (eds), *Macroeconomic Analysis: Essays in Macroeconomics and Econometrics*, 63–105. London: Croom Helm.

Davidson, J. E. H., Hendry, D. F., Srba, F., and Yeo, S. (1978), 'Econometric modelling of the aggregate time-series relationship between consumers' expenditure and income in the United Kingdom', *Economic Journal*, **88**, 661–92.

Engle, R. F., Granger, C. W. J., Hylleberg, S., and Yoo, S. (1990), 'Seasonal integration and co-integration'. *Journal of Econometrica*, **44**, 215–38.

Evans, G. B. A., and Savin, N. E. (1981), 'Testing for unit roots: 1', *Econometrica*, **49**, 753–79.

Gersovitz, M., and MacKinnon, J. G. (1978), 'Seasonality in regression: an application of smoothness priors', *Journal of the American Statistical Association*, **73**, 264–73.

Hall, R. E. (1978), 'Stochastic implications of the life cycle-permanent income hypothesis', *Journal of Political Economy*, **86**, 971–87.

—— (1981), 'Comments on "Interpreting economic evidence" by Davidson and Hendry', *European Economic Review*, **16**, 193–4.

Miron, J. A. (1986), 'Seasonal fluctuations and the life cycle-permanent income model of consumption', *Journal of Political Economy*, **94**, 1258–79.

Muellbauer, J. (1983), 'Surprises in the consumption function', *Economic Journal*, Conference Papers Supplement, **93**, 34–50.

Nankervis, J. C., and Savin, G. E. (1987), 'Finite sample distributions of t and F statistics in an AR(1) model with an exogenous variable', *Econometric Theory*, **3**, 387–408.

Osborn, D. R. (1987), 'Modelling seasonal time series and the implications of periodically varying coefficients'. Discussion Paper ES180, Department of Econometrics and Social Statistics, University of Manchester.

—— and Smith, J. P. (1989), 'The performance of periodic autoregressive models in forecasting seasonal U.K. consumption', *Journal of Business and Economic Statistics*. **7**, 117–27.

—— Chui, A. P. L., Smith, J. P., and Birchenhall, C. R. (1988), 'Seasonality and the order of integration for consumption', *Oxford Bulletin of Economics and Statistics*, **50**, 361–77.

Park, J. C., and Phillips, P. C. B. (1989), 'Statistical inference in regressions with integrated processes: part 2'. *Econometric Theory*, **5**, 95–131.

STOCK, J. H., and WEST, K. D. (1987), 'Integrated regressors and tests of the permanent income hypothesis', NBER Working Paper No. 2359.

TIAO, G. C., and GRUPE, M. R. (1980), 'Hidden periodic autoregressive-moving average models in time series data', *Biometrika*, **67**, 365–73.

WALLIS, K. F. (1974), 'Seasonal adjustment and relations between variables', *Journal of the American Statistical Association*, **69**, 18–31.

WICKENS, M. R., and MOLANA, H. (1984), 'Stochastic life cycle theory with varying interest rates and prices', *Economic Journal*, Conference Papers Supplement, **94**, 133–47.

8

Seasonality, Cost Shocks, and the Production Smoothing Model of Inventories

JEFFREY A. MIRON and STEPHEN P. ZELDES[1]

Abstract. A great deal of research on the empirical behavior of inventories examines some variant of the production smoothing model of finished goods inventories. The overall assessment of this model that exists in the literature is quite negative: there is little evidence that manufacturers hold inventories of finished goods in order to smooth production patterns.

This paper examines whether this negative assessment of the model is due to one or both of two features: cost shocks and seasonal fluctuations. The reason for considering cost shocks is that, if firms are buffeted more by cost shocks than demand shocks, production should optimally be more variable than sales. The reasons for considering seasonal fluctuations are that seasonal fluctuations account for a major portion of the variance in production and sales, that seasonal fluctuations are precisely the kinds of fluctuations that producers should most easily smooth, and that seasonally adjusted data are likely to produce spurious rejections of the production smoothing model even when it is correct.

We integrate cost shocks and seasonal fluctuations into the analysis of the production smoothing model in three steps. First, we present a general production smoothing model of inventory investment that is consistent with both seasonal and nonseasonal fluctuations in production, sales, and inventories. The model allows for both observable and unobservable changes in marginal costs. Second, we estimate this model using both seasonally adjusted and seasonally unadjusted data plus seasonal dummies. The goal here is to determine whether the incorrect use of seasonally adjusted data has been responsible for the rejections of the production smoothing model reported in previous studies. The

[1] The authors are grateful for helpful comments by Andrew Abel, Olivier Blanchard, Alan Blinder, John Campbell, Larry Christiano, Angus Deaton, Martin Eichenbaum, Stanley Fischer, Marvin Goodfriend, Tryphon Kollintzas, Louis Maccini, Trisk Mosser, Chris Sims, Larry Summers, Ken West, members of the Macro Lunch Group at the University of Pennsylvania, two referees, and seminar participants at workshops at Michigan, Princeton, Johns Hopkins, Rochester, MacMaster, Northwestern, Econometric Society/NORC, and FRB Minneapolis and Philadelphia; and for excellent research assistance by Edward Gold.

Printed with permission of: Econometrica, **56**. 877–908.

third part of our approach is to explicitly examine the seasonal movements in the data. We test whether the residual from an Euler equation is uncorrelated with the seasonal component of contemporaneous sales. Even if unobservable seasonal cost shocks make the seasonal variation in output greater than that in sales, the timing of the resulting seasonal movements in output should not necessarily match that of sales.

The results of our empirical work provide a strong negative report on the production smoothing model, even when it includes cost shocks and seasonal fluctuations. At both seasonal and nonseasonal frequencies, there appears to be little evidence that firms hold inventories in order to smooth production. A striking piece of evidence is that in most industries the seasonal in production closely matches the seasonal in shipments, even after accounting for the movements in interest rates, input prices, and the weather.

Keywords: Inventories, seasonality, production, cost shocks

Introduction

A great deal of research on the empirical behavior of inventories examines some variant of the production smoothing model of finished goods inventories. Blinder (1986a) emphasizes that, in the absence of cost shocks, the model implies that the variance of production should be less than the variance of sales, an inequality that is violated for manufacturing as a whole and most 2-digit industries. West (1986) derives a variance bounds test that extends this inequality in a number of ways and also finds that the data reject the model. Both Blinder and West conclude that there is strong evidence against the production smoothing model. Other authors, such as Blanchard (1983), Eichenbaum (1984), and Christiano and Eichenbaum (1986), present evidence that is less unfavorable to the model, but they reject it as well.

This paper examines the extent to which the negative assessment of the model is due to two features: cost shocks and seasonal fluctuations. Blinder (1986a) and West (1986) both note that the presence of cost shocks could explain the rejections and they report, and Blinder (1986b), Maccini and Rossano (1984), Eichenbaum (1984), and Christiano and Eichenbaum (1986) test the model in the presence of cost shocks, with partial success. The reason for considering these shocks is simply that if firms are buffeted more by cost shocks than demand shocks, production should optimally be more variable than sales.

Most of the empirical work on the production smoothing model uses data adjusted by the X-11 seasonal adjustment routine. This includes studies by Blinder (1986a,b), Eichenbaum (1984), and Maccini and Rossana (1984). Blanchard (1983), Reagan and Sheehan (1985), and West (1986) begin with the seasonally unadjusted data and then adjust the data with seasonal dummies. Few studies examine whether the seasonal fluctuations themselves are consistent with the model of inventories. Exceptions are Ward (1978), who finds evidence that firms alter production rates differently in response to seasonal versus nonseasonal variations in demand; West (1986), who includes a version of his variance bounds test based on both the seasonal and nonseasonal variations in the data; and Ghali (1987), who uses data from the Portland Cement industry and finds that seasonal adjustment of the data is an important factor in the rejection of the production smoothing model.[2]

There are several reasons to think that using seasonally adjusted data to test inventory models is problematic. To begin with, seasonal fluctuations account for a major portion of the variation in production, shipments, and inventories. Table 1 shows the seasonal, nonseasonal, and total variance of the logarithmic rate of growth of production and shipments, for six 2-digit manufacturing industries.[3,4] For both variables, seasonal variation accounts for more than half of the total variance in most industries. Any analysis of production/inventory behavior that excludes seasonality at best explains only part of the story and fails to exploit much of the variation in the data.

Seasonal fluctuations are likely to be particularly useful in examining the production smoothing model because they are anticipated. Any test of the production smoothing model involves a set of maintained hypotheses, one of which is the rationality hypothesis. Rejections of the model, therefore, are not usually informative as to which aspect of the joint hypothesis has been rejected. When a rational expectations model is applied to seasonal fluctuations, however, it seems reasonable to take the rationality hypothesis as correct, since if anything is correctly anticipated by agents seasonal fluctuations ought to be. Applying the production smoothing model to seasonal fluctuations may help determine which aspects of the model, if any, fail.

A final reason to avoid the use of seasonally adjusted data is that, since the true model apply to the seasonally unadjusted data, the use of adjusted data is likely to lead to rejection of the model even when it is correct.[5] This is especially the case with data adjusted by the Census X-11 method because this technique makes the adjusted data a two-

---

[2] Irvine (1981) uses seasonally unadjusted data, with no seasonal dummies, to examine retail inventory behavior and the cost of capital.

[3] Table 1 includes results based on two different measures of production. See Section 4 for details.

[4] This table is similar to Table II in Blanchard (1983). As he points out, since the seasonal component is deterministic, it has no variance in the statistical sense. The numbers reported here for the seasonal variances are the average squared deviations of the twelve seasonal dummy coefficients from the sample mean of these coefficients.

[5] Summers (1981) emphasizes this point.

TABLE 1. Summary statistics, log growth rates of production and shipments

		Food	Tobacco	Apparel	Chemicals	Petroleum	Rubber
Shipments	Mean:	0.16%	−0.09%	−0.006%	0.20%	0.16%	0.15%
	Variance:						
	Nonseasonal	5.60E−04	5.08E−03	1.74E−03	9.30E−04	5.10E−04	1.08E−03
	Seasonal	1.63E−03	1.61E−03	1.36E−02	2.86E−03	3.10E−04	4.33E−03
	Total	2.19E−03	6.69E−03	−1.54E−02	3.79E−03	8.20E−04	5.41E−03
	Seasonal/Total	75%	24%	89%	75%	38%	80%
Production, Y4	Mean:	0.13%	−0.17%	−0.04%	0.19%	0.13%	0.15%
	Variance:						
	Nonseasonal	6.10E−04	6.03E−03	3.10E−03	8.00E−04	9.80E−04	1.60E−03
	Seasonal	1.63E−03	5.26E−03	1.16E−02	2.20E−04	2.20E−04	5.13E−03
	Total	2.24E−03	1.13E−02	1.47E−02	3.00E−03	1.20E−03	6.73E−03
	Seasonal/Total	73%	47%	79%	73%	18%	76%
Production, IP	Mean:	0.22%	−0.17%	0.01%	0.36%	0.11%	0.42%
	Variance:						
	Nonseasonal	1.50E−04	2.47E−03	1.80E−03	2.70E−04	4.50E−04	1.09E−03
	Seasonal	8.50E−04	1.70E−02	4.28E−03	4.30E−04	5.10E−04	3.06E−03
	Total	1.00E−03	1.95E−02	6.08E−03	6.90E−04	9.60E−04	4.14E−03
	Seasonal/Total	85%	87%	70%	62%	53%	74%

Notes: The sample period is 1967:5–1982:12. The log growth rates are defined as $\ln x_t - \ln x_{t-1}$. They have not been annualized.

sided moving average of the underlying unadjusted data.[6,7] Therefore, the key implication of most rational expectations models, that the error term should be uncorrelated with lagged information, need not hold in the adjusted data even if it does hold in the unadjusted data.[8] If the data are adjusted by some other method, such as seasonal dummies, then the time series properties of the adjusted data are not altered as radically as they are with X-11.

We integrate cost shocks and seasonal fluctuations into the analysis of the production smoothing model in three steps. First, we present a general production smoothing model of inventory investment that is consistent with both seasonal and nonseasonal fluctuations in production, sales, and inventories. The model allows for both observable and unobservable changes in marginal costs (cost shocks). The observables include wages, energy prices, raw materials prices, and interest rates, as well as weather variables (temperature and precipitation).[9] We examine a firm's cost minimization problem, so our analysis is robust to various assumptions about the competitiveness of the firm's output market. A key implication of the model is that, for any firm that can hold finished goods inventories at finite cost, the marginal cost of producing an additional unit of output today and holding it in inventories until next period must equal the expected marginal cost of producing that unit next period. With standard types of auxiliary assumptions about functional forms and identification, the model leads to an estimable Euler equation relating the rate of growth of production to the rate of growth of input prices, the level of inventories, and the interest rate. We estimate this Euler equation and test the overidentifying restrictions implied by the model, using data on six 2-digit manufacturing industries.

The second part of our approach is to perform the exact same estimations and tests of the above model using both seasonally adjusted and unadjusted data.[10] The goal here is to determine whether the incorrect use of seasonally adjusted data is responsible for the rejections of the production smoothing model reported in previous studies.

The third part of our approach is to explicitly examine the seasonal

[6] X-11 is not literally a two-sided moving average filter. Rather, it can be well approximated by such filters. For more on this point, see Cleveland and Tiao (1976) and Wallis (1974).

[7] For example, Miron (1986) finds that the use of X-11 adjusted data is partially responsible for rejections of consumption Euler equations.

[8] See Sargent (1978).

[9] Maccini and Rossana (1984) estimate a different style model of inventory accumulation (a general flexible accelerator model) using data on aggregate durables and nondurables inventory accumulation in which they include wages, energy costs, interest rates, and raw materials prices. They found that only raw materials prices had significant effects in their model.

[10] Constant dollar, seasonally unadjusted inventory data are not available and are therefore constructed. This is discussed further in Section 4.

movements in the data. Since the predictable seasonal movement in demand is exactly the variation that should be most easily smoothed by firms, tests of the model at seasonal frequencies are particularly powerful. We therefore test whether the residual from the Euler equation is uncorrelated with the seasonal component of contemporaneous sales. Even if unobservable seasonal cost shocks make the seasonal variation in output greater than that of sales, the *timing* of the resulting seasonal movements in output should not match that of sales.

The estimation strategy that we employ involves a number of important identifying restrictions about the shifts over time in the firm's production function. We include a number of observable variables that account for the shifts in technology. There may, however, be additional shifts that are not accounted for by the measured variables, and these unobserved productivity shifts will appear in the error term of the equation that we estimate. In order to consistently estimate the Euler equation, therefore, we need to assume that this term is uncorrelated with the variables we use as instruments. Specifically, we assume that the observed productivity shifter is uncorrelated with lagged values of sales and with the part of current sales that is predictable based on lagged information, and that the growth of the unobserved productivity shifter is uncorrelated with lagged growth rates of input prices, lagged growth rates of output, and lagged interest rates. In addition, when we examine the seasonal fluctuations in production, we assume that any seasonal in unobserved productivity is uncorrelated with the seasonal in sales.

The remainder of the paper is organized as follows. Section 2 presents the basic production smoothing model that we employ throughout the paper and derives the first order condition that we estimate. In Section 3 we describe the identifying assumptions, the resulting testable implications, and the econometric techniques used to test those implications. In Section 4, we discuss the data used. Section 5 presents the basic results with seasonally adjusted and unadjusted data. In Section 6, we examine the seasonal-specific results. Section 7 concludes the paper.

2.   The Model

Consider a profit maximizing firm. Sales by the firm, the price of the firm's output, and the firm's capital stock may be exogenously or endogenously determined. The firm may be a monopolist, a perfect competitor, or something in between. The firm is, however, assumed to be a competitor in the markets for inputs. For any pattern of prices, sales and the capital stock, the firm chooses its inputs over time so as to minimize costs.

The firm's intertemporal cost minimization problem is

$$\min_{\{y_{t+j}\}} E_t \sum_{j=0}^{T} \Gamma_{t,t+j} C_{t+j}(Y_{t+j}) \tag{1}$$

subject to

$$n_{t+j} = n_{t+j-1}(1 - s'_{t+j-1}) + y_{t+j} - x_{t+j}, \quad n_{t+j} \leq 0 \ \forall_j,$$

where y_t is production in period t, x_t is sales in period t, an n_t is the stock of inventories at the end of period t, all measured in terms of the output good. The end of the firm's horizon is period T. C_t is the one period nominal cost function of the firm, to be derived shortly. $\Gamma_{t,t+j}$ is the nominal discount factor, defined as the present value at time t of one dollar at $t+j$. Thus,

$$\Gamma_{t,t+j} \equiv \left[\prod_{s=0}^{j-1} \left(\frac{1}{1 + \widetilde{R}_{t+s}} \right) \right], \quad \Gamma_{t,t} \equiv 1, \text{ and}$$

$$\widetilde{R}_{t+s} \equiv (1 - m_{t+s+1}) R_{t+s}.$$

R_t is the pretax cost of capital for the firm, and m_t is the marginal tax rate. E_t indicates expectations conditional on information available at time t.

The term s'_t is the fraction of inventories lost due to storage costs. In the case of linear storage costs, s'_t is equal to a constant (call this s_1). Some researchers have modeled storage costs as being convex in the level of inventories. For example, convex inventory costs are the key factor driving Blinder and Fischer's (1981) model of the real business cycle. We capture these types of costs here by writing $s'_t = s_1 + (s_2/2) \cdot n_t$.[11]

For any cost minimizing firm that carries inventories between two periods, the marginal cost of producing an extra unit of output this period and holding it in inventories until next period must equal the expected marginal cost of producing an extra unit of output next period. This first-order condition can be written as

$$MC_t = E_t \left[\frac{MC_{t+1}(1 - s_t)}{1 + \widetilde{R}_t} \right] \tag{2}$$

or

---

[11] If storage costs come in the form of depreciating inventories, then the accounting identity definition of output would be $y_t = x_t + (n_t - n_{t-1}(1 - s'_{t-1}))$. In this paper, we construct output in the standard way: $y_t = x_t + (n_t - n_{t-1})$. If, rather than coming in the form of depreciated stocks, storage costs are actually paid out and these costs are proportional to the replacement cost of the goods, then our model and our constructed output measure are consistent with one another. In either of these cases the equations are correct when the IP measure of output is used. If the costs are paid out in dollars, in an amount related to the goods stored, our equation is approximately correct.

$$E_t\left[\frac{MC_{t+1}}{MC_t}\cdot\frac{(1-s_t)}{1+\widetilde{R}_t}\right]=1. \tag{3}$$

Rational expectations implies

$$\frac{MC_{t+1}}{MC_t}\cdot\frac{(1-s_t)}{1+\widetilde{R}_t}=1+\varepsilon_{t+1} \tag{4}$$

where $E_t[\varepsilon_{t+1}]=0$, i.e. ε_{t+1} is orthogonal to all information available at time t. The marginal storage cost, s_t, is equal to $s_1+s_2\cdot n_t$.[12] The Euler equation (4) will not be satisfied if desired inventories are zero. We discuss this possibility below.

At this point it is worth pointing out the parallel between the production/storage problem of a cost minimizing firm and the consumption/saving problem of a utility maximizing consumer. The firm's problem is to minimize the expected discounted value of a convex cost function, subject to an expected pattern of sales and costs of holding inventories. The consumer's problem is to maximize the expected discounted value of a concave utility function, subject to an expected pattern of income and return to holding wealth. Not surprisingly, then, the solution to cost minimization yields a first-order condition analogous to the first-order condition implied by the stochastic version of the permanent income hypothesis (Hall (1978), Mankiw (1981), Hansen and Singleton (1983)), and we can apply the methods of that literature to testing the production smoothing model of inventories and output. Production, sales, inventories, the interest rate, and storage costs are analogous to consumption, income, wealth, the rate of time preference, and the return on wealth, respectively.[13] In the simplest version of this model, the real interest rate, the growth in the capital stock, and productivity growth are all constant over time. Given the production function that we employ, these assumptions imply that the expected growth in output is constant over time—i.e. real output follows a geometric random walk with drift. This is analogous to Hall's (1978) condition that consumption follows a random walk with drift.

To implement the model described above we need to specify the form of the cost function. We assume a standard Cobb–Douglas production function with m inputs (q_i, $i=1,\ldots,m$). Let the last input (q_m) be the capital stock. In each period, the firm thus solves the following (constrained) problem:

[12] If average storage costs (s_t') are equal to $s_1+(s_2/2)n_t$, this implies that marginal storage costs (s_t) are equal to $s_1+s_2n_t$.

[13] The non-negativity condition on inventories mentioned above is analogous to a borrowing constraint in the consumption literature. If time series/cross section data on firms were available, an approach similar to that of Zeldes (1985) could be applied here to test for the importance of this non-negativity constraint on inventories.

$$\min_{\{q_1, q_2, \ldots, q_{m-1}\}} \sum_{i=1}^{m} w_i \cdot q_i \qquad \text{subject to} \qquad (5)$$

$$f(q_1, \ldots, q_m) = \mu \prod_{i=1}^{m} q_i^{a_i} = \tilde{y},$$

$$q_m = Q_m,$$

where w_i and q_i are the price and quantity, respectively, of input i, and f is the production function. Note that the production function includes a productivity measure μ that may shift over time in deterministic and/or stochastic ways.[14] Define $A \equiv \sum_{i=1}^{m-1} a_i$. The one period (constrained) cost function from this problem is:

$$C(y) = w_m \cdot q_m + A \cdot q_m^{(A-1)/A} \left[\prod_{i=1}^{m-1} \left(\frac{w_i}{a_i} \right)^{a_i/A} \right] \cdot \mu^{-1/A} \cdot y^{1/A} \qquad (6)$$

and the marginal cost function MC is:

$$MC(y) = q_m^{A-1/A} \left[\prod_{i=1}^{m-1} \left(\frac{w_i}{a_i} \right)^{a_i/A} \right] \cdot \mu^{-(1/A)} \cdot y^{(1-A)/A}. \qquad (7)$$

Equation (7) can be used to calculate the ratio of marginal costs in t and $t + 1$:

$$\ln \left(\frac{MC_{t+1}}{MC_t} \right) = \left[\sum_{i=1}^{m-1} (a_i/A) \cdot \ln \left(\frac{w_{it+1}}{w_{it}} \right) \right] - \left(\frac{1-A}{A} \right) \ln \left(\frac{q_{mt+1}}{q_{mt}} \right) \qquad (8)$$

$$+ \left(\frac{1-A}{A} \right) \ln \left(\frac{Y_{t+1}}{Y_t} \right) - \frac{1}{A} \ln \frac{\mu_{t+1}}{\mu_t}.$$

The next step is to derive an expression for the growth rate of output. We do so by taking logs of the Euler equation (4), taking a first order Taylor expansion of $\ln(1 - s_t)$ around $n_t = k$ for an arbitrary value of $k \le 0$ and a second order Taylor expansion of $\ln(1 + \varepsilon_{t+1})$ around $\varepsilon_{t+1} = 0$, substituting in equation (8), and rearranging. This gives:

$$Gy_{t+1} = [(A/(1-A))(-\ln(1 - s_1 - s_2 k) - ks_2/(1 - s_1 - s_2 k) - \tfrac{1}{2}\sigma_\varepsilon^2)]$$

$$+ \left(\frac{A}{1-A} \right) \left[\ln(1 + \tilde{R}_t) - \sum_{i=1}^{m-1} (a_i/A) Gw_{it+1} \right] + Gq_{mt+1}$$

$$+ \frac{s_2}{1 - s_1 - s_2 k} \left(\frac{A}{1-A} \right) n_t + \left(\frac{1}{1-A} \right) G\mu_{t+1}$$

$$+ \left(\frac{A}{1-A} \right) [(\tfrac{1}{2}\sigma_\varepsilon^2 - \tfrac{1}{2}\varepsilon_{t+1}^2) + \varepsilon_{t+1}]$$

[14] Unlike some previous studies, we do not include costs of adjusting the level of output. As Maccini and Rossana (1984) point out, the costs of adjusting output presumably arise because of the costs of changing one or more factors of production. These costs may be important, but we do not attempt to model them here.

where for any variable Z, $GZ_{t+1} \equiv \ln(Z_{t+1}/Z_t)$. We have added and substracted $(A/(1 - A)) \frac{1}{2} \sigma_\varepsilon^2$ from the equation, so that the last term in brackets in equation (9) has mean zero.

Discussion of the model

Equation (9) is the basis of all the estimations performed in this paper. It says that the growth rate of output is a function of the real interest rate (where the inflation rate used to calculate the real rate is a weighted average of the rates of inflation of factor prices), the growth in the capital stock, the level of inventories, productivity growth, and a surprise term. The key implication that we test in this paper is that no other information known at time t should help predict output growth.

As is well known, an advantage of estimating this Euler equation is that we avoid solving for firms' closed form decision rule for production. This allows us to step outside the linear-quadratic framework, and it allows us to estimate our model that includes stochastic input prices and interest rates. In addition, the Euler equation procedure yields testable implications for the growth rate rather than the level of output, so we do not need to assume that output is stationary around a deterministic trend. Our procedure is valid even if there is a unit root in the level of output, a condition that Nelson and Plosser (1982) find, for example, characterizes aggregate output series.[15]

In setting up the model we have imposed the constraint that inventories are nonnegative, and we have indicated that the Euler equation is valid in a given period only if the nonnegativity constraint is not binding in that period. We should point out here a potential problem related to this nonnegativity constraint. Consider a certainty version of our model without the nonnegativity constraint imposed. Assuming that s_1 and s_2 are nonnegative, equation (3) implies that when inventories are positive firms want the level of marginal costs to rise over time. If the marginal cost *function* is constant or falling (due to growth in the capital stock), this implies that output rises over time, i.e. that firms push production towards the future and run down inventory stocks today. In fact, only if inventories are negative could there be a steady state with constant marginal costs. This indicates that in a model in which the nonnegativity condition *is* imposed, it will at times bind, and therefore the Euler equation will not be satisfied in some periods.[16]

---

[15] See Ghysels (1987) for an analysis of trends versus unit roots in manufacturing inventory and production data.

[16] Even under these assumptions, firms will in general choose to use inventories in some periods to smooth production, i.e. to build up positive inventories in the periods in which sales are especially high and run them down in periods in which sales are low.

To partially avoid this problem, we follow Blinder (1982) and allow s_1 to be negative. This captures the fact that at low but positive levels of inventories, increases in inventories may lower total costs, i.e. there may be a convenience yield to holding inventories. With s_1 sufficiently negative, there is a steady state in the certainty or uncertainty version of the model that has a positive level of inventories.[17] Of course, this still does not imply, in the certainty version of the model, that inventories *never* hit the constraint.[18,19]

The model that we use allows for seasonal fluctuations in output growth in several ways. First, there may be seasonal movements in the observable or unobservable component of the productivity shifter. Second, there may be seasonals in the relevant input prices. Of course, it is not entirely accurate to describe these as determining the seasonal fluctuations in output growth, since in general equilibrium the seasonals in output growth and input prices are determined simultaneously. For an individual firm, however, and even for a 2-digit industry, the degree of simultaneity is likely to be small.

Rather than assuming that the productivity shifter μ is totally unobservable to the econometrician, we allow it to be a function of some observable seasonal variables and some unobservables. The observable variables are weather related: functions of current temperature and precipitation. It seems reasonable a priori that productivity would be affected by the current local weather. We write $\mu = e^{Z\gamma + \eta}$, where Z is a matrix of observable weather variables and η is the unobservable productivity shifter.

In the absence of shifts in the cost function (i.e. changes in μ), the model presented is a simple production smoothing model. For a given path for the capital stock, the derived cost function is convex, inducing firms to try to spread production evenly over time.[20] When productivity is allowed to vary over time, the result is no longer a pure production smoothing model. Although our model is consistent with the variance of production exceeding the variance of sales, the convexity of the cost function remains and we continue to refer to the model as a type of production smoothing model.

---

[17] This can be seen by using (3), assuming no uncertainty, letting $R_t = R$, $n_t = n$, and setting $MC_{t+1} = MC_t$. Rearranging gives $n = (-R - s_1)/s_2$, which will be greater than zero if $s_1 < -R$.

[18] For a further discussion of this issue see Schutte (1983). Another factor in our model that tends to push inventories positive is sales growth, although this will be reversed to the extent that it is accompanied by growth in the capital stock.

[19] In the industries that we use to estimate the equation, industrywide inventories are always positive. This does not of course imply that inventories are always positive for every firm in these industries.

[20] This smoothing that arises from a convex cost function is different than the smoothing induced by introducing costs of adjusting output (as in, for example, Eichenbaum (1984)). For further discussion, see Blanchard (1983).

Blinder (1986a) states that introducing (unobservable) cost shocks into the analysis makes his variance bounds inequality untestable, because one could explain an arbitrarily large variance of production relative to sales by assuming unobservable cost shocks with appropriately large variance. The approach that we adopt in this paper avoids this problem in two ways. First, we include *measurements* of a number of factors that might influence the marginal cost of production, and account for these in the analysis. Second, we show that under reasonable identifying assumptions, the model described above has testable implications even in the presence of unobservable cost shocks. The most important assumption is that the unobserved component of productivity is uncorrelated with the component of sales that is predictable on the basis of information known at the time the firm makes its production decision. The testable implication is that once a number of cost variables are accounted for, the remaining movements in output should be uncorrelated with predictable movements in sales. In other words, even if production moves around a lot due to cost shocks, these movements should not be related to predictable movements in sales. This will be an especially useful test when applied to predictable *seasonal* movements in sales.

3.   Identification and Testing

A. *The general approach*

Equation (9), augmented to include the weather variables, can be written as:

$$Gy_{t+1} = (A/(1 - A)) \tag{10}$$

$$\times (-\ln (1 - s_1 - s_2 k) - (ks_2/(1 - s_2 k)) - \tfrac{1}{2}\sigma_\varepsilon^2)$$

$$+ \left(\frac{A}{1 - A}\right)\left[\ln (1 + \widetilde{R}_t) - \sum_{i=1}^{m-1} (a_i/A)Gw_{it+1}\right]$$

$$+ Gq_{mt+1} + \frac{s_2}{1 - s_1 - s_2 k}\left(\frac{A}{1 - A}\right)n_t + \left(\frac{1}{1 - A}\right)(Z_{t+1} - Z_t)\gamma$$

$$+ \left(\frac{1}{1 - A}\right)G\eta_{t+1} + \left(\frac{A}{1 - A}\right)[(\tfrac{1}{2}\sigma_\varepsilon^2 - \tfrac{1}{2}\varepsilon_{t+1}^2) + \varepsilon_{t+1}].$$

We cannot estimate this equation by OLS because the right-hand side variables are in general correlated with the expectations error. We therefore use an instrumental variables procedure to estimate the equation. To do so, we must choose instruments that are correlated with the included variables but not with the error term. Recall that the error term includes two components: the expectations error and the growth in the unobserved productivity shifter. Any variable that is known at time t will, by rational expectations, be orthogonal to ε_{t+1}.[21] However, rationality of expectations does not imply that $G\eta_{t+1}$ is orthogonal to time t information—it is possible that there are predictable movements in productivity growth. Note that a reasonable possibility is that the productivity measure follows a geometric random walk, in which case the growth in productivity is i.i.d. and therefore orthogonal to lagged information.[22]

Garber and King (1984) point out that a number of studies that estimate Euler equations assume that there are no shocks in the sector that they are estimating—effectively ignoring the identification issue. In this paper, we allow some measurable shocks to this sector, and we make the following identifying assumptions about the relationship between the unobserved cost shifter and the included instruments. (i) The unobserved productivity shifter (η) is uncorrelated with lagged values of sales and with the part of current sales that was predictable based on lagged information. (ii) The growth of the productivity shifter is uncorrelated with lagged growth rates of input prices, lagged growth rates of output, and lagged interest rates.

We thus consider the following variables to be orthogonal to the error term in the regression: lagged growth in sales, lagged growth in output, lagged interest rate, lagged growth in factor prices, and lagged inventories. In some sets of results we relax the assumption that the lagged growth rate of output is uncorrelated with the growth in the productivity shifter. To test the model, we first estimate equation (10) with instrumental variables, including as instruments the variables in the above list. Since there are more instruments than right-hand side variables, the equation is overidentified. We then test the overidentifying restrictions by regressing the estimated residuals on all of the included instruments (including the predetermined right-hand side variables). The quantity T times the R^2 from this regression is distributed X_j^2, where T is the number of observations and j is the number of overidentifying restrictions. One possible alternative hypothesis to our null is that firms simply set current output in line with current sales. In this case, we would expect the lagged growth rate of sales to enter significantly in our test of the overidentifying restrictions.

---

[21] We assume that production decisions for the month are made after information about demand and other economic variables is revealed, i.e. period t output decisions are made contingent on period t economic variables. An alternative assumption would be that production decisions are made before demand for the month is known. This creates a stockout motive for holding inventories (see Kahn (1986)). In Section 5 we also present results based on the alternative assumption that output must be chosen before demand for the period is known. For a further discussion of these timing issues, see Blinder (1986a).

[22] This is the assumption made by Prescott (1986).

B. Seasonality and identification

It is possible that there are seasonal movements in productivity that are not captured by the weather variables. One possible way to capture these would be to allow the productivity measure to be an arbitrary function of seasonal dummies. We do this in our first set of results by including seasonal dummies in the estimation of equation (10).[23] This gives the same results as first regressing all of the variables on seasonal dummies, and then using the residuals from these regressions for estimation purposes.

In order to examine whether the use of X-11 adjusted data has been responsible for the rejections by others of the production smoothing model, we compare the tests of the model using seasonally unadjusted data and seasonal dummies to the tests using X-11 seasonally adjusted data.

When we include seasonal dummies in equation (10), we lose all power to test the model at seasonal frequencies, i.e. we cannot test whether the seasonal movements in the data are consistent with the model. In the latter part of the paper, therefore, we make the stronger identifying assumption that seasonal shifts in productivity not captured by weather variables are uncorrelated with the instruments used to estimate equation (10).[24] Under this assumption, we can exclude seasonal dummies and perform two further tests that directly use seasonal fluctuations in the data. We test the implication that once the other factors in the cost functions are taken into account, the remaining movements in output should be uncorrelated with the seasonal movements in sales. This is a strong implication of the production smoothing model that has not been tested to date. In addition, we examine whether the model fits at purely seasonal frequencies. We describe these latter two tests in Section 6.

4. The Data

This section describes the data set that we employ. There are a number of technical issues to be considered with respect to both the adjusted

---

[23] The fact that we include seasonal dummies does not mean that we assume purely deterministic seasonality. Since the right-hand side variables may exhibit stochastic seasonality, our model allows for both stochastic and deterministic seasonality in output growth. We should also note that because we are working in log first differences, using additive seasonal dummies allows for multiplicative seasonality in output.

[24] In the section below on seasonal results, we discuss the circumstances under which this assumption might not hold.

and unadjusted data on inventories and production; we discuss these in detail below. Readers who are not interested in these details can skip to Section 5.

The equations are estimated using monthly data from May 1967 through December 1982.[25],[26] Data on inventories and shipments at the 2-digit SIC level for 20 industries were obtained from the Department of Commerce. We estimate the equations only on the six industries identified by Belsley (1969) as being production to stock industries. The inventory data are end of month inventories of finished goods, adjusted by the Bureau of Economic Analysis (BEA) from the book value reported by firms into constant dollars.[27],[28] We follow West (1983) and adjust the BEA series from 'cost' to 'market', so that shipments and inventories are in comparable units. Shipments data are total monthly figures in constant dollars.

Two different measures of production are used. The first comes from the identity that production of finished goods equals sales plus the change in inventories of finished goods. Commerce Department data for sales and the change in inventories are used to compute this production measure (which we call 'Y4'). The second measure of production used is the Federal Reserve Board's index of industrial production (IP), also available at the 2-digit SIC level.

In principle, the two production series measure the same variable and should therefore behave similarly over time. As documented in Miron and Zeldes (1987), however, the two series are in fact quite different. For the six industries studied here, the correlations between growth rates of the two series range from .8 to .4 for the seasonally unadjusted data, and from .4 to less than .1 for the seasonally adjusted data. The serial correlation properties and seasonal movements of the two series are also different. Since we have not resolved this discrepancy, we present results based on both output measures.

The nominal interest rate is the yield to maturity on Treasury Bills with one month to maturity as reported on the CRSP tapes. The marginal corporate tax rate series is the one calculated by Feldstein and

[25] Most of our data run through December 1984, but we only have weather data through December 1982.

[26] A month seems like a reasonable horizon for a firm, but there is no obvious reason why it need be so. For a discussion of time aggregation issues in inventory models, see Christiano and Eichenbaum (1986).

[27] This adjustment attempts to take into account whether firms used LIFO or FIFO accounting. See Hinrichs and Eckman (1981) for a description of how the constant dollar inventory series are constructed. See Reagan and Sheehan (1985) for a presentation of the stylized facts of these series at an aggregate (durables and nondurables) level.

[28] There is some disagreement over whether it is appropriate to use finished goods inventories only (West (1986)) or finished goods plus work in progress inventories (Blinder (1986a)). We estimate the equations separately for each definition. See footnote 32 in Section 5.

Summers (1979). The input price series are wages, the price of crude materials for further processing, and energy prices, representing the three largest variable inputs in the production process. Wages (average hourly earnings) and industrial production at the 2-digit SIC level, and aggregate measures of energy prices (the PPI for petroleum and coal products) and raw materials prices are available from the Citibank Economic Database.

The capital stock enters our equations as the number of machine days used per month. Since we did not have access to industry capital stock data, we model the growth in the capital stock as a constant plus a function of the growth in the number of nonholiday weekdays in the month. Any remaining month to month variation in the growth in the capital stock is included in the error term.

The weather data include estimates of total monthly precipitation and average monthly temperature. We construct a different temperature and precipitation measure for each industry, equal to weighted averages of the corresponding measures in the different states. The weights are equal to the historical share of the total shipments of the industry that originated in each state.[29] To capture nonlinearities, we also include the weighted average of squared temperature, squared precipitation, and the cross-product of temperature and precipitation. Given our functional form assumptions, the first differences of these variables enter equation (10).

Seasonality

Whenever possible, we obtained both seasonally adjusted (SA) and seasonally unadjusted (NSA) data. The BEA reports real shipments and inventories data, but these constant dollar series are only available on a SA basis.[30] The Bureau of the Census reports NSA and SA current dollar shipments series and book value inventories series. As in Reagan and Sheehan (1985) and West (1986), we estimate the real NSA inventory series by multiplying the real SA series by the ratio of book value NSA to book value SA, thus putting back in an estimate of the seasonal. (Another way of thinking of this is what we deflate the book value NSA series by the ratio of the book value SA to real SA series).

[29] The weights change every five years but always correspond to averages of previous (never future) years.

[30] The reason for this has to do with the technique used to construct the constant dollar figures. The disaggregated nominal series are first seasonally adjusted, then deflated and then aggregated.

We estimate real *NSA* shipments by multiplying the real *SA* series by the ratio of nominal *NSA* shipments to nominal *SA* shipments. These procedures assume that there are no seasonal movements in the factors that convert from book value to current dollar value or in the deflators used to convert the series from current dollar to constant dollar. An additional adjustment that we considered was to multiply the above series by the ratio of the *SA* to *NSA PPI* series for the finished goods, in order to adjust for the seasonal in the deflators. We found statistically significant evidence of seasonality in the price indexes in three out of six industries. However, the magnitudes of the seasonal movements in these prices are much smaller than in the corresponding quantities. We estimated the specifications in Tables 2 and 5 both with and without this adjustment and the results were virtually identical to each other.[31] We report only the results without this last adjustment.

The *IP* data are available both *NSA* and *SA*, and the energy price series, wage rates, raw materials prices, and interest rates are all unadjusted.

5.   Basic Results

In this section we examine the basic results from estimating equation (10) and testing the implied overidentifying restrictions. In order to determine whether the use of X-11 adjusted data has been responsible for previous rejections of the production smoothing model, we run the same set of tests with (i) the standard X-11 seasonally adjusted data, and (ii) seasonally unadjusted data plus seasonal dummies.

A summary of the results is presented in Table 2.[32] There are four sets of results, since we carry out the estimation with both unadjusted and adjusted data, and we do this for both the *Y4* and *IP* measures of output. In the first line of each set of results, we list the variables that entered equation (10) at a significance level of 5 per cent. In the second line of each set, we present the R^2 from the regression of the residuals on all the instruments. Recall that $T \cdot R^2$ is distributed χ_j^2, where j is the number of overidentifying restrictions. On the same line, we report the marginal significance level of the test statistic $T \cdot R^2$. In the last line of

[31] We estimated the equation over a shorter sample period for the food, chemicals, and petroleum industries because seasonally adjusted *PPI*'s were unavailable for part of the sample period.

[32] Most of these estimations were also done using the sum of finished goods inventories and work in progress inventories as the definition of inventories. The results were almost identical to those reported in the text.

TABLE 2. Regression results, equation (10) seasonal dummies in equation and instrument list

		Food	Tobacco	Apparel	Chemicals	Petroleum	Rubber
$Y4$, NSA	What enters (10) significantly?	sd, $-rm$	tem, $-tem2$	sd	$-sd$, tem /$-tem2$, $-pre$ $-tem2$, $-pre2$	$-w$, $-day$	sd
	R^2, Significance Level	$.17,.000$	$.23,.000$	$.09,.050$	$.15,.001$	$.13,.004$	$.16,.000$
	What is significant in test of OIR's?	we_{-1}, $-we_{-2}$	tem_{-1}	—	$-y_{-1}$, x_{-1}, $-n_{-2}$, n_{-3}, sd	we_{-2}	w, sd
$Y4$, SA	What enters (10) significantly?	—	rm, tem, $-tem2$	$-n_{-1}$, rm	rm	$-w$, $-day$ $-pre2$, tpr	w
	R^2, Significance Level	$.10,.027$	$.14,.002$	$.11,.014$	$.14,.002$	$.14,.002$	$.11,.014$
	What is significant in test of OIR's?	—	—	—	—	—	—
IP, NSA	What enters (10) significantly?	sd	$-sd$, w, $-pre2$	sd, day_{-1}	sd, rm	sd, $-pre2$	rm
	R^2, Significance Level	$.16,.000$	$.16,.000$	$.09,.050$	$.04,.583$	$.08,.090$	$.02,.926$
	What is significant in test of OIR's?	$-y_{-1}$, $-w_{-2}$	$-y_{-1}$, sd	$-y_{-1}$	—	—	—
IP, SA	What enters (10) significantly?	—	$-pre2$	$-pre2$, day_{-1}	tem, $-tem2$	$-day_{-1}$	rm, tem, $-tem2$
	R^2, Significance Level	$.15,.001$	$.28,.000$	$.09,.050$	$.13,.004$	$.09,.050$	$.06,.257$
	What is significant in test of OIR's?	$-y_{-1}$, $-we_{-2}$	$-y_{-1}$, $-y_{-2}$ $-tem_{-1}$, tpr_{-1}	$-y_{-1}$	x_{-1}, x_{-2}	—	$-n_{-1}$

Notes:

1. The sample period is 1967:5–1982:12.

2. The first line of each set of results lists the variables that entered equation (10) at the 5% significance level. We list seasonal dummies if one or more of the eleven dummies entered significantly.

3. The second line gives the R^2 from the regression of the residuals on the instruments, as well as the marginal significance level of this statistic. The quantity $T \times R^2$ is distributed X^2_j, where j is the number of overidentifying restrictions and T is the number of observations. In the results presented here, there are 9 such restrictions.

4. The third line lists the variables that entered the regression of the residuals on the instruments at the 5% significance level.

5. w = wage growth, sd = seasonal dummies, y = output growth, x = sales growth, day = number of production days, we = energy price growth, rm = raw materials price growth, n = inventories, r = interest rate, pre = change in precipitation, $pre2$ = change in precipitation squared, tem = change in temperature, $tem2$ = change in temperature squared, tpr = change in temperature × precipitation.

6. A (–) before variable indicates that the sign of the coefficient was negative.

7. A subscript of –1 on a variable means that it is dated l periods earlier than the dependent variable.

each set, we list the variables that entered this auxiliary test significantly.

We make the following observations about the results. First, in no case does the interest rate or the growth rate in energy prices enter equation (10) significantly. In about one third of the cases, the growth in raw materials prices enters significantly, but usually with the wrong sign. Wage growth enters significantly only four times, twice with the wrong sign. Thus, the signs and statistical significance of the coefficient estimates are not supportive of the model.

The second observation we make is that the data reject the overidentifying restrictions on the model in all cases using the $Y4$, and in two-thirds using the IP data. For the $Y4$ data, the rejections are about as strong using seasonally adjusted as seasonally unadjusted data. For the IP data, the rejections are not quite as strong overall using the seasonally unadjusted data. On the whole, there is little evidence that the use of unadjusted data with seasonal dummies provides better results than using seasonally adjusted data.

Finally, note that in approximately half of the cases, at least one of the five weather variables enters the equation significantly. Even after including seasonal dummies, the weather has a significant influence on production in certain industries (tobacco, chemicals, and petroleum).

Thus far, we arrive at a negative assessment of the model for two reasons. First, the overidentifying restrictions are typically rejected. Second, the signs of the coefficient estimates are not sensible and rarely significant. Proponents of the model might make the following argument against these two reasons, respectively. First, the instrument list may include variables that are correlated with the error term even under the null hypothesis, thus invalidating the tests of the overidentifying restrictions. Second, the instruments may not do a very good job of explaining the right-hand side variables. If this is the case, one should not expect the parameter estimates to be statistically significant, even under the null. We discuss each of these arguments in turn.

There are two circumstances in which the instrument list employed, consisting of lagged values of production, sales, input prices, and inventories, may be correlated with the error term. First, lagged output growth may not be a valid instrument, even if other lagged variables are, because productivity growth might be serially correlated. Since productivity growth is correlated with output growth, this implies that lagged output growth will also be correlated with contemporaneous productivity growth (a component of the error term), making it an invalid instrument.

Second, if firms do not have complete current period information when they make their output decisions for period t, then variables dated time t may not be valid instruments. This could arise because firms do not know the demand for their own products for the period before choosing output (as in Kahn (1986) or Christiano (1986)). Alternatively, firms may know the total demand for their product, but not the aggregate component of demand. Since we are using data on firms aggregated to the industry level, this too might invalidate the use of time t instruments (see Goodfriend (1986)).

In order to take account of these possibilities, we have estimated equation (10) using two alternative instrument lists. The first excludes production from the instrument list and includes extra lags of sales. The second list excludes all variables dated time t and includes extra lags of the variables at earlier dates.

When we employ the first alternative instrument list we reject the overidentifying restrictions significantly less often than with the list used in our basic results. In this case, the restrictions are rejected in a majority of cases for the $Y4$ data, but never for the IP data. When we employ the second alternative instrument list, we never reject the overidentifying restrictions. In both cases, however, we almost never find that the input price variables, the interest rate, or the level of inventories enter statistically significantly with the correct sign.

This brings us to the second issue. It is possible that we are not finding that expected changes in input prices affect the timing of production because there are no expected changes in input prices. That is, the instruments that we employ, either in our basic results or alternative results, may be of such poor quality that they have no explanatory power for the right-hand side variables in equation (10). If this is the case, the failure of these input prices to explain the pattern of production is not evidence against our model.

It is easy to check this possibility by examining directly the explanatory power of the instruments. For all three instrument lists, we find the following: there is statistically significant explanatory power in the instruments about half of the time for wages; all the time for interest rates, energy prices, and all five weather variables; and almost never for raw materials prices. Thus, with the exception of raw materials prices, the failure of input prices to explain production in any of our results is valid evidence against the model.

To summarize, with our basic instrument list the results provide evidence against the production smoothing model, even when it is expanded to incorporate a stochastic interest rate, measurable and unmeasurable cost shocks, and nonquadratic technology. When two weaker sets of identifying restrictions are used, there is substantially less statistical evidence against the model, but there is still no evidence that it describes an important aspect of firm behavior. Using seasonally unadjusted data and seasonal dummies does little better than using X-11 adjusted data.

6.   Seasonal-Specific Results

In this section we examine the extent to which the seasonal fluctuations in production, shipments and inventories are consistent with the production smoothing model. The results presented above incorporate seasonal fluctuations into the analysis by using seasonally unadjusted data and including seasonal dummies and weather variables in the equations. This approach does not tell us to what extent the seasonal movements in interest rates or input prices determine the seasonal movement in output growth, nor does it answer the question of whether the seasonal movements in the data themselves satisfy the production smoothing model. In order to answer these questions, we cannot include seasonal dummies in equation (10) and must therefore assume that any fluctuations (seasonal and nonseasonal) in the productivity measure not captured by the weather variables are orthogonal to the instruments used.

Before describing our formal tests, it is useful to consider a set of stylized facts about the seasonality in production, inventories, and sales. We saw in Table 1 that the seasonal variation in the data is large relative to the nonseasonal variation. In Table 3, we present estimates of the ratio of the variance of production to the variance of sales, and we include estimates based separately on the seasonal and nonseasonal variation. Following Blinder (1986a), these numbers are based on detrended levels rather than growth rates.[33],[34] As we have discussed above, if cost shocks are assumed to be 'small', the production smoothing model restricts these ratios to be less than one. We focus here on the ratio of the seasonal variances. For three of the six industries, we estimate this ratio to be greater than one.[35]

While one could interpret a ratio greater than one as a rejection of the production smoothing model, there is no reason to expect the above ratio to be less than one if there are seasonal shifts in the cost function.

---

[33] Along the lines of Blinder, we use the following procedure to obtain detrended levels of the data. The log of each series is regressed on a constant, time, and a dummy variable that is one beginning in October 1973. The coefficients are estimated by GLS, assuming a second order autoregressive process for the error term. The antilogs of the fitted values of this regression are then subtracted from the levels of the raw data to define the detrended data. We convert the IP measure from an index into a constant dollar figure by multiplying it by the ratio of average $Y4$ to average IP (i.e. we set the average of the two series equal to each other). We apply the detrending procedure to the resulting IP, as well as $Y4$ and shipments. We then regress the detrended series on a constant and eleven seasonal dummies. The seasonal and nonseasonal variances are estimated using the fitted and residual values of this regression, respectively.

[34] In the last section of his paper, West (1986) describes a variance bounds test that includes deterministic seasonal variations in the data. He found that the variance bounds were rejected for each of the three industries that he examined.

[35] We examine these ratios for seasonally adjusted data in Miron and Zeldes (1987) and find significant differences between the ratios based on IP and $Y4$ data.

TABLE 3. Variance of production divided by variance of sales

		Food	Tobacco	Apparel	Chemicals	Petroleum	Rubber
Y4	Nonseasonal	1.22	1.84	1.32	1.01	0.91	1.13
	Seasonal	1.71	4.71	0.58	0.72	2.73	0.99
	Total	1.50	2.53	0.80	0.89	0.94	1.09
IP	Nonseasonal	0.48	0.58	1.20	0.83	0.48	0.95
	Seasonal	1.64	6.28	0.21	0.18	7.91	0.61
	Total	1.14	1.95	0.50	0.55	0.59	0.86

Notes:
1. The sample period is 1967:5–1982:12.
2. The estimation procedure is the following. For both shipments and production, the log level is regressed on a constant, time, and a time trend that is one beginning in October, 1973. The coefficients are estimated by GLS, assuming a second order autoregressive process for the error term. The antilogs of the fitted values of this regression are then subtracted from the actual data, in levels, to define the detrended data. The seasonal and nonseasonal variances are calculated as the variance of the fitted values and residuals, respectively, of a regression of the detrended series on seasonal dummies.
3. We convert the IP measure from an index to a constant dollar figure by multiplying it by the ratio of average Y4 to average IP.

Even in this case, however, there is information to be learned from examining the seasonal movements. Whether or not seasonal shifts in productivity affect the seasonal pattern of production, there is no reason to expect that seasonal pattern to match the seasonal pattern of sales. Figures 1–6 show the seasonal patterns in output and shipments for the six industries we examine the document behavior potentially problematic for the production smoothing model.[36] The *seasonal movements in output and sales are in fact very similar*. The implication of these graphs is that inventories do not appear to be playing the role of smoothing seasonal fluctuations in sales.

In the tests we present in this section, we formalize this observation. First, we test whether the contemporaneous seasonal movement in sales growth helps predict residual output growth, once the movements in factor prices, the weather, and lagged inventories are taken into account. To do this, we use the same procedure as in Section 5, except that seasonal dummies are excluded from the regression and the instrument list, and the seasonal component of contemporaneous sales growth is added to the instrument list. It is unusual when running this type of orthogonality test to include as an instrument a contemporaneous variable, but since this series is deterministic, it is part of the

[36] The seasonal coefficient plotted for each month is the average percentage difference in that month from a logarithmic time trend.

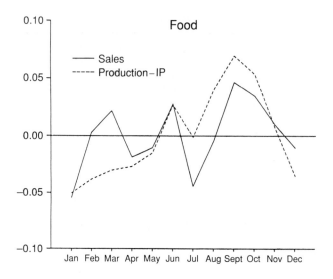

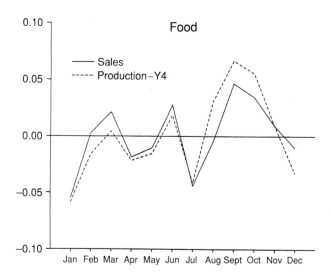

Fig. 1

lagged information set. Since it is also assumed orthogonal to the unobservable productivity shifter, it is a valid instrument.[37]

The interpretation of this procedure is the following. By excluding seasonal dummies from the equation, we force the seasonal and non-

[37] The series we actually use is, of course, the estimated rather than the true seasonal in sales growth.

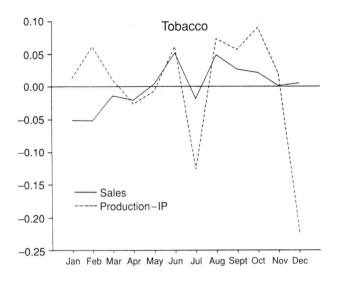

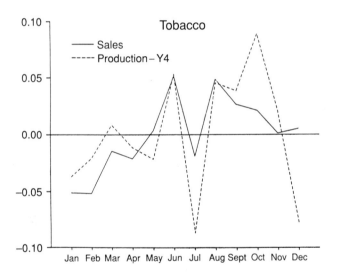

FIG. 2

seasonal movements in the right-hand side variables to affect output growth via the same coefficients. Given this restriction, we are then testing whether the part of output growth not explained by these variables is correlated with the seasonal component of sales growth. This allows us to compare the seasonals in sales and output, after taking into account the measured seasonality in factor costs, the weather, and the level of inventories.

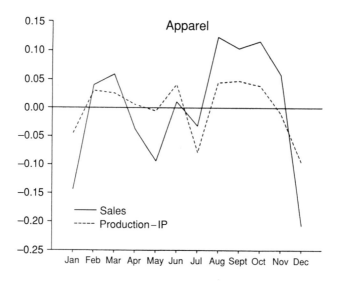

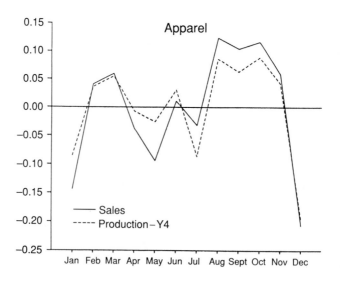

Fig. 3

This test of the production smoothing model using the seasonal fluctuations does involve one important maintained hypothesis, namely that the coefficients on the seasonal and nonseasonal components of input prices and the weather are the same. In our last set of tests, we relax this assumption and test whether the seasonal movements in the data, taken by themselves, are consistent with the model. This is

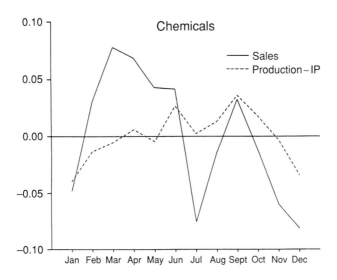

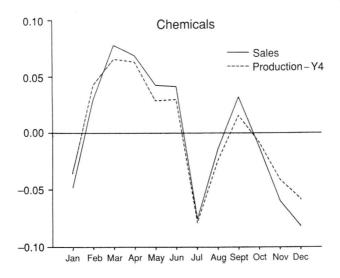

accomplished as follows. The first step is to construct the seasonal component of each of the relevant variables (output growth, input prices, weather variables, etc.) by regressing them on seasonal dummies and calculating the fitted values of these regressions. We then regress the seasonal component of output growth on the seasonal input prices, weather, the level of inventories, and the contemporaneous seasonal

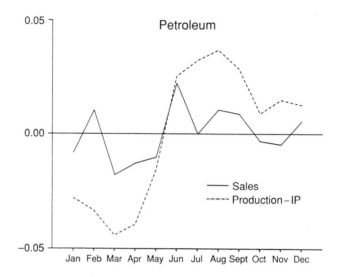

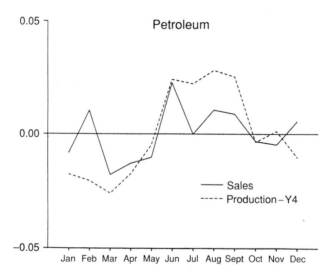

FIG. 5

component of sales, and we test the restriction implied by the model that this last coefficient should be zero.[38,39]

---

[38] Since we found there to be essentially no seasonality in energy prices, raw materials prices or interest rates, we excluded these variables.

[39] We implement the procedure above by estimating equation (10), with sales growth included, using seasonal dummies as the *only* instruments. The coefficient estimates are

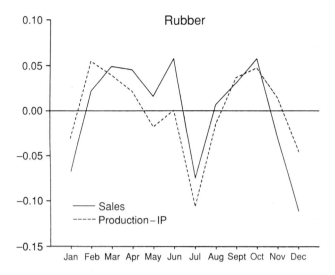

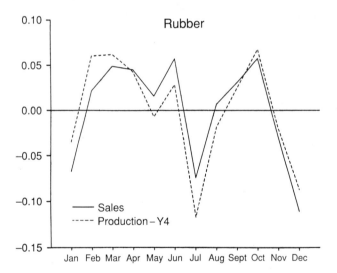

Fig. 6

The results are summarized in Tables 4 and 5. Table 4 presents the same type of information as Table 2, but it includes the t statistic on the

numerically identical to those produced by the procedure described in the text, but this instrumental variables procedure produces correct standard errors. The resulting t statistic on sales growth is reported in Table 5.

TABLE 4.   Regression results, equation (10) seasonal dummies excluded, seasonal component of sales in instrument list

		Food	Tobacco	Apparel	Chemicals	Petroleum	Rubber
Y4, NSA	What enters (10) significantly?	$-w$, tem, $-tem2$	$-w$	w, tem $-tem2$	$-w$,tem $-pre$, $-tem2$	$-w$, $-pre$ $-day$	w, tem $-tem2$, $-pre$
	R^2, Significance Level	.52,.000	.16,.001	.14,.003	.31,.000	.18,.000	.26,.000
	What is significant in test of OIR's?	tem_{-1}, $-tem2_{-1}$ $-x_{-2}$, $-rm_{-1}$ xseas	tem_{-1}	xseas	tem_{-1}, xseas	we_{-2}	xseas
	t-stat on xseas	3.51	0.51	2.84	4.14	1.87	3.41
IP, NSA	What enters (10) significantly?	$-w$, tem, $-tem2$	$-w$	w, rm tem, $-tem2$	tem, $-tem2$ $-pre$	$-w$, $-pre2$	tem, $-tem2$
	R^2, Significance Level	.30,.000	.14,.003	.12,.012	.15,.002	.13,.007	.24,.000
	What is significant in test of OIR's?	$-y_{-1}$, $-y_{-2}$, $-w_{-2}$, xseas	$-y_{-1}$, w_{-2}	$-y_{-1}$, xseas	—	$-y_{-1}$, x_{-1}, xseas	xseas
	t-stat on xseas	2.86	0.99	0.62	1.82	3.39	3.41

Notes:
1. The sample period 1967:5–1982:12.
2. The first line of each set of results lists the variables that entered equation (10) at the 5% significance level.
3. The second line gives the R^2 from the regression of the residuals on the instruments, as well as the marginal significance level of this statistic. The quantity $T \times R^2$ is distributed X_j^2, where j is the number of overidentifying restrictions and T is the number of observations. In the results presented here, there are 10 such restrictions.
4. The third line lists the variables that entered the regression of the residuals on the instruments at the 5% significance level.
5. w = wage growth, y = output growth, x = sales growth, day = number of production days, we = energy price growth, rm = raw materials price growth, n = inventories, r = interest rate, pre = change in precipitation, $pre2$ = change in precipitation squared, tem = change in temperature, $tem2$ = change in temperature squared, tpr = change in temperature* precipitation, $xseas$ = seasonal component of sales growth (defined as the fitted values from a regression on seasonal dummies).
6. A $(-)$ before variable indicates that the sign of the coefficient was negative.
7. A subscript of -1 on variable means that it is dated 1 periods earlier than the dependent variable.

TABLE 5.   Regression results, equation (10) seasonal components only

		Food	Tobacco	Apparel	Chemicals	Petroleum	Rubber
$Y4$	What enters (10) significantly?	$-n, x$	x	x	x	$-$	x
	t stat on x	9.21	4.91	1.98	11.69	1.10	19.99
IP	What enters (10) significantly?	x	$-pre, x$	$-$	x	$-$	x
	t stat on x	3.19	3.39	1.14	2.31	.62	3.97

Notes:
1. The sample period is 1967:5–1982:12.
2. The coefficients were obtained by estimating equation (10), with sales growth included, using seasonal dummies only as instruments. This gives coefficient estimates numerically identical to the procedure described in the text, but it produces correct standard errors. The t statistic on sales growth reported in the table is from this instrumental variables regression.
3. The first line of each set of results lists the variables that entered equation (10) at the 5% significance level.
4. w = wage growth, y = output growth, x = sales growth, day = change in number of production days, n = inventories, pre = change in precipitation, $pre2$ = change in precipitation squared, tem = change in temperature, $tem2$ = change in temperature squared, tpr = change in temperature* precipitation.
5. A $(-)$ before variable indicates that the sign of the coefficient was negative.

seasonal component of contemporaneous sales in the test of the over-identifying restrictions. Table 5 is also set up similarly to Table 2, but it simply reports whether the seasonal in sales significantly affects the seasonal in output growth, after controlling for the seasonal movements in input prices, the weather, and the level of inventories.

In both tables, there is striking evidence against the production smoothing model. In Table 4 we reject the overidentifying restrictions in every instance. In most cases, the seasonal component of sales is significantly correlated with the movement in output, even after taking account of any seasonals in input prices, lagged inventories, and the weather. This is true for five out of six industries using at least one of the output measures, and for three of the six industries using both output measures.

When we redo the estimates in Table 4 using the alternative instrument lists discussed above (leaving out time t variables or lagged output growth) we again reject the overidentifying restrictions and find that the seasonal in sales growth is significantly correlated with the residual output growth in most cases.

In Table 5 (the seasonal-only results) the seasonal in sales growth is statistically significant in five out of six cases for the $Y4$ measure output, and in four out of six cases for the IP measure. Variables other than sales almost never enter significantly.

These results on the behavior of production and sales at seasonal frequencies are perhaps the most problematic yet presented for the production smoothing model. To a large extent, firms appear to be choosing their seasonal production patterns to match their seasonal sales patterns, rather than using inventories to smooth production over the year. Moreover, since the seasonal variation in production and sales growth generally accounts for more than 50 per cent of the total variation in these variables, this problematic behavior is a quantitatively important feature of the data.

A key assumption that we have made here is that the seasonal in the productivity shifter is uncorrelated with the seasonal in demand. Are there circumstances under which this assumption would not hold? An example that comes to mind is the case of an economy-wide seasonal in labor supply, namely that individuals, all else equal, would rather take vacations in certain months. This would induce a corresponding seasonal in output. If each industry's output is an input into another industry, then we might expect to see a corresponding seasonal in shipments, leading optimally to the same seasonal patterns in output and shipments.

Theoretically, our approach accounts for this by including the wage as a determinant of desired production. However, if the measured wage differs from the true shadow cost of utilizing labor, then the residual will include the seasonal in labor supply and therefore will still be correlated with the seasonal in shipments. This explanation suggests that we should see the same seasonal movements in output in all industries. In Figures 1–6 we do see common seasonal patterns in output across industries, but we also see a fair amount of seasonal movement that is different across industries.

It is not clear what conclusion to draw from this discussion. It is possible that the hypothesis proposed above is the explanation for the seasonal results. If so, we should ask whether the same type of arguments could be made about nonseasonal movements, i.e. whether we believe that the failure of the production smoothing model at nonseasonal frequencies is due to economy-wide changes in desired labor supply that are not captured by measured wages.

7. Conclusions

The results presented above show a strong rejection of the production smoothing model. This is despite the fact that we have extended the standard model considerably, by allowing for nonquadratic technology, a stochastic interest rate, convex costs of holding inventories, and measurable and nonmeasurable cost shocks, and by including seasonal fluctuations explicitly. Although previous work has examined many of these features, none has simultaneously allowed for all of them.

The rejections of the basic production smoothing model that we report are robust with respect to the treatment of seasonal fluctuations. To begin with, we reject the model about as strongly when we treat seasonality in the standard way, by using adjusted data, as when we treat it more explicitly by specifying the economic sources of the seasonal movements in production and inventories. Even more surprisingly, our results show that the seasonal movements in production, inventories, and shipments are inconsistent with the basic model. Specifically, the seasonal component of output growth, even after adjusting for the seasonality in interest rates, wages, energy prices, raw materials prices, and the weather, is still highly correlated with the seasonal component of sales growth, contrary to the prediction of the model.

We conclude the paper by discussing what we believe to be the implications of our results for a number of hypotheses that have been offered for the failure of the production smoothing model. We first discuss those hypotheses on which our results provide direct evidence and then turn to more indirect implications.

Our results provide direct evidence that the limited role given to cost shocks in previous papers is not the major reason for the rejections of the model. In this paper we have included a more general set of cost shocks than in earlier work, and we still find that the data reject production smoothing. Moreover, we find relatively little evidence that cost shocks play any role in determining the optimal timing of production. It is possible, of course, that we have omitted the 'key' cost shock, or that one of our identifying assumptions is invalid. We believe, however, that the set of costs we have included covers all of the major ones, and we think that the identifying assumptions we make are minimally restrictive. It seems to us unlikely, therefore, that the treatment of cost shocks is a major factor in explaining the poor performance of the model.

The second area in which our results provide direct evidence is on whether the inappropriate use of data seasonally adjusted by X-11 has been responsible for the failure of the model. As we discussed above, X-11 data are (approximately) a two-sided moving average of the underlying seasonally unadjusted data. This means that such data likely violate the crucial orthogonality conditions that are tested in the kinds of models considered above, even if the unadjusted data satisfy them. Although it seemed likely to us on a priori grounds that the use of X-11 adjusted data was a major problem, our results indicate otherwise. The particular method of treating seasonal fluctuations does not appear crucial to an evaluation of the model.

So much for direct implications. We now turn to more indirect implications, specifically, the implications of our tests using the seasonal movements in the data. These implications are subject to the critique that the production smoothing model may fit differently at different frequencies, in which case we may not be able to learn about the validity of the model at nonseasonal frequencies from its performance at seasonal frequencies. However, to the extent that the same model is underlying the different movements in the data, we can draw the following conclusions.

To begin with, since seasonal fluctuations are anticipated, it seems unlikely that the failure of the model at seasonal frequencies could be due to any kind of irrationality or disequilibrium. If so, this rules out a large class of possible explanations of the failure of the model.

A second issue that is illuminated by our seasonal specific results is that of costs of changing production. We have omitted costs of changing production (or, more generally, costs of changing inputs) from our specifications above; the addition of these costs might 'help the data fit the model'. We regard this tactic as unsatisfactory, however. The fact that there are extremely large seasonal changes in the rate of production makes it seem quite unlikely that there are large costs of adjustment, although it is true that costs may be lower when they are anticipated.

Blinder (1986a) suggests that the production smoothing model could be saved by including persistent demand shocks and small cost shocks. Even if the nonseasonal movements in sales are very persistent, however, the same is not true of the seasonal movements. Therefore, our seasonal results suggest that Blinder's explanation will not suffice to 'save' the production smoothing model.

Finally, our seasonal specific results allow us to rule out a concern regarding the choice of appropriate instruments. In our estimation, we assume that firms know current demand, and therefore time t sales is a valid instrument. In contrast, others, such as Kahn (1986), assume that firms do not know the level of current period demand when they choose the current period level of production. If this assumption is a more appropriate abstraction, then our general results are inconsistent. When we correct for this by using only variables dated $t - 1$ and earlier as instruments, we can no longer reject the model. However, it is still valid to include the seasonal component of contemporaneous sales growth, since the seasonal component of demand would be known even if the overall level were not. Since the results from this test show a strong rejection of the model, this suggests that the assumption that firms observe demand before choosing output is not, by itself, to blame.

What remains, then, as a possible explanation for the failure of the production smoothing model? There are two main possibilities: nonconvexity of the cost function, and stockout costs. Giving up convexity of costs is unappealing because it requires also giving up much of neoclassical theory. This does not mean it is not the correct explanation; it simply suggests that we should turn to it only as a last resort. We end, therefore, by discussing the role of stockout costs.

An important maintained assumption above is that firms always hold positive inventories, which implies that firms do not stock out. Total inventories for each industry are always positive in our data, but this may not be the case for each individual firm or product. Kahn (1986) presents a model in which, because stockouts are costly, firms may not smooth production.[40] However, there is as yet relatively little direct evidence that stockout costs are high, or that firms cannot simply hold unfilled orders as a type of negative inventory. This line of research deserves further attention, in particular direct empirical testing.

References

(References marked with a * are included in this volume)

ABEL, ANDREW B. (1985), 'Inventories, stock-outs and production smoothing', *Review of Economic Studies*, **52**, 283–93.

BELSLEY, DAVID A. (1969), *Industrial Production Behavior: The Order-Stock Distinction*. Amsterdam: North-Holland.

BLANCHARD, OLIVIER J. (1983), 'The production and inventory behavior of the American automobile industry', *Journal of Political Economy*, **91**, 365–400.

BLINDER, ALAN S. (1982), 'Inventories and sticky prices: more on the microfoundations of macroeconomics', *American Economic Review*, **72**, 334–48.

—— (1986*a*), 'Can the production smoothing model of inventory behavior be saved?', *Quarterly Journal of Economics*, **101**, 431–54.

—— (1986*b*), 'More on the speed of adjustment in inventory models', *Journal of Money, Credit, and Banking*, **18**, 355–65.

—— FISCHER, STANLEY (1981), 'Inventories, rational expectations, and the business cycle', *Journal of Monetary Economics*, **8**, 277–304.

CHRISTIANO, LAWRENCE J. (1986), 'Why does inventory investment fluctuate so much?', manuscript, Federal Reserve Bank of Minneapolis.

—— and EICHENBAUM, MARTIN (1986), 'Temporal aggregation and structural inference in macroeconomics', manuscript, Carnegie–Mellon University.

CLEVELAND, W., AND TIAO G. (1976), 'Decomposition of seasonal time series: a model for the census X-11 program', *Journal of the American Statistical Association*, **71**, 581–7.

EICHENBAUM, MARTIN S. (1984), 'Rational expectations and the smoothing properties of inventories of finished goods', *Journal of Monetary Economics*, **14**, 71–96.

FELDSTEIN, MARTIN AND SUMMERS, LAWRENCE (1970), 'Inflation and the taxation of capital income in the corporate sector', *National Tax Journal*, **32**, 445–70.

---

[40] Abel (1985) also examines production smoothing in a model with stockouts.

GARBER, PETER AND KING, ROBERT (1984), 'Deep structural excavation? A critique of Euler equation methods', NBER Technical Working Paper no. 83–14.

GHALI, MOHEB (1987), 'Seasonality, aggregation, and testing of the production smoothing hypothesis', *American Economic Review*, **77**, 464–9.

GHYSELS, ERIC (1987), 'Cycles and seasonals in inventories: another look at non-stationarity and induced seasonalilty', manuscript, University of Montreal.

GOODFRIEND, MARVIN (1986), 'Information–aggregation bias: the case of consumption', manuscript, Federal Reserve Bank of Richmond.

HALL, ROBERT E. (1978), 'Stochastic implications of the life cycle-permanent income hypothesis: theory and evidence', *Journal of Political Economy*, **86**, 971–87.

HANSEN, LARS, AND SINGLETON, KENNETH J. (1983), 'Stochastic consumption, risk aversion, and the temporal behavior of asset returns', *Journal of Political Economy*, **91**, 249–66.

HINRICHS, JOHN C., AND ECKMAN, ANTHONY D. (1981), 'Constant dollar manufacturing inventories', *Survey of Current Business*, **61**, 16–23.

IRVINE, F. OWEN, JR. (1981), 'Retail inventory investment and the cost of capital', *American Economic Review*, **71**, 633–8.

KAHN, JAMES (1986), 'Inventories and the volatility of production', manuscript, University of Rochester.

MACCINI, LOUIS J., and ROSSANA, ROBERT J. (1984), 'Joint production, quasi-fixed factors of production, and investment in finished goods inventories', *Journal of Money, Credit, and Banking*, **16**, 218–36.

MANKIW, N. GREGORY (1981), 'The permanent income hypothesis and the real interest rate', *Economics Letters*, **7**, 307–11.

MIRON, JEFFREY A. (1986), 'Seasonality and the life cycle-permanent income model of consumption', *Journal of Political Economy*, **94**, 1258–79.

—— and ZELDES, STEPHEN P. (1987), 'Production, sales, and the change in inventories: an identity that doesn't add up', Rodney L. White Working Paper no. 20–87, The Wharton School, University of Pennsylvania.

NELSON, CHARLES R., AND PLOSSER, CHARLES I. (1982), 'Trends and random walks in macroeconomic time series: some evidence and implications', *Journal of Monetary Economics*, **10**, 139–62.

PRESCOTT, EDWARD C. (1986), 'Theory ahead of business cycle measurement', Carnegie–Rochester Conference Series, **25**, 11–44.

REAGAN, PATRICIA, AND SHEEHAN, DENNIS P. (1985), 'The stylized facts about the behavior of manufacturers' inventories and backorders over the business cycle: 1959–1980', *Journal of Monetary Economics*, **15**, 217–46.

SARGENT, THOMAS J. (1978): 'Rational expectations, econometric exogeneity, and consumption', *Journal of Political Economy*, **86**, 673–700.

SCHUTTE, DAVID P. (1983), 'Inventories and sticky prices: note', *American Economic Review*, **73**, 815–16.

SUMMERS, LAWRENCE (1981), 'Comment on "retail inventory behavior and business fluctuations" by Alan Blinder', *Brookings Papers on Economic Activity*, **2**, 513–17.

WALLIS, KENNETH F. (1974): 'Seasonal adjustment and the relation between variables', *Journal of the American Statistical Association*, **69**, 13–32.*

WARD, MICHAEL P. (1978), 'Optima production and inventory decisions: an analysis of firm and industry behavior', unpublished Ph.D. thesis, University of Chicago.

WEST, KENNETH, D. (1983), 'A note on the econometric use of constant dollar inventory series', *Economics Letters*, **13**, 337–41.

—— (1986), 'A variance bounds test of the linear quadratic inventory model', *Journal of Political Economy*, **94**, 374–401.

ZELDES, STEPHEN P. (1985), 'Consumption and liquidity constraints: an empirical investigation', Rodney L. White Center Working Paper no. 24–85, The Wharton School, University of Pennsylvania.

PART III
Seasonal Adjustment Procedures

Introduction

Traditionally, seasonal adjustment is undertaken for three different reasons. The two most important arguments in favour of computing and publishing seasonally adjusted data are that they are helpful in the informal appraisal of current economic conditions, and in historical studies of business cycles. Thirdly, the fact that seasonally adjusted data are used as input in econometric studies has not been of much concern for most data-collecting agencies, which often have ignored the fact that most econometricians regard seasonal adjustment as an unnecessary and unproductive removal of important information from the data.

Often an unobserved components model such as

$$x_t = T_t + C_t + S_t + \varepsilon_t \tag{1}$$

where T_t is the trend, C_t is the cycle, S_t is the seasonal and ε_t the irregular component must be considered grossly misspecified as the components are dependent and not independent as implicity assumed. In Denmark, for instance, the period of full employment in the building industries during the sixties had dramatic effects on the building techniques applied and consequently on the seasonal behaviour of that industry. Likewise, the dry summers of the mid-seventies caused a massive investment in irrigation, and permanently changed the technique and the productivity of parts of the agricultural sector.

None the less, the basic model illustrated by (1) has survived. As a result the data-collecting agencies are producing seasonally adjusted series, sometimes even without publishing the unadjusted data. One reason for this unfortunate practice is that several macroeconomic time series are constructed on the basis of seasonally adjusted components.

In the literature there exists abundant[1] evidence that the use of seasonally adjusted data may have serious effects on both estimation and model selection, i.e. on econometric modelling as such. It is therefore important that the seasonal adjustment procedures of the data-collecting agencies are well understood and their possible impact analysed. By far the most popular method for seasonal adjustment is the X-11 method developed by Julius Shiskin and associates for the US Census Bureau during the sixties (see Shiskin, Young, and Musgrave (1967)) and the further development of that method made by Estela Bee Dagum at Statistics Canada (see Dagum (1980)).

---

[1] See Nerlove (1964), Wallis (1974), Sims (1974), Davidson et al. (1978), Hylleberg (1986), Ghysels (1984), and many others.

The first article in this section is an extract from Hylleberg (1986) describing the basic features of the X-11 method. This is done by the help of a flow chart which indicates the different steps of the quite complicated procedure. The second article by Burridge and Wallis (1984) extends the analysis by Cleveland and Tiao (1976) by constructing an unobserved components time series model with component estimates which mimic the component estimates obtained by the X-11 method. The unobserved components model applied has the form $x_t = N_t + S_t$, where s_t and N_t are the seasonal and non-seasonal components, respectively, and the estimated components models are

$$U(B)S_t = \Phi(B)v_t \tag{2}$$

$$(1 - B)^2 \, N_t = \Theta(B)\eta_t$$

$$U(B) = 1 + B + B^2 + \ldots + B^{11}$$

$$v_t \sim i.i.d(0,\sigma_v^2), \qquad \eta_t \sim i.i.d(0,\sigma_\eta^2).$$

where the estimated moving average parts and the variance ratio are

$$\Phi(B) = 1 + 1.00B^{24} \tag{2.1}$$

$$\Theta(B) = 1 - 1.43B + .70B^2$$

$$\sigma_v^2/\sigma_\eta^2 = .018$$

if the one-sided filter is used,

$$\Phi(B) = 1 + .33B^{12} + .99B^{24} \tag{2.2}$$

$$\Theta(B) = 1 - 1.55B + .82B^2$$

$$\sigma_v^2/\sigma_\eta^2 = .026$$

if the asymmetric filter is used, and

$$\Phi(B) = 1 + .71B^{12} + 1.00B^{24} \tag{2.3}$$

$$\Theta(B) = 1 - 1.59B + .86B^2$$

$$\sigma_v^2/\sigma_\eta^2 = .017$$

if the symmetric filter is used. The three models mimic the X-11 filter at the end of the sample period, i.e for current data (2.1), close to the end of the sample period, i.e within one year (2.2), and when there are enough observations on both sides to compute the symmetric X-11 filter (2.3). Notice, that the three models are quite similar in spite of the apparent differences in the estimated parameters of the moving average parts. A similarity that is more easily depicted by writing the polynomials in polar form.

Another noteworthy feature is the use of the seasonal polynomial operator $U(B)$ and the application of the difference operator twice. The composite model has the form.

This implies that the X-11 program implicity assumes that the series are

$$(1 - B)^2 U(B)x_t = U(B)\Theta(B)\eta_t + (1 - B)^2\Phi(B)v_t \qquad (3)$$

integrated of order two at the zero frequency, and of order one at each of the monthly seasonal frequencies. However, the estimated moving average parts of the three models have roots on or very close to the unit circle and with angles not too far from some of the seasonal angles. This could indicate the existence of common factors, whereby the degree of integration is less than one at some seasonal frequencies. When cancelling of common factors does not take place the possible existence of unit roots slightly away from the seasonal frequencies in the moving average part could point to some less attractive features of the X-11 filter.

It is thus an important task for future research to continue this evaluation of the standard seasonal adjustment packages and in addition persuade the data-collecting agencies to produce the seasonal unadjusted data.

3.   References

(References marked with a * are included in this volume)

BURRIDGE, P., and WALLIS, K. F. (1984), 'Unobserved-components models for seasonal adjustment filters', *Journal of Business and Economic Statistics*, **2**, 350–9.*

CLEVELAND, W. P., AND TIAO, G. C. (1976), 'Decomposition of seasonal time series: a model for the census X-11 program', *Journal of the American Statistical Association*, **71**, 581–7.

DAGUM, E. B. (1980), 'The X-11–ARIMA seasonal adjustment method', *Statistics Canada, Cataloque No. 12–564E.*

DAVIDSON, J. E. H., HENDRY, D. F., SRBA, F., and YEO, S. (1978), 'Economic modelling of the aggregate time-scale relationship between consumer expenditure and income in the United Kingdom, *Economic Journal*, **88**, 661–92.

GHYSELS, E. (1984), 'The Economic of Seasonality: The Case of the Money Supply', unpublished, Ph.D. Dissertation, Northwestern University.

HYLLEBERG, S. (1986), *Seasonality in Regression.* Orlando: Academic Press.

NERLOVE, M. (1964), 'Spectral analysis of seasonal adjustment procedures', *Econometrica*, **32**, 241–84.

SHISKIN, J., YOUNG, A. H., and MUSGRAVE, J. C. (1967), 'The X-11 variant of the census method II seasonal adjustment program', *Technical Paper No. 15. Bureau of the Census.* Washington DC: Department of Commerce.

SIMS, C. A. (1972), 'Seasonality in regression', *Journal of the American Statistical Association*, **69**, 545–63.*

WALLIS, K. F. (1974), 'Seasonal adjustment and relations between variables', *Journal of the American Statistical Association*, **69**, 18–31.*

9

The X-11 Method[1]

SVEND HYLLEBERG

The Bureau of the Census method I was a seven-step program based on a refinement of the ratio-to-moving-average method developed by Macaulay (1931) at the NBER. The method was introduced in 1954 and used as a springboard for the method II of 1955 (see Shiskin and Eisenpress (1957) and Shiskin (1960, 1978)). During the following years several versions of this method were put forward. The versions were denoted X-1, X-2, etc. The last version, the X-11 method, was developed in 1965 (see Shiskin *et al.* (1967); Kallek (1978); Kuiper (1978); and Danmarks Statistik (1975)). The X-11 method has been in use since 1965, but the program has been improved by the introduction of several different options that allow the user to adhere to the special characteristics of the individual series.

The main characteristics of the X-11 method for the multiplicative model

$$X_t = TC_t \cdot S_t \cdot TD_t \cdot H_t \cdot I_t \qquad (5.1)$$

(where X_t is the observed value while TC_t, S_t, TD_t, H_t, and I_t are the unobserved trend-cycle component, the seasonal component, the trading-day component, the holiday component, and the irregular component, respectively) are described in Fig. 1.[2] The additive model can be described accordingly.

The X-11 program is divided into seven parts (A to G). The first part (A) is optional and allows the user to make prior adjustments for trading days and certain holidays. In parts E to G, summary measures, tables, and charts are produced to facilitate analyses of the filtering processes made in the parts B, C, and D, which consist of almost identical routines. The purposes of the computations made in parts B and C are to provide preliminary and final estimates, respectively, of

---

[1] A description of the version of the X-11 program applied in Denmark by Danmarks Statistik can be found in Danmarks Statistik (1975).

[2] The term SI indicates the combined seasonal-irregular component.

Printed with permission of: Seasonality in Regression, 89–93. Orlando: Academic Press.

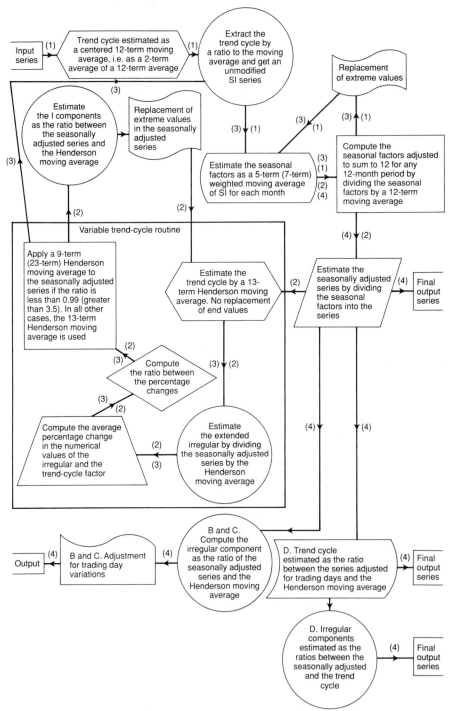

FIG. 1. The X-11 variant of the Census method II, monthly seasonal adjustment. Program parts B, C, and D.

trading-day variations and weights and to replace or smooth extreme values. In part D the series, which is finally adjusted for trading-day variation, is used as input and the final estimates of the seasonally adjusted series, the trend-cycle component, and the irregular component are made.

The computations in B, C, and D start out by estimating the trend-cycle component as a centered 12-term moving average, followed by an extraction of this component from the series, i.e. an estimation of the seasonal irregular (SI) component by computing the ratio of the series of the moving average. A set of preliminary seasonal factors is then computed by applying a weighted 5-term moving average to the estimated SI values separately for each month. The weights applied are given in Shiskin *et al.* (1967) and Danmarks Statistik (1975). The seasonal factors are adjusted to 12 for any 12-month period by dividing by a 12-term moving average. The missing 6 values at either end are replaced by the first and last available moving-average value. In order to smooth the extreme SI values, a moving 5-year standard deviation of the estimated irregular I_t and, in parts B and C, an extended irregular component $TD_tH_tI_t$ are computed, the irregular component being estimated by dividing the SI series by the preliminary adjusted seasonal factors. In the following step, irregular values beyond 2.5 times the moving standard deviations are removed and a new set of moving standard deviations is computed. This new set of standard deviations is used to assign weights to the unmodified SI series. The weighting function has the form

$$\text{weight} = \begin{cases} 1 & \text{for} \quad 0 \leqslant I^* \leqslant 1.5 \\ 2.5 - 1.0I^* & \text{for} \quad 1.5 < I^* \leqslant 2.5 \\ 0 & \text{for} \quad I^* > 2.5 \end{cases}$$

where I^* is the estimated irregular value divided by the 5-year moving standard deviation.

For SI values receiving less than full weight, the value is replaced by an average of the SI value times its weight and the two nearest preceding and the two nearest following values with full weight for that month.

The seasonal and adjusted seasonal factors are then recomputed and a preliminary estimate of the seasonally adjusted series is obtained by dividing the seasonal factors into the series. Thereafter the so-called variable trend-cycle routine is applied to the preliminary seasonally adjusted data. This routine starts out by estimating the trend-cycle component by a 13-term Henderson moving-average filter, which smooths the series by minimizing the sum of squares of the third differences. The weights applied are given in Shiskin *et al.* (1967, pp.

63–4) and Danmarks Statistik (1975) and a general discussion of the Henderson formular can be found in Macaulay (1931, chap. VI).

In the next step of the variable trend-cycle routine, the extended irregular component is estimated as the ratio of the preliminary season-ally adjusted series and the trend cycle. The ratio of the average percentage change in the extended irregular component and the average percentage change of the trend-cycle component is then used to choose between a 9-term Henderson moving-average (HMA), a 23-term Hen-derson moving-average, and the 13-term Henderson moving-average already computed. The 9-(23-) term HMA is applied if the ratio is less than or equal to 0.99 (greater than or equal to 3.5), while the 13-term HMA is applied otherwise. The output from the routine, i.e. the HMA estimates of the trend-cycle component, is then divided into the pre-liminary seasonally adjusted series in order to produce an estimate of the irregular series. By use of exactly the same procedure as before, including the weighting function, extreme values of the seasonally adjusted series are replaced and the resulting modified seasonally adjusted series is sent through the variable trend-cycle routine once more, thereby producing a new HMA estimate trend-cycle series.

The trend-cycle series is then used instead of the simple 12-term centered moving average originally applied to extract the trend-cycle component from the series, and a new set of seasonal factors is computed, but instead of the 5-term weighted-moving average of the SI values for each month, a 7-term moving-average formular is applied. The seasonal factors are adjusted to sum to 12 and extreme values are replaced as before. Finally, a series of seasonally adjusted data is obtained by dividing the input series by the new set of seasonal factors. In parts B and C this series is used in the adjustment for trading days, while the seasonally adjusted series in part D is used as a final output series together with estimates of the trend-cycle series and the irregular series.

Thus, the X-11 program consists basically of a series of moving-aver-age computations and replacements of extreme values whereby the components are isolated one by one.

3.   References

DANMARKS STATISTIK, (1975), *Saesonkorrigering a Danske Tidsserier* ('Seasonal adjustments of Danish time series'). Copenhagen: Danmarks Statistik, Statis-tike Undersøgelser nr. 32.

---

[3] Notice that a 23-term HMA smooths the series more than a 13-term HMA, which smooths the series more than a 9-term HMA.

KALLEK, S. (1978), 'An overview of the objectives and framework of seasonal adjustment', in *Seasonal Analysis of Economic Time Series*. Proceedings of the Conference on the Seasonal Analysis of Economic Time Series, Washington DC, 9–10 Sept. 1976 (A. Zellner, ed.), US Department of Commerce, Bureau of the Census, Washington DC.

KUIPER, J. (1978), 'A survey and comparative analysis of various methods of seasonal adjustment', in *Seasonal Analysis of Economic Time Series* Proceedings of the Conference on the Seasonal Analysis of Economic Time Series, Washington DC, 9–10 Sept. 1976 (A. Zellner, ed.), pp. 59–76. Washington DC: US Department of Commerce, Bureau of the Census.

MACAULAY, F. R. (1931), 'The Smoothing of Time Series'. New York: National Bureau of Economic Research.

SHISKIN, J. (1960), 'Electrical computer seasonal adjustments. Test and revision of US census methods', *Seasonal Adjustments on Electronic Computers*. Paris: Proceeding of the International Conference, OECD.

—— (1978), 'Keynote address: seasonal adjustment of sensitive indicators', in *Seasonal Analysis of Economic Time Series*. Proceedings of the Conference on the Seasonal Analysis of Economic Time Series, Washington DC, 9–10 Sept. 1976 (A. Zellner ed.), pp. 97–103. Washington DC: US Department of Commerce, Bureau of Census.

—— and EISENPRESS, H. (1957), 'Seasonal adjustments by electronic computer methods', *Journal of the American Statistical Association*, **52**, 415–49.

—— YOUNG, A. H., and MUSGRAVE J. C. (1967), 'The X-11 variant of the census method II seasonal adjustment program', *Technical Paper no. 15*. Washington DC: Bureau of the Census, US Department of Commerce.

10

Unobserved-Components Models for Seasonal Adjustment Filters

PETER BURRIDGE AND KENNETH F. WALLIS

Abstract. Time series models are presented, for which the seasonal-component estimates delivered by linear least squares signal extraction closely approximate those of the standard option of the widely-used Census X-11 program. Earlier work is extended by consideration of a broader class of models and by examination of asymmetric filters, in addition to the symmetric filter implicit in the adjustment of historical data. Various criteria that guide the specification of unobserved-components models are discussed, and a new preferred model is presented. Some nonstandard options in X-11 are considered in the Appendix.

Key words: Time series; seasonal adjustment; signal extraction; X-11 method; unobserved-components models; ARIMA models.

Introduction

Procedures for the seasonal adjustment of economic time series used by official statistical agencies are often criticized for their ad hoc nature. Whereas practical statisticians justify these procedures on intuitive and pragmatic grounds, pointing to their apparent success in satisfying the demands of users of statistics, theorists point to the absence of well-specified objectives and criteria of performance. Indeed, the very notions of the three components of a series that underlie the practical procedures—trend-cycle, seasonal, and irregular—are not well defined.

Recently developed alternative techniques rest on a more formal specification of the problem. Given stochastic models for the unobserved components and a linear least squares criterion, classical signal-extraction theory as described, for example, by Whittle (1963) can be applied to obtain an optimal estimate of the deseasonalized. The seasonal adjustment problem was formulated in this way by Grether and Nerlove (1970), who assumed stationarity of the components and hence of the observed series. Subsequent work (Cleveland (1972); Cleveland

Printed with permission of: Journal of Business and Economic Statistics, **2**. 350–9.

and Tiao (1976); Box, Hillmer, and Tiao (1978); Burman (1980); and Hillmer and Tiao (1982)) considered extensions to series that are adequately represented by models of the Box–Jenkins (1970) seasonal autoregressive integrated moving average (ARIMA) class and so can be reduced to stationarity by differencing. A practical difficulty in implementing seasonal adjustment methods based on optimal signal extraction theory is that of specifying models for the unobserved components of the observed series, and although various suggestions have been made, the resulting methods have not yet been widely adopted by official statistical agencies.

In this article we use the signal-extraction approach to study the properties of a widely used seasonal-adjustment procedure, namely the Census Bureau's X-11 method (Shiskin, Young, and Musgrave 1967), which we represent as a set of linear filters, as in Wallis (1982). These filters range from the one-sided moving average implicit in the preliminary adjustment of the current observation, through a number of asymmetric moving averages, to the symmetric moving average implicit in the adjustment of historical data. We present models whose optimal signal-extraction filters virtually coincide with certain of these moving averages and for which X-11, therefore, provides the linear least squares estimate of the seasonally adjusted series. Our analysis extends that of Cleveland and Tiao (1976), who considered only the symmetric X-11 filter (in a truncated form), and Wallis (1983), who presented seasonal ARIMA models for the observed series for which the asymmetric X-11 filters minimize revisions in the seasonally adjusted series. Many statistical agencies run the X-11 program only once a year, and at that time they project seasonal factors for the adjustment of the next 12 months' data, to be used as the data become available. Kenny and Durbin (1982) and Wallis (1982) argued that the practice of year-ahead adjustment should be replaced by running the program every month; year-ahead adjustment is not considered in this article.

The signal-extraction interpretation of the X-11 filters is described in Section 2, and the models for which X-11 represents the optimal procedure in this sense are presented in Section 3. Corresponding models for some nonstandard options of X-11 are presented in the Appendix. Section 4 contains concluding comments.

2. The X-11 Linear Filters and Signal Extraction Models

2.1 The X-11 linear filters

The X-11 procedure assumes that the observed monthly time series variable Y_t is made up of three unobserved components, namely the trend-cycle, seasonal, and irregular components, denoted by C_t, S_t, and I_t, respectively. We work with the additive decomposition

$$Y_t = C_t + S_t + I_t; \qquad (2.1)$$

the program also includes a multiplicative option, which is essentially the same as (2.1) on taking logarithms. The seasonal-adjustment problem is to obtain an estimate S_t of the seasonal component and subtract it from the original series, yielding the seasonally adjusted series

$$Y_t^a = Y_t - \hat{S}_t. \qquad (2.2)$$

In fact the X-11 program provides a decomposition of the original series into three estimated components, but we concentrate on the seasonal component; we also neglect the option of graduating extreme values of the estimated irregular component. The program comprises a sequence of moving-average or linear-filter operations, whose net effect can be represented by a single set of moving averages. For a date sufficiently far in the past, the *final* or *historical* adjusted value $Y_t^{(m)}$ is obtained by application of the symmetric filter $a_m(L)$,

$$Y_t^{(m)} = a_m(L)Y_t = \sum_{J=-m}^{m} a_{m,j} Y_{t-j},$$

where L is the lag operator, and $a_{m,j} = a_{m,-j}$ for symmetry. For current and recent data this filter cannot be applied, and truncated asymmetric filters are employed:

$$Y_t^{(k)} = a_k(L)Y_t = \sum_{j=-k}^{m} a_{k,j} Y_{t-j}, \quad K = 0, 1, \ldots, m. \qquad (2.3)$$

For the filter $a_k(L)$, the subscript k indicates the number of *future* values of Y entering the moving average; equivalently, the subscript of Y indicates that $Y_t^{(k)}$ is the adjusted value of Y_t calculated from observations Y_{t-m}, Y_{t-m+1}, $\ldots$, Y_t, $\ldots$, Y_{t+k}. Thus $Y_t^{(0)}$ is the first-*announced* or *preliminary* seasonally adjusted figure. For the standard X-11 filters considered here, $m = 84$ (it is assumed that at the stage at which the program chooses a 9-, 13-, or 23-term Henderson moving average to estimate the trend-cycle component, the 13-term average is chosen). The program is then represented as a set of 85 linear filters in which, respectively, 0, 1, $\ldots$, 84 future data points appear. Although $m = 84$ implies that seven years' past data are required to calculate a current seasonally adjusted value, after three years the weights are very small.

A useful description of the filters is provided by the frequency response function

$$a_k(\omega) = \sum a_{k,j} e^{-i\omega j} = |a_k(\omega)| e^{i\psi} k(\omega),$$

the squared gain $|a_k(\omega)|^2$, or the transfer function of the filter, representing the extent to which the contribution of the component of frequency ω to the total variance of the series is modified by the action of the filter. The weights and transfer functions of three X-11 filters of particular interest—$a_0(L)$, $a_{12}(L)$, and $a_{84}(L)$—are presented in Figures 1–3, where they act as benchmarks for the signal-extraction filters described in Section 3.2. Further details of their calculation may be found in Wallis (1982), and a listing of the coefficients is available on request.

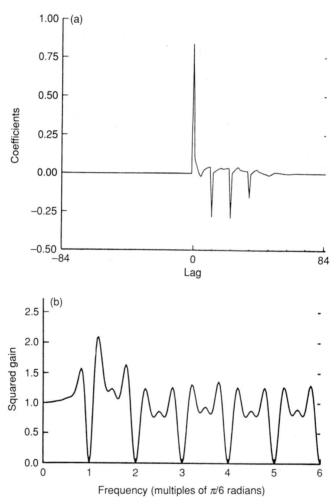

FIG. 1. Weights (a) and transfer function (b) of $a_0(L)$ for X-11.

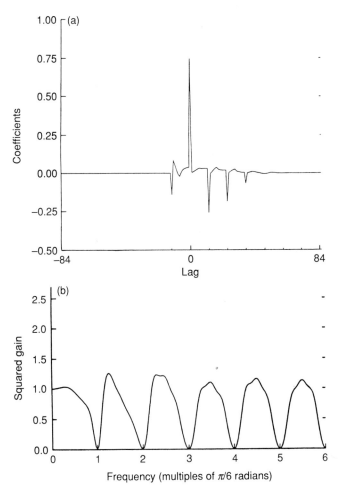

Fig. 2. Weights (a) and transfer function (b) of $a_{12}(L)$ for X-11.

2.2 Linear least squares signal extraction

In the signal-extraction literature the unobserved components introduced in (2.1) are treated as uncorrelated random processes, and the signal-extraction problem is to estimate S_t, say, from observations on Y. The linear least squares approach to this problem is to construct a linear filter,

$$\hat{S}_t = f_k(L)Y_t, \qquad (2.4)$$

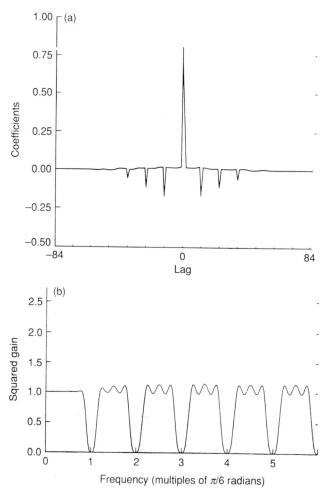

FIG. 3. Weights (a) and transfer function (b) of $a_{84}(L)$ for X-11.

to minimize the mean squared error $E(S_t - \hat{S}_t)^2$, where k again indicates that $\hat{S}_t$ is based on data through time $t + k$.

The classical theory assumes that the autocovariances of the unobserved components and hence of the observed variable are known. Both in theoretical work and in practical implementation this requirement has been met by postulating linear models for the components and expressing the autocovariances as functions of those models' parameters. Accordingly, we consider component models of the following form:

$$\phi_c(L)C_t = \theta_c(L)u_t, \quad \phi_s(L)S_t = \theta_s(L)v_t, \quad I_t = w_t, \quad (2.5)$$

where u_t, v_t and w_t are uncorrelated normally distributed white-noise series. Particular specifications are achieved by imposing restrictions on the autoregressive and moving-average lag polynomials in (2.5); these are discussed in the next section. For the moment we simply assume that each component is *parsimoniously parameterized*—that is, that each of the pairs of polynomials $\{\phi_c(L)\}$ and $\{\phi_s(L),\ \theta_s(L)\}$ has no common factors and that the pair $\{\phi_c(L),\ \phi_s(L)\}$ has no common factor. Then the composite model for Y_t is

$$\phi(L)Y_t = \beta(L)\varepsilon_t, \tag{2.6}$$

where $\phi(L) = \phi_c(L)\phi_s(L)$ and $\beta(L)$ is obtained as the canonical factorization of the autocovariance-generating function of $\phi(L)Y_t$, defined in terms of the parameters of (2.5), namely

$$\sigma_\varepsilon^2|\beta(z)|^2 = \sigma_u^2|\phi_s(z)\theta_c(z)|^2 + \sigma_v^2|\phi_c(z)|^2 + \sigma_w^2|\phi_c(z)\phi_s(z)|^2, \tag{2.7}$$

where the notations $|h(z)|^2$ denotes $h(z)h(z^{-1})$.

The signal-extraction filters depend, essentially, on the ratio of the second term on the right side of (2.7) to the complete expression. Thus

$$f_k(z) = \frac{\sigma_v^2\phi_c(z)\phi_s(z)}{\sigma_a^2\beta(z)} \times \left(\frac{\sigma_c(z^{-1})\theta_s(z)\theta_s(z^{-1})}{\beta(z^{-1})\phi_s(z)}\right)_{-k}, \tag{2.8}$$

where $[h(z)]_{-k}$ denotes that part of $h(z)$ containing powers of z greater than or equal to $-k$, and as $k \to \infty$ we obtain the symmetric filter

$$f_\infty(z) = \frac{\sigma_v^2|\phi_c(z)\theta_s(z)|^2}{\sigma_\varepsilon^2|\beta(z)|^2}. \tag{2.9}$$

These results, as treated extensively by Whittle (1963), rested initially on an assumption of stationarity and a semi-infinite sample $\{Y_\tau;\ \tau \le t + k\}$. Cleveland and Tiao (1976) and Pierce (1979) considered extensions to difference-stationary processes, and Burridge and Wallis (1988) showed that the same filters can be obtained more generally as the steady-state Kalman filters under appropriate assumptions on initial conditions.

2.3 Model specification

In seeking unobserved-components models that lend a signal-extraction interpretation to the X-11 filters, we postulate various possible forms of the component models (2.5) and in each choose particular parameter values by matching the corresponding signal-extraction filters to the X-11 filters by numerical methods. Since the signal-extraction filters are defined in (2.4) as filters that estimate the seasonal component, the correspondence we seek is

$$a_k(L) = 1 - f_k(L), \tag{2.10}$$

where the $a_k(L)$ are X-11 filters defined in (23) and where $f_k(L)$ are given, for particular component model specifications, by (2.8). In this section we discuss various criteria that guide the selection of such specifications.

First, preliminary investigation indicated the need to incorporate differencing and seasonal differencing operators, $(1 - L)$ and $(1 - L^{12})$, respectively, in accordance with the common empirical identification of the composite model (2.6) with the Box–Jenkins seasonal ARIMA model. Following Cleveland (1972), Box, Hillmer, and Tiao (1978), Burman (1980), and Hillmer and Tiao (1982), we factor the seasonal difference operator as

$$1 - L^{12} = (1 - L)(1 + L + L^2 + \ldots + L^{11})$$
$$= (1 - L)U(L), \tag{2.11}$$

and assign $(1 - L)$ and $U(L)$ to the trend-cycle and seasonal autoregressive operators, respectively. Whereas the seasonal difference operator $(1 - L^{12})$ produces spikes in the pseudospectrum at frequencies $j\pi/6$, $j = 0, \ldots, 6$, the factorization identifies the peak at the origin with the ordinary difference operator $(1 - L)$ and properly associates it with a nonseasonal component. This also conforms to the assumption of the previous section that $\phi_c(L)$ and $\phi_s(L)$ have no common factor. Pierce (1979) showed that application of a filter corresponding to (2.8) to a series in which signal and noise processes share a common unit root yields a signal estimate with unbounded variance, whereas in the Kalman-filter context Burridge and Wallis (1988) showed that conditions for the convergence of the signal-extraction error variance exclude the existence of an unstable common factor—such a factor representing an 'undetectable' case, using the state-space terminology.

A second consideration for the autoregressive specification arises from the fact that in (2.10), $a_k(L)$ is a polynomial in L of finite degree whereas $f_k(L)$ is infinite. In seeking models for which the equivalence holds we ignore the remote coefficients of $f_k(L)$ and fit only the $m + k + 1$ nonzero coefficients of $a_k(L)$. In general, models with a predominantly autoregressive specification—so called 'bottom-heavy' models—generate long signal-extraction filters that are not able to approximate the relatively rapid decline of the X-11 filter coefficients, especially at multiples of 12 lags. Thus, whereas in empirical modeling of observed time series one is often indifferent between enhancing an inadequate model on the autoregressive or the moving-average side, in the present context there is a clear preference for top-heavy or moving-average-dominated specifications. Following Cleveland (1972) and Cleveland and Tiao (1976), the moving-average operator $\theta_s(L)$ is written as a polynomial in L^{12}, as in the conventional Box–Jenkins seasonal specification, again ensuring a top-heavy specification.

Third, although in practical time-series analysis a three-component decomposition may be useful—identifying, in particular, an irregular component to assist the analysis of outliers—we note that this may not be possible in the present context. To see the difficulty, consider the symmetric filter (2.9), whose denominator is given as the right side of (2.7). The first and third terms do not appear in the numerator of the filter, and with $\phi_s(L) = U(L)$ as defined in (2.11) and $\phi_c(L) = (1 - L)^d$, we may write these as

$$\sigma_u^2|\phi_s(z)\theta_c(z)|^2 + \sigma_w^2|\phi_c(z)\sigma_s(z)|^2$$
$$= |U(z)|^2\{\sigma_u^2|\theta_c(z)|^2 + \sigma_w^2|(1 - z)^d|^2\}. \qquad (2.12)$$

The moving-average operator $\theta_c(L)$ is a polynomial of degree q with coefficients to be determined, and if $q \geq d$, then multiple sets of values of these coefficients give the same filter, in each case being accompanied by appropriate variations in the white-noise variances. That is, (2.12) is also equal to

$$|U(z)|^2\{\tilde{\sigma}_u^2|\tilde{\theta}_c(z)|^2 + \tilde{\sigma}_w^2|(1 - z)^d|^2\},$$

with $\tilde{\sigma}_u^2 > 0$, $\tilde{\sigma}_w^2 > 0$. Thus an emphasis on top-heavy or balanced models for C_t, together with a white-noise specification for I_t, precludes separate identification of their models from the filter coefficients; when this occurs, we report a model for the composite nonseasonal element $N_t = C_t + I_t$. If $q < d$, this problem does not arise, because the higher-order terms of the polynomial in braces determine σ_w^2, and there is then only one solution for σ_u^2 and $\theta_c(z)$. Equivalently, note that the sum of an ARMA (p,q) process and an independent white-noise process has an ARMA (p,q) representation provided that $p \leq q$. (The possibility of arbitrarily allocating white noise to the seasonal component, which arises in the empirical identification of components from a given composite model for an observed series, and which may be ruled out by an arbitrary *minimum variance* or 'canonical' assumption (Box, Hillmer, and Tiao (1978); Hillmer and Tiao (1982)) does not occur in the present case, where a given filter determines the variance ratio $\sigma_v^2/\sigma_\varepsilon^2$).

For each model specification of a given form, we find the parameter values that minimize the unweighted sum of squared differences between the X-11 coefficient and those of the truncated signal-extraction-based adjustment filter by numerical methods. That is, over the $m + k + 1$ coefficients of $a_k(L)$, we seek to make (2.10) hold as closely as possible in this sense. Our least squares criterion differs from those used by Cleveland (1972) and Cleveland and Tiao (1976) in two respects. First, the 'X-11' filter used by Cleveland omits the intermediate adjustments of the estimated seasonal components (steps c and g in Wallis's description) and is truncated after 42 terms. Second, Cleveland and Tiao fit their model to this truncated seasonal filter and to the corresponding trend filter simultaneously, whereas we fit only the seasonal-adjustment filter. Our results extend the work of these authors by estimating a wider class of models and by fitting these models to two of the asymmetric filters, $a_0(L)$ and $a_{12}(L)$, in addition to the symmetric filter, $a_{84}(L)$. This enables us to test whether the same model emerges from the single-extraction interpretation of these filters—hence whether the X-11 filters are internally consistent in this sense.

3.   Estimation Results

3.1 Introduction

It is clear from Figures 1–3 that the X-11 filters are dominated by their seasonal weights, so models whose optimal signal extraction filters match these principal characteristics tend to give a good overall fit. For example, the elementary model

$$(1 - L)C_t = u_t, \quad U(L)S_t = v_t, \quad I_t = w_t,$$

with appropriately chosen innovation variance ratios, achieves a residual sum of squares of .023 against the sum of squares of the $a_{84}(L)$ coefficients of .785. Although we can thus say that it accounts for 97.1 per cent of the variation in the weights, we see in Section 3.2 that slightly more elaborate models are able to reduce substantially the residual sum of squares.

Our calculations were organized as follows. Working with a three-component specification, we normalized on the irregular variance $(\sigma_w^2 = 1.0)$ and tested various seasonal and cyclical specifications, in each case calculating the values of the parameters, including σ_u^2 and σ_v^2 that gave the best fit. As noted in Section 2.3, the seasonal-component models have $\phi_s(L) = U(L)$ and $\theta_s(L)$, a polynomial of degree Q, in L^{12}. Preliminary investigations led to cyclical component models having $\phi_c(L) = (1 - L)^d$, since estimation of unrestricted autoregressions in general resulted in unit roots being found; $\theta_c(L)$ is a general (but invertible) moving-average operator of degrees q. If $q \geq d$, the decomposition of the nonseasonal into cyclical and irregular components is not unique, as noted previously, but this difficulty is avoided at the estimation stage by assigning a convenient value to the cyclical innovation variance.

Within the range of possibilities thus delineated, the choice of a final model is guided by the same considerations that conventionally apply in the empirical modeling of observed time series. A given model is extended if adding a further parameter achieves a substantial reduction in residual sum of squares. If the additional parameter, however, results only in a marginal improvement, a preference for simple, parsimonious models leads us back to the initial specification.

3.2 Models for $a_0(L)$, $a_{12}(L)$, and $a_{84}(L)$

The specification eventually chosen, for each of these three filters, has $d = 2$, $q = 2$, and $Q = 2$. Reducing the order of either moving-average specification substantially increases the residual sum of squares, whereas including a third parameter causes only a slight decrease. A closely competing specification has $d = 1$, $q = Q = 2$, but this results in a combined residual sum of squares some 10 per cent greater.

For the one-sided filter, $a_0(L)$, the preferred model is

$$U(L)S_t = (1 + 1.00L^{24})v_t,$$

$$(1 - L)^2 N_t = (1 - 1.43L + .70L^2)\eta_t,$$

$$\sigma_v^2/\sigma_\eta^2 = .018, \text{RSS} = .041$$

original sum of squares $= .931$.   (3.1)

The coefficients in $\theta_s(L)$ are estimated, but the coefficient of L^{12} is nonzero only in its fourth decimal place, aand it is not reported. The associated signal-extraction adjustment filter, $\tilde{a}_0(L)$, and its transfer function are plotted in Figure 4. We find that of the three filters considered, the goodness of fit is poorest in the one-sided case, principally because in the X-11 filter (Figure 1), the weight at lag 24 is greater than that at lag 12, whereas in the signal extraction filters such weights decline smoothly. This feature of X-11 is possibly due to the ad hoc adjustment of end weights of some of the component moving averages, which has been remarked upon elsewhere (Kenny and Durbin (1982) and Wallis (1983)).

For the asymmetric filter $a_{12}(L)$, the performed model is

$$U(L)S_t = (1 + .33L^{12} + .99L^{24})n_t,$$

$$(1 - L)^2 N_t = (1 - 1.55L + .82L^2)\eta_t,$$

$$\sigma_v^2/\sigma_\eta^2 = .026, \quad \text{RSS} = .017,$$

original sum of squares $= .717$.   (3.2)

The coefficients and transfer function of the associated filter $\tilde{a}_{12}(L)$ are plotted in Figure 5. A particular feature of the transfer function for the X-11 filter $a_{12}(L)$ (Figure 2) is that it does not appear to represent a

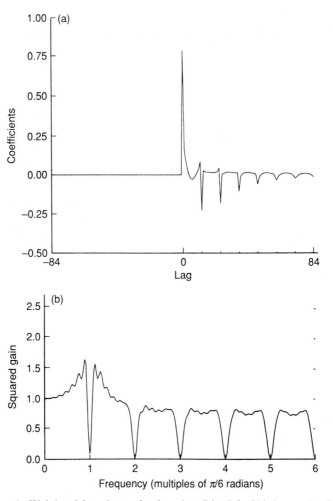

FIG. 4. Weights (a) and transfer function (b) of $\tilde{a}_0(L)$ for model (3.1).

step in a gradual transition from the one-sided to the symmetric filter: the characteristic oscillations between the seasonal frequencies are absent, the seasonal dips cover a wide frequency band, and the initial departure from 1 occurs at a lower frequency. It is interesting that the transfer function of $\tilde{a}_{12}(L)$ has the same appearance, thus these features seem to be associated with the lag-12 filter, even when it is an optimal signal extraction filter for a model of the same form as (3.1).

For the symmetric filter $a_{84}(L)$, the preferred model is

$$U(L)S_t = (1 + .71L^{12} + 1.00L^{24})v_t,$$

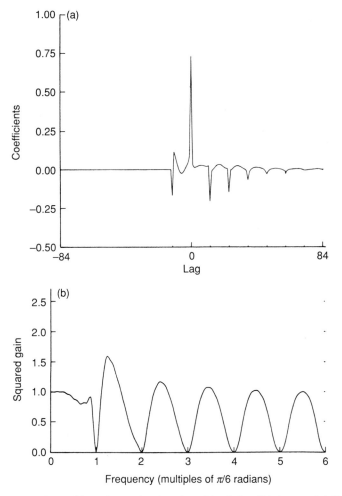

FIG. 5. Weights (a) and transfer function (b) of $\tilde{a}_{12}(L)$ for model (3.2).

$$(1 - L)^2 N_t = (1 - 1.59L + .86L^2)\eta_t,$$

$$\sigma_v^2/\sigma_\eta^2 = .017, \quad \text{RSS} = .0036,$$

$$\text{original sum of squares} = .785. \qquad (3.3)$$

It is in this case that the closest match of a signal-extraction filter to an X-11 filter is achieved, and the coefficients and transfer function of $\tilde{a}_{84}(L)$ are plotted in Figure 6 for comparison with those of $a_{84}(L)$ in Figure 3. The important coefficients in the X-11 filters and in those corresponding to models (3.1)–(3.3) are given in Table 1. Only in the

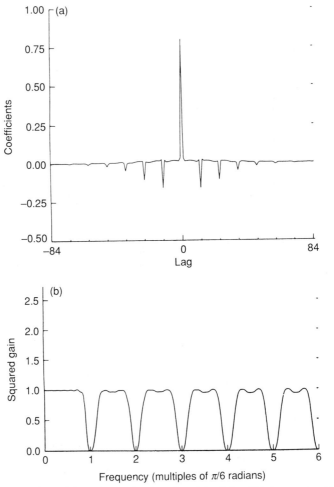

FIG. 6. Weights (a) and transfer function (b) of $\tilde{a}_{84}(L)$ for model (3.3).

lag 24 weight of $a_0(L)$ do the X-11 and the fitted weights differ in the first decimal place.

The composite model for the observed series corresponding to these unobserved-components models is

$$(1 - L)(1 - L^{12})Y_t = \beta(L)\varepsilon_t, \qquad (3.4)$$

where the moving-average operator $\beta(L)$, is of degree 26. Its coefficients are given, for each of the three cases, in Table 2. Whereas the higher-order coefficients are negligible, intermediate coefficients at lags 2–11 are not; thus the common multiplicative specification $(1 - \theta L)$ $(1 - \theta L^{12})$ can only be an approximation to $\beta(L)$. Simple specifications

TABLE 1.   Principal coefficients in X-11 and approximating filters

Lag	$a_0(L)$	$\widetilde{a}_0(L)$	$a_{12}(L)$	$\widetilde{a}_{12}(L)$	$a_{84}(L)$	$\widetilde{a}_{84}(L)$
−84					*	*
−72					*	*
−60					*	−.01
−48					*	−.02
−36					−.06	−.05
−24					−.12	−.11
−12			−.14	−.17	−.18	−.16
0	.84	.79	.75	.73	.82	.80
12	−.28	−.23	−.26	−.21	−.18	−.16
24	−.29	−.18	−.19	−.15	−.12	−.11
36	−.16	−.11	−.07	−.07	−.06	−.05
48	−.01	−.06	−.01	−.03	*	−.02
60	*	−.04	*	−.01	*	−.01
72	*	−.02	*	−.01	*	*
84	*	−.02	*	*	*	*

* A coefficient less than .01 in absolute value.

for the component models typically do not yield simple overall models! The three composite models are rather similar, and in broad outline they also correspond to the model of Cleveland and Tiao (1976) although their decomposition into seasonal and nonseasonal components is somewhat different.

Comparing the component models, we note that the moving-average specifications are more similar than might appear at first sight. Each moving-average operator has a pair of complex conjugate roots, and expressing these in polar form gives the modulus and angle as presented in Table 3. To consider the impact of these differences in parameter values together with the observed variations in variance ratios, we calculate the residual sum of squares in fitting to each of the three X-11 filters the signal extraction filters associated with each of the estimated models (3.1)–(3.3), with the results presented in Table 4. The *diagonal* element is the smallest in each column, representing the best-fitting model already chosen, but we see that the alternative estimated models fit a given filter relatively well, models (3.2) and (3.3) being rather close together and fitting better overall than model (3.1). The perceived differences between the estimated models indicate that with a signal-extraction interpretation, the X-11 filters are not internally consistent. Nevertheless, these differences are seen to be slight, indicating that the inconsistency is not great, although the fact that $a_0(L)$ is the outlier among the three filters considered is a matter for concern, given that

TABLE 2. Coefficients of the composite moving-average operator $\beta(L) = 1 + \beta_1 L + \ldots + \beta_{26} L^{26}$ for component models (3.1)–(3.3)

Lag	(3.1)	(3.2)	(3.2)
1	−.53	−.64	−.67
2	.28	.30	.29
3	.23	.23	.23
4	.23	.22	.22
5	.22	.22	.21
6	.22	.21	.20
7	.21	.20	.20
8	.21	.20	.19
9	.20	.19	.19
10	.19	.18	.18
11	.14	.13	.12
12	−.43	−.33	−.33
13	.45	.44	.45
14	*	.02	.02
15	*	*	*
16	*	*	*
17	*	*	*
18	*	*	*
19	*	*	*
20	*	*	*
21	*	*	*
22	*	*	*
23	−.01	−.01	−.01
24	.05	.05	.04
25	−.04	−.05	−.04
26	.01	.02	.01
$\sigma_v^2/\sigma_\varepsilon^2$	0.12	0.16	0.11

* A coefficient less than .01 in absolute value.

TABLE 3. Analysis of component moving-average operators

Model	Seasonal MA		Nonseasonal MA	
	Modulus	Angle	Modulus	Angle
(3.1)	.999	$.50\pi$	.824	$.83\pi$
(3.2)	.997	$.45\pi$	.910	$.82\pi$
(3.3)	.999	$.38\pi$	.930	$.83\pi$

TABLE 4. Residual sum of squares in fitting models (3.1), (3.2), and (3.3) to $a_0(L)$, $a_{12}(L)$, and $a_{84}(L)$

| Model | X-11 Filter | | |
	$a_0(L)$	$a_{12}(L)$	$a_{84}(L)$
(3.1)	.0413	.0236	.0151
(3.2)	.0547	.0168	.0043
(3.3)	.0561	.0175	.0036

public attention is usually focused most heavily on the first-announced seasonally adjusted figure and that less attention is usually given to subsequent revisions.

Our finding that models with $q = Q = 2$ and $d = 1$ are close competitors, at their best-fitting parameter values, to the models (3.1)–(3.3) and that much simpler models can also fit well suggests a certain robustness of the X-11 filters in this context. To investigate this further within the framework of our preferred model specification, we have studied the sensitivity of the residual sum of squares to parameter variation. Increasing (decreasing) the variance ratio σ_v^2/σ_η^2 both shortens (lengthens) the signal-extraction filter and decreases (increases) the weight at lag 0. This reflects two effects: first, that if the seasonal pattern changes rapidly, then observations at remote lags contain less information relevant to its estimation, and second, that as the relative contribution of the nonseasonal component to the overall variation in the series is reduced, so the lag 0 weight is driven towards zero. Since it is the rather small variance ratio that makes the higher-order coefficients in the composite moving average $\beta(L)$ negligible (Table 2), this suggests that the optimal signal-extraction interpretation of X-11 does not hold up well for composite models with moving-average specifications of an order higher than the widely used $(1 - \theta L)(1 - \theta L^{12})$. With respect to the moving-average parameters, we have considered variations in their values accompanied by compensating variations in the innovation variances that keep the variance of $U(L)S_t$ and $(1 - L)^2 N_t$ in the same proportion. Then the goodness of fit is more sensitive to changes in the nonseasonal moving-average parameters, so much so that the roots of the seasonal moving-average operator can be driven quite close to zero without dramatically worsening the fit. Again this is a reflection of the variance ratio, and corresponding variations in the nonseasonal moving-average parameters have a greater effect on the composite moving average $\beta(L)$, suggesting that the appropriateness of X-11 for a series adequately represented by the seasonal ARIMA $(0, 1, 1) \times (0, 1, 1)_{12}$

specification would depend on the similarity of its key parameters to those given in Table 2.

The X-11 program does provide some flexibility in the treatment of series with relatively stable or unstable seasonal components, however, and the importance of the variance ratio in shaping the signal-extraction filters is further illustrated by the models for two of the nonstandard X-11 options reported in the Appendix.

4. Conclusion

Models (3.1)–(3.3) represent data-generation processes for which seasonal adjustment (at lags 0, 12, and 84, respectively) is accomplished virtually optimally, in a linear least squares sense, by the X-11 program. Our analysis extends previous work by considering asymmetric X-11 filters and the symmetric 'historical' filter and by searching over a wider class of models. Some divergence from results is also expected as we concentrate exclusively on the seasonal adjustment filter, unlike Cleveland (1972) and Cleveland and Tiao (1976), who included the trend filter in their fitting exercises.

The overall model for the observed series implied by these component models is similar in broad outline to that of Cleveland and Tiao, although there are differences in detail. In particular, since in our models β_{13} is *greater* in absolute value than β_{12}, the common multiplicative specification $(1 - \theta L)(1 - \theta L^{12})$ is a less-appropriate approximation. Greater differences, however, are to be found in the specification of the components. The use of both trend and seasonal filters allows Cleveland and Tiao to specify a three-component model whereas in the context of our preferred forms fitting the seasonal filter alone permits only a two-component specification. Our seasonal component incorporates the autoregressive operator $U(L) = 1 + L + \ldots + L^{11}$, whereas theirs has the seasonal difference $1 - L^{12}$. Although the process of specifying the components has some essentially arbitrary elements, our choice avoids associating a spectral peak at the origin with the seasonal component and, given that the nonseasonal autoregression includes the factor $(1 - L)$, ensures that the signal-extraction error variance converges to a finite limit, both of which seem reasonable. Thus we suggest that the models (3.1)–(3.3) should replace that of Cleveland and Tiao as the standard interpretation of X-11 in a pure seasonal-adjustment context. Since these models are not identical and the X-11 filters are not internally consistent in a signal-extraction sense, strictly speaking, the particular model (3.1), (3.2), or (3.3) to be adopted as a justification of X-11 depends on whether one is considering the adjustment of current data, of one-year-old data, or of historical data.

When amendments or extensions to existing procedures are proposed, it is conventional to evaluate them by studying their effects on a sample of real or artificial time series. Our results enable us to predict the results of comparisons between model-based signal extraction methods of seasonal adjustment and X-11: for data well described or generated by the models of Section 3, few differences will be observed. To demonstrate an advantage of a signal extraction method over X-11, it will be necessary to choose data of a considerably different form.

Acknowledgements

The computational assistance of Paul Fisher and the helpful comments of J. P. Burman, W. P. Cleveland, and two referees are gratefully acknowledged. This research was supported by a grant from the Social Science Research Council.

Appendix

Section 3 presents the approximating models for the X-11 filters, assuming standard options. In this Appendix these models are reestimated as approximations to two nonstandard options, specifically for X-11 filters using 3×3 or 3×9 seasonal filters. In the description of Wallis (1982, p. 79), this concerns step f, in which a weighted seven-term MA (3×5) is applied to each month separately to estimate the seasonal component. Here it is replaced by a weighted five-term (3×3) or 11-term (3×9) MA respectively. The asymmetric MAs used at the ends of the series are given in Appendix B, Table 1B and 1D, respectively, of the X-11 manual (Shiskin, Young, and Musgrave (1967)). In section VIII of the manual these options arise at Table D10 and replace an automatic selection that was made in the X-10 variant basis of the moving seasonality ratio. If an estimated seasonal component is changing more (less) rapidly than is accommodated by the standard option, then the use of the shorter (longer) MA is indicated. (In the limit, if the seasonal component appears very stable, then it can be best estimated by averaging the estimated seasonal plus irregular over the whole sample for each month separately.) Since the averages are applied to each month separately, changing from a seven-term MA to a five-term or an 11-term MA changes the value of m, the half-length of the symmetric filter, from 84 to 72 or 108.

Retaining the specification $d = 2$, $qp = 2$, and $Q = 2$ and reestimating the moving average parameters and variance ratios gives the models in Table 5. In each case the best fit is achieved for the symmetric filter, and the one-sided filter fits least well, as with the standard option. The three models differ in detail, again indicating some inconsistency in these filters. In fact the variation in the variance ratio, σ_v^2/σ_η^2, across a_0, a_{12}, and a_m is greater in the 3×3 case than in the 3×9 case and the standard case of Section 3; thus the inconsistency is greatest in the shortest filter.

TABLE 5. Models for nonstandard options

Filter	TSS	RSS	Seasonal MA			Nonseasonal MA			σ_v^2/σ_η^2	RSS (standard model)	
			L^0	L^{12}	L^{24}	L^0	L^1	L^2			
3×3											
a_0	.863	.035	1	.65	.99	1	-1.33	.61	.024	.058	(3.1)
a_{12}	.574	.012	1	.85	.99	1	-1.43	.70	.063	.028	(3.2)
a_{72}	.625	.001	1	.65	.65	1	-1.53	.81	0.86	.019	(3.3)
a_0	.907	.024	1	.07	.99	1	-1.55	.80	.009	.032	(3.1)
a_{12}	.770	.013	1	-.32	1.00	1	-1.59	.86	.017	.028	(3.2)
a_{108}	.887	.007	1	-.16	.98	1	-1.62	.88	.010	.031	(3.3)

TABLE. 6. Principal Coefficients in X-11 (3 × 3 option) and Approximating Filters

Lag	$a_0(L)$	$\tilde{a}_0(L)$	$a_{12}(L)$	$\tilde{a}_{12}(L)$	$a_{72}(L)$	$\tilde{a}_{72}(L)$
−72					*	*
−60					*	*
−48					*	*
−36					−.01	−.01
−24					−.10	−.10
−12			−.15	−.18	−.20	−.20
0	.76	.73	.65	.64	.71	.71
12	−.40	−.31	−.28	−.24	−.20	−.20
24	−.23	−.17	−.13	−.11	−.10	−.10
36	−.05	−.07	−.01	−.01	−.01	−.01
48	*	−.03	*	*	*	*
60	*	−.02	*	*	*	*
72	*	−.01	*	*	*	*

* A coefficient less than .01 in absolute value.

TABLE 7. Principal coefficients in X-11 (3 × 9 option) and approximating filters

Lag	$a_0(L)$	$\tilde{a}_0(L)$	$a_{12}(L)$	$\tilde{a}_{12}(L)$	$a_{108}(L)$	$\tilde{a}_{108}(L)$
−108					*	−.01
−96					*	−.01
−84					*	−.01
−72					*	−.02
−60					−.03	−.03
−48					−.07	−.04
−36					−.10	−.06
−24					−.10	−.09
−12			−.12	−.13	−.10	−.10
0	.86	.83	.80	.79	.90	.88
12	−.23	−.19	−.19	−.16	−.10	−.10
24	−.22	−.17	−.16	−.15	−.10	−.09
36	−.17	−.12	−.13	−.10	−.10	−.06
48	−.10	−.08	−.08	−.06	−.07	−.04
60	−.05	−.06	−.03	−.04	−.03	−.03
72	*	−.04	*	−.03	*	−.02
84	*	−.03	*	−.02	*	−.01
96	*	−.02	*	−.01	*	−.01
108	*	−.01	*	−.01	*	−.01

* A coefficient less than .01 in absolute value.

The final column of Table 5 gives the residual sum of squares of the standard option filters reported in Section 3 when fitted to the nonstandard X-11 filters, indicating the improvement achieved by the new estimates and, indeed, that the nonstandard options imply different models. The main differences from the models for the standard option are in the variance ratio, in accordance with the rationale for choosing the nonstandard options, and in the lag-12 coefficient in $\theta_s(L)$. For each of three filters considered, the seasonal component has a relatively larger variance in the 3×3 case than in the standard option and a relatively smaller variance in the 3×9 case.

The important coefficients in these filters are shown in Tables 6 and 7. These again emphasize that it is the one-sided filter that is most difficult to approximate. For example, considering the lag-0 coefficient, it is a property of the model-based adjustment filters for models of this class that this leading coefficient declines in value as one moves from a_m through a_{12} to a_0, but this property is not shared by the X-11 filters.

References

(References marked with a * are included in this volume)

Box, G. E. P., Hillmer, S. C., and Tiao, G. C. (1978), 'Analysis and modeling of seasonal time series', in *Seasonal Analysis of Economic Time Series,* ed. A. Zellner. Washington, DC: US Bureau of the Census, 309–34.

—— and Jenkins, G. M. (1970), *Time Series Analysis, Forecasting and Control.* San Francisco: Holden-Day.

Burman, J. P. (1980), 'Seasonal adjustment by signal extraction', *Journal of the Royal Statistical Society,* Ser. A, **143**, 321–37.

Burridge, P., and Wallis, K. F. (1988), 'Prediction theory for autoregressive-moving average processes', *Econometric Reviews*, **7**, 65–95.

Cleveland, W. P. (1972), *'Analysis and Forecasting of Seasonal Time Series'*, Ph.D. dissertation, University of Wisconsin.

—— and Tiao, G. C. (1976), 'Decomposition of seasonal time series: a model for the census X-11 program', *Journal of the American Statistical Association*, **71**, 581–7.

Grether, D. M., and Nerlove, M. (1970), 'Some properties of "optimal" seasonal adjustment', *Econometrica*, **38**, 682–703.

Hillmer, S. C., and Tiao, G. C. (1982), 'An ARIMA-model-based approach to seasonal adjustment', *Journal of the American Statistical Association*, **77**, 63–70.*

Kenny, P. B., and Durbin, J. (1982), 'Local Trend Estimation and seasonal adjustment of economic and social time series' (with discussion), *Journal of the Royal Statistical Society*, Ser. A, **145** 1–41.

Pierce, D. A. (1979), 'Signal extraction error in nonstationary time series', *Annals of Statistics*, **7**, 1303–20.

Skiskin, J., Young, A. H., and Musgrave, J. C. (1967), *The X-11 Variant of the Census Method II Seasonal Adjustment Program,* Technical Paper 15 (revised), Washington, DC: US Bureau of the Census.

WALLIS, K. F. (1982), 'Seasonal adjustment and revision of current data: linear filters for the X-11 method', *Journal of the Royal Statistical Society*, Ser. A. **145**, 74–85.

—— (1983), 'Models for X-11 and X-11-FORECAST procedures for preliminary and revised seasonal adjustments', in *Applied Time Series Analysis of Economic Data*, ed. A. Zellner. Washington, DC: US Bureau of the Census, 3–11.

WHITTLE, P. (1963), *Prediction and Regulation by Linear Least-Square Methods* London: English Universities Press.

PART IV

MODEL-BASED PROCEDURES

Introduction

The applications of very complex seasonal adjustment procedures like the X-11 which are based on more or less *ad hoc* methods have left many statisticians working with time series uneasy for several reasons. First, the complex nature of the procedures makes it virtually impossible to evaluate the procedures except by looking at the output and input series. Secondly, the extensive use of moving average filters causes endpoint problems which in turn imply often large revisions of the seasonally adjusted data. Thirdly, the black-box nature of the procedure prevents a deeper understanding of the nature and the interdependencies of the seasonal and cyclical components.

In the now classical Box–Jenkins framework (see Box and Jenkins (1970)) the modelling of time series with seasonal components takes place by applying seasonal differences such as $1 - B^4$, $1 - B^{12}$, etc. where B is the lag operator, in addition to the first differences, $1 - B$, in the stationarity producing phase of the procedure. In the next step autoregressive and moving average factors with lags at the seasonal frequencies are added. The final model can then be written as

$$\phi(B)\Phi(B^s)(1 - B)^d(1 - B^s)^D x_t = \theta(B)\Theta(B^s)\varepsilon_t \qquad (1)$$

where $s = 4$ or 12 depending whether the data are quarterly or monthly. $\phi(B)$ and $\theta(B)$ are polynomials in the lag operator B, $\Phi(B^s)$ and $\Theta(B^s)$ are polynomials in the seasonal lag operator B^s, while $\varepsilon_t \sim \text{nid}(0,\sigma^2)$. d and D determine the order of the differencing and seasonal differencing, respectively. As $1 - B^s$ may be factorized as $(1 - B)(1 + B + \ldots B^{s-1})$ the filter $(1 - B)^d(1 - B^s)^D$ can also be written[1] as $(1 - B)^{d+D}(1 + B + \ldots + B^{s-1})^D$, which indicates the potential danger of overdifferencing when using both the filter $1 - B$ and $1 - B^s$.

A slightly different way to represent a univariate time series process was advocated by Nerlove (1967), see also Nerlove, Grether, and Carvalho (1979). Their model is the so-called unobserved components (or UC) model which may be written as

$$x_t = TC_t + S_t + N_t, \qquad N_t \sim \text{nid}(0,\sigma_3^2) \qquad (2)$$

where the trend cycle component TC_t is assumed to be generated by the ARMA process

---

[1] Notice that use of these operators implicitly assumes that the series x_t is integrated at the long-run and seasonal frequencies (see Part V).

$$\phi_c(B)TC_t = \theta_c(B)\varepsilon_{1t} \tag{3}$$

while the seasonal component is represented by

$$\phi_s(B^s)S_t = \theta_s(B^s)\varepsilon_{2t} \tag{4}$$

where $\varepsilon_{it} \sim \text{nid}(0,\sigma_i^2)$, $i = 1,2$ and where the autoregressive parts of (3) and (4) may have roots on the unit circle at the zero frequency, $B = 1$, and at the seasonal frequencies $1/s$, $2/s$, $\ldots$, $(s-1)/s$, etc. respectively. The irregular component N_t is here assumed to be white noise for simplicity, but it could have been a stationary ARMA process.

By application of the concept of an autocovariance generating function[2] it is easy to show (see for instance Hylleberg (1986)) that the UC model in (2), (3), and (4) has a corresponding ARMA representation

$$\alpha(B)x_t = \gamma(B)\varepsilon_t \qquad \varepsilon_t \sim \text{nid}(0,\sigma_\varepsilon^2) \tag{5}$$

with an autoregressive part of order equal to the sum, $p_c + p_s$ (the orders of the autoregressive parts of (3) and (4)) and a moving average part of order $q = \max[q_c + p_s, q_s + p_c, p_c + p_s]$, where the q's indicate the orders of the moving average parts of (3) and (4) respectively.[3] The UC model is thus seen to be a seasonal ARIMA model with parameter constraints which may considerably reduce the number of free parameters. For instance, the UC model of Grether and Nerlove (1970) where $s = 12$, $\phi_c(B) = (1 - \phi_{c1}B)(1 - \phi_{c2}B)$, $\theta_c(B) = 1 + \theta_{c1}B$, $\phi_s(B) = 1 - \phi_{s1}B^{12}$, $\theta_s(B) = 1 + \theta_{s1}B^{12}$ contains five unknown coefficients and two variances (see below), while the corresponding unconstrained ARMA model in (5) is of order $p = 2 + 12 = 14$ and $q = \max[2 + 12, 12 + 1, 2 + 12] = 14$.

From the autocovariance generating function the following relation between the variances can be found

$$\frac{\gamma(z)\gamma(z^{-1})}{\alpha(z)\alpha(z^{-1})}\,\sigma_\varepsilon^2 = \frac{\theta_c(z)\theta_c(z^{-1})}{\phi_c(z)\phi_c(z^{-1})}\,\sigma_1^2 + \frac{\theta_s(z)\theta_s(z^{-1})}{\phi_s(z)\phi_s(z^{-1})}\,\sigma_2^2 + \sigma_3^2 \tag{6}$$

and by inserting $z = \exp(-i2\pi\theta)$ we obtain the result that the spectrum of the observed process is the sum of the spectrum of the unobserved components. The formulation in (6) also indicates that an arbitrary choice has to be made in order to identify the parameters in cases where the ARMA processes for the components are not known. This leads to the so-called canonical decomposition, see Hillmer and Tiao (1982), reprinted below. Their suggestion is to maximize the variation in the

[2] The autocovariance generating function of an ARMA process $\alpha(B)x_t = \gamma(B)\varepsilon_t$, $\varepsilon_t \sim \text{nid}(0,\sigma_\varepsilon^2)$ is $\Gamma(z) = \sigma_\varepsilon^2\,\gamma(z)\gamma(z^{-1})/\alpha(z)\alpha(z^{-1})$, where z is the complex information bearer. In case $z = \exp(-i2\pi\theta)$ $\Gamma(z)$ gives the spectrum of the series.

[3] Notice that an ARIMA model with a lower MA order than AR order does not have a corresponding UC model, see Engle (1978) reprinted below.

irregular component and thereby make the two other components as non-varying or deterministic as possible. Notice that this view of seasonality is at odds with the view advocated in the general introduction by reference to the varying seasonal pattern of the causal variables among other things. However, an alternative procedure in this context may also be difficult to defend. Hillmer and Tiao then propose a procedure where the starting-point is a formulation and estimation of an ARIMA representation followed by an estimation of the components models applying the constraints in (6) as well as the canonical decomposition principle.

In Engle (1978) UC models or UCARIMA models are presented, both with and without exogenous variables. In addition, an ML estimation procedure is suggested based on a formulation of the state space form of the model, and use of the Kalman filter to produce innovations, where the serial correlation characteristics of the data are transformed to a heteroskedasticity problem, thereby easing the formulation of the likelihood function and its subsequent maximization. Basically, what happens is similar to what is obtained by the well-known prediction error decomposition.

In the article by Harvey and Todd (1983), the basic structure of the UC model is (2) with TC_t and S_t assumed to be of the form

$$TC_t = TC_{t-1} - \beta_{t-1} + \eta_t \tag{7}$$

$$\beta_t = \beta_{t-1} + \xi_t \tag{8}$$

$$(1 + B + \ldots B^{s-1})S_t = \omega_t \tag{9}$$

where $\eta_t \sim \text{nid}(0,\sigma_\eta^2)$, $\xi_t \sim \text{nid}(0,\sigma_\xi^2)$, and $\omega_t \sim \text{nid}(0,\sigma_\omega^2)$ are independent. The trend (cycle) component is a random walk with a drift β_{t-1} generated by a random walk mechanism as well. The form of the trend cycle component is thus allowed to change over time. The seasonal component is a seasonally integrated process, see Part V with unit roots at the frequencies $1/s, 2/s, \ldots, (s-1)/s$, which also allows the seasonal pattern to change.

This so-called structural model is also cast in state space form and Maximum Likelihood estimates obtained using the Kalman filter. Several criteria for model evaluation are presented, and especially the forecasting ability of the model is stressed.

From the above discussion of the UC models it is obvious that one of the major challenges is to be able to identify the components models from the reduced form ARIMA model in (5) and furthermore that strong and debatable assumptions must be made. In Engle (1978) and Harvey and Todd (1983) the identification is obtained by constraining coefficients to zero. In Maravall and Pierce (1987) the resolution lies in setting up linear restrictions between the coefficients. In addition,

Maravall and Pierce evaluate the revision and the revision variances caused by future values not being available in the estimation phase.

In the article by Burridge and Wallis (1990), see below, the Kalman filter implementation of the unobserved components model is discussed and compared with the usual Wiener Kolmogorov approach.[4] While the latter is only applicable in the stationary case, the Kalman filter applies even if the series is integrated. However, in order to secure convergence of the updating scheme for the covariance matrix to a unique positive definite matrix the system must be controllable and detectable. The system is controllable if all the lag polynomials in (3) and in (4) have no common factors, and it is detectable if the autoregressive parts of (3) and (4) have no unstable common factors, i.e. factors such as $(1 - \varphi B)$, where $\varphi \geq 1$. But this requirement rules out the use of $(1 - B)$ in $\varphi_c(B)$ and $(1 - B^s)$ in $\varphi_s(B)$ as $(1 - B_s)$ contains $(1 - B)$.

Burridge and Wallis also present the extension of the UC model to a periodic model. In the actual application they allow σ_2^2 to vary over the seasons.[5] The standard way to treat periodic models is to stack the observations for the year and then proceed as in the multivariate case. However, the dimensionality of the model may cause problems unless severe constraints are put on it.

As indicated, the model-based seasonal adjustment procedures have enriched our understanding of the subject of seasonality. However, progress necessitates the integration of economic theory and statistical methods in a more substantive way than has hitherto been the case. In order to accomplish that we must develop the univariate techniques of the model-based procedures into a viable multivariate framework. However, without conditioning assumptions, i.e. assumptions on exogeneity, etc., we may not get far anyway, and here economic theory can play an important role.

References

(References marked with a * are included in this volume)

Box, G. E. P., and Jenkins, G. M. (1970), *Time Series Analysis: Forecasting and Control*. San Francisco, California: Holden-Day.

Burridge, P., and Wallis, K. F. (1990), 'Seasonal adjustment and Kalman filtering: extension to periodic variances', *Journal of Forecasting*, 9, 109–18.*

Engle, R. F. (1978), 'Estimating structural models of seasonality', in *Seasonal Analysis of Economic Time Series*, Proceedings of the Conference on the Seasonal Analysis of Economic Time Series, Washington DC, 9–10 Sept. 1976 (A. Zellner, ed.), US Department of Commerce, Washington DC.

[4] See Whittle (1983).
[5] See also Osborn *et al.* (1988) reprinted in Part V and Hylleberg (1986), chapter 6.

GRETHER, D. M., and NERLOVE, M. (1970), 'Some properties of optimal seasonal adjustment, *Econometrica*, **38**, 682–703.

HARVEY, A. C. and TODD, P. H. J. (1983), 'Forecasting economic time series with structural and Box–Jenkins models: a case study', *Journal of Business and Economic Statistics*, **1**, 299–307.*

HILLMER, S. C., and TIAO, G. C. (1982), 'An ARIMA model based approach to seasonal adjustment', *Journal of the American Statistical Association*, **77**, 63–70.*

HYLLEBERG, S. (1986), *Seasonality in Regression*. Orlando: Academic Press.

MARAVALL, A., and PIERCE, D. A. (1987), 'A prototype seasonal adjustment model', *Journal of Time Series Analysis*, **8**, 177–93.*

NERLOVE, M. (1967), 'Distributed lags and unobserved components of economic time series', in *Ten Economic Essays in the Tradition of Irving Fisher* (W. Fellner *et al.*, eds), 126–69. New York: Wiley.

—— GRETHER, D. M., and CARVALHO, J. L. (1979), *Analysis of Economic Time Series; A Synthesis*. New York: Academic Press.

WHITTLE, P. (1983), *Prediction and Regulation by Linear Least Squares Methods*, 2nd rev. edn., Oxford: Blackwell.

11

Estimating Structural Models of Seasonality

ROBERT F. ENGLE*

Introduction

The intention of this paper is to define and estimate several classes of models of seasonal behavior. A stochastic model will be formulated for each of several unobserved components that then add to give an observed series. The statistical problem is first to choose the appropriate model from the class, then to estimate the unknown parameters of the model, and finally to estimate the values of the unobserved components. When one of the components is a seasonal, the end result is a seasonally adjusted data series.

There are at least three advantages of this approach to seasonal adjustment. *First*, with an explicit statistical model of the seasonal process, it is possible to calculate the properties of different methods and the variances of individual component estimates. *Second*, the method of seasonal adjustment will be tailored to the characteristics of the series, and third, it is possible to incorporate additional information about economic trends and cycles, weather, strikes, and holidays which will help distinguish seasonal from nonseasonal behavior and will provide means for automatically correcting for phenomena that are normally treated as outliers.

This approach to seasonal adjustment was introduced by Grether and Nerlove (1970), following the similar discussions in Nerlove (1967; 1972). The Grether–Nerlove study assumed that not only the true model

* The author is indebted to Edwin Kuh at the NBER Computer Research Center for research support on the Troll system, to Kent Wall for advice on the Kalman filtering facilities, and to the colleagues at UCSD for many helpful suggestions. Clive W. J. Granger, Allan Andersen, Terence Wales, and David Hendry all made particular contributions. In addition, Ken Wallis, Arnold Zellner, and my discussants, Philip Howrey and Donald Watts, made very helpful comments on the previous draft.

Printed with permission of: *Seasonal Analysis of Economic Time Series* (Zellner, (ed.)), 281–95. Bureau of the Census, Washington.

but even the parameter values were known. Based on these data, the optimum seasonal adjustment filter was calculated as a signal extraction problem.

Four problems make implementation of this procedure formidable. *First* is the assumption that the model and parameters are all known or that they are valid for every series. *Second*, the calculations involved in deriving the filter are quite difficult and are different for each model. *Third*, the technique is limited to stationary processes and will not easily incorporate causal series or nonstationary means. *Finally*, the filters are generally infinite in length so there is a truncation problem and a difficulty with the initial values.

Pagan (1973*a–c*), in extending this approach, has estimated the parameters of the Grether–Nerlove model and has suggested the desirability of using Kalman filtering techniques to estimate the unobserved components. However, he did not compare these procedures with alternatives and did not adapt his methods to problems with causal variables.

In the second section of this paper, a class of seasonal unobserved component models without causal variables is defined. The third section describes the Kalman filter and its application to extraction of seasonals. The fourth section suggests several estimation procedures which are tried on a simulated series in the fifth section. Here the data are filtered and compared with the X-11 method and with the true nonseasonal component. The sixth section introduces the class of seasonal, unobserved component models with exogenous variables. The estimation and filtering problems are discussed, and, in the seventh section, several unobserved component models are estimated and compared for seasonally unadjusted monthly retail sales.

A Class of Unobserved Component Seasonal Models Without Causal Variables

As the class of integrated autoregressive moving average models (ARIMA) have proved very fruitful for modeling univariate time series (see Box and Jenkins (1976)), they form ideal models for unobserved components. A wide class of models can be derived by assuming that a seasonal variable and a nonseasonal variable each follow an ARIMA model of some form with independent innovations, and that their sum plus, perhaps, a white-noise term, is an observable data series. This additive decomposition applies, without loss of generality, to a purely multiplicative model by letting the components be logarithms of the multiplicative factors. Thus far, the distributional properties of the disturbances have not been specified. However, mixed additive-multiplicative models or models that change over the sample period are more difficult. (See Durbin and Kenny (0000) for an example.) If a data series y is assumed to be additively composed of a seasonal component s, a nonseasonal component x and an irregular component ε_y, then in terms of the lag operator L, the model can be written

$$y = s + x + \varepsilon_y \tag{1}$$

$$(1 - L)^{d_x} A_x(L)x = B_x(L)\varepsilon_x \tag{2}$$

$$(1 - L')^{d_s} A_s(L')s = B_s(L')\varepsilon_s. \tag{3}$$

Here, the x process is ARIMA (p_x, d_x, q_x), where p_l and q_l are the orders of the lag polynomials A_x and B_x, respectively. The seasonal s also follows an ARIMA process but in terms of r-period lags where r is the period of the seasonal. A particular member of this class can be characterized by the parameters of each of the processes and the relative variances of the epsilons. The defining characteristic of the seasonal is that it depends only upon the rth lags. This turns out not to be the assumption used in the work of Grether and Nerlove, although there is no reason why one could not expand the specification of the seasonal to include a first-order moving average if there were reasonable a priori reasons to expect that the seasonal would have such a term.

This class of unobserved components autoregressive-moving average models (UCARIMA) will be considered the class of structural models. Corresponding to each structural model (which has unobserved endogenous variables) is a reduced form model that includes only observable variables. This reduced form model will also be an ARIMA model, which can be easily estimated using familiar techniques. *However, the statistical problem is to identify the form of the structural relations and to identify and estimate the parameters of these relations.* These parameters are required for the construction of the filter that will ultimately estimate the values and distribution of the unobserved components. Unlike the forecasting problem, where only the reduced form parameters are required, the seasonal adjustment process depends upon estimation of the structure.

The reduced form corresponding to the structural relations (1)–(3) is derived by premultiplying the first equation by the operators on the left of equations (2) and (3) and substituting to obtain

$$(1 - L)^{d_x}(1 - L')^{d_s} A_x(L)A_s(L')y = (1 - L)^{d_x} A_x(L)B_s(L^x)\varepsilon_s$$
$$+ (1 - L')^{d_s} A_s(L')B_x(L)\varepsilon_x$$
$$+ (1 - L)^{d_x}(1 - L')^{d_x} A_x(L)A_s(L')\varepsilon_y. \tag{4}$$

The error term of this model is a very complicated function of unknown parameters, which has been called by Pagan (1973a) a composite error term. However, it has the property that after a certain number, q_{max}, all the autocorrelations will be identically zero. Anderson (1971) has proven that any process with this characteristic has an invertible moving average representation of order q_{max}. For the UCARIMA class described here, q_{max} is given by

$$q_{max} = \max(d_x + p_x + q_s r, d_s r + p_s r + q_x, d_x + d_s r + p_x + p_s r) \quad (5)$$

as long as all of the variances are nonzero. If one of the variances is zero, then its term is merely eliminated from the maximum in obvious fashion.

Equation (4) is, therefore, a seasonal ARIMA model with differencing of orders d_I and d_s, of the nonseasonal and seasonal, respectively, multiplicative autoregressive errors of order p_I and p_s, and a moving average of order q_{max}. In Box and Jenkins' notation, this is $p = p_x$, $P = p_s$ $d = d_x$, $D = d_s$, $q = q_{max}$, $Q = 0$. It is important to notice that, although the autoregressive part is a multiplicative model, the moving average part is not a multiplicative model of seasonal and nonseasonal parts. *The normal multiplicative constraint* is not true.

How general is the class of UCARIMA models, or, in other words, is there at least one UCARIMA model corresponding to any observable ARIMA process? If the variances of the innovations are allowed to be zero, then there always exists trivially a member of UCARIMA corresponding to an ARIMA model. If, however, the variances are restricted to be nonzero, there are many ARIMA models without a structural counterpart. *In particular, any model with moving average order less than the auto-regressive order would not have an UCARIMA* counterpart. The appearance of such models in empirical work suggests that either, through the search for parsimonious models, some nonzero moving average coefficients are set to zero or that the variances of some components may be zero. Alternatively, perhaps other models, such as the causal models (to be discussed later in this paper) are the true generating equations to which the ARIMA model is merely a good approximation.

A second question is whether there may be *more than one structural relation* corresponding to a particular reduced form model, or, in other words, is the structural model always identified if the reduced form is known? There are many cases where the structural model is underidentified, either through the parameters not being uniquely derivable from the reduced form parameters or that even the form of the structural model is not identified.

Underidentified models are considered by both Pierce (1978) and Box, Hillmer, and Tiao (1978). In each case, only one structural formulation would give the observed reduced form, however, several possible parameter values were consistent with this model. Each employed the principle of minimum variance for the seasonal component to identify this parameter.

When ARIMA models of order greater than one or models with three components are used, it is quite common that the reduced form is overidentified. In this case, there are parameter restrictions among the reduced form parameters that could be imposed. If these overidentifying restrictions are imposed, generally improved estimates of the reduced form will be achieved, and a unique structural model can be obtained from the reduced form parameters. If the restrictions are not imposed, the estimation is less efficient, and the equations relating the reduced form coefficients to the structural parameters will, in general, be inconsistent, leading to no solution. By ignoring some of these equations, of course, an estimate, or several estimates, can be obtained.

In this paper, two overidentified models will be considered. In each case, the estimation problems imposing the restrictions are far greater than those without these restrictions. Furthermore, some of the equations relating the reduced form coefficients to the structural coefficients are far more complicated than the others. Thus, it is natural to ask what loss in efficiency results from not imposing these restrictions and ignoring the complicated transformation equations.

Kalman Filtering

Although the primary purpose of this paper is the estimation of the structural parameters, it is useful first to consider the problem of estimating the values of the unobserved components, *given the true structural model and values of its parameters*. The solution to this problem was initially given by Wiener (1950) and Whittle (1963) and applied by Grether and Nerlove (1970). Based upon the parameters of the model, the weights of the optimum linear time invariant signal extraction filter can be algebraically calculated. *The calculation requires factoring the covariance-generating function that is, in general, a difficult numerical procedure*. In addition, the weights, whether one sided or two sided, will, in general, extend to infinity, and, therefore, there are both truncation and initial-value problems.

Pagan (1975) has suggested that a computationally simpler way to obtain the Wiener filter is *through the use of the Kalman filter*. The Kalman filter, originally introduced into engineering by Kalman (1960) and Kalman and Bucy (1961), is now becoming familiar in economics through work by Taylor (1970), Chow (1975), and many others. It provides a set of recursive formulas which calculate the mean and variance of the unobserved components at each time conditional on a particular information set. If the information set includes all past and current data on the observable variables, then this is the *filtering problem*. If current data are not included, it is a *forecasting problem*, and if future data are included, the problem is called a *smoothing problem*. Additional information, which is generally assumed to be available, is *the mean and variance of the initial conditions*. Commonly, an informative or a diffuse prior distribution is used when such data are not available.

The filtering equations are written recursively to give the best linear unbiased estimate of the unobserved component, one period ahead, based on the similar estimate of the component this period. *In a time invariant problem, the filter weights are not time invariant, because the initial condition introduces transients*. These eventually damp out leaving the time invariant Wiener filter. The Kalman equations, however, are more general than the Wiener formulation of the problem, *since the known parameters of the problem are permitted to change over time, leading to a nonstationary output* time series and, of course, a time-varying filter. This formulation is especially useful when exogenous variables are included in the model.

A brief statement of the Kalman result may be helpful. Without loss of generality, the models in equations (1)–(3) can be rewritten in the state-space formulation. This formulation increases the dimension of the vector of unobserved components, while reducing the problem to a first-order Markov representation plus noise. Letting w_t be a k-dimensional column vector of unobserved states, ϕ a matrix of transition coefficients, and ε_t a vector of disturbances with covariance matrix Q, the state equation is written

$$w_t = \phi w_{t-1} + \varepsilon_t \tag{6}$$

and the observation equation is written

$$y_t = H w_t + \eta_t \tag{7}$$

where y_t is a vector (although, in most of these applications, it is a scalar) of observables, H is a matrix of known constants, and η_t is a vector of disturbances with covariance matrix R. The disturbances are assumed to be Gaussian white-noise processes, and ε and η are uncorrelated. If the errors are not white noise, then the dynamics of the system can be expanded to include this process as well.

As an example, consider the system

$$y = s + x + \varepsilon_y$$
$$s = \alpha s_{-4} + \varepsilon_s$$
$$x = \beta_1 x_{-1} + \beta_2 x_{-2} + \varepsilon_x. \tag{8}$$

For this system, the state vector w must be augmented to convert the transition equation into a first-order system. The matrices have the form

$$w = \begin{pmatrix} x \\ x_{-1} \\ s \\ s_{-1} \\ s_{-2} \\ s_{-3} \end{pmatrix}, \quad \phi = \begin{pmatrix} \beta_1 & \beta_2 & 0 & 0 & 0 & 0 \\ 1 & 0 & 0 & 0 & 0 & 0 \\ 0 & 0 & 0 & 0 & 0 & \alpha \\ 0 & 0 & 1 & 0 & 0 & 0 \\ 0 & 0 & 0 & 1 & 0 & 0 \\ 0 & 0 & 0 & 0 & 1 & 0 \end{pmatrix}$$

$$Q = \begin{pmatrix} \sigma^2_{\varepsilon_x} & & & & \\ & 0 & & & 0 \\ & & \sigma^2_{\varepsilon_s} & & \\ & & & 0 & \\ & 0 & & & 0 \\ & & & & & 0 \end{pmatrix}$$

$$R = \sigma^2_{\varepsilon_y}, \quad H = (101000). \tag{9}$$

Notice that although there are only two unobserved components, the state vector is six dimensional to adjust for the higher order dynamics. If the x equation were generalized to include a first-order moving-average term

$$x = \beta_1 x_{-1} + \beta_2 x_{-2} + \varepsilon_x + \gamma \varepsilon_{x_{-1}}$$

then the first three rows and columns of the w, ϕ, and Q matrices would become

$$w = \begin{pmatrix} x \\ x_y \\ \varepsilon_I \end{pmatrix}, \quad \phi = \begin{pmatrix} \beta_1 & \beta_2 & \gamma \\ 1 & 0 & 0 \\ 0 & 0 & 0 \end{pmatrix}, \quad Q = \begin{pmatrix} \sigma^2_{\varepsilon_I} & 0 & \sigma^2_{\varepsilon_I} \\ 0 & 0 & 0 \\ \sigma^2_{\varepsilon} & 0 & \sigma^2_{\varepsilon_I} \end{pmatrix}.$$

In both these examples, the Q matrix is singular, and, in the last, the ϕ matrix is also singular.

The Kalman filter calculates the conditional expectation and variance of w_t given the Gaussian data $y_1 \ldots y_t$, initial conditions w_0 and V_0 and the parameters of (6) and (7). This is the optimum estimate in terms of minimizing mean-squared error and will be linear in the data. Denoting the *conditional mean and variance* by $w_{t/t}$ and $V_{t/t}$, the essential simplification of the Kalman filtering equations is to recognize that the optimal estimate at time t depends only on the optimal estimate at time $t - 1$, $(w_{t-1/t-1})$ and the new data y_t. The equations have been derived in many sources;[1] thus, only an intuitive explanation for the procedure will be given here.

The proof, however, can be easily motivated by consideration of the joint density of w_t and y_t, conditional on $y_1, \ldots y_{t-1}$. From normality, the expectation of w_t, conditional on y_t (and $y_1, \ldots, y_{t-1}$), is a linear function of the means of w_t and the deviation of y_t from its mean.

That is

$$w_{t/t} = w_{t/t-1} + K_t(y_t - y_{t/t-1})$$

where K_t *is a matrix called the Kalman gain, which depends upon the variances and covariances of the random variables.* As all variance matrices are known at the beginning, K_t does not depend upon the data; however, it is dependent upon t, and, therefore, the Kalman filter is a time-varying linear filter.

The equations that determine K_t as well as $w_{t/t}$ and $V_{t/t}$ are—

1. $w_{t/t-1} = \phi w_{t-1/t-1}$

2. $w_{t/t} = w_{t/t-1} + K_t(y_t - Hw_{t/t-1})$

3. $V_{t/t-1} = \phi V_{t-1/t-1}\phi' + Q$

4. $V_{t/t} = V_{t/t-1} - V_{t/t-1}H'(HV_{t/t-1}H' + R)^{-1}HV_{t/t-1}$

5. $K_t = V_{t/t-1}H'(HV_{t/t-1}H' + R)^{-1}.$ \hfill (10)

For many applications in seasonal adjustment, two-sided filters are desired, since historical data must also be seasonally adjusted and it might be sensible to use subsequent information. It is easy to include a fixed number of future observations in each state estimate. In the example of equation (9), if one wished to calculate $w_{t/t+1}$ so that one future observation would be used in calculating the current estimate, the H matrix could merely be redefined as $H = (0, 1, 0, 1, 0, 0)$. Here there is not even an increase in dimension of the state vector; however, in general, there would be, and, for long fixed leads, this could be very substantial.

The best estimate, based on all the data, is the conditional expectation of the state, given $y_1, \ldots, y_t$. This optimal smoothing problem has well-known solutions (see Engle (1974) for a list of different solutions), but Fraser and Potter (1969) and Mehra (1969) were the first to note a clever formulation of this result, which is implemented in Cooley, Rosenberg, and Wall (1977). The estimate $w_{t/t}$ could be combined with the estimate of a reverse Kalman filter that uses only future data. The two estimates are Gaussian, and, because the innovations are white noise, they are independent. These estimates can be optimally com-

---

[1] See, e.g. Chow (1975).

bined, based on the variances to yield $w_{t/T}$. This estimator is demonstrated to be numerically equal to the optimal smoother. Because the variances are large at the beginning of the sample period, the reverse filter will initially receive most importance, while at the end of the period, the forward estimates will be chosen. This set of smoothed estimates is a two-sided filter, which optimally wraps itself up at each end of the sample period.

A second extension of the Kalman filter, beyond the formulation in (10), is its application to time-varying systems. The recursive formulas can be used equally if ϕ and H, and even Q and R, have time subscripts. In each place, the current matrix is used. This feature fully sets the Kalman filter apart from the signal extraction problem, which cannot deal easily with any type of nonstationarity. In particular, when exogenous variables are introduced in the sixth section, a time-varying ϕ matrix will be needed, since some of its elements will be the data on the exogenous variables.

Estimation of UCARIMA Models

The estimation of unobserved component autoregressive moving average models is a very complicated process. *Several* approaches have been suggested that might be separated into full and limited information methods. The most direct approach, following Schweppe (1965) and Sarris (1974), is to maximize the likelihood under Gaussian assumptions. A direct way to evaluate the likelihood for any set of parameters is available from the Kalman filter output. The log likelihood L is given by Schweppe (1965)

$$L = \text{const} + \sum_{t=1}^{T} (\log \det P_t^{-1} - \mu_t' P_t^{-1} \mu_t)$$

$$\mu_t = y_t - H w_{t/t-1}$$

$$P_t = HV_{t/t-1}H' + R \tag{11}$$

where μ_t is the innovation at time t and P_t is its covariance matrix.

The log likelihood can be maximized, using a variety of algorithms. Pagan (1973b) has applied this technique with a variety of nonlinear optimization methods and finds mixed results, with some preference for a modified Gauss–Newton method but also with satisfactory convergence with the Davidson–Fletcher–Powell algorithm. When the maximum is reached, the estimate is full-information-maximum likelihood, FIML.

An alternative approach, also suggested by Pagan (1973a) is to begin with the reduced form ARIMA version of the model in equation (4). If

all the constraints implicit in the formulation were imposed, the likelihood function would be identical to that in (11), except, perhaps, for
the treatment of starting values that could introduce a Jacobian,
depending on the particular assumptions used. It might be that some
constraints should sensibly be ignored for computational convenience,
since only efficiency and not consistency would be impaired. As mentioned previously, the constraints on the moving average parameters are
very complicated, and there would be substantial savings on computation from ignoring them. Zero restrictions in the moving averages can,
however, easily be imposed, although, generally, these would not be
sufficient to identify a unique structure. The suggestion made here is to
estimate the moving average terms without constraints but *draw the
parameter estimates from the autoregressive coefficients*. The estimates
are, therefore, limited information estimates, since some prior restrictions are not imposed. Pagan's results from the relaxation of the
constraints differed little from his full maximum likelihood estimates.
Although this could be a result of his particular problems, one would
expect, with a large sample, that the estimates would differ little. After
all, if they differed substantially, one might reject the specification.

An Example

In an effort to compare various methods on the same data with a
known-true decomposition, a quarterly unobserved-components time
series was artificially generated, using the following model:

$$
\begin{aligned}
y &= x + s + \varepsilon_y & \alpha &= 0.95 & \sigma_{\varepsilon_y}^2 &= 0.8 & \sigma_y^2 &= 29.3 \\
s &= \alpha s_{-4} + \varepsilon_s & \beta_1 &= 0.75 & \sigma_{\varepsilon_s}^2 &= 0.31 & \sigma_s^2 &= 4.37 \\
x &= \beta_1 x_{-1} + \beta_2 x_{-2} + \varepsilon_1, \beta_2 = 0.2 & & & \sigma_{\varepsilon_x}^2 &= 2.45 & \sigma_x^2 &= 23.4
\end{aligned} \tag{12}
$$

where each of the random variables is independent normal[2] with
observations from 1950 to 1974. An initial seasonal pattern, with a
fourth quarter peak, was used for start values. All calculations were
performed on the Troll computer system.

The Kalman filter was used to estimate the parameter values of the
transition matrix. The parameter estimates were found in five iterations
to be

$$\alpha = 0.99, \; \beta_1 = 0.69, \; \beta_2 = 0.28$$

[2] The random numbers were computed by the SNORM subroutine of the TROLL
system, which essentially uses a polar transformation of uniform variates to obtain normal
random variables. The uniform numbers are obtained from a linear bicongruential
generator that truncates a set of large numbers and then uses a second set to randomly
shuffle the first, thereby eliminating all possibilities of serial dependence.

corresponding to 0.95, 0.75, and 0.2, respectively. These estimates, however, used the true values to start the nonlinear optimization and used true relative variances. Both of these will be unavailable for real data. On the other hand, the initial state, w_0, in this application, was estimated as a parameter vector, assuming a diffuse prior. In an actual application, one could presumably do better.

Two other estimation procedures were used. The Kalman filter maximum likelihood procedure was used to estimate the two relative variances, as well as the three parameters. For this set of data, the maximization algorithm did not converge, since it drove the seasonal variance to zero as the seasonal autoregressive coefficient went to one. The difficulty in estimating the relative variance in a mixture of normal distributions is well known, since the likelihood function has a singularity where the relative variance goes to zero; this appears particularly in economics in the switching regression problem. Here the solution usually proposed is to assume that the relative variance is known or, at least, to bound it away from zero. Thus the assumptions in the estimates of the previous paragraphs seem appropriate.

An alternative solution to this divergence would be to bound the autoregressive parameter away from one. This is sometimes done by including a Jacobian term in the likelihood function, which picks up various assumptions concerning the behavior of the initial values. (See, e.g. Engle (1974).)

A second set of estimates were calculated using the ARIMA formulation of equation (4). The model in this example has a multiplicative seasonal autoregressive component with the nonseasonal of order 2 and the seasonal of order 1. The moving average portion has coefficients to order 6.[3] This process was estimated using the ESP version of Charles Nelson's time series package. The results and the associated standard errors are shown in Table 1.

Notice that the seasonal *ar* parameter is very close to the true value and the nonseasonal *ar* terms, although not very close, are within two standard deviations of the true values. The fitted model has both autoregressive roots positive, while the true model has a large positive root and a small negative one. In both cases, the spectrum has a sharp peak at low frequencies, but, in the true model, it also has a small rise at the high frequency end of the spectrum. The moving average parameters are generally significant with the first and fourth as the largest, as would be expected. The chi-squared statistic for the test of whiteness of residuals is abnormally low, suggesting overfitting of the model. Because there are several constraints overlooked in this estimation, such a result is to be expected.

---

[3] Ken Wallis has pointed out that the third-order term is not zero, as I assumed in an earlier draft.

Robert F. Engle

TABLE 1. Box–Jenkins estimates

$$(1 - \beta_1 L - \beta_2 L^2)(1 - \alpha L^4)y + \delta =$$
$$(1 - \theta_1 L - \theta_2 L^2 - \theta_3 L^3 - \theta_4 L^4 - \theta_5 L^5 - \theta_6 L^6)\varepsilon$$

Coefficient	Value	Standard error
a	0.946	0.048
B_1	1.183	.314
B_2	−.296	.329
θ_1	.738	.307
θ_2	−.286	.246
θ_3	−.031	.145
θ_4	.598	.133
θ_5	−.124	.278
θ_6	−.269	.121
δ	−.002	.049

Note: Chi-square (24) = 6.7 with 14 degrees of freedom.

The means of the unobserved component series were estimated for each of three sets of parameter values, using each of two estimation assumptions. Filtered estimates, which use only past and current data[4] and smoothed estimates that optimally use the entire data set, were used with the true coefficients (true Φ) with the Φ matrix estimated by the Kalman filter that provides full information estimates (FIML Φ) and with the coefficients estimated by Box–Jenkins methods that are limited information estimates, since some parameter restrictions are ignored (BJ Φ). In each of these six cases, the estimated seasonal component was subtracted from the original data to obtain a seasonally adjusted series. These series were compared with the known seasonally adjusted series and with the adjusted series produced by the Census X-11 program in an additive mode with no provision for the exclusion of outliers.

For each of the Kalman filter estimates, the initial values were estimated using Rosenberg's (1973) algorithm. This basically estimates the initial state by assuming a diffuse prior on the mean and then using all the data to form a posterior. The mean and variance of the posterior are then used to initiate the recursive Kalman equations.

A casual inspection of the output suggested that the X-11 method outperformed all alternatives. However, more specific comparisons do not invariably uphold this result. In Table 2, the X-11 output has nearly the highest correlation with the true adjusted series when the whole sample period is considered; however, when the first decade is eliminated, all are about the same. This points out a second characteristic of

---

[4] As will be mentioned, the entire data set is used to estimate the initial state, but, thereafter, only current and past data are used.

TABLE 2. Comparison of estimators

Measure	X-11	True Φ filtered	True Φ smoothed	FIML Φ filtered	FIML Φ smoothed	BJ Φ filtered	BJ Φ smoothed
		January 1950 to April 1974					
Correlation	0.990	0.920	0.982	0.892	0.987	0.984	0.991
Bias	-.37	1.02	1.29	3.58	4.50	-.57	-.37
Standard deviation	.71	1.96	.97	2.25	.83	.89	.69
Root mean-squared error	.80	2.21	1.61	4.23	4.58	1.06	.78
		January 1960 to April 1974					
Correlation	0.991	0.992	0.992	0.991	0.992	0.990	0.992
Bias	-.40	-.02	.86	2.72	4.22	-.84	-.30
Standard deviation	.73	.87	.72	1.58	.72	.80	.69
Root mean-squared error	.84	.87	1.13	3.14	4.28	1.16	.75

the output. The Kalman filtered estimates performed very poorly at the beginning of the sample period. This result is traceable directly to the estimation of the initial state. These estimates were invariably far from the true values and were very sensitive to parameter changes. Furthermore, they have a substantial effect on the estimates for many periods. A clear recommendation of this research will be that more informative priors be used for the initial state.

When the deviations from the true adjusted series are decomposed into bias, standard deviation and root mean-squared error, more substantial differences between the estimators appear. The FIML estimates have very substantial biases that, in turn, dominate the *rms* error figures. Presumably, these are due to the seasonal *ar* coefficient which is so close to unity that a bias in the initial state estimate never disappears. In almost all cases, the biases are significantly different from zero, which is rather surprising in that, at least, the true Φ cases should be unbiased.

In practice, one would probably be less concerned with bias than with variance. In seasonal adjustment, it would be reasonable to impose the mean of the unadjusted series on the adjusted series and, therefore, the bias would be corrected. In terms of the standard deviations, several features are prominent. In each case, the smoothed estimate is superior to the filtered, and, in each case, the results, excluding the first decade, are somewhat better than those of the whole sample period. The ranking of the estimators is, however, rather surprising. The Box–Jenkins estimator is generally better than either the true Φ or the FIML Φ, and, between the latter two, the results are ambiguous. In the standard forecasting problem, where the data being forecast are not used in the estimation, one would expect to do better with the true parameters. This is presumably the expectation here, although a case can be made by analogy with forecasting inside the sample period to expect the fitted model to do better.

In terms of standard deviation around the true value, the X-11 performs quite well in this competition. Although it is never the best, it is superior to all the filtered estimates and, at least across the whole sample period, superior to two of the three smoothed estimates, including the one based upon the true parameters. In terms of *rms* error, it is the second best in both sample periods and far superior to several of the other candidates. This suggests that, even though the X-11 is not specifically designed for the series in this example, it does almost as well as the more specific procedures.

In Table 3, these estimates are examined to see if a linear combination of the X-11 and another process would provide a superior method of seasonal adjustment to either separately. This criterion has been used by Granger (1978) and Nelson (1972). When the whole sample period is used, only the Box–Jenkins estimates contribute to the X-11. When the

TABLE 3.   Regression coefficients in explanation of true adjusted series

Range	Constant	X-11	True Φ filtered	True Φ smoothed	FIML Φ filtered	FIML Φ smoothed	BJ Φ filtered	BJ Φ smoothed
1950 to 1974	0.38	1.01	− 0.02	—	—	—	—	—
	¹(4.2)	(25.0)	(− .37)					
	.51	1.08		—	—	—	—	—
	(2.2)	(8.12)						
	.45	1.01		− .09	− .02	—	—	—
	(2.6)	(29.3)		(− .67)	(− .57)			
	.57	1.04				− .04	—	—
	(.59)	(5.06)				(− .22)		
	.42	.71		—	—	—	.29	.71
	(6.03)	(8.45)					(3.41)	(3.76)
	.38	.31		—	—	—	—	—
	(5.60)	(1.68)						
1960 to 1974	.22	.40	.66	—	—	—	—	—
	(2.1)	(2.0)	(3.1)					
	− .98	− .08		1.04	—	—	—	—
	(− 1.86)	(− .20)		(2.62)				
	− 1.35	.51			.65	—	—	—
	(− 2.3)	(3.2)			(2.9)			
	− 4.8	− .14				1.10	—	—
	(− 2.15)	(− .29)				(2.3)		
	.62	.56		—	—	—	.45	.93
	(5.15)	(4.21)					(3.17)	(2.76)
	.33	.09		—	—	—	—	—
	(3.48)	(1.26)						

— Entry represents zero.   ¹ Standard errors are shown in parentheses.

first decade is eliminated, the importance of the X-11 diminishes sharply and has negative or insignificant weight in each of the smoothed estimates.

The conclusion from this example[5] is that the various methods do relatively equivalently in the latter portion of the sample period. In the early portions, the transients give substantially increased variances to the filtered and smoothed estimates, as well as some appearance of bias. The smoothed estimates perform slighly better, which is not surprising since they use more information, and the methods with estimated parameters appear to perform as well as, if not better than, those with the true values. The Kalman filter does appear to provide a reliable method of seasonal adjustment, at least in terms of variance, but great attention should be given to finding better methods of beginning the procedure. This might substantially improve the estimation capabilities of the filter and allow more information for model identification and diagnostic checking. The nearly comparable performance of X-11, however, casts doubt on the extent of the possible improvement. All of these results, of course, are for one realization from one model and are, therefore, only suggestions for further investigation.

Models with Exogenous Variables

Many of the difficult problems in seasonal analysis have to do with the introduction of additional information about strikes, weather, trading days, holidays, model change dates, etc., as well as information about business cycles, inflation, and other causal influences for a particular series. In order to adapt the analysis of the previous sections of this paper to these fundamentally nonstationary influences, it is only necessary to expand the unobserved component models to include exogenous determinants and, then again, to estimate and infer seasonal patterns. The required tools are, however, somewhat different, especially in the estimation phase.

As an example of the type of problem, consider the seasonal adjustment of fuel oil consumption. Consumption in the winter of 1974 fell below its normal winter peak and, therefore, would appear as a decline in the seasonally adjusted series, suggesting a very large response to the sharp increase in fuel prices. On the other hand, the winter was particularly warm, and, therefore, the seasonal peak was not as high as usual, so perhaps there was very little price responsiveness.

---

[5] In an earlier draft, coherence plots for each series with the true adjusted series were included but gave little grounds for comparison. The causes for this failure are pointed out in the comments by Donald Watts.

Treating weather as a causal variable would help to discriminate between these two possibilities.

This class of models is generated by using transfer function models for each of the unobserved components. Letting Z_l and Z_s be matrices of exogenous variables that determine x and s, equations (1) to (3) can be replaced by

$$y = s + x + \varepsilon_y \tag{13}$$

$$A_x(L)x = C_x(L)Z_x + B_x(L)\varepsilon_x \tag{14}$$

$$A_s(L')S = C_s(L)Z_s + B_s(L')\varepsilon_s \tag{15}$$

where C_l and C_s are matrices of lag polynomials and now B_l and B_s must be interpreted as rational lag polynomials in order to maintain full generality. Differencing operators could still be used to induce stationarity; this is usually not necessary, since the exogenous variables will pick up nonstationarity, leaving the residuals as stationary.

Again, this set of structural equations can be put in the form of a single, more complicated, reduced-form transfer function model in the observed variable y. Premultiplying by the autoregressive operators, this becomes

$$A_x(L)A_s(L')y = A_x(L)C_s(L)Z_s + A_s(L')C_x(L)Z_x$$
$$+ A_x(L)B_s(L')\varepsilon_s + A_s(L')B_x(L)\varepsilon_l + A_x(L)A_s(L')\varepsilon_y. \tag{16}$$

This transfer function has both sets of exogenous variables in it and has constraints implicit between the autoregressive coefficients and the transfer function coefficients. The error term is now an ARMA process, since the B's were postulated to be rational functions of L, and there are likely to be constraints between the coefficients of this process and the other parameters of the model.

The estimation problem for this model might appear to be extremely complicated, and, indeed, it is if all the information is to be used efficiently. However, adopting the strategy that it may be reasonable to ignore some constraints, equation (16) can be thought of as a simple dynamic regression problem with a complicated error structure and some nonlinear constraints between regression coefficients.

Methods for estimating regression models with lagged dependent variables and stationary errors were originally developed by Hannan (1965) and given time domain interpretation by Amemiya and Fuller (1967). The procedure amounts to estimating the spectrum of the disturbances and then transforming all the data to find a regression with white-noise disturbances. To bypass the complications of the lagged dependent variable, this procedure is applied to the equation obtained when the lagged dependent variable is solved out, leaving an infinite lag distribution in the exogenous variables. More recently, Espasa (1975) and Engle (1976) have pointed out that maximum likelihood estimates of the lagged dependent variable model can be obtained directly by iterating until the coefficient estimates generate a residual spectrum, which, in turn, generates the same coefficient estimates. This estimate will be exactly maximum likelihood for some assumptions on the initial missing observation and only asymptotically maximum likelihood otherwise. Presumably, a consistent starting guess is not necessary, since any convergence of the iteration is a solution to the likelihood equations. However, it is more likely that the iterations will converge to the appropriate solution if a consistent start is used.

Having ignored the constraints on the nature of the error process, a reasonable second step consists of testing whether these constraints hold in the data. This can be done in many ways. The procedure, followed here, is rather ad hoc and consists of examining the properties of the untransformed residuals to see if they follow the stochastic process implied by the structural model. A more attractive way of formulating this procedure[6] would be to solve from the autoregressive parameters for the implied spectrum of the disturbances. The residuals transformed by this constrained estimate of their spectrum should be white.

This procedure is to estimate the model without imposing constraints on the disturbance process and then test those constraints. If the test fails, the adequacy of the model is questioned, and a new structural relation must be sought. The end result should be the identification of the structural model and estimation of its parameters.

This estimation and testing procedure is less than fully efficient since a priori information is ignored, It is, again, a limited information procedure. As before, there is surely a full-information maximum likelihood estimation procedure for this problem. One potential method of calculating this estimator is to use the Kalman filter to evaluate the likelihood and then to maximize it with respect to all the parameters. However, at this point, there are far more parameters because of the presence of the exogenous variables with their separate lag structures, and, therefore, one might hesitate to maximize such a complicated function in so many dimensions. Alternatively, Pagan (1973a) has directly calculated the constraints but finds that they help little with his parameter estimates.

Once the identification and estimation steps have been completed, the model can be used to estimate the means of the unobserved components. Again, this can simply be done by the Kalman filter, although now it must also include the exogenous variables. The presence of these variables in the transition equation can either be treated directly or can be treated as a time-varying ϕ matrix, depending on the computer programs available.

---

[6] This alternative was stimulated by Watts' comments.

An Example with Exogenous Variables

As an example, several models of seasonally unadjusted monthly retail sales will be analyzed. The series, titled 'U.S. Total, All Stores', series 0A0100, was for 1953 through the first half of 1975. It was deflated by the trading days of the month, including Saturdays and excluding all major holidays. This was then logged, since the seasonal appeared clearly to be multiplicative.

Two models were postulated and fitted, neither of which appears fully adequate in view of the residuals, but they suggest a range of possibilities. The first assumes that the seasonal has a deterministic portion with some spreading of the spectrum around the seasonals. Twelve seasonal dummies, a twelfth-order autoregression, and the timing of Easter were assumed to reduce the seasonal component to white noise. The seasonal pattern is so regular that a purely nondeterministic model, such as that simulated for the previous example, did not appear appropriate. The nonseasonal component was assumed to depend upon a constant and the log of monthly personal income in current dollars (seasonally adjusted). If the series were not seasonally adjusted, a long moving average or computation of a permanent income measure would be appropriate. In this case, the results, using current income or permanent income, were indistinguishable.

The model is, therefore, written

$$y = x + s + \varepsilon_y$$

$$I \qquad\qquad x = \gamma_0 + \gamma_1 \log(PY) + \varepsilon_x$$

$$s = \alpha s_{-12} + \sum_{j=0}^{10} \delta_j \mathrm{Dec}_{t-j} + \delta_{11}\mathrm{Easter} + \varepsilon_s \qquad (17)$$

where Dec is a dummy for the month of December, Easter is a variable which is zero, except in March when it takes on a value between 0 and 12, depending on how many of the 2 weeks of shopping days before Easter occurred in March. The γ_0s are normalized to sum to zero, although this only affects the simulation when they must be separated from y_0.

The regression form of the model is

$$y = \alpha y_{-12} + \gamma_1 \log(PY) - \alpha\gamma_1 \log(PY_{-12})$$

$$+ \sum_{j=0}^{10} \delta_j \mathrm{Dec}_{t-j}$$

$$+ \delta_{11}\mathrm{Easter} + \gamma_0 + u$$

$$u = (1 - (L^{12}))(\varepsilon_x + \varepsilon_y) + \varepsilon_s. \qquad (18)$$

There are 15 exogenous variables, a lagged dependent variable, and a nonlinear constraint. The error process is a MA(12), with a negative coefficient that would bias α downwards under ordinary least squares. All autocovariances, except the 12th, should be zero.

The second model assumes that the 12th difference of the seasonal model is white noise, except for the effect of the Easter dummy. The nonseasonal component is, however, assumed to have an AR(1) component. This model is

$$y = x + s + \varepsilon_y$$

$$\text{II} \qquad x = \beta x_{-1} + \gamma_1 \log(PY) + \gamma_0 + \varepsilon_x$$

$$s = s_{-12} + \delta \text{Easter} + \varepsilon_s \qquad (19)$$

that can be written in the regression formulation as

$$\Delta_{12} y = \beta \Delta_{12} y_{-1} + \delta \text{Easter} - \beta \delta \text{Easter}_{-1}$$
$$+ \gamma_1 \Delta_{12} \log(PY) + \gamma_0 + u$$
$$u = (1 - L^{12})(1 - \beta L)\varepsilon_y + (1 - L^{12})\varepsilon_x$$
$$+ (1 - \beta L)\varepsilon_s. \qquad (20)$$

This is a regression model in the 12th differences of y, with 1 lagged dependent variable, 4 exogenous variables, a nonlinear constraint, and a complicated error term. The error term is 13-order moving average with nonzero autocorrelations only at lags 1, 12, and 13.

Many other models could easily be formulated by taking any acceptable nonseasonal model from the economic literature, where most analysis is performed with seasonally adjusted data, and one of several seasonal models, suggested by Granger (1978). Here, a more complicated model is formulated that consists of the seasonal part of model I and the nonseasonal part of model II. There are consequently autoregressive components from each of the component models. The regression formulation of this model is

$$y = \beta y_{-1} + \alpha y_{-12} - \alpha \beta y_{-13} + \gamma_1 \log(PY)$$
$$- \alpha \gamma_1 \log(PY_{-12}) + \delta_{11} \text{Easter} - \beta \delta_{11} \text{Easter}_{-1}$$
$$\text{III} \qquad + \sum_{j=1}^{10} (\delta_j - \beta \delta_{j-1}) \text{Dec}_{-j} + \delta_0 \text{Dec}$$
$$- \beta \delta_{10} \text{Dec}_{-10} + \gamma_0 + u$$
$$u = (1 - \beta L)\varepsilon_s + (1 - \alpha L^{12})\varepsilon_x$$
$$+ (1 - \beta L)(1 - \alpha L^{12})\varepsilon_y. \qquad (21)$$

This model now has 17 regressors, 3-lagged dependent variables, many nonlinear constraints, and an error term with a 13-order moving average that has nonzero autocorrelations at 1, 12, and 13 lags.

Several computational methods were used for each of these models, all of which were performed on the Troll computer system. The instrumental variable estimator of Liviatan (1963) is consistent, regardless of the error structure. This is easily calculated without the constraints but can also be calculated when the nonlinear constraints are imposed by minimizing the sum of squares in the metric of the projection on the instrument list, as discussed by Amemiya (1974) for two-stage least squares.

To achieve a more efficient estimation, the residual spectrum can be used to correct for the stochastic properties, and this procedure, iterated to convergence, will be maximum likelihood subject of the constraints imposed. Further estimates can, therefore, be computed by iterating from either OLS or INST starting-points without the nonlinear constraints or by imposing these constraints within the spectral estimation. The latter was not done in these examples.

The iterative Hannan efficient estimator was calculated using the fast fourier transform with the series extended to 3×2^n for some n. The factor of 3 is important when using monthly data so that spectra are calculated at the exact seasonal frequencies. The iterative procedure calculates the spectrum of the residuals, transforms all the data by taking the fourier transform, dividing by the square root of the spectral estimate, and then taking the inverse fourier transform to obtain a time-domain data vector. The residuals of this process should be white noise if convergence has occurred. If they are not, their spectral estimate is multiplied times the previous estimate and the process repeated. The estimates are said to converge when the scaled log likelihood changes by less than 0.0001.

In Table 4 estimates are presented for model I. Six estimates are tabulated that correspond to the various options previously mentioned. The results are, in many cases, quite similar. Of particular interest is the 12th-order autoregressive coefficient. It ranges from 0.2 to 0.42 over the methods. That is the largest variation, but all of these values are small enough that such differences would not substantially affect the behavior of the model. The nonlinear constraint is only roughly satisfied. When it is imposed, the largest values of the autoregressive parameter are coupled with the smallest values of $\log(PY)$ and the highest standard error of the regression. One would expect from economic theory that the elasticity of retail expenditure concerning personal income would be one, or maybe slightly less, if the goods are predominantly necessities rather than luxuries. This is precisely observed in the iterated methods, and, altogether, the results are rather encouraging. The main disappointment with these estimates is that the final iterative results differ

TABLE 4. Estimates of model I: April 1954 to June 1975

Variable	OLS	INST	Nonlinear	Nonlinear INST	Iterate from OLS	Iterate from INST
Y_{-12}	[1]0.38(0.06)	0.22(0.13)	0.42(0.06)	0.40(0.13)	0.30(0.06)	0.23(0.06)
log(PY)	1.22(.08)	1.23(.08)	.83(.006)	.83(.006)	1.00(.11)	1.01(.11)
log(PY$_{-12}$)	−.72(.09)	−.61(.12)		—	−.43(.13)	−.37(.13)
Easter	.004(.001)	.004(.001)	004(.001)	.004(.001)	.003(.0007)	.003(.0007)
December	.09(.01)	.11(.02)	.09(.01)	.09(.02)	.09(.02)	.10(.010)
January	−.10(.01)	−.12(.02)	−.09(.01)	−.10(.02)	−.11(.011)	−.12(.011)
February	−.09(.01)	−.12(.02)	−.09(.01)	−.09(.02)	−.10(.010)	−.11(.010)
March	−.07(.01)	−.08(.02)	−.06(.01)	−.06(.017)	−.08(.009)	−.08(.009)
April	−.06(.01)	−.07(.01)	−.06(.01)	−.06(.008)	−.07(.008)	
May	−.03(.008)	−.04(.01)	−.03(.008)	−.03(.010)	−.03(.006)	−.04(.006)
June	−.01(.007)	−.02(.008)	−.01(.008)	−.01(.008)	−.02(.005)	−.02(.006)
July	−.05(.009)	−.07(.01)	−.05(.009)	−.05(.01)	−.06(.008)	−.07(.008)
August	−.05(.009)	−.06(.01)	−.05(.009)	−.05(.01)	−.05(.007)	−.06(.007)
September	−.03(.008)	−.03(.009)	−.02(.008)	−.02(.009)	−.03(.006)	−.03(.006)
October	−.04(.008)	−.05(.01)	−.04(.008)	−.04(.01)	−.05(.006)	−.05(.006)
Constant	1.11(.10)	1.37(.23)	.96(.11)	.99(.22)	1.15(.118)	1.27(.12)
Standard Error	.0235	.0239	.0245	.0345	.0200	.0203
Durbin–Watson	1.31	1.24	1.16	1.16	1.99	1.99

— Entry represents zero.
[1] Standard errors are shown in parentheses.

depending upon the starting-point. This is mainly true of the auto-regressive coefficient and suggests that the likelihood function is relatively flat regarding this parameter. Perhaps, more efficient algorithms or better criteria for termination would minimize this discrepancy. Generally, the likelihood is slightly larger for the OLS-starting values, and thus, these will be reported subsequently.

In Table 5 the iterated Hannan estimates are presented for models II and III. In model II, the first-order autoregression is significant but not very large. Economic theory might suggest that this should be very close to one to construct a measure of permanent income, however, the data support a model that says people consume out of transitory income as well. (This has also been found in other contexts; see Engle (1976).) The long run elasticity is about unity as expected. The constraint on Easter is not supported, but the standard errors are large. Probably, the 12th difference of Easter should be used anyway. The standard error of this model is substantially larger than model I, and, on that ground alone, one might prefer I.

Model III is the same as model I except with an autoregressive term introduced into the nonseasonal component. The results are basically similar to those found above with significant, but not very large, autoregressive coefficients for both the seasonal and nonseasonal components. The autoregressive and Easter constraints are satisfied almost exactly, while the income constraint is only roughly true. The standard error of this model is substantially lower than the 2 per cent of model I.

Part of the diagnostic checking of these models must be examination of the residuals to see if they satisfy the processes assumed for them. For all of these models, there should be a negative autocorrelation coefficient at lag 12, for some a nonzero coefficient at lags 1, 11, and 13, but always zero for the other lags. The most cursory check of the autocorrelations of the raw residuals (the difference between the original data and the fitted values, before transformation to whiten the regression residuals, labelled u) shows this not to be true. In Figure 1, the autocorrelations are shown for model I, but they look much the same for the others. There are substantial autocorrelations at 3, 6, and 9 but not for 12. The pattern appears to repeat with diminished amplitude. This suggests a third-order autogression. Furthermore, the spectrum of the raw residuals has a slight negative seasonal pattern, but with a large positive peak at about 0.35, or roughly 3 months per cycle. Since this is a seasonal harmonic, it seems reasonable to attribute this missing autoregression to the seasonal component.

A third-order autoregression in the twelfth differences of the seasonal, plus the twelfth difference in Easter, are used as the seasonal model with the simple nonseasonal of model I to get model IV. The regression form is, therefore,

TABLE 5.   Iterated estimates using OLS starting values: April 1954 to June 1975

Model II $\Delta_{12}y = 0.29\ \Delta_{12}y_{-1} + 0.77\ \Delta_{12}\log(PY) + 0.0005$ Easter
$\quad\quad\quad\quad\ \ (0.06)\quad\quad\quad (0.10)\quad\quad\quad\quad (0.0004)$

$\quad\quad\quad\ + 0.0001$ Easter$_{-1} - 0.012$
$\quad\quad\quad\quad (0.0004)\quad\quad\quad (0.006)$

Model III $y = 0.40\ y_{-1} + 0.26\ y_{-12} - 0.12\ y_{-13} + 0.69\ \log(PY) - 0.31\ \log(PY_{-12})$
$\quad\quad\quad\ \ (0.06)\quad (0.06)\quad\ /(0.06)\quad\quad (0.10)\quad\quad\quad (0.10)$

$\quad\quad\ + 0.003$ Easter $-\quad\quad 0.001$ Easter$_{-1} + 0.09$ Dec $- 0.18$ Jan $- 0.08$ Feb
$\quad\quad\quad (0.0001)\quad\quad\quad (0.0007)\quad\quad\quad\quad (0.01)\quad\quad\quad (0.02)\quad\quad (0.01)$

$\quad\quad\ - 0.06$ Mar $- 0.05$ Apr $- 0.03$ May $- 0.02$ Jun $- 0.08$ July $- 0.05$ Aug
$\quad\quad\quad (0.01)\quad\quad (0.008)\quad\quad (0.007)\quad\quad (0.006)\quad\quad (0.010)\quad\quad (0.006)$

$\quad\quad\ - 0.03$ Sept $- 0.06$ Oct $+ 0.80$
$\quad\quad\quad (0.006)\quad\quad (0.008)\quad\ (0.14)$

$\quad\quad\quad$ SER = 0.0181, DW = 1.98

Model IV $\Delta_{12}y = 0.37\ \Delta_{12}y_{-3} + 0.94\ \Delta_{12}\log(PY) - 0.33\ \Delta_{12}\log(PY_{-3})$
$\quad\quad\quad\quad\ \ (0.06)\quad\quad\quad (0.15)\quad\quad\quad\quad (0.15)$

$\quad\quad\ + 0.003\ \Delta_{12}$Easter $-\quad 0.005$
$\quad\quad\quad (0.0005)\quad\quad\quad (0.0006)$

$\quad\quad\quad$ SER = 0.0208, DW = 1.99

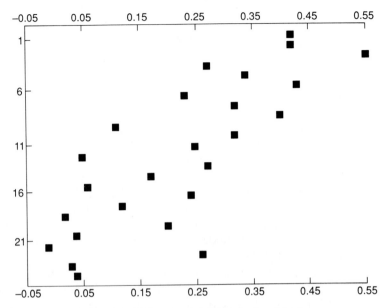

FIG. 1. Model I, autocorrelations of residuals

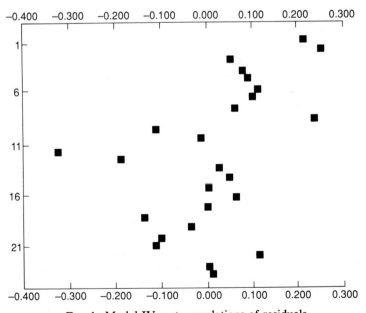

FIG. 1. Model IV, autocorrelations of residuals

$$\Delta_{12}y = \alpha\Delta_{12}y_{-3} + \gamma_1\Delta_{12}\log(PY)$$

$$\text{IV} \qquad - \alpha\gamma_1\Delta_{12}\log(PY_{-3})$$

$$+ \delta\Delta_{12}\text{Easter} + \gamma_0 + u$$

$$u = (1 - L^{12})(1 - \alpha L^3)(\varepsilon_x + \varepsilon_y) + \varepsilon_s. \qquad (22)$$

This is now one of the simplest models in that there are only five regressors. There are still a nonlinear constraint and an error process, which has third-, twelfth-, and fifteenth-order moving average terms. The estimates of this model look quite encouraging. The constraint is almost exactly satisfied, and income has nearly a unit elasticity. The standard error is between model I and model II, but the structure is far more parsimonious. The autocorrelation of the residuals looks substantially better with the expected negative term at 12. Various alternative means of respecifying the model to capture the unexplained seasonal part might prove still better.

The technique of model identification is, therefore, an iterative one. The autoregressive parameters are estimated, assuming a general stationary error structure. The residuals are then examined to see if they obey the prescribed process. If not, a respecification of the model is required. The mechanics of this search procedure are yet to be worked out, but this example may be a helpful illustration.

This discussion has suggested several types of unobserved component models with exogenous variables and various estimation methods. The estimation difficulties do not appear particularly great, but some of the specification choices may be difficult. It is quite possible that the seasonally adjusted series would not be very sensitive to the model specification, just as in the simulated series in the fifth section. Only further study of this problem can provide the answer.

Conclusion

This paper has proposed a method of seasonal adjustment, based upon specifying and estimating a structural unobserved components model, and then using this model to optimally filter the data to remove the seasonal component. The computational problems in estimating the models using asymptotically efficient procedures are quite severe. In this paper, it has been argued that some constraints on parameters can be relaxed to yield less efficient, but still consistent, structural estimates. In this fashion, model estimation becomes feasible, although the identification problems remain very complicated.

The model is then used to optimally filter the data, using the Kalman version of the Wiener filter. Both a one-sided filter and a two-sided smoother were used on artificial data. Empirically, even when the true model parameters were employed, the X-11 performed nearly as well as the optimal filter. In terms of variance, the differences between results using estimated models and the true model were not great, although one of the estimated models was badly biased. The filtered and smoothed results were generally inferior at the beginning of the sample period, reflecting a badly estimated initial condition. Improvement in the performance would surely be expected from imposing a proper prior on this state.

The relative success of the X-11 in a situation where it should be dominated suggests that, perhaps, the structural approach to seasonal adjustment, based entirely on a single series, should not be recommended. However, when causal variables are introduced, there is no alternative, to the estimation of a structural model and inference about the seasonal characteristics from this model. The second example presents estimation methods and results for a model of monthly retail sales. Here, the timing of holidays and trading days were shown to influence the seasonal component, while personal income influenced the nonseasonal.

In this case, one would expect the Kalman filter to more efficiently utilize the information in the causal series and provide superior estimates of the adjusted series than the X-11, which can only, in simplistic fashions, make use of causal information.

References

AMEMIYA, T., and FULLER, W. A. (1967), 'A comparative study of alternative estimators in a distributed lag model', *Econometrica*, **35**, 509–29.

—— (1974), 'The nonlinear limited information maximum likelihood estimator and the modified nonlinear two-stage least-squares estimator'. Working Paper No. 52. Palo Alto, Calif. Institute for Mathematical Studies in the Social Sciences, Stanford University.

ANDERSON, T. W. (1971), *The Statistical Analysis of Time Series*. New York: John Wiley and Sons, Inc.

BOX, G. E. P., and JENKINS, G. M. (1976), *Time Series Analysis: Forecasting and Control*. San Francisco: Holden Day.

——, HILLMER, S. C., and TIAO, G. C. (1978), 'Analysis and modelling of seasonal time series', in Zellner (ed.), *Seasonal Analysis of Time Series*, 309–33. Bureau of the Census.

CHOW, G. C. (1975), *Analysis and Control of Dynamic Economic Systems*. New York: John Wiley and Sons, Inc.

COOLEY, T. F., ROSENBERG, B., AND WALL, K. D. (1977), 'A Note on Optimal

Smoothing for Time Varying Coefficient Problems', *Annals of Economic and Social Measurement*, **6**, 453–6.

DURBIN, J., and KENNY, P. B. (1978), 'Seasonal adjustment when the seasonal component behaves neither purely multiplicatively nor purely additively', in Zellner (ed.), *Seasonal Analysis of Time Series*, 173–85. Bureau of the Census.

ENGLE, R. F. (1974), 'Band spectrum regression', *International Economic Review*, **15**, 1–11.

—— (1976), 'Band spectrum regression methods with lagged dependent variables and stationary errors—an iterated instrumental variables approach'. Paper presented to Symposium on Current Directions in Applied Time Series Analysis, Tulsa, Okla.

ESPASA, A. (1975), 'The estimation of the multiple regression model with stationary errors and lagged endogenous variables'. London School of Economics. (Unpublished manuscript.)

FRASER, D. C., and POTTER, J. E. (1969), 'The optimum linear smoother as a combination of two optimum linear filters', *IEEE Transaction on Automatic Control*, **AS14** 387–90.

GRANGER, C. W. J. (1978), 'Seasonality: causation, interpretation and implications', in Zellner (ed.), *Seasonal Analysis of Time Series*, 33–46. Bureau of the Census.

GRETHER, D. M., and NERLOVE, M. (1970), 'Some properties of "optimal" seasonal adjustment', *Econometrica*, **38**, 686–703.

HANNAN, E. J. (1965), 'The estimation of relationships involving distributed lags', *Econometrica*, **35**, 206–24.

KALMAN, R. E. (1960), 'A new approach to linear filtering and prediction problems', *Journal of Basic Engineering*, **82D**, 33–45.

—— and BUCY, R. S. (1961), 'New results in linear filtering and prediction theory', *Journal of Basic Engineering*, **83**, 95–108.

LIVIATAN, N. (1963), 'Consistent estimation of distributed lags', *International Economic Review*, **4**, 44–52.

MEHRA, R. K. (1969), 'On a limiting procedure in linear recursive estimation theory', *Journal of Mathematical Analysis and Applications*, **26**, 1–8.

—— (1976), *A Note on Optimal Smoothing for Time Varying Coefficient Problems*, by T. F. Cooley and K. D. Wall. Working Paper No. 128. New York: National Bureau of Economic Research.

NELSON, C. R. (1972), 'Prediction performance of the FRB–MIT–PENN model of the U.S. economy', *American Economic Review*, **62**, 902–17.

NERLOVE, M. (1967), 'Distributed lags and unobserved components in economic time series', *Ten Economic Studies in the Tradition of Irving Fisher* (W. Fellner *et al.*). New York: John Wiley and Sons, Inc.

—— (1972), 'Lags in economic behavior', *Econometrica*, **40**, 221–51.

Pagan, A. (1973*a*), 'Efficient estimation of models with composite disturbance terms', *Journal of Econometrics*, **1**, 329–40.

—— (1973*b*), 'Estimation of an evolving seasonal pattern as an application of stochastically varying parameter regression'. Princeton University, Econometric Research Program. Research Memorandum No. 153.

—— (1973*c*), 'A note on the extraction of components from time series'.

Princeton University, Econometric Research Program. Research Memorandum No. 148.

—— (1975), 'A note on the extraction of components from time series', *Econometrica*, **43**, 163–8.

PIERCE, D. A. (1978), 'Seasonal adjustment when both deterministic and stochastic seasonality are present', in Zellner (ed.), *Seasonal Analysis of Economic Time Series*, 242–64. Bureau of the Census.

ROSENBERG, B. (1973), 'A survey of stochastic parameter regression', *Annals of Economic and Social Measurement*, **2**, 381–97.

SARRIS, A. H. (1974), *A general Algorithm of Simultaneous Estimation of Constant and Randomly-Varying Parameters in Linear Relations*. National Bureau of Economic Research. Working Paper No. 38. New York: National Bureau of Economic Research.

SCHWEPPE, F. C. (1965), 'Evaluation of likelihood function for Gaussian signals', *IEEE Transactions in Information Theory*, **11**, 61–70.

TAYLOR, L. (1970), 'The existence of optimal distributed lags', *Review of Economic Studies*, **37**, 95–106.

WHITTLE, P. (1963), *Prediction and Regulation by Linear Least-Square Methods*. London: The English Universities Press, Ltd.

WIENER, N. (1950). *Extrapolation, Interpolation, and Smoothing of Stationary Time Series*. Cambridge and New York: Massachusetts Institute of Technology Press and John Wiley and Sons. Inc.

12

An ARIMA-Model-Based Approach to Seasonal Adjustment

S. C. HILLMER and G. C. TIAO*

Abstract. This article proposes a model-based procedure to decompose a time series uniquely into mutually independent additive seasonal, trend, and irregular noise components. The series is assumed to follow the Gaussian ARIMA model. Properties of the procedure are discussed and an actual example is given.

Keywords: ARIMA model; seasonal adjustment; Census X-11 program; pseudospectral density function; model-based decomposition; canonical decomposition.

1. Introduction

Business and economic time series frequently exhibit seasonality –periodic fluctuations that recur with about the same intensity each year. It has been argued (cf. Nerlove, Grether and Carvalho 1979, p. 147) that seasonality should be removed from economic time series so that underlying 'business cycles' can be more easily studied and current economic conditions can be appraised. Of the large number of seasonal adjustment procedures, the most widely used is the Census X-11 method described in Shiskin, Young, and Musgrave (1967). The X-11 program and other methods that have been empirically developed tend to produce what their developers feel are desirable seasonal adjustments, but their statistical properties are difficult to assess from a theoretical

* S. C. Hillmer is Assistant Professor, School of Business, University of Kansas, Lawrence, KS 66044. G. C. Tiao is Professor of Statistics and Business, Department of Statistics, University of Wisconsin, Madison, WI 53706. This research was partially supported by the U.S. Bureau of the Census, Washington, DC under JSA No. 80-10; Army Research Office, Durham under grant No. DAAG29-78-G-0166; the ALCOA Foundation; and University of Kansas research allocation 3139-X0-0038. The article was completed when G. C. Tiao was on leave at the University of Chicago.

Printed with permission of: *Journal of the American Statistical Association, 77*. 63–70.

view-point. Recently, there has been considerable interest in developing model-based procedures for the decomposition and seasonal adjustment of time series (see, e.g., the work of Grether and Nerlove 1970; Cleveland and Tiao 1976; Pierce 1978, 1980; Box, Hillmer, and Tiao 1978; Tiao and Hillmer 1978; and Burman 1980). Following this line of work and motivated in part by the considerations in the X-11 program, this article proposes a model-based approach that decomposes a time series into seasonal, trend, and irregular components.

We suppose that an observable time series at time t, Z_t, can be represented as

$$Z_t = S_t + T_t + N_t, \tag{1.1}$$

where S_t, T_t, and N_t are unobservable seasonal, trend, and noise components. It may be the case that a more accurate representation for Z_t would be as the product of S_t, T_t, and N_t. In that situation the model (1.1) would be appropriate for the logarithms of the original series. We assume that each of the components follows an ARIMA model,

$$\phi_S(B)S_t = \eta_S(B)b_t$$

$$\phi_T(B)T_t = \eta_T(B)c_t \tag{1.2}$$

$$\phi_N(B)N_t = \eta_N(B)d_t$$

where B is the backshift operator such that $BS_t = S_{t-1}$, each of the pairs of polynominals $\{\phi_S(B), \eta_S(B)\}$, $\{\phi_T(B), \eta_T(B)$, and $\{\phi_N(B), \eta_N(B)\}$ have their zeros lying on or outside the unit circle and have no common zeros, and b_t, c_t, and d_t are three mutually independent white noise processes, identically and independently distributed as $N(0, \sigma_b^2)$, $N(0, \sigma_{kc}^2)$, and $N(0, \sigma_d^2)$, respectively. Then it is readily shown that the overall model for Z_t is the ARIMA model

$$\varphi(B)Z_t = \theta(B)a_t, \tag{1.3}$$

where $\varphi(B)$ is the highest common fator of $\phi_s(B)$, $\phi_T(B)$, and $\varphi_N(B)$, and $\theta(B)$ and σ_a^2 can be obtained from the relationship

$$\frac{\theta(B)\theta(F)\sigma_a^2}{\varphi(B)\varphi(F)} = \frac{\eta_S(B)\eta_S(F)\sigma_b^2}{\phi_S(B)\phi_S(F)} + \frac{\eta_T(B)\eta_T(F)\sigma_c^2}{\phi_T(B)\phi_T(F)} + \frac{\eta_N(B)\eta_N(F)\sigma_d^2}{\sigma_N(B)\phi_N(F)},$$

$$\tag{1.4}$$

where $F = B^{-1}$. We also assume that the parameters in (1.3) are known. In practice a model for the observable series Z_t can be built from the data, and the estimated parameter values used as if they were the true values.

The ARIMA form has been found flexible enough to describe the behavior of many actual nonstationary and seasonal time series (Box and Jenkins 1970). There are situations in which such models by themselves may not be adequate; for example, a series describing employment may be dramatically affected by a strike and the model (1.3) does not cover such contingencies. However, in these situations ARIMA models can frequently be modified to approximate reality; for instance, intervention analysis techniques described in Box and Tiao (1975) might be used to account for the effects of strikes and other exogenous events.

Given the observable Z_t and the structure in (1.1), (1.2), and (1.3), the problem is to decompose Z_t into S_t, T_t and N_t. Our approach is as follows: (a) We first impose restrictions on $\phi_S(B)$ and $\phi_T(B)$ for the component models (1.2) based in part on considerations in the Census X-11 program. (b) A model for Z_t is derived from observable data. (c) A principle is adopted that uniquely specifies the component models in a manner consistent with the imposed restrictions and the model derived for Z_t. (d) Given the component models, known signal extraction methods are applied to decompose Z_t into (estimates of) the components. Properties of the procedure are explored and an illustration using an actual time series is presented.

2.   Decomposition when the Component Models are Known

If in (1.1) the stochastic structures of S_t, T_t, and N_t in (1.2) are known, then estimates of S_t and T_t can be readily obtained (see, e.g., Whittle 1963 and Cleveland and Tiao 1976). Specifically, Cleveland and Tiao have shown that, when all the zeros of $\phi_S(B)$, $\phi_T(B)$, and $\phi_N(B)$ are on or outside of the unit circle, the minimum mean squared estimates of the seasonal and trend components S_t and T_t are, respectively,

$$\hat{S}_t = W_S(B)Z_t \quad \text{and} \quad \hat{T}_t = W_t(B)Z_t, \tag{2.1}$$

where

$$W_S(B) = \frac{\sigma_b^2}{\sigma_a^2} \frac{\sigma(B)\varphi(F)\eta_S(B)\eta_S(F)}{\theta(B)\theta(F)\phi_S(B)\phi_S(F)}$$

and

$$W_T(B) = \frac{\sigma_c^2}{\sigma_a^2} \frac{\varphi(B)\varphi(F)\eta_T(B)\eta_T(F)}{\theta(B)\theta(F)\phi_T(B)\phi_T(F)}.$$

Because in practice the S_t, T_t and N_t series are unobservable, it is usually unrealistic to assume that the component models in (1.2) are known. As a result, the weight functions $W_S(B)$ and $W_T(B)$ cannot be determined and the values $\hat{S}_t$ and $\tilde{T}_t$ cannot be calculated. We can, however, get an accurate estimate of the model (1.3) from the observable Z_t series. Consequently, it is of interest to investigate to what extent a known model for Z_t will determine the models for the component series.

3.   Properties of Seasonal and Trend Components

It is well known that the Census X-11 procedure may be approximated by a linear filter (for instance see Young 1968 and Wallis 1974). One important feature of the X-11 filter weights for the trend and the seasonal components is that the weights applied to observations more removed from the current time period decrease. This feature was incorporated into the X-11 program probably because of the belief that the trend and seasonal components of many series change over time; consequently the information about the current trend or seasonal is contained in the values of Z_t close to current time. Therefore, in developing a decomposition procedure we should allow for evolving trend and seasonal components.

Stochastic trend

Economic data often exhibit underlying movements that drift over time. While *locally* such movements might be adequately modeled by a polynomial in time, a fixed polynomial time function is clearly inappropriate over the *entire* time span. Thus a stochastic trend model is needed, and we assume that the trend component, T_t, follows the nonstationary model

$$(1 - B)^d T_t = \eta_T(B)c_t, \qquad (3.1)$$

where $\eta_T(B)$ is a polynomial in B of degree at most d, and c_t are iid $N(0, \sigma_c^2)$. Box and Jenkins (1970, p. 149) have shown that the minimum mean squared error forecast function of (3.1) is a polynomial time function as of degree $(d - 1)$ whose coefficients are updated as the origin of forecast is advanced; therefore (3.1) can be regarded as a polynomial model with stochastic coefficients.

It is also of interest to consider the trend component in the frequency domain. Intuitively, the spectral density function of a trend component should be large for the low frequencies and small for higher frequencies. Since the model (3.1) is nonstationary, the spectral density function is strictly speaking not defined. However, we can define a pseudospectral density function (psdf) for (3.1) by

$$f_T(w) = \sigma_c^2 \eta_T(e^{iw}) \eta_T(e^{-iw})/(1 - e^{iw})^d (1 - e^{-iw})^d, \; 0 \leq w \leq \pi. \quad (3.2)$$

Now the psdf (3.2) is infinite at $w = 0$ and very large for small w. This is consistent with what could be viewed as a stochastic trend component.

Stochastic seasonal

A deterministic seasonal component S_t of period s would have the property that it repeats itself every s periods and that the sum of any s consecutive components should be a constant, that is,

$$S_t = S_{t-s} \quad \text{and} \quad U(B)S_t = c, \quad (3.3)$$

where $U(B) = 1 + B + \ldots + B^{s-1}$ and c is an arbitrary constant that can be taken as zero. Such a model, however, implies that the seasonal pattern is fixed over time. For business and economic time series, it seems reasonable to require that the seasonal component should be capable of revolving over time but that *locally* a regular seasonal pattern should be preserved. In other words, $U(B)S_t$ should be random but cluster about zero. Consider the nonstationary model

$$U(B)S_t = \eta_S(B)b_t, \quad (3.4)$$

where $\eta_S(B)$ is a polynomial in B of degree at most $s - 1$ and b_t are iid $N(0, \sigma_b^2)$. That is, the consecutive moving sum of s components, $U(B)S_t$, follows a moving average model of order (at most) $s - 1$. It is readily shown that the forecasting function of (3.4) at a given time origin follows a fixed seasonal pattern of period s, but the pattern is updated as the origin is advanced. Also, $EU(B)S_t = E\eta_S(B)b_t = 0$. Thus, the model (3.4) preserves a local cyclical pattern but allows seasonality to evolve over time.

It is also informative to consider the psdf, $f_s(w)$, of the model in (3.4)

$$f_s(w) = \sigma_b^2 \frac{\eta_S(e^{iw})\eta_S(e^{-iw})}{U(e^{iw})U(e^{-iw})}. \quad (3.5)$$

It can be shown that $f_S(w)$ has the following properties: (a) $f_S(w)$ is infinite at the seasonal frequencies $w = 2k\pi/s$ for $k = 1, \ldots, [s/2]$, where $[x]$ denotes the greatest integer less than or equal to x; (b) $f_S(w)$ has relative minimum at $w = 0$ and near the frequencies $w = ((2k - 1)\pi)/s$ for $k = 2, \ldots, [s/2]$. Therefore, the psdf of (3.4) has infinite power at the seasonal frequencies and relatively small power away from the seasonal frequencies.

4. Model-based Seasonal Decomposition

From considerations in the previous section, we require $\varphi(B)$ to contain the factor $U(B)$ before we impose a seasonal component S_t and to contain the factor $(1 - B)^d$ before we impose a trend component T_t for Z_t. We further require that in (1.2) the autoregressive polynomial of N_t, $\phi_N(B)$, has no common zeros with either $(1 - B)^d$ or $U(B)$, because otherwise it would imply the existence of additional seasonal and trend components that could then be absorbed into S_t and T_t. Thus, we shall suppose that in (1.3)

$$\varphi(B) = (1 - B)^d U(B)\phi_N(B), \qquad (4.1)$$

where the three factors on the right side have no common zeros. In other words, knowing the model for Z_t and assuming that a decomposition is possible, the autoregressive polynomials of S_t, T_t and N_t can be uniquely determined. Also, the relationship (1.4) becomes

$$\frac{\theta(B)\theta(F)}{\varphi(B)\varphi(F)} \sigma_a^2 = \frac{\eta_S(B)\eta_S(F)}{U(B)U(F)} \sigma_b^2$$

$$+ \frac{\eta_T(B)\eta_T(F)}{(1 - B)^d(1 - F)^d} \sigma_c^2 + \frac{\eta_N(B)\eta_N(F)}{\phi_N(B)\phi_N(F)} \sigma_d^2. \qquad (4.2)$$

The more difficult task is to determine the moving average polynomials and the innovation variances. Within the class of $\eta_S(B)$ and $\eta_T(B)$ whose degrees are at most $(s - 1)$ and d as required by (3.1) and (3.4), any choice of the three moving average polynomials $\eta_S(B)$, $\eta_T(B)$, and $\eta_N(B)$ and the three variances σ_b^2, σ_c^2, and σ_d^2 satisfying (4.2) will be called an *acceptable* decomposition because it is consistent with information provided by the model for the observed data Z_t.

We now give a necessary and sufficient condition for the existence of an acceptable decomposition. Assuming that $\varphi(B)$ takes the form (4.1), we may perform a unique partial fraction decomposition of the left side of (4.2) to yield

$$\frac{\theta(B)\theta(F)}{\varphi(B)\varphi(F)} \sigma_a^2 = \frac{Q_S(B)}{U(B)U(F)}$$

$$+ \frac{Q_T(B)}{(1 - B)^d(1 - F)^d} + \frac{Q_N(B)}{\phi_N(B)\phi_N(F)}, \qquad (4.3)$$

where

$$Q_S(B) = q_{0S} + \sum_{i=1}^{s-2} q_{iS}(B^i + F^i),$$

$$Q_T(B) = q_{0T} + \sum_{i=1}^{d-1} q_{iT}(B^i + F^i),$$

and $Q_N(B)$ can be obtained by subtraction. The uniqueness in (4.3) results from the fact that the degrees of $Q_S(B)$ and $Q_T(B)$ are lower than the degrees of the corresponding denominator. Now for $0 \leqslant w \leqslant \pi$, let

$$\epsilon_1 = \min_w \frac{Q_S(e^{-iw})}{|U(e^{-iw})|^2},$$

$$\epsilon_2 = \min_w \frac{Q_T(e^{-iw})}{|1 - e^{-iw}|^{2d}}, \qquad (4.4)$$

and

$$\epsilon_3 = \min_w \frac{Q_N(e^{-iw})}{|\phi_N(e^{-iw})|^2}.$$

We now show that an acceptable decomposition exists if and only if $\epsilon_1 + \epsilon_2 + \epsilon_3 \geqslant 0$.

Proof. By writing $B = e^{-iw}$, $0 \leqslant w \leqslant \pi$, each of the three terms on the right side of (4.2) is a psdf.

Since $\eta_S(B)$ is of degree at most $s - 1$ and $\eta_T(B)$ is of degree at most d, by comparing (4.2) with (4.3) we can write

$$\frac{|\eta_S(e^{-iw})|^2 \sigma_b^2}{|U(e^{-iw})|^2} = \frac{Q_S(e^{-iw})}{|U(e^{-iw})|^2} + \gamma_1,$$

$$\frac{|\eta_T(e^{-iw})|^2 \sigma_c^2}{|1 - e^{-iw}|^{2d}} = \frac{Q_T(e^{-iw})}{|1 - e^{-iw}|^{2d}} + \gamma_2, \qquad (4.5)$$

and

$$\frac{|\eta_N(e^{-iw})|^2 \sigma_d^2}{|\phi_N(e^{-iw})|^2} = \frac{Q_N(e^{-iw})}{|\phi_N(e^{-iw})|^2} + \gamma_3,$$

where γ_1, γ_2, and γ_3 are three constants such that $\gamma_1 + \gamma_2 + \gamma_3 = 0$. The constants γ_i provide a means to change from the initial partial fractions decomposition (4.2) to an acceptable decomposition if one exists. Thus, an acceptable decomposition implies and is implied by the fact that $\gamma_i + \epsilon_i \geqslant 0$ for $i = 1, 2, 3$ or equivalently that $\epsilon_1 + \epsilon_2 + \epsilon_3 \geqslant 0$.

From the previous discussion, when $\epsilon_1 + \epsilon_2 + \epsilon_3 \geqslant 0$, every set of γ_i's corresponds to a unique acceptable decomposition; thus a unique decomposition exists if and only if $\epsilon_1 + \epsilon_2 + \epsilon_3 = 0$. On the other hand, when $\epsilon_1 + \epsilon_2 + \epsilon_3 > 0$, there are an infinite number of ways of adding constants to the three terms on the right side of (4.3) to obtain acceptable decompositions.

5. A Canonical Decomposition

In the absence of prior knowledge about the precise stochastic structure of the trend and seasonal components, all of the information in the known model of Z_t, (1.3), about S_t and T_t is embodied in (4.2). However, when $\epsilon_1 + \epsilon_2 + \epsilon_3 > 0$, this information is not sufficient to uniquely determine the models for S_t and T_t. To perform seasonal adjustment of the data, an arbitrary choice must be made. Considering that the seasonal and trend components should be slowly evolving, it seems reasonable to extract as much white noise as possible from the seasonal and trend components subject to the restrictions in (4.2). Thus, we seek to maximize the innovation variance σ_d^2 of the noise component N_t. Therefore, we define the *canonical decomposition* as the decomposition that maximizes σ_d^2 subject to the restrictions in (4.2).

Properties of the canonical decomposition

In the following we denote the canonical seasonal component by $\bar{S}_t$, the canonical trend component by $\bar{T}_t$, and use the same convention when referring to the moving average polynomials and innovation variances of the canonical decompositions. We prove the following properties of the canonical decomposition in the appendix. (a) The canonical decomposition is unique. (b) It minimizes the innovation variances σ_b^2 and σ_c^2. (c) The polynomials $\bar{\eta}_S(B)$ and $\bar{\eta}_T(B)$ have at least one zero on the unit circle so that the models for $\bar{S}_t$ and $\bar{T}_t$ are noninvertible. (d) If $\tilde{S}_t$ and $\tilde{T}_t$ are any acceptable seasonal and trend components other than the canonical decomposition, then $\tilde{S}_t = \bar{S}_t + e_t$ and $\tilde{T}_t = \bar{T}_t + \alpha_t$, where e_t and α_t are white noise series. (e) The variance of $U(B)S_t$ is minimized for the canonical decomposition.

One may lend justification of the (arbitrary) choice of the canonical decomposition on the basis of these properties. In particular, property (b) is intuitively pleasing since the randomness in S_t arises from the sequence of b_t's and the randomness in T_t arises from the sequence of c_t's. Thus, minimizing σ_b^2 and σ_c^2 makes the seasonal and trend components as deterministic as possible while remaining consistent with the information in the observable Z_t series. Also, from property (d) any acceptable seasonal component can be viewed as the sum of the canonical seasonal and white noise. But $\bar{S}_t$ is a highly predictable component that accounts for all of the seasonality in the original series and e_t is a completely unpredictable component. Thus, one might argue that the choice of an acceptable decomposition other than the canonical decomposition only produces a more confused seasonal component than necessary. Finally, property (e) is intuitively pleasing since

$E[U(B)S_t] = 0$ and a small value for $\text{var}[U(B)S_t]$ will help ensure that the sum of s consecutive seasonal components remains close to zero.

6. Application to some Special Seasonal Models

We now illustrate the results in the preceding sections with the following three special cases of (1.3). These models have been frequently used in practice to fit seasonal data (see, e.g., Box and Jenkins 1970, and Tiao, Box, and Hamming 1975).

$$(1 - B^s)Z_t = (1 - \theta_2 B^s)a_t, \tag{6.1}$$

$$(1 - B)(1 - B^s)Z_t = (1 - \theta_1 B)(1 - \theta_2 B^s)a_t, \tag{6.2}$$

and

$$(1 - B^s)Z_t = (1 - \theta_1 B)(1 - \theta_2 B^s)a_t. \tag{6.3}$$

Without loss of generality, we assume that $\sigma_a^2 = 1$. For these models, the general approach is as follows. We first divide the denominator of the left side of (4.3) into the numerator to obtain $Q_N(B)$ and a remainder term $R(B)$; we then perform a partial fractions expansion of $R(B)/\varphi(B)\varphi(F)$ to obtain $Q_s(B)$ and $Q_T(B)$; and finally we find the minimum values ϵ_1, ϵ_2, and ϵ_3 in order to investigate whether an acceptable decomposition exists.

The model (6.1)

In this case, $d = 1$ and $\phi_N(B) = 1$. By partial fractions (4.3) becomes

$$\frac{(1 - \theta_2 B^s)(1 - \theta_2 F^s)}{(1 - B^s)(1 - F^s)} = \frac{Q_S(B)}{U(B)U(F)} + \frac{Q_T(B)}{(1 - B)(1 - F)} + \theta_2, \tag{6.4}$$

where

$$Q_T(B) = \frac{1}{s^2}(1 - \theta_2)^2$$

and

$$Q_S(B) = (1 - \theta_2)^2 \left[1 - \frac{1}{s^2} U(B)U(F) \right] \bigg/ (1 - B)(1 - F)$$

$$= \frac{1}{6s^2}(1 - \theta_2)^2 \times \left[\sum_{l=2}^{s-1} (l - 1)l(l + 1)(B^{s-l} + F^{s-l}) \right.$$

$$+ (s - 1)s(s + 1) \bigg].$$

For the trend component, we see that $Q_T(e^{-iw})|1-$ where $e^{-iw}|^{-2}$ is monotonically decreasing in w and

$$\epsilon_2 = \frac{1}{4s^2}(1 - \theta_2)^2.$$

For the seasonal component, it is easy to show that $Q_S(e^{-iw})|U(e^{-iw})|^{-2} \geq 0$ and has local minimum at $w = 0$. Also, we conjecture that $w = 0$ is in fact the global minimum. This conjecture is verified analytically for $s \leq 3$ and numerically for s from 4 to 20. Assuming this is true for all s we find that

$$\min_w \left\{ 1 - \frac{1}{s^2}|U(e^{-iw})|^2 \right\} \Big/ |1 - e^{-iw}|^2$$

$$= (s^2 - 1)/12 \tag{6.5}$$

so that $\epsilon_1 = (1 - \theta_2)^2(s^2 - 1)/12s^2$. Since $\epsilon_3 = \theta_2$, for an acceptable decomposition to exist it is required that

$$\epsilon_1 + \epsilon_2 + \epsilon_3 = \theta_2 + \frac{(1 - \theta_2)^2}{4s^2} + \frac{(s^2 - 1)(1 - \theta_2)^2}{12s^2} \geq 0$$

or equivalently

$$\theta_2 \geq -\frac{(5s^2 - 2) + 2s\sqrt{6(s^2 - 1)}}{(s^2 + 2)}. \tag{6.6}$$

Values of the lower bound of θ_2 for selected values of s are given in the following tabulation:

s	2	4	6
1.b. θ_2	$-.1716$	$-.1170$	$-.1080$
8	10	12	∞
$-.1049$	$-.1035$	$-.1027$	$-.1010$

Therefore, there are values of θ_2 for which the model (6.1) is not consistent with an additive decomposition as we have defined it; however, a value of $\theta_2 > -.1010$ will always lead to an acceptable decomposition.

When strict inequality is obtained in (6.6), there will be an infinite number of acceptable decompositions. The canonical decomposition corresponds to

$$\frac{\bar{\sigma}_b^2 \bar{\eta}_S(B)\bar{\eta}_S(F)}{U(B)U(F)} = \frac{Q_S(B)}{U(B)U(F)} - \frac{s^2 - 1}{12s^2}(1 - \theta_2)^2 \tag{6.7}$$

and

$$\frac{\bar{\sigma}_c^2 \bar{\eta}_T(B)\bar{\eta}_T(F)}{(1 - B)(1 - F)} = \frac{1}{4_s^2}(1 - \theta_2)^2 \frac{(1 + B)(1 + F)}{(1 - B)(1 - F)}.$$

The model (6.2)

For this model, $d = 2$ and $\phi_N(B) = 1$. After some algebraic reduction, we find

$$\frac{(1 - \theta_1 B)(1 - \theta_2 B^S)(1 - \theta_1 F)(1 - \theta_2 F^S)}{(1 - B)(1 - B^S)(1 - F)(1 - F^S)}$$

$$= \frac{Q_S(B)}{U(B)U(F)} + \frac{Q_T(B)}{(1 - B)^2(1 - F)^2} + \theta_1\theta_2, \qquad (6.8)$$

where

$$Q_T(B) = \frac{(1 - \theta_1)^2(1 - \theta_2)^2}{s^2}$$

$$\times \left\{1 + \left[\frac{\theta_2 s^2}{(1 - \theta_2)^2} + \frac{(s^2 - 4)}{12} + \frac{(1 + \theta_1)^2}{4(1 - \theta_1)^2}\right]\right.$$

$$\left.\times(1 - B)(1 - F)\right\}$$

and

$$(1 - \theta_2)^2(1 - B)^2(1 - F)^2 Q_S(B)$$

$$= (1 - \theta_1)^2\left\{1 - \frac{1}{s^2} U(B)U(F)\right\} + \theta_1(1 - B)(1 - F)$$

$$- \left\{\frac{s^2 - 4}{12 s^2}(1 - \theta_1)^2 + \frac{(1 + \theta_1)^2}{4 s^2}\right\}(1 - B^S)(1 - F^S).$$

We now show that an acceptable decomposition exists if $\theta_2 \geq 0$.

Proof. First, setting $B = -1$ (or $w = \pi$ in $B = e^{-iw}$) in $Q_T(B)(1 - B)^{-2}(1 - F)^{-2}$, we have

$$\frac{Q_T(- 1)}{16} = \frac{(1 - \theta_2)^2}{48 s^2}\{(1 - \theta_1)^2(s^2 - 1) + 3(1 + \theta_1)^2\}$$

$$+ \frac{\omega_2(1 - \theta_1)^2}{4} = C \qquad (6.9)$$

say. The right side of (6.8) can now be written as

$$\frac{Q_S^*(B)}{U(B)U(F)} + \frac{Q_T^*(B)}{(1 - B)^2(1 - F)^2} + \theta_2\frac{(1 + \theta_1)^2}{4}, \qquad (6.10)$$

where

$$Q_W^*(B) = Q_T(B) - C(1 - B)^2(1 - F)^2$$

and

$$Q_S^* = Q_S(B) + U(B)U(F) \left\{ C - \frac{\theta_2(1 - \theta_1)^2}{4} \right\}.$$

Also, it can be verified that

$$(1 - \theta_2)^{-2}(1 - B)^2(1 - F)^2 Q_S^*(B) = \frac{(1 - \theta_1)^2}{4}(1 + B)(1 + F)$$

$$\times \left\{ 1 - \frac{1}{s^2} U(B)U(F) \right.$$

$$- \frac{s^2 - 1}{12s^2}(1 - B^s)(1 - F^s) \bigg\}$$

$$+ \frac{(1 + \theta_1)^2}{4}(1 - B)(1 - F)$$

$$\times \left\{ 1 - \frac{1}{4s^2} U(B)U(F)(1 + B)(1 + F) \right\}. \qquad (6.11)$$

When $\theta_2 \geq 0$, one can readily show that $Q_T(e^{-iw})|1 - e^{-iw}|^{-2}$ is monotonically decreasing in w so that the second term in (6.10) is non negative for all w. Now, on the right side of the equation in (6.11), the second term with $B = e^{-iw}$ is clearly non negative for all w and, from (6.5), so is the first term. Thus, an acceptable decomposition exists and is given by (6.10).

The model (6.3)

In this case, $d = 1$ and $\phi_N(B) = 1$. By partial fraction, we find

$$\frac{(1 - \theta_1 B)(1 - \theta_1 F)(1 - \theta_2 B^s)(1 - \theta_2 F^s)}{(1 - B^s)(1 - F^s)}$$

$$= \frac{Q_S(B)}{U(B)U(F)} + \frac{Q_T(B)}{(1 - B)(1 - F)} + Q_N(B), \qquad (6.12)$$

where

$$Q_T(B) = \frac{1}{s^2}(1 - \theta_1)^2(1 - \theta_2)^2,$$

$$(1 - \theta_2)^{-2}(1 - B)(1 - F)Q_S(B)$$

$$= \frac{(1 + \theta_1)^2}{4}(1 - B)(1 - F)$$

$$+ (1 - \theta_1)^2 \left\{ \frac{1}{4}(1 + B)(1 + F) - \frac{1}{s^2} U(B)U(F) \right\},$$

and

$$Q_N(B) = \theta_2(1 - \theta_1 B)(1 - \theta_1 F).$$

Noting that

$$\min_w Q_T(e^{-iw})|1 - e^{-ie}|^2 = \frac{1}{4s^2}(1 - \theta_1)^2(1 - \theta_2)^2,$$

we can express the right side of (6.12) alternatively as

$$\frac{Q_S^*}{U(B)U(F)} + \frac{Q_T^*(B)}{(1 - B)(1 - F)} + Q_N^*(B), \qquad (6.13)$$

where

$$Q_T^*(B) = Q_T(B) - \frac{1}{4s^2}(1 - \theta_1)^2(1 - \theta_2)^2(1 - B)(1 - F),$$

$$Q_N^*(B) = Q_N(B) + \frac{1}{4s^2}(1 + \theta_1)^2(1 - \theta_2)^2,$$

and

$$(1 - \theta_2)^{-2}(1 - B(1 - F)Q_S^*(B)$$

$$= (1 - \theta_1 B)(1 - \theta_1 F)\left\{1 - \frac{1}{s^2}U(B)U(F)\right\}.$$

Similar to the model (6.2), when $\theta_2 \geq 0$, all three terms in (6.13) are nonnegative for all w so that acceptable decompositions exist.

For the models (6.2) and (6.3), acceptable decompositions also exist for negative values of θ_2 near zero. The precise lower bounds are difficult to determine analytically. However, for these as well as for any model of the form (1.3) satisfying the condition (4.1), the existence of acceptable decompositions and the corresponding canonical form can always be determined by numerical methods. A computer program to determine the canonical component models and to compute the estimates $\hat{S}_t$, $\hat{T}_t$, and $\hat{N}_t$ is available on request.

7.   An Example

We now apply the model-based decomposition procedure to the monthly series US unemployment males aged 16 to 19 from January 1965 to August 1979, obtained from the Bureau of Labor Statistics. The series is a component used in constructing the monthly unemployment index.

The series is plotted in Figure 1. The variability of the series appears relatively constant over time; thus we decided to model the series in the

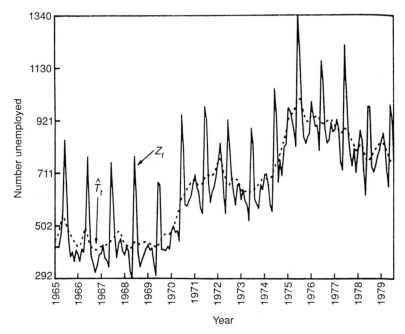

FIG. 1. Monthly unemployed males aged 16 to 19 (January 1971–August 1979)
and the estimated trend component series

original metric. It is found that the data can be adequately represented
by the model (6.2) with

$$s = 12, \quad \hat{\theta}_1 = .313 \text{ , and } \hat{\theta}_2 = .817 \text{ ,} \qquad (7.1)$$
$$\quad\quad (.075) \qquad\qquad (.035)$$

with the standard errors of the parameter estimates given in parentheses
below the estimates.

Assuming the estimates in (7.1) are the true values, we computed the
corresponding canonical decomposition and, from (2.3), the associated
weights for the estimates of the seasonal and trend components. These
weights are given in Tables 1 and 2 from the center through lag 47. In
both cases the remaining weights can be obtained by using the equation
$w_j = .313 \, s_{j-1} + .817 \, w_{j-12} - .256 \, w_{j-13}$. We observe that the weights
associated with the seasonal component die out slowly and span a large
number of years. This is in contrast to the weights associated with the
standard Census X-11 program whose weights die out in about three
years (see, e.g., Wallis 1974). We note that the rate at which the weight
in the model-based approach decreases is primarily determined by the
value of the parameter $\hat{\theta}_2 = .817$, which is determined from the original
series.

TABLE 1. Weight function for estimating the seasonal component: unemployed males data

Lag j	w_j											
0–11	.085	−.007	−.008	−.008	−.008	−.008	−.008	−.007	−.007	−.007	−.007	−.007
12–23	.076	−.007	−.007	−.007	−.006	−.006	−.006	−.006	−.006	−.006	−.006	−.006
24–35	.062	−.006	−.005	−.005	−.005	−.005	−.005	−.005	−.005	−.005	−.005	−.005
36–47	0.51	−.005	−.004	−.004	−.004	−.004	−.004	−.004	−.004	−.004	−.004	−.004

TABLE 2. Weight function for estimating the trend component: unemployed males data

Lag j	w_j											
0–11	.318	.212	.072	.028	.014	.010	.008	.008	.007	.005	.001	−.012
12–23	−.021	−.012	.001	.005	.006	.006	.006	.006	.006	.004	.001	−.009
24–35	−.018	−.010	.001	.004	.005	.005	.005	.005	.005	.004	.001	−.008
36–47	−.014	−.008	.001	.003	.004	.004	.004	.004	.004	.003	.001	−.006

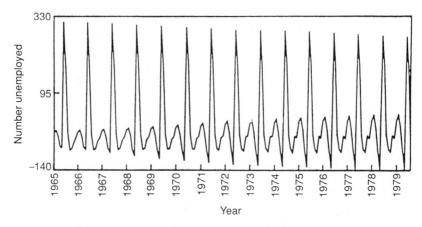

Year

FIG. 2. Estimated seasonal component series for the unemployed males data

The estimated trend component $\hat{T}_t$ is shown in Figure 1 and the estimated seasonal component $\hat{S}_t$ is plotted in Figure 2. We make the following observations. (a) The estimated trend component appears to capture the basic underlying movements of the series. (b) The seasonal component seems to have been adequately removed by the model-based decomposition. (c) The estimated seasonal component varies around a zero level and it is slowly changing over time. Therefore, for this particular series it appears that the model-based seasonal adjustment procedure has led to intuitively pleasing results.

8. Discussion

In this article, we have proposed a model-based procedure to decompose a time uniquely into mutually independent seasonal, trend, and irregular noise components. The method can be readily extended to models other than the ones discussed. For example, when $s = 12$, the autoregressive part of the seasonal component need not be $U(B)$, but can be any product of the factors $(1 + B)$, $(1 + B^2)$, $(1 + B + B^2)$, $(1 - B + B^2)$, $(1 + \sqrt{3}B + B^2)$, and $(1 - \sqrt{3}B + B^2)$. Also, the trend component may be augmented into a 'trend-cycle' component by allowing the autoregressive part to take the form $(1 - B)^d \phi_T^*(B)$, where $\phi_T^*(B)$ has all its zeros lying on the unit circle (but distinct from $B = 1$ and those of the seasonal component). The possibilities are unlimited, depending on the form of the known model of Z_t and the nature of the problem.

Finally, we remark here that in illustrating the decomposition procedure with the models (6.1) to (6.3), in each case the values of θ_2 are

restricted essentially to be nonnegative to yield acceptable decompositions. While we have rarely seen in practice a negative estimate of θ_2,
it is conceivable that this could happen. One possible explanation for a
negative θ_2 is that the white noise b_t and c_t for the seasonal and trend
components are correlated. As an extreme example of the model (6.1)
with $s = 2$, suppose the component models are

$$(1 + B)S_t = (1 - B)b_t,$$
$$(1 - B)T_t = (1 + B)c_t, \tag{8.1}$$

and

$$N_t \equiv 0.$$

The reader can readily verify that if $\sigma_b^2 = \sigma_c^2$ and b_t and c_t are perfectly
positively correlated, then $\theta_2 = -1$. Thus, by allowing the component
models to be dependent, we could increase the range of the models of
Z_t for which acceptable decompositions exist. This seems to be an
interesting topic for further study.

Appendix

In this appendix we sketch the proof of the properties of the canonical
decomposition given in Section 5. Upon multiplying each expression in (4.5) by
the denominator on the left side of the corresponding equation, we obtain

$$|\eta_S(e^{-iw})|^2 \sigma_b^2 = Q_S(e^{-iw}) + \gamma_1 |U(e^{-iw})|^2$$
$$= f_S(w, \gamma_1),$$
$$|\eta_T(e^{-iw})|^2 \sigma_c^2 = Q_T(e^{-iw}) + \gamma_2 |1 - e^{-iw}|^{2d}$$
$$= f_T(w, \gamma_2),$$
$$|\eta_N(e^{-iw})|^2 \sigma_d^2 = Q_N(e^{-iw}) + \gamma_3 |\phi_N(e^{-iw})|^2$$
$$= f_N(w, \gamma_3). \tag{A.1}$$

Using a result of Hannan (1970, p. 137) we have that

$$\sigma_b^2(\gamma_1) = \exp\left\{\frac{1}{2\pi} \int_{-\pi}^{\pi} \ln f_S(w, \gamma_1) dw\right\},$$
$$\sigma_c^2(\gamma_2) = \exp\left\{\frac{1}{2\pi} \int_{-\pi}^{\pi} \ln f_T(w, \gamma_2) dw\right\}, \tag{A.2}$$
$$\sigma_d^2(\gamma_3) = \exp\left\{\frac{1}{2\pi} \int_{-\pi}^{\pi} \ln f_N(w, \gamma_3) dw\right\}.$$

Now in (A.1), $f_N(w, \gamma_3)$ does not depend on γ_3 if $\phi_N(e^{-iw}) = 0$ and is otherwise
strictly increasing in γ_3; thus σ_d^2 is maximized when $\gamma_3 = \epsilon_1 + \epsilon_2$. From the
restrictions that $\gamma_1 + \gamma_2 + \gamma_3 = 0$ and $\gamma_i + \epsilon_i \geq 0$, $i = 1, 2, 3$, we have that for
the canonical decomposition $\gamma_1 = -\epsilon_1$ and $\gamma_2 = -\epsilon_2$. Therefore, the canonical

decomposition is unique and furthermore, from (A.1) and (A.2), the innovation variances $\sigma_b^2(\gamma_1)$ and $\sigma_c^2(\gamma_2)$ are minimized for the canonical decomposition. In addition, if we take $\gamma_1 = -\epsilon_1$ and $\gamma_2 = -\epsilon_2$ in (A.1), both $f_S(w, -\epsilon_1)$ and $f_S(w, -\epsilon_2)$ are zero for some $0 \leq w \leq \pi$ implying that $\bar{\eta}_S(B)$ and $\bar{\eta}_T(B)$ are not invertible.

If we let

$$f_{\bar{S}}(w) = Q_S(e^{-iw})|U(e^{-iw})|^{-2} - \epsilon_1$$

denote the psdf of $\bar{S}_t$ and let $f_{\tilde{S}}(w)$ denote the pdsf of any other acceptable decomposition $\tilde{S}_t$, then it follows that

$$f_{\tilde{S}}(w) = f_{\bar{S}}(w) + \sigma_e^2 \tag{A.3}$$

with $\sigma_e^2 > 0$. Equation (A.3) implies $\tilde{S}_t = \bar{S}_t + e_t$, where e_t is white noise with variance σ_e^2.

Finally, from (4.5) the variance of $U(B)S_t$ is $\text{var}[U(B)S_t]$

$$= \frac{1}{2\pi} \int_{-\pi}^{\pi} [Q_S(e^{-iw}) + \gamma_1|U(e^{-iw})|^2]dw. \tag{A.4}$$

It is evident that (A.4) is minimized when γ_1 is made as small as possible or $\gamma_1 = -\epsilon_1$, the value corresponding to the canonical decomposition.

References

(References marked with a * are included in this volume)

Box, G. E. P., Hillmer, S. C., and Tiao, G. C. (1978). 'Analysis and modeling of seasonal time series', in *Seasonal Analysis of Economic Time Series*, ed. Arnold Zellner. US Department of Commerce, 309.

—— and Jenkins, G. M. (1970), *Time Series Analysis: Forecasting and Control*. San Francisco: Holden-Day.

—— and Tiao, G. C. (1975). 'Intervention analysis with applications to economic and environmental problems', *Journal of the American Statistical Association*. **70**, 70.

Burman, J. P. (1980), 'Seasonal adjustment by signal extraction', *Journal of the Royal Statistical Society*, Ser. A, **143**, 321.

Cleveland, W. P., and Tiao, G. C. (1976), 'Decomposition of seasonal time series: a model for the census X-11 program', *Journal of the American Statistical Association*, **71**, 581.

Grether, D. M., and Nerlove, M. (1970), 'Some properties of "optimal" seasonal adjustment', *Econometrica*, **38**, 682.

Hannan, E. J. (1970), *Multiple Time Series*, New York: John Wiley.

Nerlove, M., Grether, D. M., and Carvalho, J. L. (1979), *Analysis of Economic Time Series*, New York, Academic Press.

Pierce, D. A. (1978), 'Seasonal adjustment when both deterministic and stochastic seasonality are present', in *Seasonal Analysis of Economic Time Series*, ed. Arnold Zellner. US Department of Commerce, 242.

—— (1980). 'Data revisions with moving average seasonal adjustment procedures', *Journal of Econometrics*, **14**, 95.

SHISKIN, J., YOUNG, A. H., and MUSGRAVE, J. C. (1967), 'The X-11 variant of census method II seasonal adjustment program'. Technical Paper 15, Bureau of the Census, US Dept. of Commerce.

TIAO, G. C., and HILLMER, S. C. (1978), 'Some consideration of decomposition of a time series', *Biometrika*, **65**, 497.

—— BOX, G. E. P., and HAMMING, W. (1975), 'A statistical analysis of the Los Angeles ambient carbon monoxide data 1955–1972', *Journal of the Air Pollution Control Association*, **25**, 1130.

WALLIS, K. F. (1974), 'Seasonal adjustment and the relations between variables', *Journal of the American Statistical Association*, **69**, 18.*

WHITTLE, P. (1963), *Prediction and Regulation*, New York: D. Van Nostrand.

YOUNG, A. H. (1968), 'Linear approximations to the census and BLS seasonal adjustment methods', *Journal of the American Statistical Association,* **63**, 445.

13

Forecasting Economic Time Series with Structural and Box–Jenkins Models: A Case Study

A. C. HARVEY and P. H. J. TODD

Abstract. The basic structural model is a univariate time series model consisting of a slowly changing trend component, a slowly changing seasonal component, and a random irregular component. It is part of a class of models that have a number of advantages over the seasonal ARIMA models adopted by Box and Jenkins (1976). This article reports the results of an exercise in which the basic structural model was estimated for six UK macroeconomic time series and the forecasting performance compared with that of ARIMA models previously fitted by Prothero and Wallis (1976).

KEY WORDS: Forecasting; ARIMA models; structural models; unobserved components; Kalman filter; macroeconomic time series.

Introduction

The autoregressive-integrated-moving average (ARIMA) processes introduced by Box and Jenkins (1976) provide a wide class of models for univariate time series forecasting. In the traditional Box–Jenkins framework, the main tools for specifying a suitable model are the correlogram and, to a lesser extent, the sample partial autocorrelation function. However, the correlogram and sample partial autocorrelation function are not always very informative, particularly in small samples. Furthermore, the difficulties in interpretation are compounded when a series has been differenced, and differencing is the rule rather than the exception in economic time series. The result is that inappropriate

Printed with permission of: *Journal of Business and Economic Statistics*, **1**. 299–307.

models are often fitted. Attempts to select ARIMA models by an automatic procedure, based on, say, the Akaike Information Criterion can lead to even worse results; see the examples cited by Jenkins (1982).

Experienced ARIMA model builders usually take into account the type of forecast function that their models imply; see Box, Hillmer, and Tiao (1978) and Jenkins (1982). They also tend to be aware of the type of time series structure that their models imply. Hillmer and Tiao (1982) attempt to make this last point more explicit by defining what constitutes an acceptable decomposition into trend, seasonal, and irregular components. They examine three of the ARIMA models commonly fitted to economic time series and show that certain restrictions must be placed on the range of parameter values for such a decomposition to exist. However, anyone reading the Hillmer and Tiao article, or the related article by Burman (1980), will realize that the relationship between an ARIMA model and the corresponding decomposition is often complex.

An alternative way of proceeding is to formulate models directly in terms of trend, seasonal, and irregular components. This necessarily limits the choice to those models that have forecast functions satisfying any prior considerations. Such models will be termed *structural* models. The fact that the individual components in a structural model have a direct interpretation opens up the possibility of employing a more formal model selection strategy. The question of developing such a strategy will not, however, be pursued in this article. For many economic time series we believe that one of the simplest structural models, which we call the basic structural model, will be adequate.

In this article we report the results of fitting the basic structural model to a number of economic time series, and then compare the predictions with those obtained using the Box–Jenkins models selected by Prothero and Wallis (1976). The idea of the exercise is not to prove that one method yields better forecasts than the other, but rather to show that for these series at least, the forecasts given by the two methods are comparable. Having demonstrated the viability of one of the simplest models within the structural class, we feel that the case for using this class as the basis for univariate time series modeling is a strong one.

From the technical point of view, all aspects of structural models can be handled by putting them into state space form. In particular, the likelihood function can be constructed in terms of the prediction error decomposition by using the Kalman filter; see Harvey (1982). Once estimates of the parameters have been computed, optimal predictions of future observations, together with their conditional mean square errors, can be obtained using the Kalman filter. Finally, optimal estimates of the individual components can be computed using a smoothing algorithm.

2. Structural Models

Let y_t be the observed variable. The basic structural model has the form

$$y_t = \mu_t + \gamma_t + \varepsilon_t, \quad t = 1, \ldots, T, \tag{2.1}$$

where μ_t, γ_t, and ε_t are trend, seasonal, and irregular components, respectively.

The process generating the trend is of the form

$$\mu_t = \mu_{t-1} + \beta_{t-1} + \eta_t, \quad t = 1, \ldots, T \tag{2.2a}$$

and

$$\beta_t = \beta_{t-1} + \zeta_t, \quad t = 1, \ldots, T, \tag{2.2b}$$

where η_t and ζ_t are normally distributed independent white noise processes with zero means and variances σ_η^2 and σ_ζ^2, respectively. The essential feature of this model is that it is a local approximation to a linear trend. The level and slope both change slowly over time according to a random walk mechanism.

The process generating the seasonal component is

$$\gamma_t = -\sum_{j=1}^{s-1} \gamma_{t-j} + \omega_t, \quad t = 1, \ldots, T, \tag{2.3}$$

where $\omega_t \sim \text{NID}(0, \sigma_\omega^2)$, and s is the number of 'seasons' in the year. The seasonal pattern is thus slowly changing but by a mechanism that ensures that the sum of the seasonal components over any s consecutive time periods has an expected value of zero and a variance that remains constant over time. This specification could be modified by replacing the white noise disturbance term by a moving average process.[1] The advantage of doing this is that it allows a smoother change in the seasonal pattern than that permitted by (2.3). However, for the small sample sizes considered in this article we felt it best to restrict our attention to one simple model.

The disturbances η_t, ζ_t, and ω_t are independent of each other and of the irregular component that is a normally distributed white noise process, that is, $\varepsilon_t \sim \text{NID}(0, \sigma^2)$. Although the model as a whole is relatively simple, it contains the main ingredients necessary for a time series forecasting procedure in that it projects a local linear trend and a

---

[1] The coefficients of the moving average model can be specified on a priori grounds or treated as additional parameters to be estimated. In the latter case the order of the process must be restricted to $s - 2$ or the model as a whole ceases to be identifiable. In the acceptable decomposition of Hillmer and Tiao (1982) the order of the MA component can be $s - 1$, but only because of the introduction of an additional restriction requiring that the variances of the trend and seasonal disturbance terms be minimized.

local seasonal pattern into the future.[2] It will be adequate for many economic time series, and it has the attraction that it involves no model selection procedure whatsoever.

The model can be written in the form

$$y_t = \frac{\xi_t}{\Delta^2} + \frac{\omega_t}{S(L)} + \varepsilon_t, \quad t = 1, \ldots, T, \tag{2.4}$$

where L is the lag operator, Δ is the first difference operator, $S(L)$ is the seasonal operator

$$S(L) = \sum_{j=0}^{s-1} L^j, \tag{2.5}$$

and ξ_t is equivalent to an MA(1) process since it is defined by

$$\xi_t = \eta_t - \eta_{t-1} + \zeta_{t-1}. \tag{2.6}$$

The first component on the right side of (2.4) is the trend, while the second is the seasonal component. The fact that the operators Δ^2 and $S(L)$ do not have a root in common is important, because it means that the minimum mean square estimates of both components have finite variance; see Pierce (1979). Put in a more informal way this amounts to saying that changes in the seasonal pattern are not confounded with changes in the trend. Note that the same operators are used in the decompositions proposed by Hillmer and Tiao (1982) and Burman (1980).

Expressing the model the form (2.4) makes it clear that it belongs to the class of unobserved component ARIMA (UCARIMA) models; compare Engle (1978). Models of this kind are discussed at some length in the book by Nerlove, Grether, and Carvalho (1979), but in their work attention is focused on stationary models fitted to the residuals from a polynomial regression. Thus a deterministic trend is adopted as a matter of course. In (2.2), on the other hand, a deterministic (linear) trend only emerges as a limiting case when $\sigma_\eta^2 = \sigma_\zeta^2 = 0$.

2.1 State space form

Suppose for simplicity that $s = 4$. The trend and seasonal components can be written in the form

$$
\begin{bmatrix} \mu_t \\ \beta_t \\ \gamma_t \\ \gamma_{t-1} \\ \gamma_{t-2} \end{bmatrix} =
\begin{bmatrix} 1 & 1 & & & 0 \\ 0 & 1 & & & \\ & & -1 & -1 & -1 \\ & 0 & 1 & 0 & 0 \\ & & 0 & 1 & 0 \end{bmatrix}
\begin{bmatrix} \mu_{t-1} \\ \beta_{t-1} \\ \gamma_{t-1} \\ \gamma_{t-2} \\ \gamma_{t-3} \end{bmatrix} +
\begin{bmatrix} \eta_t \\ \xi_t \\ \omega_t \\ 0 \\ 0 \end{bmatrix} \tag{2.7}
$$

[2] A similar model is employed by Kitagawa (1984) except that he has σ_η^2 constrained to be zero.

or, more compactly, as

$$\alpha_t = C\alpha_{t-1} + \tau_t, \tag{2.8}$$

where $\alpha_t = (\mu_t, \beta_t, \gamma_t, \gamma_{t-1}, \gamma_{t-2})'$, and so on. Defining

$$z_t = (1 \quad 0 \quad 1 \quad 0 \quad 0)', \tag{2.9}$$

(2.1) can be written as

$$y_t = z_t'\alpha + \varepsilon_t, \quad t = 1, \ldots, T. \tag{2.10}$$

Equations (2.8) and (2.10) can be regarded as the transition and measurement equations of a state space model; see, for example, Harvey (1981a, ch. 4).

2.2   Estimation

Maximum likelihood estimators of the parameters in structural models can be computed either in the time domain or in the frequency domain. The most attractive time domain procedure is based on the state space representation of the model. As (2.7) makes clear, the state vector in the basic structural model is nonstationary, but starting values for the Kalman filter can be constructed from the first $s + 1$ observations. The likelihood function for $y_{s+2}, \ldots, y_T$ is then given by the prediction error decomposition, that is,

$$\log L = -\frac{(T - s - 1)}{2} \log 2\pi - \tfrac{1}{2} \sum_{t=s+2}^{T} \log f_t^* - \tfrac{1}{2} \sum_{t=s+2}^{T} \frac{v_t^2}{f_t^*}, \tag{2.11}$$

where v_t is the one-step-ahead prediction error at time t, and f_t^* is its variance; compare Harvey (1981a, pp. 204–7). From the practical point of view an easy way of calculating close approximations to the starting values is to initiate the Kalman filter at $t = 0$ with a diagonal covariance matrix in which the diagonal elements are large but finite numbers.

If the variances of η_t, ζ_t, and ω_t are expressed relative to σ^2, the variance of ε_t (i.e. σ_η^2/σ^2, σ_ζ^2/σ^2 and σ_ω^2/σ^2), then the likelihood function can be written in the form

$$\log L = -\frac{(T - s - 1)}{2} \log 2\pi - \frac{(T - s - 1)}{2} \log \sigma^2$$

$$- \tfrac{1}{2} \sum_{t=s+2}^{T} \log f_t - \frac{1}{2\sigma^2} \sum_{t=s+2}^{T} \frac{v_t^2}{f_t}, \tag{2.12}$$

where the variance of v_t is $\sigma^2 f_t$. It now becomes possible to concentrate σ^2 out of the likelihood function, leaving

$$\log L = -\frac{(T-s-1)}{2}(\log 2\pi + 1) - \frac{(T-s-1)}{2}\log \tilde{\sigma}^2$$

$$-\frac{1}{2}\sum_{t=s+2}^{T}\log f_t, \tag{2.13}$$

where

$$\tilde{\sigma}^2 = (T-s-1)^{-1}\sum_{t=s+2}^{T}\frac{v_t^2}{f_t}. \tag{2.14}$$

The advantage of concentrating σ^2 out of the likelihood function is that numerical optimization can be carried out with respect to three parameters rather than four. The disadvantage is that the ML estimator of σ^2 is sometimes equal to zero. When this is the case, the relative variances in the concentrated likelihood tend to infinity.

Approximate ML estimates[3] can be obtained by expressing the likelihood function in terms of the periodogram of the differenced observations, $\Delta\Delta_s y_t$. These differenced observations are stationary and can be expressed as

$$\Delta\Delta_s y_t = \Delta_s \eta_t + (1 + L + \ldots + L^{s-1})\zeta_{s-1} + \Delta^2 w_t + \Delta\Delta_s \varepsilon_s. \tag{2.15}$$

The spectral density of the right side of (2.15) is relatively easy to construct using the autocovariance generating function. Frequency domain methods of this kind have been used quite successfully in the estimation of UCARIMA models; see Nerlove, Grether, and Carvalho (1979).

The autocorrelation structure implied by the basic structural model can be derived directly from (2.15). If $\gamma(\tau)$ denotes the autocovariance of $\Delta\Delta_s y_t$ at lag τ, then for quarterly data

$$\gamma(0) = 2\sigma_\eta^2 + 4\sigma_\zeta^2 + 6\sigma_\omega^2 + 4\sigma^2,$$

$$\gamma(1) = \qquad 3\sigma_\zeta^2 - 4\sigma_\omega^2 - 2\sigma^2,$$

$$\gamma(2) = \qquad 2\sigma_\zeta^2 + \sigma_\omega^2,$$

$$\gamma(3) = \qquad \sigma_\zeta^2 \qquad + \sigma^2,$$

$$\gamma(4) = -\sigma_\eta^2 \qquad - 2\sigma^2,$$

$$\gamma(5) = \qquad \sigma^2,$$

$$\gamma(\tau) = 0, \qquad \tau \geq 6. \tag{2.16}$$

These equations can be used as the basis for constructing estimators of the unknown parameters from the sample autocovariance function or

---

[3] The likelihood in (2.11) is exact if the first $s+1$ observations are taken to be fixed, although other assumptions can be made; see Harvey (1982). The frequency domain likelihood would be exact if the differenced observed were generated by a circular process.

from the correlogram. However, since there are six nonzero auto-covariances and only four unkown parameters, there is no unique way of forming such estimators. Even in special cases where the number of parameters is equal to the number of nonzero autocovariances, efficient estimators cannot be obtained, just as they cannot be obtained for an MA model. Nevertheless, estimates computed from the correlogram may still be useful as preliminary estimates in a maximum likelihood procedure.

2.3 Prediction and signal extraction

Once the parameters in the model have been estimated, predictions of future values, together with their conditional mean square errors, can be made from the state space form. The forecast function consists of the local trend with the local seasonal pattern superimposed upon it. If y_t is in logarithms, the estimator of β_t at time T can be regarded as the current estimator of the growth rate. This is of considerable importance to policy markers. The fact that it is immediately available in the structural model, together with its conditional MSE, is a great advantage.

Optimal estimates of the trend and seasonal components throughout the series can be obtained by applying a smoothing algorithm. This is sometimes known as signal extraction. In the present context it can be used to provide a method of model-based seasonal adjustment.

2.4 A class of structural models

Although this article is primarily concerned with the basic structural model, it is worth noting how the model can be generalized. In the first place the trend component can be extended so that it yields a local approximation to any polynomial; see Harrison and Stevens (1976). Second, a more elaborate seasonal model can be fitted, as was observed in the discussion after Equation (2.3). In addition, the seasonal pattern in the eventual forecast function can be made to change over time by adding to (2.3) a component, γ_t^*, which satisfies the condition that $S(L)\gamma_t^*$ is white noise. In the third place the irregular component can be modeled by any stationary ARMA process. Finally, a cyclical component can be brought into the model. This can be done by adding it directly to (2.1) or by incorporating it into the trend.[4]

---

[4] In a study of annual US economic time series over a period of 100 years, Nelson and Plosser (1982) found that the correlograms had a pattern consistent with the first differences being stationary about a non-zero mean. In all cases the lag one autocorrelation

3.   Criteria for Model Evaluation

Models can be evaluated and compared on the basis of goodness of fit both inside and outside the sample period. The criteria employed in our study are set out in this section.

3.1   Prediction error variance

The prediction error variance, that is, the variance of the one-step-ahead prediction errors in the models, is a basic measure of goodness of fit within the sample. For an ARIMA model, the prediction error variance is given directly by the estimator of the variance of the disturbances. For a structural model, the corresponding estimator is given by

$$\tilde{\sigma}_p^2 = \tilde{\sigma}^2 \, \bar{f}, \tag{3.1}$$

where $\tilde{\sigma}^2$ is given by (2.14) and $\bar{f}$ is defined by

$$\bar{f} = \lim_{t \to \infty} f_t. \tag{3.2}$$

The value of $\bar{f}$ can be found by running the Kalman filter until it reaches a steady state. It can usually be approximated by f_T, although there is an important distinction between $\sigma^2 \bar{f}$ and $\sigma^2 f_\tau$ in that the latter is the *finite* sample prediction error variance.

If the variances in the model are not expressed relative to σ^2, as in (2.11), then $\tilde{\sigma}_p^2 = \bar{f}^*$, where $\bar{f}^*$ is defined analogously to $\bar{f}$.

3.2   Post-sample predictions

Once the parameters of a model have been estimated within the sample period, predictions can be made in a post-sample period. The sum of squares of the one-step prediction errors then gives a measure of forecasting accuracy. These quantities can then be compared for rival models.

of first differences was positive. A referee has pointed out that series with this property could not have been generated by an annual structural model in which the trend is (2.2) with $\sigma_\zeta^2 = 0$, and the irregular component is white noise. However, for the UK series studies later in this paper, we found that the lag one sample autocorrelation for differenced annual data was negative for all series but one, and in that particular case it was less that .05. This behaviour is probably accounted for by the relative stability of the UK economy over the relatively short sample period covered (the 1950s and 1960s). Were we to consider modeling longer time series of the kind studied by Nelson and Plosser, we would probably do so by setting up a model in which a stochastic cyclical component was built into the trend.

The prediction errors in the post-sample period can also be compared with the prediction errors within the sample. A test statistic can be employed to test whether the prediction errors in the post-sample period are significantly greater than the prediction errors within the sample period. If they are, we can draw three possible conclusions:

1. The variances of the disturbances are increasing over time;
2. The process generating the observations has changed in some way, possibly due to the impact of certain outside interventions; or
3. The fit achieved in the sample period is to some extent a product of data mining.

If the variances of the disturbances are increasing over time, this should normally be detected within the sample period when the residuals are examined. The heteroscedasticity can often be removed by a suitable transformation such as taking logarithms. Predictive failure due to a changing data generation process simply shows up the weakness of univariate time series models, and there is little that can be done about it apart from extending the models to include explanatory variables. The third reason for predictive failure is the most relevant in the present context, since one of the objections to the Box–Jenkins methodology is that the cycle of identification, estimation, and diagnostic checking can lead to models that, while they give a good fit in the sample period, are inappropriate for making predictions in the future. Such models are usually, though not necessarily, overparameterized.

The mechanics of carrying out a post-sample predictive test are as follows. Consider the basic structural model and suppose that the relative variances of η_t, ζ_t, and ω_t are *known*. In this case $v_t \sim \text{NID}(0, \sigma^2 f_t)$ for $t = s + 2, \ldots, T$. If the model is correct, the prediction errors in the post-sample period, v_t, $t = T + 1, \ldots, T + l$, are distributed in a similar way and so

$$\xi(l) = \frac{(\sum_{t=T+1}^{T+l} v_t^2/f_t)/l}{\sum_{t=s+2}^{T} (v_t^2/f_t)/(T - s - 1)} \sim F_{l,T-s-1}. \qquad (3.3)$$

In the special case when $\sigma_\eta^2 = \sigma_\zeta^2 = \sigma_\omega^2 = 0$, the model is a linear regression with time trend and seasonal dummies, and the test based on (3.3) is then identical to the Chow test.

If T is reasonably large, the Kalman filter will be virtually in a steady state with $f_{T+j} \simeq \bar{f}$ for $j = 1, \ldots, l$. Therefore,

$$\xi(l) \simeq \sum_{t=T+1}^{T+l} \frac{v_t^2}{l\tilde{\sigma}_p^2}. \qquad (3.4)$$

When the relative variances are estimated, the statistic $l \cdot \xi(l)$ has a χ_l^2 distribution under the null hypothesis. However, testing $\xi(l)$ against an

F-distribution is still legitimate and may be more satisfactory in small samples.

A post-sample predictive test statistic for an ARIMA model can be derived in a similar way; compare Box and Tiao (1976). The distinction between (3.3) and (3.4) can again be made if a finite sample prediction algorithm is employed; see Harvey (1981b).

3.3 *Unconditional post-sample predictions*

Another useful measure of forecasting performance is the sum of squares of the prediction errors in the post-sample period for the unconditional predictions. The unconditional predictions are the predictions made for $t = T + 1$ to $T + l$ using the observations up to time $t = T$ only. As pointed out by Box and Tiao (1976), the only formal statistical test of the adequacy of the model is the one based on one-step-ahead predictions. However, looking at predictions several steps ahead is useful as a check that the form of the forecast function is sensible.

4.   Modeling Macroeconomic Time Series

Prothero and Wallis (1976) fitted Box–Jenkins' seasonal ARIMA models to quarterly observations on a number of UK economic time series. Their purpose was to compare the performance of these models with that of a small-scale econometric model devised by Hendry. Our purpose is to compare their models with the basic structural model. A subsidiary aim was simply to gain some experience of the problems involved in fitting structural models to relatively short time series.

For each series, Prothero and Wallis presented results for a number of models. In most cases they do not state unequivocally that any one of the models is the preferred specification. However, in light of their comments we have chosen one model in each case. Note that it is the ambiguity surrounding the choice of a suitable ARIMA model that is one of the weaknesses of the whole Box–Jenkins approach. The cycle of identification, estimation, and diagnostic checking is not only time consuming, but it can also on occasion produce poor results through an excess of data mining. The results for Series 5 (Imports) provide a good example.

We must stress again that only one structural model, the basic structural model, was fitted to each series. Hence no model selection was involved at all. It is quite likely that we could have obtained an even better performance by working with the wider class of models sketched out at the end of Section 2. However, in only one case, Series 4, did we feel that restricting ourselves to the basic model was a significant limitation and even in that case the performance of the model was quite reasonable.

4.1 The data

The data used in the study by Prothero and Wallis (1976) consisted of various UK economic time series published in *Economic Trends*. They fitted models to 42 quarterly observations covering the period 1957/3 to 1967/4. In 1969 the Central Statistical Office changed the data base, and this altered the characteristics of the series. This meant that only the first three observations in 1968 could be used for post-sample predictive testing. It was therefore decided to reestimate the preferred ARIMA specifications over the 37 observations from 1957/3 to 1966/3. The same observations were used to fit the basic structural model, while the eight observations 1966/4 to 1968/3 were used for post-sample predictive testing.

Prothero and Wallis fitted their models without taking logarithms. This was done for comparability with Hendry's econometric model. However, there is evidence of heteroscedasticity in some of the series and, other things being equal, one would almost certainly want to consider taking logarithms in these cases. This should be borne in mind when evaluating the results.

4.2 Estimation

The structural model was estimated via the prediction error decomposition using the concentrated form of the likelihood given in (2.13). The likelihood was maximized using the variable metric Gill–Murray–Pitfield algorithm, E04JBP in the NAG library. Analytic derivatives were not used.

The ARIMA models were reestimated using Prothero's own exact ML program, FMLAMS. The randomness of the residuals was assessed by reference to the values of the Box–Pierce Q-statistic.

4.3 Results

The results of fitting basic structural models and the preferred ARIMA specifications of Prothero and Wallis—hereafter denoted as P–W are summarized in Tables 1 and 2. The following points need to be made for the results on individual series.

A. C. Harvey and P. H. J. Todd

TABLE 1. Estimates of parameters for the basic structural model and for the preferred specification of the ARIMA model

Series	Structural model				ARIMA model[a] and Q-statistic	
	$\tilde{\sigma}^2_\eta$	$\tilde{\sigma}^2_\xi$	$\tilde{\sigma}^2_\omega$	$\tilde{\sigma}^2$		
1. Consumer durables	408.20	.00	181.42	.03	(a)	$\Delta\Delta_4 y_t = (1 - .27L^4)\epsilon_t$, Q(15) = 10.02
2. Other expenditure	305.51	.00	30.01	181.87	(a)	$\Delta\Delta_4 y_t = (1 - .59L^4)\epsilon_t$, Q(15) = 7.48
3. Investment	1,392.00	.00	.82	111.90	(d)	$(1 - .27L^4 - .05L^8 - .12L^{12} - .43L^{16})\Delta y_t = \epsilon_t$, Q(12) = 6.90
4. Inventory investment	1,204.08	.00	168.89	371.06	(a)	$\Delta\Delta_4 y_t = (1 - .35L^4 + .36L^2)(1 - .60L^4)\epsilon_t$, Q(13) = 5.17
					(e)	$(1 - .25L - .37L^2)(1 - .20L^4 - .06L^8 - .14L^{12} - .51L^{16})y_t = \epsilon_t$, Q(10) = 4.32
5. Imports	879.74	.00	.00	268.02	(c)	$(1 + .91L^4 + .94L^8 + .89L^{12} + .21L^{16})\Delta_4 y_t = 219.33 + \epsilon_t$, Q(11) = 12.13
6. GDP	3,375.47	.00	599.71	.20	(a)	$\Delta\Delta_4 y_t = (1 - .30L)(1 - .79L^4)\epsilon_t$, Q(14) = 9.48

[a] Letters in parentheses denote the specification in Prothero and Wallis (1976).

TABLE 2. Forecasting performance of the basic structural model and the preferred specification of the ARIMA model

Series	Prediction error variance		Post-sample prediction sum of squares		Predictive F-test[a]		Unconditional post-sample prediction sum of squares for structural mode
	Structural	ARIMA	Structural	ARIMA	Structural	ARIMA	
1. Consumer durables	1,349	1,509	71,705	78,372	6.67	6.49	46.218
2. Other expenditure	924	1,084	20,211	18,868	2.75	2.17	22,054
3. Investment	1,823	1,745	13,651	12,065	.95	.86	7,551
4. Inventory investment	3,274	(a)3,162 (e)2,157	62,683	(a)59,596 (e)43,381	2.40	(a)2.36 (e)2.51	76,929
5. Imports	1,532	1,259	57,428	604,080	4.75	59.98	34,223
6. GDP	7,663	7,733	47,794	33,020	.78	.53	56,091

a5% critical value for $F_{8,32}$ is approximately 2.25.

1. *Consumers' expenditure on durable goods*. The P–W specification (a) was chosen because P–W considered it to be 'an obvious choice'. The structural model gave a slightly better fit both within and outside the sample period. Both models clearly fail the post-sample predictive test, but the reason for this is almost certainly the change in vehicle registration policy introduced in 1967; see Prothero and Wallis (1976, p. 484).

2. *Consumer's expenditure on all other goods and services*. Again the preferred ARIMA model is of the simple form adopted in the first series. As before the structural model gives a slightly better fit inside the sample period, but the ARIMA model does better outside the sample period. However, the differences are not great, and as with Series 1, the overall conclusion must be that there is little distinction between the two methods in terms of forecasting performance. The relatively high values of the post-sample predictive test statistics are almost certainly explained by the heteroscedasticity in the series. This could probably be rectified by modeling the observations in logarithms.

3. *Investment*. P–W considered four models and chose (d) as being the 'most reasonable'. Unlike the preferred ARIMA models for the previous two series it contains more parameters than the structural model. Perhaps as a result of this it fits slightly better in the sample period. However, it also fits better in the postsample period, although as with the other two series, the difference in forecasting performances is not great.

Although the preferred ARIMA model appears to be satisfactory for one-step-ahead forecasting (at least for the post-sample period considered), it is less impressive over a longer time horizon. The sum of squares of the unconditional predictions over the sample period was 15,942, which is approximately twice the figure obtained with the structural model. Furthermore, the eventual forecast function is horizontal, and it seems unlikely that one would want a forecast function of this kind for a series that shows a clear upward movement over time. The forecast function for the structural model over the post-sample period is shown in Figure 1, and one can see that it tracks the series quite well.

4. *Inventory investment*. P–W observed that an examination of the sample autocorrelation function for various differences of the series suggests the operator $\Delta\Delta_4$. However, the preferred model was one fitted to the undifferenced observations. An examination of the series indicates that this is probably not unreasonable as there are no strong upward or downward movements in the series. Table 1 shows the models P–W fitted to both the differenced ($\Delta\Delta_4$) and undifferenced series. The differenced model has a similar performance to the structural model, but the undifferenced model is clearly superior to both. For this

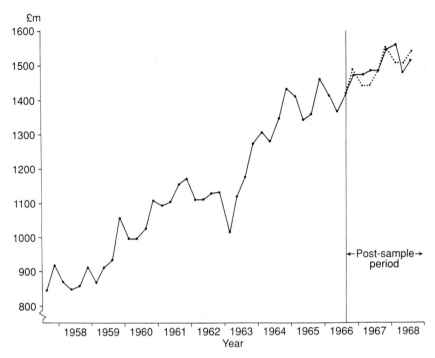

FIG. 1. Unconditional forecasts for investment using the basic structural model

series, therefore, the basic structural model is inadequate and a more general model, in which the irregular component is modeled by an autoregressive process, needs to be employed.

5. *Imports of goods and services.* For this series the preferred specification of P–W was their model (c) 'on account of its small residual variance and small value[5] of the Q-statistic'. This model has a smaller prediction error variance than the structural model, but its forecasting performance is disastrous. The devaluation of the pound in 1967 meant that any univariate model would have difficulty in forecasting over the post-sample period with any reasonable degree of accuracy, and this is apparent from the post-sample F-statistic value of 4.75 for the structural model. However, the F-statistic of 59.98 achieved with the ARIMA model is of a completely different order of magnitude. The performance of this model is therefore a particularly dramatic example of the dangers inherent in the Box–Jenkins methodology. We should, however, add that P–W's (e) and (f) specifications—which are some-

---

[5] P–W had $Q(11) = 4.79$. Our estimates are based on fewer observations and Q is rather larger, although still not significant at the 5% level.

what more conventional forms—forecasted in much the same way as the basic structural model.

6. *Gross Domestic Product.* P–W's model (a) is one of the standard forms of an ARIMA model. The prediction error variance is similar to the one obtained in the structural model, and both perform rather well in the post-sample period.

Overall, the performance of the basic structural model is quite good. For Series 1, 2, 3, and 6, its forecasting performance both inside and outside the sample period is similar to that achieved by the preferred ARIMA model. For Series 4, the ARIMA model is clearly better, but in this case a more general form of the structural model is called for. For Series 5, on the other hand, the forecasting performance of the preferred ARIMA model is disastrous while that of the basic structural model is quite reasonable.

For all of the series, the basic structural model produced a sensible forecast function. This is reflected in the last column in Table 2, which shows the sum of squares of the unconditional predictions over the post-sample period. In half the cases it is actually smaller than the sum of squares of the conditional forecast!

As regards the estimated variances in the structural model, it is interesting to note that in all cases the estimate of σ_ζ^2 is consistent with a steady increase over time, which all of the series display. However, the fact that the estimate goes right to zero may be a reflection of the small sample size and the method of estimation. When exact ML estimation is carried out in the time domain, it is not unusual to find some of the estimates ending up on the boundary of the parameter space; see Sargan and Bhargava (1983) and our Appendix for further details. The properties of approximate ML estimates computed in the frequency domain may be quite different, but this is a matter for future investigation.

5. Conclusions

The forecast function for a structural model can always be reproduced by an ARIMA model. For example, it is clear from (2.15) and (2.16) that the basic structural model is equivalent to an MA$(s + 1)$ model for $\Delta\Delta_s y_t$ in which the parameters are subject to nonlinear restrictions. The attraction of specifying models in terms of a well-defined structure is that attention is more likely to be confined to models that yield forecast functions of an acceptable form.

The basic model we propose has a similar structure to the Bayesian model of Harrison and Stevens (1976). However, while Harrison and Stevens make assumptions about plausible values for the variances of the disturbances, this article has shown that it is possible to estimate these variances even with a relatively small number of observations. In all the cases examined this led to a sensible forecast function. Furthermore, the forecasting performance of the estimated models compared well with the forecasting performance of ARIMA model selected after the usual process of identification, estimation, and diagnostic checking. Given these results, we feel that the conceptual advantages of structural models make them attractive as a class of univariate time series models.

Appendix: Boundary Solutions of Maximum Likelihood Estimates in Structural Models

Consider a simple case of the structural model in which there is no seasonal component and no slope; that is,

$$y_t = \mu_t + \varepsilon_t, \quad \varepsilon_t \sim \text{NID}(0, \sigma^2) \tag{A.1a}$$

and

$$\mu_t = \mu_{t-1} + \eta_t, \eta_t \sim \text{NID}(0, \sigma_\eta^2). \tag{A.1b}$$

This model is equivalent to an ARIMA (0, 1, 1) model

$$\Delta y_t = \xi_t + \theta \xi_{t-1}, \xi_t \sim \text{NID}(0, \sigma_\xi^2), \tag{A.2}$$

in which

$$\theta = [(q^2 + 4q)^{1/2} - 2 - q]/2,$$

where $q = \sigma_\eta^2/\sigma^2$; see Harvey (1981a, p. 170).

For an MA(1) model, Sargan and Bhargava (1983) have shown that there is a relatively high probability that an exact ML estimate of θ will be *exactly* equal to -1, even when the true value is some distance from -1. In model (A.1), a relatively low value of σ_η^2 corresponds to a value of θ close to -1 in (A.2). In these circumstances, ML estimates of zero will not be uncommon for σ_η^2.

Acknowledgements

An earlier version of this article was presented at the Second International Symposium on Forecasting, Istanbul, July 1982. We would like to thank the two referees of this journal for their useful comments on the first draft. The views expressed in this article are not necessarily those of HM Treasury.

References

(References marked with a * are included in this volume)

Box, G. E. P., Hillmer, S. C., and Tiao, G. C. (1978), 'Analysis and modelling of seasonal time series', in *Seasonal Analysis of Economic Time Series*, ed. A. Zellner. Washington, DC: Bureau of the Census, 309–334.

—— and JENKINS, G. M. (1976), *Time Series Analysis: Forecasting and Control* (revised edn.). San Francisco: Holden-Day.

—— and TIAO, G. C. (1976), 'Comparison of forecasts with actuality', *Applied Statistics*, **25**, 195–200.

BURMAN, J. P. (1980), 'Seasonal adjustment by signal extraction', *Journal of the Royal Statistical Society*, Series A, **143**, 321–37.

ENGLE, R. F. (1978), 'Estimating structural models of seasonality', in *Seasonal Analysis of Economic Time Series*, A. Zellner (ed.). Washington DC: Bureau of the Census, 281–308.*

HARRISON, P. J., and STEVENS, C. F. (1976), 'Bayesian forecasting', *Journal of the Royal Statistical Society,* Series B, **38**, 205–47.

HARVEY, A. C. (1981a), *Time Series Models*. Deddington: Philip Allan, and New York: John Wiley.

—— (1981b), 'Finite sample prediction and overdifferencing', *Journal of Time Series Analysis*, **2**, 221–32.

—— (1982), 'Estimation procedures for a class of univariate time series models', LSE Econometrics Program Discussion Paper No. 32.

HILLMER, S. C., and TIAO, G. C. (1982), 'An ARIMA-model-based approach to seasonal adjustment', *Journal of the American Statistical Association*, **77**, 63–70.*

JENKINS, G. M. (1982), 'Some practical aspects of forecasting in organizations', *Journal of Forecasting*, **1**, 3–21.

KITAGAWA, G. (1989), 'State space modelling of nonstationary time series'. *Time Series Analysis of Irregularly Observed Data*, 189–210. New York: Springer Verlag.

NELSON, C. R., and PLOSSER, C. I. (1982), 'Trends and random walks in macroeconomic time series: some evidence and implications', *Journal of Monetary Economics*, **10**, 139–62.

NERLOVE, M., GRETHER, D. M., and CARVALHO, J. L. (1979), *Analysis of Economic Time Series*. New York: Academic Press.

PIERCE, D. A. (1979), 'Signal extraction error in nonstationary time series', *Annals of Statistics*, **7**, 1303–20.

PROTHERO, D. L., and WALLIS, K. F. (1976), 'Modelling macroeconomic time series', *Journal of the Royal Statistical Society*, Series A, **139**, 468–500.

SARGAN, J. D., and BHARGAVA, A. (1983), 'Maximum likelihood estimation of regression models with first-order moving average errors when the root lies on the unit circle', *Econometrica*, **40**, 617–36.

14

A Prototypical Seasonal Adjustment Model

AGUSTIN MARAVALL, DAVID A. PIERCE

Abstract. The paper analyses unobserved-components modelling and estimation for the simplest ARIMA process that accepts a full decomposition into trend, seasonal and irregular components. This prototypical model exemplifies many features of and issues arising in model-based seasonal adjustment that are less transparent in more complex seasonal time series models. In particular the analysis illuminates the major issues surrounding the specification of the component models and the identification of a unique structure for them. In so doing, the relationship between reduced- and structural-form approaches to unobserved components estimation is illustrated within an ARIMA-modelling framework. Finally, the properties of the minimum mean-squared-error estimators of the unobserved components are examined and the two main types of estimation error, revisions in the preliminary estimator and error in the final estimator, are analysed.

Keywords. Time series; ARIMA models; unobserved-components models; model-based seasonal adjustment; signal extraction; trend estimation.

1. Introduction

Model-based seasonal adjustment has been increasingly developed over the past several years, primarily as an alternative to the Census X-11 method (Shiskin *et al.*, 1967) or its ARIMA variant (Dagum, 1975), which have been by far the most common procedures for producing published seasonally adjusted series. A number of approaches have involved expressing an observed seasonal series as the sum of unobserved components generated by ARIMA models, one of which is the seasonal component; see. e.g., Bell and Hillmer (1984), Box *et al.* (1978), Burman (1980), Hillmer and Tiao (1982), Pierce (1978). The process of seasonal adjustment is then the estimation (by signal extraction) and removal of this component.

Printed with permission of: *Journal of Time Series Analysis*, **8**. 177–93.

By far the most difficult task in developing such a procedure is the specification of the model for the seasonal component, which requires a statement (even if implicit) about what we mean by seasonality and what we want to remove in seasonally adjusting a series. In many approaches, including the use of unobserved-components ARIMA models, the embodiment of such a statement in the model specification can be a complex and unintuitive process. Thus we believe it is of value to examine the issues arising and the decisions required within the context of a very simple model, which can then serve as a prototype for more complex applications.

The model for the observable series which we have chosen for this purpose is one that we believe to be the simplest possible ARIMA model which possesses a non-trivial decomposition into trend, seasonal and irregular components—namely, the model $x_t - x_{t-2} = a_t$, for the observable series x_t in terms of white noise a_t. This model is appropriate for semiannual data or other periodic data of period 2. Section 2 develops this model and the corresponding component-model specifications which embody our usual concepts of seasonality and trend. However, there are an infinite number of such specifications consistent with the assumed model x_t, and Section 3 characterizes the class of all admissible decompositions. Section 4 then focuses on one of these, the 'canonical' decomposition, discusses some of its most relevant properties and presents a structural interpretation of the decomposition. In Section 5 the decomposition problem is analysed in the frequency domain.

Having solved the identification/specification problem, Section 6 considers estimation of the unobserved components, and discusses properties of the derived estimators. The last section analyses the two implied types of estimation error: revision error contained in the preliminary estimator and error still present in the final estimator.

2.   The Model

Numerous recent applications of signal extraction consist of two-component decompositions such as into signal plus noise, or into seasonal plus non-seasonal. However, frequently there are reasons for desiring a separation of the non-seasonal component into trend and irregular components as well. Purposes given for seasonal adjustment are typically that seasonality is extraneous to and interferes with what we want to observe in a series, so that its removal facilitates interpretation of the remainder of the series. But then, insofar as the irregular component may also be extraneous, its removal should still further aid in these goals, as the remaining component (the trend) would then represent the long-term evolution of the series, which is presumably of greater interest. The estimation of trend has in fact been recommended for years as an alternative or adjunct to seasonal adjustment, a few of the more recent examples being Moore *et al.* (1981), Kenny and Durbin (1982), Box *et al.* (1987), Maravall and Pierce (1986).

It should be noted that always is a separation into additive components desired or desirable; for some applications (an obvious example is forecasting) the overall model's relatively simple form and interpretation may suffice. We are addressing situations where a separation into components is useful (such as, for example, whenever seasonal adjustment is desired.) Thus we focus our attention on the three-component model

$$x_t = p_t + s_t + u_t \tag{2.1}$$

where p_t, s_t, and u_t are respectively the unobserved trend, seasonal and irregular components of the observable series x_t, at time t.

For x_t, we require a seasonal ARIMA model which admits a decomposition such that the components themselves have ARIMA-model specifications and, moreover, reflect the essential properties ordinarily associated with them, namely, 'periodicity' for the seasonal and low frequency dominance for the trend. We consider the simplest model to do so, given by

$$\nabla_2 x_t = a_t, \tag{2.2}$$

where $\nabla_2 = 1 - B^2 = (1 - B)(1 + B)$, and where a_t is white noise.

It is illuminating to examine the frequency-domain behaviour of this series. The model (2.2) is non-stationary so that the spectrum of x_t is not defined. However, it is customary to define the 'pseudospectrum' of this series by

$$g_x(\omega) = \left| \frac{\sigma_a}{1 - e^{2i\omega}} \right|^2 = \frac{\sigma_a^2}{2(1 - \cos 2\omega)} \tag{2.3}$$

for $0 \leq \omega \leq \pi$ where $|z|^2 = z\bar{z}$ for a complex number z with conjugate $\bar{z}$. This spectrum is graphed in Figure 1 where it is seen to be symmetric about $\omega = \pi/2$. The low-frequency behaviour can be associated with trend, and the frequencies near π with seasonal behaviour (π is the single seasonal frequency, corresponding to a seasonal cycle of period 2).

Since: (i) the autoregressive polynomial in the model for x_t is $\nabla_2 = (1 + B)(1 - B)$, and (ii) the peaks for $\omega = 0$ and $\omega = \pi$ are associated with the roots $B = 1$ and $B = -1$ of ∇_2, respectively, from the additive relation (2.1) it follows that acceptable trend and seasonal component models are of the form

$$p_t = \frac{\beta(B)}{1 - B} b_t \tag{2.4}$$

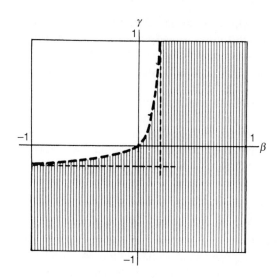

FIG. 1. Pseudospectrum of series x_t obeying model $\nabla_2 x_t = a_t$ and canonical components.

and

$$s_t = \frac{\gamma(B)}{1 + B} c_t, \tag{2.5}$$

where b_t and c_t are white noise and $\beta(B)$ and $\gamma(B)$ are polynomials in B. Multiplying both sides of (2.1) by ∇_2, we obtain

$$a_t = (1 + B)\beta(B)b_t + (1 - B)\gamma(B)c_t + \nabla_2 u_t. \tag{2.6}$$

Since the lag-two autocorrelation of the r.h.s. of (2.6) has to be equal to zero, reasonable models for the components are of the form

$$(1 - B)p_t = (1 - \beta B)b_t, \tag{2.7}$$

$$(1 + B)s_t = (1 - \gamma B)c_t, \tag{2.8}$$

$$u_t = \text{white noise}, \tag{2.9}$$

where, in order to avoid model multiplicity (see Box and Jenkins, 1970, pp. 195–200), we assume

$$|\beta| \leq 1, \qquad |\gamma| \leq 1. \tag{2.10}$$

Recapitulating, in this model the seasonality is of period 2, appropriate for semi-annual data. The trend p_t is an integrated process, reduced to stationarity by the ordinary difference operator; and the seasonal component s_t is summed to attain stationarity. These specifications are consistent with those of several recently developed model-based seasonal adjustment procedures, including Burman (1980), Hillmer and Tiao (1982) and Bell and Hillmer (1984).

We note that the same component specifications as (2.7) through (2.9) (though with different parameter values) are consistent with a slightly more general IMA (2, 2) model for x_t,

$$\nabla_2 x_t = (1 - \theta_1 B - \theta_2 B^2) a_t, \qquad (2.11)$$

which reduces to (2.2) by taking $\theta_1 = \theta_2 = 0$. Another point is that the irregular component u_t is required to be white noise. This is not always imposed, though two of the procedures where u_t is allowed to be serially correlated (Burman, 1980; Hillmer and Tiao, 1982) do produce a white noise irregular for this example. In general, having specified the seasonal component, one can define the trend to have certain properties and the irregular as the residual, which could then be autocorrelated; or alternatively one could specify the irregular as white noise and the trend as the residual, which could then exhibit features in addition to the smooth, low-frequency behaviour ordinarily associated with this component. Our prototypical model is sufficiently well behaved that such a choice is not necessary.

3. Autocovariance Equations and Admissible Decompositions

Given the difference/summation specifications for p_t and s_t and the white noise u_t, the models (2.7)-(2.9) are the most general first-order component models which imply the overall model (2.2) for x_t. As we shall see in this section, they are in fact too general, as an infinite number of models (2.7)-(2.9) are compatible with (2.2), and the components p_t, s_t, and u_t are thus unidentified.

Given $x_t = p_t + s_t + u_t$, if we multiply through by $(1 - B)(1 + B)$ and use the model specification (2.7) through (2.9), we obtain

$$
\begin{aligned}
a_t &= (1 - B)(1 + B)x_t \\
&= (1 - B)(1 - \beta B)b_t + (1 - B)(1 - \gamma\beta)c_t + (1 - B^2)u_t \\
&= b_t + (1 - \beta)b_{t-1} - \beta b_{t-2} + c_t - (1 + \gamma)c_{t-1} + \gamma c_{t-2} + u_t - u_{t-2}.
\end{aligned}
$$
$$(3.1)$$

The system of equations used to determine relationships among the parameters is obtained by equating autocovariances on the left and right sides of (3.1). In particular, for $k = 0, 1, 2$ we have

$$\sigma_a^2/2 = (1 - \beta + \beta^2)\sigma_b^2 + (1 + \gamma + \gamma^2)\sigma_c^2 + \sigma_u^2, \qquad (3.2)$$

$$0 = (1 - \beta)^2 \sigma_b^2 - (1 + \gamma)^2 \sigma_c^2, \tag{3.3}$$

$$0 = -\beta \sigma_b^2 + \gamma \sigma_c^2 - \sigma_u^2. \tag{3.4}$$

Adding the first and third equations gives

$$\sigma_a^2/2 = (1 - \beta)^2 \sigma_b^2 + (1 + \gamma)^2 \sigma_c^2 \tag{3.5}$$

which together with the second suggests expressing σ_b^2 and σ_c^2 as functions of β and γ. Adding and then subtracting (3.3) and (3.5), we obtain

$$\sigma_b^2 = \frac{\sigma_a^2}{4(1 - \beta)^2}, \quad \sigma_c^2 = \frac{\sigma_a^2}{4(1 + \gamma)^2}, \tag{3.6}$$

and, after substitution into (3.4)

$$\sigma_u^2 = \left(\frac{-\beta}{4(1 - \beta)^2} + \frac{\gamma}{4(1 + \gamma)^2} \right) \sigma_a^2. \tag{3.7}$$

Equations (3.6) and (3.7) show the dependence of the component-model innovation variances on the moving average parameters β and γ, so that the specification of values β and γ suffices to determine (identify) the system. However, in addition to (2.10) these parameters must satisfy the restriction that the variances σ_b^2, σ_c^2, and σ_u^2 be non-negative. Equation (3.6) ensures that $\sigma_b^2 \geqslant 0$, $\sigma_c^2 \geqslant 0$; it is the non-negativity of σ_u^2 that is at issue, which from (3.7) is equivalent to the constraint

$$-\beta(1 + \gamma)^2 + \gamma(1 - \beta)^2 \geqslant 0. \tag{3.8}$$

Figure 2 shows the graph of the region (not shaded) where the constraints (3.8) and (2.10) are satisfied. All points (β, γ) in this region (and only those points) correspond to an admissible decomposition of x_t in (2.2) into components p_t, s_t, and u_t as given by (2.7) through (2.9). In the next section, we shall be interested in the decomposition which corresponds to the upper left corner of the graph.

4. Identification and the Canonical Decomposition

The identification of the seasonal, trend and irregular components of x_t in (2.2) is tantamount to the selection of a point in the space of admissible (β, γ) values given in Figure 2. Several approaches to the resolution of this problem are possible. One often employed is to restrict the order of the MA polynomials, which in our cases means setting $\beta = \gamma = 0$ in (2.7) and (2.8) (see Maravall, 1985). More generally, specifying in advance the model forms for p_t, and s_t and a sufficient number of parameter values is what the 'structural' approach

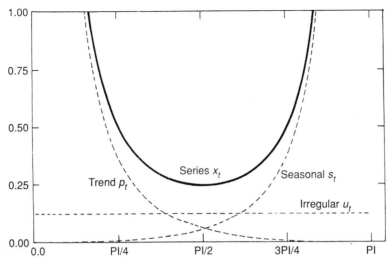

FIG. 2. Admissible parameter region.

would entail (see, for example, Engle, 1978, or Harvey and Todd, 1983.)

The identification problem encountered here is similar to the one that appears in standard econometric models. The model for the observed series is the reduced form, while the models for the components represent the associated structural form. For a particular reduced form, there are an infinite number of structures from which it can be generated. In order to select one, additional information has to be incorporated. The traditional approach in econometrics has been to set a priori some parameters in the structural model equal to zero (see Fisher, 1966). These zero-parameter restrictions reflect a priori econometric theory information, for example that some variables that affect demand of a commodity do not affect supply and vice versa.

In the case of our unobserved-components model, such a priori information is not available. We follow instead an alternative approach, originally suggested by Box, Hillmer, and Tiao (1978) and Pierce (1978). The additional information will be the requirement that separable white noise should not be a part of either the trend or the seasonal, and should instead be regarded as irregular; thus the irregular-component variance is maximized and the resulting decomposition has been termed 'canonical' by Hillmer and Tiao (1982). We now show that in the present example maximizing the variance of the irregular component u_t results in determining unique values for both β and γ and thus identifies the system (2.7) through (2.9).

By differentiation of (3.7) it is seen that the maximum of σ_u^2 occurs at $\beta = -1$, $\gamma = +1$, values which, in view of (3.6), also minimize σ_b^2 and σ_c^2, the variances of the trend and seasonal innovations. Thus in the canonical decomposition of a series generated by (2.2) into $p_t + s_t + u_t$, the models (2.7) and (2.8) for the trend and seasonal components are given by

$$(1 - B)p_t = (1 + B)b_t \tag{4.1}$$

and

$$(1 + B)s_t = (1 - B)c_t, \tag{4.2}$$

where, moreover, from (3.6) and (3.7) the innovation variances are seen to satisfy

$$\sigma_b^2 = \sigma_c^2 = \sigma_a^2/16, \quad \sigma_u^2 = \sigma_a^2/8. \tag{4.3}$$

Let $h(z)$ denote a spectrum (or pseudospectrum) $g(\omega)$ as a function of $z = \cos \omega$. An important property of the canonical model is the following. If s_t represents any admissible seasonal component, and s_t^* denotes the canonical one, the spectra of the two are given by

$$h_s(z) = \frac{\sigma_a^2}{8(1 + \gamma)^2} \left(\frac{1 + \gamma^2 - 2\gamma z}{1 + z} \right),$$

$$h_s^*(z) = \frac{\sigma_a^2}{16} \left(\frac{1 - z}{1 + z} \right),$$

where use has been made of (3.6). Then, it is easily seen that $h_s(z) = h_s^*(z) + k_o$, where $k_o = (1 - \gamma)^2/16(1 + \gamma)^2$ is a constant, and hence the two spectra are parallel. Since a similar result holds for the trend, any admissible trend or seasonal component—of the type (2.7) or (2.8)—is equal to the canonical one plus orthogonal white noise.

The manner in which maximizing the variance of the irregular identifies the component models is easily understood by considering the following. For our simple model (2.1) and (2.2), the spectra of the trend and seasonal components are decreasing and increasing functions, respectively, of ω. Hence the minimum is obtained, in the trend case, at $\omega = \pi$ and, in the seasonal case, at $\omega = 0$. Since for the canonical decomposition these minima are zero, it follows that $g_p(\omega = \pi) = 0$ and $g_s(\omega = 0) = 0$, where $g_p(\omega)$ and $g_s(\omega)$ are the trend and seasonal spectra. The first condition implies that $B = -1$ is a root of the moving average polynomial $(1 - \beta B)$ in the trend model; and similarly, the second condition implies that the $B = 1$ is a root of the moving average polynomial $(1 - \gamma B)$ in the seasonal model. In terms of (2.4) and (2.5), these two restrictions are equivalent to $\beta(-1) = \gamma(1) = 0$, or, in our model, to the linear constraints $1 + \beta = 1 - \gamma = 0$.

It follows that identification is attained by, instead of setting coefficients equal to zero, imposing linear constraints on them, reflecting the minima of zero in the trend and seasonal component spectra. There is thus a close relationship between the ARIMA-based decomposition and the structural approach. The requirement of noise-free components can be easily incorporated into the latter, and equations (4.1) to (4.3) represent the structural form associated with the reduced form (2.2).

Since, as noted before, equations (2.7)-(2.9) are consistent with the more general reduced form (2.11), equations (4.1) and (4.2) and a white-noise irregular will also represent the canonical components associated with the model (2.11). The three innovation variances, however, would not be given by (4.3) but would, instead, be functions of the parameters θ_1 and θ_2.

5.   The Decomposition in the Frequency Domain

The preceding sections have illustrated the decomposition of a time series into trend, seasonal and irregular components in the time domain. It is also of interest to examine this problem in the frequency domain, which we do with a development similar to Burman (1980). Since the components p_t, s_t and u_t are orthogonal, an admissible decomposition is characterized by a partition of the spectrum of x_t into three additive component spectra, which we write as

$$h_x(z) = h_p(z) + h_s(z) + h_u(z). \qquad (5.1)$$

From (2.3), the l.h.s. of (5.1) is

$$h_x(z) = \frac{1}{4(1 - z^2)} = \frac{1}{4(1 - z)(1 + z)},$$

where, without loss generality, we set $\sigma_a^2 = 1$. The factors $(1 - z)$ and $(1 + z)$ are associated with the trend and seasonal roots ($B = 1$ and $B = -1$), respectively, of the AR polynomial in (2.2), and $h_u(z)$ is constant. Thus an admissible decomposition can be obtained from the identity

$$\frac{1}{4(1 - z)(1 + z)} = \frac{n_p(z)}{1 - z} + \frac{n_s(z)}{1 + z} + k, \qquad (5.2)$$

where the three terms of the r.h.s. represent the trend, seasonal and irregular spectra, which are non-negative. For $|z| \leqslant 1$, the minimum of $h_x(z)$ is greater than zero; hence at least one of the three quantities (k, min $h_p(z)$, min $h_s(z)$) will be positive. Since a positive constant can be interchanged among the three component spectra without violating the admissibility constraints, it follows that the decomposition given by (5.2) will not be unique: an infinite number of combinations of non-negative $n_p(z)$, $n_s(z)$ and k exist which satisfy (5.2). This is the frequency domain equivalent of the existence of an infinite number of component models satisfying the system of covariance equations (3.2)-(3.4). It implies, as before, that, without additional assumptions, the overall model does not identify unique models for the components.

In order to derive the canonical solution, the partial fraction expansion of $h_x(z)$ provides an easy to compute two-stage procedure. First, to obtain simply an admissible decomposition, we seek values a and b such that

$$\frac{1}{(1-z)(1+z)} = \frac{a}{1-z} + \frac{b}{1+z}, \qquad (5.3)$$

which are obtained by noting that, from (5.3), $a(1+z) + b(1-z) = 1$ so that $a = b = \frac{1}{2}$. Consequently, from (5.2) and (5.3)

$$h_x(z) = \frac{1}{8}\left(\frac{1}{1-z} + \frac{1}{1+z}\right)$$

hence

$$h_p(z) = \frac{1}{8(1-z)}, \quad h_s(z) = \frac{1}{8(1+z)}, \quad h_u(z) = 0,$$

with analogous component spectra

$$g_p(\omega) = \frac{\sigma_a^2}{8(1-\cos\omega)}, \quad g_s(\omega) = \frac{\sigma_a^2}{8(1+\cos\omega)}, \quad g_u(\omega) = 0.$$

Since the two minima

$$\min_{0\leqslant\omega\leqslant\pi} g_p(\omega) = g_p(\pi) = \sigma_a^2/16, \qquad (5.4)$$

$$\min_{0\leqslant\omega\leqslant\pi} g_s(\omega) = g_s(0) = \sigma_a^2/16, \qquad (5.5)$$

are both strictly positive, the decomposition obtained in the first stage is not a canonical one. Thus in the second stage the constants (5.4) and (5.5) are subtracted from the trend and seasonal spectra, respectively, and added to the irregular. Consequently, for the canonical decomposition

$$g_p^*(\omega) = g_p(\omega) - \frac{\sigma_a^2}{16} = \frac{\sigma_a^2}{16}\frac{1+\cos\omega}{1-\cos\omega}, \qquad (5.6)$$

$$g_s^*(\omega) = g_s(\omega) - \frac{\sigma_a^2}{16} = \frac{\sigma_a^2}{16}\frac{1-\cos\omega}{1+\cos\omega}, \qquad (5.7)$$

and

$$g_u^*(\omega) = \frac{\sigma_a^2}{8}. \tag{5.8}$$

These spectra imply the same component processes and variances as previously derived, given by (4.1) through (4.3). Notice that the first stage of the procedure is equivalent to decreasing the order of the moving averages in (2.7)-(2.8), and hence the admissible decomposition obtained in the first stage is the one that results from identifying the component models by a priori setting $\beta = \gamma = 0$.

The graph of $g_x(\omega)$ is given in Figure 1, which also shows the spectra of the three canonical components. Figure 3 illustrates the two stages of the decomposition. For the canonical components, the height of $g_u(\omega)$ is maximized, and the minima of $g_p(\omega)$ and of $g_s(\omega)$ are both zero.

6.   Estimation

The foregoing has been concerned with specification of the model forms assumed to generate the series x_t and its components. The components are unobservable and, having resolved the identification/specification problem, we proceed to obtain estimates of p_t, s_t, and u_t given a realization of $\{x_t\}$.

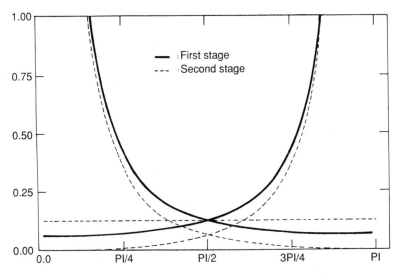

FIG. 3. Decomposition of $\nabla_2 x_t = a_t$: first and second stages.

6.1. Signal extraction

Consider an admissible decomposition, given by equations (2.7) to (2.9), and let

$$\psi_p(B) = (1 - \beta B)/(1 - B)$$
$$\psi_s(B) = (1 - \gamma B)/(1 + B)$$
$$\psi_x(B) = 1/(1 - B^2) \qquad (6.1)$$

denote the polynomials in B of the moving average representations of p_t, s_t and x_t. Using well-known results (see Cleveland and Tiao, 1976, or Bell, 1984), the minimum mean squared error (MMSE) estimators of the three components are given by

$$\hat{p}_t = v_p(B)x_t, \qquad (6.2)$$
$$\hat{s}_t = v_s(B)x_t, \qquad (6.3)$$
$$\hat{u}_t = [1 - v_p(B) - v_s(B)]x_t, \qquad (6.4)$$

where the v-polynomials represent the two-sided symmetric filters

$$v_p(B) = \frac{\sigma_b^2}{\sigma_a^2} \left| \frac{\psi_p(B)}{\psi_x(B)} \right|^2, \quad v_s(B) = \frac{\sigma_c^2}{\sigma_a^2} \left| \frac{\psi_s(B)}{\psi_x(B)} \right|^2, \qquad (6.5)$$

where the convention

$$|h(B)|^2 = h(B)h(F)$$

is employed, $F = B^{-1}$ denoting the forward shift operator.

For the trend component estimator, (6.1) and (6.5) eventually yield,

$$v_p(B) = \frac{\sigma_b^2}{\sigma_a^2} |(1 + B)(1 - \beta B)|^2 = v_{p0} + v_{p1}(B + F) + v_{p2}(B^2 + F^2),$$

where $v_{p0} = (\sigma_b^2/\sigma_a^2)(2 - 2\beta + 2\beta^2)$, $v_{p1} = (\sigma_b^2/\sigma_a^2)(1 - \beta)^2$, $v_{p2} = - (\sigma_b^2/\sigma_a^2)\beta$, and, from (3.6), $\sigma_b^2/\sigma_a^2 = 1/4(1 - \beta)$. Similarly, for the seasonal component estimator, given by (6.3),

$$v_s(B) = \frac{\sigma_c^2}{\sigma_a^2} |1 - \gamma B|^2 |1 - B|^2 = v_{s0} + v_{s1}(B + F) + v_{s2}(B^2 + F^2),$$

where $v_{s0} = (\sigma_c^2/\sigma_a^2)(2 + 2\gamma + 2\gamma^2)$, $v_{s1} = - (\sigma_c^2/\sigma_a^2)(1 + \gamma)^2$, $v_{s2} = (\sigma_c^2/\sigma_a^2)\gamma$, and, from (3.6), $\sigma_c^2/\sigma_a^2 = 1/4(1 + \gamma)^2$.

As is the case whenever the model for the observed series is a finite autoregression, the two filters are finite, depending in this case only on values x_{t-2} through x_{t+2}. Furthermore, they satisfy the conditions $v_p(1) = v_s(-1) = 1$ and $v_p(-1) = v_s(1) = 0$.

6.2. The models for the estimators

For the canonical decomposition, $\beta = -1$ and $\gamma = 1$, so that $v_{p0} = v_{s0} = 6/16$, $v_{p1} = -v_{s1} = 4/16$, $v_{p2} = v_{s2} = 1/16$; and in compact form

$$v_p(B) = \tfrac{1}{16}|1 + B|^4, \ v_s(B) = \tfrac{1}{16}|1 - B|^4. \tag{6.6}$$

In order to analyse the estimators, it will prove helpful to obtain the models that express the three components as functions of the innovations a_t. Using (6.6) in (6.2)–(6.4), and then considering that $x_t = (1 - B^2)^{-1} a_t$, the estimators of the components can be expressed as

$$(1 - B)\hat{p}_t = (1 + B)(1 + F)^2 a_t/16, \tag{6.7}$$

$$(1 + B)\hat{s}_t = (1 - B)(1 - F)^2 a_t/16, \tag{6.8}$$

$$\hat{u}_t = (1 - F^2)a_t/8. \tag{6.9}$$

Comparing these three expressions with the models for the components, given by (4.1)–(4.3), it is seen that the model for the MMSE estimator of a component is different from the model for the component itself (see Grether and Nerlove, 1970). There are some similarities: first, the same stationarity-inducing transformations are required; second, since the models for $\hat{p}_t$ and $\hat{s}_t$ contain the moving average factor $(1 + B)$ and $(1 - B)$, respectively, estimation preserves the canonical properties of the trend and seasonal components.

From (6.7)–(6.9), the spectra of the three estimators are found to be

$$g_{\hat{p}}(\omega) = \sigma_a^2(1 + \cos \omega)^3/[64(1 - \cos \omega)],$$

$$g_{\hat{s}}(\omega) = \sigma_a^2(1 - \cos \omega)^3/[64(1 + \cos \omega)],$$

$$g_{\hat{u}}(\omega) = \sigma_a^2(1 - \cos^2 \omega)/16,$$

and comparing them with the true-component spectra, given by (5.6)–(5.8), it is found that, when $0 \leqslant \omega \leqslant \pi$, $g_p^*(\omega) \geqslant g_p(\omega)$, $g_s^*(\omega) \geqslant g_s(\omega)$, $g_u^*(\omega) > g_u(\omega)$; hence, in each of the three cases and for all frequencies, the spectrum of the estimator is smaller than that of the component.

Figure 4 compares the two spectra for the three components. The 'distortion' induced by MMSE estimation is seen to affect mostly, the spectrum of the irregular component, which shows dips for $\omega = 0$ and $\omega = \pi$. These dips reflect the fact that, in extracting the noise from the x_t series, the MMSE ignores the frequencies dominated by the trend and seasonal components (notice that, for $\omega = 0$ and $\omega = \pi$, the ratio of the irregular variance to that of the trend plus seasonal becomes zero). As a result, the spectrum of the irregular estimator displays a peak for

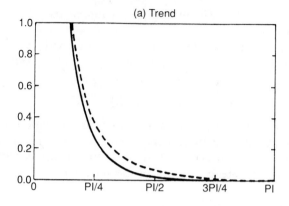

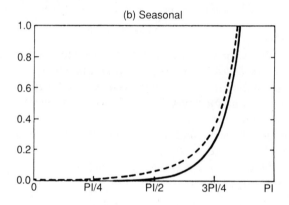

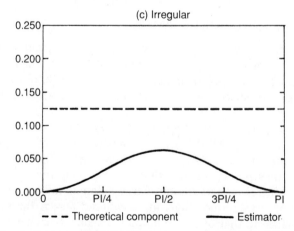

FIG. 4. Spectra of theoretical components and their estimators.

$\omega = \pi/2$, which implies a periodic effect (in semi annual data associated with a two-year period).

From equations (6.7)–(6.9), the autocovariance functions of the (stationary transformation of the) component estimators can also be computed. As shown in Table 1, MMSE estimation induces additional autocorrelation in the models for the three estimators. Furthermore, the variances of the theoretical components are larger than those of their estimators, particularly concerning the irregular component. Finally, the correlations between the estimators can be computed. It is seen that estimation preserves orthogonality of the trend and seasonal component estimators, although the two are correlated with the estimator of the irregular ($\rho = 0.316$ in both cases). By comparing the properties of the empirical estimates with those implied by the models for the estimators, the model-based approach provides a natural way for evaluating the results of a particular application.

7.   Estimation Errors

7.1 Revisions

The preceding has assumed that both future and past data are available, whereas this is not the case for the current time period, which is in practice often with the most important application. Consider, for example, the trend estimator associated with an admissible decomposition, given by

$$\hat{p}_t = v_{p0}\, x_t + \sum_{i=1,2} v_{pi}(x_{t-i} + x_{t+i}) \qquad (7.1)$$

where the v coefficients were given in Section 6.1. At time t, $\hat{p}_t$ cannot be computed since x_{t+1}, and x_{t+2} are not yet known. The MMSE

TABLE 1.   Variances and non-zero autocorrelations of the stationary components and their estimators

		Variance	ρ_1	ρ_2	ρ_3
Trend	Component	0.125	0.50	–	–
	Estimator	0.078	0.75	0.30	0.05
Seasonal	Component	0.125	−0.50	–	–
	Estimator	0.078	− .75	0.30	−0.05
Irregular	Component	0.125	–	–	–
	Estimator	0.031	–	−0.50	–

'concurrent' estimator of p_t, denoted $\hat{p}_t^0$, is the conditional expectation of p_t at time t. Since (for $i > 1$)

$$E_t p_t = E_t E_{t+i} p_t = E_t \hat{p}_t,$$

taking expectations in both sides of (7.1) yields

$$\hat{p}_t^0 = v_{p0} \, x_t + \sum_{i=1,2} v_{pi}(x_{t-i} + \hat{x}_t(i)), \qquad (7.2)$$

where $\hat{x}_t(i) = E_t x_{t+i}$ denotes the origin-t lead-i forecast of x. Therefore, the concurrent estimator is obtained by applying the two-sided filter $v_p(B)$ to a forecast augmented series (see Cleveland and Tiao, 1976). This concurrent estimator will be revised in future periods, as forecasts are either updated or replaced with new observations until the historical or final estimator can be computed.

Substracting (7.2) from (7.1) shows that the total revision in the concurrent trend estimator is

$$r_{pt} = \hat{p}_t - \hat{p}_t^0 = v_{1p} e_t(1) + v_{2p} e_t(2),$$

with $e_t(j) = x_{t+j} - \hat{x}_t(j)$ denoting the corresponding forecast error. Since $e_t(1) = a_{t+1}$ and (for this model) $e_t(2) = a_{t+2}$, we have

$$r_{pt} = [(1 - \beta)^2 a_{t+1} - \beta a_{t+2}] \sigma_b^2 / \sigma_a^2$$

so that r_{pt} is a first-order moving average. Using (3.6),

$$r_{pt} = \frac{1}{4}\left(a_{t+1} - \frac{\beta}{(1 - \beta)^2} \, a_{t+2}\right), \qquad (7.3)$$

whence

$$\text{var}(r_{pt}) = \frac{\sigma_a^2}{16}\left(1 + \frac{\beta^2}{(1 - \beta)^4}\right). \qquad (7.4)$$

Similarly, the revision in a concurrent seasonal estimate $\hat{s}_t^0$ is

$$r_{st} = \frac{\sigma_c^2}{\sigma_a^2} [- (1 + \gamma)^2 a_{t+1} + \gamma a_{t+2}]$$

$$= \frac{1}{4}\left(- a_{t+1} + \frac{\gamma}{(1 + \gamma)^2} \, a_{t+2}\right), \qquad (7.5)$$

with variance

$$\text{var}(r_{st}) = \frac{\sigma_a^2}{16}\left(1 + \frac{\gamma^2}{(1 + \gamma)^4}\right). \qquad (7.6)$$

It is of interest to examine the revision variances in terms of the chosen decomposition. In Section 3 we derived the admissible space for the parameters β and γ. On its boundary, where (3.8) holds as an equality, at $\beta = -1$, we have $\gamma = -3 + 2\sqrt{2}$, and, at $\gamma = 1$, $\beta = 3 - 2\sqrt{2}$. Hence for all admissible decompositions (see Figure 2):

$$-1 \leqslant \beta \leqslant 3 - 2\sqrt{2} \text{ and } -3 + 2\sqrt{2} \leqslant \gamma \leqslant 1.$$

Figure 5 shows the variances of the trend and seasonal revisions as functions of the respective parameters, β and γ, over their admissible range. The figure suggests, and equations (7.4) and (7.6) show, that the revision variances are maximized at the canonical-decomposition values, $\beta = -1$, $\gamma = 1$. The occurrence of larger revisions may indicate a price paid for choosing the canonical decomposition (i.e. a trade-off between size of the revision and cleanness of signal).

For the canonical model the revision variance is

$$\sigma_r^2 = \frac{\sigma_a^2}{16}(1 + \tfrac{1}{16}) \tag{7.7}$$

for either trend or seasonal revisions, a value which is slightly above the innovation variance of the trend or seasonal models (see (4.3)), and well below the one-step-ahead forecast error variance σ_a^2. Also, from (7.3) and (7.5) the correlation between r_{pt} and r_{st} is seen to be $(-15/17)$, so that joint confidence intervals, based on these revisions, can be built around the concurrent estimates of the trend and seasonal components.

7.2. Final estimation error

Revisions may be regarded as measurement errors in the concurrent estimate of a component, caused by limitations on the availability of

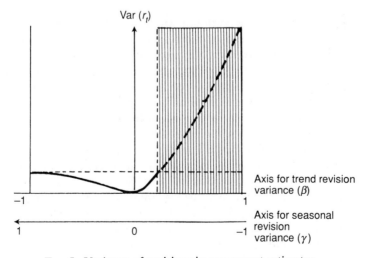

FIG. 5. Variance of revisions in concurrent estimates.

data. But even if an infinite length of data is assumed (and the models known exactly), the final or historical estimate still contains an error. For the historical seasonal estimate $\hat{s}_t$ in (6.3), let the error be $\delta_t = s_t - \hat{s}_t$. Then

$$\delta_t = - v_s(B)(p_t + u_t) + [1 - v_s(B)]s_t \qquad (7.8)$$

where, for the canonical decomposition,

$$v_s(B) = \tfrac{1}{16}(1 - B)^2(1 - F)^2. \qquad (7.9)$$

Using (4.1), (4.2) and (7.9) in (7.8), it is found that

$$\delta_t = \tfrac{1}{16}[-(1 - B^2)(1 - F)^2 b_t$$

$$+ (1/k)(1 + F)(1 - B)(1 - kB)(1 - kF)c_t$$

$$+ (1 - B)^2(1 - F)^2 u_t].$$

with $k = 3 - 2\sqrt{2}$. Thus

$$\mathrm{var}(\delta_t) = \tfrac{1}{256}(10\sigma_b^2 + 74\sigma_c^2 + 70\sigma_u^2),$$

and, using (4.3), we obtain

$$\mathrm{var}(\delta_t) = \sigma_\delta^2 = \frac{\sigma_a^2}{16}(1 - \tfrac{1}{8}). \qquad (7.10)$$

(The value (7.10) may alternatively be derived by obtaining the stochastic process followed by $n_t = p_t + u_t$ and applying the results of Pierce, 1979.)

Therefore, most of the variation in the seasonal's final estimate is induced by the irregular and by the seasonal innovation. The variance of the error in the historical estimate, given by (7.10), is slightly less than the innovation variance σ_b^2 in (4.3), whereas the revision variance σ_r^2 in (7.7) is slightly larger. Roughly, the three standard deviations σ_b, σ_r and σ_δ, are of similar magnitudes and all approximately one-fourth the standard deviation σ_a of the innovation of the series.

Having obtained expressions for the errors and their associated standard deviations, the model-based procedure permits us to analyze the precision of the estimates, a major point of concern (see Moore *et al.*, 1981). Combining the revision and final-data error results, an approximate 95 per cent confidence interval for p_t based on the concurrent measurement is given by $\hat{p}_t^0 + 0.70\sigma_a$; when the final measurement is available, the interval narrows to $\hat{p}_t + 0.46\sigma_a$. The corresponding confidence intervals for the true seasonal component s_t would be of the same width.

Acknowledgements

Any views expressed are those of the authors and not necessarily related to those of any central bank. Helpful comments on an earlier version were provided by W. P. Cleveland, D. F. Findley, A. Espasa, and an anonymous referee.

References

(References marked with a * are included in this volume)

BELL, W. R. (1984), 'Signal extraction for nonstationary time series', *Ann. Statist.* **12**, 646–64.

—— and HILLMER, S. C. (1984), 'Issues involved with the seasonal adjustment of economic time series', *J. Bus. Econ. Statist.* **2**, 291–320.

BOX, G. E. P., HILLMER, S. C., and TIAO, G. C. (1978), 'Analysis and modelling of seasonal time series', in *Seasonal Analysis of Economic Time Series* (ed. A. Zellner). Washington, DC: US Department of Commerce, Bureau of the Census, pp. 309–34.

—— and JENKINS, G. M. (1970), *Time Series Analysis, Forecasting and Control*. San Francisco: Holden Day.

—— PIERCE, D. A., and NEWBOLD, P. (1987), 'Estimating Current Trend and Growth Rates in Seasonal Time Series', *J. Amer. Statist. Ass.* **82**, 276–82.

BURMAN, J. P. (1980), 'Seasonal adjustment by signal extraction', *J. Roy. Statist. Soc. A.* **13**, 321–37.

CLEVELAND, W. P., and TIAO, G. C. (1976), 'Decomposition of seasonal time series: A model for the X-11 Program', *J. Amer. Statist. Ass.* **71**, 581–7.

DAGUM, E. B. (1975), 'Seasonal factors forecasts from ARIMA models', *Proc. International Statistical Institute.*, 40th Session, 3. Warsaw, pp. 206–19.

ENGLE, R. F. (1978), 'Estimating structural models of seasonality', in *Seasonal Analysis of Economic Time Series* (ed. A. Zellner). Washington, DC: US Department of Commerce, Bureau of the Census, pp. 281–97.*

FISHER, F. M. (1966), *The Identification Problem in Econometrics*. New York: McGraw Hill.

GRETHER, D. M., and NERLOVE, M. (1970), 'Some properties of "optimal" seasonal adjustment', *Econometrica*, **38**, 682–703.

HARVEY, A. C., and TODD, P. H. J. (1983) 'Forecasting economic time series with structural and Box–Jenkins models: A case study', *J. Bus. Econ. Statist.* **1**, 299–306.*

HILLMER, S. C., and TIAO, G. C. (1982), 'An ARIMA model-based approach to seasonal adjustment', *J. Amer. Statist. Ass.* **77**, 63–70.*

KENNY, P., and DURBIN, J. (1982), 'Local trend estimation and seasonal adjustment of economic and social time series', *J. Roy. Statist. Soc. A*, **145**, 1–28.

MARAVALL, A. (1985), 'On structural time series models and the characterization of components', *J. Bus. Econ. Statist.* **3**: 4, 350–5.

—— and PIERCE, D. A. (1986), 'The transmission of data noise into policy noise in US monetary control', *Econometrica*, **54**, 961–79.

MOORE, G. H., BOX, G. E. P., KAITZ, H. B., STEPHENSON, J. A., and ZELLNER, A. (1981), *Seasonal Adjustment of the Monetary Aggregates: Report of the Committee of Experts on Seasonal Adjustment Techniques.* Washington, DC: Board of Governors of the Federal Reserve System.

PIERCE, D. A. (1978), 'Seasonal adjustment when both deterministic and stochastic seasonality are present', in *Seasonal Analysis of Economic Time Series* (ed. A. Zellner). Washington, DC: US Department of Commerce, Bureau of the Census, pp. 242–73.

—— (1979), 'Signal extraction error in nonstationary time series', *Ann. Statist.* **7**, 1303–20.

SHISKIN, J., YOUNG, A. H., and MUSGRAVE, J. C. (1967), 'The X-11 variant of the census method-II seasonal adjustment program', Technical Paper No. 15, US Bureau of the Census.

15

Seasonal Adjustment and Kalman Filtering: Extension to Periodic Variances

PETER BURRIDGE and KENNETH F. WALLIS

Abstract. This paper reviews the relations between the methods of seasonal adjustment used by official statistical agencies and the 'model-based' methods that postulate explicit stochastic models for the unobserved components of a time series and applying optimal signal extraction theory to obtain a seasonal adjusted series. The Kalman filter implementation of the model-based methods is described and some recent results on its properties are reviewed. The model-based methods employ homogeneous or time-invariant models that assume in particular that the autocovariance structure does not vary with the season. Relaxing this leads to the class of models known as periodic models, and an example of a seasonally heteroscedastic unobserved-components ARIMA (SHUCARIMA) model is presented. The calculation of the standard error of a seasonally adjusted series via the Kalman filter is extended to this periodic model and illustrated for a monthly rainfall series.

Key words: Seasonal adjustment; signal extraction; Kalman filter; periodic models; seasonally heteroscedastic unobserved-components autoregressive-integrated-moving average; (SHUCARIMA) models

Seasonal adjustment procedures aim to remove from an observed time series the unobserved component associated with its regular periodic variation, and hence to display more clearly the remaining non-seasonal variation. Methods of seasonal adjustment used by official statistical agencies, of which the best known is the US Census Bureau's X-11 method (Shiskin *et al.*, 1967), do not employ explicit statistical models for the unobserved components; their performance is evaluated in relation to various criteria for assessing the quality of their results in practical applications. An alternative approach is to postulate explicit stochastic models for the unobserved components, and to apply linear least squares (LLS) signal extraction theory to obtain the 'optimal'

Printed with permission of: *Journal of Forecasting*, **9**. 109–18.

seasonally adjusted series. Such 'model-based' methods have not been widely adopted by official statistical agencies, but have proved helpful in increasing understanding of the properties of the more traditional methods and of the various criteria for assessing their performance.

   In this paper we review the relations between the two approaches, considering in particular the Kalman filter implementation of the model-based methods. This has been shown to provide a natural solution to the problem of calculating the standard error of a seasonally adjusted series, either to indicate the likely magnitude of revisions to preliminary seasonally adjusted data or to show the inherent uncertainty of their final values (Burridge and Wallis, 1985). A common practical finding, however, is that some months are inherently more variable than others, and we show how this feature can be accommodated by an appropriate extension of the methods.

Seasonal Adjustment and Kalman Filtering

The observed variable is denoted y_t, and is assumed to comprise three unobserved components, respectively seasonal, trend cycle and irregular components, as follows:

$$y_t = S_t + C_t + I_t. \tag{1}$$

An additive decomposition is employed in this paper; a multiplicative decomposition can be approximated by working with the logarithm of the observed variable. The seasonal adjustment problem is to estimate the seasonal component and remove it from the original series, yielding the seasonally adjusted series. For an adjustment performed by using information available at time $t + k$, the adjusted value may be written as

$$y^a_{t,t+k} = y_t - \hat{S}_{t,t+k}. \tag{2}$$

The traditional methods comprise a sequence of moving-average or linear filter operations which, by neglecting some non-linear aspects, can be represented as a single set of linear filters $a_k(L)$, $k = 0, \ldots, m$, where L is the lag operator, thus

$$y^a_{t,t+k} = a_k(L)y_t = \sum_{j=-k}^{m} a_{kj}y_{t-j} \qquad k = 0, \ldots, m. \tag{3}$$

The linear filter representation of the X-11 method is presented by Wallis (1982). The filters range from one-sided $a_0(L)$ used to obtain preliminary adjustment of current data, through the asymmetric filters used to obtain revised estimates as more data become available, to the symmetric filter $a_m(L)$, with $a_{mj} = a_{m,-j}$, that gives the final or 'historical' seasonally adjusted values. After m periods have elapsed, no further revisions to the adjusted values occur. For the standard options in the monthly X-11 filters, the value of m is 84, although the revisions that occur after $k = 36$ are negligible.

Model-based seasonal adjustment methods require the specification of stochastic (or mixed stochastic-deterministic) models for the unobserved components, assumed to be independent. In a widely used framework, also employed in this paper, it is assumed that the unobserved components follow autoregressive-moving average (ARMA) processes, thus

$$\phi_s(L)S_t = \theta_s(L)w_{1t}, \qquad \phi_c(L)C_t = \theta_c(L)w_{2t}, \qquad I_t = v_t \qquad (4)$$

where w_{1t}, w_{2t} and v_t are uncorrelated white-noise random variables. Application of the classical prediction theory developed by Wiener and Kolmogorov (see, for example, Whittle, 1963, chapter 6) yields the LLS estimate of the 'signal', S_t, as a linear filter of the observations

$$\hat{S}_{t,t+k} = f_k(L)y_t \qquad (5)$$

from which the optimal seasonal adjustment follows immediately.

The first use of this approach, by Grether and Nerlove (1970), was to provide a benchmark for interpreting practical criteria for the evaluation of existing, more pragmatically based, seasonal adjustment procedures. Thus Grether and Nerlove asked, if optimal seasonal adjustment were used, what we would observe on comparing spectral densities of original and adjusted series. The answer that the adjusted series would exhibit spectral dips at seasonal frequencies then led to a revision of earlier criticism of practical methods (Nerlove, 1964) for producing exactly this phenomenon.

A subsequent use of model-based methods was to provide a direct interpretation of the practical methods. For example, one might ask, given the linear filter representation of the X-11 method, for what unobserved-components ARMA model would the optimal seasonal adjustment filter be the same. This question was addressed by Cleveland and Tiao (1976), who fitted a model to a truncated symmetric X-11 seasonal filter and to the corresponding trend filter simultaneously. Burridge and Wallis (1984) consider the X-11 seasonal adjustment filters and fit unobserved-component ARMA models to two of the asymmetric filters, $a_0(L)$ and $a_{12}(L)$, in addition to the symmetric filter $a_{84}(L)$. The resulting models represent data-generation processes for which seasonal adjustment is accomplished virtually optimally, in a linear least squares sense, by the X-11 program. For the symmetric filter, the model written in terms of a seasonal component, S_t, and a combined non-seasonal component, $N_t = C_t + I_t$, is

$$(1 + L + L^2 + \ldots + L^{11})S_t = (1 + 0.71L^{12} + 1.00L^{24})w_{1t}$$

$$(1 - L)^2 N_t = (1 - 1.59L + 0.86L^2)\eta_t \tag{6}$$

$$\sigma_{w1}^2/\sigma_\eta^2 = 0.071.$$

The composite model for the observed series corresponding to this unobserved-components model is

$$(1 - L)(1 - L^{12})y_t = \beta(L)\varepsilon_t \tag{7}$$

where the moving-average operator, $\beta(L)$, is of degree 26, its complexity countering the relative simplicity of the component models.

Burman (1980) and Hillmer and Tiao (1982) propose the use of the model-based approach for practical seasonal adjustment. The additional problem that this faces is that of identifying the ARMA model for the unobserved components. The usual starting point is an ARMA model for the observed series, obtained by conventional Box–Jenkins methods, and various additional assumptions about the nature of the components are then necessary to achieve a unique decomposition. Considerable room for debate thus exists, since no objective model-selection criteria are available to discriminate between different component models that correspond to the same model for the observed variable. The element of judgement required at this stage, together with that needed at the earlier stage of model identification for the observed series, explains why these methods have not been widely adopted by official statistical agencies, who retain a preference for more automated seasonal adjustment procedures.

Much of the discussion of model-based approaches uses the classical Wiener–Kolmogorov prediction theory, as noted above, which is restricted to stationary stochastic processes. While Grether and Nerlove (1970) similarly restrict attention to stationary ARMA models, most of the subsequent work has considered non-stationary integrated or ARIMA models, given the common finding that economic time series need to be differenced at least once before appearing stationary. The standard Wiener–Kolmogorov apparatus continued to be applied, however, despite the difficulties caused by the assumption of a semi-infinite sample and the theoretically infinite range of the filter (equation (5)). However, the recursive techniques known as the Kalman filter give a satisfactory treatment of the difference-stationary case, provided that appropriate attention is given to initial conditions. Burridge and Wallis (1988) show how, in the limit, the steady-state Kalman filter coincides with the Wiener–Kolmogorov filter in the cases in which the latter is defined, but is valid in more general cases, including unobserved component ARIMA models.

We consider the preceding models in their state-space form, writing the state transition equation and the measurement equation as

$$x_t = Fx_{t-1} + Gw_t$$
$$y_t = H'x_t + v_t. \tag{8}$$

In general, x_t and y_t denote the state vector and output vector, respectively, and w_t and v_t are independent serially uncorrelated random variables with zero means and covariance matrices Q and R. Here y_t is a scalar, and denoting the degrees of the lag polynomials in equation (4) by m, n, p and q, respectively, a convenient state-space representation of the unobserved-components model is obtained through the following definitions and equivalences:

$$x_t = (x'_{1t}, x'_{2t})'$$

$$x_{1t} = (S_t, S_{t-1}, \ldots, S_{t-m+1}, w_{1,t}, w_{1,t-1}, \ldots, w_{1t-n+1})'$$

$$x_{2t} = (C_t, C_{t-1}, \ldots, C_{t-p+1}, w_{2,t}, w_{2,t-1}, \ldots, w_{2t-q+1})'$$

$$F = \text{block diagonal } (F_1, F_2)$$

$$
\begin{pmatrix}
\phi_{s,1} & \phi_{s,2} & \cdots & \phi_{s,m-1} & \phi_{s,m} & -\theta_{s,1} & -\theta_{s,2} & \cdots & -\theta_{s,n-1} & \theta_{s,n} \\
1 & 0 & \cdots & 0 & 0 & 0 & 0 & \cdots & 0 & 0 \\
0 & 1 & \cdots & 0 & 0 & 0 & 0 & \cdots & 0 & 0 \\
\vdots & & \ddots & \vdots & \vdots & \vdots & \vdots & \ddots & \vdots & \vdots \\
0 & 0 & \cdots & 1 & 0 & 0 & 0 & \cdots & 0 & 0 \\
0 & 0 & \cdots & 0 & 0 & 0 & 0 & \cdots & 0 & 0 \\
0 & 0 & \cdots & 0 & 0 & 1 & 0 & \cdots & 0 & 0 \\
0 & 0 & \cdots & 0 & 0 & 0 & 1 & \ddots & 0 & 0 \\
\vdots & \vdots & \ddots & \vdots & \vdots & \vdots & \vdots & \ddots & & \vdots \\
0 & 0 & \cdots & 0 & 0 & 0 & 0 & \cdots & 1 & 0
\end{pmatrix}
$$

F_2 similarly matches coefficients in the model for C_t to elements of x_{2t}

$$G' = \begin{pmatrix} 1 & 0 & \cdots & 0 & 1 & 0 & \cdots & 0 & 0 & 0 & \cdots & 0 & 0 & 0 & \cdots & 0 \\ 0 & 0 & \cdots & 0 & 0 & 0 & \cdots & 0 & 1 & 0 & \cdots & 0 & 1 & 0 & \cdots & 0 \end{pmatrix}$$

$$H' = (1 \quad 0 \quad \cdots \quad 0 \quad 0 \quad 0 \quad \cdots \quad 0 \quad 1 \quad 0 \quad \cdots \quad 0 \quad 0 \quad 0 \quad \cdots \quad 0)$$

$$w_t = (w_{1t}, w_{2t})'$$

$$Q = \text{diag}(\sigma^2_{w_1}, \sigma^2_{w_2}$$

$$R = \sigma^2_v \text{ (scalar).} \tag{9}$$

The specification is completed by the assumed initial conditions that, in advance of any observations, x_0 is known to be randomly distributed with mean $\hat{x}_{0,-1}$ and variance $P_{0,-1}$. Denoting by Ω_{t+k} the information set comprising the initial conditions together with the observations y_0, $y_1, \ldots, y_{t+k}$, the Kalman filter equations give the LLS estimate of x_t conditional on Ω_{t+k}, denoted by $\hat{x}_{t,t+k}$, together with its covariance matrix,

$$P_{t,t+k} = E(x_t - \hat{x}_{t,t+k})(x_t - \hat{x}_{t,t+k})'.$$

The *filtering* recursions give $\hat{x}_{t,t-1}$, $\hat{x}_{t,t}$, $P_{t,t-1}$ and $P_{t,t}$ for $t = 0, 1, 2,$

..., and the *smoothing* recursions give $\hat{x}_{t,t+k}$ and $P_{t,t+k}$ for t fixed and $k = 0, 1, \ldots$. Burridge and Wallis (1985) show that this set-up provides a computationally convenient implementation of model-based seasonal adjustment, the preliminary estimate $\hat{S}_{t,t}$ of the seasonal component and its subsequent revisions $S_{t,t+k}$, $k = 1, 2, \ldots$ being given by appropriate elements of the state estimate $\hat{x}_{t,t+k}$, $t = 0, 1, \ldots, k = 0, 1, \ldots$. An important by-product is the calculation of the variance of seasonally adjusted data, given by the appropriate diagonal elements of the P-matrices. These provide $\text{var}(\hat{S}_{t,t+k})$, $k = 0, 1, \ldots$ and hence show how the variance of the seasonally adjusted data is reduced from a preliminary value, through subsequent revisions as more data become available, to a final or historical value, $\text{var}(\hat{S}_{t,t+h})$, say. Attention might alternatively be focused on the revision process, and at some intermediate point a user might wish to know the likely size of further revisions in the adjusted value. Since the revision is independent of the error in the final estimate, its variance is

$$\text{var}(y^a_{t,t+h} - y^a_{t,t+k}) = \text{var}(\hat{S}_{t,t+k}) - \text{var}(\hat{S}_{t,t+h}), \qquad k = 0, 1, \ldots, h.$$

An important question is whether the Kalman filter recursions converge to a steady state, for which a sufficient condition is that the sequence $P_{t,t-1}$, $t = 0, 1, \ldots$ tends to a unique positive definite steady-state covariance matrix P, given as the solution of the Riccati equation

$$P = FPF' - FPH(H'PH + R)^{-1} H'PF' + GQG'.$$

Burridge and Wallis (1988) adapt relevance existence and convergence conditions from the control theory literature, namely controllability and detectability, to the present problem. The system (9) is controllable if each of the pairs of polynomials $\{\phi_s(L), \theta_s(L)\}$ and $\{\phi_c(L), \theta_c(L)\}$ has no common factors, and it is detectable if the autoregressive lag polynomials $\phi_s(L)$ and $\phi_c(L)$ have no unstable common factor (that is, a common factor $(1 - \lambda L)$ with $|\lambda| \geqslant 1$); no further 'stationarity' conditions are imposed on the autoregressive polynomials. Under these conditions the covariance sequence $P_{t,t-1}$, $t = 0, 1, \ldots$ converges to a limit; in this steady state the filtering and smoothing recursions are also time-invariant. The steady-state Kalman filter corresponds to the Wiener–Kolmogorov filter whenever the latter is defined, that is, when the series is stationary.

In the unobserved-components model, the controllability condition simply requires that each component ARMA model is parsimoniously parameterized, in the usual sense. Of greater practical significance is the detectability condition. Whereas a common factor $(1 - \lambda L)$ with $|\lambda| > 1$ in the seasonal and trend-cycle autoregressive polynomials might be considered a numerical coincidence unlikely to occur, common factors

$(1 - L)$ might be found in the context of seasonal ARIMA models. Since the use of both seasonal and non-seasonal difference operators is common, and the seasonal difference operator can be factored as

$$(1 - L^{12}) = (1 - L)(1 + L + L^2 + \ldots + L^{11})$$

the detectability condition requires that the second factor on the right-hand side, an annual summation operator, and not the seasonal difference operator, be associated with the seasonal component. This condition is satisfied in the model (6) above. It also represents an intuitively appealing model identification: whereas the seasonal difference operator produces spikes in the pseudospectrum at seasonal frequencies and at the zero frequency, the factorization identifies the peak at the origin with the ordinary difference operator and associates it with the non-seasonal component. If, despite these considerations, a common unit root does exist, Burridge and Hall (1987) show that, although the covariance sequence does not converge, the state estimate recursions do converge to a steady state. This strengthens the result of Pierce (1979), that application of the Wiener–Kolmogorov filter to a series in which signal and noise processes share a common unit root yields a signal estimate with unbounded variance.

Periodic Variances

All the literature on model-based seasonal adjustment employs models that are homogeneous or time invariant. However, the assumption that the autocovariance structure does not vary with the season may be unduly restrictive for series exhibiting strong seasonality, and relaxing this assumption leads to the class of models known as periodic models. The literature on such models includes general discussion of their properties (Jones and Brelsford, 1967; Pagano, 1978; Cleveland and Tiao, 1979; Troutman, 1979; Tiao and Grupe, 1980) together with applications in meteorology (Jones and Brelsford) and hydrology (Thompstone et al., 1987, and references therein); periodic models appear to have been little used in economics. In an exception to this general statement, however, Osborn and Smith (1989) find that the use of periodic autoregressions for the components of UK consumers' expenditure may improve forecast accuracy, especially at short horizons. Their results indicate seasonal variation in the residual variance of these models, and it is this feature of the general periodic model on which we focus our attention.

Users of the X-11 program often find that the final estimates of the seasonal component or seasonal factor exhibit variation over time, to an extent that differs across months. An implication is that if it were desired to attach a standard error to the seasonally adjusted data, this standard error should itself vary with the seasons, unlike the treatment of Burridge and Wallis (1985) discussed above, in which such quantities are assumed constant. To capture the possibility that some monthly effects are easier to estimate than others, we provide a simple generalization of the models (4) and (9) to the case of periodic variances.

In difference to the usual definitions of seasonal and non-seasonal components, we restrict attention to the innovation variance of the seasonal component, σ_{w1}^2, and now allow this to assume twelve different values, one for each month. This simple generalization produces a non-homogeneous model, and even if the autoregressive polynomials $\phi_s(L)$ and $\phi_c(L)$ do not indicate non-stationarity in the usual sense, the observed series y_t is no longer stationary. The standard device for analysing periodic models, following Gladysev (1961), is to stack the observations for a complete period, in our case a year, into a vector, giving a homogeneous vector process that can be analysed in the usual way. Thus if each month's model is stationary, but different, then although the monthly time series y_t is not stationary, the vector series z_T indexed in years, where

$$z_T = (y_{12(T-1)+1}, y_{12(T-1)+2}, \ldots, y_{12T})'$$

is stationary.

For the unobserved-components ARMA model in its state space representation (9), stacking the periodic models increases the dimensions of the system, in particular the first diagonal element of the matrix Q is expanded to a diagonal array of twelve different seasonal innovation variances. Since convergence of the Kalman filter to its steady state depends only on detectability, which is not affected by the form of the state noise covariance matrix, Q, the stacked system has the same limiting properties as the system (9), except that the steady-state covariance matrix P is now itself periodic. The implications of this for the calculation of the estimation variance of seasonally adjusted data are illustrated in the following example.

We consider a meterological time series, namely monthly rainfall in Penzance, 1967–86, working with the natural logarithm of the variable to respect its positivity. The data are plotted in Figure 1. The X-11 program finds evidence of stable, not moving, seasonality, and the sample variances of the estimated seasonal components for each month (that is, the variance within each column of Table D10 in the X-11 output) are in the following proportions (scaled to average 1.00):

Jan.	0.13	May	0.37	Sept.	0.55
Feb.	1.88	June	0.85	Oct.	2.10
March	1.47	July	0.53	Nov.	0.49
April	0.43	Aug.	0.68	Dec.	2.04

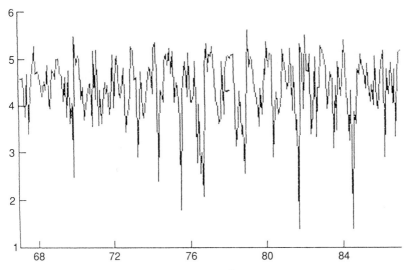

FIG. 1. Penzance rainfall (natural log) 1967–86

These results indicate that the standard error of the seasonally adjusted series varies from month to month, most notably being reduced by a factor of four between December and January.

To illustrate the generalization of the Kalman filter implementation of model-based seasonal adjustment to the present case, we use the X-11 model previously identified (Burridge and Wallis, 1984), equation (6), with the variance σ_{w1}^2 scaled monthly according to the proportions presented above. Before using the steady-state covariance matrix, P, to calculate the variance of seasonally adjusted series, Burridge and Wallis (1985) assess the practical significance of the theoretical convergence results by studying the rate of convergence of the covariance sequence from its initial value, $P_{0,-1}$. The standard procedure in practical applications is to assign a very large value to $P_{0,-1}$: this not only reflects uncertainty about the initial state but also delivers acceptable filter performance in practice. In Figure 2 we present the corresponding results for $\operatorname{var}(\hat{S}_{t,t})$, $t = 0, 1, \ldots,$ for the periodic version of the model: it is seen that the steady-state values are quickly reached, but, of course, the steady state is itself periodic.

Finally, the steady-state covariance matrices can be used to study the improvement in the seasonal adjustment of a given data point as more data are obtained by calculating $\operatorname{var}(\hat{S}_{t,t+k})$, $k = 0, 1, \ldots$ for different months: results for December and January are shown in Figure 3. In each case the profile corresponds to that of the non-periodic model, in that there is a small reduction in variance as each of the next two

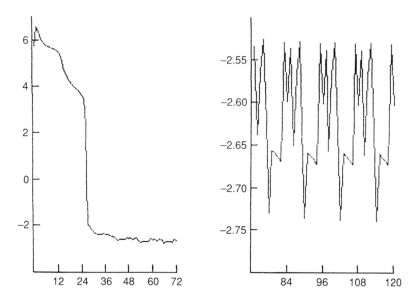

FIG. 2. Convergence of covariance sequence: $\log_{10}$ var $S_{t,t}$, $t = 0, 1, \ldots$ (scale change at $t = 72$)

observations arrive, followed by a pause until the next observation on the same month is obtained, when there is a significant fall. Further reductions to the historical values principally occur at $k = 24$ and $k = 36$, again indicating that additional observations on the month in question are particularly informative; subsequent reductions are negligible, reflecting the property of the X-11 procedure that the revision process is virtually complete after three years. For the two different months, however, this general pattern occurs at a different overall level, reflecting the seasonal heteroscedasticity of the periodic model.

Conclusion

In this paper we review model-based seasonal adjustment and its Kalman filter implementation, and show how the models can be generalized to incorporate seasonal heteroscedasticity, or periodic variances. This is a limited use of the general class of periodic models, but represents a first step away from the restrictive assumption of homogeneous or non-periodic models. Further applications, in particular to empirically identified models, will tell whether the advantages indicated here can be realized in practical situations.

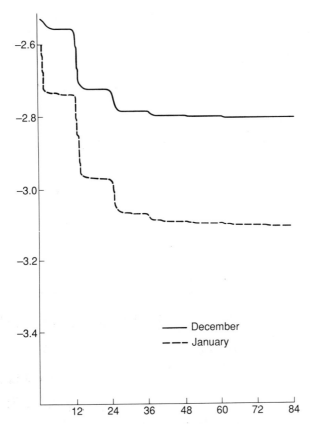

FIG. 3. Variance of revised estimates: $\log_{10} \operatorname{var} S_{t,t+k}$, $k = 0, 1, \ldots$, in steady state, for different months

References

(References marked with a * are included in this volume)

BURMAN, J. P. (1980), 'Seasonal adjustment by signal extraction', *Journal of the Royal Statistical Society*, Series A, **143**, 321–37.

BURRIDGE, P., and HALL, A. R. (1987), 'Convergence of the Kalman filter gain for a class of non-detectable signal extraction problems', *IEEE Transactions on Automatic Control*, **32**, 1036–9.

—— and WALLIS, K. F. (1984), 'Unobserved-components models for seasonal adjustment filters', *Journal of Business and Economic Statistics*, **2**, 350–59.*

—— —— (1985), 'Calculating the variance of seasonally adjusted series', *Journal of the American Statistical Association*, **80**, 541–52.

—— —— (1988), 'Prediction theory for autoregressive-moving average process', *Econometric Reviews*, **7**, 65–95.

390   Peter Burridge and Kenneth F. Wallis

CLEVELAND, W. P., and TIAO, G. C. (1976), 'Decomposition of seasonal time series: a model for the Census X-11 program', *Journal of the American Statistical Association*, **71**, 581–7.

—— —— (1979), 'Modeling seasonal time series', *Economic Appliquée*, **32**, 107–29.

GLADYSEV, E. G. (1961), 'Periodically correlated random sequences', *Soviet Mathematics*, **2**, 385–8.

GRETHER, D. M., and NERLOVE, M. (1970), 'Some properties of optimal seasonal adjustment', *Econometrica*, **38**, 682–703.

HILLMER, S. C., and TIAO, G. C. (1982), 'An ARIMA-model-based approach to seasonal adjustment', *Journal of the American Statistical Association*, **77**, 63–70.*

JONES, R. H., and BRELSFORD, W. M. (1967), 'Time series with periodic structure', *Biometrika*, **54**, 403–8.

NERLOVE, M. (1964), 'Spectral analysis of seasonal adjustment procedures', *Econometrica*, **32**, 241–86.

OSBORN, D. R., and SMITH, J. P. (1989), 'The performance of periodic autoregressive models in forecasting seasonal U.K. consumption', *Journal of Business and Economic Statistics*, **7**, 117–27.

PAGANO, M. (1978), 'On periodic and multiple autoregressions', *Annals of Statistics*, **6**, 1310–17.

PIERCE, D. A. (1979), 'Signal extraction error in nonstationary time series', *Annals of Statistics*, **7**, 1303–20.

SHISKIN, J., YOUNG, A. H., and MUSGRAVE, J. C. (1967), *The X-11 Variant of the Census Method II Seasonal Adjustment Program*, Technical Paper 15 (revised), Washington, DC: US Bureau of the Census.

THOMPSTONE, R. M., HIPEL, K. W., and McLEOD, A. I. (1987), 'Simulation of monthly hydrological time series', in I. B. MacNeill and G. J. Umphrey (eds), *Advances in the Statistical Sciences: Volume IV. Stochastic Hydrology*, pp. 57–71, Dordrecht: D. Reidel.

TIAO, G. C., and GRUPE, M. R. (1980), 'Hidden periodic autoregressive-moving average models in time series data', *Biometrika*, **67**, 365–73.

TROUTMAN, B. M. (1979), 'Some results in periodic autoregression', *Biometrika*, **66**, 219–28.

WALLIS, K. F. (1982), 'Seasonal adjustment and revision of current data: linear filters for the X-11 method', *Journal of the Royal Statistical Society*, Series A, **145**, 74–85.

WHITTLE, P. (1963), *Prediction and Regulation by Linear Least-Square Methods*, London: English Universities Press: 2nd edn, Minneapolis: University of Minnesota Press (1983).

PART V

SEASONAL INTEGRATION and COINTEGRATION

Introduction

One of the most common and oldest prescriptions for the treatment of seasonality is to consider the difference between a given quarter or month of the current year and the same quarter or month of last year. This has led to the use of seasonal differences such as $\Delta_4 = 1-B^4$ and $\Delta_{12} = 1-B^{12}$ where B is the lag operator (see Box and Jenkins (1970)). In the aftermath of the development of tests for unit roots at the zero frequency (i.e. processes such as $(1 - \phi B)y_t = \varepsilon_t \sim \text{nid}(0, \sigma^2)$ where $\phi = 1$) in the late seventies and early eighties by Dickey, Fuller, Evans, and Savin among others,[1] a natural extension to processes such as $(1 - \phi B^s)y_t = \varepsilon_t \sim \text{nid}(0, \sigma^2)$, where $\phi = 1$ and $s = 2$, 4, 12 was proposed by Dickey, Hasza, and Fuller (DHF) (1984) who developed the distributional properties and suggested a test following the tradition of the so-called Dickey–Fuller test. The test is based on an auxiliary regression of the form

$$(1 - B^s)y_t = \pi y_{t-s} + \varepsilon_t, \quad s = 2, 4, 12 \tag{1}$$

and the test statistic is the 't-value' corresponding to π. Due to the non-standard distributional properties of the t-value under the null H_0: $\pi = 0$, Dickey et al. provides the fractiles of simulated distributions, which may give us the critical values to be applied when testing the null against the stationary alternative H_1: $\pi < 0$. In order to whiten the errors the auxiliary regression may be augmented by lagged values of $(1 - B_s)y_t$ without any effect on the asymptotic distribution, and with deterministic parts as intercept, seasonal dummies, and trend. Unfortunately, this changes the distribution of the test statistics. In addition, use of the 'correct' augmentation is of paramount importance for the size and power of the test in finite samples.

The limitation of the DHF test is that it is a joint test for roots at long-run and seasonal frequencies, and that the alternative is a specific sth order autoregression. For instance, the polynomium $1 - B^4$ can be written as $(1 - B)(1 + B + B^2 + B^3) = (1 - B)(1 + B)(1 + B^2) = (1 - B)(1 + B)(1 - iB)(1 + iB)$ with roots $B = 1 \pm 1, \pm i$ all of length 1. These roots correspond to the zero frequency ($B = 1$), the semi-annual ($B = -1$), and the annual ($B = \pm i$) frequency if the data are quarterly. This is the basis for the extension of the DHF test by Hylleberg, Engle, Granger, and Yoo (HEGY) (1990) who propose a test for the quarterly case based on the auxiliary regression

---

[1] See Fuller (1976), Dickey and Fuller (1979, 1981), and Evans and Savin (1981, 1984).

$$(1 - B^4)y_t = \pi_1 y_{1t-1} + \pi_2 y_{2t-1} + \pi_3 y_{3t-2} + \pi_4 y_{3t-1} + \varepsilon_t \qquad (2)$$

where $y_{1t} = (1 + B + B^2 + B^3)y_t$ removes the seasonal unit roots and leave in the zero frequency unit root, $y_{2t} = -(1 - B + B^2 - B^3)y_t$ and $y_{3t} = -(1 - B^2)y_t$ leave in the root at the semi-annual frequency and the annual frequency, respectively.

The existence of unit roots of the long-run, semi-annual, and annual frequencies implies that $\pi_1 = 0$, $\pi_2 = 0$, and $\pi_3 = \pi_4 = 0$, respectively. The t-values on π_1 and π_2 are shown to have a Dickey–Fuller distribution under the null of $\pi_1 = 0$ or $\pi_2 = 0$, respectively, while the t-value on π_3 has a DHF distribution with $s = 2$ conditional on $\pi_4 = 0$. A joint test of $\pi_3 = \pi_4 = 0$ is proposed based on the F-value and the critical values of the distribution are tabulated. Again the auxiliary regression has to be augmented with lagged values of the dependent variables in order to whiten the errors. The HEGY test for roots in quarterly data has been extended to the monthly case by Franses (1990) and Beaulieu and Miron (1990 a, b, c).

Processes that become stationary apart from deterministic non-stationarities when first differenced are called integrated (see Engle and Granger (1987)), and in HEGY this concept of integration is extended to cover also the seasonal frequencies by defining an integrated series at frequency θ as a series with a pseudo-spectrum of $f(\omega) = \text{const}/(\omega - \theta)^2$ for ω close to θ. This implies that a process such as $(1 - B^4)y_t = \varepsilon_t$, $\varepsilon_t \sim \text{nid}(o, \sigma^2)$ is integrated at the frequency $\theta = 0, \frac{1}{2}, \frac{1}{4}\ (\frac{3}{4})$.

In the article by Osborn et al. (1988) the different tests are applied to test for the integration properties of UK consumption and income, and it is found that while income seems to be integrated at zero frequency only consumption may be integrated at the seasonal frequencies as well. However, it is argued that a periodically integrated process defined as a non-stationary process y where $(1 - \varphi_q B)y_t$ is stationary, φ_q, $q = 1, 2, \ldots, s$ with $|\varphi_1 \varphi_2 \ldots \varphi_s| = 1$ better describes the UK consumption series. In addition it is shown that such a process closely resembles that of a seasonally integrated series, and it is argued that such a process better describes the UK consumption series. These results underline what practitioners of these tests also have experienced. Namely, that it is extremely difficult to choose between different simple univariate seasonal representations such as a stationary stochastic model with a deterministic seasonal part (seasonal dummies), seasonally integrated or nearly integrated processes and a periodically integrated process.

However, it should be realized first, that any simple univariate representation can at best be only a crude approximation to the Data Generating Process. Secondly, what is compared in a world of finite, and often small samples, are models which allow for a different degree of variation in the seasonal pattern. At one end is the seasonal dummy model which allows some variation but no persistent change in the seasonal pattern, and at the other end the seasonally integrated process, which allows a very changing seasonal pattern.

Where to draw the borderline between the different processes may therefore be debatable, but it is obvious that a careful analysis and modesty in drawing the conclusion are called for. Recently, the question has been addressed in several articles such as Barsky and Miron (1989), Beaulieu and Miron (1990 a, b, c), Ghysels (1990 a, b), Osborn (1990), and Hylleberg, Jørgensen, and Sørensen (1991), but it is fair to conclude that no simple class of univariate models has been shown to properly describe the seasonal pattern in macroeconomic time series as a whole. Most importantly, this line of research also indicates the limitations of univariate analysis.[2]

In the article by Hylleberg et al. (1990) the notion of a cointegrated system put forward by Granger (1983) and Engle and Granger (1987) is extended to the cases of seasonally integrated series. Two series integrated at frequency φ are said to be cointegrated if a linear combination possibly with lags is stationary at frequency θ. Seasonal cointegration exists if series with a varying and changing seasonal pattern exhibit a parallel movement in a seasonal component. In Engle et al. (1991) critical values for the tests of seasonal cointegration in quarterly data are presented. In addition, a weak indication of seasonal cointegration at the annual frequency in the Japanese consumption–income relation is found. In Lee (1989) and Lee and Siklos (1990) the maximum likelihood method for estimating a cointegrated system proposed by Johansen (1988) is extended to the seasonal case.[3]

The articles presented in this section are best seen in the light of two important aspects of seasonality. First, the seasonal movements are often varying and changing, and in addition interdependent with the non-seasonal parts. Secondly, the seasonal variation accounts for a major part of the variation in many economic time series. The two taken

---

[2] In a recent paper by Canova and Hansen (1991) results similar to those obtained by Hylleberg, Jørgensen, and Sørensen (1991) are obtained based on a test, which have the deterministic seasonal as the null and the alternative being a varying seasonal pattern. Consider the multivariate linear regression

$$y_t - \alpha_t + x_t \beta \mid e_t$$

where y_t is a $s \times 1$ vector of observations on the dependent variable for the s seasons, x_t is a $k \times s$ matrix containing the observations on the regressors in the s seasons. The intercept is described by the process

$$\alpha_t = \alpha + \tau \xi_t, \qquad \xi_t = \xi_{t-1} + \varepsilon_t$$

where ε_t is a martingale difference process, while α_t, α, and ξ_t are $s \times 1$ vectors, and τ a scalar.

The null hypothesis of τ equal to 0 is then tested against the alternative that τ is positive.

[3] See Kunst (1990) for an application.

together imply that seasonal modelling is worthwhile, but not straight-forward. It is therefore necessary to further develop tools for detecting the varying and changing nature of seasonality and to integrate the available information from the data and the economic theory in a multivariate structural modelling of all components of the data. The concept of seasonal integration and cointegration, periodic models, and so on constitutes a step in this direction.

References

(References marked with a * are included in this volume)

BARSKY, R. B., and MIRON, J. A. (1989), 'The seasonal cycle and the business cycle', *Journal of Political Economy*, **97**, 503–34.

BEAULIEU, J. J., and MIRON, J. A. (1990a), 'Evidence on unit roots and zero frequencies'. Mimeo. Boston University and NBER.

—— —— (1990b), 'A cross-country comparison of seasonal cycles and business cycles', *NBER Working Paper 3459*.

—— —— (1990c), 'The seasonal cycle in U.S. manufacturing', *NBER Working Paper 3450*.

BOX, G. E. P., and JENKINS, G. M. (1970), *Time Series Analysis: Forecasting and Control* San Francisco: Holden-Day.

CANOVA F., and HANSEN, B. E. (1991), 'Are seasonal patterns constant over time? A test for seasonal stability'. Mimeo, University of Rochester.

DICKEY, D. A., and FULLER, W. A. (1979), 'Distribution of the estimators for autoregressive time series with a unit root', *Journal of the American Statistical Association,* **84**, 427–31.

—— —— (1981), 'Likelihood ratio statistics for autoregressive time series with a unit root', *Econometrica*, **49**, 1057–72.

—— HASZA, D. P., and FULLER, W. A. (1984), 'Testing for unit roots in seasonal time series', *Journal of American Statistical Association,* **79**, 335–67.* [Part V this volume.]

ENGLE, R. F., and GRANGER, C. W. J. (1987), 'Co-integration and error correction: representation, estimation and testing', *Econometrica*, **55**, 251–76.

—— —— HYLLEBERG, S. and LEE, H. S. (1991), 'Seasonal cointegration: the Japanese consumption function', *Journal of Econometrics,* forthcoming.

EVANS, G. B. A., and SAVIN, N. E. (1981), 'Testing for unit roots: 1', *Econometrica*, **49**, 753–79.

—— —— (1984), 'Testing for unit roots: 2', *Econometrica*, **52**, 1241–69.

FRANSES, P. H., (1990), 'Testing for seasonal unit root in monthly data', *Report 9032A*. Amsterdam: Econometric Institute, ERASMUS University.

FULLER, W. A., (1976), *Introduction to Statistical Time Series*. New York: John Wiley and Sons.

GHYSELS, E., (1990a), 'On the economics and econometrics of seasonality', *Discussion Paper 2990*, CRDE, Université de Montréal (revised 1991).

—— (1990b), 'On seasonal asymmetries and their implications for stochastic and deterministic models of seasonality', Mimeo, CRDE, Université de Montréal.

GRANGER, C. W. J. (1983), 'Cointegrated variables and error correction models', *UCSD Discussion Paper 83–13a*.

HYLLEBERG, S., ENGLE, R. F., GRANGER, C. W. J., and YOO, B. S. (1990), 'Seasonal integration and cointegration', *Journal of Econometrics*, **44**, 215–38.*

—— JØRGENSEN, C. and SØRENSEN, N. K. (1991), 'Seasonality in macroeconomic time series', Memo 1991-9, Institute of Economics, University of Aarhus.

JOHANSEN, S. (1988), 'Statistical analysis of cointegrated vectors', *Journal of Economic Dynamics and Control*, **12**, 231–54.

KUNST, R. M., (1990), 'Seasonal cointegrated in macroeconomic systems: case studies for small and large european countries', *Research Memorandum 271*. Institute for Advanced Studies, Vienna.

LEE, H. S. (1989), 'Maximum likelihood inference of cointegration and seasonal cointegration.' Ph.D Dissertation, Department of Economics, UCSD.

—— and SIKLOS, P. L. (1990), 'The influence of seasonal adjustment on unit roots and cointegration: the case of the consumption function for Canada: 1947–1987.' Mimeo, Wilfred Laurier University.

MIRON, J. A. (1990), 'The economics of seasonal cycles 2.' Mimeo. Boston University and NBER.

OSBORN, D. R. (1990), 'A survey of seasonality in UK macroeconomic variables', *International Journal of Forecasting*, **6**, 327–36.

—— CHUI, A. P. L., SMITH, J. P., and BIRCHENHALL, C. R. (1988), 'Seasonality and the order of integration for consumption', *Oxford Bulletin of Economics and Statistics,* **50** 361–77.*

16

Testing for Unit Roots in Seasonal Time Series

D. A. DICKEY, D. P. HASZA, and W. A. FULLER*

Abstract. Regression estimators of coefficients in seasonal autoregressive models are described. The percentiles of the distributions for time series that have unit roots at the seasonal lag are computed by Monte Carlo integration for finite samples and by analytic techniques and Monte Carlo integration for the limit case. The tabled distributions may be used to test the hypothesis that a time series has a seasonal unit root.

Key words: Time series; seasonal; nonstationary; unit root.

1. Introduction

Let the time series Y_t satisfy

$$Y_t = \alpha_d Y_{t-d} + e_t, \ t = 1, 2, \ldots, \tag{1.1}$$

where Y_{-d+1}, Y_{-d+2}, $\ldots$, Y_0 are initial conditions and the e_t are iid $(0, \sigma^2)$ random variables. Model (1.1) is a simple seasonal time series model in which monthly data are represented by $d = 12$, quarterly data by $d = 4$, and so on.

We consider several regression-type estimators of α_d and compute percentiles of their distributions under the hypothesis that $\alpha_d = 1$. This hypothesis states that the seasonal difference $Y_t = Y_t - Y_{t-d}$ is white noise for model (1.1). Extensions of model (1.1) permit a variety of applications.

* D. A. Dickey is Professor, Department of Statistics, North Carolina State University, Raleigh, NC 27695-8203. D. P. Hasza is a statistician at Boeing Computer Services, P.O. Box 7730, Wichita, KS 67277-7730. W. A. Fuller is Distinguished Professor, Department of Statistics, Iowa State University, Ames, IA 50011. The authors are indebted to an anonymous referee for helpful suggestions.

Printed with permission of: *Journal of the American Statistical Association*, **79**. 355–67.

2. Estimators

Our first estimator of α_d is the least squares estimator defined as

$$\hat{\alpha}_d = \left(\sum_{t=1}^{n} Y_{t-d}^2 \right)^{-1} \sum_{t=1}^{n} Y_{t-d} Y_t. \tag{2.1}$$

If the initial conditions are fixed and e_t is normal, $\hat{\alpha}_d$ is the maximum likelihood estimator. The Studentized regression statistic for testing the hypothesis $H_0: \alpha_d = 1$ is

$$\hat{\tau}_d = \left[\left(\sum_{t=1}^{n} Y_{t-d}^2 \right)^{-1} S^2 \right]^{1/2} (\hat{\alpha}_d - 1), \tag{2.2}$$

where

$$S^2 = (n - 1)^{-1} \sum_{t=1}^{n} (Y_t - \hat{\alpha}_d Y_{t-d})^2. \tag{2.3}$$

The statistics $\hat{\alpha}_d - 1$ and $\hat{\tau}_d$ are standard output from a computer regression of $Y_t = Y_t - Y_{t-d}$ on Y_{t-d}. Dickey (1976), Fuller (1976), and Dickey and Fuller (1979) discussed $\hat{\alpha}_1$ and $\hat{\tau}_1$; M. M. Rao (1978) and Evans and Savin (1981) discussed $\hat{\alpha}_1$.

An alternative model for seasonal data is the stationary model in which the observations satisfy

$$Y_t = \alpha_d Y_{t-d} + e_t, \quad |\alpha_d| < 1. \tag{2.4}$$

Furthermore, for normal stationary Y_t satisfying (2.4), $Y_t - \alpha_d Y_{t+d}$ is a NID$(0, \sigma^2)$ time series. That is,

$$Y_t = \alpha_d Y_{t+d} + v_t, \quad v_t \sim \text{NID}(0, \sigma^2). \tag{2.5}$$

Motivated by (2.4) and (2.5), we suggest an alternative estimator of α_d, which we call the symmetric estimator. The symmetric least squares estimator, $\tilde{\alpha}_d$, pools information from the regression of Y_t on Y_{t+d} and the regression of Y_t on Y_{t-d}. Let

$$\tilde{\alpha}_d = \left(2 \sum_{t=1}^{n} Y_t Y_{t-d} \right) \Big/ \left(\sum_{t=1}^{n} (Y_t^2 + Y_{t-d}^2) \right), \tag{2.6}$$

and define the associated Studentized statistic as

$$\tilde{\tau}_d = 2^{1/2} \left[\left\{ \sum_{t=1}^{n} (Y_t^2 + Y_{t-d}^2) \right\}^{-1} S^2 \right]^{1/2} (\tilde{\alpha}_d - 1), \tag{2.7}$$

where

$$S^2 = (2n - 1)^{-1} \sum_{t=1}^{n} [(Y_t - \tilde{\alpha}_d Y_{t-d})^2 + (Y_{t-d} - \tilde{\alpha}_d Y_t)^2]. \tag{2.8}$$

It follows from the definitions that $-1 \leqslant \tilde{\alpha}_d \leqslant 1$ and that

$$2^{-1/2}\tilde{\tau}_d = -[(2n-1)(1-\tilde{\alpha}_d)]^{1/2}(1+\tilde{\alpha}_d)^{-1/2},$$

where $\tilde{\tau}_d$ is a monotone function of $\tilde{\alpha}_d$. Thus tests based on $\tilde{\tau}_d$ will be equivalent to tests based on $\tilde{\alpha}_d$.

The statistics $\tilde{\alpha}_d$ and $2^{-1/2}\tilde{\tau}_d$ can be obtained using standard regression programs. Table 1 gives two columns appropriate for the regression computation when $d = 2$ and $n = 5$. A · indicates a missing value. Thus an observation with a missing value for either the independent or the dependent variable is not used in the regression. The Independent Variable column is the Dependent Variable column lagged by the seasonal d. The ordinary regression of the first column on the second column gives the estimator $\tilde{\alpha}_2$.

Models (1.1) and (2.4) have the property that $E(Y_t) = 0$. A stationary time series with zero mean is seldom encountered in practice. An alternative to H_0: $\alpha_d = 1$, which is reasonable for much real data, is the stationary model in which $E(Y_t)$ is nonzero. We therefore consider the regression model

$$Y_t = \sum_{i=1}^{d} \theta_i \delta_{it} + \alpha_d Y_{t-d} + e_t, \quad t = 1, 2, \ldots, \tag{2.9}$$

where

TABLE 1. Regression variables used to construct $\tilde{\alpha}_2$ with $n = 5$

Dependent variable	Independent variable
Y_{-1}	·
Y_0	·
Y_1	Y_{-1}
Y_2	Y_0
Y_3	Y_1
Y_4	Y_2
Y_5	Y_3
·	Y_4
·	Y_5
Y'_5	·
Y_4	·
Y_3	Y_5
Y_2	Y_4
Y_1	Y_3
Y_0	Y_2
Y_{-1}	Y_1
·	Y_0
·	Y_{-1}

$$\delta_{it} = 1 \quad \text{if} \quad t = i \ (\text{mod } d)$$

$$= 0 \quad \text{otherwise,}$$

and $\{e_t\}$ is a sequence of iid $(0, \sigma^2)$ random variables. The regression of Y_t on $\delta_{1t}, \delta_{2t}, \ldots, \delta_{d,t}, Y_{t-d}$ for $t = 1, 2 \ldots, n$, produces coefficients $\hat{\theta}_1, \hat{\theta}_2, \ldots, \hat{\theta}_d, \hat{\alpha}_{\mu d}$. We denote the Studentized regression statistic associated with $\hat{\alpha}_{\mu d} - 1$ by $\hat{\tau}_{\mu d}$.

If we assume that $|\alpha_d| < 1$, a reparameterized version of model (2.9) is

$$Y_t - \sum_{i=1}^{d} \delta_{it}\mu_i = \alpha_d \left(Y_{t-d} - \sum_{i=1}^{d} \delta_{it}\mu_i \right) + e_t, \tag{2.10}$$

where

$$\theta_i = (1 - \alpha_d)\mu_i, \quad i = 1, 2, \ldots, d.$$

Under model (2.10) the hypothesis $\alpha_d = 1$ implies that $\theta_i = 0$ regardless of the value of μ_i. Thus, specifyng $\alpha_d = 1$ in the model (2.10) allows μ_i to assume any value. Under the alternative of $|\alpha_d| < 1$, however, μ_i is an identified parameter and should be estimated.

Two estimators of μ_i can be considered for the stationary model. The first is that defined by the regression estimators for (2.9), and the second is the seasonal mean $\tilde{\mu}_i$ defined by

$$\tilde{\mu}_i = (n_i + 1)^{-1} \sum_{j=0}^{n_i} Y_{-d+i+dj}, \quad i = 1, 2, \ldots, d, \tag{2.11}$$

where n_i is the greatest integer not exceeding $(n + d - i)/d$. The estimator $\tilde{\mu}_i$ can be used to define a symmetric estimator of α_d analogous to (2.6). We define

$$\tilde{\alpha}_{\mu d} = \left\{ \sum_{t=1}^{n} (y_t^2 + y_{t-d}^2) \right\}^{-1} 2 \sum_{t=1}^{n} y_t y_{t-d}, \tag{2.12}$$

where

$$y_t = Y_t - \sum_{i=1}^{d} \tilde{\mu}_i \delta_{it}.$$

If the initial conditions are fixed, the θ_i (r μ_i) should be estimated using the regression model.

Finally, we consider a model in which the seasonal means μ_i are equal to a constant μ. For the model with constant mean, the ordinary regression estimators are defined by

$$\begin{bmatrix} \hat{\theta}^* \\ \hat{\alpha}_d^* \end{bmatrix} = \begin{bmatrix} n & \sum_{t=1}^{n} \\ \sum_{t=1}^{n} Y_{t-d} & \sum_{t=1}^{n} Y_{t-d} \end{bmatrix}^{-1} \begin{bmatrix} \sum_{t=1}^{n} Y_t \\ \sum_{t=1}^{n} Y_{t-d} Y_t \end{bmatrix} \tag{2.13}$$

and the Studentized statistic for H_0: $\alpha_d = 1$ is

$$\hat{\tau}_d^* = \left\{ \left[\sum_{t=1}^{n} Y_{t-d}^2 - n^{-1} \left(\sum_{t=1}^{n} Y_{t-d} \right)^2 \right]^{-1} S_*^2 \right\}^{-1/2} (\hat{\alpha}_d^* - 1),$$

where

$$S_*^2 = (n - 2)^{-1} \sum_{t=1}^{n} (Y_t - \hat{\theta}^* - \hat{\alpha}_d^* Y_{t-d})^2.$$

The symmetric estimator of α_d for the stationary constant-mean model is defined by

$$\tilde{\alpha}_{\mu d}^* = \left\{ \sum_{t=1}^{n} [(y_t^*)^2 + (y_{t-d}^*)^2] \right\}^{-1} 2 \sum_{t=1}^{n} y_t^* y_{t-d}^*, \tag{2.14}$$

where

$$\tilde{\mu}_* = (n + d)^{-1} \sum_{t=-d+1}^{n} Y_t,$$

$$y_t^* = Y_t - \tilde{\mu}_*. \tag{2.15}$$

3.   Limiting Representation of Regression Statistics

The error in the estimator $\hat{\alpha}_1$ is

$$\hat{\alpha}_1 - 1 = \left\{ \sum_{t=1}^{n} Y_{t-1}^2 \right\}^{-1} \sum_{t=1}^{n} Y_{t-1} e_t$$

when $\alpha_1 = 1$ in model (1.1) Dickey (1976) obtained a representation for the joint limiting distribution of

$$\left(n^{-2} \sum_{t=1}^{n} Y_{t-1}^2, \quad n^{-1} \sum_{t=1}^{n} Y_{t-1} e_t \right)$$

and used it to calculate percentiles of the limit distributions of $n(\hat{\alpha}_1 - 1)$, $\hat{\tau}_1$, $n(\tilde{\alpha}_{\mu 1} - 1)$, and $\hat{\tau}_{\mu 1}$ by Monte Carlo integration. This approach is now extended to the model with $d > 1$.

Consider the case $d = 2$ and the estimator $\hat{\alpha}_2$. Letting $n = 2m$, we have

$$\hat{\alpha}_2 = \left[\sum_{t=1}^{n} Y_{t-2}^2 \right]^{-1} \left[\sum_{t=1}^{n} Y_t Y_{t-2} \right]$$

$$= \left[\sum_{j=1}^{m} Y_{2j-2}^2 + \sum_{j=1}^{m} Y_{2j-3}^2 \right]^{-1}$$

$$\times \left[\sum_{j=1}^{m} Y_{2j} Y_{2j-2} + \sum_{j=1}^{m} Y_{2j-1} Y_{2j-3} \right]. \tag{3.1}$$

Each summation involves only Y's whose subscripts are even or only Y's whose subscripts are odd. Because

$$Y_{2j} = e_0 + e_2 + \cdots + e_{2j}$$

and

$$Y_{2j-1} = e_{-1} + e_1 + \cdots + e_{2j-1}$$

for all j, we see that summations on even subscripts are independent of summations on odd subscripts. That is,

$$\hat{\alpha}_2 = [D_1 + D_2]^{-1}[N_1 + N_2],$$

where

$$N_j = \sum_{t=1}^{m} X_{jt}X_{j,t-1}, \quad j = 1, 2, \tag{3.2}$$

$$D_j = \sum_{t=1}^{m} X_{j,t-1}^2, \quad j = 1, 2, \tag{3.3}$$

$$X_{jt} = Y_{2t-j+1},$$

and the vector (N_1, D_1) is independent of the vector (N_2, D_2). The argument extends immediately to the dth order process with estimated means. We have

$$\hat{\alpha}_{\mu d} = \left[\sum_{j=1}^{d} D_{\mu j}\right]^{-1} \sum_{j=1}^{d} N_{\mu j},$$

where

$$N_{\mu j} = \sum_{t=1}^{m} X_{jt}(X_{j,t-1} - \bar{X}_{j(-1)}), \quad j = 1, 2, \ldots, d,$$

$$D_{\mu j} = \sum_{t=1}^{m} (X_{j,t-1} - \bar{X}_{j(-1)})^2, \quad j = 1, 2, \ldots, d,$$

$$X_{jt} = Y_{dt-j+1},$$

$$\bar{X}_{j(-1)} = m^{-1} \sum_{t=1}^{m} X_{j,t-1},$$

and $n = md$. Therefore, the representations for the limit distributions given in Theorem 1 follow from the results of Dickey (1976). The asymptotic distributions of the symmetric estimators for $\alpha_d = 1$ depend only on the asymptotic distributions of their denominators because, for example,

$$n(\tilde{\alpha}_d - 1) = \frac{-n^{-1} \sum\limits_{t=1}^{n} (Y_t - Y_{t-d})^2}{n^{-2} \sum\limits_{t=1}^{n} (Y_t^2 + Y_{t-d}^2)}$$

$$= \frac{-n^{-1} \sum\limits_{t=1}^{n} e_t^2}{n^{-2} \sum\limits_{t=1}^{n} (Y_t^2 + Y_{t-d}^2)},$$

$$n^{-1} \sum_{t=1}^{n} e_t^2 \xrightarrow{P} \sigma^2, \tag{3.4}$$

and $n^{-2} \sum_{t=1}^{n} (Y_t^2 + Y_{t+d}^2)$ has a limiting distribution.

Theorem 1. Let Y_t satisfy (1.1), where $\alpha_d = 1$ and $\{e_t\}$ is a sequence of iid $(0, \sigma^2)$ random variables. Let $\hat{\alpha}_d$ be defined by (2.1), $\hat{\alpha}_{\mu d}$ by regression equation (2.9), $\hat{\alpha}_{\mu d}^*$ by (2.13), $\tilde{\alpha}_d$ by (2.6), $\tilde{\alpha}_{\mu d}$ by (2.12), and $\tilde{\alpha}_{\mu d}^*$ by (2.14). Then

$$n(\hat{\alpha}_d - 1) \xrightarrow{L} \frac{1}{2} \left(\sum_{j=1}^{d} L_j \right)^{-1} d \sum_{j=1}^{d} (T_j^2 - 1),$$

$$\hat{\tau}_d \xrightarrow{L} \frac{1}{2} \left(\sum_{j=1}^{d} L_j \right)^{-1/2} \sum_{j=1}^{d} (T_j^2 - 1),$$

$$n(\hat{\alpha}_{\mu d} - 1) \xrightarrow{L} \left[\sum_{j=1}^{d} (L_j - W_j^2) \right]^{-1} \times d \sum_{j=1}^{d} \left[\frac{1}{2} (T_j^2 - 1) - T_j W_j \right],$$

$$\hat{\tau}_{\mu d} \xrightarrow{L} \left[\sum_{j=1}^{d} (L_j - W_j^2) \right]^{-1/2} \sum_{j=1}^{d} \left[\frac{1}{2} (T_j^2 - 1) - T_j W_j \right],$$

$$n(\hat{\alpha}_{\mu d}^* - 1) \xrightarrow{L} d \left\{ d \sum_{j=1}^{d} L_j - \left(\sum_{j=1}^{d} W_j \right)^2 \right\}^{-1}$$

$$\times \left\{ d \sum_{j=1}^{d} \frac{1}{2} (T_j^2 - 1) - \left(\sum_{j=1}^{d} T_j \right) \left(\sum_{j=1}^{d} W_j \right) \right\},$$

$$\hat{\tau}_{\mu d}^* \xrightarrow{L} d^{-1/2} \left\{ d \sum_{j=1}^{d} L_j - \left(\sum_{j=1}^{d} W_j \right)^2 \right\}^{1/2}$$

$$\times \left\{ d \sum_{j=1}^{d} \frac{1}{2} (T_j^2 - 1) - \left(\sum_{j=1}^{d} T_j \right) \left(\sum_{j=1}^{d} W_j \right) \right\},$$

$$n(\tilde{\alpha}_d - 1) \xrightarrow{L} -\frac{1}{2} d^2 \left(\sum_{j=1}^{d} L_j \right)^{-1},$$

$$n(\tilde{\alpha}_{\mu d} - 1) \xrightarrow{L} -\frac{1}{2} d^2 \left[\sum_{j=1}^{d} (L_j - W_j^2) \right]^{-1},$$

$$n(\tilde{\alpha}_{\mu d}^* - 1) \overset{L}{\to} -\frac{1}{2} d^2 \left[\sum_{j=1}^{d} L_j - d^{-1} \left(\sum_{j=1}^{d} W_j \right)^2 \right]^{-1},$$

where

$$W_j = 2^{1/2} \sum_{k=1}^{\infty} \gamma_k^2 Z_{jk},$$

$$T_j = 2^{1/2} \sum_{k=1}^{\infty} \gamma_k Z_{jk},$$

$$L_j = \sum_{k=1}^{\infty} \gamma_k^2 Z_{jk}^2,$$

$$\gamma_k = 2(-1)^{k+1}[(2k-1)\pi]^{-1},$$

and Z_{jk} are normal independent $(0, 1)$ random variables.

4. Alternative Representations for the Limit Distributions of the Symmetric Statistics

In Theorem 1 we gave the limiting distribution of all statistics as functions of certain random variables. In this section we present expressions for the limit cumulative distribution functions of the symmetric statistics. These results follow the work of Anderson and Darling (1952), Sargan (1973), Bulmer (1975), and McNeill (1978). The proofs of Theorems 2–4 are given in Appendix A.

Theorem 2. Let

$$X_{jt} = \sum_{k=1}^{t} e_{jk},$$

$$L_{jm} = m^{-2} \sum_{t=1}^{m} X_{jt}^2,$$

where e_{jk} are iid $(0, 1)$ random variables. Then the limiting distribution of $[2nd^{-2}(1 - \tilde{\alpha}_d)]^{-1}$ is the limiting distribution of $\Sigma_{j=1}^{d} L_{jm}$, and

$$F_L(l) = \lim_{m \to \infty} P \left\{ \sum_{j=1}^{d} L_{jm} \le l \right\}$$

$$= 2^{1/2(2+d)}[\Gamma(\tfrac{1}{2}d)]^{-1} \sum_{j=1}^{\infty} (-1)^j [\Gamma(j+1)]^{-1}$$

$$\times \Gamma(j + \tfrac{1}{2}d)[1 - \Phi\{\tfrac{1}{2}l^{-1/2}(4j + d)\}]$$

for $l > 0$, where $\Phi(x)$ is the probability that a normal $(0, 1)$ random variable is less than x.

Theorem 3. Let X_{jt} and L_{jm} be as defined in Theorem 2. Let

$$V_{jm} = L_{jm} - W_{jm}^2,$$

$$W_{jm} = m^{-3/2} \sum_{t=1}^{m} X_{jt},$$

$$F_{Vd}(l) = \lim_{m \to \infty} P\left\{\sum_{j=1}^{d} V_{jm} \leq l\right\}, \quad l > 0.$$

Then the limiting cumulative distribution function of $[2d^{-2}n(1 - \tilde{\alpha}_{\mu d})]^{-1}$ is $F_{Vd}(l)$, and

$$F_{V2}(l) = 4(2\pi l)^{-1/2} \sum_{j=0}^{\infty} \exp\left\{-\tfrac{1}{2}l^{-1}(2j + 1)^2\right\},$$

$$F_{V4}(l) = 16(2\pi l^3)^{-1/2} \sum_{j=1}^{\infty} j^2 \exp\left\{- 2l^{-1}j^2\right\},$$

$$F_{V6}(l) = 8(2\pi l^5)^{-1/2} \sum_{j=0}^{\infty} (j + 1)(j + 2)$$

$$\times [(2j + 3)^2 - l]\exp\left\{- (2l)^{-1}(2j + 3)^2\right\}$$

$$F_{V12}(l) = 32(15)^{-1}(2\pi l^{11})^{-1/2} \sum_{j=3}^{\infty} \Gamma(j + 3)[\Gamma(j - 2)]^{-1}$$

$$\times j(15l^2 - 40j^2l + 16j^4)\exp\left\{-2l^{-1}j^2\right\}.$$

Theorem 4. Let the definitions of Theorems 2 and 3 hold. Then the limiting distribution of $[2d^{-2} n(1 - \tilde{\alpha}_{\mu d}^*)]^{-1}$ is that of

$$u_{md} = \sum_{j=1}^{d} L_{jm} - W_{1m}^2.$$

The limiting cumulative distribution function of u_{md} is

$$F_{ud}(l) = 2^{1/2(d-1)}\pi^{-1}l^{-1/2} \sum_{j=0}^{\infty} A_j(4j + d)^{1/2}$$

$$\times \exp\left\{-(16l)^{-1}(4j + d)^2\right\}K_{1/4}[(16l)^{-1}(4j + d)^2],$$

where

$$A_j = \pi^{-1/2}[\Gamma\{\tfrac{1}{2}(d-1)\}]^{-1} \sum_{k=0}^{j} (-1)^k [k!(j-k)!]^{-1}$$

$$\times \Gamma\{k + \tfrac{1}{2}(d-1)\}\Gamma\{j - k + \tfrac{1}{2}\}, \quad j = 0, 1, \ldots,$$

and $K_{1/4}$ is the modified Bessel function of the second kind of order one-fourth.

5. Percentiles of Sampling Distributions

Tables of percentiles for the statistics discussed in this article are given in Tables 2–10. For the ordinary regression statistics, the representation in Theorem 1 and the simulation method described by Dickey (1976), and used in Dickey and Fuller (1979), 1981) and Hasza (1977), were

TABLE 2.   Percentiles for $n(\hat{\alpha}_d - 1)$; the ordinary regression coefficient for the zero mean model

		Probability of a smaller value									
	$n = md$	.01	.025	.05	.10	.50	.90	.95	.975	.99
	20	−12.20	−9.66	−7.70	−5.62	−.67	1.83	2.43	3.02	3.74
	30	−12.67	−9.93	−7.83	−5.71	−.71	1.72	2.28	2.79	3.43
	40	−12.98	−10.11	−7.94	−5.78	−.73	1.67	2.21	2.69	3.30
$d = 2$	100	−13.63	−10.50	−8.23	−5.93	−.76	1.58	2.10	2.54	3.07
	200	−13.88	−10.65	−8.34	−5.99	−.77	1.56	2.06	2.50	3.01
	400	−14.01	−10.73	−8.41	−6.02	−.77	1.54	2.04	2.48	2.97
	∞	−14.14	−10.81	−8.47	−6.06	−.78	1.53	2.02	2.46	2.94
	40	−13.87	−10.89	−8.67	−6.40	−.61	2.86	3.69	4.41	5.29
	60	−14.10	−11.09	−8.86	−6.51	−.65	2.68	3.47	4.13	4.97
	80	−14.31	−11.23	−8.94	−6.54	−.67	2.60	3.38	4.02	4.82
$d = 4$	200	−14.82	−11.57	−9.08	−6.59	−.70	2.50	3.23	3.85	4.55
	400	−15.04	−11.70	−9.12	−6.59	−.71	2.47	3.19	3.80	4.47
	800	−15.15	−11.77	−9.14	−6.59	−.71	2.46	3.17	3.78	4.43
	∞	−15.27	−11.85	−9.16	−6.59	−.71	2.45	3.15	3.76	4.39
	120	−18.10	−14.25	−11.51	−8.76	−.53	5.54	7.02	8.09	9.70
	180	−18.04	−14.31	−11.55	−8.74	−.62	5.25	6.66	7.82	9.17
	240	−18.02	−14.33	−11.56	−8.73	−.65	5.13	6.52	7.69	8.97
$d = 12$	600	−18.00	−14.35	−11.57	−8.72	−.69	4.97	6.34	7.49	8.71
	1,200	−18.00	−14.35	−11.58	−8.72	−.69	4.93	6.30	7.42	8.65
	2,400	−18.00	−14.35	−11.58	−8.72	−.69	4.92	6.28	7.39	8.63
	∞	−17.99	−14.35	−11.58	−8.72	−.69	4.90	6.27	7.36	8.61

TABLE 3.   Percentiles for 174_d, the Studentized statistic for the ordinary regression coefficient of the zero mean model

	n = md	.01	.025	.05	.10	.50	.90	.95	.975	.99
						Probability of a smaller value				
	20	−2.69	−2.27	−1.94	−1.57	−.29	1.07	1.48	1.85	2.28
	30	−2.64	−2.24	−1.93	−1.58	−.31	1.04	1.43	1.79	2.21
	40	−2.62	−2.23	−1.93	−1.58	−.32	1.03	1.42	1.76	2.18
$d = 2$	100	−2.58	−2.22	−1.92	−1.59	−.34	1.01	1.39	1.72	2.12
	200	−2.57	−2.22	−1.92	−1.59	−.35	1.00	1.38	1.71	2.10
	400	−2.56	−2.22	−1.92	−1.59	−.35	1.00	1.38	1.70	2.09
	∞	−2.55	−2.22	−1.92	−1.60	−.35	.99	1.38	1.69	2.08
	40	−2.58	−2.20	−1.87	−1.51	−.20	1.14	1.53	1.86	2.23
	60	−2.57	−2.20	−1.89	−1.52	−.20	1.10	1.49	1.82	2.20
	80	−2.56	−2.20	−1.89	−1.53	−.22	1.09	1.47	1.80	2.18
$d = 4$	200	−2.56	−2.20	−1.90	−1.53	−.23	1.07	1.45	1.78	2.17
	400	−2.56	−2.20	−1.90	−1.53	−.24	1.07	1.44	1.77	2.16
	800	−2.56	−2.20	−1.90	−1.53	−.24	1.07	1.44	1.77	2.16
	∞	−2.56	−2.20	−1.90	−1.53	−.24	1.07	1.44	1.77	2.16
	120	−2.50	−2.08	−1.77	−1.39	−.10	1.20	1.55	1.87	2.24
	180	−2.49	−2.09	−1.77	−1.41	−.12	1.17	1.53	1.85	2.22
	240	−2.49	−2.10	−.177	−1.42	−.13	1.16	1.53	1.85	2.21
$d = 12$	600	−2.49	−2.10	−1.79	−1.43	−.14	1.15	1.52	1.84	2.20
	1,200	−2.49	−2.10	−1.79	−1.43	−.14	1.15	1.52	1.84	2.20
	2,400	−2.49	−2.10	−1.80	−1.43	−.14	1.15	1.52	1.84	2.20
	∞	−2.49	−2.10	−1.80	−1.44	−.14	1.15	1.52	1.84	2.20

used to construct limit percentiles. For these limit distributions and for all finite sample sizes, the programs described in Dickey (1981) were used for the Monte Carlo integration. For all combinations of $d = 1, 2,$ 4, 12 and $m = 10, 15, 20, 50, 100, 200$ and for the limit case, two replications of d^{-1} 60,000 statistics were run. Normal time series were used for all finite sample sizes. The empirical percentiles were smoothed by regression on n^{-1}. For the symmetric estimators, the regression-smoothed percentiles were forced through the known limit percentiles. The smoothing procedure involved 234 regressions. A lack-of-fit statistic was computed for each regression. Of these, 12 were significant at the 5 per cent level, and four were also significant at 1 per cent.

The leftmost column in each table is headed by $n = md$, which is the total number of observations. The other column headings are probabilities of obtaining a value smaller than the tabulated value under the model with a $\alpha_d = 1$. Percentiles for the Studentized statistics in the

TABLE 4. Percentiles for $n(\hat{\alpha}_{\mu d}{}^* - 1)$, the ordinary regression coefficient for the single mean model

	n = md	.01	.025	.05	.10	.50	.90	.95	.975	.99
					Probability of a smaller value					
	20	−15.57	−13.15	−11.12	−8.97	−2.74	.99	1.75	2.41	3.19
	30	−16.82	−13.91	−11.17	−9.36	−2.84	.88	1.60	2.21	2.92
	40	−17.50	−14.36	−12.04	−9.56	−2.89	.84	1.54	2.12	2.79
d = 2	100	−18.81	−15.29	−12.68	−9.96	−2.96	.76	1.44	1.97	2.59
	200	−19.27	−15.63	−12.90	−10.10	−2.98	.74	1.41	1.93	2.53
	400	−19.50	−15.81	−13.02	−10.18	−2.99	.73	1.39	1.91	2.50
	∞	−19.74	−15.99	−13.14	−10.25	−3.00	.72	1.38	1.89	2.47
	40	−17.40	−14.16	−11.66	−9.14	−2.06	2.16	3.10	3.87	4.78
	60	−17.85	−14.59	−12.01	−9.27	−2.10	1.98	2.86	3.60	4.45
	80	−18.16	14.80	−12.17	−9.35	−2.12	1.91	2.77	3.49	4.31
d = 4	200	−18.90	−15.19	−12.45	−9.52	−2.17	1.81	2.64	3.33	4.11
	400	−19.19	−15.32	−12.54	−9.58	−2.19	1.79	2.61	3.29	4.05
	800	−19.35	−15.38	−12.58	−9.62	−2.20	1.78	2.60	3.27	4.02
	∞	−19.50	−15.44	−12.62	−9.65	−2.21	1.78	2.59	3.25	4.00
	120	−20.16	−16.35	−13.43	−10.50	−1.67	4.77	6.44	7.63	9.03
	180	−20.28	−16.42	−13.55	−10.47	−1.73	4.52	6.01	7.21	8.65
	240	−20.35	−16.47	−13.59	−10.45	−1.76	4.41	5.85	7.05	8.48
d = 12	600	−20.47	−16.60	−13.64	−10.44	−1.81	4.27	5.69	6.84	8.19
	1,200	−20.52	−16.65	−13.65	−10.44	−1.82	4.23	5.66	6.80	8.10
	2,400	−20.54	−16.68	−13.65	−10.44	−1.83	4.21	5.66	6.78	8.06
	∞	−20.56	−16.71	−13.65	−10.44	−1.84	4.20	5.66	6.77	8.02

symmetric case are not given because the Studentized statistics are simple transformations of the $\tilde{\alpha}$ statistics. The percentiles for $d = 1$ are not included in Table 10 because they are identical to those for $d = 1$ in Table 9.

The limiting distribution of the symmetric statistic with the mean removed is the same for $d = 2$ and $\alpha_2 = 1$ as for $d = 1$ and $\alpha_1 = 1$. The distribution is also similar for finite n. To see the reason for the similarity, let $Y_t = \Sigma_{j=1}^t e_j$ and consider the sum of squares for a sample of $2n$,

$$\sum_{t=1}^{2n}(Y_t - \bar{Y})^2 = \sum_{t=1}^{2n}[Y_t - Y_n - (\bar{Y} - Y_n)]^2$$

$$= \sum_{t=1}^{2n}(Y_t - Y_n)^2 - 2n(\bar{Y} - Y_n)^2$$

TABLE 5. Percentiles for $\tau_{\mu d}{}^*$, the Studentized test for the single mean model

		Probability of a smaller value							
$n = md$	.01	.025	.05	.10	.50	.90	.95	.975	.99
20	−3.54	−3.08	−2.72	−2.32	−.97	.49	.92	1.31	1.76
30	−3.44	−3.02	−2.69	−2.31	−1.01	.46	.88	1.25	1.68
40	−3.40	−3.00	−2.68	−2.31	−1.02	.44	.86	1.22	1.65
$d = 2$ 100	−3.31	−2.95	−2.65	−2.31	−1.05	.41	.83	1.19	1.61
200	−3.28	−2.93	−2.64	−2.31	−1.05	.40	.83	1.19	1.60
400	−3.25	−2.92	−2.63	−2.31	−1.06	.40	.82	1.18	1.59
∞	−3.25	−2.92	−2.63	−2.31	−1.06	.40	.82	1.18	1.59
40	−3.14	−2.73	−2.38	−2.00	−.60	.80	1.19	1.54	1.94
60	−3.11	−2.71	−2.38	−2.00	−.63	.76	1.15	1.49	1.89
80	−3.09	−2.71	−2.38	−2.01	−.64	.74	1.13	1.47	1.87
$d = 4$ 200	−3.07	−2.70	−2.38	−2.02	−.66	.72	1.11	1.46	1.86
400	−3.06	−2.70	−2.38	−2.02	−.67	.72	1.11	1.45	1.85
800	−3.06	−2.70	−2.38	−2.02	−.67	.72	1.10	1.45	1.85
∞	−3.05	−2.70	−2.38	−2.03	−.67	.72	1.10	1.45	1.85
120	−2.73	−2.33	−2.01	−1.65	−.31	1.02	1.38	1.71	2.08
180	−2.73	−2.35	−2.02	−1.66	−.33	.99	1.35	1.68	2.06
240	−2.73	−2.36	−2.02	−1.66	−.34	.98	1.34	1.67	2.05
$d = 12$ 600	−2.73	−2.37	−2.04	−1.66	−.35	.97	1.34	1.66	2.03
1,200	−2.73	−2.37	−2.05	−1.66	−.35	.96	1.33	1.65	2.02
2,400	−2.74	−2.37	−2.06	−1.66	−.36	.96	1.33	1.65	2.02
∞	−2.74	−2.37	−2.06	−1.66	−.36	.96	1.33	1.65	2.01

$$= \sum_{r=1}^{n-1} \left(\sum_{j=0}^{r-1} e_{n-j} \right)^2 + \sum_{r=1}^{n} \left(\sum_{j=1}^{r} e_{n+j} \right)^2$$

$$- (2n)^{-1} \left[\sum_{t=1}^{2n} \left(\sum_{j=1}^{t} e_j - \sum_{j=1}^{n} e_j \right) \right]^2$$

$$= \sum_{r=1}^{n-1} \left(- \sum_{j=0}^{r-1} e_{n-j} \right)^2 + \sum_{r=1}^{n} \left(\sum_{j=1}^{r} e_{n+j} \right)^2$$

$$- (2n)^{-1} \left[\sum_{r=1}^{n-1} \sum_{j=0}^{r-1} (-e_{n-j}) + \sum_{r=1}^{n} \sum_{j=1}^{r} e_{n+j} \right]^2 .$$

If $2n$ is replaced by $(2n - 1)$ in the final sum of squares, the resulting quantity has the same distribution as the sum of squares for a sample of $2n - 1$ from model (1.1) with $d = 2$ and $\alpha_2 = 1$.

TABLE 6. Percentiles for $n(\hat{\alpha}_{\mu d} - 1)$, the ordinary regression coefficient for the seasonal mean model

		Probability of a smaller value							
	$n = md$ .01	.025	.05	.10	.50	.90	.95	.975	.99
	20	−18.98	−16.75	−14.96	−12.78	−6.48	−1.94	−.83	.10	1.16
	30	−20.89	−18.19	−16.01	−13.62	−6.76	−2.11	−1.01	−.11	.92
	40	−22.02	−19.03	−16.64	−14.09	−6.91	−2.18	−1.10	−.21	.79
$d = 2$	100	−24.32	−20.76	−17.95	−15.05	−7.20	−2.31	−1.25	−.40	.55
	200	−25.17	−21.39	−18.44	−15.40	−7.30	−2.35	−1.30	−.46	.46
	400	−25.62	−21.72	−18.69	−15.58	−7.35	−2.37	−1.33	−.49	.42
	∞	−26.07	−22.06	−18.95	−15.76	−7.41	−2.39	−1.35	−.52	.38
	40	−28.78	−25.59	−23.10	−20.40	−11.89	−5.40	−3.90	−2.51	−1.05
	60	−30.63	−27.18	−24.49	−21.42	−12.33	−5.73	−4.15	−2.81	−1.33
	80	−31.79	−28.12	−25.27	−22.00	−12.58	−5.87	−4.28	−2.96	−1.47
$d = 4$	200	−34.26	−30.03	−26.78	−23.15	−13.06	−6.09	−4.51	−3.20	1.74
	400	−35.20	−30.73	−27.32	−23.56	−13.23	−6.15	−4.59	−3.28	−1.83
	800	−35.69	−31.10	−27.60	−23.78	−13.32	−6.18	−4.63	−3.32	−1.87
	∞	−36.19	−31.47	−27.88	−24.00	−13.41	−6.21	−4.67	−3.35	−1.92
	120	−60.72	−55.63	−51.22	−46.98	−33.65	−22.13	−19.46	−17.09	−14.25
	180	−63.40	−57.83	−53.57	−49.14	−34.95	−23.06	−20.00	−17.44	−14.57
	240	−64.90	−59.21	−54.89	−50.28	−35.57	−23.48	−20.31	−17.70	−14.86
$d = 12$	600	−67.87	−62.16	−57.52	−52.44	−36.65	−24.16	−20.92	−18.34	−15.57
	1,200	−68.93	−63.29	−58.47	−53.19	−36.99	−24.37	−21.14	−18.60	−15.87
	2,400	−69.48	−63.87	−58.95	−53.57	−37.16	−24.47	−21.26	−18.74	−16.03
	∞	−70.04	−64.48	−59.45	−53.95	−37.33	−24.56	−21.37	−18.88	−16.20

6. Higher Order Models

A popular model for seasonal time series is the multiplicative model

$$(1 - \alpha_d B^d)(1 - \theta_1 B - \ldots - \theta_p B^p)Y_t = e_t, \tag{6.1}$$

where B is the backshift operator defined by $B(Y_t) = Y_{t-1}$ and e_t is a sequence of iid $(0, \sigma^2)$ random variables.

We assume that all roots of

$$m^p - \theta_1 m^{p-1} - \ldots - \theta_p = 0 \tag{6.2}$$

are less than one in absolute value and that $Y_0, Y_{-1}, \ldots, Y_{-p-d+1}$ are initial values. Hasza and Fuller (1981) considered tests of the hypothesis that $\alpha_d = 1$ and that one of the roots of (6.2) is one. Model (6.1) defines e_t as a nonlinear function of (α_d, θ) where $\theta' = (\theta_1, \theta_2, \ldots, \theta_p)$. Define this function, evaluated at $(\hat{\alpha}_d, \theta)$, by $e_t(\hat{\alpha}_d, \theta)$. Expanding in Taylor's series, we obtain

$$e_t(\hat{\alpha}_d, \hat{\theta}) = e_t(\alpha_d, \theta)$$

$$- (1 - \hat{\theta}_1 B - \hat{\theta}_2 B^2 - \ldots - \hat{\theta}_p B^p)\, Y_{t-d}(\hat{\alpha}_d - \alpha_d)$$

TABLE 7.   Percentiles of $\tau_{\mu d}{}^*$, the Studentized statistic for the seasonal mean model

	$n = md$	.01	.025	.05	.10	.50	.90	.95	.975	.99
						Probability of a smaller value				
	20	−4.46	−3.98	−3.60	−3.18	−1.92	−.66	−.29	.03	.42
	30	−4.25	−3.84	−3.50	−3.13	−1.95	−.73	−.36	−.04	.34
	40	−4.15	−3.77	−3.45	−3.11	−1.96	−.76	−.40	−.08	.29
$d = 2$	100	−4.00	−3.66	−3.38	−3.07	−1.99	−.81	−.46	−.15	.21
	200	−3.95	−3.63	−3.36	−3.05	−1.99	−.83	−.48	−.18	.18
	400	−3.93	−3.62	−3.35	−3.05	−2.00	−.83	−.49	−.19	.17
	∞	−3.90	−3.60	−3.34	−3.04	−2.00	−.84	−.50	−.20	.15
	40	−5.01	−4.57	−4.21	−3.83	−2.55	−1.30	−.94	−.61	−.26
	60	−4.85	−4.46	−4.14	−3.79	−2.58	−1.36	−1.01	−.70	−.35
	80	−4.78	−4.41	−4.11	−3.78	−.260	−1.40	−1.05	−.74	−.39
$d = 4$	200	−4.67	−4.34	−4.06	−3.75	−2.63	−1.45	−1.11	−.81	−.46
	400	−4.64	−4.32	−4.05	−3.74	−2.64	−1.47	−1.14	−.84	−.48
	800	−4.62	−4.31	−4.04	−3.74	−2.65	−1.48	−1.15	−.85	−.49
	∞	−4.61	−4.30	−4.04	−3.73	−2.65	−1.49	−1.16	−.86	−.50
	120	−6.63	−6.20	−5.86	−5.49	−4.21	−2.97	−2.62	−2.35	−1.95
	180	−6.52	−6.15	−5.84	−5.49	−4.27	−3.06	−2.71	−2.39	−2.01
	240	−6.47	−6.13	−5.83	−5.49	−4.30	−3.10	−2.75	−2.43	−2.05
$d = 12$	600	−6.39	−6.09	−5.82	−5.49	−4.34	−3.17	−2.83	−2.52	−2.18
	1,200	−6.37	−6.07	−5.82	−5.49	−4.35	−3.19	−2.86	−2.56	−2.23
	2,400	−6.36	−6.07	−5.82	−5.49	−4.36	−3.20	−2.87	−2.58	−2.26
	∞	−6.35	−6.06	−5.82	−5.49	−4.36	−3.22	−2.88	−2.60	−2.29

$$- \sum_{i=1}^{p} (Y_{t-i} - \hat{\alpha}_d Y_{t-d-i})(\hat{\theta}_i - \theta_i) + r_t,$$

where r_t is the Taylor series remainder. This suggests the following estimation procedure (where $\dot{Y}_t = Y_t - Y_{t-d}$ corresponds to the initial estimate $\hat{\alpha}_d = 1$):

(1) Regress $\dot{Y}_t$ on $\dot{Y}_{t-1}, \ldots, \dot{Y}_{t-p}$ to obtain an initial estimator of $\boldsymbol{\theta}$ that is consistent for $\boldsymbol{\theta}$ under the null hypothesis that $\alpha_d = 1$.

(2) Compute $e_t(1, \hat{\boldsymbol{\theta}})$ and regress $e_t(1, \hat{\boldsymbol{\theta}})$ on

$$[(1 - \hat{\theta}_1 B - \hat{\theta}_2 B^2 - \cdots - \hat{\theta}_p B^p) Y_{t-d}, \dot{Y}_{t-1}, \dot{Y}_{t-2}, \ldots, \dot{Y}_{t-p}]$$

to obtain estimates of $(\alpha_d - 1, \boldsymbol{\theta} - \hat{\boldsymbol{\theta}})$. The estimator of $\alpha_d - 1$ may be used to test $H_0: \alpha_d = 1$.

Theorem 5. If $\alpha_d = 1$ in model (6.1), the two-step regression procedure suggested earlier results in an estimator $\hat{\alpha}_d$ and a corresponding Studentized statistic with the same limit distribution as that of the statistic one would obtain by regressing $Z_t - Z_{t-d} = \dot{Z}_t$ on Z_{t-d}, where $2 - \theta_p Y_{t-p}$. The estimators $\hat{\theta}_i$, obtained by adding the estimates of

TABLE 8. Percentiles of $n(\tilde{\alpha}_d - 1)$, the symmetry estimator for the zero model

	$n = md$	.01	.025	.05	.10	.50	.90	.95	.975	.99
			Probability of a smaller value							
$d = 1$	10	−9.98	−8.31	−6.92	−5.37	−1.57	−.42	−.33	−.27	−.22
	15	−11.18	−9.12	−7.48	−5.71	−1.62	−.42	−.31	−.25	−.21
	20	−11.89	−9.59	−7.79	−5.90	−1.64	−.42	−.31	−.25	−.20
	50	−13.38	−10.54	−8.40	−6.27	−1.69	−.42	−.30	−.24	−.19
	100	−13.93	−10.89	−8.63	−6.40	−1.71	−.42	−.30	−.24	−.18
	200	−14.22	−11.07	−8.74	−6.46	−1.71	−.42	−.30	−.24	−.18
	∞	−14.51	−11.26	−8.86	−6.53	−1.72	−.42	−.30	−.23	−.18
$d = 2$	20	−12.94	−10.62	−8.71	−6.82	−2.50	−1.01	−.82	−.70	−.60
	30	−13.83	−11.11	−9.12	−7.09	−2.54	−.99	−.79	−.67	−.56
	40	−14.29	−11.40	−9.34	−7.24	−2.56	−.98	−.78	−.66	−.54
	100	−15.16	−12.01	−9.75	−7.50	−2.61	−.97	−.77	−.64	−.52
	200	−15.46	−12.24	−9.90	−7.59	−2.62	−.97	−.76	−.63	−.51
	400	−15.61	−12.36	−9.97	−7.64	−2.63	−.97	−.76	−.63	−.51
	∞	−15.76	−12.48	−10.05	−7.68	−2.64	−.97	−.76	−.63	−.51
$d = 4$	40	−16.21	−13.61	−11.45	−9.38	−4.46	−2.35	−2.01	−1.77	−1.57
	60	−16.77	−13.86	−11.73	−9.57	−4.49	−2.31	−1.96	−1.71	−1.49
	80	−17.10	−14.06	−11.90	−9.68	−4.51	−2.29	−1.93	−1.68	−1.45
	200	−17.77	−14.55	−12.23	−9.89	−4.55	−2.27	−1.90	−1.65	−1.41
	400	−18.02	−14.74	−12.35	−9.97	−4.57	−2.26	−1.90	−1.64	−1.40
	800	−18.15	−14.85	−12.41	−10.01	−4.58	−2.26	−1.89	−1.63	−1.39
	∞	−18.28	−14.95	−12.48	−10.05	−4.59	−2.26	−1.89	−1.63	−1.39
$d = 12$	120	−26.43	−23.58	−21.29	−18.78	−12.42	−8.57	−7.82	−7.25	−6.64
	180	−27.39	−24.02	−21.56	−19.04	−12.49	−8.43	−7.65	−7.06	−6.35
	240	−27.77	−24.26	−21.72	−19.18	−12.52	−8.38	−7.58	−6.98	−6.25
	600	−28.29	−24.70	−22.07	−19.44	−12.55	−8.32	−7.48	−6.85	−6.13
	1,200	−28.42	−24.86	−22.20	−19.53	−12.55	−8.31	−7.46	−6.82	−6.12
	2,400	−28.47	−24.94	−22.27	−19.57	−12.55	−8.31	−7.45	−6.80	−6.11
	∞	−28.52	−25.02	−22.34	−19.62	−12.55	−8.30	−7.44	−6.78	−6.11

$\theta_i - \hat{\theta}_i$ to $\hat{\theta}_i$, have the same asymptotic distribution as the coefficients in a regression of $\dot{Y}_t$ on $\dot{Y}_{t-1}, \dot{Y}_{t-2}, \ldots, \dot{Y}_{t-p}$.

The proof of Theorem 5 is given in Appendix B. Theorem 5 implies that the tabulated limit percentiles for estimators in model (1.1) are applicable in the multiplicative model for large sample sizes.

The extension of Theorem 5 to estimators with seasonal means or a single mean is immediate. Let

$$y_t = Y_t - \sum_{i=1}^{d} \delta_{it} \tilde{\mu}_i. \qquad (6.3)$$

Replacing Y_t by y_t in the two-step estimation procedure results in the regression of $e_t(1, \hat{\boldsymbol{\theta}})$ on

$$(1 - \hat{\theta}_1 B - \hat{\theta}_2 B^2 - \cdots - \hat{\theta}_p B^p) y_{t-d},$$

$$\dot{Y}_{t-1}, \dot{Y}_{t-2}, \ldots, \dot{Y}_{t-d}.$$

TABLE 9. Percentiles of $n(\tilde{\alpha}_d^* - 1)$, the symmetric estimator for the single mean model

		Probability of a smaller value							
	$n = md$	.01	.025	.05	.10	.50	.90	.95	.975	.99
	10	−12.64	−11.28	−9.92	−8.38	−3.84	−1.51	−1.20	−1.01	−.86
	15	−14.77	−12.71	−11.01	−9.14	−3.96	−1.47	−1.15	−.96	−.78
	20	−15.97	−13.55	−11.62	−9.55	−4.02	−1.46	−1.13	−.93	−.75
$d = 1$	50	−18.38	−15.30	−12.81	−10.32	−4.13	−1.45	−1.10	−.88	−.70
	100	−19.25	−15.95	−13.24	−10.59	−4.17	−1.44	−1.09	−.86	−.69
	200	−19.70	−16.28	−13.45	−10.73	−4.19	−1.44	−1.09	−.85	−.68
	∞	−20.16	−16.62	−13.68	−10.87	−4.21	−1.44	−1.08	−.84	−.67
	20	−15.88	−13.48	−11.57	−9.51	−4.02	−1.46	−1.13	−.93	−.75
	30	−17.23	−14.45	−12.24	−9.95	−4.08	−1.45	−1.11	−.90	−.72
	40	−17.93	−14.97	−12.59	−10.18	−4.11	−1.45	−1.11	−.89	−.71
$d = 2$	100	−19.25	−15.94	−13.23	−10.59	−4.17	−1.44	−1.09	−.86	−.69
	200	−19.70	−16.28	−13.45	−10.73	−4.19	−1.44	−1.09	−.85	−.68
	400	−19.93	−16.45	−13.56	−10.80	−4.20	−1.44	−1.09	−.85	−.68
	∞	−20.16	−16.62	−13.68	−10.87	−4.21	−1.44	−1.08	−.84	−.67
	40	−18.97	−16.13	−13.86	−11.45	−5.46	−2.74	−2.32	−2.02	−1.76
	60	−19.62	−16.51	−14.08	−11.65	−5.51	−2.70	−2.26	−1.97	−1.68
	80	−20.03	−16.79	−14.26	−11.17	−5.53	−2.69	−2.24	−1.94	−1.64
$d = 4$	200	−20.89	−17.47	−14.70	−12.05	−5.59	−2.67	−2.21	−1.89	−1.60
	400	−21.21	−17.74	−14.88	−12.16	−5.61	−2.67	−2.20	−1.87	−1.59
	800	−21.38	−17.88	−14.98	−12.21	−5.62	−2.66	−2.20	−1.86	−1.58
	∞	−21.56	−18.03	−15.08	−12.27	−5.63	−2.66	−2.20	−1.85	−1.58
	120	−28.27	−25.14	−22.77	−20.09	−13.15	−9.01	−8.16	−7.51	−6.98
	180	−28.91	−25.63	−22.96	−20.28	−13.24	−8.87	−8.01	−7.38	−6.70
	240	−29.25	−25.92	−23.12	−20.41	−13.28	−8.82	−7.95	−7.30	−6.59
$d = 12$	600	−29.94	−26.49	−23.51	−20.70	−13.31	−8.76	−7.86	−7.16	−6.45
	1,200	−30.18	−26.69	−23.67	−20.81	−13.32	−8.75	−7.84	−7.11	−6.42
	2,400	−30.31	−26.80	−23.76	−20.87	−13.32	−8.75	−7.83	−7.08	−6.40
	∞	−30.43	−26.91	−23.85	−20.93	−13.32	−8.75	−7.82	−7.06	−6.39

Notice that $\dot{Y}_t = \dot{y}_t$ and that derivatives with respect to μ_i in the Taylor series get multiplied by zero, so that no adjustments to $\tilde{\mu}_i$ are made in the second step. Using the arguments of Theorem 5, it follows that the first coefficient $\hat{\alpha}_{\mu d}$ and its Studentized statistic converge to the limit distributions of the corresponding estimators in model (1.1).

Finally, we extend the results for our symmetric statistics to the multiplicative model. If $|\alpha_d| < 1$ in (6.1), then

$$(1 - \alpha_d F^d)(1 - \theta_1 F - \cdots - \theta_p F^p)Y_t$$

is a white noise series with the same variance as e_t, where F denotes the forward shift operator $F(Y_t) = Y_{t+1}$. To compute a symmetric estimator for the model with seasonal means, first compute the deviations from seasonal means defined in (6.3). Then create the column vector

TABLE 10. Percentiles of $n(\tilde{\alpha}_d - 1)$, the symmetric estimator for the seasonal means model

		Probability of a smaller value								
	$n = md$	.01	.025	.05	.10	.50	.90	.95	.975	.99
	20	−19.24	−16.90	−14.97	−12.86	−6.85	−3.46	−2.92	−2.55	−2.22
	30	−21.01	−18.22	−16.04	−13.61	−6.96	−3.39	−2.82	−2.44	−2.07
	40	−22.00	−18.96	−16.58	−13.99	−7.02	−3.36	−2.78	−2.38	−2.01
$d = 2$	100	−23.95	−20.45	−17.59	−14.67	−7.13	−3.32	−2.71	−2.28	−1.91
	200	−24.65	−20.99	−17.93	−14.90	−7.17	−3.31	−2.69	−2.25	−1.89
	400	−25.01	−21.26	−18.10	−15.01	−7.19	−3.30	−2.68	−2.23	−1.87
	∞	−25.37	−21.54	−18.28	−15.13	−7.21	−3.29	−2.68	−2.22	−1.86
	40	−28.95	−26.00	−23.23	−20.59	−12.83	−7.88	−6.95	−6.28	−5.58
	60	−30.89	−27.35	−24.41	−21.44	−12.90	−7.72	−6.74	−6.03	−5.32
	80	−31.85	−28.06	−24.98	−21.84	−12.95	−7.66	−6.65	−5.92	−5.21
$d = 4$	200	−33.53	−29.41	−25.97	−22.52	−13.08	−7.57	−6.53	−5.74	−5.03
	400	−34.08	−29.88	−26.29	−22.74	−13.13	−7.54	−6.49	−5.68	−4.98
	800	−34.35	−30.12	−26.45	−22.84	−13.16	−7.53	−6.48	−5.65	−4.95
	∞	−34.63	−30.36	−26.61	−22.95	−13.19	−7.53	−6.47	−5.63	−4.93
	120	−60.83	−56.03	−52.50	−48.69	−36.64	−27.56	−25.69	−24.02	−22.39
	180	−63.22	−58.06	−54.17	−49.67	−36.74	−27.20	−25.14	−23.50	−21.62
	240	−64.30	−59.02	−54.89	−50.17	−36.81	−27.05	−24.92	−23.25	−21.32
$d = 12$	600	−66.06	−60.63	−56.02	−51.07	−37.00	−26.87	−24.61	−22.79	−20.90
	1,200	−66.59	−61.14	−56.35	−51.37	−37.08	−26.82	−24.54	−22.64	−20.81
	2,400	−66.85	−61.39	−56.50	−51.52	−37.12	−26.81	−24.50	−22.57	−20.76
	∞	−67.10	−61.64	−56.65	−51.67	−37.16	−26.79	−24.47	−22.49	−20.73

$$\mathbf{Z}' = (y_{-p-d+1}, y_{-p-d+2}, \ldots, y_n, M, M, \ldots, M, y_n, \ldots, y_{-p-d+1}).$$

Here the M's denote a string of $p + d$ missing values. Let the elements of $\mathbf{Z}$ be denoted by z_t, $t = -p - d + 1, \ldots, 2n + 2(p + d)$. Now create

$$\hat{e}_t = e_t(1, \hat{\theta}_1, \hat{\theta}_2, \ldots, \hat{\theta}_p) = (1 - \hat{\theta}_1 B - \hat{\theta}_2 B^2 - \cdots - \hat{\theta}_p B^p)\dot{z}_t,$$

and regress $\hat{e}_t$ on

$$(1 - \hat{\theta}_1 B - \hat{\theta}_2 B_2 - \cdots - \hat{\theta}_p B^p)z_{t-d}, \dot{z}_t, \dot{z}_{t-1}, \ldots, \dot{z}_{t-p}.$$

If the first coefficient in this regression is denoted by $(\tilde{\alpha}_{\mu d} - 1)$, the percentiles of the limit distribution of $n(\tilde{\alpha}_{\mu d} - 1)$ are those given in Table 9.

7. Power Study

Using the Monte Carlo method, we computed power curves for the eight test statistics discussed in this paper. Power curves were generated for all combinations of $m = 10, 15, 20, 50, 100$, and 200, with $d = 2, 4$, and 12. In all cases, the hypothesis that $\alpha_d = 1$ was tested at the .05

level against the alternative that $\alpha_d < 1$. The power was evaluated for stationary time series satisfying $Y_t = \alpha Y_{t-d} + e_t$, where e_t are NI(0, 1) random variables for $\alpha =$ .995, .99, .95, .90, .85, .70, .60, .50, and .30. The empirical power is the fraction of the samples in which the statistic was in the rejection region. The number of replications was 24,000 for $d = 2$, 12,000 for $d = 4$, and 4,000 for $d = 12$. The power for the eight statistics is given in Table 11 for $m = 20$ and $d = 4$.

For $m \geq 100$, all statistics have power exceeding .90 for coefficients less than .85. The power increases with d and, of course, with m.

It is interesting that tests based on $\hat{\alpha}_d$, $\hat{\alpha}_{\mu d}^*$, and $\tilde{\alpha}_{\mu d}^*$ are seriously biased for the stationary alternative with small m and α_d close to one. The bias is clear in Table 11. The bias is associated with the properties of stationary time series. For example, if $\alpha_d = .99$, the variance of the stationary time series is $50.25\ \sigma^2$ and the initial value can be far from zero. In small samples with large Y_0, the variance of the estimator of α_d is smaller than the variance of $\hat{\alpha}_d$ under the null distribution. The τ statistics show less bias because these statistics reflect the fact that samples with large Y_0 have small variance. Note, however, that $\tau_{\mu4}^*$ is also slightly biased for $m = 20$ and $\alpha_4 = .995$.

Tests based on statistics constructed with seasonal means removed displayed little bias. For $m = 10$ and $\alpha_d = .995$, the null was rejected by the statistic $\hat{\alpha}_{\mu4}$ about 4.8% of the time. For larger m, little or no bias was observed. The power of the statistic $\hat{\alpha}_{\mu4}$ was similar to that of $\tilde{\alpha}_{\mu4}$, with $\tilde{\alpha}_{\mu4}$ displaying a slight advantage.

To summarize, if the alternative model is the zero mean or single mean stationary model, the $\hat{\tau}$ and τ_{μ}^* statistics are preferred. If the alternative model is the stationary process with seasonal means, $\hat{\alpha}_{\mu}$ and $\tilde{\alpha}_{\mu}$ are the most powerful of the statistics studied.

TABLE 11. Empirical power of tests against the stationary alternative for 20 years of quarterly data

Statistic	α_4								
	.995	.99	.98	.95	.90	.85	.80	.70	.60
$\hat{\alpha}_4$	.001	.003	.018	.13	.47	.81	.96	1.00	1.00
$\hat{\tau}_4$	.090	.114	.170	.35	.66	.88	.97	1.00	1.00
$\hat{\alpha}_{\mu4}^*$	.001	.005	.017	.09	.35	.65	.88	1.00	1.00
$\tau_{\mu4}^*$	.044	.062	.102	.22	.47	.72	.90	1.00	1.00
$\hat{\alpha}_{\mu4}$	.054	.057	.064	.10	.19	.32	.50	.84	.97
$\hat{\tau}_{\mu4}$	.054	.054	.059	.08	.13	.20	.33	.65	.89
$\tilde{\alpha}_{\mu4}^*$	.000	.002	.005	.04	.21	.50	.79	.99	1.00
$\tilde{\alpha}_{\mu4}$	.054	.055	.064	.10	.19	.34	.53	.86	.99

Appendix A. Proofs of Limit Results for Symmetric Statistics

Proof of Theorem 2. White (1958) showed that

$$E\{\exp(2tL_1)\} = [\cos h(2t^{1/2})]^{-1/2}.$$

Thus

$$E\{\exp(-tL_1)\} = [\cos h(2t)^{1/2}]^{-1/2},$$

and for $L = \sum_{i=1}^{d} L_i$,

$$E\{\exp(-tL)\} = [\cos h(2t)^{1/2}]^{-d/2}$$

$$= \int_0^\infty \exp(-lt)dF_L(l),$$

where, for notational convenience, we omit the subscript d. Integrating by parts, we have

$$\int_0^\infty \exp(-lt)dF_L(l) = t\int_0^\infty \exp(-lt)F_L(l)dl,$$

so that

$$\int_0^\infty \exp(-lt)F_L(l)dl = t^{-1}[\cos h(2t)^{1/2}]^{-d/2}.$$

By the theory of Laplace transforms, $F_L(l)$ is the inverse Laplace transform, $\mathcal{L}^{-1}(\cdot)$ given by

$$F_L(l) = \mathcal{L}^{-1}\{t^{-1}[\cos h(2t)^{1/2}]^{-d/2}\}.$$

Now

$$t^{-1}[\cos h(2t)^{1/2}]^{-1/2d} = 2^{d/2}t^{-1}\exp[-\tfrac{1}{2}d(2t)^{1/2}][1 + \exp(-2(2t)^{1/2})]^{-d/2}$$

$$= 2^{d/2}t^{-1}\exp[-\tfrac{1}{2}d(2t)^{1/2}]\sum_{j=0}^{\infty}(-1)^j[\Gamma(\tfrac{1}{2}d)$$

$$\times \Gamma(j+1)]^{-1}\Gamma(j+\tfrac{1}{2}d)\exp\{-2j(2t)^{1/2}\}.$$

Therefore,

$$F_L(l) = [\Gamma(\tfrac{1}{2}d)]^{-1}2^{d/2}\sum_{j=0}^{\infty}(-1)^j[\Gamma(j+1)]^{-1}\Gamma(j+\tfrac{1}{2}d)\mathcal{L}^{-1}[f(t)],$$

where

$$f(t) = t^{-1}\exp\{-2^{-1/2}(4j+d)t^{1/2}\}.$$

From standard tables (Selby 1968, p. 476, No. 83),

$$\mathcal{L}^{-1}[t^{-1}\exp\{-kt^{1/2}\}] = 2[1 - \Phi(k(2l)^{-1/2})],$$

where Φ is the standard normal cumulative distribution function.

Proof of Theorem 3. We show the general result for $V_i = L_i - W_i^2$, $V = \sum_{i=1}^{d}V_i$, and d even. Then for every $l > 0$,

$$F_V(l) = C2^{-3/2} \sum_{j=0}^{\infty} W_j(4j + d)$$

$$\times \frac{\partial^i}{\partial l^i} [\alpha^{-3/2} \exp\{-(8l)^{-1}(4j + d)^2\}], \quad d \equiv 0 \pmod 4,$$

$$= C \sum_{j=0}^{\infty} W_j \frac{\partial^k}{\partial l^k} [l^{-1/2} \exp\{-(8l)^{-1}(4j + d)^2\}], \quad d \equiv 2 \pmod 4,$$

where

$$C = [\pi^{1/2}\Gamma(\tfrac{1}{2}d)]^{-1} 2^{3d/4},$$
$$W_j = [\Gamma(j + 1)]^{-1}\Gamma(j + \tfrac{1}{2}d),$$
$$(i, k) = ((d - 4)/4, (d - 2)/4).$$

Proof. Using results of Anderson and Darling (1952),

$$E\{\exp(-tV_1)\} = [(\sin h(2t)^{1/2})^{-1}(2t)^{1/2}]^{1/2},$$

and thus

$$E\{\exp(-tV)\} = [(\sin h(2t)^{1/2})^{-1}(2t)^{1/2}]^{d/2}$$
$$= \int_0^{\infty} \exp\{-lt\} dF_V(l).$$

By the Laplace transform theory,

$$F_V(l) = \mathcal{L}^{-1}\{[t(\sin h(2t)^{1/2})^{d/2}]^{-1}(2t)^{d/4}\}.$$

We have

$$[\sin h(2t)^{1/2}]^{-d/2} t^{-1}(2t)^{d/4}$$
$$= 2^{3d/4} t^{(d-4)/4} \exp[-d(2t)^{1/2}2^{-1}][1 - \exp\{-2(2t)^{1/2}\}]^{-d/2}$$
$$= 2^{3d/4} t(d-4)/4 \exp[-d(2t)^{1/2}2^{-1}]$$
$$\times \sum_{j=0}^{\infty} [\Gamma(j + 1)\Gamma(\tfrac{1}{2}d)]^{-1}\Gamma(j + \tfrac{1}{2}d) \exp\{-2j(2t)^{1/2}\}.$$

Thus

$$F_V(l) = \pi^{1/2}C \sum_{j=0}^{\infty} W_j \mathcal{L}^{-1}\{t^{(d-4)/4} \exp[-2^{1/2}(2j + \tfrac{1}{2}d)t^{1/2}]\}.$$

The inverse transforms

$$\mathcal{L}^{-1}\{\exp(-bt^{1/2})\} - [2\pi^{1/2} l^{3/2}]^{-1} b \exp\{-b^2(4l)^{-1}\},$$
$$\mathcal{L}^{-1}\{t^{-1/2} \exp(-bt^{1/2})\} = (\pi l)^{-1/2} \exp\{-b^2(4l)^{-1}\},$$

along with the usual formula for differentiation of Laplace transforms, give the result.

Proof of Theorem 4. Let

$$U = \sum_{i=1}^{d} L_i - W_1^2 = (L_1 - W_1^2) + \sum_{i=2}^{d} L_i,$$

where $d \geq 2$ is an integer. Letting $\mathcal{L}\{\cdot\}$ denote the Laplace transform and $F_U(l) = P(U \leq l)$, we have

$$\mathcal{L}\{F_U(l)\} = t^{-1}\{\tfrac{1}{2}[\exp\{(2t)^{1/2}\} + \exp\{-(2t)^{1/2}\}]\}^{(1-d)/2}$$

$$\times \{2(2t)^{1/2}[\exp\{(2t)^{1/2}\} - \exp\{-(2t)^{1/2}\}]^{-1}\}^{1/2}$$

$$= 2^{(2d+1)/4} t^{-3/4} \exp\{-d(2t)^{1/2}2^{-1}\}$$

$$\times [1 + \exp\{-2(2t)^{1/2}\}]^{(1-d)/2}[1 - \exp\{-2(2t)^{1/2}\}]^{-1/2}$$

$$= 2^{(2d+1)/4} t^{-3/4} \exp\{-d(2t)^{1/2}2^{-1}\}$$

$$\times \sum_{k=0}^{\infty} (-1)^k [k!\Gamma((d-1)/2)]^{-1}$$

$$\times \Gamma(k + (d-1)/2) \exp\{-2k(2t)^{1/2}\}$$

$$\times \sum_{j=0}^{\infty} [j!\Gamma(\tfrac{1}{2})]^{-1}\Gamma(j + \tfrac{1}{2}) \exp\{-2j(2t)^{1/2}\}$$

$$= 2^{(2d+1)/4} \sum_{j=0}^{\infty} \omega_j t^{-3/4} \exp\{-t^{1/2}(4j + d)2^{-1/2}\},$$

where

$$\omega_j = \pi^{-1/2}[\Gamma((d-1)/2)]^{-1} \sum_{k=0}^{j} (-1)^k [k!(j-k)!]^{-1}$$

$$\times \Gamma(k + (d-1)/2)\Gamma(j - k + \tfrac{1}{2}).$$

The result follows because

$$\mathcal{L}^{-1}\{t^{-3/4}\exp(-t^{1/2}b)\} = \pi^{-1}b^{1/2}(2l)^{-1/2}\exp\{-(8l)^{-1}b^2\}K_{1/4}((8l)^{-1}b^2).$$

We now establish the relationship between U and $n(1 - \tilde{\alpha}_{\mu d}^*)$. Let $\mathbf{Q}$ be a $d \times d$ orthonormal matrix with $1j$th entry $q_{1j} = d^{-1/2}$. Let $\mathbf{X}_t = (X_{1t}, X_{2t}, \ldots, X_{dt})'$. Let $\mathbf{Z}_t = \mathbf{Q}\mathbf{X}_t$. Notice that

$$\sum_{j=1}^{d}\sum_{t=1}^{m} X_{jt}^2 = \sum_{t=1}^{m} \text{tr}(\mathbf{X}_t\mathbf{X}_t') = \sum_{t=1}^{m} \text{tr}(\mathbf{Q}\mathbf{X}_t\mathbf{X}_t'\mathbf{Q}') = \sum_{j=1}^{d}\sum_{t=1}^{m} Z_{jt}^2,$$

where $\mathbf{Z}_t = (Z_{1t}, Z_{2t}, \ldots, Z_{dt})'$. Furthermore,

$$\sum_{j=1}^{d}\sum_{t=1}^{m} X_{jt} = d^{1/2} \sum_{t=1}^{m} Z_{1t},$$

so that

$$\sum_{j=1}^{d}\sum_{t=1}^{m} X_{jt}^2 - (dm)^{-1}\left(\sum_{j=1}^{d}\sum_{t=1}^{m} X_{jt}\right)^2 = \sum_{j=1}^{d}\sum_{t=1}^{m} Z_{jt}^2 - (dm)^{-1}d\left(\sum_{t=1}^{m} Z_{1t}\right)^2.$$

Since the covariance matrix of $\mathbf{X}_t$ is of the form $\sigma^2\mathbf{I}$, so is that of $\mathbf{Z}_t$. Thus, the sum of squared deviations of Y_t from the single mean

$$\bar{Y} = (md)^{-1}\sum_{t=1}^{md} Y_t$$

is

$$\sum_{t=1}^{md} Y_t^2 - (md)^{-1} \left(\sum_{t=1}^{md} Y_t \right)^2$$

$$= \sum_{j=1}^{d} \sum_{t=1}^{m} X_{jt}^2 - (md)^{-1} \left(\sum_{j=1}^{d} \sum_{t=1}^{m} X_{jt} \right)^2$$

$$= \sum_{j=1}^{d} \sum_{t=1}^{m} Z_{jt}^2 - m^{-1} \left(\sum_{t=1}^{m} Z_{1t} \right)^2.$$

It follows that the limit distribution of $n(1 - \tilde{\alpha}_{\mu d}^*)$ is the same as that of $\frac{1}{2} d^2 \{ \sum_{j=1}^{d} L_j - W_1^2 \}^{-1}$.

Appendix B

To prove the results for extension to higher order models, simply note that if

$$(1 - B^d)(1 - \theta_1 B - \theta_2 B^2 - \cdots - \theta_p B^p) Y_t = e_t$$

and if $\dot{Y}_t = Y_t - Y_{t-d}$, then $\dot{Y}_t$ is stationary, except for effects of initial conditions, so that

$$[n^- \sum \dot{Y}_t^2 - E(\dot{Y}_n^2)] = O_p(n^{-1/2})$$

and

$$\sum e_t \dot{Y}_{t-1} = O_p(n^{1/2}),$$

and by standard theory of stationary time series, $\hat{\theta}_i - \theta_i = O_p(n^{-1/2})$ when $\hat{\theta}_i$ is estimated by ordinary least squares from the $\dot{Y}_t$ series.

Now the series

$$\hat{e}_t = (1 - \hat{\theta}_1 B - \hat{\theta}_2 B^2 - \cdots - \hat{\theta}_p B^p) \dot{Y}_t,$$

regressed on

$$(1 - \hat{\theta}_1 B - \hat{\theta}_2 B^2 - \cdots - \hat{\theta}_p B^p) Y_{t-d},$$

yields an estimator of $\lambda = \alpha_d - 1$, denoted by $\hat{\lambda}$, and the regression of

$$e_t = (1 - \theta_1 B - \cdots - \theta_p B^p) \dot{Y}_t$$

on

$$(1 - \theta_1 B - \cdots - \theta_p B^p) Y_{t-d}$$

yields the estimator $\tilde{\lambda}$, where the limit distribution of $n \tilde{\lambda}$ is known.

Now

$$2^{-2} \{ \sum [(1 - \hat{\theta}_1 B - \cdots - \hat{\theta}_p B^p) Y_{t-d}]^2$$

$$- \sum [(1 - \theta_1 B - \cdots - \theta_p B^p) Y_{t-d}]^2 \} = O_p(n^{-1/2})$$

because

$$(\hat{\theta}_i\hat{\theta}_j - \theta_i\theta_j) \sum_{t=1}^{n} Y_t^2 = O_p(n^{3/2}).$$

Similarly,

$$n^{-1} \sum \hat{e}_t(1 - \hat{\theta}_1 B - \hat{\theta}_2 B^2 - \cdots - \hat{\theta}_p B^p)Y_{t-d}$$

$$= n^{-1} \sum e_t(1 - \theta_1 B - \cdots - \theta_p B^p)Y_{t-d} + O_p(n^{-1/2}).$$

Thus $n(\hat{\lambda} - \lambda) = O_p(n^{-1/2})$, so by Slutzky's theorem, the limit distribution for $n\hat{\lambda}$ is the same as that of $n\tilde{\lambda}$. The removal of an overall mean $\bar{Y}$ at the outset does not affect the estimation of the θ_i because $(Y_t - \bar{Y}) - (Y_{t-d} - \bar{Y}) = Y_t - Y_{t-d} = \dot{Y}_t$, as before. Similarly, $\hat{e}_t$ is unchanged but is regressed on $(1 - \hat{\theta}_1 B - \cdots - \hat{\theta}_p B^p)(Y_{t-d} - \bar{Y})$. Comparison of this regression coefficient to that in the regression of e_t on $(1 - \hat{\theta}_1 B - \cdots - \hat{\theta}_p B^p)(Y_{t-d} - \bar{Y})$ shows, in exactly the same manner as before, that the estimators differ by $O_p(n^{-1/2})$.

The inclusion of $Y_{t-1}, Y_{t-2}, \ldots, Y_{t-p}$ in the regressions allows for Gauss–Newton improvements of $\hat{\theta}_i$ but does not affect the limit distribution of $n(\hat{\alpha}_d - 1)$, since $\sum Y_{t-d}Y_{t-j} = O_p(n)$.

References

ANDERSON, T. W., and DARLING D. A. (1952), 'Asymptotic theory of certain "goodness of fit" criteria based on stochastic processes', *Annals of Mathematical Statistics*, **23**, 193–212.

BULMER, M. G. (1975), 'The statistical analysis of density population', *Biometrics*, **31**, 901–11.

DICKEY, D. A. (1976), 'Estimation and hypothesis testing in non-stationary time series', unpublished Ph.D. thesis. Iowa State University.

— (1981), 'Histograms, percentiles, and moments', *The American Statistician*, **35**, 164–5.

— and FULLER, W. A. (1979), 'Distribution of the estimators for autoregressive time series with a unit root', *Journal of the American Statistical Association*, **74**, 427–31.

— (1981), 'Likelihood ratio statistics for autoregressive time series with a unit root', *Econometrica*, **49**, 1057–72.

EVANS, G. B. A., and SAVIN, N. E. (1981), 'The calculation of the limiting distribution of the least squares estimator of the parameter in a random walk model', *Annals of Statistics*, **5**, 1114–18.

FULLER, W. A. (1976), *Introduction to Statistical Time Series* New York: John Wiley.

— (1979), 'An estimator for the parameters of the autogressive process with application to testing for a unit root', Report to the US Census Bureau.

HASZA, D. P. (1977), 'Estimation in nonstationary time series', unpublished Ph.D. thesis. Iowa State University.

— and FULLER, W. A. (1981), 'Testing for nonstationary parameter specifications in seasonal time series models', *Annals of Statistics,* **10**, 1209–16.

MCNEILL, I. B. (1978), 'Properties of sequences of partial sums of polynomial regression residuals with application to tests for change of regression at unknown time', *Annals of Statistics*, **6**, 422–33.

RAO, M. M. (1978). 'Asymptotic distribution of an estimator of the boundary parameter of an unstable process', *Annals of Statistics*, **6**, 185–90.

SARGAN, J. D. (1973), 'The Durbin–Watson ratio of the Gaussian random walk', unpublished manuscript. London School of Economics Forms the basis for: Sargan, J. D., and A. Bhargava (1983), 'Testing Residuals from Least Squares Regression for Being Generated by the Gaussian Random Walk', *Econometrica*, **51**, 153–74.

SELBY, S. M. (1968), *Standard Mathematics Tables* (6th edn.). Cleveland: Chemical Rubber Company.

WHITE, J. S. (1958), 'The limiting distribution of the serial correlation coefficient in the explosive case', *Annals of Mathematical Statistics*, **29**, 118–97.

17

Seasonal Integration and Cointegration*

S. HYLLEBERG, R. F. ENGLE, C. W. J. GRANGER, and B. S. YOO

Abstract. This paper develops tests for roots in linear time series which have a modulus of one but which correspond to seasonal frequencies. Critical values for the tests are generated by Monte Carlo methods or are shown to be available from Dickey–Fuller or Dickey–Hasza–Fuller critical values. Representations for multivariate processes with combinations of seasonal and zero-frequency unit roots are developed leading to a variety of autoregressive and error-correction representations. The techniques are used to examine cointegration at different frequencies between consumption and income in the UK.

1. Introduction

The rapidly developing time-series analysis of models with unit roots has had a major impact on econometric practice and on our understanding of the response of economic systems to shocks. Univariate tests for unit roots were first proposed by Fuller (1976) and Dickey and Fuller (1979) and were applied to a range of macroeconomic data by Nelson and Plosser (1982). Granger (1981) proposed the concept of cointegration which recognized that even though several series all had unit roots, a linear combination could exist which would not. Engle and Granger (1987) present a theorem giving several representations of cointegrated series and tests and estimation procedures. The testing is a direct generalization of Dickey and Fuller to the hypothesized linear combination.

* The research was carried out while the first author was on sabbatical at UCSD and the last author was completing his dissertation. The authors are indebted to the University of Aarhus, NSF SE587-05884, and SES87-04669 for financial support. The data will be made available through the Inter-university Consortium for Political and Social Research at the University of Michigan.

Printed with permission of: *Journal of Econometrics,* **44**. 215–38.

All of this work assumes that the root of interest not only has a modulus of one, but is precisely one. Such a root corresponds to a zero-frequency peak in the spectrum. Furthermore, it assumes that there are no other unit roots in the system. Because many economic time series exhibit substantial seasonality, there is a definite possibility that there may be unit roots at other frequencies such as the seasonals. In fact, Box and Jenkins (1970) and the many time-series analysts influenced by their work implicitly assume that there are seasonal unit roots by using the seasonal differencing filter.

This paper describes in section 2 various classes of seasonal processes and in section 3 sets out to test for seasonal unit roots in time-series data both in the presence of other unit roots and other seasonal processes. Section 4 defines seasonal cointegration and derives several representations. Section 5 gives an empirical example and section 6 concludes.

2.   Seasonal Time-series Processes

Many economic time series contain important seasonal components and there are a variety of possible models for seasonality which may differ across series. A seasonal series can be described as one with a spectrum having distinct peaks at the seasonal frequencies $\omega_S \equiv 2\pi j/s$, $j = 1, \ldots, s/2$, where s is the number of time periods in a year, assuming s to be an even number and that a spectrum exists. In this paper, quarterly data will be emphasised so that $s = 4$, but the results can be *naturally* extended in a straightforward fashion to monthly data, for example.

Three classes of time-series models are commonly used to model seasonality. These can be called:

(a) Purely deterministic seasonal processes,
(b) Stationary seasonal processes,
(c) Integrated seasonal processes.

Each is frequently used in empirical work often with an implicit assumption that they are all equivalent. The first goal of this paper is to develop a testing procedure which will determine what class of seasonal processes is responsible for the seasonality in a univariate process. Subsequently, this approach will deliver multivariate results on cointegration at seasonal frequencies.

A purely deterministic seasonal process is a process generated by seasonal dummy variable such as the following quarterly series:

$$x_t = \mu_t \quad \text{where} \quad \mu_t = m_0 + m_1 S_{1t} + m_2 S_{2t} + m_3 S_{3t}. \quad (2.1)$$

Notice that this process can be perfectly forecast and will never change its shape.

A stationary seasonal process can be generated by a potentially infinite autoregression

$$\varphi(B)x_t = \varepsilon_t, \qquad \varepsilon_t \text{ i.i.d.},$$

with all of the roots of $\varphi(B) = 0$ lying outside the unit circle but where some are complex pairs with seasonal periodicities. More precisely, the spectrum of such a process is given by

$$f(\omega) = \sigma^2 / |\varphi(e^{i\omega})|^2,$$

which is assumed to have peaks at some of the seasonal frequencies ω_s. An example for quarterly data is

$$x_t = \rho x_{t-4} + \varepsilon_t,$$

which has a peak at both the seasonal periodicities $\pi/2$ (one cycle per year) and π (two cycles per year) as well as at zero frequency (zero cycles per year).

A series x_t is an integrated seasonal process if it has a seasonal unit root in its autoregressive representation. More generally it is integrated of order d at frequency θ if the spectrum of x_t takes the form

$$f(\omega) = c(\omega - \theta)^{-2d},$$

for ω near θ. This is conveniently denoted by

$$x_t \sim I_\theta(d).$$

The paper will concentrate on the case $d = 1$. An example of an integrated quarterly process at two cycles per year is

$$x_t = -x_{t-1} + \varepsilon_t, \tag{2.2}$$

and at one cycle per year it is

$$x_t = -x_{t-2} + \varepsilon_t. \tag{2.3}$$

The very familiar seasonal differencing operator, advocated by Box and Jenkins (1970) and used as a seasonal process by Grether and Nerlove (1970) and Bell and Hillmer (1984) for example, can be written as

$$(1 - B^4)x_t = \varepsilon_t = (1 - B)(1 + B + B^2 + B^3)x_t$$
$$= (1 - B)(1 + B)(1 + B^2)x_t$$
$$= (1 - B)S(B)x_t, \tag{2.4}$$

which therefore has four roots with modulus one: one is a zero frequency, one at two cycles per year, and two complex pairs at one cycle per year.

The properties of seasonally integrated series are not immediately obvious but are quite similar to the properties of ordinary integrated processes as established for example by Fuller (1976). In particular they have 'long memory' so that shocks last forever and may in fact change permanently the seasonal patterns. They have variances which increase linearly since the start of the series and are asymptotically uncorrelated with processes with other frequency unit roots.

The generating mechanisms being considered, such as (2.2) or (2.4), are stochastic difference equations. They generalize the ordinary $I(1)$, or $I_0(1)$ in the present notation, process. It is well known that an equation of the form

$$(1 - B)x_t = \varepsilon_t \tag{2.5}$$

has two components to its solution: the homogeneous solution x_{1t} where

$$(1 - B)x_{1t} = 0$$

and the particular solution x_{2t} given by

$$x_{2t} = (1/(1 - B))\varepsilon_t.$$

Thus $x_t = x_{1t} + x_{2t}$, where $x_{1t} = x_0$ (the starting value) and $x_{2t} = \sum_{j=0}^{t-1}\varepsilon_{t-j}$.

Clearly, if $E[\varepsilon_t] = m \neq 0$, then x_{2t} will contain a linear trend mt.

The equation with $S(B) = (1 + B)(1 + B^2)$,

$$S(B)x_t = \varepsilon_t, \tag{2.6}$$

also has a solution with two components. The homogeneous solution is

$$x_{1t} = c_1(-1)^t + c_2(i)^t + c_3(-i)^t,$$

where c_1, c_2, c_3 are determined from the starting conditions, plus the requirement that x_{1t} is a real series, i.e. c_2 and c_3 are complex conjugates. If $x_{-2} = x_{-1} = x_0 = 0$ so that the starting values contain no seasonal, then $x_{1t} \equiv 0$.

The particular solution is

$$x_{2t} = [S(B)]^{-1}\varepsilon_t,$$

and noting that

$$[S(B)]^{-1} = \tfrac{1}{2}[1/(1 + B) + (1 - B)/(1 + B^2)],$$

some algebra gives

$$x_{2t} = \tfrac{1}{2}\sum_{j=0}^{t-1}(-1)^j\varepsilon_{t-j} + \tfrac{1}{2}\sum_{j=0}^{\mathrm{int}[(t-1)/2]}(-1)^j\Delta\varepsilon_{t-2j},$$

where $\Delta = 1 - B$ and $\mathrm{int}[z]$ is the largest integer in z. The two parts of this solution correspond to the two seasonal roots and to eqs. (2.2) and (2.3).

The homogeneous solution to eqs. (2.5), (2.2), and (2.3) are given, respectively, by

$$s_{1t} = \sum_{j=0}^{t-1} \varepsilon_{t-j} \qquad \text{for zero-frequency root,}$$

$$s_{2t} = \sum_{j=0}^{t-1} (-1)^j \varepsilon_{t-j} \qquad \text{for the two-cycle-per-year root,}$$

$$s_{3t} = \sum_{j=0}^{\text{int}[(t-1)/2]} (-1)^j \lambda \varepsilon_{t-2j} \qquad \text{for the one-cycle-per-year root.}$$

The variances of these series are given by

$$V(s_{1t}) = V(s_{2t}) = V(s_{3t}) = t\sigma^2,$$

so that all of the unit roots have the property that the variance tends to infinity as the process evolves. When the series are excited by the same $\{\varepsilon_t\}$ and t is divisable by four, the covariances are all zero. At other values of t the covariances are at most σ^2, so the series are asymptotically uncorrelated as well as being uncorrelated in finite samples for complete years of data.

It should be noted that, if $E[\varepsilon_t] = m \neq 0$, all t, then the first term in x_{2t} will involve an oscillation of period 2. The complete solution to (2.6) contains both cyclical deterministic terms, corresponding to 'seasonal dummies' plus long nondeclining sums of past innovations or their changes. Thus, a series generated by (2.6) will have a component that is seasonally integrated and may also have a deterministic seasonal component, largely depending on the starting values. A series generated by (2.6) will be inclined to have a seasonal with peak that varies slowly through time, but if the initial deterministic component is large, it may not appear to drift very fast.

If x_t is generated by

$$(1 - B^4)x_t = \varepsilon_t, \qquad (2.7)$$

the equation will have solutions that are linear combinations of those for (2.5) and (2.6).

A series with a clear seasonal may be seasonally integrated, have a deterministic seasonal, a stationary seasonal, or some combination. A general class of linear time-series models which exhibit potentially complex forms of seasonality can be written as

$$d(B)a(B)(x_t - \mu_t) = \varepsilon_t, \qquad (2.8)$$

where all the roots of $a(z) = 0$ lie outside the unit circle, all the roots of $d(z) = 0$ lie on the unit circle, and μ_t is given as above. Stationary seasonality and other stationary components of x are absorbed into $a(B)$, while deterministic seasonality is in μ_t when there are no seasonal unit roots in $d(B)$. Section 3 of this paper considers how to test for seasonal unit roots and zero-frequency unit roots when other unit roots are possibly present and when deterministic or stochastic seasonals may be present.

A pair of series each of which are integrated at frequency ω are said to be cointegrated at that frequency if a linear combination of the series is not integrated at ω. If the linear combination is labelled α, then we use the notation

$$x_t \sim CI_\omega \quad \text{with cointegrating vector } \alpha.$$

This will occur if, for example, each of the series contains the same factor which is $I_\omega(1)$. In particular, if

$$x_t = \alpha v_t + \bar{x}_t, \qquad y_t = v_t + \bar{y}_t,$$

where v_t is $I_\omega(1)$ and $\bar{x}_t$ and $\bar{y}_t$ are not, then $z_t \equiv x_t - \alpha y_t$ is not $I_\omega(1)$, although it could be still integrated at other frequencies. If a group of series are cointegrated, there are implications about their joint generating mechanism. These are considered in section 4 of this paper.

3. Testing for Seasonal Unit Roots

It is the goal of the testing procedure proposed in this paper to determine whether or not there are any seasonal unit roots in a univariate series. The test must take seriously the possibility that seasonality of other forms may be present. At the same time, the tests for conventional unit roots will be examined in seasonal settings.

In the literature there exist a few attempts to develop such tests. Dickey, Hasza, and Fuller (1984), following the lead suggested by Dickey and Fuller for the zero-frequency unit-root case, propose a test of the hypothesis $a = 1$ against the alternative $a < 1$ in the model $x_t = ax_{t-s} + \varepsilon_t$. The asymptotic distribution of the least-squares estimator is found and the small-sample distribution obtained for several values of s by Monte Carlo methods. In addition the test is extended to the case of higher-order stationary dynamics. A major drawback of this test is that it doesn't allow for unit roots at some but not all of the seasonal frequencies and that the alternative has a very particular form, namely that all the roots have the same modulus. Exactly the same problems are encountered by the tests proposed by Bhargava (1987). In Ahtola and Tiao (1987) tests are proposed for the case of complex roots in the quarterly case but also their suggestion may at best be a part of a more comprehensive test strategy. In this paper we propose a test and a general framework for a test strategy that looks at unit roots at all the seasonal frequencies as well as the zero frequency. The test follows the Dickey–Fuller framework and in fact has a well-known distribution possibly on transformed variables in some special cases.

For quarterly data, the polynomial $(1 - B^4)$ can be expressed as

$$(1 - B^4) = (1 - B)(1 + B)(1 - iB)(1 + iB)$$
$$= (1 - B)(1 + B)(1 + B^2), \qquad (3.1)$$

so that the unit roots are 1, -1, i, and $-i$ which correspond to zero frequency, $\frac{1}{2}$ cycle per quarter or 2 cycles per year, and $\frac{1}{4}$ cycle per quarter or one cycle per year. The last root, $-i$, is indistinguishable from the one at i with quarterly data (the aliasing phenomenon) and is therefore also interpreted as the annual cycle.

To test the hypothesis that the roots of $\varphi(B)$ lie on the unit circle against the alternative that they lie outside the unit circle, it is convenient to rewrite the autoregressive polynomial according to the following proposition which is originally due to Lagrange and is used in approximation theory.

Proposition. Any (possibly infinite or rational) polynomial $\varphi(B)$, which is finite-valued at the distinct, nonzero, possibly complex points $\theta_1, \ldots, \theta_p$, can be expressed in terms of elementary polynomials and a remainder as follows:

$$\varphi(B) = \sum_{k=1}^{p} \lambda_k \Delta(B)/\delta_k(B) + \Delta(B)\varphi^{**}(B), \qquad (3.2)$$

where the λ_k are a set of constants, $\varphi^{**}(B)$ is a (possibly infinite or rational) polynomial, and

$$\delta_k(B) = 1 - \frac{1}{\theta_k}B, \qquad \Delta(B) = \prod_{k=1}^{p} \delta_k(B).$$

Proof. Let λ_k be defined to be

$$\lambda_k = \varphi(\theta_k)/\prod_{j \neq k} \delta_j(\theta_k),$$

which always exists since all the roots of the δ's are distinct and the polynomial is bounded at each value by assumption. The polynomial

$$\varphi(B) - \sum_{k=1}^{p} \lambda_k \Delta(B)/\delta_k(B) = \varphi(B) - \sum_{k=1}^{p} \varphi(\theta_k)\prod_{j \neq k} \delta_j(B)/\delta_j(\theta_k)$$

will have zeroes at each point $B = \theta_k$. Thus it can be written as the product of a polynomial, say $\varphi^{**}(B)$, and $\Delta(B)$. QED

An alternative and very useful form of this expression is obtained by adding and subtracting $\Delta(B)\sum\lambda_k$ to (3.2) to get

$$\varphi(B) = \sum_{k=1}^{p} \lambda_k \Delta(B)(1 - \delta_k(B))/\delta_k(B) + \Delta(B)\varphi^*(B), \quad (3.3)$$

where $\varphi^*(B) = \varphi^{**}(B) + \sum\lambda_k$. In this representation $\varphi(0) = \varphi^*(0)$ which is normalized to unity.

It is clear that the polynomial $\varphi(B)$ will have a root at θ_k if and only if $\lambda_k = 0$. Thus testing for unit roots can be carried out equivalently by testing for parameters $\lambda = 0$ is an appropriate expansion.

To apply this proposition to testing for seasonal unit roots in quarterly data, expand a polynomial $\varphi(B)$ about the roots $+1$, -1, i, and $-i$ as θ_k, $k = 1, \ldots, 4$. Then, from (3.3),

$$\begin{aligned}
\varphi(B) = {} & \lambda_1 B(1 + B)(1 + B^2) + \lambda_2(-B)(1 - B)(1 + B^2) \\
& + \lambda_3(-iB)(1 - B)(1 + B)(1 - iB) \\
& + \lambda_4(iB)(1 - B)(1 + B)(1 + iB) \\
& + \varphi^*(B)(1 - B^4).
\end{aligned}$$

Clearly, λ_3 and λ_4 must be complex conjugates since $\varphi(B)$ is real. Simplifying and substituting $\pi_1 = -\lambda_1$, $\pi_2 = -\lambda_2$, $2\lambda_3 = -\pi_3 + i\pi_4$, and $2\lambda_4 = -\pi_3 - i\pi_4$, gives

$$\begin{aligned}
\varphi(B) = {} & -\pi_1 B(1 + B + B^2 + B^3) - \pi_2(-B)(1 - B + B^2 - B^3) \\
& - (\pi_4 + \pi_3 B)(-B)(1 - B^2) + \varphi^*(B)(1 - B^4). \quad (3.4)
\end{aligned}$$

The testing strategy is now apparent. The data are assumed to be generated by a general autoregression

$$\varphi(B)x_t = \varepsilon_t, \quad (3.5)$$

and (3.4) is used to replace $\varphi(B)$, giving

$$\varphi^*(B)y_{4t} = \pi_1 y_{1t-1} + \pi_2 y_{2t-1} + \pi_3 y_{3t-2} + \pi_4 y_{3t-1} + \varepsilon_t, \quad (3.6)$$

where

$$\begin{aligned}
y_{1t} &= (1 + B + B^2 + B^3)x_t = S(B)x_t, \\
y_{2t} &= -(1 - B + B^2 - B^3)x_t, \\
y_{3t} &= -(1 - B^2)x_t, \\
y_{4t} &= (1 - B^4)x_t = \Delta_4 x_t.
\end{aligned} \quad (3.7)$$

Eq. (3.6) can be estimated by ordinary least squares, possibly with additional lags of y_4 to whiten the errors. To test the hypothesis that $\varphi(\theta_k) = 0$, where θ_k is either 1, -1, or $\pm i$, one needs simply to test that

λ_k is zero. For the root 1 this is simply a test for $\pi_1 = 0$, and for -1 it is $\pi_2 = 0$. For the complex roots λ_3 will have absolute value of zero only if both π_3 and π_4 equal zero which suggests a joint test. There will be no seasonal unit roots if π_2 and either π_3 or π_4 are different from zero, which therefore requires the rejection of both a test for π_2 and a joint test for π_3 and π_4. To find that a series has no unit roots at all and is therefore stationary we must establish that each of the π's is different from zero (save possibly either π_3 or π_4). A joint test will not deliver the required evidence.

The natural alternative for these tests is stationarity. For example, the alternative to $\varphi(1) = 0$ should be $\varphi(1) > 0$ which means $\pi_1 < 0$. Similarly, the stationary alternative to $\varphi(-1) = 0$ is $\varphi(-1) > 0$ which corresponds to $\pi_2 < 0$. Finally, the alternative to $|\varphi(i)| = 0$ is $|\varphi(i)| > 0$. Since the null is two-dimensional, it is simplest to compute an F-type of statistic for the joint null, $\pi_3 = \pi_4 = 0$, against the alternative that they are not both equal to zero. An alternative strategy is to compute a two-sided test of $\pi_4 = 0$, and if this is accepted, continue with a one-sided test of $\pi_3 = 0$ against the alternative $\pi_3 < 0$. If we restrict our attention to alternatives where it is assumed that $\pi_4 = 0$, a one-sided test for π_3 would be appropriate with rejection for $\pi_3 < 0$. Potentially this could lack power if the first-step assumption is not warranted.

In the more complex setting where the alternative includes the possibility of deterministic components it is necessary to allow $\mu_t \neq 0$. The testable model becomes

$$\varphi^*(B)y_{4t} = \pi_1 y_{1t-1} + \pi_2 y_{2t-1} + \pi_3 y_{3t-2} + \pi_4 y_{3t-1} + \mu_t + \varepsilon_t, \quad (3.8)$$

which can again be estimated by OLS and the statistics on the π's used for inference.

The asymptotic distribution of the t-statistics from this regression were analyzed by Chan and Wei (1988). The basic finding is that the asymptotic distribution theory for these tests can be extracted from that of Dickey and Fuller (1979) and Fuller (1976) for π_1 and π_2, and from Dickey, Hasza, and Fuller (1984) for π_3 if π_4 is assumed to be zero. The tests are asymptotically similar or invariant with respect to nuisance parameters. Furthermore, the finite-sample results are well approximated by the asymptotic theory and the tests have reasonable power against each of the specific alternatives.

It is clear that several null hypotheses will be tested for each case of interest. These can all be computed from the same least-squares regression (3.6) or (3.8) unless the sequential testing of π_3 and π_4 is desired.

To show intuitively how these limiting distributions relate to the standard unit-root tests consider (3.6) with $\varphi^*(B) = 1$. The test for

$\pi_1 = 0$ will have the familiar Dickey–Fuller distribution if $\pi_2 = \pi_3 = \pi_4 = 0$ since the model can be written in the form

$$y_{1t} = (1 + \pi_1)y_{1t-1} + \varepsilon_t.$$

Similarly,

$$y_{2t} = -(1 + \pi_2)y_{2t-1} + \varepsilon_t,$$

if the other π's are zero. This is a test for a root of -1 which was shown by Dickey and Fuller to be the mirror of the Dickey–Fuller distribution. If y_{2t} is regressed on $-y_{2t-1}$, the ordinary DF distribution will be appropriate. The third test can be written as

$$y_{3t} = -(1 + \pi_3)y_{3t-2} + \varepsilon_t,$$

assuming $\pi_4 = 0$ which is therefore the mirror of the Dickey–Hasza–Fuller distribution for biannual seasonality. The inclusion of y_{3t-1} in the regression recognizes potential phase shifts in the annual component. Since the null is that $\pi_3 = \pi_4 = 0$, the assumption that $\pi_4 = 0$ may merely reduce the power of the test against some alternatives.

To show that the same distributions are obtained when it is not known *a priori* that some of the π's are zero, two cases must be considered. First, if the π's other than the one being tested are truly nonzero, then the process does not have unit roots at these frequencies and the corresponding y's are stationary. The regression is therefore equivalent to a standard augmented unit-root test.

If, however, some of the other π's are zero, there are other unit roots in the regression. However, it is exactly under this condition that it is shown in section 2 that the corresponding y's are asymptotically uncorrelated. The distribution of the test statistic will not be affected by the inclusion of a variable with a zero coefficient which is orthogonal to the included variables. For example, when testing $\pi_1 = 0$, suppose $\pi_2 = 0$ but y_2 is still included in the regression. Then y_1 and y_2 will be asymptotically uncorrelated since they have unit roots at different frequencies and both will be asymptotically uncorrelated with lags of y_4 which is stationary. The test for $\pi_1 = 0$ will have the same limiting distribution regardless of whether y_2 is included in the regression. Similar arguments follow for the other cases.

When deterministic components are present in the regression even if not in the data, the distributions change. Again, the changes can be anticipated from this general approach. The intercept and trend portions of the deterministic mean influence only the distribution of π_1 because they have all their spectral mass at zero frequency. Once the intercept is included, the remaining three seasonal dummies do not affect the limiting distribution of π_1. The seasonal dummies, however, do affect the distribution of π_2, π_3, and π_4.

Table 1a gives the Monte Carlo critical values for the one-sided 't' tests on π_1, π_2, and π_3 in the most important cases. These are very close to the Monte Carlo values from Dickey–Fuller and Dickey–Hasza –Fuller for the situations in which they tabulated the statistics.

In Table 1B we present the critical values of the two-sided 't' test on $\pi_4 = 0$ and the critical values for the 'F' test on $\pi_3 \cap \pi_4 = 0$. Notice that the distribution of the 't' statistic is very similar to a standard normal except when the auxiliary regression contains seasonal dummies, in which case it becomes fatter-tailed. The distribution for the 'F' statistic also looks like an F distribution with degrees of freedom equal to two and T minus the number of regressors in (3.6). However, when seasonal dummies are present, the tail becomes fatter here as well.

4.   Error-correction Representation

In this section, an error-correction representation is derived which explicitly takes the cointegrating restrictions at the zero and at the seasonal frequencies into account. As the time series being considered has poles at different locations on the unit circle, various cointegrating situations are possible. This naturally makes the general treatment mathematically complex and notationally involved. Although we treat the general case we will present the special cases considered to be of most interest.

Let x_t be an $N \times 1$ vector of quarterly time series, each of which potentially has unit roots at zero and all seasonal frequencies, so that each component of $(1 - B^4)x_t$ is a stationary process but may have a zero on the unit circle. The Wold representation will thus be

$$(1 - B^4)x_t = C(B)\varepsilon_t, \qquad (4.1)$$

where ε_t is a vector white noise process with zero mean and covariance matrix Ω, a positive definite matrix.

There are a variety of possible types of cointegration for such a set of series. To initially examine these, apply the decomposition of (3.2) to each element of $C(B)$. This gives

$$C(B) = \sum_{k=1}^{p} \Lambda_k \Delta(B)/\delta_k(B) + C^{**}(B)\Delta(B),$$

where $\delta_k(B) = 1 - (1/\theta_k)B$ and $\Delta(B)$ is the product of all the $\delta_k(B)$. For quarterly data the four relevant roots, θ_k, are 1, -1, i, and $-i$, which after solving for the Λ's becomes

$$C(B) = \Psi_1[1 + B + B^2 + B^3] + \Psi_2[1 - B + B^2 - B^3]$$
$$+ (\Psi_3 + \Psi_4 B)[1 - B^2] + C^{**}(B)(1 - B^4), \qquad (4.2)$$

TABLE 1A. Critical values from the small-sample distributions of test statistics for seasonal unit roots on 24000 Monte Carlo replications; data-generating process $\Delta_4 x_t = \varepsilon_t \sim \text{nid}(0,1)$.

Auxiliary regressions	T	$t:\pi_1$				$t:\pi_2$				$t:\pi_3$			
		0.01	0.025	0.05	0.10	0.01	0.025	0.05	0.10	0.01	0.025	0.05	0.10
No intercept	48	-2.72	-2.29	-1.95	-1.59	-2.67	-2.27	-1.95	-1.60	-2.66	-2.23	-1.93	-1.52
No seas. dum.	100	-2.60	-2.26	-1.97	-1.61	-2.61	-2.22	-1.92	-1.57	-2.55	-2.18	-1.90	-1.53
No trend	136	-2.62	-2.25	-1.93	-1.59	-2.60	-2.23	-1.94	-1.61	-2.58	-2.21	-1.92	-1.56
	200	-2.62	-2.23	-1.94	-1.62	-2.60	-2.24	-1.95	-1.61	-2.58	-2.24	-1.92	-1.55
Intercept	48	-3.66	-3.25	-2.96	-2.62	-2.68	-2.27	-1.95	-1.60	-2.64	-2.23	-1.90	-1.55
No seas. dum.	100	-3.47	-3.14	-2.88	-2.58	-2.61	-2.24	-1.95	-1.60	-2.61	-2.23	-1.90	-1.54
No trend	136	-3.51	-3.17	-2.89	-2.58	-2.60	-2.21	-1.91	-1.58	-2.53	-2.18	-1.88	-1.53
	200	-3.48	-3.13	-2.87	-2.57	-2.58	-2.22	-1.92	-1.59	-2.57	-2.21	-1.90	-1.53
Intercept	48	-3.77	-3.39	-3.08	-2.72	-3.75	-3.37	-3.04	-2.69	-4.31	-3.92	-3.61	-3.24
Seas. dum.	100	-3.55	-3.22	-2.95	-2.63	-3.60	-3.22	-2.94	-2.63	-4.06	-3.72	-3.44	-3.14
No trend	136	-3.56	-3.23	-2.94	-2.62	-3.49	-3.15	-2.90	-2.59	-4.06	-3.72	-3.44	-3.11
	200	-3.51	-3.18	-2.91	-2.59	-3.50	-3.16	-2.89	-2.60	-4.00	-3.67	-3.38	-3.07
Intercept	48	-4.23	-3.85	-3.56	-3.21	-2.65	-2.24	-1.91	-1.57	-2.68	-2.27	-1.92	-1.52
No seas. dum.	100	-4.07	-3.73	-3.47	-3.16	-2.58	-2.24	-1.94	-1.60	-2.56	-2.19	-1.89	-1.54
Trend	136	-4.09	-3.75	-3.46	-3.16	-2.65	-2.25	-1.96	-1.63	-2.56	-2.20	-1.90	-1.52
	200	-4.05	-3.70	-3.44	-3.15	-2.59	-2.25	-1.95	-1.62	-2.58	-2.21	-1.92	-1.56
Intercept	48	-4.46	-4.04	-3.71	-3.37	-3.80	-3.41	-3.08	-2.73	-4.46	-4.02	-3.66	-3.28
Seas. dum.	100	-4.09	-3.80	-3.53	-3.22	-3.60	-3.22	-2.94	-2.63	-4.12	-3.76	-3.48	-3.14
Trend	136	-4.15	-3.80	-3.52	-3.21	-3.57	-3.18	-2.93	-2.61	-4.05	-3.72	-3.44	-3.12
	200	-4.05	-3.74	-3.49	-3.18	-3.52	-3.18	-2.91	-2.60	-4.04	-3.69	-3.41	-3.10

TABLE 1B. Critical values from the small-sample distributions of test statistics for seasonal unit roots on 24000 Monte Carlo replications; data-generating process $\Delta_4 x_t = \varepsilon_t \sim \text{nid}(0,1)$.

Auxiliary regressions	Fractiles												
		't':π_4								'F':$\pi_3 \cap \pi_4$			
	T	0.01	0.025	0.05	0.10	0.90	0.95	0.975	0.99	0.90	0.95	0.975	0.99
No Intercept	48	−2.51	−2.11	−1.76	−1.35	1.33	1.72	2.05	2.49	2.45	3.26	4.04	5.02
No seas. dum.	100	−2.43	−2.01	−1.68	−1.32	1.31	1.67	2.00	2.40	2.39	3.12	3.89	4.89
No trend	136	−2.44	−1.99	−1.68	−1.31	1.30	1.66	1.99	2.38	2.41	3.14	3.86	4.81
	200	−2.43	−1.98	−1.65	−1.30	1.29	1.67	1.97	2.36	2.42	3.16	3.92	4.81
Intercept	48	−2.44	−2.06	−1.72	−1.33	1.30	1.68	2.04	2.41	2.32	3.04	3.78	4.78
No seas. dum.	100	−2.38	−1.99	−1.68	−1.30	1.28	1.65	1.97	2.32	2.35	3.08	3.81	4.77
No trend	136	−2.36	−1.98	−1.68	−1.31	1.27	1.65	1.97	2.31	2.36	3.00	3.70	4.73
	200	−2.36	−1.98	−1.66	−1.29	1.28	1.65	1.96	2.30	2.37	3.12	3.86	4.76
Intercept	48	−2.86	−2.37	−1.98	−1.53	1.54	1.96	2.35	2.81	5.50	6.60	7.68	9.22
Seas. dum.	100	−2.78	−2.32	−1.96	−1.53	1.52	1.93	2.29	2.73	5.56	6.57	7.72	8.74
No trend	136	−2.72	−2.31	−1.96	−1.52	1.51	1.92	2.28	2.71	5.56	6.63	7.66	8.92
	200	−2.74	−2.33	−1.96	−1.54	1.53	1.95	2.32	2.78	5.56	6.61	7.53	8.93
Intercept	48	−2.41	−2.05	−1.70	−1.33	1.26	1.64	1.96	2.37	2.23	2.95	3.70	4.64
No seas. dum.	100	−2.38	−1.97	−1.65	−1.28	1.28	1.65	1.98	2.32	2.31	2.98	3.71	4.70
Trend	136	−2.36	−1.97	−1.64	−1.29	1.26	1.62	1.92	2.31	2.33	3.04	3.69	4.57
	200	−2.35	−1.97	−1.66	−1.29	1.26	1.64	1.96	2.30	2.34	3.07	3.76	4.66
Intercept	48	−2.75	−2.26	−1.91	−1.48	1.51	1.97	2.34	2.78	5.37	6.55	7.70	9.27
Seas. dum.	100	−2.76	−2.32	−1.94	−1.51	1.51	1.92	2.28	2.69	5.52	6.60	7.52	8.79
Trend	136	−2.71	−2.78	−1.94	−1.51	1.53	1.96	2.31	2.78	5.55	6.62	7.59	8.77
	200	−2.65	−2.27	−1.92	−1.48	1.55	1.97	2.31	2.71	5.56	6.57	7.56	8.96

where $\Psi_1 = C(1)/4$, $\Psi_2 = C(-1)/4$, $\Psi_3 = \text{Re}\,[C(i)]/2$, and $\Psi_4 = \text{Im}\,[C(i)]/2$. Multiplying (4.1) by a vector α' gives

$$(1 - B^4)\alpha'x_t = \alpha'C(B)\varepsilon_t.$$

Suppose for some $\alpha = \alpha_1$, $\alpha_1'C(1) = 0 = \alpha'\Psi_1$, then there is a factor of $(1 - B)$ in all terms, which will cancel out giving

$$(1 + B + B^2 + B^3)\alpha_1'x_t = \alpha_1'\{\Psi_2[(1 + B^2)] + (\Psi_3 + \Psi_4B)[1 + B] \\ + C^{**}(B)[1 + B + B^2 + B^3]\}\varepsilon_t,$$

so that $\alpha_1'x_t$ will have unit roots at the seasonal frequencies but not at zero frequency. Thus x is cointegrated at zero frequency with cointegrating vector α_1, if $\alpha_1'C(1) = 0$. Denote these as

$$x_t \sim CI_0 \text{ with cointegrating vector } \alpha_1.$$

Notice that the vector $y_{1t} = S(B)x_t$ is $I_0(1)$ since $(1 - B)y_{1t} = C(B)\varepsilon_t$, while $\alpha_1'y_{1t}$ is stationary whenever $\alpha_1'C(1) = 0$ so that y_{1t} is cointegrated in exactly the sense described in Engle and Granger (1987). Since y_{1t} is essentially seasonally adjusted x_t, it follows that one strategy for estimation and testing for cointegration at zero frequency in seasonal series is to first seasonally adjust the series.

Similarly, letting $y_{2t} = -(1 - B)(1 + B^2)x_t$, $(1 + B)y_{2t} = -C(B)\varepsilon_t$ so that y_{2t} has a unit root at -1. If $\alpha_2'C(-1) = 0$, then $\alpha_2'\Psi_2 = 0$ and $\alpha_2'y_{2t}$ will not have a unit root at -1. We say then that x_t is cointegrated at frequency $\omega = \frac{1}{2}$, which is denoted.

$$x_t \sim CI_{1/2} \text{ with cointegrating vector } \alpha_2.$$

Finally, denote $y_{3t} = -(1 - B^2)x_t$, which satisfies $(1 + B^2)y_{3t} = -C(B)\varepsilon_t$ and therefore includes unit roots at frequency $\frac{1}{4}$. If $\alpha_3'C(i) = 0$ which implies that $\alpha_3'\Psi_3 = \alpha_3'\Psi_4 = 0$, then $\alpha_3'y_{3t}$ will not have a unit root at $\frac{1}{4}$, implying that

$$x_t \sim CI_{1/4} \text{ with cointegrating vector } \alpha_3.$$

Cointegration at frequency $\frac{1}{4}$ can also occur under weaker conditions. Consider the bivariate system:

$$(1 + B^2)x_t = \begin{bmatrix} 1 & 0 \\ B & 1 + B^2 \end{bmatrix}\varepsilon_t,$$

in which both series are $I_{1/4}(1)$ and there is no fixed cointegrating vector. However, the polynomial cointegrating vector (PCIV), as introduced by Yoo (1987), of $(-B, 1)$ will generate a stationary series. It is not surprising with seasonal unit roots, that the timing could make a difference. We now show that the need for PCIV is a result purely of the fact that one vector is sought to eliminate two roots $(\pm i)$ and that one lag in the cointegrating polynomial is sufficient.

Expanding the PCIV $\alpha(B)$ about the two roots $(\pm i)$ using (3.2) gives

$$\alpha(B) = \text{Re}\,[\alpha(i)] + B\,\text{Im}\,[\alpha(i)] + \alpha^{**}(B)(1 + B^2)$$
$$\equiv (\alpha_3 + \alpha_4 B) + \alpha^{**}(B)(1 + B^2),$$

so that the condition that $\alpha'(B)\ C(B)$ have a common factor of $(1 + B^2)$ depends only on α_3 and α_4. The general statement of cointegration at frequency $\frac{1}{2}$ then becomes

$$x_t \sim CI_{1/4} \quad \text{with polynomial cointegrating vector } \alpha_3 + \alpha_4 B,$$

$$\text{if and only if} \quad (\alpha_3' + \alpha_4' i)(\Psi_3 - \Psi_4 i) = 0,$$

which is equivalent to $\alpha(i)'C(i) = 0$.

There is no guarantee that x_t will have any type of cointegration or that these cointegrating vectors will be the same. It is however possible that $\alpha_1 = \alpha_2 = \alpha_3$, $\alpha_4 = 0$, and therefore one cointegrating vector could reduce the integration of the x series at all frequencies. Similarly, if $\alpha_2 = \alpha_3$, $\alpha_4 = 0$, one cointegrating vector will eliminate the seasonal unit roots. This might be expected if the seasonality in two series is due to the same source.

A characterization of the cointegrating possibilities has now been given in terms of the moving-average representation. More useful are the autoregressive representations and in particular, the error-correction representation. Therefore, if $C(B)$ is a rational matrix in B, it can be written (using the Smith–McMillan decomposition (Kailath (1980), as adapted by Yoo (1987), and named the Smith–McMillan–Yoo decomposition by Engle (1987)) as follows:

$$C(B) = U(B)^{-1}M(B)V(B)^{-1}, \tag{4.3}$$

where $M(B)$ is a diagonal matrix whose determinant has roots only on the unit circle, and the roots of the determinants of $U^{-1}(B)$ and $V(B)^{-1}$ lie outside the unit circle. This diagonal could contain various combinations of the unit roots. However, assuming that the cointegrating rank at each frequency is r, the matrix can be written without loss of generality as

$$M(B) = \begin{bmatrix} I_{N-r} & 0 \\ 0 & \Delta_4 I_r \end{bmatrix}, \tag{4.4}$$

where I_k is a $k \times k$ unit matrix. The following derivation of the error-correction representation is easily adapted for other forms of $M(B)$.

Substituting (4.3) into (4.1) and multiplying by $U(B)$ gives

$$\Delta_4 U(B)x_t = M(B)V(B)^{-1}\varepsilon_t. \tag{4.5}$$

The first $N - r$ equations have a Δ_4 on the left side only while the final r equations have Δ_4 on both sides which therefore cancel. Thus (4.5) can be written as

$$\bar{M}(B)U(B)x_t = V(B)^{-1}\varepsilon_t, \qquad (4.6)$$

with

$$\bar{M}(B) = \begin{bmatrix} \Delta_4 I_{N-r} & 0 \\ 0 & I_r \end{bmatrix}. \qquad (4.7)$$

Finally, the autoregressive representation is obtained by multiplying by $V(B)$ to obtain

$$A(B)x_t = \varepsilon_t, \qquad (4.8)$$

where

$$A(B) = V(B)\bar{M}(B)U(B). \qquad (4.9)$$

Notice that at the seasonal and zero-frequency roots, $\det[A(\theta)] = 0$ since $A(B)$ has rank r at those frequencies. Now, partition $U(B)$ and $V(B)$ as

$$U(B) = \begin{bmatrix} U_1(B)' \\ \alpha(B)' \end{bmatrix}, \qquad V(B) = [V_1(B), \gamma(B)],$$

where $\alpha(B)$ and $\gamma(B)$ are $N \times r$ matrices and $U_1(B)$ and $V_1(B)$ are $N \times (N - r)$ matrices. Expanding the autoregressive matrix using (3.3) gives

$$A(B) = \Pi_1 B[1 + B + B^2 + B^3] - \Pi_2 B[(1 - B)(1 + B^2)] \\ + (\Pi_4 - B\Pi_3)B[1 + B^2] + A^*(B)[1 - B^4],$$

with $\Pi_1 = -\gamma(1)\alpha'(1)/4 \equiv -\gamma_1\alpha_1'$, $\Pi_2 = -\gamma(-1)\alpha(-1)'/4 \equiv -\gamma_2\alpha_2'$, $\Pi_3 = \text{Re}[\gamma(i)\alpha(i)']/2$, and $\Pi_4 = \text{Im}[\gamma(j)\alpha(i)']/2$. Letting $\alpha_1 = \alpha(1)/4$, $\alpha_2 = \alpha(-1)/4$, $\alpha_3 = \text{Re}[\alpha(i)]/2$, and $\alpha_4 = \text{Im}[\alpha(i)]$ while $\gamma_1 = \gamma(1)$, $\gamma_2 = \gamma(-1)$, $\gamma_3 = \text{Re}[\gamma(i)]$, and $\gamma_4 = \text{Im}[\gamma(i)]$, the general error-correction model can be written

$$A^*(B)\Delta_4 x_t = \gamma_1\alpha_1' y_{1t-1} + \gamma_2\alpha_2' y_{2t-1} - (\gamma_3\alpha_3' - \gamma_4\alpha_4') y_{3t-2} \\ + (\gamma_4\alpha_3' + \gamma_3\alpha_4') y_{3t-1} + \varepsilon_t, \qquad (4.10)$$

where $A^*(0) = C(0) = I_N$ in the standard case. This expression is an error-correction representation where both α, the cointegrating vector, and γ, the coefficients of the error-correction term, may be different at different frequencies and, in one case, even at different lags. This can be written in a more transparent form by allowing more than two lags in the error-correction term. Add $\Delta_4(\gamma_3\alpha_4' + \gamma_4\alpha_3' + \gamma_4\alpha_4' B)x_{t-1}$ to both sides and rearrange terms to get

$$\tilde{A}^*(B)\Delta_4 x_t = \gamma_1 \alpha_1' y_{1t-1} + \gamma_2 \alpha_2' y_{2t-1}$$

$$- (\gamma_3 + \gamma_4 B)(\alpha_3' + \alpha_4' B) y_{3t-2} + \varepsilon_t, \qquad (4.11)$$

where $\tilde{A}^*(B)$ is a slightly different autoregressive matrix from $A^*(B)$. The error-correction term at the annual seasonal enters potentially with two lags and is potentially a polynomial cointegrating vector. When $\alpha_4 = 0$ or $\gamma_4 = 0$ or both, the model simplifies so that, respectively, cointegration is contemporaneous, the error correction needs only one lag, or both.

Notice that all the terms in (4.11) are stationary. Estimation of the system is easily accomplished if the α's are known *a priori*. If they must be estimated, it appears that a generalization of the two-step estimation procedure proposed by Engle and Granger (1987) is available. Namely, estimate the α's using prefiltered variables y_1, y_2, and y_3, respectively, and then estimate the full model using the estimates of the α's. In the PCIV case this regression would include a single lag. It is conjectured that the least-squares estimates of the remaining parameters would have the same limiting distribution as the estimator knowing the true α's just as in the Engle–Granger two-step estimator. The analysis by Stock (1987) suggests that although the inference on the α's can be tricky due to their nonstandard limiting distributions, inference on the estimates of $A^*(B)$ and the γ's can be conducted in the standard way.

The following generalizations of the above analysis are discussed formally in Yoo (1987). First, if $r > 1$ but all other assumptions remain as before, the error-correction representation (4.11) remains the same but the α's and γ's now become $N \times r$ matrices. Second, if the cointegrating rank as the long-run frequency is r_0, which is different from the cointegrating rank at the seasonal frequency, r_s, (4.11) is again legitimate with the sizes of the matrices on the right-hand side appropriately redefined. Thirdly, if the cointegrating vectors α_1, α_2, and α_3 coincide, equalling say, α, and $\alpha_4 = 0$, a simpler error-cointegrating model occurs:

$$A^*(B)\Delta_4 x_t = \gamma(B)\alpha' x_{t-1} + \varepsilon_t, \qquad (4.12)$$

where the degree of $\gamma(B)$ is at most 3, as can be seen either from (4.10) or from an expansion of $\gamma(B)$ using (3.2). For four roots there are potentially four coefficients and three lags.

Finally, some of the cointegrating vectors may coincide but some do not. A particularly interesting case is where a single linear combination eliminates all seasonal unit roots. Thus suppose $\alpha_2 = \alpha_3 \equiv \alpha_s$ and $\alpha_4 = 0$. Then (4.10) becomes

$$A^*(B)\Delta_4 x_t = \gamma_1 \alpha_1' S(B) x_{t-1} + \gamma_s(B)\alpha_s' \Delta x_{t-1} + \varepsilon_t, \qquad (4.13)$$

where $\gamma_s(B)$ has potentially two lags. Thus zero-frequency cointegration occurs between the elements of seasonally adjusted x, while seasonal cointegration occurs between the elements of differenced x. This is the case examined by Engle, Granger, and Hallman (1989) for electricity demand. There monthly electricity sales were modeled as cointegrated with economic variables such as customers and income at zero frequency and possibly at seasonal frequencies with the weather. The first relation is used in long-run forecasting, while the second is mixed with the short-run dynamics for short-run forecasting.

Although an efficiency gain in the estimates of the cointegrating vectors is naturally expected by checking and imposing the restrictions between the cointegrating vectors, there should be no efficiency gain in the estimates of the 'short-run parameters', namely $A^*(B)$ and γ's, given the superconsistency of the estimates of the cointegrating vectors. Hence, the representation (4.11) is considered relatively general and the important step of model-building procedure is then to identify the cointegratedness at the different frequencies. This question is considered in the next section.

5.   Testing for Cointegration: An Application

In this section it is assumed that there are two series of interest, x_{1t} and x_{2t}, both integrated at some of the zero and seasonal frequencies, and the question to be studied is whether or not the series are cointegrated at some frequency. Of course, if the two series do not have unit roots at corresponding frequencies, the possibility of cointegration does not exist. The tests discussed in section 3 can be used to detect which unit roots are present.

Suppose for the moment that both series contain unit roots at the zero frequency and at least some of the seasonal frequencies. If one is interested in the possibility of cointegration at the zero frequency, a strategy could be to form the static O.L.S. regression

$$x_{1t} = Ax_{2t} + \text{residual},$$

and then test if the residual has a unit root at zero frequency, which is the procedure in Engle and Granger (1987). However, the presence of seasonal unit roots means that A may not be consistently estimated, in sharp contrast to the case when there are no seasonal roots when $\hat{A}$ is estimated superefficiently. This lack of consistency is proved in Engle, Granger, and Hallman (1989). If, in fact, x_{1t} and x_{2t} are cointegrated at both the zero and the seasonal frequencies, with cointegrating vectors α_1 and α_s and with $\alpha_1 \neq \alpha_s$, it is unclear what value of A would be chosen by the static regression. Presumably, if $\alpha_1 = \alpha_s$, then $\hat{A}$ will be an estimate of this common value. These results suggest that the standard procedure for testing for cointegration is inappropriate.

An alternative strategy would be to filter out unit-root components other than the one of interest and to test for cointegration with the filtered series. For example, to remove seasonal roots, one could form

$$\tilde{x}_{1t} = S(B)x_{1t}, \qquad \tilde{x}_{2t} = S(B)x_{2t},$$

where $S(B) = (1 - B^s)/(1 - B)$, and then perform a standard cointegration test, such as those discussed in Engle and Granger (1987), on $\tilde{x}_{1t}$ and $\tilde{x}_{2t}$. If some seasonal unit roots were thought to be present in x_{1t} and x_{2t}, this procedure could be done without testing for which roots were present, but the filtered series could have spectra with zeros at some seasonal frequencies, and this may introduce problems with the tests. Alternatively, the tests of section 3 could be used, appropriate filters applied just to remove the seasonal roots indicated by these tests, and then the standard cointegration tests applied. For zero-frequency cointegration, this procedure is probably appropriate, although the implications of the pretesting for seasonal roots has not yet been investigated.

To test for seasonal cointegration the corresponding procedure would be to difference the series to remove a zero-frequency unit root, if required, then run a regression of the form

$$\Delta x_{1t} = \sum_{j=0}^{s-2} \alpha_j \Delta x_{2t-j} + \text{residual},$$

and test if the residual has any seasonal unit roots. The tests developed in section 3 could be applied, but will not have the same distribution as they involve estimates of the α_j. The correct test has yet to be developed.

A situation where the tests of section 3 can be applied directly is where $\alpha_1 = \alpha_s$ and some theory suggests a value for this α, so that no estimation is required. One merely forms $x_{1t} - \alpha x_{2t}$ and tests for unit roots at the zero and seasonal frequencies.

An example comes from the permanent income hypothesis where the log of income and the log of consumption may be thought to be cointegrated with $\alpha = 1$. Thus $c - y$ should have no unit roots using a simplistic form of this theory, as discussed by Davidson et al. (1978), for instance.

To illustrate the tests, quarterly United Kingdom data for the period 1955.1 to 1984.4 were used with $y = $ log of personal disposable income and $c = $ log of consumption expenditures on nondurables. The data are shown in Fig. 1.

From the Figure, it is seen that both series may have a random-walk character implying that we would expect to find a unit root at the zero

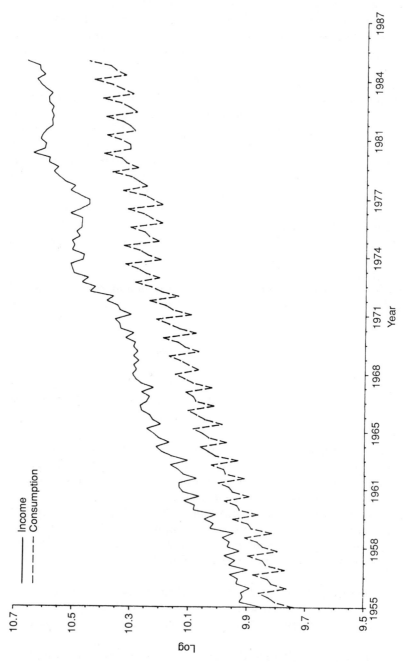

Fɪɢ. 1. Income and consumption in the UK.

frequency. However, the two series seem to drift apart whereby cointegration at the zero frequency with cointegrating vector $(1, -1)$ is less likely. For the seasonal pattern, it is clear that c contains a much stronger and less changing seasonal pattern than y, although even the seasonal consumption pattern changes over the sample period. Based on these preliminary findings, one may or may not find seasonal unit roots in c and y or both, but cointegration at the seasonal frequencies cannot be expected.

The tests are based on the auxiliary regression (3.6) where $\phi(B)$ is a polynomial in B. The deterministic term is a zero, an intercept (I), an intercept and seasonal dummies (I, SD), an intercept and a trend (I, Tr), or an intercept, seasonal dummies, and a trend (I, SD, Tr).

In the augmented regressions nonsignificant lags were removed, and for c and y this implied a lag polynomial of the form $1 - \phi_1 B - \phi_4 B^4 - \phi_5 B^5$, where ϕ_1 was around 0.85, ϕ_4 around -0.32, and ϕ_5 around 0.25. For $c - y$ the lag polynomial was approximately $1 - 0.29B - 0.22B^2 + 0.21B^4$. The '$t$' statistics from these augmented regressions are shown in Table 2.

TABLE 2. Tests for seasonal unit roots in the log of UK consumption expenditure on nondurables c, in the log of personal disposable income y, and in the difference $c - y$; 1955.1–1984.4.

VAR	Auxiliary regression[a]	't':π_1 (zero frequency)	't':π_2 (biannual)	't':π_3 (annual)	't':π_4	'F':$\pi_3 \cap_4$
	—	2.45	-0.31	0.22	-0.84	0.38
	I	-1.62	-0.32	0.22	-0.87	0.40
c	I, SD	-1.64	-2.22	-1.47	-1.77	2.52
	I, Tr	-2.43	-0.35	0.18	-0.85	0.38
	I, SD, Tr	-2.33	-2.16	-1.53	-1.65	2.43
	—	2.61	-1.44	-2.35^b	-2.51^b	5.68^b
	I	-1.50	-1.46	-2.38^b	-2.51^b	5.75^b
y	I, SD	-1.56	-2.38	-4.19^b	-3.89^b	14.74^b
	I, Tr	-2.73	-1.46	-2.52^b	-2.23^b	5.46^b
	I, SD, Tr	-2.48	-2.30	-4.28^b	-3.46^b	13.74^b
	—	1.54	-1.10	-0.98	-1.17	1.19
	I	-1.24	-1.10	-1.03	-1.16	1.22
$c - y$	I, SD	-1.19	-2.64	-2.55	-2.79^b	8.25^b
	I, Tr	-2.40	-1.21	-1.05	-1.04	1.12
	I, SD, Tr	-2.48	-2.84	-2.72	-2.48^b	7.87^b

[a] The auxiliary regressions were augmented by significant lagged values of the fourth difference of the regressand.

[b] Significant at the 5% level.

The results indicate strongly a unit root at the zero frequency in both c, y, and $c - y$ implying that there is no cointegration between c and y at the long-run frequency, at least not for the cointegrating vector $[1, -1]$.

Similarly, the hypothesis that c, y, and $c - y$ are $I_{1/2}(1)$ cannot be rejected implying that c and y are not cointegrated at the biannual cycle either. The results also indicate that the log of consumption expenditures on nondurables are $I_{1/4}(1)$ as neither the 'F' test nor the two 't' tests can reject the hypothesis that both π_4 and π_3 are zero. Such hypotheses are, however, firmly rejected for the log of personal disposable income and conditional on these results, c and y cannot possibly be cointegrated at this frequency or at the frequency corresponding to the complex conjugate root, irrespective of the forms of the cointegrating vectors. In fact, conditional on π_4 being zero, the 't' test on π_3 cannot reject a unit root in $c - y$ at the annual frequency in any of the auxiliary regressions. The assumption that $\pi_4 = 0$ is not rejected when seasonal dummies are absent and the joint 'F' test cannot reject in these cases either. When the auxiliary regression contains deterministic seasonals, both $\pi_4 = 0$ and $\pi_3 \cap \pi_4 = 0$ are rejected leading to a theoretical conflict which can of course happen with finite samples.

6.   Conclusion

The theory of integration and cointegration of time series is extended to cover series with unit roots at frequencies different from the long-run frequency. In particular, seasonal series are studied with a focus upon the quarterly periodicity. It is argued that the existence of unit roots at the seasonal frequencies has similar implications for the persistence of shocks as a unit root at the long-run frequency. However, a seasonal pattern generated by a model characterized solely by unit roots seems unlikely as the seasonal pattern becomes too volatile, allowing 'summer to become winter'.

A proposition on the representation of rational polynomials allows reformulation of an autoregression isolating the key unit-root parameters. Based on least-squares fits of univariate autoregressions on transformed variables, similar to the well-known augmented Dickey–Fuller regression, tests for the existence of seasonal as well as zero-frequency unit roots in quarterly data are presented and tables of the critical values provided.

By extending the definition of cointegration to occur at separate frequencies, the error-correction representation is developed by use of the Smith–McMillan lemma and the proposition on rational lag polynomials. The error-correction representation is shown to be a direct generalization of the well-known form, but on properly transformed variables.

The theory is applied to the UK consumption function and it is shown that the unit-elasticity error-correction model is not valid at any frequency as long as we confine ourselves to only the consumption and income data.

References

(References marked with a * are included in this volume)

AHTOLA, J., and TIAO, G. C. (1987), 'Distributions of least squares estimators of autoregressive parameters for a process with complex roots on the unit circle', *Journal of Time Series Analysis,* **8**, 1–14.

BELL, W. R., and HILLMER, S. C. (1984), 'Issues involved with the seasonal adjustment of economic time series', *Journal of Business and Economic Statistics,* **2**, 291–320.

BHARGAVA, A. (1987), 'On the specification of regression models in seasonal differences'. Mimeo. (Department of Economics, University of Pennsylvania, Philadelphia, PA).

BOX, G. E. P., and JENKINS, G. M. (1970), *Time Series Analysis, Forecasting and Control.* San Francisco: Holden-Day.

CHAN, N. H., and WEI, C. Z. (1988), 'Limiting distributions of least squares estimates of unstable autoregressive processes', *Annals of Statistics,* **16**, 367–401.

DAVIDSON, J. E., HENDRY, D. F., SRBA, F., and YEO, S. (1978), 'Econometric modelling of aggregate time series relationships between consumer's expenditure and income in the U.K.', *Economic Journal,* **91**, 704–15.

DICKEY, D. A., and FULLER, W. A. (1979), 'Distribution of the estimators for autoregressive time series with a unit root', *Journal of the American Statistical Association,* **84**, 427–31.

—— HASZA, D. P., and FULLER, W. A. (1984), 'Testing for unit roots in seasonal times series', *Journal of the American Statistical Association,* **79**, 355–67.*

—— and GRANGER, C. W. J. (1987), 'Co-integration and error correction: Representation, estimation and testing', *Econometrica,* **55**, 251–76.

—— —— and HALLMAN, J. (1989), 'Merging short- and long-run forecasts: An application of seasonal co-integration to monthly electricity sales forecasting', *Journal of Econometrics,* **40**, 45–62.

FULLER, W. A. (1976), *Introduction of Statistical Time Series.* New York: Wiley.

GRANGER, C. W. J. (1981), 'Time series data and econometric model specification', *Journal of Econometrics,* **16**, 121–30.

GRETHER, D. M., and NERLOVE, M. (1970), 'Some properties of optimal seasonal adjustment', *Econometrica,* **38**, 682–703.

HYLLEBERG, S. (1986), *Seasonality in Regression.* New York: Academic Press.

KAILATH, T. (1980), *Linear Systems.* Englewood Cliffs: Prentice-Hall.

NELSON, C. R., and PLOSSER, C. I. (1982), 'Trends and random walks in macroeconomic time series', *Journal of Monetary Economics,* **10**, 129–62.

STOCK, J. H. (1987), 'Asymptotic properties of least squares estimates of cointegrating vectors', *Econometrica*, **55**, 1035–56.

YOO, S. (1987), 'Co-integrated time series: Structure, forecasting and testing', Ph.D. dissertation University of California, San Diego.

18

Seasonality and the Order of Integration for Consumption*

DENISE R. OSBORN, A. P. L. CHUI, JEREMY P.
SMITH, AND C. R. BIRCHENHALL

1. Introduction

Cointegration has aroused considerable interest in the recent literature of dynamic modelling for economic time series. Nevertheless, despite the importance of seasonal movements as a feature of economic data, seasonality has received relatively little attention in the cointegration analysis. A notable exception to this lack of attention, however, is the paper by Engle *et al.* (1987).

In a companion paper, Birchenhall *et al.* (1989), we use cointegration as the bases for a dynamic analysis of non-durable consumption in the UK. There we take the view that consumer preferences are seasonal, which implies the equilibrium relationship between consumption and its explanatory variables has a seasonal structure. The equilibrium used, in its non-seasonal form, is based on

$$C = KY^{\alpha}(1 + \pi)^{\beta}(W_{-1})^{\gamma} \tag{1}$$

where C is real non-durable consumers' expenditure, Y is real personal disposable income, π is the rate of inflation and W is the end-of-period real liquid assets. All analysis is carried out with the data in logarithms, converting (1) to a linear function. This equilibrium equation is a generalization of that used by Davidson *et al.* (1978) and Hendry and von Ungern-Sternberg (1981) for modelling UK consumption.

* This work is based on research funded by the Economic and Social Research Council (ESRC), reference number B00232124. We are grateful to our project colleague Robin Bladen–Hovell, who suggested the form of the equilibrium equation used here. Our thanks also go to the editors, particularly David Hendry, for their helpful comments. Jeremy Smith is now at the Australian National University.

Printed with permission of: *Oxford Bulletin of Economics and Statistics*, **50**. 361–77.

Prior to examining the relationships between variables, however, univariate time series properties need to be established. This is important because if this equation is to represent a long-term relationship, or cointegrating regression, the left- and right-hand sides of (1) must have compatible long-run properties: that is, they must be integrated to the same order (see Granger, 1981). The purpose of this paper is to investigate these univariate properties in the light of the pronounced seasonality in consumption.

In Section 2 the concept of integration is broadened to allow for a mixture of one-period (or unit) and seasonal differencing. A number of tests, including that recently proposed by Engle *et al.* (1987), are used to decide on the combination required for each of the variables in (1). An apparent conflict arises here between the levels of integration consumption and the right-hand side variables, with both unit and seasonal differences being indicated for the former, but only one level of differencing is needed for each of the latter. Conventional differencing does not, however, capture the dynamics of consumption, since seasonal preferences generally imply seasonally varying coefficients. Section 3 then examines the non-stationary structure of consumption in the context of a periodic or seasonally-varying specification, and defines periodic integration. We conclude that consumption is periodically integrated of order one. This classification of consumption allows us to maintain (1) as an equilibrium relationship, albeit in a periodic form.

2.   Integration and Seasonality

To study the degree of integration for strongly seasonal variables, such as consumption, we amend the standard terminology (used by Granger, 1986; Engle and Granger, 1987, and others) as follows:

Definition. A non-deterministic series X_t is said to be *integrated* of order (d, D), denoted $X_t \sim I(d, D)$, if the series has a stationary, invertible ARMA representation after one-period differencing d times and seasonally differencing D times.

This terminology is directly in the seasonal time series modelling tradition of Box and Jenkins.

Seasonality, as considered in this paper, may have both deterministic and stochastic components. Thus, if the observed series is Y_t, then it is assumed that

$$Y_t = X_t + k_q \tag{2}$$

where X_t is purely stochastic and k_q is the deterministic seasonal component for season q. We remove deterministic seasonality by a prior regression of the levels series on four quarterly dummy variables; the residuals for this regression are then treated in the subsequent analysis as if they are the true X_t. This procedure is justified by Dickey, Hasza, and Fuller (1984) for testing a unit root at a seasonal lag and by Dickey, Bell, and Miller (1986) for testing a non-seasonal unit root in the presence of deterministic seasonality.

It is important that deterministic seasonality be considered when testing whether the stochastic seasonal autoregressive polynomial includes a unit root; otherwise, seasonal differencing may be indicated simply because of the failure to eliminate deterministic seasonal movements. This is discussed, in a related context, by Wallis (1976).

The details of our testing for $I(d, D)$ integration are presented below.

2.1 Integration tests

The tests used here, with quarterly data, are:

(i) Augmented Dickey–Fuller [$ADF(p)$]: the t-statistic for β in

$$\Delta X_t = \beta X_{t-1} + \alpha_1 \Delta X_{t-1} + \ldots + \alpha_p \Delta X_{t-p} + u_t$$

H_0: $X_t \sim I(1,0)$ with H_a: $X_t \sim I(0,0)$. The critical values used are given in Fuller (1976, Table 8.5.2) for the regression including an intercept: justification for using these values when seasonal means are removed is provided by Dickey, Bell, and Miller (1986, Appendix B).

(ii) Dickey–Hasza–Fuller [$DHF(p)$]: the t-statistic for β in the regression

$$\Delta_4 X_t = \beta Z_{t-4} + \alpha_1 \Delta_4 X_{t-1} + \ldots + \alpha_p \Delta_4 X_{t-p} + u_t$$

where $Z_t = \hat{\lambda}(L) X_t = (1 - \hat{\lambda}_1 L - \ldots - \hat{\lambda}_p L^{\,p}) X_t$ and L is the lag operator. The $\hat{\lambda}_i$ are the coefficient estimates obtained in the prior regression of $\Delta_4 X_t$ on $\Delta_4 X_{t-1}, \ldots, \Delta_4 X_{t-p}$. H_0: $X_t \sim I(0,1)$, H_a: $X_t \sim I(0,0)$; critical values are given in Table 7 of Dickey, Hasza and Fuller (1984).

(iii) Engle–Granger–Hylleberg–Yoo* [$EGHY(p)$]: the t-statistics on π_1, π_2 and π_3 in

$$\Delta_4 X_t = \pi_1 Z_{1,t-1} + \pi_2 Z_{2,t-1} + \pi_3 Z_{3t-2} + \alpha_1 \Delta_4 X_{t-1} + \ldots$$
$$+ \alpha_p \Delta_4 X_{t-p} + u_t$$

*This test is further developed in Hylleberg et al. (1990) which is the published version of $EGHY$ (1987). See the Introduction.

where

$$Z_{1t} = \hat{\lambda}(L)(1 + L + L^2 + L^3)X_t$$
$$Z_{2t} = -\hat{\lambda}(L)(1 - L + L^2 - L^3)X_t$$
$$Z_{3t} = -\hat{\lambda}(L)(1 - L^2)X_t$$

and $\hat{\lambda}(L)$ is obtained as for the $DHF(p)$ statistic. The overall null hypothesis here is $H_o: X_t \sim I(0, 1)$, but this is broken up using

$$1 - L^4 = (1 - L)(1 + L)(1 + L^2)$$
$$= (1 - \gamma_1 L)(1 + \gamma_2 L)(1 + \gamma_3 L^2)$$

with $\gamma_i = 1$, $i = 1, 2, 3$. Each π_i represents the difference between the corresponding γ_i and its value under H_o. The alternative hypotheses are $X_t \sim I(1, 0)$, corresponding to $\pi_1 = 0$ with π_2 or π_3 non-zero, or $X_t \sim I(0, 0)$, when $\pi_1 \neq 0$ and π_2 or π_3 is also non-zero.[1] The critical values are given by Engle et al. (1987).

(iv) $HF(p)$: the F statistic for testing $\beta = 0$ in

$$\Delta\Delta_4 X_t = \beta_1 Z_{4,t-1} + \beta_2 Z_{5,t-4} + \alpha_1 \Delta\Delta_4 X_{t-1} + \ldots$$
$$+ \alpha_p \Delta\Delta_4 X_{t-p} + u_t \tag{3}$$

where $Z_{4t} = \hat{\lambda}(L)\Delta_4 X_t$ and $Z_{5t} = \hat{\lambda}(L)\Delta X_t$. In this case the $\hat{\lambda}_i$ are the coefficient estimates of $\Delta\Delta_4 X_t$ on $\Delta\Delta_4 X_{t-1}, \ldots, \Delta\Delta_4 X_{t-p}$. The null hypothesis here is $H_o: X_t \sim I(1, 1)$, with alternative $H_a: X_t \sim I(0, 0)$ or $I(1, 0)$ or $I(0, 1)$; critical values are obtained by simulation.

(v) The t-ratios on β_1 and β_2 in equation (3), with the same null and alternative hypotheses as in (iv). We refer to these as $OCSB$ t-ratios: the rationale for examining these is discussed below. Critical values are again obtained by simulation.

Hasza and Fuller (1982) discuss using F-type statistics, as in (iv) above, for testing the $I(1, 1)$ null hypothesis. They do not, however, consider the case of interest to us, where there is deterministic seasonality but no time trend under the alternative hypothesis. In any case, as Dickey and Pantula (1987) point out, such F statistics are inappropriate in that they are two-sided in nature, whereas the alternative of stationarity is one-sided.

For the non-seasonal case Dickey and Pantula propose starting from the highest level of differencing to be contemplated and testing down to lower levels using a sequence of one-sided t-tests, rather than starting from the lowest level and testing up. Our $OCSB$ t-tests follow the former route. That is, under the $I(1, 1)$ null, β_1 provides a test of the

---

[1] The other case of interest might be $\pi_1 \neq 0$ with $\pi_2 = \pi_3 = 0$: this may indicate that unit differences had previously been taken whereas seasonal differences were appropriate.

non-seasonal unit root, while β_2 examines the unit root at the seasonal lag. Indeed, with $\beta_2 = 0$ the t-ratio on β_1 is an ADF test on the need for a first-order difference in addition to a seasonal difference; similarly, with $\beta_1 = 0$ the t-ratio on β_2 is a DHF test of the seasonal unit root after first differencing.

The two-stage regression carried out for (iv) and (v) results from considering a Taylor series expansion of

$$\lambda(L)(1 - \gamma_1 L)(1 - \gamma_4 L^4)X_t = u_t$$

about $\gamma_1 = \gamma_4 = 1$, with $\beta_1 = -(1 - \gamma_1)$ and $\beta_2 = -(1 - \gamma_4)$. Our proposed test statistics for β_1 and β_2 are analogous to the EGHY t-ratios, although we do not examine the separate roots of $1 - \gamma_4 L^4$.

Below we use critical values for the F and t-statistics of (iv) and (v) obtained using 10,000 replications of 100 observations (approximately our sample size) for the process with true $\lambda(L) = 1$ and seasonal means of zero. Zero starting values were used in generating the series. In these simulations $\lambda(L)$ was not estimated, but the seasonal means were subtracted before calculation of the test statistics. Our simulations are discussed in further detail in Appendix I.

Despite this prior subtraction of seasonal means, the critical values obtained for our t-ratios (see Table 1) are not very different from the value of -1.95 tabulated by Fuller for the case of testing a unit root with no intercept. Also, our F-test value is similar to 3.26 given by Hasza and Fuller for their two-coefficient F-test without an intercept. Thus, it appears the adjustment for seasonal means has relatively little influence on the distribution of the t-ratios when ΔX_t or $\Delta_4 X_t$ is used in place of X_t and tested for an additional unit root at a lag of a year or a quarter respectively.

It should be made clear that there is an important potential problem in the generality of the ADF test when applied to seasonal data. That is, the ADF statistic with $p \geqslant 3$ is sufficiently general to include the simple non-stationary seasonal process

$$\Delta_4 X_t = \Delta X_t + \Delta X_{t-1} + \Delta X_{t-2} + \Delta X_{t-3} = u_t$$

so that the ADF statistic on β in (i) above may test $H_o: X_t \sim I(0, 1)$ instead of $H_o: X_t \sim I(1, 0)$. Admittedly this problem is ruled out in the theory of the test by the assumption that the roots, other than the one being tested, are stationary: clearly, however, this cannot be guaranteed in practice. Similarly, because a unit root at lag four also implies a non-seasonal unit root, acceptance of the $I(0, 1)$ null hypothesis for the DHF test may, in fact, be due to a $I(1, 0)$ process.

The $EGHY$ test, in looking at the three distinguishable roots implied by Δ_4, separates the non-stationary seasonal and non-seasonal polynomials: therefore, it should assist in interpreting the ADF and DHF test results. Similarly, our *OCSB* *t*-ratios should be helpful, since this test regression also embeds the two competing hypotheses.

Notice that our implementation of the *DHF* and *EGHY* tests, as outlined above, is different in one respect from that proposed by the original, respective, sets of authors. That is, we use the variable as defined under H_o as the dependent variable, rather than this variable transformed using $\hat{\lambda}(L)$. The test statistics are invariant to this change, since the p lags indicated by $\lambda(L)$ are explanatory variables in the regression. However, where $\lambda(L)$ is unknown, our form has the advantage of being able to indicate over-specification of p.

2.2   Empirical results

An important problem in the practical implementation of the integration tests is, indeed, the value of p to be used: too low a value leads to invalid statistics due to autocorrelation remaining in the residuals, while an excessively high order implies a reduction in power. Based on a preliminary time series analysis of the series, p was initially set to 8 for the *ADF*, *DHF*, and *EGHY* tests, with 4 lags used in the *HF* and *OCSB* tests. For the wealth variables, where fewer observations are available, an initial $p = 4$ set for all four tests. The procedure was then to calculate a Lagrange Multiplier test for residual autocorrelation up to order four in each test regression: significant autocorrelation at the 5 per cent level led to p being increased. On the other hand, when no significant autocorrelation was detected and the original test regression suggested that p was unnecessarily high,[2] the order was reduced and the autocorrelation properties were again checked.

Four of the series analysed here correspond directly to the variables of equation (1): these are non-durable consumption, income, wealth (all in logarithms) and inflation. Following Davidson *et al.* (1978), we use the annual change in log prices to represent inflation.[3] In addition, we include the wealth/income and income/consumption ratios (also in logarithms) in our analysis, because of their importance in the analyses of Davidson *et al.* and Hendry and von Ungern-Sternberg (1981).

Because discussing the test results, it is worthwhile pausing to consider the broad characteristics of the series being analysed: to this end, time series plots are included as Figures 1 to 3. (The data are detailed in Appendix II.) Although consumption trends upwards over the period, it does not do so as strongly as income (Figure 1), resulting

---

[2] A conservative strategy is adopted in that a lower order was considered only if each individual *t*-ratio was less than 1.65 in absolute terms.

[3] We also analysed the original price series (in logs): this was classified as $I(1, 1)$, which also implies that $\Delta_4 P$ is $I(1, 0)$. The results for P are not reported to conserve space.

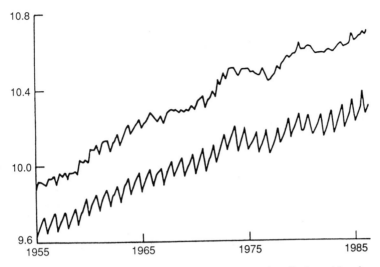

FIG. 1. Real income and non-durable consumption (in logarithms).

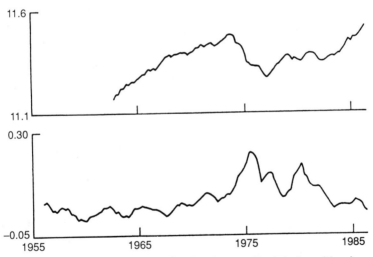

FIG. 2. Real wealth and annual price changes (both in logarithms).

in a general decrease over time in the average propensity to consume non-durables, C/Y (Figure 3). It is clear from Figure 2 that the high inflation rates of the mid-1970s and early 1980s had a substantial influence on real wealth. Since the growth in income is not matched by a corresponding growth in wealth, W/Y declines over our data period.

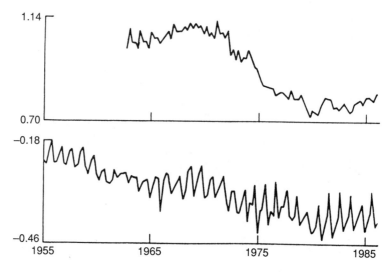

FIG. 3. Wealth/income and consumption/income ratios (in logarithms).

Notice also that the seasonal movements in consumption are very marked, but there does not appear to be any explanation for these in terms of the seasonal characteristics of income, wealth or inflation. One consequence of this is the seasonality evident in the average propensity to consume.

Numerical results for the integration tests are presented in Table 1. These calculations, and all those of the paper, have been carried out using *RATS* (Doan and Litterman, 1984). The level of significance throughout is a nominal 5 per cent: the critical values corresponding to a sample size of 100 are included in the table to simplify interpretation.

TABLE 1.   *Testing orders of integration*

	C	Y	W	$\Delta_4 P$	W/Y	C/Y	5% c.v.
$ADF(p)$	−0.35(8)	−0.67(5)	−1.76(4)	−1.45(8)	−0.81(4)	−1.54(5)	−2.89
$DHF(p)$	−1.97(5)	−2.99(9)	−4.73(2)	−5.06(20)	−4.37(12)	−3.44(9)	−4.11
$EGHY$:							
$\pi_1(p)$	−0.36(5)	−0.75(7)	−1.50(2)	−1.68(8)	−0.71(4)	−1.61(2)	−2.96
π_2	−1.85	−2.37	−2.18	−3.92	−1.77	−2.56	−2.95
π_3	−1.37	−3.59	−4.63	−6.43	−5.42	−3.63	−3.51
$HF(p)$	3.15(4)	12.19(4)	7.89(4)	51.39(7)	13.62(5)	16.58(4)	3.56
$OCSB: \beta_1$	−0.57	0.45	0.02	1.47	0.80	−2.61	−1.83
β_2	−2.05	−4.43	−3.47	−8.68	−4.73	−4.07	−2.03

The results for wealth, inflation and the wealth/income ratio are straightforward in terms of the statistical tests: they are all unambiguously $I(1,0)$.

Income certainly has a unit root, but the need for both unit and seasonal diffencing is decisively rejected. The (very marginal) rejection of the $I(0,1)$ hypothesis by π_3 suggests that the unit root may be at a lag of one quarter rather than a year; this is confirmed by the acceptance of the first-order unit root and rejection of the seasonal lag unit root by the $OCSB$ t-ratios. Thus, the acceptance of the $I(0,1)$ null hypothesis using the DHF statistic is presumably reflecting the non-stationary unit lag polynomial. We conclude income is $I(1,0)$.

For consumption, on the other hand, firm conclusions are more difficult. Looking at unit and seasonal differencing together, the F statistic for testing the overall $I(1,1)$ null marginally indicates acceptance. Similarly, although the t-statistic for β_1 is clear-cut, that for β_2 falls almost exactly on its simulated critical value. These results lead to a tentative classification of consumption as $I(1,1)$. Although it is the seasonal difference which is called into question by β_2, the $EGHY$ test indicates that taking unit differences is not sufficient to induce stationarity in consumption. Thus, the alternative to $I(1,1)$ appears to be $I(0,1)$.

Except for the t-ratio on β_1, the test statistics calculated for the income/consumption ratio are broadly similar to those for income. That is, the $I(1,1)$ null hypothesis is firmly rejected, so the lower order tests need to be examined. Here the $EGHY$ statistics indicate unit differencing, in that π_3 again marginally rejects seasonal differencing. Unlike the case with income, however, both unit and seasonal differencing are individually rejected by the $OCSB$ t-ratios. Thus, it remains unclear whether this variable is $I(1,0)$ or $I(0,1)$.

The conclusion that the average propensity to consume is non-stationary is uncomfortable from an economic viewpoint. Although they use total consumption, Engle et al. (1987) also find that C/Y has a unit root. As it is known that these tests of unit roots are not powerful against 'nearly stationary' alternatives, researchers with strong priors may be tempted to argue that this classification of C/Y is an error and that in truth it is $I(0,0)$. Nevertheless, the statistical result is not surprising for this particular data period (Figure 3). From our current interests we would also draw attention to the fact that there is no suggestion that C/Y is $I(1,1)$. However, if the classifications of C as $I(1,1)$ and Y and $I(1,0)$ are valid, then any linear combination will be dominated by the higher order process: recalling the log transform applied to all variables, this implies that C/Y will also be $I(1,1)$. Thus, there is a tension in the statistical results here.

Table 2 summarizes the classification of the variables that appear in

TABLE 2.   *Orders of integration: summary*

Variable	Order
C	$I(1, 1)^m$
Y	$I(1, 0)$
W	$I(1, 0)$
$\Delta_4 P$	$I(1, 0)$

m indicates a marginal result.

our equation (1). It can be seen that all the right-hand side variables have one non-stationary unit root at a lag of one quarter, while consumption itself may have two (that is, non-seasonal and seasonal) unit roots. Consequently, according to the theory of cointegration (see Granger, 1981), (1) cannot represent a valid cointegrating regression. Put differently, the orders given in Table 2 would imply that consumption can move far away from these variables in the long run, so that they cannot explain all the non-stationarity in consumption. This we find unacceptable on economic grounds, since income is the principal determinant of expenditure.

Thus the tension implied by the classification of C/Y in relation to those of consumption and income is compounded by our unease, based on strong economic priors, about the nature of these variables. Our explanation of these difficulties lies in the idea that the conventional view of unit and seasonal differencing may be not appropriate when dealing with seasonal consumers' expenditure. This is explored in the next section.

3.   Periodic Integration

In addition to the conventional view of differencing for seasonal data, considered in Section 2, we examine in this section a type of generalized first difference operator. This operator arises naturally from the class of periodic processes, which have parameters varying across the seasons. Tiao and Grupe (1980) examine the properties of periodic *ARMA* processes, while Osborn and Smith (1989) find that periodic autoregressions perform well, relative to other time series models, in forecasting UK non-durable consumers' expenditure. Our hypothesis is that seasonality, and seasonally varying coefficients in particular, may cause a process requiring this generalized differencing to appear as if it were $I(1, 1)$.

Due to the relative novelty of periodic processes, we briefly review the periodic autoregression before moving on to empirical results.

3.1   The periodic autoregressive model

The non-deterministic periodic $AR(1)$ is sufficiently general for illustrative purposes. This is given by

$$X_t = \sum \phi_q D_{qt} X_{t-1} + u_t, \tag{4}$$

or

$$X_t = \phi_q X_{t-1} + u_t \qquad q = 1, \ldots, s \tag{5}$$

when t falls in season q. In (4) D_{qt} is the zero/one dummy variable corresponding to 'season' q and the summation is over the s 'seasons', $q = 1, \ldots, s$ (in our case $q = 1, \ldots, 4$). Here X_t is seasonal, but this is due to the annual variation in the autoregressive coefficients ϕ_q rather than any direct dependence of X_t on X_{t-s}.

As discussed in Osborn (1987), the stationarity condition for the periodic $AR(1)$ process is $|\phi_1 \ldots \phi_s| < 1$. The product being equal to one is analogous to the unit root non-stationarity investigated in the $I(d, D)$ tests. Important for our analysis here is the possibility, considered by Osborn, that a single non-stationary root in a periodic process may make the series appear as $I(1, 1)$ when analysed as a constant parameter process. This arises because the non-stationary periodic process gives rise to a unit root at the seasonal lag, and hence is $I(0, 1)$ according to the definition above, but with a moving average coefficient polynomial similar to the summing operator $(1 + L + \ldots + L^{s-1})$. Taking first differences may then act to simplify this moving average so that the data generating process (DGP) appears to be

$$\Delta_1 \Delta_s X_t = \varepsilon_t - \theta \varepsilon_{t-s} \tag{6}$$

with $\theta < 1$.

Indeed, although annual data is usually thought to remove seasonality, the effects of periodic autoregressive coefficients are pervasive and are not necessarily removed by taking annual sums; see Osborn (1987). Thus, for example, if X_t is closely approximated by (6), then the annual sum of X_t may appear to be $I(2)$. This suggests that we need to proceed with care when identifying the degree of integration of a strongly seasonal variable, such as consumption.[4]

---

[4] Systematic annual sampling, in treating data relating to the four quarters as separate series, can give us information about the level of differencing appropriate. To test the $I(2)$ null hypothesis, the $ADF(0)$ statistic was calculated for each of the quarters: in no case was autocorrelation indicated. The resulting values were -2.73, -2.27, -2.56 and -1.79 corresponding to quarters 1 to 4 respectively. Compared with the -1.95 critical value, the null hypothesis is accepted for the Christmas quarter and rejected in favour of the $I(1)$ alternative for the others. Since it is difficult to rationalize the quarters being integrated to different orders, and $I(1)$ conclusion seems reasonable.

To cope with a non-stationary periodic process we require a concept of periodic integration. Consider, then, the following seasonally varying parameter or periodic type of differencing. With a sequence $\phi_q(q = 1, \ldots s)$ whose product $\phi_1 \ldots \phi_s$ is equal to one, we define the generalized difference operator δ_q in the obvious way from (5) as:

$$\delta_q X_t = X_t - \phi_q X_{t-1}. \tag{7}$$

Definition. We say X_t is *periodically integrated* of order one, or $X_t \sim PI(1)$, if X_t is non-stationary and $\delta_q X_t$ is stationary.

This concept is related to Granger's *TVP I*(1), see Granger (1986, p. 224).

Clearly, the standard constant parameter notion of $I(1,0)$ integration is the special case with all ϕ_q equal to one. This corresponds to $\theta = 1$ in (6), and hence that representation being over-differenced. Therefore, where there is little periodic variation in the autoregressive coefficients, it may be anticipated that the conventional tests will often indicate an $I(1,0)$ process. As the periodic nature of the autoregressive coefficients becomes more important, then θ moves further away from unity. Then, as noted by Hendry (1986) in relation to the simulation results of Molinas (1986), the probability of accepting $I(1,1)$ or rejecting it in favour of $I(1,0)$ will be a function of $1 - \theta$. Therefore, the results to be anticipated from the application of conventional tests (as in Section 2) to a $PI(1)$ variable will depend on the degree to which the parameters do, in fact, change from season to season.

Although the periodic $AR(1)$ process has been used here for illustrative purposes, it should be noted that it is a special case. Therefore, $\delta_q X_t$ is not necessarily white noise. For example, if the *DGP* is

$$(1 - \phi_q L)\lambda(L)X_t = u_t$$

with the polynomial $\lambda(L)$ non-periodic, then $\delta_q X_t$ will follow a conventional autoregressive process.

Non-durable consumption is the only variable of real interest from the viewpoint of periodic integration, because all the right-hand side variables of the equilibrium relationship have already been shown to have one unit root. If consumption is $PI(1)$, the apparent need to difference this variable twice arises from the inappropriate assumption of constant coefficient stochastic, rather than periodic, seasonality. This is not to say that the variables are necessarily non-periodic, but merely that any seasonal variation in their coefficients has not led to a conflict in the orders of integration for the right-hand side of (1).

A conventional view of stochastic and deterministic seasonality was taken in Section 2. Instead of the assumption embodied in equation (2), consider the inclusion of a deterministic component in a periodic $AR(1)$ process, giving

$$Y_t = \psi_q + \phi_q Y_{t-1} + u_t, \qquad q = 1, \ldots, s \tag{8}$$

which is written in terms of the original observations, Y. If $\phi_1 \ldots \phi_s = 1$, then this represents the periodic analogue of a random walk with drift. This process is of particular interest here because Osborn (1988) analyses seasonality in consumption starting from a seasonal utility function and derives equation (8) with the restriction $\phi_1 \ldots \phi_s = 1$.

Deterministic seasonality is treated in two ways. Firstly, as in Section 2, conventional deterministic seasonality is removed by using the residuals from the prior regression of the levels series on four seasonal dummy variables: a non-deterministic periodic $AR(1)$ model is then fitted to the residuals. Secondly, equation (8) is used: this latter case is referred to below as included deterministic seasonality.

To allow for the possibility of a periodic disturbance variance, the periodic model is estimated by a two-step procedure. In the first step, the appropriate equation (4) or (8), is estimated by ordinary least squares applied to observations on each of the four quarters separately. The equation is then transformed by dividing each variable by the appropriate quarterly residual standard deviation estimated from this first-stage regression. Using the transformed data, the periodic $AR(1)$ model is estimated with the imposition of the restriction $\phi_1 \phi_2 \phi_3 \phi_4 = 1$ in the second step.

3.2   Empirical results

Table 3 records the results of applying the integration tests to the residuals of the non-stationary periodic model. Specification of the lag p for each test is carried out in the same manner as previously, beginning with $p = 8$: once again, the regressions corresponding to quoted statistics have passed a Lagrange Multiplier test for autocorrelation to order four.

When deterministic seasonality has been removed by a prior regression, this is ignored as far as the critical values are concerned and the values quoted are appropriate when the mean is zero. The rationalization for this lies in our empirical finding, in relation to the distributions of our $OCSB$ t-ratios in Section II, that this adjustment to the levels series for seasonal means has little influence on the distributions of the test statistics when testing for a second level of differencing. When seasonal dummies are included in the periodic model, the critical values for regressions including an intercept (ADF) or seasonal dummies (DHF and $EGHY$) are quoted.

TABLE 3.   *Testing periodic AR residuals for consumption*

| | Deterministic seasonality | | | |
	Removed	5% c.v.	Included	5% c.v.
ADF(3)	−2.71	−1.95	−4.28	−2.89
DHF(5)	−4.03	−1.90	−5.14	−4.11
EGHY(5) π_1	−1.84	−1.94	−3.51	−2.96
π_2	−1.73	−1.95	−2.61	−2.95
π_3	−3.11	−1.91	−3.34	−3.51

Only the *ADF*, *DHF* and *EGHY* test statistics are calculated for the periodic residuals, since differences have already been taken through the periodic model estimation.

Under either treatment of deterministic seasonality, the computed test statistics show little evidence of non-stationarity remaining in the periodic residuals. Although the *EGHY* π_2 and either π_1 or π_3 statistics marginally accept non-stationary roots, the *ADF* and *DHF* statistics comfortably reject the need for conventional unit or seasonal differencing.

4.   Conclusions

This paper is concerned with identifying the degrees of integration of the variables that appear in the long run consumption function (1). This classification of variables is preliminary to an analysis of the cointegration properties of those variables. As with most workers in this area we have a prior belief that consumption, income and wealth should share a common degree on integration. More specifically we would expect all of them to be integrated to order one. To put these priors to the test in the context of a strongly seasonal variable such as consumption requires us to clarify what we mean when we say a variable is integrated. For example when we say consumption is integrated to degree one do we mean that there is a unit root over a one period lag or over a seasonal lag? A more interesting option arises when we allow the process to be inherently seasonal, that is, to be periodic.

Working with 'standard', non-periodic integration tests and allowing unit roots at a seasonal lag, UK real non-durable consumers' expenditure is found to be 'close' to $I(1, 1)$, which suggests that both seasonal and one-period differencing may be needed to render the series stationary. This evidence that consumption is on the margin of being classified as integrated to degree two conflicts with our priors, in particular with the single unit root found for each of the right-hand side variables in the equilibrium relationship (1).

Happily, however the periodic analysis of Section 3 offers a resolution of the conflict and shows that the second level of differencing marginally indicated for consumption is due to an appropriate treatment of seasonality. In particular, when stochastic seasonality is generalized to allow seasonally varying autoregressive coefficients, only one unit root is indicated. In this way we can say all the variables in (1) are unambiguously integrated to degree one, albeit in a periodic fashion.

These results raise a large number of interesting questions about the cointegration of variables where one or more are periodically integrated while others are non-periodically integrated. We finish here with the suggestion that, in such a case, the cointegrating equation will itself have a periodic structure. In other words, we believe that the periodic structure of consumption, which here arises as a statistical feature of the data, in fact has an underlying economic cause. In so far as preferences are seasonal (Osborn, 1988) we would anticipate that the relationship between consumption and the explanatory variables will vary across seasons, that is, the structure will be periodic. This in turn suggests a modelling strategy which relaxes the constant parameter (i.e. non-periodic) restrictions implicitly imposed in the models of Davidson et al. (1978) and Hendry and von Ungern-Sternberg (1981). We pursue these ideas of periodic cointegration and periodic dynamics in Birchenhall et al. (1987).

References

(References marked by a * are included in this volume)

BIRCHENHALL, C. R., BLADEN-HOVELL, R., CHUI, A. P. L., OSBORN, D. R. and SMITH, J. P. (1989), 'A seasonal model of consumption', (Revised version) Discussion Paper ES215, Department of Econometrics and Social Statistics, University of Manchester.

BOX, G. E. P., and JENKINS, G. M. (1970), Time Series Analysis: Forecasting and Control San Francisco: Holden-Day.

DAVIDSON, J. E. H., HENDRY, D. F., SRBA, F., and YEO, S. (1978), 'Econometric modelling of the aggregate time-series relationship between consumers' expenditure and income in the United Kingdom', Economic Journal, 88, 661–92.

DICKEY, D. A., BELL, W. R., and MILLER, R. B. (1986), 'Unit roots in time series models: tests and implications', The American Statistician, 40, 12–26.

—— HASZA, D. P., and FULLER, W. A. (1984), 'Testing for unit roots in seasonal time series', Journal of the American Statistical Association, 79, 355–67.*

—— and PANTULA, S. G. (1987), 'Determining the order of differencing in autoregressive processes', *Journal of Business and Economic Statistics*, **5**, 455–61.

DOAN, T. A., and LITTERMAN, R. B. (1984), *RATS User's Manual*, Version 4.3, Minneapolis: VAR Econometrics.

ENGLE, R. F., and GRANGER, C. W. J. (1987), 'Co-integration and error correction: representation, estimation and testing', *Econometrica*, **55**, 251–76.

—— —— HYLLEBERG, S., and YOO, B. S. (1987), 'Seasonal integration and co-integration', unpublished paper, Department of Economics, University of California, San Diego.

FULLER, W. A. (1976), *Introduction to Statistical Time Series*. New York: Wiley.

GRANGER, C. W. J. (1981), 'Some properties of time series data and their use in econometric model specification', *Journal of Econometrics*, **16**, 121–30.

—— (1986), 'Developments in the study of cointegrated economic variables', *Oxford Bulletin of Economics and Statistics*, **48**, 213–28.

HASZA, D. P., and FULLER, W. A. (1982), 'Testing for nonstationary parameter specifications in seasonal time series models', *Annals of Statistics*, **10**, 1209–16.

HENDRY, D. F. (1986), 'Econometric modelling with cointegrated variables: an overview', *Oxford Bulletin of Economics and Statistics*, **48**, 201–12.

—— and VON UNGERN-STERNBERG, T. (1981), 'Liquidity and inflation effects on consumers' expenditure', in Deaton, A. (ed.), *Essays in the Theory and Measurement of Consumer Behaviour*. Cambridge: Cambridge University Press, 237–60.

HYLLEBERG, S., ENGLE, R. F., GRANGER, C. W. J., and YOO B. S. (1990), 'Seasonal Integration and Cointegration' *Journal of Econometrics*, **99**, 215–238.

MOLINAS, C. (1986), 'A note on spurious regressions with integrated moving average errors', *Oxford Bulletin of Economics and Statistics*, **48**, 279–82.

OSBORN, D. R. (1987). 'Modelling seasonal time series and the implications of periodically varying coefficients', Discussion Paper ES180, Department of Econometrics and Social Statistics, University of Manchester.

—— (1988), 'Seasonality and habit persistence in a life cycle model of consumption', *Journal of Applied Econometrics*, **3**, 255–66.*

—— and SMITH, J. P. (1989), 'The performance of periodic autoregressive models in forecasting seasonal UK consumption', *Journal of Business and Economic Statistics* **7**, 117–27.

TIAO, G. C., and GRUPE, M. R. (1980), 'Hidden periodic autoregressive-moving average models in time series data', *Biometrika*, **67**, 365–73.

WALLIS, K. F. (1976), 'Seasonal adjustment and multiple time series analysis', in Zellner, A. (ed.), *Seasonal Analysis of Economic Time Series*. Washington DC: Bureau of the Census, 347–57.

Appendix 1: Simulations

As mentioned in the text, the critical values of the *HF* and *OCSB* statistics have been obtained by simulation. The data generating process corresponding to the 5

TABLE A1. *Simulated Critical Values*

Statistic	Case 1	Case 2	Case 3	Case 4	Previously tabulated
HF: 10%	2.52	2.66	2.55	2.88	2.53
5%	3.20	3.56	3.24	3.81	3.26
1%	4.99	5.74	4.86	5.98	4.92
OCSB β_1: 10%	−1.52	−1.53	−1.59	−1.65	−1.61
5%	−1.87	−1.83	−1.94	−1.95	−1.95
1%	−2.48	−2.44	−2.61	−2.61	−2.60
OCSB β_2: 10%	−1.57	−1.63	−1.65	−1.68	−1.53
5%	−1.93	−2.03	−1.93	−2.05	−1.89
1%	−2.59	−2.77	−2.50	−2.79	−2.56

per cent critical values quoted in Table 1 contained no deterministic seasonality, but simple seasonal means were subtracted before calculation of the sample test statistics. As noted, the subtraction of seasonal means appears to have had relatively little impact on the critical values compared to the case, for which tables are available, of no deterministic component.

Consider, therefore, four cases of interest:

Case 1: No deterministic seasonality, no seasonal mean subtraction.
Case 2: No deterministic seasonality, seasonal means subtracted.
Case 3: Deterministic seasonality present, no seasonal mean subtraction.
Case 4: Deterministic seasonality present, seasonal means subtracted.

Fuller (1976), Dickey, Hasza, and Fuller (1984), Hasza and Fuller (1982) provide tables appropriate for Case 1, while we have used the results from Case 2 in Table 1.

Our simulations cover, however, all four cases. Table A1 details the results of our simulations, recording the 1 per cent and 10 per cent critical values, in addition to the 5 per cent ones. The Case 1 critical values previously tabulated are also included: these are either for a sample size of 100 or the nearest sample size given by the authors.

The empirical critical values here are based on 10,000 replications of samples of 100 observations using zero starting values for the stochastic process. As in the applications of the text, no degrees of freedom adjustment is made for the prior subtraction of seasonal means. In the notation of equation (2), the deterministic component k_q is added after the generation of X_t for Cases 3 and 4. In each case, we have used $k_q = q$ for $q - 1, 2, 3, 4$.

The impression from this table is that conventional deterministic seasonality has relatively little influence on these test statistics.

Appendix 2: The Data

We use seasonally unadjusted UK data, mainly from *Economic Trends Annual Supplement, 1987*. Data on non-durable consumers' expenditure in both current and 1980 prices are available in seven categories, namely: food; alcoholic drink and tobacco; clothing and footwear; energy products; other goods; rent, rates and water charges; other services. We exclude rent, rates and water charges from the analysis and our total non-durable consumers' expenditure (C) is defined as the sum of the remaining six components' series. Rent, rates and water charges is omitted because it is an annual series interpolated quarterly; this is discussed further in Osborn and Smith (1987).

Y is real personal disposable income in 1980 prices, and P is the retail price index. The wealth (W) variable is end-of-period net liquid assets deflated by the non-durable consumers' expenditure deflator, where net liquid assets is the total identified net of bank borrowing. Data on total identified and bank borrowing are taken from *Financial Statistics 1971*, 1979 editions and more recent data from the CSO data bank. Total identified liquid assets is defined as the sum of national savings, tax instruments, local authority temporary debt, deposits with the monetary sector and other financial institutions. The deflator used is the implicit deflator for total non-durable consumers' expenditure.

Except for the wealth variable, all series extend from 1955(i) to 1986(ii), yielding 126 observations. Our wealth series can be constructed back only to 1962(iv), giving 95 observations. Results reported here are always based on the longest sample period over which the particular test regression can be calculated for the series being analysed.

Index of Names

Lancaster 27, 57
Laroque, G. 9, 13
Lee, H. S. 142, 143, 395, 396, 397
Litterman, R. B. 456, 464
Liviatan, N. 311, 318
Ljung, G. M. 122, 134
Lomholt, E. 18, 25
Lovell, M. C. 21, 24, 28, 58, 61, 81,
  97, 106, 134
Lucas, R. E. 181, 189, 190

Macauley, F. R. 20, 24, 90, 93, 134,
  253, 256, 257
Maccini, L. J. 209, 210, 213, 217, 244
McKenzie, S. 117, 135
MacKinnon, J. G. 21, 22, 193, 207
McLeod, A. I. 385, 390
McNeill, I. B. 406, 423
Makridakis, S. 105, 134
Malinvaud, E. 38, 58
Mankiw, N. G. 216, 244
Mann, H. B. 93, 135
Maravall, A. 10, 13, 287, 288, 289,
  359, 361, 364, 377
March, L. 89, 135
Marris, S. N. 92, 135
Martin, R. D. 95, 132, 135
Mehra, R. K. 298, 318
Melnick, E. L. 97, 135
Mendershausen, H. 19, 20, 24, 90, 97,
  103, 135
Meyer, R. A. 55, 57
Miller, R. B. 451, 463
Mills, F. C. 18, 24
Miron, J. A. 11, 13, 142, 143, 144,
  194, 205, 207, 209, 213, 223, 230,
  244, 394, 395, 396, 397
Mitchell, W. C. 21, 22
Modigliani, F. 57, 58
Molana, H. 194, 198, 208
Molinas, C. 460, 464
Moore, G. H. 21, 24, 361, 377
Moran, P. A. P. 94, 135
Morris, M. J. 183, 190
Mosser, T. 209
Moussourakis, J. 97, 135
Muellbauer, J. 194, 203, 205, 207
Musgrave, J. C. 9, 14, 21, 24, 27, 29,

58, 91, 108, 136, 249, 251, 255, 257,
  260, 277, 280, 321, 339, 359, 377,
  379, 390

Nankervis, J. C. 202, 205, 207
Nelson, C. R. 218, 244, 301, 304, 318,
  347, 358, 425, 447
Nerlove, M. 4, 10, 13, 14, 15, 17, 21,
  24, 27, 28, 40, 42, 43, 56, 57, 58, 61,
  75, 77, 78, 80, 83, 88, 106, 108, 113,
  133, 135, 249, 251, 259, 280, 285,
  286, 289, 291, 293, 295, 318, 321,
  322, 338, 344, 346, 358, 371, 377,
  381, 382, 390, 427, 447
Newbold, P. 19, 23, 107, 108, 135

Orcutt, G. H. 94, 131
Osborn, D. R. 11, 14, 142, 144, 193,
  197, 200, 203, 204, 207, 385, 390,
  394, 395, 397, 449, 458, 459, 461,
  463, 464, 466

Pagan, A. 10, 14, 292, 294, 299, 300,
  308, 318
Pagano, M. 385, 390
Palm, F. C. 142, 144
Pantula, S. G. 452, 464
Park, J. C. 202, 207
Perazzelli, P. 98, 126, 131
Perron, P. 9, 12
Persons, W. M. 18, 20, 24, 89, 90, 91,
  135
Phillips, P. C. B. 202, 205, 207
Pierce, D. A. 10, 13, 21, 24, 88, 98,
  117, 128, 135, 265, 266, 287, 288,
  289, 294, 319, 322, 338, 344, 358,
  359, 361, 365, 377, 385, 390
Plosser, C. I. 104, 105, 135, 181, 182,
  190, 218, 244, 347, 358, 425, 447
Potter, J. E. 298, 318
Power, E. A. 171, 180
Prescott, E. C. 189, 190, 221, 244
Priestley, M. B. 95, 135
Prothero, D. L. 341, 342, 350, 351,
  352, 354, 358

Rao, M. M. 400
Reagan, P. 210, 223, 244

Index of Subjects